About the Authors

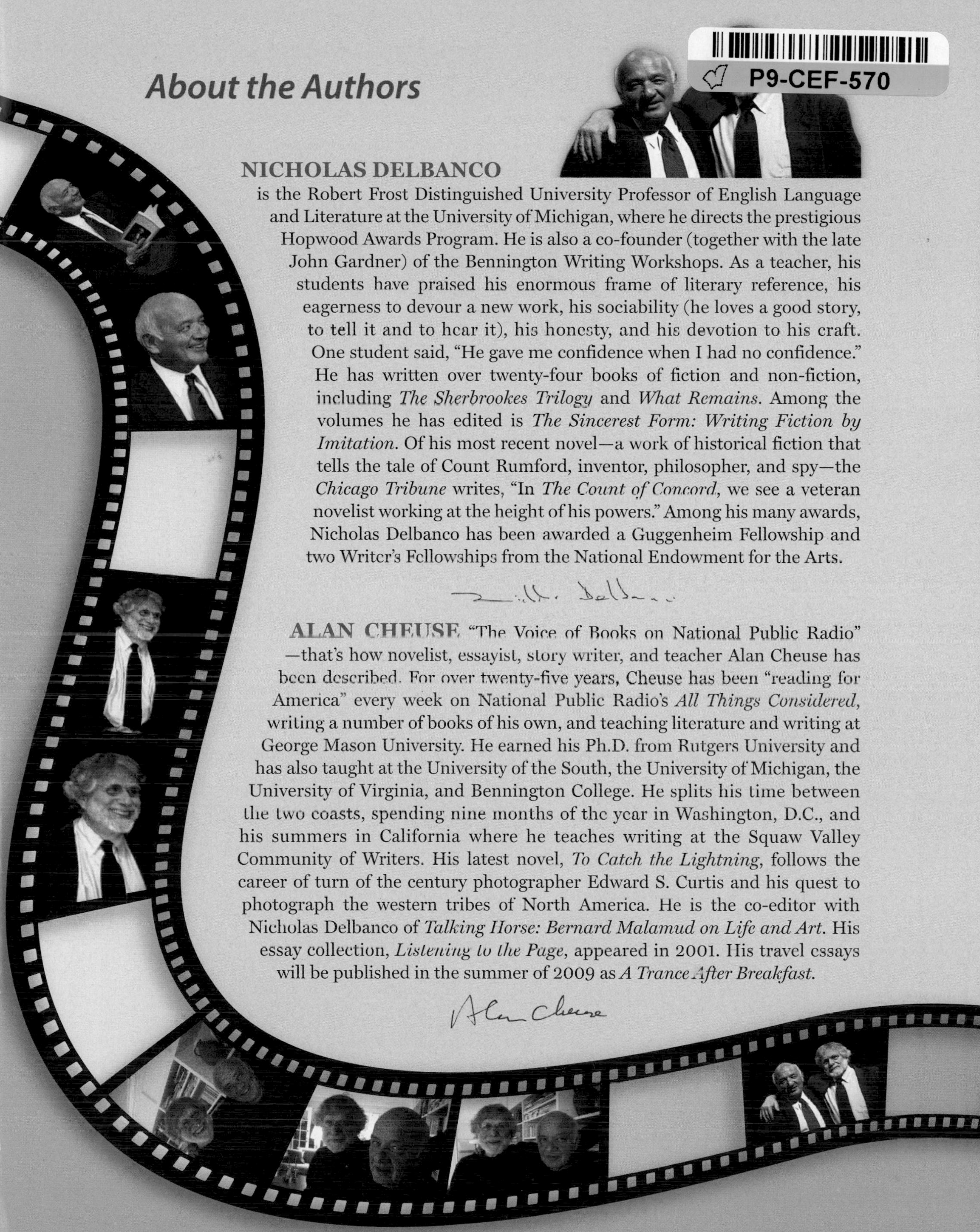

P9-CEF-570

NICHOLAS DELBANCO is the Robert Frost Distinguished University Professor of English Language and Literature at the University of Michigan, where he directs the prestigious Hopwood Awards Program. He is also a co-founder (together with the late John Gardner) of the Bennington Writing Workshops. As a teacher, his students have praised his enormous frame of literary reference, his eagerness to devour a new work, his sociability (he loves a good story, to tell it and to hear it), his honesty, and his devotion to his craft. One student said, "He gave me confidence when I had no confidence." He has written over twenty-four books of fiction and non-fiction, including *The Sherbrookes Trilogy* and *What Remains*. Among the volumes he has edited is *The Sincerest Form: Writing Fiction by Imitation*. Of his most recent novel—a work of historical fiction that tells the tale of Count Rumford, inventor, philosopher, and spy—the *Chicago Tribune* writes, "In *The Count of Concord*, we see a veteran novelist working at the height of his powers." Among his many awards, Nicholas Delbanco has been awarded a Guggenheim Fellowship and two Writer's Fellowships from the National Endowment for the Arts.

ALAN CHEUSE "The Voice of Books on National Public Radio" —that's how novelist, essayist, story writer, and teacher Alan Cheuse has been described. For over twenty-five years, Cheuse has been "reading for America" every week on National Public Radio's *All Things Considered*, writing a number of books of his own, and teaching literature and writing at George Mason University. He earned his Ph.D. from Rutgers University and has also taught at the University of the South, the University of Michigan, the University of Virginia, and Bennington College. He splits his time between the two coasts, spending nine months of the year in Washington, D.C., and his summers in California where he teaches writing at the Squaw Valley Community of Writers. His latest novel, *To Catch the Lightning*, follows the career of turn of the century photographer Edward S. Curtis and his quest to photograph the western tribes of North America. He is the co-editor with Nicholas Delbanco of *Talking Horse: Bernard Malamud on Life and Art*. His essay collection, *Listening to the Page*, appeared in 2001. His travel essays will be published in the summer of 2009 as *A Trance After Breakfast*.

Literature

Poetry: Craft and Voice

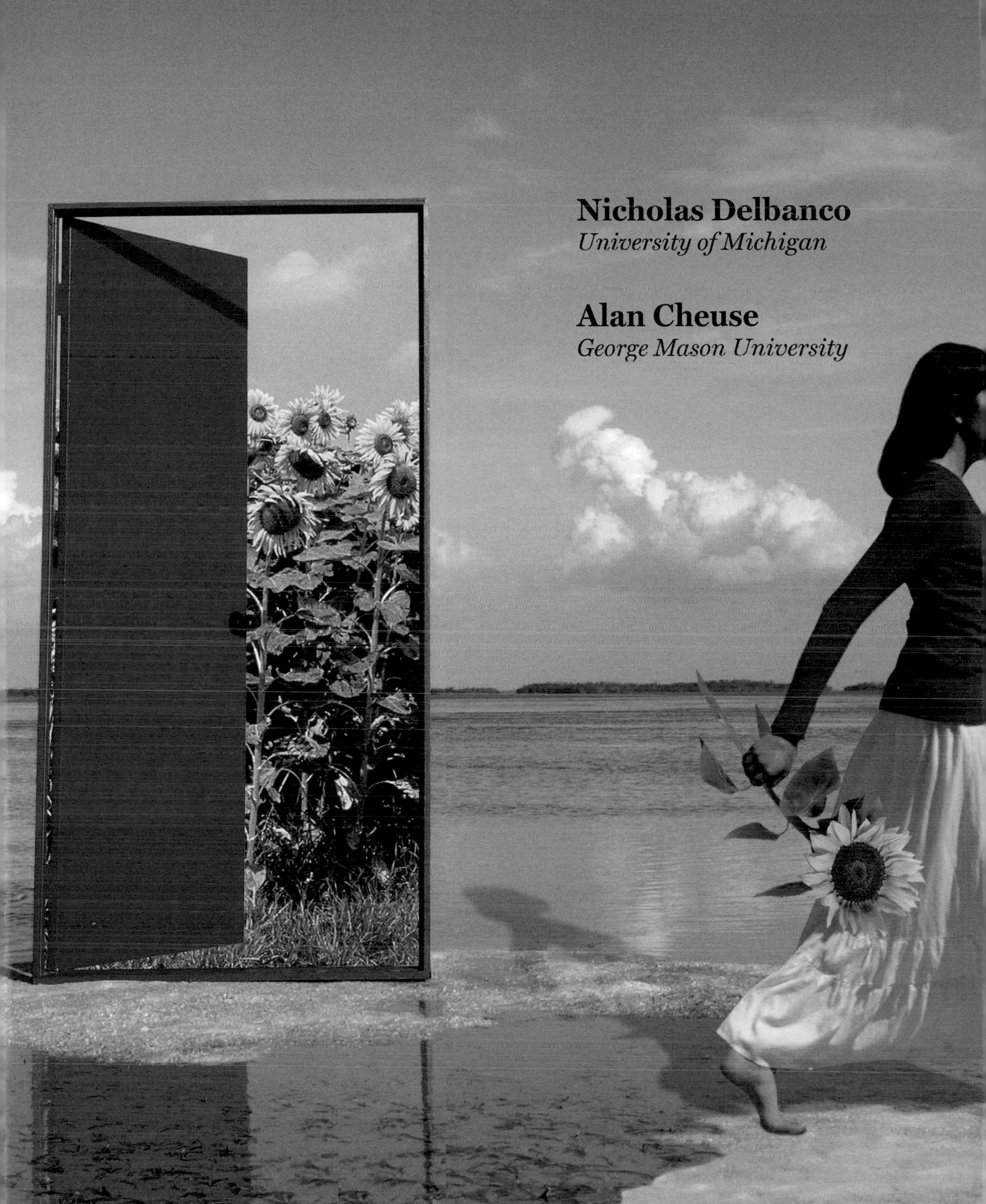

Nicholas Delbanco
University of Michigan

Alan Cheuse
George Mason University

To Our Students

Mc Graw Hill **Higher Education**

Published by McGraw-Hill, an imprint of The McGraw-Hill Companies, Inc., 1221 Avenue of the Americas, New York, NY 10020. Copyright © 2010. All rights reserved. No part of this publication may be reproduced or distributed in any form or by any means, or stored in a database or retrieval system, without the prior written consent of The McGraw-Hill Companies, Inc., including, but not limited to, in any network or other electronic storage or transmission, or broadcast for distance learning.

This book is printed on acid-free paper.

5 6 7 8 9 0 DOW/DOW 0

ISBN: 978-0-07-721424-1
MHID: 0-07-721424-2

Editor in Chief: *Michael Ryan*
Publisher: *Lisa Moore*
Executive Marketing Manager: *Allison Jones*
Editorial Coordinator: *Stephen Sachs*
Production Editor: *Jasmin Tokatlian*
Manuscript Editor: *Susan Norton*
Cover Designer: *Jeanne Schreiber*
Interior Designers: *Jeanne Schreiber and Linda Robertson*
Senior Photo Research Coordinator: *Nora Agbayani*
Lead Media Project Manager: *Ron Nelms*
Production Supervisor: *Louis Swaim*
Composition: *9.25/11.25 Miller Roman by Thompson Type*
Printing: *45# NewPage Orion Gloss, R. R. Donnelley & Sons/Willard, OH*

Cover: © picturegarden/The Image Bank/Getty Images.

Credits: The credits section for this book begins on page C-1 and is considered an extension of the copyright page.

Library of Congress Cataloging-in-Publication Data

Delbanco, Nicholas.
Literature : craft and voice / Nicholas Delbanco, Alan Cheuse.—1st ed.
p. cm.
Includes index.
3 vols. planned.
ISBN-13: 978-0-07-721424-1 (v. 1 : acid-free paper)
ISBN-10: 0-07-721424-2 (v. 1 : acid-free paper) 1. Literature. I. Cheuse, Alan. II. Title.
PN45.D457 2009
800—dc22

2008051003

The Internet addresses listed in the text were accurate at the time of publication. The inclusion of a Web site does not indicate an endorsement by the authors or McGraw-Hill, and McGraw-Hill does not guarantee the accuracy of the information presented at these sites.

Contents

POETRY

Video interview with the authors available online at www.mhhe.com/delbancopreview

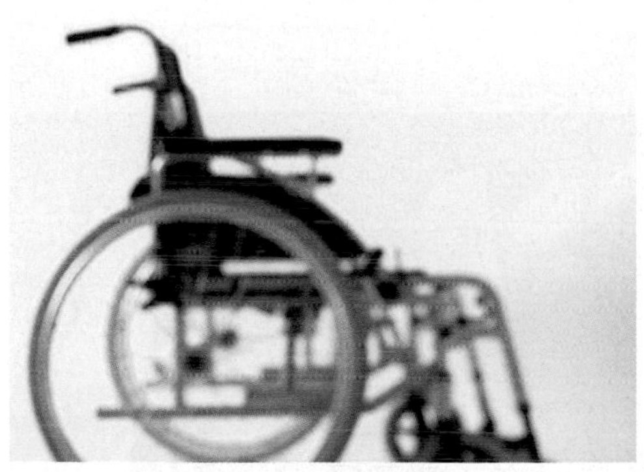

20 Imagery and Symbol 144

21 Figures of Speech 176

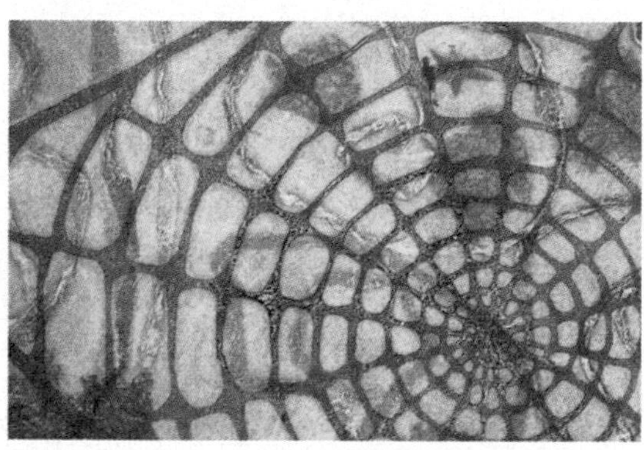

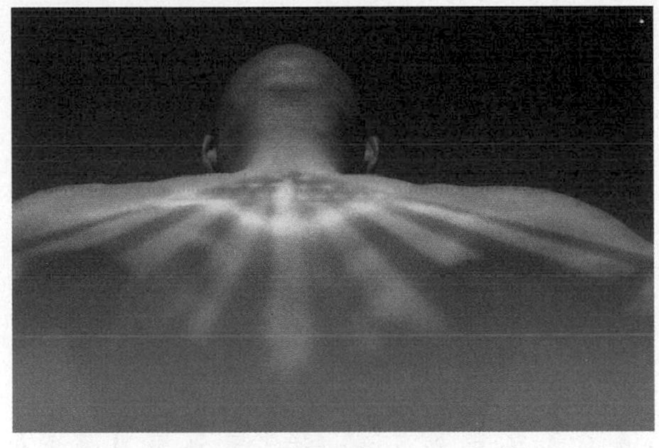

26 Langston Hughes 356

27 Art and Poetry 380

A HANDBOOK FOR WRITING FROM READING H-1

1 Critical Approaches to Literature H-3

2 Writing from Reading H-25

15 Reading a Poem in Its Elements

THIS is your museum of stones, assembled in matchbox and tin,
collected from roadside, culvert, and viaduct,
battlefield, threshing floor, basilica, abattoir,
stones loosened by tanks in the streets
of a city whose earliest map was drawn in ink on linen,
schoolyard stones in the hand of a corpse,
pebble from Apollinaire's *oui*,
stone of the mind within us
carried from one silence to another . . .

—from "The Museum of Stones," by Carolyn Forché

NOWADAYS more people read fiction or go to the movies (our contemporary version of the theater) than read poetry. However, most writers think of poetry as the purest example of verbal expression; all of us acknowledge it as the mother form. Short stories and novels are relatively recent genres, but poetry has been a hallmark of civilization since civilization began. The earliest singers and bards expressed themselves in rhythm and rhyme long before prose was composed. When the first drum sounded or the first string was plucked, its verbal companion or accompaniment was what we have come to call verse.

While we may be more familiar with the techniques of prose fiction, the language of poetry is often where we turn to better express the emotion of a great occasion or a deeply personal one. At weddings and funerals everywhere, poems are being recited; they remain the "touchstones" of experience relived. Carolyn Forché tells us that "The Museum of Stones" is a memorial tribute to a dead friend—a man who kept a collection of

"The more we know about how a poem makes its rhythms and musics and patternings, the more deeply we can enter into the poem. It doesn't mean that we can't read the poem with great pleasure knowing very little about those matters, it means that we'll have much more pleasure if we know more."

Conversation with Carolyn Forché, available on video at www.mhhe.com/delbanco1e

stones to remind him of his travels. The long list of places where the stones in the poem were found provides a kind of encyclopedia of buildings seen and countries visited. This general human history is made vivid for the poet through personal loss. If we can open ourselves to the experience of reading poetry, its special language—its lists and repetitions—can touch our lives more deeply than ordinary speech.

A FIRST READING: "DUFFING INTO IT"

When reading a poem for the first time, remember: We may start anywhere. As the great American poet Robert Frost expresses it, "We *duff* into our first reading of a poem. We read that poem imperfectly (thoroughness with it would be fatal), but the better to read the second. We read the second the better to read the third . . . ." A "duffer" is a beginner, and everyone who reads a poem for the first time duffs his or her way into it.

All children are alive to rhyme, the pleasures of repeated sound, and it's one of the ways we learn language: *pretty* rhymes with *witty, hiss* with *kiss* or *miss.* (Think of those nursery rhymes that have remained intact across the ages.) When you read a poem for the first time, it's that childhood pleasure you're after. Notice the way words edge up against each other, the way they match and shift. Let your mind drift, enjoy the words, and listen to the sound of the lines. What do the sounds make you think of? What words stand out for you? What associations does the poem have?

In her interview, Carolyn Forché says "as the reader" you should read the first time "without a preconception." As you begin to read poems in this chapter you will notice that some of them are easier to understand than others; some seem transparent with respect to their meaning while others may appear flat-out incomprehensible. Some will please you; some will not. Upon first reading, don't make finding the poem's meaning your sole aim. The sound and the shape of a poem will be as important as the final interpretation.

CONTINUED ON PAGE 6

The poet is imagining you . . .

You are as much this poem's important reader as the very first person who read it.

Q & A

A Conversation on Writing

Carolyn Forché

Reading Poetry

A poet will tell you this if you ask. They go where the poem takes them, and they don't know in advance where the poem is going when they are writing it the first time. They don't know what the poem is going to be about, often. They certainly don't know what its destination is. So, your experience as the reader is also to go without a preconception, and to enter the poem and to read freshly. You are as much this poem's important reader as the very first person who read it. Writing does not recur. The poem is written and finished and goes into the world. But reading recurs, and you are a fresh reader.

Interpreting Poetry

The poet is imagining you . . . and is attempting to become present to you and to celebrate your presence. . . . You are making a reading of the poem. If you are sitting in a circle of students, you will find that there might be six or seven different readings of this poem. Often the way to really solve the puzzle is to talk about all the different readings. Some of them might contradict each other and some of them might complement each other, but eventually you'll arrive at a full appreciation of what's before you on the page, and it's delightful.

The Story of "The Museum of Stones"

I had a friend who, when he was traveling around the world, decided that instead of going to souvenir shops . . . would choose a little stone . . . from each place he visited. . . . He would put it on a little prong or block and he would label it. "Stone from beneath the Eiffel Tower, 1993, spring" . . . "Stone from the Banks of the Nile," "Stone from Hector's Garage in Illinois." You know, he had all kinds of different stones, and he called it his museum. I wrote this poem for him . . . after he died.

Known as a "poet of witness," Carolyn Forché (b. 1950)—a native of Detroit, Michigan—became a spokesperson for human rights through her poetry after traveling to El Salvador. Forché had a consciousness of atrocities from the time she was a young girl—she discovered a copy of *Look* magazine with pictures of the Holocaust, which her mother promptly hid—but it wasn't until her second book of poetry, *The Country Between Us* (1981), that she stirred controversy by dealing with political violence overtly. Her first collection, *Gathering the Tribes* (1976), won the Yale Series of Younger Poets Prize, and she has continued to receive prestigious awards and fellowships, including the Guggenheim and National Endowment of the Arts Creative Writing Fellowship. She has taught at George Mason University and Skidmore College; she now is a member of the faculty at Georgetown University.

To watch this entire interview and hear the author read from her work, go to www.mhhe.com/delbanco1e.

RESEARCH ASSIGNMENT Watch the interview and explain what Forché means when she says "form and content are intertwined." How does this relate to the word *stone* in the poem "The Museum of Stones"?

AS YOU READ Duff your way into the poem in a first reading. Notice the different stones mentioned in this poem.

The Museum of Stones

(2007)

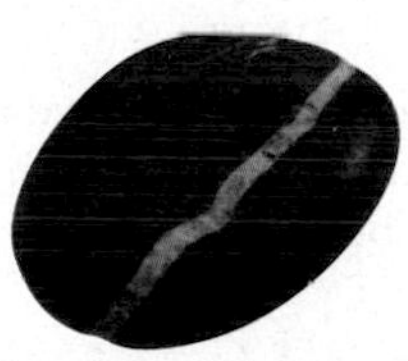

This is your museum of stones, assembled in matchbox and tin,
collected from roadside, culvert, and viaduct,
battlefield, threshing floor, basilica, abattoir,
stones loosened by tanks in the streets
of a city whose earliest map was drawn in ink on linen,
schoolyard stones in the hand of a corpse,
pebble from Apollinaire's *oui,*
stone of the mind within us
carried from one silence to another,
stone of cromlech and cairn, schist and shale, hornblende,
agate, marble, millstones, and ruins of choirs and shipyards,
chalk, marl, and mudstone from temples and tombs,
stone from the silvery grass near the scaffold,
stone from the tunnel lined with bones,
lava of the city's entombment,
chipped from lighthouse, cell wall, scriptorium,
paving stones from the hands of those who rose against the army,
stones where the bells had fallen, where the bridges were blown,
those that had flown through windows and weighted petitions,
feldspar, rose quartz, slate, blueschist, gneiss, and chert,
fragments of an abbey at dusk, sandstone toe
of a Buddha mortared at Bamiyan,
stone from the hill of three crosses and a crypt,
from a chimney where storks cried like human children,
stones newly fallen from stars, a stillness of stones, a heart,
altar and boundary stone, marker and vessel, first cast, lode, and hail,
bridge stones and others to pave and shut up with,
stone apple, stone basil, beech, berry, stone brake,
stone bramble, stone fern, lichen, liverwort, pippin, and root,
concretion of the body, as blind as cold as deaf,
all earth a quarry, all life a labor, stone-faced, stone-drunk
with hope that this assemblage, taken together, would become
a shrine or holy place, an ossuary, immovable and sacred,
like the stone that marked the path of the sun as it entered the human dawn.

"When we read a poem maybe the mind of the reader is a kind of solvent, like you drop the DNA, which is the poem, in the mind of the reader, and the poem begins to blossom, to bloom with all these meanings. Of course the information I'm talking about in a poem isn't just data, and it's not necessarily biographical information. It's emotional information, spiritual information, soulful information, erotic information, intellectual information, all of that stuff packed into a poem." Conversation with Li-Young Lee

Writing from Reading

Summarize

1 List the stones included here and describe how "this assemblage, taken together" can help us to understand the world.

Analyze Craft

2 In her interview, Forché says, "In our culture it becomes more and more difficult for us to enter into, imaginatively at least, the consciousness of others. Literature is a way of doing that." How do you share in the speaker's experience of mourning by reading this poem? What in the poem makes that sadness clear?

3 Why do you think the speaker plays with the different *stone* words? What effect does the wordplay have on your reading of the poem?

4 Do the references to Apollinaire and Bamiyan require research on your part, or do they seem like private allusions?

Analyze Voice

5 In her interview, Forché also indicates that "The first level of [a poem's] meaning is simply to be moved and to hear a speaker, to hear a voice giving voice to what is within the poet." In this poem, does "your museum of stones" mean the poet is talking to herself, or is she addressing someone else, or both?

Synthesize Summary and Analysis

6 There is a great deal of information in this poem. Compare it to the listing technique of O'Brien's "The Things They Carried" (*Fiction,* chapter 10). In both instances, what is the effect of the writers' doing this?

Interpret the Poem

7 Why do you think the poet uses the image of a "museum" in this poem; what about a museum lends additional meaning to the poem?

(CONTINUED FROM PAGE 3)

A CRITICAL READING

In ways we'll come to understand, poetry often manages to use everyday language in uncommon ways—to rise above the commonplace and avoid cliché. A thing that's said too frequently can feel unimportant, and if we repeat the same phrase again and again its meaning empties out. Certain expressions—or words like *like*—come to us on automatic pilot, and we barely notice what we're saying or reading. When people say "No problem" now, they tend to mean "You're welcome," but neither of those phrases means precisely what the words say, and both of them get used with something less than conscious attention to word choice. "Good-bye," for example, is a contraction of "God be with ye," but which of us who shouts "Good-bye!" is conscious of its original meaning? "Farewell"—a slightly more formal expression at parting—has also been stripped of its resonance until we stop and think about what "fare well" might mean. To the poet—and poetry's careful reader—each word has its own history and every syllable counts.

"You have to read the way a cook eats. How is it done? How is that put together?" Conversation with Robert Pinsky

> "Be completely open—innocent, if you will, of the poem. Walk in, just like it's water, and say, "What is this?" And read it over and over again. . . . [Read] with that kind of ignorant joy, and [let] yourself be bewildered when you're bewildered."
>
> Conversation with Marie Howe

Although such an assertion—that every syllable counts—seems simple and even self-evident, it involves a host of elements the following chapters will discuss in detail. No one element works in isolation from the others. Rather, rhythm depends on word choices, and word choices conjure up a speaker's voice; that voice will be inflected by the use of images, symbols, or figures of speech. These will be made shapely and arranged into a form, either a formal prescribed structure or one that emerges from the content and cadence of the words themselves. All these elements work together to create the effect the poem makes.

- **Words** are the language of poetry; a poet chooses "the best words" and puts them in "the best order" to describe an experience or feeling. Choices may be playful, lofty, direct, or unusual, and they lead directly to voice.
- **Voice** refers to every poem's speaker. The words and the order of the words that the poet chooses determine that speaker's tone of voice (stately, mournful, tender, angry). The speaker may or may not be the poet.
- **Images** in poetry transform the everyday thing that is experienced for itself into a vivid sensory impression.
- **Symbols** transcend the thing itself (a tree) and suggest a larger meaning (nature). Imagery and symbolism work in the service of word choice and tone of voice to generate emotion and establish the mood of the poem. Like language itself, they are a sign for something not present on the page.
- **Figures of speech** most commonly compare two unlike objects, such as "the sun" and "the face of the beloved," to condense and heighten the effect of language, particularly the effect of the imagery or symbolism used in a poem.
- **Sound,** the rhythmic structure of the lines that draws the reader in, often utilizes rhyme and is created through word choice and word order.
- **Form,** either formal or open, distinguishes poetry from prose through its arrangement in rhythmic lines of words.

As Carolyn Forché says in her interview, every reader gets to have a fresh reading. Forché also indicates that as her work on "The Museum of Stones" progressed, she went to the dictionary, to the thesaurus, to various sources of information on the sound and shape and look of these particular objects (she's not a geologist and had no previous expertise with rocks). The words became a kind of game for her, and she began to link

> "Everybody plays with language, with the rhythms of language as part of what they do, you know, it's sort of our fundamental act of learning." Conversation with Robert Hass

three categories—animal, vegetable, and mineral—from the game "Twenty Questions." You do not need to know these things to read her poem critically, but do be mindful of the pleasure in the playfulness in the poet's language. Here is a sample reading of "The Museum of Stones" in which the reader looks at how the poet's choices helped create the experience of the first reading.

An Interactive Reading of "The Museum of Stones"

This is your museum of stones, assembled in matchbox and tin,
collected from roadside, culvert, and viaduct,
battlefield, threshing floor, basilica, abattoir,
stones loosened by tanks in the streets
of a city whose earliest map was drawn in ink on linen,
schoolyard stones in the hand of a corpse,
pebble from Apollinaire's *oui*,
stone of the mind within us
carried from one silence to another,
stone of cromlech and cairn, schist and shale, hornblende,
agate, marble, millstones, and ruins of choirs and shipyards,
chalk, marl, and mudstone from temples and tombs,
stone from the silvery grass near the scaffold,
stone from the tunnel lined with bones,
lava of the city's entombment,
chipped from lighthouse, cell wall, scriptorium,
paving stones from the hands of those who rose against the army,
stones where the bells had fallen, where the bridges were blown,
those that had flown through windows and weighted petitions,
feldspar, rose quartz, slate, blueschist, gneiss, and chert,
fragments of an abbey at dusk, sandstone toe
of a Buddha mortared at Bamiyan,
stone from the hill of three crosses and a crypt,
from a chimney where storks cried like human children,
stones newly fallen from stars, a stillness of stones, a heart,
altar and boundary stone, marker and vessel, first cast, lode, and hail,
bridge stones and others to pave and shut up with,
stone apple, stone basil, beech, berry, stone brake,
stone bramble, stone fern, lichen, liverwort, pippin, and root,
concretion of the body, as blind as cold as deaf,
all earth a quarry, all life a labor, stone-faced, stone-drunk
with hope that this assemblage, taken together, would become
a shrine or holy place, an ossuary, immovable and sacred,
like the stone that marked the path of the sun as it entered the human dawn.

Image: very violent—war; I'm picturing a dusty landscape.

Interpret: References to something outside the poem? What?

Image: Suddenly really abstract, in the middle of all this physical imagery . . .

Interpret: a long list of rock types. Can picture a ruined shipyard, but a ruined choir?

Interpret: Is this a story or a progression of related images? What's tying it all together?

Words: Look up "scriptorium"—what do these three words have in common?

Words: Another list of rock types . . . a break? or a type of momentum?

Sound: Repetition of "s" sounds . . . slows the line down—emphasis?

Interpret: She is clearly not talking just about stones—"all earth, all life" means this is about everything.

Image: Unexpected words . . . words for a person, not nature.

Interpret: Does "museum" equal "rock collection"?

Words: look up "culvert" and "abbatoir." Why such complicated words?

Image: shift in image . . . tanks on rock to ink on cloth. Change to softer tone?

Words: Types of rocks, I think—but why these? Sound of the words, maybe, more than the rocks themselves.

Words: "tomb" repeated, and lots of "grave" imagery. Is the collection a "museum" because something/someone has died?

Rhyme: "sandstone toe"—the sounds of the words are the same—almost a relief after the list of weird rock names.

Interpret: Significance of two different religious references in a row?

Words: repetition of "stone"—gives the impression of hardness over and over, even though basil, beech, and berry are nice images. But then, liverwort, lichen, and bramble aren't so pretty.

Interpret: great image!—a stone catching the sunlight in the morning. But here, it's not just any morning—it's the beginning of the whole human race. So maybe even though there is so much death and war earlier, it shows these stones and the human race still go on? I never quite figured out who the poet was addressing—"this is *your* museum of stones." The textbook says it's a dead friend of the poet, but I didn't get many clues about the "you." Still, the poem seems less personal and more universal to me.

THE CRAFT OF POETRY

Robert Burns is perhaps best known for his work with Scottish folk songs, and what we first notice in the seemingly simple work that follows is the rhythm and rhyme in the four-line stanzas of "O my luve's like a red, red rose." The poem is more a description of an emotion than an emotion itself. The only three-syllable word in the sixteen lines is "melodie"—a somewhat formal way of saying *song*. Burns wrote in Scottish dialect; the poem can be (and has been) set to music.

Robert Burns (1759–1796)

One of Scotland's greatest poets, Robert Burns was born to a struggling tenant farm family. At age fifteen, Burns fell in love and consequently wrote his first poem. He became notorious for his love affairs, which shocked the Calvinist society surrounding him, and he cultivated his poetry based on his own broad reading. He published *Poems* in 1786 and became immensely popular in Edinburgh. But perhaps his greatest achievement was his preservation and creation of folk songs, which he did formally for two anthologies, *The Scots Musical Museum* and *Select Collection of Original Scottish Airs.* Burns is known for writing in Scots, an English dialect spoken by commoners and by eighteenth-century nobility. Burns's songs are still widely known today, especially "Auld Lang Syne."

AS YOU READ Note that the speaker addresses both his lover and an audience over her shoulder; the first stanza is a kind of general declaration, and the next three are specific to "my bonnie lass" herself.

O my luve's like a red, red rose (1794)

O my luve's like a red, red rose,
  That's newly sprung in June.
O my luve's like the melodie
  That's sweetly play'd in tune.

As fair art thou, my bonnie lass,
  So deep in luve am I;
And I will luve thee still, my dear,
  Till a' the seas gang dry.

Till a' the seas gang dry, my dear,
  And the rocks melt wi' the sun;
And I will luve thee still, my dear,
  While the sands o' life shall run.

And fare thee weel, my only luve!
  And fare thee weel awhile!
And I will come again, my luve,
  Tho' it were ten thousand mile.

Writing from Reading

Summarize

1 If this poem is a declaration, what is the speaker declaring? How long does he indicate his love will last?

2 How far would he be willing to travel to see his love again?

Analyze Craft

3 Burns compiled and created Scottish folk songs in the Scots dialect. What about this poem seems musical to you?

4 What two things does the poet compare to his "luve" in the first stanza? What do those comparisons help him accomplish in this poem? How does it set the stage for the rest of the poem?

5 When is the rose that he compares his love to "sprung"? Why would the month be significant?

Analyze Voice

6 What words does the speaker use that show how "deep in luve am I"?

Synthesize Summary and Analysis

7 Burns has chosen the form of a song to declare his love. How does this choice make his declaration convincing?

Interpret the Poem

8 Although the poem is clearly a love poem, how would you characterize the love here? Do we know why the speaker is leaving his lover? Do we need to?

Here's a very different kind of love poem—one written by a son to the memory of his father. For Robert Burns, the problem with his "luve" is one of distance, and he promises he will return; for Robert Hayden, in the twentieth century, the distance is unbridgeable because his parent is dead. This is never made *explicit* in the fourteen lines that follow, but the sense of loss is *implicit* throughout, a muted if not mute regret that the poet failed to tell his father, "Thanks."

Robert Hayden (1913–1980)

Though uneducated themselves, Robert Hayden's parents encouraged their son's intellectual efforts in his childhood spent in Detroit, Michigan. Of African-American descent, Hayden resisted a narrow view of his work as that of a "black" poet, even though it frequently engages with African-American history and experience. Hayden earned a bachelor's degree from Wayne State University in Detroit. He then worked for the Federal Writers' Project, published his first collection of poems in 1940, and married before earning his master's degree at the University of Michigan, where he studied with W. H. Auden. Known for his formal poetry on a range of subjects—including historical figures like Phillis Wheatley and Malcolm X—Hayden earned the position of Poet Laureate from 1976 to 1978. Aside from poetry, Hayden made his career as a professor of English at Fisk University and the University of Michigan.

AS YOU READ Try to hear the speaker's tone of voice, the sorrow here expressed.

Those Winter Sundays (1962)

Sundays too my father got up early
and put his clothes on in the blueblack cold,
then with cracked hands that ached
from labor in the weekday weather made
banked fires blaze. No one ever thanked him.

I'd wake and hear the cold splintering, breaking.
When the rooms were warm, he'd call,
and slowly I would rise and dress,
fearing the chronic angers of that house,

Speaking indifferently to him,
who had driven out the cold
and polished my good shoes as well.
What did I know, what did I know
of love's austere and lonely offices?

Writing from Reading

Summarize

1 The poem's first two words are "Sundays too." This suggests that what he does on Sunday morning he does the other six days of the week. What evidence do we have of the socio-economic circumstance of this family? Is there a furnace, for instance?

2 What might be some of "the chronic angers of that house"?

Analyze Craft

3 Imagine for a moment that the poem has been written in the present tense. Its title would be "These Winter Sundays," and the first line would report "my father gets up early." How does the use of the past tense instead suggest that these are memories, and that "No one ever thanked him" means they cannot do so now?

Analyze Voice

4 Notice the way the poet repeats his regretful, "What did I know, what did I know . . ." Does this provide a kind of emphasis, and, if you were to read it aloud, where would the emphasis change?

Synthesize Summary and Analysis

5 We know that this is a Sunday and that the father polishes his son's "good shoes." Does this suggest the family will soon go to church?

Interpret the Poem

6 What does the poet mean by, and what do we learn about, "love's austere and lonely offices"? And why did Hayden choose to use that final word?

Ezra Pound writes in his eccentric but illuminating study *ABC of Reading*, "That poetry is best which is closest to music. . . ." Most people think of "lyric" as the words to a song, yet it is, in fact, a form of poetry, playing the same music from the ancient time of Sappho to the present moment: a song of love and loss. The speaker of the following fragment finds herself in darkness, in the middle of the night. She yearns for company (with the presence in the visible sky of the constellation known as the Pleiades, or the Seven Sisters, suggesting it might be female company she desires). Here too the subject is isolation, some twenty-five hundred years before "Those Winter Sundays," and here too the context is different—but the tone of the two poems is in many ways the same.

> "I just was entranced by [the poetry] I read, and I read it with a kind of fury. I felt kind of saved by it. Then I began to read poems that made a tremendous difference to me; I felt almost as if I had written them." Conversation with Edward Hirsch

Sappho (c. 630–570 B.C.E.)

Although much of her biography is speculation rather than fact, we know Sappho lived on the island of Lesbos in ancient Greece. She was exiled to Sicily for a time before returning to Lesbos, where she had a husband and daughter. She also ran a school for girls. Sappho has been recognized throughout the centuries as the greatest ancient female poet, one whom Plato referred to as the "tenth muse" (in Greek mythology, there are nine). Her verse, which would have been sung to the accompaniment of the lyre, is direct and simple but overflows with emotion. Today, only fragments of Sappho's work survive, although in her lifetime, she likely produced nine collections of poetry. Sappho died either of old age or, according to legend, from jumping off a cliff for love of Phaon, a young boatman.

AS YOU READ Notice the way the last line rises up and sweeps back against the first few lines, qualifying what went before.

A Fragment (c. 600 B.C.E.)

The moon has set,
The Pleiades have gone,
Midnight, and the hours pass,
I lie in my bed alone . . .

—adapted by Alan Cheuse

Writing from Reading

Summarize

1 Where is the speaker, and what time is it?

Analyze Craft

2 What significance does the time have?

Analyze Voice

3 Who is the speaker? What is her lament?

Synthesize Summary and Analysis

4 What are the Pleiades? How do the night sky, the moon, and the Pleiades support the mood of the poem?

5 How would you describe the tone of the poem?

6 How does the setting of the poem reflect the loneliness of the speaker?

Interpret the Poem

7 This is only a fragment, which has been recovered, of a longer work by Sappho. Many of her fragments, on similar themes, are all that we have of Sappho's work. Judging from this brief work, is her loneliness temporary, or will it be relieved?

There is more than mere sentiment or sentimentality in this poem. Everyone feels this variety of loneliness at some point in a lifetime. The poet finds a way to give that shared feeling or emotion a particular expression. If Sappho had written "with you" as opposed to "alone," the whole feel of the poem would change, and the mood of melancholy would likely be supplanted by one of celebration. If the last line read "with my dog Spot" or "with my daughter" or "with a man I met an hour ago," the tone would also shift; each word *matters,* and the word *alone* gives the fragment its negative force.

> "Reading good poetry helps a person feel less lonely. It's the evidence that someone else has felt what we feel, knowing what we know." Conversation with Jane Hirshfield

William Wordsworth, the nineteenth-century British poet, defined the essence of a poem as "the spontaneous overflow of powerful feelings . . . recollected in tranquility." Traditionally, the **lyric** poem speaks of the poet's misery over the loss of love or the loss of his or her affections toward the object of his or her love. Wordsworth dramatizes in the poem that follows the process by which a past event becomes transformed. The poet can nonetheless remember from his "couch" what it felt like to be out on a hillside, surrounded by flowers. (This poem is also known by the alternative title "The Daffodils.") The twentieth-century American poet John Ciardi spoke about the movement at the end of a poem as the "wave" that doubles back and breaks against all the lines that come before it. By reconstructing what he felt, the poet helps us as readers feel it anew: an experience described is an experience shared.

William Wordsworth (1770–1850)

One of the major British Romantic poets, Wordsworth was born—and lived most of his life—in the Lake District of England. He and Samuel Taylor Coleridge developed a close friendship built on mutual admiration of each other's poetry. Together, they published *Lyrical Ballads* (1798), which contained one of Wordsworth's major poems, "Tintern Abbey." A poet with a deep reverence for nature and an interest in the individual, Wordsworth's touchstone work is "The Prelude" (1850), a long autobiographical poem full of reflections on past emotions. Although Wordsworth grew in stature and was named Poet Laureate in 1848, the quality of his poetry declined after 1810, perhaps because he relied on remembered emotions of his youth—an exhaustible resource—to fuel his poetry. Still, he shaped the course of British poetry with his famous "Preface" to *Lyrical Ballads* in which he argued that poetry should be about emotions and everyday experience, rather than the intellect and classical forms—a dictum Wordsworth followed in his own work.

AS YOU READ **Notice how perfect yet casual the rhyme appears to be. No one without conscious intention and considerable effort could shape past emotion into such a work of art.**

I Wandered Lonely As a Cloud (1804)

I wandered lonely as a cloud
That floats on high o'er vales and hills,
When all at once I saw a crowd,
A host, of golden daffodils;
Beside the lake, beneath the trees,
Fluttering and dancing in the breeze.

Continuous as the stars that shine
And twinkle on the milky way,
They stretched in never-ending line
Along the margin of a bay:
Ten thousand saw I at a glance,
Tossing their heads in sprightly dance.

The waves beside them danced, but they
Out-did the sparkling leaves in glee;
A poet could not be but gay,
In such a jocund company;
I gazed—and gazed—but little thought
What wealth the show to me had brought:

For oft, when on my couch I lie
In vacant or in pensive mood,
They flash upon that inward eye
Which is the bliss of solitude;
And then my heart with pleasure fills,
And dances with the daffodils.

Writing from Reading

Summarize

1 What does the speaker mean by "that inward eye/ Which is the bliss of solitude"?

Analyze Craft

2 Which words are formal here ("sprightly," "jocund," "pensive," etc.) and which ones less so ("lonely," "twinkle," "pleasure," etc.)?

3 How do the words chosen in the rhymes convey a casualness that supports the idea of "wandering" on a hill?

Analyze Voice

4 Why does the speaker begin by mentioning he is lonely? Where does the tone change? What is the overall tone of this poem?

Synthesize Summary and Analysis

5 Where does the poet locate himself in the first three stanzas; where is he in the fourth?

6 How does Wordsworth's loneliness compare with that of Sappho?

Interpret the Poem

7 Why are daffodils a consolation?

Next come two examples of the art of "shaping" personal expression to suggest more than what the words say. In each case the poet addresses both the self and the reader, describing an encounter—with a body of water as well as a journey—in language that might seem casual but is carefully arranged. As Mary Oliver writes in her *Rules for the Dance: A Handbook for Writing and Reading Metrical Verse:* "Every poem is music—a determined, persuasive, reliable, enthusiastic, and crafted music. Without an understanding of this music, Shakespeare is only the sense we can make of him; he is the wisdom without the shapeliness, which is one half of the poem."

> "I've been looking for a safe place all my life, a refuge. . . . It might have something to do with the possibility that my own identity was nearly erased when I was born. Many Chinese lost their lives in Indonesia. . . . Maybe that's what . . . poetry is about ultimately . . . discovering who we are, being friends with who we are, getting friendly with your own mind."
>
> Conversation with Li-Young Lee

The music of "At Blackwater Pond" is easily "one half of the poem"; read it to yourself aloud and notice where your breath starts, stops. When the poet asks "what is that beautiful thing that just happened?" is she describing a cold drink of water or perhaps the effect of poetry itself? The "tossed waters" that "have settled after a night of rain" are similar to Wordsworth's "powerful feelings . . . recollected in tranquility"; here the natural world is, again, full of mystery for the poet who observes it, and one poem responds to the other.

Mary Oliver (b. 1935)

Mary Oliver was born in Maple Heights, Ohio, and spent part of her teenage years living in the home of Edna St. Vincent Millay, where she helped organize the poet's remaining papers. She attended Ohio State University and Vassar College but received a degree from neither. Oliver's first collection of poetry, *No Voyage, and Other Poems,* was published in 1963. Since then she has published more than a dozen books of poetry, winning such prestigious honors as the Pulitzer Prize for Poetry for *American Primitive* (1983), the L. L. Winship/PEN New England Award for *House of Light* (1990), and the National Book Award for *New and Selected Poems* (1992). Oliver has taught at several institutions, including Case Western Reserve University, Bucknell University, and Bennington College in Vermont; she currently lives in Massachusetts.

AS YOU READ What "voice" are you hearing in the poem—who speaks to whom, and why? As in the case of Wordsworth, this poet also addresses both the self and the reader, describing an encounter—with a lake as well as a poem.

At Blackwater Pond (1993)

At Blackwater Pond the tossed waters have settled
after a night of rain.
I dip my cupped hands. I drink
a long time. It tastes
like stone, leaves, fire. It falls cold
into my body, waking the bones. I hear them
deep inside me, whispering
oh what is that beautiful thing
that just happened?

Writing from Reading

Summarize

1 What did the speaker literally do at the pond?

2 What did the water taste like?

3 Drinking from the lake awakened "the bones . . . deep inside me." What kind of experience is the poet having as she drinks from the pond?

Analyze Craft

4 In six lines, this poem includes six sentences. Given the experience the poet recalls, should the poem have been longer?

5 Discuss the tenses in this poem—what happens when.

Analyze Voice

6 The poem is, in some ways, like a prayer. How does the poet establish a spiritual or meditative tone?

Synthesize Summary and Analysis

7 What do you think "stone, leaves, fire" taste like, and how do bones wake and whisper? Describe what's "normal" in this poem and what seems most strange.

Interpret the Poem

8 What is transformed in the speaker?

William Butler Yeats (1865–1939)

An Irish poet of unparalleled importance to twentieth-century British literature, William Butler Yeats spent his childhood in Dublin, Sligo, and London. Of a religious nature but not devoted to one religion, Yeats explored folklore, mysticism, and neoplatonism, which enabled him to create a set of unique symbols and imagery in his poems. Yeats managed to combine a sense of Romantic dreaminess with colloquialism, clarity, and Celtic influence, making his poetry unlike any other. Also unlike most other poets, Yeats perfected his style in his later years, bringing his talent to full fruition in collections such as *The Tower* (1928) and *The Winding Stair* (1933). Yeats led an active life, taking part in the movement for Irish nationalism and co-founding the Irish National Theatre, in addition to writing plays. He was awarded the Nobel Prize in Literature in 1923.

AS YOU READ **Consider the poem in terms of time, not space. What refers to the past, the present, and what will happen in the future?**

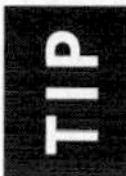

FOR INTERACTIVE READING . . . Note each time the word *song* or *singing* is used. Track the changes in the way the word *song* is used in the poem.

Sailing to Byzantium (1927)

I

That is no country for old men. The young
In one another's arms, birds in the trees
—Those dying generations—at their song,
The salmon-falls, the mackerel-crowded seas,
Fish, flesh, or fowl, commend all summer long
Whatever is begotten, born, and dies.
Caught in that sensual music all neglect
Monuments of unaging intellect.

II

An aged man is but a paltry thing,
A tattered coat upon a stick, unless
Soul clap its hands and sing, and louder sing
For every tatter in its mortal dress,
Nor is there singing school but studying
Monuments of its own magnificence;
And therefore I have sailed the seas and come
To the holy city of Byzantium.

III

O sages standing in God's holy fire
As in the gold mosaic of a wall,
Come from the holy fire, perne in a gyre,
And be the singing-masters of my soul.
Consume my heart away; sick with desire
And fastened to a dying animal
It knows not what it is; and gather me
Into the artifice of eternity.

IV

Once out of nature I shall never take
My bodily form from any natural thing,
But such a form as Grecian goldsmiths make
Of hammered gold and gold enameling
To keep a drowsy Emperor awake;
Or set upon a golden bough to sing
To lords and ladies of Byzantium
Of what is past, or passing, or to come.

Writing from Reading

Summarize

1 As a "voyage" poem, what journey does it describe the poet taking? Where does he arrive?

Analyze Craft

2 How does the use of the triad (three terms in a row)—"what is past, or passing, or to come," "fish, flesh, or fowl"—affect the music of the poem? Can you point to other triads in the poem, where phrases repeat each other or vary only slightly?

3 How is the idea of a song used in this poem? In stanza I, for example, there's a "song" of "sensual music"; in stanza II this modulates to "sing, and louder sing" and "singing school." The "singing-masters" of line 20 instruct the poet how "to sing" and "keep a drowsy Emperor awake."

Analyze Voice

4 What does Yeats feel about the journey to Byzantium?

Synthesize Summary and Analysis

5 What does Yeats mean by "*That* is no country for old men"? Does he mean his native Ireland or also life in the world at his age?

Interpret the Poem

6 What is meant by "the artifice of eternity"? How is eternity artificial instead of natural?

This is one of the most important and complex poems in Yeats's career; we can only scratch its surface here. Look at the way Yeats modulates from "old men" in the first stanza to "a tattered coat upon a stick" in the second, in which the "aged man" has become a scarecrow. In the third stanza, the scarecrow is burned up and melted down; the poet asks the "sages" (wise men) to "consume my heart away." By the last stanza, however, far from frightening the birds away, the poet has joined up with them and been "set upon a golden bough to sing." So the transformation of the "dying animal" into "such a form as Grecian goldsmiths make" is a journey *out* of nature and "into the artifice of eternity." The poem's subject is, appropriately enough, the very life cycle he will leave behind: "whatever is begotten, born, and dies."

In "Sailing to Byzantium," Yeats refers to the absence in Ireland of a "singing school." By the time of his death, he had gone a good distance to remedying that absence and was recognized worldwide as a major representative—perhaps the twentieth century's foremost practitioner—of the art of poetry. So one way to read his poems, as was the case with Mary Oliver, is to think about the way he built them word by word, and what the artifact itself reveals about its making. Poets often write about the art of poetry, addressing or revising or invoking their great predecessors, and in the chapters that follow there are several examples of this variety of conversation. The first comes from a poet featured in chapter 19.

Stephen Dunn (b. 1939)

For a brief biography and A Conversation on Writing with Stephen Dunn, see chapter 19.

AS YOU READ Notice the use of humor and then the "awful" shift in the last lines of the poem.

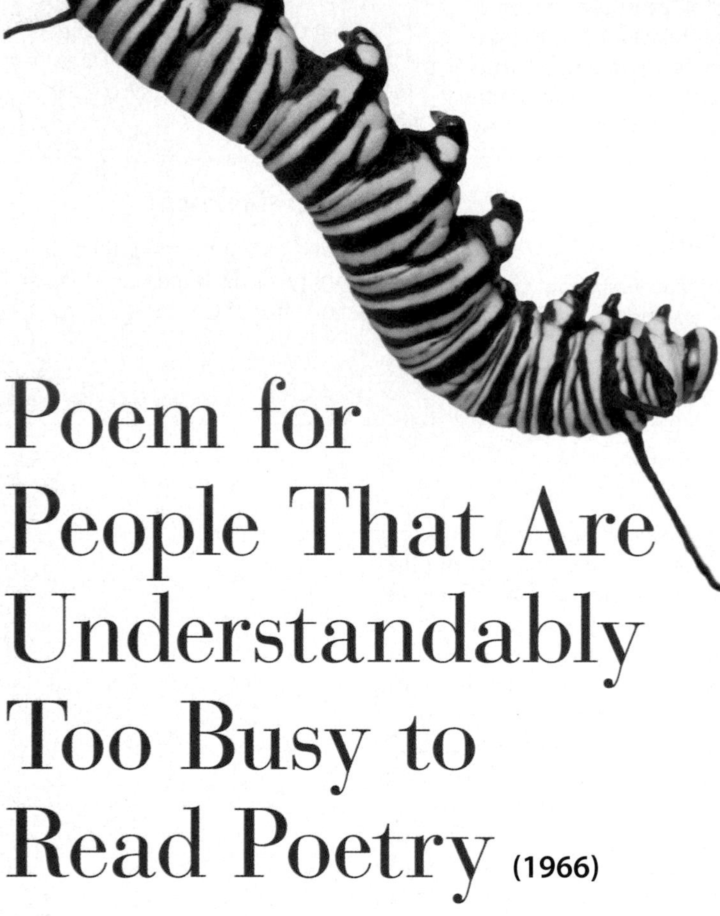

Poem for People That Are Understandably Too Busy to Read Poetry (1966)

Relax. This won't last long.
Or if it does, or if the lines
make you sleepy or bored,
give in to sleep, turn on
the T.V., deal the cards.
This poem is built to withstand
such things. Its feelings
cannot be hurt. They exist
somewhere in the poet,
and I am far away.
Pick it up anytime. Start it
in the middle if you wish.
It is as approachable as melodrama,
and can offer you violence
if it is violence you like. Look,
there's a man on a sidewalk;
the way his leg is quivering
he'll never be the same again.
This is your poem
and I know you're busy at the office
or the kids are into your last good nerve.
Maybe it's sex you've always wanted.
Well, *they lie together*
like the party's unbuttoned coats,
slumped on the bed,
waiting for drunken arms to move them.
I don't think you want me to go on;
everyone has his expectations, but this
is a poem for the entire family.
Right now, Budweiser
is dripping from a waterfall,
deodorants are hissing into armpits
of people you resemble,
and *the two lovers are dressing now,*
saying farewell.
I don't know what music this poem
can come up with, but clearly
it's needed. For it's apparent
they will never see each other again

and we need music for this
because there never was music when he or she
left *you* standing on that corner.
You see, I want this poem to be nicer
than life. I want you to look at it
when anxiety zigzags your stomach
and the last tranquilizer is gone
and you need someone to tell you
I'll be here when you want me
like the sound inside a shell.
The poem is saying that to you now.
But don't give up anything for this poem.
It doesn't expect much. It will never say more
than listening can explain.
Just keep it in your attache case
or in your house. And if you're not asleep
by now, or bored beyond sense,
the poem wants you to laugh. Laugh at
yourself, laugh at this poem, at all poetry.
Come on:

Good. Now here's what poetry can do.
Imagine you're a caterpillar:
There's an awful shrug and, suddenly,
you're beautiful for as long as you live.

Writing from Reading

Summarize

1 The poet says of his work that "It doesn't expect much. It will never say more / than listening can explain." What does that mean about poetry in general and "this poem" in particular?

Analyze Craft

2 Discuss the language of this poem—sophisticated or familiar?—and how it achieves its effects.

Analyze Voice

3 Who is the speaker addressing?

4 Is the speaker serious? Point to places in the poem that indicate the speaker is serious or, conversely, playful.

Synthesize Summary and Analysis

5 You might want to look at the poem "Leda and the Swan" by William Butler Yeats, in the next chapter, and contrast and compare the two poets' uses of tone and imagery.

Interpret the Poem

6 "This is your poem," says the speaker, and then compares his reader to a caterpillar. What does he mean by "awful shrug," and what will happen next?

16 Going Further with Reading

Reading in Context

"THE way to read a poem," Robert Frost wrote, "is in the light of all the other poems ever written." Though none of us will ever know all the other poems ever written, it helps to have some sense of what went before. Understanding its tradition and **context**—the situation of, or reason for, the writing—also makes poetry richer. A first reading can bring you close to the music of speech. A second critical reading can help you see how the work has been constructed to achieve that music. A contextual reading will situate the poem for you; as is the case with fiction or drama, poems hold clues to their meaning embedded in each line.

Some of our most beautiful poetry was written in a different context from our own. William Shakespeare, the "Bard of Avon," was at work four hundred years ago, and much of our language has changed. He was writing for *his* audience, and the Elizabethan diction (or choice of words) that he and they found natural no longer sounds natural to us. The Elizabethan language in the following poem goes against the grain of the modern ear, and its diction may present a barrier to understanding. The strategy behind the poem—especially the way Shakespeare praises his lady love's qualities by playing them down—may seem confusing as well. This interactive reading can provide some tips for understanding the words artists used in other centuries and seeing the craft at work in poetry outside our own day.

CONTINUED ON PAGE 24

"I read it over and over . . . at the end it seemed to me that the poet had written something that was not [just] literature, that this man had really seen something . . . and if I could understand what he had seen, I would have a way of dealing with this pain in my heart. . . . It felt like listening to the most profound, gorgeous music. I could hear it and know that it was crucial to my life."

Conversation with Stephen Mitchell, available on video at www.mhhe.com/delbanco1e

An Interactive Reading of William Shakespeare's "My mistress' eyes are nothing like the sun"

My mistress' eyes are nothing like the sun;
Coral is far more red than her lips' red;
If snow be white, why then her breasts are dun;
If hairs be wires, black wires grow on her head.
I have seen roses damasked, red and white,
But no such roses see I in her cheeks;
And in some perfumes is there more delight
Than in the breath that from my mistress reeks.
I love to hear her speak, yet well I know
That music hath a far more pleasing sound;
I grant I never saw a goddess go;
My mistress when she walks treads on the ground.
  And yet, by heaven, I think my love as rare
  As any she belied with false compare.

Paraphrase: My lover's eyes are different from the sun. *Different how?*

Words: Coral is bright . . . he's saying her lips are less bright than coral?

Voice: "be white" and "be wires" . . . this is how Elizabethans spoke naturally, ok.

Interpret: Black wires grow on her head? No roses in her cheeks? Not the romantic comparisons I expected from Shakespeare.

Words: ???—look this up. I think it's a patterned kind of linen.

Rhyme: same sounds as "cheeks" and "reeks"—ties all of it together.

Context: means "has." Sounds old-fashioned, but was it back then?

Interpret: This last line is hard. What does "any" refer to? Maybe any of his other loves: "my love is as rare as any other lover . . ."?

Words: Look up "belied." "False compare" is maybe short for comparison? So, a false comparison?

Figures of Speech: Poem seems to mostly be a list of comparisons.

Words: I don't know this word, but it must describe her body.

Rhyme: "dun" rhymes with "sun" here . . . and "red" rhymes with "head." I can hear the rhythm.

Rhyme: "white" and "delight"; "cheeks" and "reeks" . . . more rhyming words.

Voice: inverted words here . . . common back then, or done on purpose?

Context: "reeks"—does that mean the same thing in Shakespeare's time as now?!

Interpret: all these negative comparisons are funny—a poem making fun of love poems: an anti-love Poem.

Interpret: not sure I get this line—a goddess go? go where?

Words: means walking, I guess. Elizabethan word.

Interpret: Last lines set apart—probably tie up the whole poem.

"I think my love as rare"—if something is rare, it's usually treasured because it's one of a kind. So . . . he's saying, 'I think my mistress, whom I love, is one of a kind in a way that makes me value her.'

"And yet" means "despite all that preceded." So, she's *different* from all the other poets' lovers . . . but he loves her because of that.

CONTINUED FROM PAGE 22

What Shakespeare suggests here is that too many poets indulge in "false compare." You don't need to belie the facts by comparing your mistress's eyes to the sun, her lips to coral, her body to snow—and so on and so forth. Her cheeks contain no actual roses; her breath is not actual perfume. She is *human*, not a goddess, and real love consists of recognizing and admitting this; the genuine commitment to truth telling is one of the hallmarks of art. It's not an accident that the two uses of the crucial word and the two phrases in which it's embedded—"I *love* to hear her speak" and "I think my *love* as rare . . ."—are reality based and straightforward in the choice of words.

A world away from Shakespeare's formal approach to the question of love is singer-songwriter-novelist-poet Leonard Cohen's brief contemporary poem that plays off against the Shakespearean sonnet. It's possible the language here will sound obscure to some English speaker four hundred years in the future—but to our ears the diction is natural and plain. Maybe the word *compare*—used three times in the poem's six lines—will confuse a future reader, but the idea of comparison is likely to endure. Poets often write this sort of echoing response to previous poems; it's a kind of conversation with what went before.

Leonard Cohen (b. 1934)

Poet, novelist, and singer-songwriter, Leonard Cohen was born in Montreal, Canada, to Jewish parents. He attended McGill University in Montreal and published his first book of poetry, *Let Us Compare Mythologies* (1956), while still an undergraduate. His next collection, *The Spice-Box of Earth* (1961), earned him wide recognition throughout Canada. Cohen spent much of the sixties living on Hydra, a Greek island, where he enjoyed semi-isolation and published one more collection of poetry, *Flowers for Hitler* (1964), and two novels. In 1967, he relocated to New York City to pursue a music career. He has since produced eleven albums, and at age seventy-four continues to write, record, and perform music.

AS YOU READ Note the reference to Shakespeare's poem "My mistress' eyes are nothing like the sun"—as well, no doubt, as the sonnet "Shall I compare thee to a summer's day?"(chapter 18)—and the twist in the last lines.

For Anne (1961)

With Annie gone,
Whose eyes to compare
With the morning sun?

Not that I did compare,
But I do compare
Now that she's gone.

Writing from Reading

Summarize

1 What does the speaker think about now that his love has left? And what does the shift in naming—the title uses the formal "Anne," the poem itself calls her "Annie"—suggest?

Analyze Craft

2 Cohen is using Shakespeare's famous comparison as a starting point. How does the comparison change over the course of "For Anne"?

Analyze Voice

3 Cohen is a songwriter. The music suggests a rhythm and you move to it, sometimes silently, internally, sometimes by snapping your fingers and stamping your feet to the beat. Can you imagine this poem sung?

Synthesize Summary and Analysis

4 Would you be able to understand this poem without knowledge of what went before—Shakespeare's poems, for example?

Interpret the Poem

5 Would it affect your hearing of the voice of the speaker if the poem were set to music? Does the speaker want his lost love to come back to him? How do we know?

FORMS OF POETRY

We are much the richer for literature's variety and range. In James Joyce's novel *A Portrait of the Artist As a Young Man,* the main character—an intense young writer in the making named Stephen Dedalus—lectures his schoolmates about the three modes of creative expression. These are, according to him, lyric, epic, and dramatic. Of the epic and dramatic modes we'll have more to say later on; lyric—according to Joyce

> "The way to study a poem is to read the poem as you would anything else. There's not necessarily a code or a puzzle. You take in the lines and often read it aloud and pause at the end of the lines just a little so that you get a sense of . . . the music that the lines establish in the poem. Then read it again, and think about it, and let your mind drift and be open. A reading will become available to you." Conversation with Carolyn Forché

and Dedalus—comes first. It is "the simplest verbal vesture of an instant of emotion, a rhythmical cry such as ages ago cheered on the man who pulled at the oar or dragged stones up a slope. He who utters it is more conscious of the instant of emotion than of himself as feeling emotion."

Lyric

A **lyric** is a short poem with a central pictorial image written in an *uninflected* voice—by which we mean a voice that's both direct and personal (usually using the first-person pronoun to create an intimate point of view). As the name implies, a lyric was originally sung to the accompaniment of a lyre; this was surely the case with the following work, from the Song of Solomon. A lyric poem relies on music, but it also conjures up a series of visual emblems—images to which our emotions adhere. In this way, whatever feelings the words of the poem create for you become crystallized in pictorial terms: we *see* as well as *hear* what the poet tries to say. The great love poem that follows was translated by a committee of scholars, under the sponsorship of King James I and for the King James Version of the Bible.

"I didn't start learning to read poetry in English—although I was reading the Bible, I guess. I was reading the Psalms and the Gospels and Genesis and Exodus, and those books just knocked me out. I thought they were weird and mysterious and otherworldly." Conversation with Li-Young Lee

In addition to considering the audience for whom a work was written, we have the added consideration that this is a sacred work, a poem written in celebration of God. (Indeed, the love of God and the secular devotion to "my love" become somehow *conflated,* or made one and the same; the singer celebrates both. There's no separation of body and soul or sacred and profane; this lyric conjoins them in praise.) How does such knowledge deepen our reading of this work? Does it feel modern? If so, what makes it feel modern? The answers to these questions help us place a poem in the context of its own tradition, in this case the tradition of lyric poetry, and help us read other lyric poems in the light of at least this one poem, if not "in the light of all the other poems ever written."

AS YOU READ **Imagine that you hold a lyre—or, in the contemporary moment, a guitar—and sing these lines. What kind of melody would be most fitting here?**

Song of Solomon 4:1–7

—from the King James Bible *[Behold, thou art fair, my love]* (1611)

Behold, thou art fair, my love; behold, thou art fair; thou hast doves' eyes within thy
locks: thy hair is as a flock of goats, that appear from mount Gilead.
Thy teeth are like a flock of sheep that are even shorn, which came up from the
washing; whereof every one bear twins, and none is barren among them.
Thy lips are like a thread of scarlet, and thy speech is comely: thy temples are like a
piece of a pomegranate within thy locks.
Thy neck is like the tower of David builded for an armoury, whereon there hang a
thousand bucklers, all shields of mighty men.

Thy two breasts are like two young roes that are twins, which feed among the lilies.
Until the day break, and the shadows flee away, I will get me to the mountain of
myrrh, and to the hill of frankincense.
Thou art all fair, my love; there is no spot in thee.

Writing from Reading

Summarize

1 What kinds of comparisons does the poet-singer use to address his God?

Analyze Craft

2 The poet compares parts of his beloved's body to various animals. List these. What is the effect of comparing his love this way?

Analyze Voice

3 How does the poet's deep love affect the way he sings? Can the poem be read the way such poems as William Shakespeare's and Leonard Cohen's can be read—as the specific discussion of an individual "she"?

Synthesize Summary and Analysis

4 Singing to his God, the poet dramatizes his emotion by a series of striking images. What does this technique accomplish?

Interpret the Poem

5 What is the context for this poem? Why do you imagine the singer-poet chooses to express his love in this way?

We looked at D. H. Lawrence's short story "Odour of Chrysanthemums" (chapter 9); now consider a poem by the same author. (Many other authors in this volume—Margaret Atwood, Joyce Carol Oates, and John Updike, for example—write both prose fiction and verse.) "Piano" attests to the power of music and how it takes a listener back to "the old Sunday evenings at home."

D. H. Lawrence (1885–1930)

David Herbert Lawrence was born in the coal mining district of Eastwood, Nottinghamshire, in the center of England, his father a hard-drinking coal miner and his mother a schoolteacher. He attended high school there and went on to Nottingham University, from which he graduated in his early twenties with a teaching certificate. A few years later, after he had moved to London and taken up a teaching position, he came under the tutelage of writer and magazine editor Ford Madox Ford, who published Lawrence in the English Review (see below). By 1910 Lawrence had published his first novel, The White Peacock, and was entirely committed to the writing life. After the death of his mother from cancer, he published his autobiographical masterpiece *Sons and Lovers* (1913), and this was followed by other major titles such as *The Rainbow* (1915), *Women in Love* (1920), *Aaron's Rod* (1922), *The Plumed Serpent* (1926) and, perhaps most notoriously, *Lady Chatterly's Lover*, in 1928. This last book created a scandal, because of its frank sexuality as well as its discussion of class; the "lady's" lover is a gardener, a man beneath her standing in society. In his personal life, as well, Lawrence broke social taboos; he ran off with

Frieda von Richthofen Weekley, the wife of his university language professor. Thus began a period of extended travel with only occasional trips back to England; after the end of World War I, he and Frieda embraced a life of self-imposed exile. Mediterranean Europe, Australia, North America and Mexico became Lawrence's shifting home grounds. While living outside of England a torrent of language poured forth from his pen; story after story, poem after poem, novel after novel appeared in rapid succession. He wrote travel books and articles and social tracts and plays. Lawrence used Aztec mythology, British social class distinctions, modern history—just about everything in modern life seemed useful to him in the composition of his work. Above all else—and this is truly why he matters to readers and writers of modern fiction—he found a forceful, direct, and appropriate diction by which to dramatize in physical form the volatile nature of interior states of mind and feeling. Upon his death from tuberculosis at the age of only forty-four he left behind one of the great modern bodies of work.

AS YOU READ **Notice that the title of the poem gets repeated in each of the three stanzas; notice how a musical instrument organizes the dozen lines that constitute the poem.**

Piano (1918)

Softly, in the dusk, a woman is singing to me;
Taking me back down the vista of years, till I see
A child sitting under the piano, in the boom of the tingling strings
And pressing the small, poised feet of a mother who smiles as she sings.

In spite of myself, the insidious mastery of song
Betrays me back, till the heart of me weeps to belong
To the old Sunday evenings at home, with winter outside
And hymns in the cozy parlor, the tinkling piano our guide.

So now it is vain for the singer to burst into clamour
With the great black piano appassionato. The glamour
Of childish days is upon me, my manhood is cast
Down in the flood of remembrance, I weep like a child for the past.

Writing from Reading

Summarize

1 Do these three stanzas tell a story? Summarize the action in each.

Analyze Craft

2 How is the present linked to the past?

Analyze Voice

3 What does the speaker feel toward his remembrance? What words give you clues as to his feeling?

4 Who is speaking in the poem?

Synthesize Summary and Analysis

5 Compare the two experiences of music here, the two pianos, the two musicians.

Interpret the Poem

6 What does the speaker mean by "my manhood is cast down"? What in his childhood does he long for?

The speaker connects the occasion of the woman singing to him in the twilight hour and the set of emotions it calls up: his adult attention to the singer, his child's love for his mother, his deeply felt memories of long-ago evenings—all of this comes together in the image of the "Piano." The musical instrument he looks at and the one the poet remembers are both different and the same. When the speaker weeps "like a child for the past," it's clear that memory takes precedence; "the flood of remembrance" carries him away. So "the glamour" that would seem to attach to a woman "singing to me" in "the great black piano appassionato" in fact belongs to the recollection of past childhood, and the singer who begins "Softly, in the dusk," bursts merely into "clamour" in the present scene.

An image such as "the piano" is central to any lyric poem, and one of the first things to consider is the image pattern you discover as you read. An indelible part of the following poem by William Butler Yeats is the image of a swan, its "feathered glory." Were the poem about Leda to involve the kind of bird Yeats wrote of in "Sailing to Byzantium" (in chapter 15), or if that poem had involved a flock of swans, the poems would be less distinctive. This swan is thoroughly physical, not something "out of nature," and it's useful to contrast the two varieties of birds.

> "I can't imagine any writer or any artist doing anything of any good without knowing some or a lot of what preceded him." Conversation with Stephen Dunn

According to Greek myth, the swan is actually the god Zeus who has descended to earth, and this narrative focuses on a violent act, the disguised god's rape of a human woman. There's a complicated history here, as is often the case in Yeats's work. According to the Greeks, Leda gave birth to two sets of children after having been raped. One egg produced the twins Castor and Pollux, rendered immortal and "heavenly" in the night sky; out of the other came her daughters, Helen and Clytemnaestra—the wives of Menelaeus and Agamemnon respectively. The Trojan War resulted from Helen's abduction by Paris, and "the broken wall, the burning roof and tower, and Agamemnon dead" is how Yeats refers to the nine-year-long siege of the Greeks. This poem talks about "A sudden blow" and "a white rush"; the moment "engenders" consequences that will last long after this particular action is done.

William Butler Yeats (1865–1939)

For a biography of William Butler Yeats, see chapter 15.

AS YOU READ Think about the differences between this bird and the birds described in "Sailing to Byzantium."

Leda and the Swan (1924)

A sudden blow: the great wings beating still
Above the staggering girl, her thighs caressed
By the dark webs, her nape caught in his bill,
He holds her helpless breast upon his breast.

How can those terrified vague fingers push
The feathered glory from her loosening thighs?
And how can body, laid in that white rush,
But feel the strange heart beating where it lies?

A shudder in the loins engenders there
The broken wall, the burning roof and tower
And Agamemnon dead.
Being so caught up,
So mastered by the brute blood of the air,
Did she put on his knowledge with his power
Before the indifferent beak could let her drop?

Writing from Reading

Summarize

1 The poet takes a story from Greek mythology and describes it in close detail. What kind of picture does he paint, and what is going on?

Analyze Craft

2 Parts of this poem are "descriptive" and parts ask questions. What kind of questions get asked?

Analyze Voice

3 The voice has a kind of overview of history—looking back on what would happen as a result of the act described. In terms of point of view, is the speaker omniscient or merely informed? How does this affect the speaker's tone?

Synthesize Summary and Analysis

4 "Knowledge" and "power" would seem to be opposing qualities. Is there a moment when they become one and the same?

Interpret the Poem

5 The "strange heart" and "brute blood" and "indifferent beak" all belong to the animal kingdom. What is the poet saying about the part that animal behavior plays in human behavior?

Because the poet helps us visualize the event, the reader *sees* the questions the poem raises about the relation of wisdom and power, of frailty and strength. Notice also the frank—and frankly daring—sexuality of words like "laid in that white rush" or "the indifferent beak" and how the rhythms of the poem manage to suggest the physical encounter in and of itself. When it's over it's over for Zeus; he simply "let her drop." Yeats creates an image that stays in our mind of this unequal meeting between heaven and earth, this fusion of power and knowledge. If that pictorial image had been presented as an abstraction only, it would not stay with us long.

Epic

Although the image is central to most modern verse, it's important to remember that this was not always the case. Poetry was originally very different. The first widespread use of poetry in Western culture comes in the form of the **epic,** a long narrative poem recited publicly. The earliest audiences took in these poems with their ears, not their eyes. Poetry was an oral and aural (spoken and heard) art form rather than a visual entity or a series of lines transcribed. The audience listened to but could not read them because until the late fourth century B.C. these epics were not written down.

> "Before television and before radio, and really, before typewriters and computers and all of that . . . the ability to stand up in public and speak was very important. . . . The teaching of poetry . . . had to do with learning to recite it, to say it in public." Conversation with Robert Hass

One function of the epic narrative derives from or is connected to the notion of community and a collective hearing. This sort of poem is more *public* rather than *private;* its intended audience is less the individual than the group. Bards called upon the goddess Memory to send down the words of the poem. The values of a culture—its sense of tradition, its very existence—were incorporated and communicated in the medium of poetry. "Voice" is crucial to the form—but less as individual intonation than as a communal voice, a kind of chanted chorus in which everybody learns to "sing along."

In Greece, *rhapsodes,* or reciters of poetry, performed by reciting the thousands and thousands of lines of the Homeric epics of the *Iliad* and the *Odyssey,* the earliest stories to arise in our civilization—with their heroes at the center, their large groups of secondary characters, their multiple sequences of events in war and peace. Great narrative poems such as these may contain powerful images—such as the intricately described shield of Achilles in the *Iliad* and the monstrous Cyclops in the *Odyssey*—but these poems usually derive their power from the strength of the language and the story's sound and flow.

After the two major Greek epic poems, the *Iliad* and the *Odyssey,* comes the *Aeneid,* the epic of the founding of Rome. Each of these three long narratives deals with the relationship between the gods and human beings, the past and present, the values, rules, laws, and customs of civilizations and empires, and the variety of heroes who keep them vital. Several long poems in old English also attempt this fusion of nature and culture. *Beowulf, Sir Gawain and the Green Knight,* and *Le Morte d'Arthur,* the story of Sir King Arthur and the knights of the fabled Round Table, all instruct their audience in the "proper" way to behave.

"Li-Young Lee says . . . memorizing poems . . . is a kind of yoga where you assume the same position, if you will, as the poet. When you memorize a poem . . . you actually inhabit the mind and heart of the poet, and every turn that poet has taken, and it's a remarkably great thing to do. It doesn't seem like it's going to help your writing, but of course it does. It provides syntactical moves and ways of thinking and feeling . . . that would never occur to you on your own. That's what all reading does." Conversation with Marie Howe

The extended poems that come later (such as Geoffrey Chaucer's *Canterbury Tales* and the early Italian Renaissance poet Dante Alighieri's *Divine Comedy*) build on the same principles as those of the ancient epic poets. In *Paradise Lost,* John Milton, the last great poet to create a Christian epic, describes it as justifying God's ways to man, an attempt to clarify the nature of religious and social relations. After Milton this variety of poem more or less disappears, although there do continue to be narratives in verse.

Ironically enough, the epic is the form least natural to modern culture. (Although some contemporary movies have been described as "epic," and may require years to produce and cost hundreds of millions of dollars, they take barely two hours of screen time and are not the kind of art form we mean here.) George Gordon, Lord Byron, takes a sardonic and comical approach to the genre, working with the epic but with a lighter touch. The Greeks traditionally invoked a goddess when they began to sing—and Milton, too, provided a Christian version of "the Goddess of Memory," calling her "Heavenly Muse." Byron, however, starts his long narrative poem "Don Juan" with an insulting address to one of his contemporaries.

George Gordon, Lord Byron (1788–1824)

One of the great English Romantic poets, Lord Byron enjoyed a larger-than-life celebrity status after the publication of the first cantos of "Childe Harold's Pilgrimage" in 1811. His fame came largely from the public conflation of Byron himself with his character creation, the Byronic hero. The Byronic hero is one who stands apart from society, brooding and hating the rest of humankind, whom he considers unable to equal his capacity for passion. Byron's poetry ranges from lyrics that mimic older styles of complimenting women in verse to satires in the style of Pope, to extended poems like his capstone "Don Juan." Byron led a turbulent life up to his death at age thirty-six, while helping Greece gain its independence.

AS YOU READ Enjoy the way the poet in the dedication calls out one of his contemporaries and then calls for a real hero as the poem proper begins.

[Bob Southey! You're a poet]

—*from the Dedication to Don Juan* (1819)

Bob Southey! You're a poet—Poet-laureate,
And representative of all the race;
Although 'tis true that you turn'd out a Tory at
Last,—yours has lately been a common case;
And now, my Epic Renegade! what are ye at?
With all the Lakers, in and out of place?
A nest of tuneful persons, to my eye
Like "four and twenty Blackbirds in a pye;

"Which pye being open'd they began to sing"
(This old song and new simile holds good),
"A dainty dish to set before the King,"
Or Regent, who admires such kind of food;
And Coleridge, too, has lately taken wing,
But like a hawk encumber'd with his hood,
Explaining Metaphysics to the nation—
I wish he would explain his Explanation.

Writing in a time when, as he sees it, poets lack inspiration from the Goddess and in which great heroes no longer can be found, Bryon relies on humor to create a personal epic for his age. Notice how he plays with the nursery rhyme about blackbirds in a pie—saying that "This old song and new simile holds good"—turning the blackbirds into poets. Robert Southey and Samuel Taylor Coleridge, two of Byron's contemporaries, need to have their politics and metaphysics explained, and though he dedicates his lines to them, he does so tongue in cheek.

Here again, context helps. When Byron refers to "the Lakers," he's reporting not on a basketball team but on poets such as William Wordsworth, who liked to walk in England's Lake District. It may also help to know that the name *Southey* would have been pronounced *Suhthee* and that the Poet-laureate holds a position of honor—one that Byron with his scandalous private life could never expect to attain.

[I want a hero]

—*from Don Juan, Canto the First* (1819)

I want a hero: an uncommon want,
When every year and month sends forth a new one,
Till, after cloying the gazettes with cant,
The age discovers he is not the true one;
Of such as these I should not care to vaunt,
I'll therefore take our ancient friend Don Juan—
We all have seen him, in the pantomime,
Sent to the devil somewhat ere his time.

Writing from Reading

Summarize

1 The poet opens a long poem with a dedication and the first stanza. Who and what is he making fun of?

Analyze Craft

2 The Greek epics narrate the deeds of heroes. How does Byron twist the form of an ancient Greek epic?

Analyze Voice

3 What kind of tone does the mix of satire and elevated language create?

Synthesize Summary and Analysis

4 Why does Byron use the epic form in a time when epic has fallen out of fashion?

Interpret the Poem

5 What does the poet have in mind when he speaks of a "hero"? Why does he choose this particular figure—Don Juan—as his subject? Research this figure in the library or on the Internet.

Dramatic

The dramatic poem, also called the **dramatic monologue,** in which a character addresses another character, or the reader, is an offshoot of the epic form and the third of James Joyce's three categories. The notion of "voice" in this case has more to do with impersonation than the personal or lyric "cry" of an individual; the poet assumes the "mask" or "persona" of a character not his or her own (for more on persona, see chapter 19, Voice). In the case of "My Last Duchess," Robert Browning becomes someone altogether other than the poet Robert Browning, creating a character engaged in soliloquy much as might a playwright. What we learn of the Duke here is more than the Duke might wish to confess—his pride and temper, his murderous distrust of his young wife, his chilly desire (stated almost unconsciously in the first line, with the possessive pronoun "my") to treat people as possessions. The "scene" (in Ferrara, Italy) is swiftly set; the speaker walks a silent witness—a kind of stand-in for the reader—through a picture gallery. By the second line, we learn what the title already suggests, that his "last duchess" is dead; near the poem's end, we learn that he's planning to marry again. The man who listens is a negotiator from "the Count your master," a rich man whose daughter the speaker intends to acquire as his next wife.

"In our culture it becomes more and more difficult for us to enter into, imaginatively at least, the consciousness of others. Literature is a way of doing that." Conversation with Carolyn Forché

Robert Browning (1812–1889)

Robert Browning was one of the great Victorian poets, but his fame was eclipsed by that of Elizabeth Barrett (his wife) in his own time; today, however, he is recognized for his innovative use of the dramatic monologue. Browning's poems explore faith, doubt, crime, and madness using speakers who lived in past times, frequently from the Renaissance era. Browning was educated mostly at home and traveled little until he and Barrett eloped to Italy, where they lived for sixteen years (until Barrett's death). Among Browning's more famous poems are "Porphyria's Lover," "My Last Duchess," and "Fra Lippo Lippi," but his masterpiece is a four-volume dramatic monologue, *The Ring and the Book* (1868), that tells the story of a murder trial in seventeenth-century Italy.

AS YOU READ Listen in your mind's ear to the way in which the statements overlap the ends of lines and continue on to complete their meanings.

My Last Duchess (1842)

Ferrara

That's my last Duchess painted on the wall,
Looking as if she were alive. I call
That piece a wonder, now: Frà Pandolf's hands
Worked busily a day, and there she stands.
Will't please you sit and look at her? I said
"Frà Pandolf" by design, for never read
Strangers like you that pictured countenance,
The depth and passion of its earnest glance,
But to myself they turned (since none puts by
The curtain I have drawn for you, but I)
And seemed as they would ask me, if they durst,
How such a glance came there; so, not the first
Are you to turn and ask thus. Sir, 'twas not
Her husband's presence only, called that spot
Of joy into the Duchess' cheek: perhaps
Frà Pandolf chanced to say "Her mantle laps
Over my lady's wrist too much," or "Paint
Must never hope to reproduce the faint
Half-flush that dies along her throat." Such stuff
Was courtesy, she thought, and cause enough
For calling up that spot of joy. She had
A heart—how shall I say?—too soon made glad,
Too easily impressed; she liked whate'er
She looked on, and her looks went everywhere.
Sir, 'twas all one! My favour at her breast,
The dropping of the daylight in the West,
The bough of cherries some officious fool
Broke in the orchard for her, the white mule
She rode with round the terrace—all and each
Would draw from her alike the approving speech,

Or blush, at least. She thanked men—good! but thanked
Somehow—I know not how—as if she ranked
My gift of a nine-hundred-years-old name
With anybody's gift. Who'd stoop to blame
This sort of trifling? Even had you skill
In speech—(which I have not)—to make your will
Quite clear to such an one, and say, "Just this
Or that in you disgusts me; here you miss,
Or there exceed the mark"—and if she let
Herself be lessoned so, nor plainly set
Her wits to yours, forsooth, and make excuse,
—E'en then would be some stooping; and I choose
Never to stoop. Oh sir, she smiled, no doubt,
Whene'er I passed her; but who passed without
Much the same smile? This grew; I gave commands;
Then all smiles stopped together. There she stands
As if alive. Will't please you rise? We'll meet
The company below, then. I repeat,
The Count your master's known munificence
Is ample warrant that no just pretense
Of mine for dowry will be disallowed;
Though his fair daughter's self, as I avowed
At starting, is my object. Nay we'll go
Together down, sir. Notice Neptune, though,
Taming a sea-horse, thought a rarity,
Which Claus of Innsbruck cast in bronze for me!

Writing from Reading

Summarize

1 Who is the speaker of the poem? To whom does he give the tour? What brings the visitor to the viewing?

Analyze Craft

2 The speaker is not the poet—the poet creates a character here, and a story. Can you describe the two characters in the poem and the woman in the painting whom the speaker describes?

Analyze Voice

3 What are your first impressions of the speaker, and what are your final ones? How and where do they begin to change?

Synthesize Summary and Analysis

4 What do you learn about his "last Duchess," and how do you imagine she felt about her husband?

Interpret the Poem

5 When "all smiles stopped together," what do you think happened? Did he have her killed? Was she perhaps a suicide? Or did she simply—as old stories have it—"die of grief"?

The more we "listen" to this speaker, the more we come to mistrust him. Even such a simple word as "now" in the third line suggests its opposite, "then"; quite probably he wasn't as pleased by the smile of his living wife as he is by the portrait behind the curtain, which he alone is permitted to "draw." He keeps her beauty hidden, in effect, and for his private pleasure; soon enough we learn he was unable to do so while she was alive. She smiled at the painter, at other men, at common folk, and the proud duke did not approve of this. The lines "I gave commands; / Then all smiles stopped together" is bone chilling in its suggestiveness. At the very least he commanded his wife to stop smiling at and thanking other people; possibly he ordered her death. There's a long short story embedded in this narrative, and the dramatic monologue reveals an attitude and a situation the speaker tries to hide.

AROUND THE WORLD

It's important early on to stress how many different languages enable creative expression, and how many of the world's masterworks were composed in other tongues. As we suggested at this chapter's start, the English of Shakespeare or the King James Version of the Bible (and, to a lesser degree, the English of Lord Byron and Robert Browning) can seem foreign to a modern reader; their language is not quite the one we use in daily speech. When we deal with foreign languages, that's literally the case. The poet Li-Young Lee (in chapter 17) describes his first experience of hearing and then speaking English; born in Indonesia, of Chinese ancestry, he came to this country when young. Having been exposed from infancy to his parents' love of ancient Chinese poetry, he grew up to write poetry himself, but he does so in his non-native English. We are more and more citizens of the world, and poetry and its global traditions are part of the context of reading.

The three poems that follow are translations, which means the translators did research in the language, the culture, the traditions—the context—that brought these works into being. Stephen Mitchell, in his interview, describes his experience of translating sacred texts almost as a spiritual journey. While translations have issues that

> "Translation makes the world accessible to us."
>
> Conversation with Robert Hass

are special to any work that links languages, all poetry is enhanced by an understanding of its context and history. In the previous chapter, you examined the language of poetry from your first experience to reading for word choices, patterns of images and sounds, and considerations of the way the structure of a poem supports your interpretation. In this chapter, we've examined very briefly the context of major traditions of poetry—the lyric, epic, and dramatic modes. While we might not all be multilingual, reading a poem is a little like doing a translation of your own, going on your own journey into language.

There's a whole world of beauty . . . out there for people who don't know poetry . . .

Q&A

. . . I needed to know what that God was all about.

A Conversation on Translation

Stephen Mitchell

Born in Brooklyn, New York, in 1943, Stephen Mitchell went to Amherst College as a pre-med student. However, while studying in Paris, he was introduced to Rainer Maria Rilke's poetry. Mitchell learned German simply to read Rilke in his original language, and it was his translation of Rilke's poems that would launch his publishing career in 1982 with *The Selected Poems of Rainer Maria Rilke.* Although he has published original poetry in the collection *Parables and Portraits* (1990), he is best known for the poetry of his translations of ancient and modern texts. Mitchell is concerned with spirituality and religious wisdom, as is seen in his acclaimed translations *Bhagavad Gita* (2002), *The Book of Job* (1992), and *Tao Te Ching* (1988). He has also published a number of children's books, among them *Jesus: What He Really Said and Did* (2002), which presents his collection of sayings that he believes are authentic to the historical Jesus. Mitchell, who holds a degree in comparative literature from Yale, has an interest in Zen Buddhism, and he has collaborated with his wife, Byron Katie, on her books devoted to helping people achieve inner peace.

To watch the entire video and hear the author read from his work, go to www.mhhe.com/delbanco1e.

RESEARCH ASSIGNMENT For Mitchell, translating texts has been a spiritual journey. Watch the interview and describe his writing and research process. What spiritual truths draw him to the texts he chooses to translate? What has Zen meant to his ability to translate texts effectively?

Falling in Love, Learning Languages, and Reading Poetry

I've always learned a language because I've fallen in love with a consciousness. So I learned German because of Rilke, I learned Hebrew because of Job. And that was my focus. It wasn't to learn a language. It was so I could become intimate with a consciousness that I love very deeply. The value is indescribable. It's like if you ask the question, Why should I read poetry? Why should I learn Latin and other languages? It's like asking, Why should I listen to music? I mean, what would your life be without music? What an impoverishment. There's a whole world of beauty and profundity out there for people who don't know poetry, that's just waiting for you.

A Love Song to God

The Bhagavad Gita is . . . a love song to God, and that's actually a possible translation of the title. It is the central text of Hinduism . . . a very wise text, and also a very beautiful text. It's a book that I again fell in love with . . . and it astonished me to read a book with such a vast conception of God . . . It is really a hair-raising verse and the God who appears in the Bhagavad Gita says . . . in his most dreadful compassionate form . . . "I am death, I am what lies beyond all your small concepts of what should be and what is right and good." Anyway, this was a great riddle for me at first. . . . I needed to know what that God was all about.

AS YOU READ Compare the approach to deity in these lines to the approach in the Song of Solomon.

[The Secret of Life]

—from the Bhagavad Gita (“Love Song to God”) (c. 500–200 B.C.E.)

THE BLESSED LORD SAID:

Because you trust me, Arjuna,
I will tell you what wisdom is,
the secret of life: know it
and be free of suffering, forever.

This is the supreme wisdom,
the knowing beyond all knowing,
experienced directly, in a flash,
eternal, and a joy to practice.

Those who are without faith
in my teaching, cannot attain me;
they endlessly return to this world,
shuttling from death to death.

I permeate all the universe
in my unmanifest form.
All beings exist within me,
yet I am so inconceivably

vast, so beyond existence,
that though they are brought forth
and sustained by my limitless power,
I am not confined within them.

Just as the all-moving wind,
wherever it goes, always
remains in the vastness of space,
all beings remain within me.

They are gathered back into my womb
at the end of the cosmic cycle—
a hundred fifty thousand
billion of your earthly years—
and as a new cycle begins
I send them forth once again,
pouring from my abundance
the myriad forms of life.

These actions do not bind me, Arjuna.
I stand apart from them all,
indifferent to their outcome,
unattached, serene.

Under my guidance, Nature
brings forth all beings, all things
animate or inanimate,
and sets the whole universe in motion.

Foolish people despise me
in the human form that I take,
blind to my true nature
as the Lord of all life and death.

Their hopes and actions are vain,
their knowledge is sheer delusion;
turning from the light, they fall
into cruelty, selfishness, greed.

But the truly wise, Arjuna,
who dive deep into themselves,
fearless, one-pointed, know me
as the inexhaustible source.

Always chanting my praise,
steadfast in their devotion,
they make their lives an unending
hymn to my endless love.

—translated by Stephen Mitchell

Writing from Reading

Summarize

1 The Hindu God speaks, recounting his nature and his accomplishments. What does he say about the nature of those who worship him?

Analyze Craft

2 Does this scripture resemble a drama in any way?

Analyze Voice

3 Can you characterize the voice of the deity?

Synthesize Summary and Analysis

4 The God speaks. What makes it possible for us to listen in?

Interpret the Poem

5 In what ways are ideas in this poem similar to or different from those in the writings of your religion?

Rumi (c. 1207–1273)

A Persian mystic and poet, Jalal al-Din Rumi was born in what is now Afghanistan and lived most of his life in present-day Turkey. Rumi was a well-respected teacher and theologian until 1244, when he met Shams of Tabriz, a wandering dervish (an Islamic mystic). Shams inspired Rumi to devote his life to Sufism (Islamic mysticism), and Rumi began to write mystical verse, much of it in praise of Shams. When Shams was murdered, Rumi continued to write in his praise. He also wrote the *Mathnawi,* an epic poem important to the Islamic world. Beyond his verse, Rumi is known as the founder of the whirling dervishes sect of Islam, a group that uses song, dance, and spinning as a means of reaching God. His verse remains widely known, particularly in Iran, and it has enjoyed a resurgence of popularity in the United States since the 1990s.

AS YOU READ **Ask yourself if this is another hymn, in the form of a love poem, or a love poem in the form of a hymn.**

Some Kiss We Want (c. mid-thirteenth century)

There is some kiss we want
with our whole lives, the touch

of spirit on the body. Seawater
begs the pearl to break its shell.

And the lily, how passionately
it needs some wild darling!

At night, I open the window and ask
the moon to come and press its
face against mine.

Breathe into me. Close
the language-door and open the love-window.
The moon won't use the door,
only the window.

—translated by Coleman Barks

Writing from Reading

Summarize

1 To whom does the poet admit a desire? Who does he ask to come to him?

Analyze Craft

2 How does the poet turn love of his God into a poem that seems to be about human love?

Analyze Voice

3 How would you describe this voice? How is this similar to, or distinct from, the voice in the Song of Solomon?

Synthesize Summary and Analysis

4 The poet seeks union with his beloved, expressing this need in language beyond the literal. What does he mean by "the moon won't use the door"?

Interpret the Poem

5 What does the speaker want as expressed in such lines as ". . . Sea-water / begs the pearl to break its shell" or "the lily, how passionately . . . it needs some wild darling!"?

Pablo Neruda (1904–1973)

Ricardo Eliecer Neftalí Reyes Basoalto was born in southern Chile. He adopted the pen name Pablo Neruda to avoid conflict with his family, who disapproved of his poetic activity. Abandoning his studies at age twenty in order to devote himself to poetry, Neruda embarked on a diplomatic career that took him to Argentina, Spain, Mexico, and France. He became politically controversial when he supported the republican side of the Spanish Civil War, publishing the collection *España en el corazón* (1937), which forced him to end his period in Spain and return to Chile. He supported communism in Chile and was exiled as a result; during this time he wrote his keystone work *Canto General* (1950), an epic poem cataloguing the South American continent. A celebrated poet, Neruda won the Nobel Prize in Literature in 1971.

AS YOU READ Ask yourself what life must be like for a poet as passionate as Neruda describes himself here. Compare the passion in this poem to that of, say, Shakespeare or Leonard Cohen.

I Do Not Love You Except Because I Love You (1959)

I do not love you—except because I love you;
and from loving you to not loving you,
from waiting to not waiting for you
my heart moves from the cold into
the fire. I love you only because it's you
I love; I hate you no end, and hating you
bend to you, and the measure of my changing love for you
is that I do not see you but love you

blindly. Maybe the January light will consume
my heart with its cruel
ray, stealing my key to true

calm. In this part of the story I am the one who
dies, the only one, and I will die of love because I love you
because I love you, Love, in fire and in blood.

—translated by Gustavo Escobedo

Writing from Reading

Summarize

1 To whom is this passionate poem about love and its power addressed?

Analyze Craft

2 The poem seems to be so plain in its attitude: "I love you because I love you." How does the poet create the intensity of the poem? What emotionally charged words does he use?

Analyze Voice

3 What is the emotional state of the speaker? How do you know?

Synthesize Summary and Analysis

4 Why is it only the speaker who dies in this poem?

Interpret the Poem

5 What is it that the speaker longs for?

For Review and Further Study

Elizabeth Barrett Browning (1806–1861)

For a brief biography of Elizabeth Barrett Browning, see chapter 24.

Go From Me (1850)

Go from me. Yet I feel that I shall stand
Henceforth in thy shadow. Nevermore
Alone upon the threshold of my door
Of individual life, I shall command
The uses of my soul, nor lift my hand
Serenely in the sunshine as before,
Without the sense of that which I forbore—
Thy touch upon the palm. The widest land
Doom takes to part us, leaves thy heart in mine
With pulses that beat double. What I do
And what I dream include thee, as the wine
Must taste of its own grapes. And when I sue
God for myself, He hears that name of thine,
And sees within my eyes the tears of two.

Questions for Interactive Reading and Writing

1. Try to reconstruct the context, the situation, in which the poet might feel this sense of being deeply bound to the beloved but also wanting to separate. Recall out of your own experience the deep sense of being bound to someone you love even after you part.

2. Read the poem aloud without pausing at the end of each line. Which do you believe controls the poem, the thoughts the poet expresses or the rhymes?
3. Can you paraphrase this sensual image: ". . . as the wine / Must taste of its own grapes . . ."?
4. List the series of orders the speaker issues to the beloved. What does the poet mean by saying, "I sue" God?
5. Does the beloved, whom the poet addresses, have any choice about whether to leave or stay in the poet's memory?

Robert Browning (1812–1889)

For a brief biography of Robert Browning, see the discussion of dramatic monologue earlier in this chapter.

Love Among the Ruins (1855)

I

Where the quiet-coloured end of evening smiles
  Miles and miles
On the solitary pastures where our sheep
  Half-asleep
Tinkle homeward thro' the twilight, stray or stop
  As they crop—
Was the site once of a city great and gay,
  (So they say)
Of our country's very capital, its prince
  Ages since
Held his court in, gathered councils, wielding far
  Peace or war.

II

Now—the country does not even boast a tree,
  As you see,
To distinguish slopes of verdure, certain rills
  From the hills
Intersect and give a name to, (else they run
  Into one)
Where the domed and daring palace shot its spires
  Up like fires
O'er the hundred-gated circuit of a wall
  Bounding all,
Made of marble, men might march on nor be pressed,
  Twelve abreast.

III

And such plenty and perfection, see, of grass
  Never was!
Such a carpet as, this summer-time, o'erspreads
  And embeds
Every vestige of the city, guessed alone,
  Stock or stone—
Where a multitude of men breathed joy and woe
  Long ago;
Lust of glory pricked their hearts up, dread of shame
  Struck them tame;
And that glory and that shame alike, the gold
  Bought and sold.

IV

Now,—the single little turret that remains
  On the plains,
By the caper overrooted, by the gourd
  Overscored,
While the patching houseleek's head of blossom winks
  Through the chinks—
Marks the basement whence a tower in ancient time
  Sprang sublime,
And a burning ring, all round, the chariots traced
  As they raced,
And the monarch and his minions and his dames
  Viewed the games.

V

And I know, while thus the quiet-coloured eve
  Smiles to leave
To their folding, all our many-tinkling fleece
  In such peace,
And the slopes and rills in undistinguished grey
  Melt away—
That a girl with eager eyes and yellow hair
  Waits me there
In the turret whence the charioteers caught soul
  For the goal,
When the king looked, where she looks now, breathless, dumb
  Till I come.

VI

But he looked upon the city, every side,
  Far and wide,
All the mountains topped with temples, all the glades'
  Colonnades,
All the causeys, bridges, aqueducts,—and then,
  All the men!
When I do come, she will speak not, she will stand,
  Either hand,
On my shoulder, give her eyes the first embrace
  Of my face,
Ere we rush, ere we extinguish sight and speech
  Each on each.

VII

In one year they sent a million fighters forth
South and north,
And they built their gods a brazen pillar high
As the sky,
Yet reserved a thousand chariots in full force—
Gold, of course.
Oh, heart! oh, blood that freezes, blood that burns!
Earth's returns
For whole centuries of folly, noise and sin!
Shut them in,
With their triumphs and their glories and the rest!
Love is best!

Questions for Interactive Reading and Writing

1. What are the two story lines that coincide in this poem? Is the poem primarily about war and empire or about love?
2. How does the story about war and empire affect the love story?
3. To whom is the poet speaking? How does that affect the way he tells the poem?
4. What does the poem suggest about the relation of individuals, their lives and loves, in the context of the social situation of the state, of the country?
5. Does the way the poem sounds—its particular music as you read it aloud—contribute anything to the meaning?

William Dickey (1928–1994)

Therefore (1994)

Nothing exists that is not marred; therefore
we are obliged to imagine how things might be:
the sea
at its green uttermost, the shore
white to exaggeration, white before
it was checked and clouded by its spent debris.

Nothing exists that does not end, and so
to knowledge we must deliberately be untrue:
you
murmuring that you will not go, when you will go,
promising to do always what you cannot do:
hold the sun steady, and the sky new.

No one exists who can be loved the same
by day as by dark; it is that sleeping place,
lame,
we attempt to follow into, and cannot trace,
that makes us lie, saying we know his face,
as if we knew even half of his true name.

Questions for Interactive Reading and Writing

1. Does the poet have an "argument" he is trying to put forward?
2. What is the relation, in the last two lines, of the words "lie" and "true"?
3. Who is the "we" in the poem?
4. How does the poet seem to marry his personal quest for happiness and a philosophical quest to understand human feelings? Try to imagine the personal situation that gave rise to these lines.

Edna St. Vincent Millay (1892–1950)

Not in a silver casket cool with pearls (1931)

Not in a silver casket cool with pearls
Or rich with red corundum or with blue,
Locked, and the key withheld, as other girls
Have given their loves, I give my love to you;
Not in a lovers'-knot, not in a ring
Worked in such fashion, and the legend plain—
Semper fidelis, where a secret spring
Kennels a drop of mischief for the brain:
Love in the open hand, no thing but that,
Ungemmed, unhidden, wishing not to hurt,
As one should bring you cowslips in a hat
Swung from the hand, or apples in her skirt,
I bring you, calling out as children do:
"Look what I have!—And these are all for you."

Questions for Interactive Reading and Writing

1. Why does the poet choose to begin with a series of negative statements?
2. The Latin words *semper fidelis*—also the motto of the Marine Corps—mean "forever faithful." How does that connect to this poem's theme?
3. Do you like the phrase "love in the open hand"? Why does it please?

4. What does the image "apples in her skirt" conjure up? How does it compare with the opening image of "a silver casket cool with pearls"?
5. How would you feel if you were the recipient of this poem?

Adrienne Rich (b. 1929)

Living in Sin (1955)

She had thought the studio would keep itself;
no dust upon the furniture of love.
Half heresy, to wish the taps less vocal,
the panes relieved of grime. A plate of pears,
a piano with a Persian shawl, a cat
stalking the picturesque amusing mouse
had risen at his urging.
Not that at five each separate stair would writhe
under the milkman's tramp; that morning light
so coldly would delineate the scraps
of last night's cheese and three sepulchral bottles;
that on the kitchen shelf among the saucers
a pair of beetle-eyes would fix her own—
envoy from some village in the moldings . . .
Meanwhile, he, with a yawn,
sounded a dozen notes upon the keyboard,
declared it out of tune, shrugged at the mirror,
rubbed at his beard, went out for cigarettes;
while she, jeered by the minor demons,
pulled back the sheets and made the bed and found
a towel to dust the table-top,
and let the coffee-pot boil over on the stove.
By evening she was back in love again,
though not so wholly but throughout the night
she woke sometimes to feel the daylight coming
like a relentless milkman up the stairs.

Questions for Interactive Reading and Writing

1. What makes the poet feel particularly uncomfortable in her current living arrangement?
2. How does the reference to the vermin—"a pair of beetle-eyes"—add to her feeling of being ill at ease?
3. Does the reference to the out-of-tune piano increase the discomfort?
4. Does the man feel as the poet-speaker does? What makes us able to move from a description of the piano to a description of the poet's feelings?
5. What supposedly new state does she find herself in at the end of the day?
6. Can you call this a love poem, or is it a poem of another sort?

Rainer Maria Rilke (1875–1926)

Archaic Torso of Apollo (1908)

We cannot know his legendary head
with eyes like ripening fruit. And yet his torso
is still suffused with brilliance from inside,
like a lamp, in which his gaze, now turned to low,

gleams in all its power. Otherwise
the curved breast could not dazzle you so, nor could
a smile run through the placid hips and thighs
to that dark center where procreation flared.

Otherwise this stone would seem defaced
beneath the translucent cascade of the shoulders
and would not glisten like a wild beast's fur:

would not, from all the borders of itself,
burst like a star: for here there is no place
that does not see you. You must change your life.

—translated by Stephen Mitchell

Questions for Interactive Reading and Writing

1. While living in Paris, Rilke worked as a kind of private secretary to the sculptor Auguste Rodin. What does the poet look at when he sees "this stone"?
2. Look up the Greek god Apollo and make a list of his qualities. Relate them to what the poet sees here.
3. Who is the "you" in this poem, and does it also mean "I"?
4. Which images are "surface" images, and which relate to depths?
5. The poet lives in the present moment, but what he's looking at is "archaic" and comes from a civilization that flourished thousands of years before. Discuss this as an example of both "tradition" and "translation."
6. What does the last sentence of this poem mean, and who gives the order that "You must change your life"?

17

Writing about Poetry

I'VE pulled the last of the year's young onions.
The garden is bare now. The ground is cold,
brown and old. What is left of the day flames
in the maples at the corner of my
eye. I turn, a cardinal vanishes.
By the cellar door, I wash the onions,
then drink from the icy metal spigot.

—from "Eating Alone" by Li-Young Lee

"'Eating Together' or 'Eating Alone'—those are about eating and all those other things—but . . . [when we write about poetry] we should be interrogating the quality of the imagination in the poem, the quality of the mind, the heart, the soul in the poem."

Conversation with Li-Young Lee, available on video at www.mhhe.com/delbanco1e

HOW do we write about poetry? We do it in ways similar to writing about fiction, by analyzing the writer's craft and voice in terms of its technical aspects, in order to get closer to the meaning.

As suggested in the preceding chapters, there are many ways to **think about** and read poetry, based on your own thoughts and your eventual understanding of traditional techniques. First you read the poem to yourself, let the language flow over you and find general associations that the images and words bring up. This is your **first reading,** and it's not meant to be final or thorough, more a general impression that's a springboard to the work. In your first reading of "Eating Alone," you may notice how forlorn the speaker seems and how important onions are in the first and final stanzas. It's useful if you try your **second reading** out loud, the better to catch the sounds clearly and see what kind of rhythm has enforced its structure on the poem.

A **critical reading,** one in which you begin to apply various ways of looking at a poem, helps you fully understand a poem and may require a line-by-line **explication,** an examination of how the elements of craft work in each line. This kind of reading prepares you to write a **text-based argument.** Writing a text-based argument is a skill you will need for many of your college courses, and it's quite likely you will need such skill for your work and career outside of college. Lawyers, journalists, police detectives, managers of many varieties—all those who have to examine what is said between the lines—need to be able to look closely at how language works and find evidence in the text itself that supports an argument about the meaning of the work.

This chapter follows the development of a sample student essay from the earliest stages to the final draft. Emma Baldwin, a student, uses several of the prewriting and writing strategies that we discuss in depth in the Handbook for Writing from Reading at the end of this volume (see chapter 3 in the handbook on "Common Writing Assignments"). As was the case with fiction, we emphasize that most literary works don't possess a single meaning but rather offer multiple meanings and interpretations of the work.

. . . I do think that writing poems is dealing with language on a quantum level . . .

I don't blame . . . people for being intimidated by poetry . . .

Q&A
A Conversation on Writing

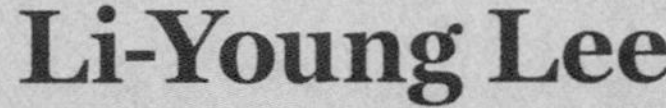

Li-Young Lee

The Strangeness of Poetry

I don't blame . . . people for being intimidated by poetry—especially lyric poetry. I'm not sure that poems belong in the same category as novels and essays and short stories. Poems are strange; they belong in a whole category of synchronicity or coincidence.

Coincidence and Poetic Order

I think [the] experience of coincidence is the closest thing we have to [the] experience of poetry. . . . Things emerge simultaneously and we can't quite account for that particular emergence of simultaneous things at the same time. So I think [that] the most radical thing about poetry is that it proposes this other order. You know, I think other kinds of writing, ultimately they participate in and examine causal orderedness: cause and effect. And maybe poetry proposes that cause and effect aren't the only lord and lady ruling the universe. . . . I think that's ultimately what lyric poetry attempts to manifest.

Language on a Quantum Level

What's so fascinating is this: I think one has to inhabit a particular state of consciousness in order to notice coincidence or synchronicity in the world. And it could be in fact that the more open we are to it, the more we realize, the more we maybe begin to notice that that's the deepest thing going on at any particular time, that cause and effect is a type of surface condition. Maybe down deep, at a deeper level, a quantum level of reality (and I do think that writing poems is dealing with language on a quantum level) . . . the synchronicities and coincidences begin to emerge, begin to yield themselves, begin to reveal themselves in language.

Li-Young Lee was born in 1957 to Chinese parents in Indonesia and came to this country when young. As he reports in his interview, the refugee experience—his family was persecuted, forced into exile—has deeply influenced his way of looking at the world; if the poet is always, to some degree, an "outsider," this one is literally so. Much of his writing has to do with tradition, the presence of the past—and what is lost, what remains. The growing and cooking and eating of food, for example, has a resonance beyond the merely literal, and for Lee such everyday procedures all partake of pilgrimage and even of the sacred. His language—direct and straightforward diction—celebrates the ordinary and sanctifies everyday life. For this, his work has received many honors, including three Puschart Prizes, the Lannan Literary Award, and the American Book Award. Lee's collection *Book of My Nights* was the winner of the Poetry Society of America's William Carlos Williams Award. His other books include *The City in Which I Love You, Rose, The Winged Seed: A Remembrance,* and, in 2008, *Behind My Eyes.*

To view this entire interview and hear the author read from his work, go to www.mhhe.com/delbanco1e.

RESEARCH ASSIGNMENT In his interview, Li-Young Lee talks about being a refugee. What happened to Li-Young Lee, and what does he think this meant for his poetry?

AS YOU READ Observe the way in which the poet focuses on two important aspects of life: first solitude and then companionship.

Two Poems by Li-Young Lee

Eating Alone (1986)

I've pulled the last of the year's young onions.
The garden is bare now. The ground is cold,
brown and old. What is left of the day flames
in the maples at the corner of my
eye. I turn, a cardinal vanishes.
By the cellar door, I wash the onions,
then drink from the icy metal spigot.

Once, years back, I walked beside my father
among the windfall pears. I can't recall
our words. We may have strolled in silence. But
I still see him bend that way—left hand braced
on knee, creaky—to lift and hold to my
eye a rotten pear. In it, a hornet
spun crazily, glazed in slow, glistening juice.

It was my father I saw this morning
waving to me from the trees. I almost
called to him, until I came close enough
to see the shovel, leaning where I had
left it, in the flickering, deep green shade.

White rice steaming, almost done. Sweet green peas
fried in onions. Shrimp braised in sesame
oil and garlic. And my own loneliness.
What more could I, a young man, want.

Eating Together (1986)

In the steamer is the trout
seasoned with slivers of ginger,
two sprigs of green onion, and sesame oil.
We shall eat it with rice for lunch,
brothers, sister, my mother who will
taste the sweetest meat of the head,
holding it between her fingers
deftly, the way my father did
weeks ago. Then he lay down
to sleep like a snow-covered road
winding through pines older than him,
without any travelers, and lonely for no one.

A Guide to Writing from Reading

Here are some guidelines for reading that will support your writing.

Summarize the poem.	Some poems are more transparent than others, but poetic language is nevertheless different from everyday speech. Make sure you understand what is going on in the poem. A poem may have dramatic action, a plot almost, but it's just as likely to be a description. After you have gotten your first impressions, depending on the difficulty of the language, you may need to write in your own prose (**paraphrase**) what each line or stanza means.
Analyze its craft.	A poem works differently from prose, so how language pushes and pulls the prose meaning of the poem is critical to an analysis. Look for patterns of images or sounds, such as the images of stones in Carolyn Forché's "The Museum of Stones" or the rhymes in Shakespeare's "My mistress' eyes are nothing like the sun." Look for other kinds of patterns (like the clustering into threes—*begotten, born, and dies*—of Yeats's "Sailing to Byzantium") and for interesting or unusual word choices, word order, or rhythms. You may want to organize your paper as a walk-through of the lines of the poem.
Analyze its voice.	Each poem has a speaker; in your writing you shouldn't assume the speaker is the poet, even though the speaker in the poem uses an "I." Don't write "In Li-Young Lee's 'Eating Together' he finds fulfillment in the family meal." Instead write "In Li-Young Lee's 'Eating Together,' he creates *a speaker* who finds fulfillment in the family meal." In Li-Young Lee's interview, he tells us that the real subject of any poem is the speaker. Ask yourself who the speaker is, what motivated the speaker to tell the "story" in the poem, and why the speaker uses the kind of rhythm, sound, and imagery in a poem the way he or she (or it) does.
Synthesize the summary and analysis.	What are the larger issues in the poem? What themes are present, what conflicts or issues are dramatized? Describe the situation of the speaker. Think about how craft is used to tell the story of the poem, where sounds, for example, reflect happiness, mourning, or wonder. How do these sounds work together? Are the image patterns most important? Is it an intimate tone that gives the poem its power? You can use your synthesis to organize your thoughts, and this may become the way you organize your paper.
Interpret the poem.	Here is your argument. Two crucial components of writing effectively are discovering something meaningful to you and maintaining a questioning, thoughtful attitude in your exploration of the poem. You will need to make a claim about the poem, and the lines from the poem will be the evidence that supports your claim. If you're using outside sources, other critics' voices should be included only as a jumping-off point for your own interpretation. Do not end your paper with a quotation from an outside critic. Learning to support your own interpretation, based on your synthesis and analysis, is the point of writing about poetry.

"Well, the writerly impulse—at least for me—proceeds from a readerly impulse." Conversation with Thomas Lynch

(CONTINUED FROM PAGE 47)

A SAMPLE STUDENT ESSAY IN PROGRESS

Everyone has his or her own way of writing. Some think it all the way through before putting pen to paper; others create numerous notes and organize those notes into an outline before they begin. Whatever your process is, there is a sequence that can help break down the writing tasks into digestible chunks and keep the dreaded "blank screen" from causing writer's block. Here you can follow Emma Baldwin through the steps of her writing process to see how her understanding of the poem evolves as she responds to this assignment: *In 2–3 pages, do a close reading of Li-Young Lee's poem "Eating Alone" in which you analyze one or more elements of the poem.*

- Interact with the Reading
- Explore Your Ideas
- Develop a Thesis
- Create a Plan for Your Paper
- Generate a First Draft
- Revise Your Draft
- Edit and Format Your Paper

> "I almost . . . never have the lines that I think are the good lines in the poem prior to the act of writing. They occur in the act of. And when you're good that day, you can be a little bit better than yourself." Conversation with Stephen Dunn

Interact with the Reading

When Emma Baldwin read "Eating Alone," she annotated the poem and took notes on her initial responses. Both her annotations and notes, reproduced here, show how she engaged with the text.

Initial Response

Overall, this poem seems very sad to me. I know that the young man is gardening and cooking, which are both fun hobbies, so it seems like the poem should be happier than it is. But I think he misses his father, since that is the only other person mentioned in the poem. I don't understand the significance of the hornet spinning in the rotten pear, but I can picture it exactly. I also don't understand the last lines—why would anyone want to be lonely? I did notice that the poem jumps around in time. Those jumps seem to occur with each stanza, so it seems like that is significant too. I think the thing I understood best in the poem was the imagery—I could relate to the smell of onions, icy cold water, the cardinal and maple trees. It was easy to picture everything in the poem, even the flickering shade and the shovel in the ground, and so I'd like to understand what it all means.

After a first reading of "Eating Alone," Emma reread the poem, scanned the first few lines to determine the meter, and made annotations. Her annotations are a combination of personal reaction and notation of formal elements, like rhyme and rhythm. At this stage in our discussion of the **craft** of poetry, you won't yet be familiar in detail with the formal elements of rhythm, rhyme, and structure—we simply allude to them here—but they are discussed in the chapters that follow. "A sonnet," for example, is a poetic "fixed form" examined at length in chapter 22. It's early innings yet, and we won't go into elaborate discussions of technique.

TIPS

FOR INTERACTIVE READING . . .

Number the lines—This will help you refer to specific details as you begin your writing process. It will also help you discover whether the poem follows a particular format; for example, if you find there are fourteen lines, chances are the poem is a sonnet.

Scan the first several lines—This allows you to determine if there is a set rhythm or if the poem is written in free verse (see chapter 22). The first three lines of the following poem have been annotated for scansion of the rhythm, marking ´ for stressed and ˘ for unstressed syllables.

Identify rhyme—This is another tactic that will enable you to know the form of the poem. If you find no consistent rhyme scheme, noting internal rhyme, assonance, and consonance will help you understand the emphasis on certain words.

An Interactive Reading of "Eating Alone"

Ĭ've púlled thĕ *lást* ŏf thĕ yeár's yóung óniŏns.
Thĕ gárdĕn ĭs *báre nŏw*. Thĕ groúnd ĭs *cóld,*
brówn ănd *óld. Whăt ĭs léft* ŏf thĕ dáy flámes
in the maples at the corner of my
eye. I turn, a cardinal vanishes.
By the cellar door, I wash the onions,
then drink from the icy metal spigot.

Once, years back, I walked beside my father
among the windfall pears. I can't recall
our words. We may have strolled in silence. But
I still see him bend that way—left hand braced
on knee, creaky—to lift and hold to my
eye a rotten pear. In it, a hornet
spun crazily, glazed in slow, glistening juice.

It was my father I saw this morning
waving to me from the trees. I almost
called to him, until I came close enough
to see the shovel, leaning where I had
left it, in the flickering, deep green shade.

White rice steaming, almost done. Sweet green peas
fried in onions. Shrimp braised in sesame
oil and garlic. And my own loneliness.
What more could I, a young man, want.

Image: Imagery is barren, desolate

Setting: Present; pulling onions from garden

Image: Imagery brightens with "flames" and "cardinal"

Rhyme: Internal rhyme, wind*fall* and re*call*. knee and creaky. crazily and glazed

Setting: Past; "once, years back . . ."; walking with father, who is old

Setting: Earlier in the present day; "this morning"; mistakes a shovel for his father

Setting: Present; cooking the onions he has pulled from the garden in a meal

Interpret: Explicit statement of who narrator is (although I felt like I already knew—not sure why)

Rhyme:—cold/old

Words: Assonance: *day flames*

Rhyme: No formal rhyme scheme or set meter

Image: "Icy metal spigot"—striking; I can taste it and feel it

Interpret: Father must be old—creaky, difficulty moving

Image: Striking image—metaphor for something?

Intepret: A very sad moment—father is not there; dead, perhaps? shovel makes me think of burial

Image: Words engage sense of smell, taste, visual: very crisp and *present*

Interpret: Confusing last line . . . seems like a contradiction

"This notion of discovery is really important. It's something that's very difficult to remember. I've been writing now for twenty-five years; it's still hard for me to remember that I have to constantly go into the new. Stanley [Kunitz] used to say, he was about ninety, 'I go to write a poem, it's not where the last one was.'" Conversation with Marie Howe

Explore Your Ideas

Although Emma did a great job annotating the poem, her confusion over the last lines suggests that she still does not have a full grasp on its meaning. There are several ways you might be able to refine your own ideas for your paper. Here are some examples of freewriting, journaling, and brainstorming. Choose what works best for you.

Freewriting

The saddest moment in the poem is when he mistakes the shovel for his father. I think it means his father is dead, right? Because the poem is so sad, and also the idea of being alone is there from the very beginning, and when someone dies, you feel left alone. I also think he's dead because he seems very old in the flashback where he bends to pick up a pear; my grandpa moved like that towards the end of his life, so it definitely means the father is old. So then the situation is a son doing his normal routine of cooking and eating but without his father there because he is dead. I still don't get the hornet in the pear, but since the father showed it to him, maybe it has to do with the father? Or maybe it's just a vivid image and that's why Lee went with it. It's strange that this poem is hard to understand because the language is pretty simple. I didn't have to look anything up. Spigot is definitely the coolest word in here. Those last lines are still really confusing, too, because they seem to contradict each other. In the one, he talks about "loneliness," but then the next second, he's saying what more could he want? No one wants to be lonely, right? So how does that make sense? It seems like what he really wants is to have his father with him again.

Journaling

In Li-Young Lee's poem, a son misses his father, who is apparently dead. The situation is pretty straightforward, but it does jump around a lot in time. At first the son is in the garden; then he remembers something about his father from a long time ago; then he talks about that morning; then he's cooking at the end.

One appealing aspect of the poem is the imagery. You can practically see, taste, and smell the very things the son sees, tastes, and smells. Some of the imagery is very pleasant, like the cooking smells and tastes at the end, but other imagery is not very attractive. Especially in the first stanza, there's a lot of detail about the garden being cold, brown, and old. And empty, since the son has pulled the "last" of the onions. I don't know if the hornet in the pear is an attractive image or not—the juice is cool, but a hornet and a rotten pear are not things you like to encounter. In any case, some of the images seem to be full of life—like the cooking at the end—but others seem to be dead—like the garden.

In a poem that's easy to understand in terms of the words themselves, the last lines are really hard to figure out. The last lines contradict each other, but I realize now that he's not asking a question. The last line says, "What more could I, a young man, want." So he's telling us he is satisfied somehow, even though his father is not with him. If it had been an actual question, I would have answered that he wants his father back—so maybe his statement means he has learned to be content despite his grief over his father's death.

Brainstorming

LIFE	DEATH
son/speaker	father
young onions	bare garden—cold, brown, old
hornet	rotten pear
father waving	shovel
eating	eating alone

"[Write] about something that really moves you and engages you; you must be there on the page." Conversation with Carolyn Forché

Develop a Thesis

In your responses, annotations, and explorations, you have concentrated on the parts of the poem that make up the whole. At this point, you have an idea of the larger conflicts or issues the poem dramatizes. In developing a thesis, it helps if you choose something personally meaningful. Your thesis is your claim that the poem works a certain way or means a certain thing. It isn't a general statement with which no one can disagree, such as information on what you personally like or feel about a poem. Your thesis is a thoughtful and specific assertion that will organize your paper and for which you can provide support and evidence from the poem itself.

First draft: The imagery and the contrast in the last lines suggest contradictory feelings, although it is mostly sad.

Second draft: In a poem about a son missing his dead father, there are many contrasting elements.

Third draft: This poem, which is an expression of grief over a dead father, relies on contrasting elements like imagery, tone, and time in order to make us feel the narrator's loss.

Final draft: A close reading shows the entire poem is created out of contradictory elements. Through contrasts of imagery, tone, and the literal events of the poem, Lee uses paradox to give full expression to the grief his speaker feels about his father's death.

Create a Plan for Your Paper

In any paper, your first paragraph sets up the issues that you will explore. There are as many ways to organize your paper as there are lines in the poem, but some general guidelines might help. You can examine the poem line by line, focus on the conflicts that are dramatized in the poem, or look at patterns, types of images, themes, or repeated words. When you are organizing your paper, advance your argument with evidence from the poem to avoid creating a laundry list that leads nowhere. Your paper will focus on the text itself, but your conclusion can make connections and raise questions and emphasize crucial issues. You do not need to repeat your thesis in your concluding paragraph. Sometimes an outline will help you plan your paper.

Outlining

I. Introduction
   A. confusing because last lines contradict
   B. thesis: A close reading shows the entire poem is created out of contradictory elements. Through contrasts of imagery, tone, and the literal events of the poem, Lee uses paradox to give full expression to the grief his speaker feels about his father's death.

II. Imagery
   A. imagery that suggests life
   B. imagery that suggests death

III. Tone
   A. plain language
   B. syntax is not complicated . . .
   C. . . . but subject matter is. This = understatement

IV. Time/Literal Events
   A. present, past "years back," past "this morning"
   B. talk about contrast in time

VI. Conclusion
   A. address contrast in last lines
   B. we can understand them in context of poem

Generate a First Draft

A first draft is just that: the *first*. Often you find clearer ways to express your thoughts as you go along. Sometimes you change your mind. With poetry, as with all literature, write in the present tense (He *misses* his father; not he *missed* his father). The event that the poem describes never changes, so it is the convention to use present tense when writing about literature.

First Draft

Baldwin 1

Emma Baldwin

Professor Stoller

English 102

September 22, 2008

Paradox in "Eating Alone"

On first reading Li-Young Lee's poem "Eating Alone," it doesn't make much sense. The speaker's conclusion that he is lonely *and* has everything he wants isn't logical. But on a closer reading, the entire poem is created out of contradictory elements. Through contrasts of imagery, tone, and the literal events of the poem, Lee uses paradox to give full expression to the grief his speaker feels about his father's death.

There is lots of imagery throughout the poem. A lot of it has to do with being alive, like the smell and taste of "sesame oil / and garlic" (lines 21–22). But a lot of it also has to do with death. The poem begins with the speaker picking "the last" (1) produce so that, "The garden is bare now" (2), and Lee further describes the ground as "cold, / brown and old" (2–3). These things remind the reader of death. The images seem to contradict themselves; on the one hand, they make the reader feel connected to the physical world, but on the other hand, they are cold, fleeting images that are related to death.

The father is dead, even though the poem doesn't state that. But it's obvious from the creaky way he bends that he is old. Since that is in a memory from years ago, chances are he has since passed away if he was so old to begin with.

Baldwin 2

In a poem about death, you might expect the words to be flowery, or even like passages from the Bible. You might also expect that the narrator is outwardly sad, or might even cry. But that doesn't happen. Instead, statements like "Once, years back, I walked beside my father / among the windfall pears" (8–9) sound as though they are said in casual conversation. By understating the situation of death, there is a contrast between the level of subject matter and the way that subject matter is expressed. This contrast highlights that even though death is a major and mystical event, it has become a fact of daily life for this speaker. The understated tone of the poem shows that grief is part of everyday life.

Several other contrasts are embedded in the poem. First is the matter of time. The young man in the present talks about a memory in the past. But beyond a simple past/present contrast, there's an immediate past in addition to a farther away past. The present action is the young man picking the onions, cleaning them, then using them to cook. The distant past is the memory that takes place in the second stanza, "years back," (8) while the immediate past is the occurrence recounted in the third stanza that occurred "this morning" (15). The purpose of the immediate past is that it links the past and present. In that stanza, he sees his father waving at him in the current moment; then he recognizes it is only a shovel in the shade, making the speaker painfully aware in the present of all he has lost from the past. In this way, that painful moment of father and shovel confusion highlights how the father was once alive but is now dead.

In summation, there are contradictory elements in almost every aspect of his poem. Because of this, I can come to understand the last stanza: "Shrimp braised in sesame / oil and garlic. And my own loneliness. / What more could I, a young man, want" (21–23). As noted previously, the fact that loneliness is part of what the young man wants is confusing. But since the whole poem is built on contrasts, the last contrast somehow seems to make sense.

Work Cited

Lee, Li-Young. "Eating Alone." *Literature: Craft & Voice.* Eds. Nicholas Delbanco and Alan Cheuse. New York: McGraw-Hill, 2009. 49. Print.

Revise Your Draft

Before beginning her second draft, Emma looked back at her notes and annotations and compared those to her draft. She found that her notes frequently mentioned the image of the hornet in the pear, but that her final paper left out that image. She also found that the paper did not explicitly highlight the life-and-death contrast she had found so important to furthering her understanding of the poem. While you certainly do not need to incorporate every idea into the final version, Emma thought it would help her argument to include these elements in her paper.

"Here I have a tremendous kind of furious argument, and here I've got to try and tame it. I've got to enact it. I've got to find a way to formalize it so that someone else can experience what I experienced." Conversation with Edward Hirsch

In the second draft, look for how Emma (1) clarifies her argument by pointing out the life in death imagery; (2) adds textual support to her discussion of imagery; (3) works towards making her conclusion more related to her thesis; (4) adds citations.

Second Draft

Baldwin 1

Emma Baldwin

Professor Stoller

English 102

September 27, 2008

Paradox in Li-Young Lee's "Eating Alone"

On first reading Li-Young Lee's poem "Eating Alone," it doesn't make much sense. The speaker's conclusion that he is lonely *and* has everything he wants is not logical because loneliness means something is missing. In this case, it's the father, who is dead. The entire poem is created out of contradictory elements. Through contrasts of imagery, tone, and the literal events of the poem, Lee uses paradox to give full expression to the grief his speaker feels about his father's death.

Clarifies why the conclusion is not logical, which is an important facet of the thesis.

There is lots of imagery throughout the poem. A lot of it has to do with the different parts of being alive. There is sight when Lee describes "the shovel, leaning where I had / left it, in the flickering, deep green shade" (lines 18–19). There is sound from "the icy metal spigot" (7). There is touch when Lee talks about the cold ground and the cold water (2, 7). There is both taste and smell with the cooking, like with "sesame / oil and garlic" (21–22). But a lot of it also

Added textual support gives a solid basis for the argument. Emma has fleshed out the idea from the first draft with added examples.

Baldwin 2

has to do with death. The poem begins with the speaker picking "the last" produce so that, "The garden is bare now" (1, 2), and Lee further describes the ground as "cold, / brown and old" (2–3). Such images suggest that all has been harvested and that winter is coming, and this is linked to death. Even the image in line 5, "I turn, a cardinal vanishes," suggests the fleeting, changeable nature of all that surrounds the speaker, who himself is shown in the act of turning. The images seem to contradict themselves; on the one hand, they make the reader feel connected to the physical world, but on the other hand, they are cold, fleeting images that are related to death.

The father is dead, even though the poem doesn't state that. But it's obvious from the creaky way he bends that he is old. Since that is a memory from years ago, chances are he has since passed away if he was so old to begin with. In a poem about death, you might expect the words to be flowery, or even like passages from the Bible. You might also expect that the narrator is outwardly sad, or might even cry. But that doesn't happen. Instead, the syntax is straightforward, so that statements like "Once, years back, I walked beside my father / among the windfall pears" (8–9) sound as though they are said in casual conversation. By understating the situation of death, there is a contrast between the level of subject matter and the way that subject matter is expressed. This contrast highlights that even though death is a major and mystical event, it has become a fact of daily life for this speaker. The understated tone of the poem shows that grief is part of everyday life.

This paragraph was already well expressed, so Emma opted for no changes.

Several other contrasts are embedded in the poem. First is the matter of time. The young man in the present talks about a memory in the past. But beyond a simple past/present contrast, Lee adds an immediate past in addition to a farther away past. The present action is the young man picking the onions, cleaning them, then using them to cook. The distant past is the memory that takes place in the second stanza, "years back" (8), while the immediate past is the occurrence recounted in the third stanza that occurred "this morning." The purpose of the immediate past is that it links the past and present. In that stanza, he sees his father waving at him in the current moment; then he recognizes it is only a shovel in the shade, making the speaker painfully aware

More formal language added—tenses clarified.

Refined language more clearly articulates the importance of the moment described.

Added paragraph to highlight additional contrasts in the poem. Since the thesis statement is about contrast, this new paragraph lends further support to the argument.

Further refinement of the thesis. The previous draft asked the reader to make too many leaps in figuring out what Emma was trying to say; here she has made her argument clear.

Baldwin 2

in the present of all he has lost from the past. In this way, that painful moment of father and shovel confusion encapsulates two realities—the past reality that his father was once alive, and the present reality that the father is dead.

Life and death is another contrast placed in the poem. The title, "Eating Alone," and the fact that the poem ends with the speaker preparing his food, emphasizes the act of eating. Eating sustains life; therefore, the speaker engages in an action that highlights his state as a living being, even as he thinks of his father, who is dead. The hornet in the rotten pear is another expression of life and death in the same space. A rotten pear connotes decay, which equates with death, while the spinning hornet is clearly alive.

In summation, there are contradictory elements in almost every aspect of his poem. Because of this, I can come to understand the last stanza: "Shrimp braised in sesame / oil and garlic. And my own loneliness. / What more could I, a young man, want" (21–23). As noted previously, the fact that loneliness is part of what the young man wants is confusing. But in the context of a poem where Lee has shown death alongside life, past and present brushing shoulders in the same instant, and everyday speech coupled with as great an event as death, we instinctively understand that it is in the intersection of contradictory elements that fullness is achieved—whether that be a full life, or a full expression of grief.

Work Cited

Lee, Li-Young. "Eating Alone." *Literature: Craft & Voice.* Eds. Nicholas Delbanco and Alan Cheuse. New York: McGraw-Hill, 2009. 49. Print.

Edit and Format Your Paper

When you're ready to create your final draft, carefully go back and edit your sentences. Make sure your punctuation is correct, your spellings are accurate, and your grammar is in order. These formal considerations are not as much about the meaning of your thesis, but they are the clothes you put on it. After inserting additional content in the second draft, Emma refined her language and made sure her points were as clear as possible in the final draft. She also double-checked that she added all the missing citations, and she made sure to format the paper correctly, with a title, a standard 12-point font, and double spacing.

"Words are about experience." Conversation with Robert Pinsky

Final Draft

Baldwin 1

Proper heading: Name, Prof., Class, Date

Emma Baldwin

Professor Stoller

English 102

3 October 2008

Title that includes author and work

The Power of Paradox in Li-Young Lee's "Eating Alone"

On a first reading, Li-Young Lee's poem "Eating Alone" seems to make little sense. The speaker's conclusion that he is lonely *and* has everything he wants is not logical, as loneliness implies a lack of fulfillment. However, a closer reading shows that the entire poem is created out of contradictory elements. Through contrasts of imagery, tone, and the literal events of the poem, Lee uses paradox to fully express the speaker's grief over the father's death.

Thesis statement

Discussion of first of three elements mentioned in thesis statement

Perhaps the most striking feature of the poem is its imagery. Lee uses precise imagery that appeals to all five senses: we see, along with the speaker, "the shovel, leaning where I had / left it, in the flickering, deep green shade" (lines 18–19); we hear the water from "the icy metal spigot" (7); we feel the cold ground and the cold water (2, 7); we taste and smell "sweet green peas / fried in onions. Shrimp braised in sesame / oil and garlic" (20–22). Yet while the images reaffirm a living being's ability to see, hear, touch, taste, and smell, they also suggest death. The poem begins with the speaker picking "the last" produce so that "The garden is bare now" (1, 2), and Lee further describes the ground as "cold, / brown and old" (2–3). Such images suggest that all has been harvested and that winter is coming—traditional ways of symbolizing death. Even the image in line 5, "I turn, a cardinal vanishes," suggests the fleeting, changeable nature of all that surrounds the speaker, who himself is shown in the act of turning. Thus, the images seem to contradict themselves: on the one hand, they make the reader feel connected to the physical world, but on the other hand, they are cold, fleeting images that connote death.

textual support

textual support

Conclusion about significance of imagery

Baldwin 2

Discussion of second of three elements mentioned in thesis statement

Although the poem never directly states that the father is dead, the imagery, the speaker's act of remembering in the second stanza, and details like the father's difficulty bending years ago suggest the father's age and his subsequent passing. In a poem about death, one might expect the diction to be elevated, perhaps even to the level of Biblical language. One might also expect overt sadness or lamentation over the death of a family member. Lee follows neither of these expectations. Instead, the syntax is straightforward, so that statements like "Once, years back, I walked beside my father / among the windfall pears" sound as though they are said in casual conversation (8–9). This technique of understatement creates a contrast between the level of subject matter and the way that subject matter is expressed. The contrast highlights that even though death is a major and mystical event, it has become a fact of daily life for this speaker. The understated tone of the poem, then, creates the sense that the speaker's grief is so constant and present that he has integrated it into his everyday life.

textual support

Conclusion about significance of tone

Discussion of third of three elements mentioned in thesis statement

Several other contrasts are embedded in the poem. First is the matter of time. Lee presents a young man speaking in the present while remembering a scene from his past. But beyond a simple past/present contrast, Lee adds the element of immediate past versus distant past. The present action is the young man picking the onions, cleaning them, then using them to cook. The distant past is the memory that takes place in the second stanza, "years back" (8), while the immediate past is the occurrence recounted in the third stanza that happened "this morning" (15). The purpose of the immediate past is that it links the past and present. In that stanza, he sees his father waving at him in the current moment; then he recognizes it is only a shovel in the shade, making the speaker painfully aware in the present of all he has lost from the past. In this way, the moment of father and shovel confusion

Conclusion about significance of events in poem

Baldwin 3

encapsulates two realities—the past reality that his father was once alive, and the present reality that the father is dead.

Further discussion of third element mentioned in thesis statement

Similarly, there are other instances where life and death are placed in immediate proximity to highlight the contradicting halves. The title, "Eating Alone," and the fact that the poem ends with the speaker preparing his food, emphasizes the act of eating. Eating sustains life; therefore, the speaker engages in an action that highlights his state as a living being, even as he thinks of his father, who is dead. The hornet in the rotten pear also places life and death in the same space. A rotten pear connotes decay, which equates with death, while the spinning hornet is clearly alive.

Conclusion paragraph

Restatement of thesis, but with further nuance than in intro

Lee, then, builds contradictory elements into every aspect of his poem—within the imagery, between tone/syntax/diction and subject, and in the timing of the literal events of the poem. By using so many contrasts, Lee sets us up to understand the paradoxical last lines: "Shrimp braised in sesame / oil and garlic. And my own loneliness. / What more could I, a young man, want" (21–23). That loneliness is necessary to complete what the young man wants is difficult to reconcile. But in the context of a poem where Lee has shown death alongside life, past and present brushing shoulders in the same instant, and everyday speech coupled with as great an event as death, we instinctively understand that it is in the intersection of contradictory elements that fullness is achieved—whether that be a full life, or a full expression of grief.

Broadening of argument to entire poem

Shows how all three elements mentioned in thesis lead to understanding the poem as a whole

Work Cited

Lee, Li-Young. "Eating Alone." *Literature: Craft & Voice*. Eds. Nicholas Delbanco and Alan Cheuse. New York: McGraw-Hill, 2009. 49. Print.

18

Words

Johnny, the kitchen sink has been clogged for days,
  some utensil probably fell down there.
And the Drano won't work but smells dangerous,
  and the crusty dishes have piled up

waiting for the plumber I still haven't called. This
  is the everyday we spoke of.
It's winter again: the sky's a deep headstrong
  blue, and the sunlight pours through

the open living room windows because the heat's
  on too high in here, and I can't turn it off.
For weeks now, driving, or dropping the bag of
  groceries in the street, the bag breaking,

I've been thinking: This is what the living do. . . .

—from "What the Living Do" by Marie Howe

"I love Anglo-Saxon. I just like 'rock,' 'stone,' 'dirt,' 'blood.' . . . I would much prefer the four-letter word quite literally like 'rock' to 'boulder' even. I love the simplicity of those words, the thing closest to the thing."

Conversation with Marie Howe, available on video at www.mhhe.com/delbanco1e

IN the autobiographical poem "What the Living Do," Marie Howe reflects on the aftermath of her brother's death, personally addressing him as if she were writing a letter. She catalogs the details of everyday existence, its mundane irritations as well as its surprising beauty. The poem is a testament both to remembrance and to continuity. The series of observations culminates in the quiet recognition that these commonplace tasks constitute the way that life, in its varying majesty and modesty, continues for the bereaved.

Poets try to find and then select language appropriate to their subject matter. The resulting selection is called **diction,** the choice of words by an author or speaker. A poem about war might sound percussive, even violent. A love poem's language can seem as lush and comforting as an embrace. So, *how* an experience or feeling is expressed in language is just as important to the poet as *what* that experience or feeling consists of.

This poet writes with great clarity. She chooses language immediately understood by the attentive reader. It's almost as though we're eavesdropping on the speaker as she voices these intimate thoughts to her deceased brother. Look at how plainspoken and declarative the language is: "the kitchen sink has been clogged for days," "the heat's on too high," and "I've been thinking: This is what the living do."

In her interview, Marie Howe expresses fondness for the blunt words we've inherited from Anglo-Saxon (or Old English), the language spoken in Britain centuries ago—before the introduction of Latinate words on the heels of the Norman Conquest in 1066. "I just like 'rock,' 'stone,' 'dirt,' 'blood.' . . . I love the simplicity of those words, the thing closest to the thing." This respect for simplicity is reflected in the precision and candor of "What the Living Do." It's a poem committed to honest contemplation and emotion. "I . . . decided to write—to give myself a break—a letter to my brother John, who I missed," Howe says. "So I just wrote 'Johnny, the kitchen sink has been clogged for days,' because it actually was. 'And the Drano won't work,' because it didn't. And I kept going and just kept writing and writing."

The British poet Samuel Taylor Coleridge defined poetry, in 1835, as "the best words in the best order." More than a century later, American poet William Carlos Williams remarked that a poem is "a machine made of words." Both of these quotes wryly reiterate the necessity for language to fit and work properly within a particular poem's context and meaning. (This is also true for writers of prose fiction and drama, of course; every artist hates imprecision and strives to be exact. But it's particularly the case in poetry, where diction takes pride of place.) When you read poetry, you will want to consider how writers choose the kind of language they do, and how they go about fitting words together and putting them in the "best order."

(CONTINUED ON PAGE 68)

. . . when something huge happens, people don't use big language.

Q&A

. . . I fear for the actual.

A Conversation on Writing

Marie Howe

Writing As Discovery

I want to make one thing perfectly clear. I don't know what I'm doing when I'm writing. . . . For me at least, that a [writer] starts off knowing what she's going to say is something I thought for a long time. Now I know that . . . it's quite the opposite—that the writing itself brought me into an experience I didn't know I was going to have. My brother had died. He was my dearest friend. He was twenty-eight years old.

Poetry in Real Time

I really wanted "What the Living Do" to have . . . the startling reality of the actual. . . . I fear for the actual. It's losing to the virtual. . . . [Think about] what we're able to do with computer technology without having to see or hear anybody. . . . I think that poetry reminds us [of the actual]—it has to do with time as well, right? Why it's difficult to read poetry [i]s not because it's hard to understand, at least for me, it's because it's so painful to slow down. To . . . read a poem is to live in time in a way that is almost unbearable . . . to be all here, this very moment.

Advice on Reading Poetry

Plunge, don't be embarrassed. . . . When I got out of graduate school, I moved to Cambridge. There were all these other writers and poets living there, and . . . we would say to each other "I don't get Wallace Stevens." . . . And someone would say, "I do. Let's meet Thursday at three." . . . Every week we would meet with our friends and just talk about poems we didn't understand. And it was such a joy not to be embarrassed.

The oldest of nine children, Marie Howe (b. 1950) grew up in Rochester, New York. After teaching high school for a time, Howe earned her master of fine arts degree in poetry from Columbia University, where she studied with poet laureate Stanley Kunitz. Her first major success came in 1987 when Margaret Atwood selected Howe's *The Good Thief* (1988) as the winner of the National Poetry Series. Her next collection of poems, *What the Living Do* (1997), was written after her brother's death from AIDS, and is largely an elegy for him. Her third book of poetry, *The Kingdom of Ordinary Time,* was published in 2008. Howe's work is characterized by an open avowal of emotion—the sense of loss as well as hope; she's a thoroughly *personal* poet with an uninflected voice.

To watch this entire interview and hear the author read from her poetry, go to www.mhhe.com/delbanco1e.

RESEARCH ASSIGNMENT In her interview, Howe mentions "what happens, happens in between" in language. Listen to her interview. What does Howe mean by this? How does her example relate to "What the Living Do"?

AS YOU READ Pay close attention to the kind of language Howe uses. Be aware of how her fondness for simple, direct words (rock, stone, dirt, and blood) affects her diction and attitude to the subject of this poem. Think about the way "the everyday we spoke of" appears here again and again.

What the Living Do (1997)

Johnny, the kitchen sink has been clogged for days,
some utensil probably fell down there.
And the Drano won't work but smells dangerous,
and the crusty dishes have piled up

waiting for the plumber I still haven't called. This is
the everyday we spoke of.
It's winter again: the sky's a deep headstrong blue,
and the sunlight pours through

the open living room windows because the heat's
on too high in here, and I can't turn it off.
For weeks now, driving, or dropping a bag of
groceries in the street, the bag breaking,

I've been thinking: This is what the living do. And
yesterday, hurrying along those
wobbly bricks in the Cambridge sidewalk, spilling
my coffee down my wrist and sleeve,

I thought it again, and again later, when buying a
hairbrush: This is it.
Parking. Slamming the car door shut in the cold.
What you called *that yearning.*

What you finally gave up. We want the spring to
come and the winter to pass. We want
whoever to call or not call, a letter, a kiss—we want
more and more and then more of it.

But there are moments, walking, when I catch a
glimpse of myself in the window glass,
say, the window of the corner video store, and I'm
gripped by a cherishing so deep

for my own blowing hair, chapped face, and
unbuttoned coat that I'm speechless:

I am living, I remember you.

Writing from Reading

Summarize

1 List the activities that "the living do."

Analyze Craft

2 Contrast the shorter sentences with the longer ones. Do they serve different purposes?

3 Why do you think Howe uses familiar nouns like "Drano" or "video store"?

Analyze Voice

4 Discuss how tone informs or helps to convey the emotions in this poem. How would you characterize the tone?

5 Notice how many gerunds—present participles such as "driving," "dropping," "hurrying," "walking"—she employs. What does that do to the tense of the action, and what would happen to this "conversation" if it were in the past?

Synthesize Summary and Analysis

6 In this poem, Howe lists the activities of everyday life. How does her choice of words reinforce the subject of the poem?

Interpret the Poem

7 What is Howe trying to say about the living as opposed to those who are no longer with us?

8 Howe indicates she is "speechless" when she sees her reflection in a storefront window. What does her speechlessness represent?

9 How would you describe the main theme or themes of "What the Living Do"?

CONTINUED FROM PAGE 65

WORD CHOICE: VARIETIES OF DICTION

Poetic diction describes an especially lofty and elevated language characteristic of poetry written before the nineteenth century. A tradition inherited from the classical verse of Greek and Latin, poetic diction was used to separate poetic speech from common speech. Poets believed that verse, in its ambition to demonstrate the full power of language, demanded its own heightened vocabulary. As such, ordinary objects received flowery and exotic description. Britain's most famous poet of the Victorian era, Alfred, Lord Tennyson, uses this diction when he calls grass "the herb" and a horse a "charger." In this same vein, the eighteenth-century British poet and critic Alexander Pope memorably names a pair of scissors "the glitt'ring Forfex." Pope's example of poetic diction (represented here by an apostrophe) employs **elision,** the omission of a vowel or consonant sound within or between words. Words like "o'er" were substituted for "over" and "ne'er" for "never." In addition to dramatizing the language, this also allowed for added flexibility within a poem's meter.

"This is the secret of poets. . . . They actually read the dictionary the way some people would read spy novels."

Conversation with Carolyn Forché

A BRIEF HISTORY OF POETIC DICTION

Neoclassical poets (c. 1600–1800) chose subjects and words they felt were refined and therefore appropriate for serious poetry, often relying on Greek and Latin (*classical*) verse for inspiration. The Romantic movement in poetry inaugurated a steady change from poetic diction to more everyday modes of speech. William Wordsworth, a leading British Romantic poet, wrote in 1802 in a preface to his celebrated collection of poems *Lyrical Ballads,* "There will also be found in these volumes little of what is usually called poetic diction; I have taken as much pains to avoid it as others ordinarily take to produce it." In the United States in the twentieth century, Robert Frost notably adopted a similar poetic stance, seeking to voice his poems with what he called the "sound of sense," a phrase Frost used to mean the actual sound of spoken language. From the Romantic era of Wordsworth to Frost's modern period to the present moment, poets have chosen their words with increasing freedom.

While there is no strict line clearly separating divisions of diction, poets' selection of language can be divided into three levels, from the most extravagantly phrased lines of poetic diction to the direct and straightforward. These levels of speech are generally referred to as

- Formal (flowery, grand, and elaborate)
- Middle (educated standard English)
- Informal (everyday speech)

Formal diction refers to complex, grammatically proper, and often polysyllabic language in writing. It sounds grandiloquent—a "formal" word—and tends not to resemble the sort of talk we hear in our daily lives. Listen to the speaker in John Keats's "Ode on a Grecian Urn." He stands, likely in a museum, before an ancient Greek vase and becomes captivated, stanza after stanza, by the different rural scenes painted on its sides: images of men pursuing women, of lovers, of trees, of religious rituals.

John Keats (1795–1821)

Although John Keats died of tuberculosis at age twenty-five, he had already composed poetry of such a caliber that he remains one of the best-known and most admired British Romantic poets. Though he believed himself a failure and wanted his epitaph to read "Here lies one whose name is writ in water," nothing could be further from the truth; "Posthumous Keats," as one of his biographers, the poet Stanley Plumly, puts it, lives on. His actual life, however, was never an easy one; his parents died when he was young, he watched his brother Tom die of tuberculosis, his poetry was generally unsuccessful until after his own demise, and he was unable to marry the woman he loved because of his poverty and failing health. Having studied to be a doctor, he could recognize "arterial blood" when he coughed it up in Rome and pronounced his own death sentence there; the house where he died (by the Spanish Steps) as well as the last house where he lived in London are both museums now. John Keats combined a nature deeply sensitive to beauty with a literary talent that allowed him to render his verses with a grace and eloquence paralleled perhaps only by Shakespeare. His celebrated poems "Lamia" and "La Belle Dame sans Merci" and his odes were all written in a great burst of creativity in 1819.

AS YOU READ Note the first word of the poem, "Thou." Words like "Thou," "Thee," and "Thy" suggest an archaic form of "You" and "Your" that was seldom heard in Keats's day. Note also how the poem argues that what's lost remains, what's gone endures, and ask yourself how this relates to the poet's illness and premonition of death.

FOR INTERACTIVE READING . . . As you read "Ode on a Grecian Urn," circle or write down other words that you would characterize as formal.

Ode on a Grecian Urn (1819)

I.

Thou still unravished bride of quietness,
Thou foster-child of silence and slow Time,
Sylvan historian, who canst thus express
A flowery tale more sweetly than our rhyme:
What leaf-fringed legend haunts about thy shape
Of deities or mortals, or of both,
In Tempe or the dales of Arcady?
What men or gods are these? What maidens loth?
What mad pursuit? What struggle to escape?
What pipes and timbrels? What wild ecstasy?

II.

Heard melodies are sweet, but those unheard
Are sweeter; therefore, ye soft pipes, play on;
Not to the sensual ear, but, more endear'd,
Pipe to the spirit ditties of no tone:
Fair youth, beneath the trees, thou canst not leave
Thy song, nor ever can those trees be bare;
Bold Lover, never, never canst thou kiss,
Though winning near the goal—yet, do not grieve;
She cannot fade, though thou hast not thy bliss,
For ever wilt thou love, and she be fair!

III.

Ah, happy, happy boughs! that cannot shed
Your leaves, nor ever bid the Spring adieu;
And, happy melodist, unweariѐd,
For ever piping songs for ever new;
More happy love! more happy, happy love!
For ever warm and still to be enjoy'd,
For ever panting, and for ever young;
All breathing human passion far above,
That leaves a heart high-sorrowful and cloy'd,
A burning forehead, and a parching tongue.

IV.

Who are these coming to the sacrifice?
To what green altar, O mysterious priest,
Lead'st thou that heifer lowing at the skies,
And all her silken flanks with garlands drest?
What little town by river or sea shore,
Or mountain-built with peaceful citadel,
Is emptied of its folk, this pious morn?
And, little town, thy streets for evermore
Will silent be; and not a soul to tell
Why thou art desolate, can e'er return.

V.

O Attic shape! Fair attitude! with brede
Of marble men and maidens overwrought,
With forest branches and the trodden weed;
Thou, silent form, dost tease us out of thought
As doth eternity: Cold Pastoral!
When old age shall this generation waste,
Thou shalt remain, in midst of other woe
Than ours, a friend to man, to whom thou say'st,
"Beauty is truth, truth beauty,"—that is all
Ye know on earth, and all ye need to know.

Writing from Reading

Summarize

1 Rewrite each stanza in a couple of sentences using everyday speech.

2 Who or what is the poet addressing in the poem?

Analyze Craft

3 Why do you think Keats uses the word "still" in the first line of the poem? Does the word supply more than one meaning? And what does he mean by "unravished"?

4 List examples of elision in the poem.

5 In the final stanza the speaker calls the urn a "Cold Pastoral!" Look up the word *pastoral* in a dictionary. Which definition, the adjective or noun, do you think Keats intends to invoke? Why do you think he chooses this word?

Analyze Voice

6 Describe the mood conveyed in the poem. What words has Keats chosen to evoke this particular mood?

7 How does the use of formal diction help establish a sense of the speaker's attitude?

Synthesize Summary and Analysis

8 Compare the formal diction in Keats's poem to your rewritten stanzas from question 1. What does Keats accomplish by choosing the kinds of words he does in this poem?

9 How does the formal poetic diction add to the theme of beauty in this poem?

Interpret the Poem

10 Why do you think Keats decided to use a Grecian urn as opposed to pottery from other time periods?

11 Explain why you agree or disagree with the famous last lines of this poem,

"Beauty is truth, truth beauty,"—
that is all Ye know on earth,
and all ye need to know.

Missing the showy grandiosity of formal diction, **middle diction** is characterized by sophisticated word usage and grammatical accuracy. It is educated language, but not extravagant—a blend of "common" speech and "elevated" diction, sometimes within the same line. Mostly, however, the language is simple and straightforward. At this point in our discussion of diction, it seems appropriate to repeat a pair of points made previously.

1. Every English poem is a blend of formal and informal speech, but
2. No "natural" speaker would be able to rhyme words such as "telephone" with "bone" or "drum" with "come" so effortlessly. So there is craft involved in this particular voice.

In W. H. Auden's "Funeral Blues," the poet goes from realistic (Unplug the clocks, give the dog a bone, quit playing the piano or talking on the phone) to romantic and excessive—from requiring the plausible to asking the impossible.

W. H. Auden (1907–1973)

Wystan Hugh Auden is one of the most important British poets of the twentieth century (he became an American citizen, but he was born in England and lived there for the majority of his life). With great technical agility and a near-total command of poetic form, Auden could have been a kind of erudite "ivory-tower" artist, remaining aloof from the world. But he allowed his own time to color his poetry, writing about the literal wasteland created by the Great Depression, using the ideas of Sigmund Freud and Karl Marx to examine England's political problems, and gathering the rhythms of colloquial speech alongside his masterful versification. In later life, his poetry moved from the social consciousness of his early work to more personal and even religious poems; both serious and playful, W. H. Auden was continually able to put craft in the service of voice, and to put both craft and voice to use in the hunt for wisdom. After the following poem was featured in the movie "Four Weddings and a Funeral," this lament for a friend's death was widely read again.

AS YOU READ Note the role of sound in this poem—the perfect rhymes in couplets (up till the very last line). Though seemingly casual, rhymes such as "overhead/Dead" and "doves/gloves" in the second stanza reveal how well wrought Auden's lines are. Notice, for example, how the only rhyme that's less than true is the final one; the poet surely could have written "wood," not "woods," or found some other way to make the end rhyme absolute. Ask yourself why the speaker doesn't make the last line a true rhyme and if this poem is understated or overstated as an expression of grief.

FOR INTERACTIVE READING . . . Auden uses several images in this poem. List these images.

Funeral Blues (1940)

Stop all the clocks, cut off the telephone,
Prevent the dog from barking with a juicy bone,
Silence the pianos and with muffled drum
Bring out the coffin, let the mourners come.

Let aeroplanes circle moaning overhead
Scribbling on the sky the message He is Dead.
Put crêpe bows round the white necks of the public doves,
Let the traffic policemen wear black cotton gloves.

He was my North, my South, my East and West,
My working week and my Sunday rest,
My noon, my midnight, my talk, my song;
I thought that love would last forever: I was wrong.

The stars are not wanted now; put out every one,
Pack up the moon and dismantle the sun,
Pour away the ocean and sweep up the woods;
For nothing now can ever come to any good.

Writing from Reading

Summarize

1 What is the speaker responding to in this poem, and what does the title convey?

2 How does the speaker feel about the subject of the poem?

3 How do such phrases as "muffled drum," "mourners," and "crêpe bows," the traditional trappings of a funeral, contrast with the actual occasion of the poem?

Analyze Craft

4 Describe the diction in this poem. When does it seem formal or informal?

5 What emotions or meaning come to mind when you read "the white necks of the public doves"? What comes to mind when you read other images?

Analyze Voice

6 Describe tone in the poem. Is it uniformly mournful? If not, where does the tone shift, and where does it remind you of the blues?

7 There's wild exaggeration in the last stanza's set of instructions: "pack up the moon and dismantle the sun"—as if we could indeed "pour away the ocean" and "put out" the stars. What does this tell us about the emotion of the speaker?

Synthesize Summary and Analysis

8 How many sentences make up this poem? Discuss the consistency of the arrangement of sentences—how do they affect or reflect the poem's subject?

Interpret the Poem

9 Compare the last lines of this poem to "What the Living Do." What does this poem say about death? Explain how it is the same as or different from Howe's "What the Living Do."

10 Look at John Donne's "A Valediction: Forbidding Mourning" in the "For Review and Further Study" section of this chapter. Compare Auden's use of the compass with that of Donne's.

A majority of poets today compose in language that sounds like the speech we hear in daily life. **Informal diction** is conversational, plainspoken language and often makes use of slang, contractions, and mainstream expressions. It might sound like a remark across a dinner table, or resemble something you overhear in the course of a regular day.

Gwendolyn Brooks grew up on Chicago's South Side, and many of her poems describe and explore the lives of everyday African Americans in urban twentieth-century America. The following poem, "We Real Cool," speaks in the collective voice of a group of young men shooting pool. Not only does the poem employ informal diction, it simultaneously exemplifies **dialect,** the variety of language spoken by a particular group of people (in this case, young black men during the 1960s). In turn, dialect usually features **colloquial language,** familiar and conversational speech. Lastly, we can see in this poem a bit of **jargon,** words with specific meaning for a particular group of people. Poets assign language like this to speakers in order to convey a vivid sense of who inhabits a poem, what that person is like or what he or she wants.

> "Gwendolyn Brooks is one of my favorite poets and what I particularly love about her besides the musicality of her poems—because she works quite often with formal structures—are the voices. She has so many different voices that she can write in." Conversation with Al Young

Gwendolyn Brooks (1917–2000)

Born in Topeka, Kansas, and raised in Chicago, Gwendolyn Brooks would grow up to become the first African-American woman to win the Pulitzer Prize for poetry. Her early work, such as *A Street in Bronzeville* (1945), took for its subject the frustrated hopes of urban blacks; her later work became increasingly concerned with black identity, particularly the female perspective. Brooks is known for her bold use of language, often in new applications of old forms like the sonnet.

AS YOU READ Notice the diction Brooks uses to form our sense of these individuals and their lives. Notice also how much gets compressed into and expressed by twenty-four words.

We Real Cool (1960)

The Pool Players.
Seven at the Golden Shovel.

We real cool. We
Left school. We

Lurk late. We
Strike straight. We

Sing sin. We
Thin gin. We

Jazz June. We
Die soon.

Writing from Reading

Summarize

1 Who is the "We" of the poem? What happens to this "We"?

Analyze Craft

2 How does the informal diction of the poem affect your sense of the speaker? What does the poet mean by such phrases as "thin gin" and "jazz June"?

Analyze Voice

3 Advising readers on how to recite this poem aloud, Brooks wrote, "Say the 'We' softly." Why do you think she wanted this word quieter than others? What does it reveal about the confidence of the speaker?

Synthesize Summary and Analysis

4 Describe the author's attitude toward the pool players.

Interpret the Poem

5 How is the name of the pool hall meaningful?

6 How does the final line affect (and change) the poem's meaning?

GENERAL VS. SPECIFIC LANGUAGE

Also at work within any poet's choice of diction is the decision to lean toward language that is specific or language that is more general. **Concrete** diction is language referring to a specific, definite thing. Words like "lawn mower," "beer bottle," and "streetlight" are concrete because they represent actual objects you can perceive with your senses. **Abstract** diction is language referring to a more general or conceptual thing or quality. Because words like "progress," "justice," and "calm" do not refer to things you can see or touch, they are abstractions. Your sense of what constitutes "calm" may be slightly or even radically different from the next person's. An abstraction is, thus, an idea that means something a little different to everyone.

Most poets find that concrete language can help make an abstraction come more vividly to life for a reader. Rather than say, abstractly, "Now that the night becomes calm . . ." poet Richard Jackson writes, "Now that the earth, sky and wind settle into night's still pool. . . ." His line gives us concrete language (earth, sky, wind, pool) in order to more tangibly embody his particular idea of "calm."

> "I think . . . that there's a mastery over [language] once you name [something]. So yes, once I have got it down, once I have got it right, it's not as frightening anymore." Conversation with Thomas Lynch

Most poets do not use abstract or concrete diction uniformly. They make their selection word by word, moving back and forth between the general and the particular, in order to best serve their purposes. Note how in Auden's "Funeral Blues," the poet blends the metaphoric and specific with the declarative and abstract statement. By saying "He was my North, my South, my East and West," the poet suggests that his dead friend was a kind of compass, encircling the whole world; later, that the dead man "was" every day of the week and every hour of each day ("My noon, my midnight"), both "talk" and "song."

Here are two celebrated poems that incorporate both concrete and abstract language. In the first, a speaker commemorates his devotion by comparing his love to the elements of a season. In the second, a speaker stands next to his love and looks out onto England's ocean cliffs, lamenting his loss of faith in the world's goodness.

William Shakespeare (1564–1616)

The truth is we actually know more about the historical figure called William Shakespeare than about most other men or women of the period. He was born in Stratford, England, in April 1564. His father was a successful merchant of the town who later fell on hard times; he attended local schools. In November 1582 he married Anne Hathaway, who was eight years his senior; six months later she bore him a daughter and, in 1585, a pair of twins. In 1597, the playwright purchased New Place, a fine house in Stratford-on-Avon—a sign that he had prospered in his own chosen career. Shakespeare spent most of his working life in the city of London, as one of a troupe of "players" called the Lord Chamberlain's Men. He was an actor in the group, as well as its principal playwright. This was the troupe that in 1599 built the great Globe Theater, which stood on the south bank of the Thames outside city regulations and housed the performances of a number of Shakespeare's plays. Under the patronage of King James I (King of England from 1603 to 1625, following the death of Elizabeth I), the company became known as The King's Men. Shakespeare's poetry includes long narrative poems such as "Venus and Adonis" and "The Rape of Lucrece," and the 154 sonnets. By most counts he also composed some 37 plays. A few fragments of disputed authorship survive, but Shakespeare's pre-eminence as playwright is based on the work produced between 1591 and 1611—twenty years of unmatched productivity and enduring art. A collection of 35 plays appeared posthumously in 1623, published by two other members of The King's Men, John Heminge and Henry Condell. Shakespeare retired to New Place, most likely in 1611, and died on April 23, 1616. Contemporaries wrote often about him—competitively, at first, then respectfully, and after his death, in terms of extravagant praise.

AS YOU READ Try to identify Shakespeare's use of general and specific language. Consider why he chose the abstract or concrete language that you find. It's worth mentioning here also that "Thou" was a more common form of address in the early seventeenth century—a singular and intimate form of the plural "You"—than would have been the case for Keats two centuries later.

Shall I compare thee to a summer's day?

(1609)

Shall I compare thee to a summer's day?
Thou art more lovely and more temperate:
Rough winds do shake the darling buds of May,
And summer's lease hath all too short a date;
Sometime too hot the eye of heaven shines,
And often is his gold complexion dimmed,
And every fair from fair sometime declines,
By chance, or nature's changing course, untrimmed:
But thy eternal summer shall not fade,
Nor lose possession of that fair thou ow'st,
Nor shall death brag thou wand'rest in his shade,
When in eternal lines to time thou grow'st.
    So long as men can breathe, or eyes can see,
    So long lives this, and this gives life to thee.

Writing from Reading

Summarize

1 List the ways the speaker's beloved is lovelier than a summer day.

Analyze Craft

2 Compare the language in the final couplet to the language that precedes it. Where does the diction seem concrete? Where does it seem abstract?

Analyze Voice

3 How does the praise set the tone for the poem? What is the speaker's attitude in the poem? What does he mean by such phrases as "the darling buds of May" or "the eye of heaven"?

Synthesize Summary and Analysis

4 Explain how the poet uses comparison in the poem.

Interpret the Poem

5 What is the "this" the speaker mentions in the final line? How does it "give life"?

6 It could be argued that the closing statement here is boastful (as well as, it turns out, correct). Remember that the poem's subject has to do with life's and beauty's brevity. Is there a kind of consolation in the statement that art lasts?

Matthew Arnold (1822–1888)

The British poet Matthew Arnold was also a literary critic and a commentator on society and education. Interestingly, Arnold stopped writing poetry after 1850, turning more and more to "public" matters under discussion in England. The poetry he did create was principally about the individual in a modern, industrial world, often marked by a melancholy tone. "Dover Beach," widely read during Arnold's lifetime, survives as his best-known poem, and despite its bleak outlook, it was written while he was on his honeymoon. (The next poem here, "The Dover Bitch," makes ironic use of that fact.) Though influential and much honored, Arnold did not make his living as a writer; instead, he worked first as a secretary, then as an inspector of schools, and wrote his poetry and essays on the side.

AS YOU READ Consider how the poet's use of concrete and abstract imagery establishes mood within the poem. What, for instance, does Arnold mean by "the sea of faith," and who might he describe as "ignorant armies" that clash? It might help to know that the "white cliffs of Dover" bear roughly the same relation to the idea of England as the Statue of Liberty or the Grand Canyon do to the idea of the United States. For more on Sophocles and the Aegean Sea, look at chapter 32 on Greek drama.

Dover Beach (1867)

The sea is calm tonight.
The tide is full, the moon lies fair
Upon the straits; on the French coast the light
Gleams and is gone; the cliffs of England stand,
Glimmering and vast, out in the tranquil bay.
Come to the window, sweet is the night-air!
Only, from the long line of spray
Where the sea meets the moon-blanched land,
Listen! you hear the grating roar
Of pebbles which the waves draw back, and fling,
At their return, up the high strand,
Begin and cease, and then again begin,
With tremulous cadence slow, and bring
The eternal note of sadness in.

Sophocles long ago
Heard it on the Aegean, and it brought
Into his mind the turbid ebb and flow
Of human misery; we
Find also in the sound a thought,
Hearing it by this distant northern sea.

The Sea of Faith
Was once, too, at the full, and round earth's shore
Lay like the folds of a bright girdle furled.
But now I only hear
Its melancholy, long, withdrawing roar,
Retreating, to the breath
Of the night-wind, down the vast edges drear
And naked shingles of the world.

Ah, love, let us be true
To one another! for the world which seems
To lie before us like a land of dreams,
So various, so beautiful, so new,
Hath really neither joy, nor love, nor light,
Nor certitude, nor peace, nor help for pain;
And we are here as on a darkling plain
Swept with confused alarms of struggle and flight,
Where ignorant armies clash by night.

Writing from Reading

Summarize

1 What is meant by "the turbid ebb and flow / Of human misery"?

Analyze Craft

2 How does the concrete description of the sea ("long line of spray," "pebbles") compare or contribute to the speaker's more abstract thoughts?

Analyze Voice

3 Describe how the speaker's mood changes throughout the poem. What does he want, and when?

Synthesize Summary and Analysis

4 Describe how word choice in the poem contributes to the overall mood of the poem.

Interpret the Poem

5 What might the poet mean by "the eternal note of sadness" in the first stanza?

6 Look up the word *elegy*. Is this an elegy? If so, to what?

ALLUSION

Poets often refer or allude to the work of other poets; it is, after all, a way of maintaining tradition and tipping a cap to the past. Matthew Arnold's nineteenth-century poem refers to "Sophocles long ago" and compares the present world situation to what the Greek dramatist once heard and thought; "The Dover Bitch" refers to Dover Beach in a less serious but similar way. Both poets and poems are allusive; there's an added dimension to and pleasure in the reading when you know what went before.

Anthony Hecht (1923–2004)

As an undergraduate at Bard College in New York, Anthony Hecht fell in love with poetry, but his pursuit of it was interrupted by World War II, in which he served as an army infantryman. After the war, he studied at Kenyon College in Ohio and at Columbia University, where he received his master's degree. He spent the majority of his teaching career at the University of Rochester in upstate New York. His poetry consciously engages in the broader literary traditions, which means his poems are more formal than those of most of his contemporaries and often include references to other works of literature and art. His second collection of poetry, *The Hard Hours* (1967), won the Pulitzer Prize, and Hecht counted among his many honors the position of Poet Laureate from 1982 to 1984.

AS YOU READ Refer to Matthew Arnold's poem "Dover Beach." What has changed in "The Dover Bitch," and what stays the same? As you consider the allusion to Dover Beach in the title, ask yourself why Hecht might have responded to Arnold's poem as he did.

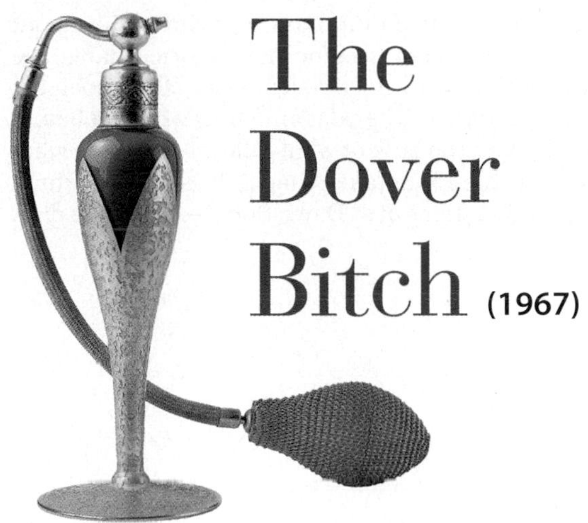

The Dover Bitch (1967)

A Criticism of Life: for Andrews Wanning

So there stood Matthew Arnold and this girl
With the cliffs of England crumbling away behind them,
And he said to her, "Try to be true to me,
And I'll do the same for you, for things are bad
All over, etc., etc."
Well now, I knew this girl. It's true she had read
Sophocles in a fairly good translation
And caught that bitter allusion to the sea,
But all the time he was talking she had in mind
The notion of what his whiskers would feel like
On the back of her neck. She told me later on
That after a while she got to looking out
At the lights across the channel, and really felt sad,
Thinking of all the wine and enormous beds
And blandishments in French and the perfumes.
And then she got really angry. To have been brought
All the way down from London, and then be addressed
As a sort of mournful cosmic last resort
Is really tough on a girl, and she was pretty.
Anyway, she watched him pace the room
And finger his watch-chain and seem to sweat a bit,
And then she said one or two unprintable things.
But you mustn't judge her by that. What I mean to say is,
She's really all right. I still see her once in a while
And she always treats me right. We have a drink
And I give her a good time, and perhaps it's a year
Before I see her again, but there she is,
Running to fat, but dependable as they come.
And sometimes I bring her a bottle of *Nuit d'Amour.*

Writing from Reading

Summarize

1 This poem could be looked at as a variation of "Dover Beach" by Matthew Arnold. In your own words, write a few sentences in prose that summarize what happens in each poem.

Analyze Craft

2 Take your summary of the two poems and look at the differences between your prose language, Hecht's humorous diction, and Arnold's high diction. Point to the differences.

Analyze Voice

3 Does the tone of this poem change as it proceeds? (*Nuit d'Amour,* which means "Night of Love," is a cheap perfume.)

Synthesize Summary and Analysis

4 To what extent does this poem echo Arnold's "Dover Beach," and to what extent does it merely parody (comically imitate) it?

Interpret the Poem

5 How is this poem "a criticism of life," as the dedication states?

Sometimes allusiveness can be confined to a title. Philip Larkin's grim plaint about the approaching (and unavoidable) reality of death uses no metaphorical language and seems in opposition to the fancy titular word *aubade* (traditionally associated with a poem or song about lovers parting at dawn). The poet announces he's up before dawn, "waking at four to soundless dark," and the bulk of what follows describes what he fears. As "slowly light strengthens, and the room takes shape," he speaks without adornment—with none of the romantic associations of a "Dawn Song"—about the dark to come.

Philip Larkin (1922–1985)

Philip Larkin, perhaps the most influential British poet since World War II, bears a literary kinship to his predecessor Thomas Hardy (see Hardy's "The Convergence of the Twain" in chapter 19 and "The Darkling Thrush" in the Anthology of Poems for Further Reading): both are marked by a pessimistic outlook expressed in unsentimental lines that present the mundane details of daily life. Also like Hardy, Larkin wrote novels in addition to his poetry—*Jill* (1946) and *A Girl in Winter* (1947). Larkin is chiefly remembered for his verse, however, and he was part of a group of poets called "The Movement," who embraced poetry that confronted the current day head-on. Larkin, who made his career as a librarian, was well appreciated in his lifetime; collections like *The Less Deceived* (1955) and *High Windows* (1974) cemented his reputation and led to his being offered the position of Poet Laureate—an honor he refused because of the public attention such a post would bring.

AS YOU READ **Ask yourself why this poem is written in the present tense, and if the speaker's feelings change as the lines proceed. Look for both hopelessness and any signs of hope.**

Aubade (1980)

I work all day, and get half drunk at night.
Waking at four to soundless dark, I stare.
In time the curtain-edges will grow light.
Till then I see what's really always there:
Unresting death, a whole day nearer now,
Making all thought impossible but how
And where and when I shall myself die.
Arid interrogation: yet the dread
Of dying, and being dead,
Flashes afresh to hold and horrify.

The mind blanks at the glare. Not in remorse
—The good not used, the love not given, time
Torn off unused—nor wretchedly because
An only life can take so long to climb
Clear of its wrong beginnings, and may never:
But at the total emptiness forever,
The sure extinction that we travel to
And shall be lost in always. Not to be here,
Not to be anywhere,
And soon; nothing more terrible, nothing more true.

This is a special way of being afraid
No trick dispels. Religion used to try,
That vast moth-eaten musical brocade
Created to pretend we never die,
And specious stuff that says *No rational being*
Can fear a thing it cannot feel, not seeing
that this is what we fear—no sight, no sound,
No touch or taste or smell, nothing to think with,
Nothing to love or link with,
The anesthetic from which none come round.

And so it stays just on the edge of vision,
A small unfocused blur, a standing chill
That slows each impulse down to indecision.
Most things may never happen: this one will,
And realization of it rages out
In furnace-fear when we are caught without
People or drink. Courage is no good:
It means not scaring others. Being brave
Lets no one off the grave.
Death is no different whined at than withstood.

Slowly light strengthens, and the room takes shape.
It stands plain as a wardrobe, what we know,
Have always known, know that we can't escape
Yet can't accept. One side will have to go.
Meanwhile telephones crouch, getting ready to ring
In locked-up offices, and all the uncaring
Intricate rented world begins to rouse.
The sky is white as clay, with no sun.
Work has to be done.
Postmen like doctors go from house to house.

Writing from Reading

Summarize

1 In a dictionary or literature glossary, look up the word *aubade.* How does this poem resemble and/or differ from the definition?

Analyze Craft

2 Would you characterize this poem's diction as formal, middle, or informal? What word choices inform your answer?

3 Describe the kind of word choice you observe in the second-to-last line of each stanza.

Analyze Voice

4 What is the speaker's attitude toward his subject matter? What mood pervades the poem, and where does the poet insist on that mood? What emotions does it represent?

Synthesize Summary and Analysis

5 How is the title of the poem reflected in the mood of the poem? What words reinforce this mood?

Interpret the Poem

6 What do you think "that vast moth-eaten musical brocade" and "the uncaring intricate rented world" mean?

7 To what is the poet referring when he writes "It stands plain as a wardrobe, what we know"?

DENOTATION AND CONNOTATION

Poets choose language based not only on what their diction as a whole will evoke but also on the associations offered by individual words. Selecting language for this additional purpose further distinguishes poetry from non-literary writing. Poets bring to their work a complicated and varied set of perceptions tied to particular word meanings. When you read the instructions in a recipe, for instance, the words hold true to their most apparent, literal meanings. The honey you add to a cookie recipe doesn't *imply* anything or suggest some veiled association. This wouldn't necessarily be the case, however, if you saw the word *honey* in a poem.

"I love it when someone says something, and someone else says another thing and that's all there is. And what happens, happens in between." Conversation with Marie Howe

Most words contain both denotation and connotation. Denotation is the most direct and specific meaning of a word. In its denotative meaning, honey is a sugary, sticky liquid substance produced by bees from flower nectar. The same word also carries connotation, meanings and implications that are suggested beyond a word's literal definition. These associations come from the history of a word's past usage, the circumstances in which it has been spoken and understood. By connotation, honey suggests sweetness and richness, and perhaps something highly prized. Or take the word *snake.* In its simplest dictionary definition, it's a long, legless reptile. However, the connotations expressed by "snake" might include associations of sneakiness, danger, or even evil.

We process denotation and connotation constantly in our lives. From the world of marketing and advertising, products and services are offered to us with careful attention paid to the wider, connotative possibilities of language. We are not just sold products themselves; we are also sold the associations they communicate. A salesperson might suggest a more "affordable" item rather than calling it "cheap" because of the negative connotations of that latter word. An "assisted living community" sounds more welcoming and pleasant than "nursing home" because words like "assist," "living," and "community" connote a much more positive and supportive atmosphere than the worrisome medical implications of "nursing." In the business world, "downsizing" implies, through connotation, associations of efficiency and productivity. For some managers, this word is preferable to terms like "laying off" or "firing," which suggest a bleaker outcome.

Connotation is crucial in poetry because it enriches words' meanings; it widens their perceived associations. In a writing genre where language is compact and economical, connotative meaning further extends a poem's potential scope and meaning.

"Most things are not going to be, as we know, new; but the way they are phrased, the way they are positioned in context might make us and should make us re-engage our lives." Conversation with Stephen Dunn

In the following two poems, notice how the speakers' word choice suggests a kind of transformation. In "The Fish," Elizabeth Bishop gives us a speaker intently observing a fish she has just caught. The poem shows us the intensity and specificity of her observation, and the meditation such observation inspires. Note the kind of image-heavy language Bishop uses throughout the poem to describe her subject. She introduces the animal as a "grunting . . . battered" creature, but by the end of the poem, the speaker has come to see the fish as resilient and strong. For James Wright's "A Blessing," a phrase like "I would like to hold the slenderer one in my arms" connotes a kind of reverence bordering on love. This change in the speaker in both poems is illustrated, in part, by word choice and its connotations.

Elizabeth Bishop (1911–1979)

An interest in geography and exploration, a tendency toward quiet understatement, and an unflinching sense of honesty make Elizabeth Bishop a unique and much-celebrated poet, a recipient of both the Pulitzer Prize and the National Book Award. She never saw her parents after the age of five—her father had died when she was an infant and her mother was permanently institutionalized—and she moved from Massachusetts to Nova Scotia, then back to Massachusetts while still a child. Later in life, she settled in Brazil for nearly two decades before moving back to the States and taking a professorship at Harvard. Her work includes *North & South—A Cold Spring* (1955), *Questions of Travel* (1965), *The Complete Poems* (published in 1969 although she continued to publish poetry after that), and her more autobiographical work *Geography III* (1976).

AS YOU READ Focus on Bishop's diction, particularly her descriptive language. Circle or make note of adjectives in the poem that describe the fish.

The Fish (1946)

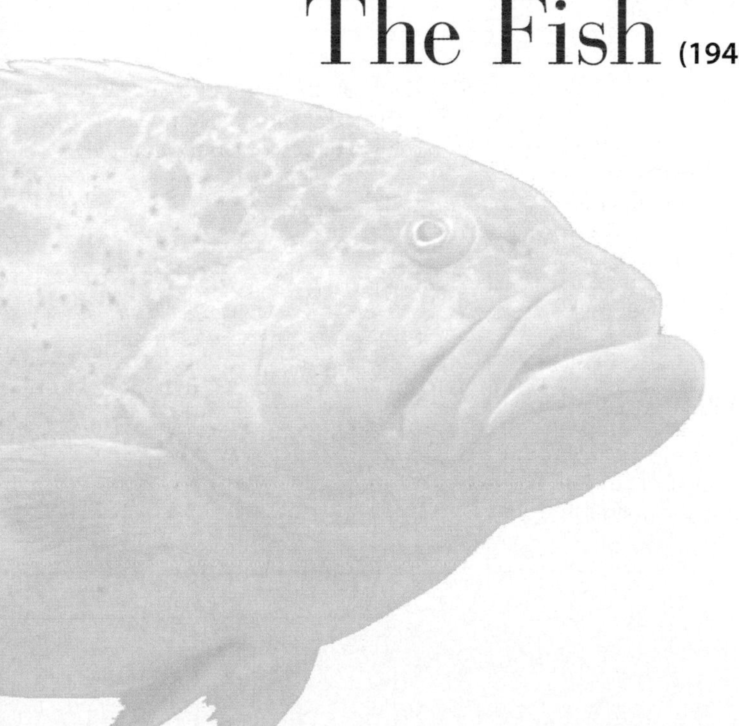

I caught a tremendous fish
and held him beside the boat
half out of water, with my hook
fast in a corner of its mouth.
He didn't fight.
He hadn't fought at all.
He hung a grunting weight,
battered and venerable
and homely. Here and there
his brown skin hung in strips
like ancient wallpaper,
and its pattern of darker brown
was like wallpaper:
shapes like full-blown roses
stained and lost through age.
He was speckled with barnacles,
fine rosettes of lime,
and infested
with tiny white sea-lice,
and underneath two or three
rags of green weed hung down.
While his gills were breathing in

the terrible oxygen
—the frightening gills,
fresh and crisp with blood,
that can cut so badly—
I thought of the coarse white flesh
packed in like feathers,
the big bones and the little bones,
the dramatic reds and blacks
of his shiny entrails,
and the pink swim-bladder
like a big peony.
I looked into his eyes
which were far larger than mine
but shallower, and yellowed,
the irises backed and packed
with tarnished tinfoil
seen through the lenses
of old scratched isinglass.
They shifted a little, but not
to return my stare.
—It was more like the tipping
of an object toward the light.
I admired his sullen face,
the mechanism of his jaw,
and then I saw
that from his lower lip
—if you could call it a lip—
grim, wet, and weaponlike,
hung five old pieces of fish-line,
or four and a wire leader
with the swivel still attached,
with all their five big hooks
grown firmly in his mouth.
A green line, frayed at the end
where he broke it, two heavier lines,
and a fine black thread
still crimped from the strain and snap
when it broke and he got away.
Like medals with their ribbons
frayed and wavering,
a five-haired beard of wisdom
trailing from his aching jaw.
I stared and stared
and victory filled up
the little rented boat,
from the pool of bilge
where oil had spread a rainbow
around the rusted engine
to the bailer rusted orange,
the sun-cracked thwarts,
the oarlocks on their strings,
the gunnels—until everything
was rainbow, rainbow, rainbow!
And I let the fish go.

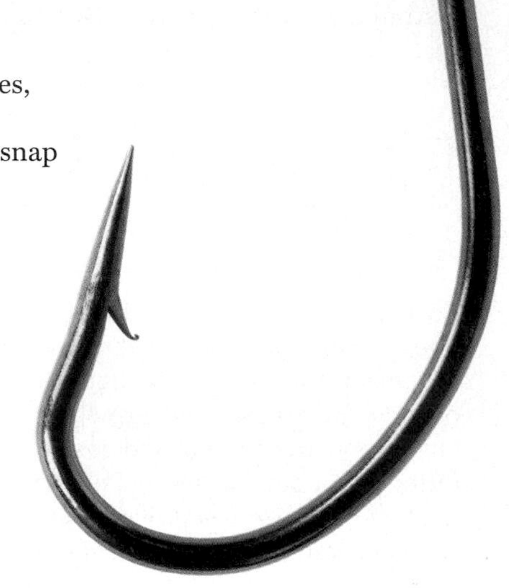

Writing from Reading

Summarize

1 In a few sentences, write the facts of what has happened in this poem.

Analyze Craft

2 How does Bishop describe the fish? What connotations do these adjectives express?

Analyze Voice

3 In a dictionary, look up the word *terrible,* which Bishop uses in line 23. In what ways does it differ from—or reinforce—the word *tremendous* in line 1? How do its meanings—primary and secondary—reflect the speaker's attitude toward the fish?

Synthesize Summary and Analysis

4 How does the speaker's attitude change through the poem?

5 Contrast the basic denotative title ("The Fish") with the language Bishop uses to describe the creature. Why do you think she uses such a simple designation?

Interpret the Poem

6 Explore why the speaker in the poem lets the fish go.

James Wright (1927–1980)

James Wright was born into a working-class family in the steel-making town of Martin's Ferry, Ohio. He began writing poetry in high school and went on to earn degrees at Kenyon College, the University of Vienna, and the University of Washington. Wright won the Yale Series of Younger Poets award in 1957 with his collection of poems *The Green Wall.* Stylistically, in the 1960s Wright moved from a formal style to a more open form of verse. His subject matter often focused on issues of social concern, particularly the divide between the working and middle classes. In 1971 he won a Pulitzer Prize for his *Collected Poems.* Wright's life was cut short at age fifty-two by cancer; in 2004 his son, Franz Wright, won the Pulitzer Prize for Poetry for his book *Walking to Martha's Vineyard.*

AS YOU READ **Consider how nature relates to the animal world and how two kinds of animals—pony and poet—relate to each other. It might also be useful to consult the interview with Robert Hass, who talks of another of Wright's works, "Autumn Begins in Martin's Ferry, Ohio," in chapter 25.**

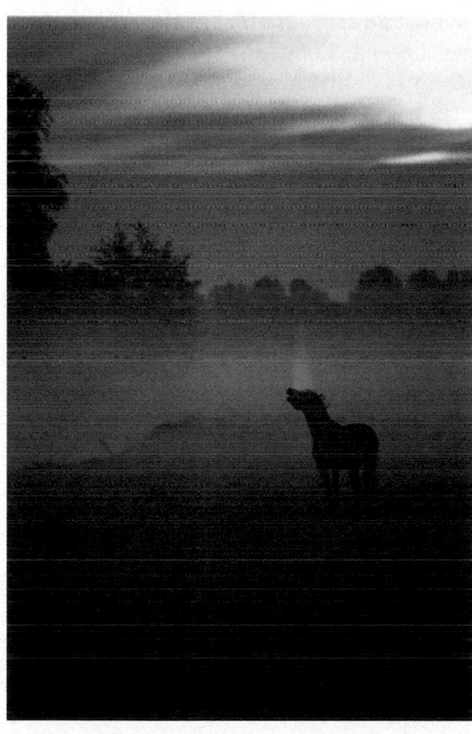

A Blessing (1963)

Just off the highway to Rochester, Minnesota,
Twilight bounds softly forth on the grass.
And the eyes of those two Indian ponies
Darken with kindness.
They have come gladly out of the willows
To welcome my friend and me.
We step over the barbed wire into the pasture
Where they have been grazing all day, alone.
They ripple tensely, they can hardly contain their happiness
That we have come.
They bow shyly as wet swans. They love each other.
There is no loneliness like theirs.
At home once more,
They begin munching the young tufts of spring in the darkness.
I would like to hold the slenderer one in my arms,
For she has walked over to me
And nuzzled my left hand.
She is black and white,
Her mane falls wild on her forehead,
And the light breeze moves me to caress her long ear
That is delicate as the skin over a girl's wrist.
Suddenly I realize
That if I stepped out of my body I would break
Into blossom.

Writing from Reading

Summarize

1 The speaker in this poem is describing a natural setting. Describe that setting in your own words.

Analyze Craft

2 Characterize the language of the poem. How does Wright describe nature? Why do you think Wright chooses this kind of language?

Analyze Voice

3 How specific is the speaker about the poem's setting? How does the sense of place change as the poem progresses?

Synthesize Summary and Analysis

4 How does the poem prepare the reader for the final three lines?

Interpret the Poem

5 What is the "blessing" in the poem? What realization does the speaker arrive at, and when?

WORD ORDER

In committing their ideas to the page, poets must do more than consider just the formality, denotations, and connotations of their speech. They must also decide how to arrange words within the lines of a poem. **Syntax** is this arrangement, the way that words and phrases combine to form sentences and make meaning. Syntax can refer to individual word placement and order, as well as the overall length and shape of a sentence. At its simplest, English grammar is grounded in word order that follows the sequence of *subject + verb + object,* as in a basic statement like "The man ate a hamburger." Changing the order of such a sentence ("A hamburger ate the man") will dramatically alter its implications.

"All the time, from when I can remember, from when I was a child, I thought obsessively about the sounds of words—the cad*ences* of *sentences*, cad*ence* of *sentence ess*. Take a word at random, 'carpet.' . . . What if you turn it inside out: 'predicate' or 'particle'? That's what my mind does, compulsively. And I can't remember a time in my life when I didn't do it." Conversation with Robert Pinsky

So, word order is another potentially powerful tool for the fashioning of meaning. Take a famous example from Robert Frost. He begins "Stopping by Woods on a Snowy Evening" with a sentence whose syntax may seem strange: "Whose woods these are I think I know." A reader might expect the speaker to say, "I think I know whose woods these are." Frost, however, sets up an **inversion,** a reversal of expected or traditional word order. Partially this choice aids the poem's sounds, its rhyme and meter.

But the unexpected syntax additionally allows Frost some extra nuance of meaning. *Ending* the line with "I think I know" instead of *opening* with it contributes to the poem's sense of uncertainty—as well as to a gathering certainty, because the speaker moves from the half-convinced "think" to the decisive "know."

> "That's another aspect of poetry. I just love to say [the words]. I love to have the words in my mouth. I love those cadences . . . the . . . music, sound, and . . . rather exotic diction . . . speaking quite directly to my life and my concerns."
>
> Conversation with Stephen Dunn

Robert Frost (1874–1963)

For a brief biography of Robert Frost, see the Casebook on American Plain Style, chapter 27.

AS YOU READ Ask yourself what this poem would sound and look like if it didn't rhyme, and look for the complex simplicities of the structure here.

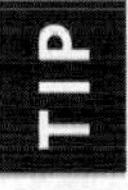

FOR INTERACTIVE READING . . . Underline or list the examples of repetition in the poem.

Stopping by Woods on a Snowy Evening (1923)

Whose woods these are I think I know.
His house is in the village though;
He will not see me stopping here
To watch his woods fill up with snow.

My little horse must think it queer
To stop without a farmhouse near
Between the woods and frozen lake
The darkest evening of the year.

He gives his harness bells a shake
To ask if there is some mistake.
The only other sound's the sweep
Of easy wind and downy flake.

The woods are lovely, dark and deep,
But I have promises to keep,
And miles to go before I sleep,
And miles to go before I sleep.

Writing from Reading

Summarize

1 Describe the situation and the landscape, the weather and the time of day.

2 To whom is the speaker in the poem speaking?

Analyze Craft

3 Why do you think Frost inverts word order in the first line of the poem? Are there additional examples of this technique, and if not, why not?

4 The title word is "Stopping"—a gerund—but the speaker and the horse have already stopped. What does this suggest about this particular journey? Has it, for example, happened before and might it happen again?

Analyze Voice

5 How would you describe the mood conveyed in the poem? What words has Frost chosen to evoke this mood, and what does the word *queer* suggest?

6 How does the use of informal diction establish a sense of the speaker's attitude?

Synthesize Summary and Analysis

7 There's not a single tri-syllabic (three-syllable) word in the four stanzas. How does this support the casual/conversational feel of the whole?

8 Discuss the "music" in this poem—in terms of both the imagery of the harness bells and the actual rhyme scheme.

Interpret the Poem

9 Why do you think Frost decides to attribute thoughts to the horse, and what does this suggest about the "natural" world?

10 What "promises" do you think the speaker might be bound to keep? Is there a suggestion that sleep equals death?

In each of the examples that follow, keep an eye (and ear) out for word order, the particular sequence of words—what's predictable and what's surprising in the poets' choices. Punctuation, too, can change the way a poem *sounds* as well as how it *looks;* consider, for example, the way that the formality of diction in Wallace Stevens' peom contrasts with the lowercase (uncapitalized) language of Lucille Clifton. Pay particular attention to the way a change of emphasis suggests a change of tone.

Wallace Stevens (1879–1955)

Wallace Stevens's conventional life seems at odds with the stunning imagery and unexpected moves of his poetry. He spent years struggling in New York, eventually bowing to his father's disapproval of the literary life and going late to law school. Ultimately, he settled in Hartford, Connecticut, and worked as an executive at the Hartford Accident and Indemnity Company for nearly forty years. He published in literary journals and corresponded with poets such as William Carlos Williams but largely led a life apart from literary circles. Stevens's business life restricted his writing to evenings and summers, but despite this, he cemented his reputation as one of the most important twentieth-century American poets with collections including *Harmonium* (1923, 1931), *Ideas of Order* (1935), *The Man with the Blue Guitar* (1937), and *The Auroras of Autumn* (1950).

AS YOU READ Underline or make note of examples of unusual word order, and imagine the poem if it had been written without these constructions.

The Emperor of Ice-Cream

(1923)

Call the roller of big cigars,
The muscular one, and bid him whip
In kitchen cups concupiscent curds.
Let the wenches dawdle in such dress
As they are used to wear, and let the boys
Bring flowers in last month's newspapers.
Let be be finale of seem.
The only emperor is the emperor of ice-cream.

Take from the dresser of deal,
Lacking the three glass knobs, that sheet
On which she embroidered fantails once
And spread it so as to cover her face.
If her horny feet protrude, they come
To show how cold she is, and dumb.
Let the lamp affix its beam.
The only emperor is the emperor of ice-cream.

Writing from Reading

Summarize

1 Who are the various people assembled in this poem? Why are they there together? What is the occasion in this poem?

2 Try to put "Let be be finale of seem" in your own words.

3 What do you think is being described in the lines "And spread it so as to cover her face. / If her horny feet protrude, they come / To show how cold she is, and dumb"?

4 Rewrite the poem in plain English.

Analyze Craft

5 How would you describe Stevens's syntax (the way the words are arranged) throughout the poem? Does its style serve a point or purpose?

Analyze Voice

6 What is the mood of the poem? How does the title contribute to this mood? How does word order? Word choice? (Why, for example, might he have chosen words like "concupiscent" and "wenches"?) Be specific.

Synthesize Summary and Analysis

7 What is the function of humor in this poem? How do subject, word choice, and word order contribute to the humor in the poem?

8 Stevens puts words in unusual order. What is the effect of this order on the poem's tone? How would the poem be different if the words were put in more ordinary sequence? What do you gain? What do you lose?

Interpret the Poem

9 What does ice cream represent to the speaker in the poem?

10 Who is the emperor of ice cream?

Lucille Clifton (b. 1936)

Born in Depew, New York, Lucille Clifton is the author of nine collections of poetry as well as a prolific author of children's books. In a plainspoken manner, Clifton writes about her personal history as a woman and African American, at times using her own family's genealogy to give voice to common issues of identity. Her poems reflect a pared-down style, bypassing conventional forms of capitalization, punctuation, and line length. Currently she is Distinguished Professor of the Humanities at St. Mary's College in Maryland, a post she has held since 1991. A former poet laureate of the state of Maryland, in 2007 Clifton became the first black woman to win the Lilly Poetry Prize for lifetime achievement in poetry.

AS YOU READ Consider how Clifton's use or lack of use of capitalization and punctuation affects your sense of the poet's voice.

Homage to my hips (1991)

these hips are big hips
they need space to
move around in.
they don't fit into little
petty places, these hips
are free hips.
they don't like to be held back.
these hips have never been enslaved,
they go where they want to go
they do what they want to do.
these hips are mighty hips.
these hips are magic hips.
i have known them
to put a spell on a man and
spin him like a top!

Writing from Reading

Summarize

1 Describe what the poem says hips need.

2 Describe what hips do.

3 What does it mean that hips can "put a spell on a man"?

Analyze Craft

4 Discuss the use of words like "free," "enslaved," "mighty," and "magic." What connotative meanings do these words evoke? How do they contribute to the poem's central meaning?

Analyze Voice

5 How does the speaker's tone create a sense of defiance alongside the celebration in this poem? Note how the title word "Homage" affects everything that follows.

Synthesize Summary and Analysis

6 What aspects of word choice and syntax contribute to the poem's humor?

Interpret the Poem

7 What do hips represent to the speaker?

Walt Whitman (1819–1892)

It is almost impossible to overestimate Walt Whitman's influence on American poetry, and indeed on the American spirit. Born on Long Island, New York, Whitman held a variety of jobs including office clerk, journalist, teacher, printer, and carpenter. He created one work of poetry, *Leaves of Grass,* first published in 1855; with each subsequent edition, Whitman added more poems, eventually titling each group of poems, among them the Calamus poems, Children of Adam, and Drum Taps. Known for its freedom of line, optimism, and expansiveness, his poetry celebrates many occupations and classes of people, thus making him a poet inextricably linked to the spirit of democracy and the broad frontier of the West (even though he lived most of his life on the East Coast). His poetry is also marked by an admiration of physicality and the body, which made his work seem scandalous to many nineteenth-century Americans. His darkest poems are those he wrote during the Civil War and after the death of his hero, Abraham Lincoln. Whitman served as a nurse for the Union troops, but his expansive compassion extends to all soldiers, regardless of their allegiance. Perhaps his greatest legacy to future poets was his unconventional abandoning of established poetic form—Whitman wrote in long, confident lines—and his free use of subject matter that made all aspects of life fair game for inclusion.

AS YOU READ Notice how the speaker starts by addressing the tide and the clouds; next he addresses "crowds of men and women" as well as the voyagers of the future ("years hence"). If Marie Howe's "What the Living Do" is a "private" poem, and Whitman's is a "public" one, look at the difference here between the "I"s.

Crossing Brooklyn Ferry (1891–1892)

1

Flood-tide below me! I see you face to face!
Clouds of the west—sun there half an hour high—I see you also face to face.
Crowds of men and women attired in the usual costumes, how curious you are to me!
On the ferry-boats the hundreds and hundreds that cross, returning home, are more curious to me than you suppose,
And you that shall cross from shore to shore years hence are more to me, and more in my meditations, than you might suppose.

2

The impalpable sustenance of me from all things at all hours of the day,
The simple, compact, well-join'd scheme, myself disintegrated, every one disintegrated yet part of the scheme,
The similitudes of the past and those of the future,
The glories strung like beads on my smallest sights and hearings, on the walk in the street and the passage over the river,
The current rushing so swiftly and swimming with me far away,
The others that are to follow me, the ties between me and them,
The certainty of others, the life, love, sight, hearing of others.

Others will enter the gates of the ferry and cross from shore to shore,
Others will watch the run of the flood-tide,
Others will see the shipping of Manhattan north and west, and the heights of Brooklyn to the south and east,

Others will see the islands large and small;
Fifty years hence, others will see them as they cross, the sun half an hour high,
A hundred years hence, or ever so many hundred years hence, others will see them,
Will enjoy the sunset, the pouring-in of the flood-tide, the falling-back to the sea of the ebb-tide.

3

It avails not, time nor place—distance avails not,
I am with you, you men and women of a generation, or ever so many generations hence,
Just as you feel when you look on the river and sky, so I felt,
Just as any of you is one of a living crowd, I was one of a crowd,
Just as you are refresh'd by the gladness of the river and the bright flow, I was refresh'd,
Just as you stand and lean on the rail, yet hurry with the swift current, I stood yet was hurried,
Just as you look on the numberless masts of ships and the thick-stemm'd pipes of steamboats, I look'd.

I too many and many a time cross'd the river of old,
Watched the Twelfth-month sea-gulls, saw them high in the air floating with motionless wings, oscillating their bodies,
Saw how the glistening yellow lit up parts of their bodies and left the rest in strong shadow,
Saw the slow-wheeling circles and the gradual edging toward the south,
Saw the reflection of the summer sky in the water,
Had my eyes dazzled by the shimmering track of beams,
Look'd at the fine centrifugal spokes of light round the shape of my head in the sunlit water,
Look'd on the haze on the hills southward and south-westward,
Look'd on the vapor as it flew in fleeces tinged with violet,
Look'd toward the lower bay to notice the vessels arriving,
Saw their approach, saw aboard those that were near me,
Saw the white sails of schooners and sloops, saw the ships at anchor,
The sailors at work in the rigging or out astride the spars,
The round masts, the swinging motion of the hulls, the slender serpentine pennants,
The large and small steamers in motion, the pilots in their pilot-houses,
The white wake left by the passage, the quick tremulous whirl of the wheels,
The flags of all nations, the falling of them at sunset,
The scallop-edged waves in the twilight, the ladled cups, the frolicsome crests and glistening,
The stretch afar growing dimmer and dimmer, the gray walls of the granite storehouses by the docks,

On the river the shadowy group, the big steam-tug closely flank'd on each side
by the barges, the hay-boat, the belated lighter,
On the neighboring shore the fires from the foundry chimneys burning high
and glaringly into the night,
Casting their flicker of black contrasted with wild red and yellow light over
the tops of houses, and down into the clefts of streets.

4

These and all else were to me the same as they are to you,
I loved well those cities, loved well the stately and rapid river,
The men and women I saw were all near to me,
Others the same—others who look back on me because I look'd forward to them,
(The time will come, though I stop here to-day and to-night.)

5

What is it then between us?
What is the count of the scores or hundreds of years between us?

Whatever it is, it avails not—distance avails not, and place avails not,
I too lived, Brooklyn of ample hills was mine,
I too walk'd the streets of Manhattan island, and bathed in the waters
around it,
I too felt the curious abrupt questionings stir within me,
In the day among crowds of people sometimes they came upon me,
In my walks home late at night or as I lay in my bed they came upon me,
I too had been struck from the float forever held in solution,
I too had receiv'd identity by my body,
That I was I knew was of my body, and what I should be I knew I should be
of my body.

6

It is not upon you alone the dark patches fall,
The dark threw its patches down upon me also,
The best I had done seem'd to me blank and suspicious,
My great thoughts as I supposed them, were they not in reality meagre?
Nor is it you alone who know what it is to be evil,
I am he who knew what it was to be evil,
I too knitted the old knot of contrariety,
Blabb'd, blush'd, resented, lied, stole, grudg'd,
Had guile, anger, lust, hot wishes I dared not speak,
Was wayward, vain, greedy, shallow, sly, cowardly, malignant,
The wolf, the snake, the hog, not wanting in me,
The cheating look, the frivolous word, the adulterous wish, not wanting,
Refusals, hates, postponements, meanness, laziness, none of these wanting,
Was one with the rest, the days and haps of the rest,
Was call'd by my nighest name by clear loud voices of young men as they saw
me approaching or passing,
Felt their arms on my neck as I stood, or the negligent leaning of their flesh
against me as I sat,
Saw many I loved in the street or ferry-boat or public assembly, yet never told
them a word,
Lived the same life with the rest, the same old laughing, gnawing, sleeping,
Play'd the part that still looks back on the actor or actress,
The same old role, the role that is what we make it, as great as we like,
Or as small as we like, or both great and small.

7
Closer yet I approach you,
What thought you have of me now, I had as much of you—I laid in my stores in advance,
I consider'd long and seriously of you before you were born.

Who was to know what should come home to me?
Who knows but I am enjoying this?
Who knows, for all the distance, but I am as good as looking at you now, for all you cannot see me?

8
Ah, what can ever be more stately and admirable to me than mast-hemm'd Manhattan?
River and sunset and scallop-edg'd waves of flood-tide?
The sea-gulls oscillating their bodies, the hay-boat in the twilight, and the belated lighter?
What gods can exceed these that clasp me by the hand, and with voices I love call me promptly and loudly by my nighest name as I approach?
What is more subtle than this which ties me to the woman or man that looks in my face?
Which fuses me into you now, and pours my meaning into you?

We understand then do we not?
What I promis'd without mentioning it, have you not accepted?
What the study could not teach—what the preaching could not accomplish is accomplish'd, is it not?

9
Flow on, river! flow with the flood-tide, and ebb with the ebb-tide!
Frolic on, crested and scallop-edg'd waves!
Gorgeous clouds of the sunset! drench with your splendor me, or the men and women generations after me!
Cross from shore to shore, countless crowds of passengers!
Stand up, tall masts of Mannahatta! stand up, beautiful hills of Brooklyn!
Throb, baffled and curious brain! throw out questions and answers!
Suspend here and everywhere, eternal float of solution!
Gaze, loving and thirsting eyes, in the house or street or public assembly!
Sound out, voices of young men! loudly and musically call me by my nighest name!
Live, old life! play the part that looks back on the actor or actress!
Play the old role, the role that is great or small according as one makes it!
Consider, you who peruse me, whether I may not in unknown ways be looking upon you;

Be firm, rail over the river, to support those who lean idly, yet haste with the hasting current;
Fly on, sea-birds! fly sideways, or wheel in large circles high in the air;
Receive the summer sky, you water, and faithfully hold it till all downcast eyes have time to take it from you!
Diverge, fine spokes of light, from the shape of my head, or any one's head, in the sunlit water!
Come on, ships from the lower bay! pass up or down, white-sail'd schooners, sloops, lighters!
Flaunt away, flags of all nations! be duly lower'd at sunset!
Burn high your fires, foundry chimneys! cast black shadows at nightfall! cast red and yellow light over the tops of the houses!
Appearances, now or henceforth, indicate what you are,
You necessary film, continue to envelop the soul,
About my body for me, and your body for you, be hung our divinest aromas,
Thrive, cities—bring your freight, bring your shows, ample and sufficient rivers,
Expand, being than which none else is perhaps more spiritual,
Keep your places, objects than which none else is more lasting.

You have waited, you always wait, you dumb, beautiful ministers,
We receive you with free sense at last, and are insatiate hence forward,
Not you any more shall be able to foil us, or withhold yourselves from us,
We use you, and do not cast you aside—we plant you permanently within us,
We fathom you not—we love you—there is perfection in you also,
You furnish your parts toward eternity,
Great or small, you furnish your parts toward the soul.

Writing from Reading

Summarize

1 What is your first impression of this poem? What is the speaker doing?

2 In one paragraph, recount what happens here.

Analyze Craft

3 Find descriptions that seem characteristic of the poem's diction. How would you characterize them? How does the language differ from other poets you've read?

Analyze Voice

4 Describe your sense of the speaker. What is his tone? What is important to him and how can you tell?

5 How does Whitman establish a relationship between his poetic voice and the reader? What is this relationship like?

Synthesize Summary and Analysis

6 Do the long lines and the diction contribute to the tone of the poem? Explain how they do or do not reinforce the subject of the poem.

Interpret the Poem

7 What do you think Whitman means by the following lines?

"Flow on, river! flow with the flood-tide, and ebb with the ebb-tide!
Frolic on, crested and scallop-edg'd waves!
Gorgeous clouds of the sunset! drench with your splendor me, or the men and women generations after me!"

8 Can you say that the poem demonstrates a particularly American way of seeing the world? Why?

Reading for Words

When reading for words, ask yourself what kind of diction the poet has used and how the poet's diction helps to convey a poem's style.

Formal Diction	Lofty, ceremonial, and explicitly serious word choice in poetry	EXAMPLE "Thou still unravished bride of quietness"
Middle Diction	A blend of "common" speech and "elevated" diction	EXAMPLE "Let aeroplanes circle moaning overhead"
Informal Diction	Conversational, plainspoken language; often makes use of slang, contractions, and mainstream expressions	EXAMPLE "Johnny, the kitchen sink has been clogged for days"
Are there specialized uses of language in a poem?	*Dialect:* A style of language spoken by and associated with a particular region or group of people *Colloquial Language:* Familiar, conversational language	EXAMPLE "We real cool" EXAMPLE "We / Thin gin. We / Jazz June."
How does the writer mix concrete and abstract words?	*Concrete:* Specific, physical language describing something perceivable to the senses *Abstract:* Vocabulary referring to something conceptual, not physically material	EXAMPLE "Rough winds do shake the darling buds of May" EXAMPLE "The sea of faith . . ."
What connotations do the words evoke beyond their denotations?	*Denotation:* The literal, dictionary definition of a word *Connotation:* The non-literal associations and impressions a word conveys to a reader.	EXAMPLE "Snake: A long, legless reptile" EXAMPLE "The wolf, the snake, the hog, not wanting in me. The cheating look, the frivolous word, the adulterous wish, not wanting."

How does the order of the words, the punctuation, and the syntax (the rhythm and shape of the sentence) enhance the meaning of the poem?	*Inversion:* A change in the normal, expected order of words	EXAMPLE "Whose woods these are I think I know" versus "I think I know whose woods these are."

Writing about Words

1. Write an analysis of the spiritual conflicts imagined in Stevens's "The Emperor of Ice Cream."
2. Compare attitudes toward religion and/or spirituality between any of the following poems: Arnold's "Dover Beach," Hecht's "The Dover Bitch," Stevens's "The Emperor of Ice-Cream," and Wright's "A Blessing."
3. Both Stevens's "The Emperor of Ice-Cream" and Larkin's "Aubade" deal with the theme of death and mortality. Contrast the tone and meaning by describing the differences between the two poets' language choices. If you wish, you can add Auden's "Funeral Blues" to this mix.
4. Address similarities and differences between tone and language in Brooks's "We Real Cool" and Clifton's "Homage to my hips."
5. Compare the connotations in word choices associated with Robert Frost's horse and speaker in "Stopping by Woods on a Snowy Evening" to those in James Wright's "A Blessing."

For Review and Further Study

Wanda Coleman (b. 1946)

The ISM (1983)

tired i count the ways in which it determines my life
permeates everything. it's in the air
lives next door to me in stares of neighbors
meets me each day in the office. its music comes out the
radio
drives beside me in my car. strolls along with me
down supermarket aisles
it's on television
and in the streets even when my walk is casual/undefined
it's overhead flashing lights
i find it in my mouth
when i would speak of other things

Questions for Interactive Reading and Writing

1. What does this title suggest, and why does the poet declare it "permeates everything"?
1. Why is there a slash between the words "casual" and "undefined"?
2. Why is the last line italicized?
3. Would you call this poem an example of high, mid-level, or informal diction? Why?

Billy Collins (b. 1941)

The Names (2002)

Yesterday, I lay awake in the palm of the night.
A fine rain stole in, unhelped by any breeze,
And when I saw the silver glaze on the windows,
I started with A, with Ackerman, as it happened,
Then Baxter and Calabro,
Davis and Eberling, names falling into place
As droplets fell through the dark.

Names printed on the ceiling of the night.
Names slipping around a watery bend.
Twenty-six willows on the banks of a stream.

In the morning, I walked out barefoot
Among thousands of flowers
Heavy with dew like the eyes of tears,
And each had a name—
Fiori inscribed on a yellow petal
Then Gonzalez and Han, Ishikawa and Jenkins.

Names written in the air
And stitched into the cloth of the day.
A name under a photograph taped to a mailbox.
Monogram on a torn shirt,
I see you spelled out on storefront windows
And on the bright unfurled awnings of this city.
I say the syllables as I turn a corner—
Kelly and Lee,
Medina, Nardella, and O'Connor.

When I peer into the woods,
I see a thick tangle where letters are hidden
As in a puzzle concocted for children.
Parker and Quigley in the twigs of an ash,
Rizzo, Schubert, Torres, and Upton,
Secrets in the boughs of an ancient maple.

Names written in the pale sky.
Names rising in the updraft amid buildings.
Names silent in stone
Or cried out behind a door.
Names blown over the earth and out to sea.

In the evening—weakening light, the last swallows.
A boy on a lake lifts his oars.
A woman by a window puts a match to a candle,
And the names are outlined on the rose clouds—
Vanacore and Wallace,
(let X stand, if it can, for the ones unfound)
Then Young and Ziminsky, the final jolt of Z.

Names etched on the head of a pin.
One name spanning a bridge, another undergoing
a tunnel.
A blue name needled into the skin.
Names of citizens, workers, mothers and fathers,
The bright-eyed daughter, the quick son.
Alphabet of names in a green field.
Names in the small tracks of birds.
Names lifted from a hat
Or balanced on the tip of the tongue.
Names wheeled into the dim warehouse of memory.
So many names, there is barely room on the walls
of the heart.

Questions for Interactive Reading and Writing

1. Why does Collins first select the names, from "Ackerman" to "Eberling," and what do they convey?
2. In the sequence of names that follow, "Gonzalez and Han," and so on, what is he trying to say—if anything—about the nature of America?
3. Is a phrase like "the walls of the heart" concrete or abstract? Or both?

Questions for Interactive Reading and Writing

1. Discuss the line arrangements here, and the use of lowercase letters.
2. Why does e. e. cummings conjoin the names of the marble-playing boys, the dancing girls, and the balloonman?
3. What does the repetition of "far and wee" suggest, and did he mean to say, instead, "far and wide"?

e. e. cummings (1894–1962)

For a biography of e. e. cummings, see chapter 25.

in Just- (1920)

in Just-
spring   when the world is mud-
luscious the little
lame balloonman

whistles   far   and wee

and eddieandbill come
running from marbles and
piracies and it's
spring

when the world is puddle-wonderful

the queer
old balloonman whistles
far   and   wee
and bettyandisbel come dancing

from hop-scotch and jump-rope and

it's
spring
and
     the

          goat-footed

balloonMan   whistles
far
and
wee

John Donne (1572–1631)

For a biography of John Donne, see chapter 22.

A Valediction: Forbidding Mourning (1633)

As virtuous men pass mildly away,
  And whisper to their souls to go,
Whilst some of their sad friends do say,
  "Now his breath goes," and some say, "No."
So let us melt, and make no noise,
  No tear-floods, nor sigh-tempests move;
'Twere profanation of our joys
  To tell the laity our love.
Moving of th' earth brings harms and fears;
  Men reckon what it did, and meant;
But trepidation of the spheres,
  Though greater far, is innocent.
Dull sublunary lovers' love
  —Whose soul is sense—cannot admit
Of absence, 'cause it doth remove
  The thing which elemented it.
But we by a love so much refined,
  That ourselves know not what it is,
Inter-assurèd of the mind,
  Care less, eyes, lips and hands to miss.
Our two souls therefore, which are one,
  Though I must go, endure not yet
A breach, but an expansion,
  Like gold to aery thinness beat.
If they be two, they are two so
  As stiff twin compasses are two;
Thy soul, the fix'd foot, makes no show
  To move, but doth, if th' other do.
And though it in the centre sit,
  Yet, when the other far doth roam,
It leans, and hearkens after it,
  And grows erect, as that comes home.

Such wilt thou be to me, who must,
Like th' other foot, obliquely run;
Thy firmness makes my circle just,
And makes me end where I begun.

Questions for Interactive Reading and Writing

1. See the extended image of the compass here. The Metaphysical poets—of whom Donne was a leading member—called such extended comparison a "conceit." Point out its several uses in the text.
2. To whom is the poet speaking when he writes, "Our two souls"? What's concrete, what abstract in Donne's word choice here?
3. The poet begins by discussing death and ends by celebrating life—is all this signaled by the four words of the title? If so, how?

Alan Dugan (1923–2003)

Love Song: I and Thou (1961)

Nothing is plumb, level or square:
the studs are bowed, the joists
are shaky by nature, no piece fits
any other piece without a gap
or pinch, and bent nails
dance all over the surfacing
like maggots. By Christ
I am no carpenter. I built
the roof for myself, the walls
for myself, the floors
for myself, and got
hung up in it myself. I
danced with a purple thumb
at this house-warming, drunk
with my prime whiskey: rage.
Oh, I spat rage's nails
into the frame-up of my work:
it held. It settled plumb,
level, solid, square and true
for that great moment. Then
it screamed and went on through,
skewing as wrong the other way.
God damned it. This is hell,
but I planned it, I sawed it,
I nailed it, and I
will live in it until it kills me.
I can nail my left palm
to the left-hand crosspiece but
I can't do everything myself.
I need a hand to nail the right,
a help, a love, a you, a wife.

Questions for Interactive Reading and Writing

1. What is the speaker's attitude toward himself in this poem? Is this a flattering self-portrait? What is the effect of that?
2. Discuss the extended metaphor in this poem. In what ways does the house reveal the character of the speaker? How would you describe the speaker's looks, character, and personality based on what you know about this house?
3. Discuss the references to Christ in the poem. How does the crucifixion reference at the end affect the tone of the poem?

Louise Glück (b. 1943)

Song of Obstacles (1985)

When my lover touches me, what I feel in my body
is like the first movement of a glacier over the earth,
as the ice shifts, dislodging great boulders, hills
of solemn rock: so, in the forests, the uprooted trees
become a sea of disconnected limbs—
And, where there are cities, these dissolve too,
the sighing gardens, all the young girls
eating chocolates in the courtyard, slowly
scattering the colored foil: then, where the city was,
the ore, the unearthed mysteries: so I see
that ice is more powerful than rock, than mere
resistance—

Then for us, in its path, time doesn't pass,
not even an hour.

Questions for Interactive Reading and Writing

1. This poem is written in the first person. Who is the "I," the "us," and how do these individuals connect to such large entities as "glacier," "sea," and "city"?
2. Discuss the diction here—high, middle, low?—and give examples of each.
3. In this short poem, Louise Glück manages to talk of "young girls / eating chocolates" as well as "unearthed mysteries"—what's abstract, what's concrete, and why?

Samuel Hazo (b. 1928)

Just Words (1999)

In Arabic a single word
describes the very act
of taking a position.
Greeks
pronounce three syllables
to signify the sense of doom
that all Greeks fear when things
are going very well.
As for
the shameful ease we feel
when bad news happens
to someone else, including
friends?
In Greek—one word.
To designate a hose that funnels
liquid fire down the turret
of a tank in battle, the Germans
speak one word.
It's three
lines long but still one word.
And as for John, Matthew,
Mark and Luke?
There's not
a surname in the lot.
With just
one name they match in memory
the immortality of martyrs.
The longer
they're dead, the more they live. . . .
I praise whatever mates
perception with precision!
It asks
us only to be spare and make
the most of least.
It simplifies
and lets each word sound final
as a car door being shut
but perfect as a telegram to God.

Questions for Interactive Reading and Writing

1. Does Hazo intend a pun in his title's first word? Discuss the two possible meanings of "just."
2. This brief poem refers to "Arabic," "Greeks," "Germans," and the long reach of history. How do the lines and particular words support this wide range of referents, and does Hazo succeed?
3. Of the four gospel-writers, the speaker says "There's not a surname in the lot." What is he suggesting here, and what do you make of the arrangement of the poem's last three words?

Naomi Shihab Nye (b. 1952)

The World in Translation (1995)

It was a long climb out of the soil.
She counted off whole continents
as she lifted each foot,
imagined her dark years falling away like husks.
Soon she could feel objects come to life
in her hand, the peel of banana,
a lightly waxed pepper,
she accepted these into her home,
placed them in bowls where they could be watched.
There was nothing obscure about melons,
nothing involved about yams.
If she were to have anything to do with the world,
these would be her translators,
through these she would learn secrets of dying,
how to do it gracefully as the peach,
softening in silence,
or the mango, finely tuned to its own skin.

Questions for Interactive Reading and Writing

1. Consider the specificity of "she lifted each foot" and the improbable generality of "She counted off whole continents." Does the juxtaposition (the placing of one line right after the other) work?
2. List the fruits and vegetables named here. What is it about the changing condition of a piece of fruit that teaches the poet about living and dying?
3. How does the title organize Nye's poem, and what are "the secrets of dying"?

19

Voice

Tone, Persona, and Irony

JACK and Jill at home together after their fall,
the bucket spilled, her knees badly scraped,
and Jack with not even an aspirin for what's broken.
We can see the arduous evenings ahead of them.
And the need now to pay a boy to fetch the water.
Our mistake was trying to do something together,
Jill sighs. Jack says, If you'd have let go for once
you wouldn't have come tumbling after.
He's in a wheelchair, but she's still an item—
for the rest of their existence confined
to a little, rhyming story . . .

—from "After" by Stephen Dunn

"Tone is the author's attitude toward subject, but it's a rather large scaffolding or coloring of subject matter that when you're listening to someone talk—if you're like me, you're making judgments about that person: Would I want to go out to dinner with him, let's say. What kind of guy is he? . . . You do that with inflection, with pauses, irony."

Conversation with Stephen Dunn, available on video at http://www.mhhe.com/delbanco1e

HERE'S a poem that reports on conversation and relies on **voice.** The poet speaks to us as readers; at the same time he speaks to himself. His diction is as informal as was Marie Howe's in "What the Living Do." Note the contractions ("He's in a wheelchair"), the slang ("she's still an item"), and the general flavor of written language as speech. Stephen Dunn wittily imagines the repercussions for two famous nursery rhyme characters "after" their untimely fall down a hill. The premise here, of course, is comic and even a bit bizarre. Jack and Jill sit at home after their accident like an old married couple, aching and depressed, blaming one another for their predicament. The "little, rhyming story" with which all of us are familiar—"Jack and Jill went up the hill / to fetch a pail of water"—becomes something unfamiliar, *new,* and that unfamiliarity has much to do with **tone.**

Despite his humorous premise, Dunn manages to use the tale of Jack and Jill to reflect on multifaceted themes of intimacy, transgression, and fate. Notice how Jack's "in a wheelchair" because—according to the original poem—he's the one who "fell down / and broke his crown," and her knees are "badly scraped." As you'll see, by the end of "After" the "fallout" of their story has something to say to all of us about coping with misfortune. "The fundamental business of making do," as the poet puts it, transforms what we take for granted—a childhood nursery rhyme—into something with which we must deal.

The lines seem wry, and a little cynical, and matter-of-fact, or all these things at once. Whenever you think about the attitude expressed, you're undoubtedly thinking about the poem's tone. Whenever you consider whose voice you're hearing as you read, you're thinking about the poem's **persona,** the speaker delivering his or her language to the audience.

On the subject of rendering voice in a poem, Stephen Dunn acknowledges the power of **irony,** the use of words to indicate an opposite or unexpected meaning. As he puts it, "irony is a way of managing experience, and thus keeping it at a distance, while at its best being a way of recognizing and opening up experience by delivering simultaneous awareness." A poem like "After" asks us to ponder the emotional lives of a pair of nursery rhyme characters, and asks us to smile at and simultaneously sympathize with the ways we confront our own hardship.

By looking carefully at the artist's choice of tone, persona, and irony, we can improve our sense of the ways poets manage our experience as readers.

CONTINUED ON PAGE 106

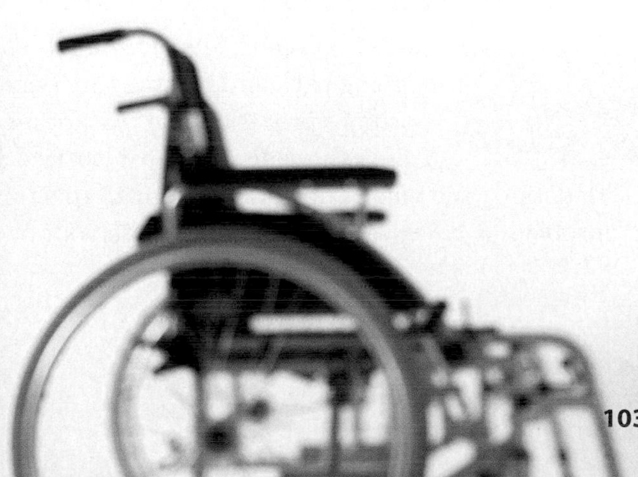

I was a very silent child and boy and even grown-up for a while . . .

Literature brought the world to me.

Q&A
A Conversation on Writing

Stephen Dunn

Poetry Makes Us Part of the World

I think one of the reasons people don't get into poetry . . . [is] they don't quite believe it has anything to do with their lives. Certainly for me, that was the case, and I didn't come to poetry seriously till after college when I started to find those poems that addressed . . . the things that I had inklings about that I was largely inarticulate about. When we find those stories or poems or novels that make us feel part of the world, [we find] . . . the things that we say are secret . . . the things we've not confessed to anybody. Good literature, whether it's poetry or any of the other genres, has a way of bringing us into the common fold, of making us part of the world.

Poetry As a Challenge to Personal Experience

I'm sure you all have heard this, when somebody says, "Oh, I can relate to that." They like to relate to that rather than be subverted, rather than to have their ideas challenged. . . . What I want from good poems is to be offered another way into experience. I don't want to have my experience confirmed.

Revision and Our Own Invention

Lots of revisions, lots of false moves, lots of altering, lots of going back and rearranging—essentially, the [composition] process is like that for me. When I'm working from experience I'm most worried about my selection of details, and when I'm working from an imaginative premise, the problem is how not to be too in love with your own invention.

Born in Forest Hills, New York (1939), Stephen Dunn quit a corporate job to try his hand at writing. Early on, he was an accomplished basketball player, and there's a way in which his skills as athlete translate into the effortless grace of his diction; there's a fluid ease of motion in the lines. He earned a master's in creative writing from Syracuse University, and has taught creative writing at Richard Stockton University in New Jersey since 1974. The author of a collection of essays on craft and a dozen books of poetry, Dunn won the Pulitzer Prize in 2001 for his collection *Different Hours.* Dunn's poetry takes the everyday for its subject; as he puts it in an interview, "I think most of our lives are made up of both things visible and things interior, with a large chunk of them being interior. So whenever I've been able to arrive at clarities about that which is elusive about dailyness, that has pleased me."

To watch this entire interview and hear the author read from his work, go to www.mhhe.com/delbanco1e.

RESEARCH ASSIGNMENT After you have watched the interview, comment on Dunn's attitude toward irony in poetry. How does he describe the way irony functions in his poem "After"? What part does irony play in Dunn's idea of engagement with poetry? How does he (or how doesn't he) achieve this ironic engagement in his poem "After"?

AS YOU READ In "After," Dunn delivers a humorous narrative. At first you may find this poem, a sort of sequel to the old Jack and Jill nursery rhyme, merely funny. As you read more deeply, look for ways the poem reveals an intricate sympathy, a seriousness, and the narrator's darker, ironic attitude.

After (2002)

Jack and Jill at home together after their fall,
the bucket spilled, her knees badly scraped,
and Jack with not even an aspirin for what's broken.
We can see the arduous evenings ahead of them.
And the need now to pay a boy to fetch the water.
Our mistake was trying to do something together,
Jill sighs. Jack says, If you'd have let go for once
you wouldn't have come tumbling after.
He's in a wheelchair, but she's still an item—
for the rest of their existence confined
to a little rhyming story. We tell it to our children,
who laugh, already accustomed to disaster.
We'd like to teach them the secrets
of knowing how to go too far,
but Jack is banging with his soup spoon,
Jill is pulling out her hair. Out of decency
we turn away, as if it were possible to escape
the drift of our lives, the fundamental business
of making do with what's been left us.

Writing from Reading

Summarize

1 What has Dunn added to or altered in the story of the nursery rhyme?

Analyze Craft

2 How does Dunn introduce irony into the nursery rhyme?

3 What makes this poem feel so playful? Compare its use of a previous text, the nursery rhyme about Jack and Jill, with Anthony Hecht's treatment of Matthew Arnold's "Dover Beach" (chapter 18).

Analyze Voice

4 Who is "we" in this poem? Why does Dunn use "we"?

5 Describe the speaker's tone in this poem. Why does Dunn choose this kind of voice for the subject matter?

Synthesize Summary and Analysis

6 How does Dunn marry a playful tone with a melancholy message?

Interpret the Poem

7 When the poem says "we turn away," what do you think "we" turn away *from*?

(CONTINUED FROM PAGE 103)

"The first level of [a poem's] meaning is simply to be moved and to hear a speaker, to hear voice giving voice to what is within the poet." Conversation with Carolyn Forché

TONE

On a daily basis, sometimes hardly conscious of it, we interpret the language we hear. We know to listen for clues that indicate to us exactly how people intend their language. By putting extra emphasis on one word in a sentence, the ordinary question "Are you going to eat that?" can suddenly become the more surprised "Are you going to *eat* that?" If, instead, the speaker asks "Are you going to eat *that?*" the question focuses on the thing about to be eaten rather than the act of consumption. The word choice is exactly the same, but the meaning is quite different. If the emphasis falls on the word *you,* a fourth meaning may become central: how come *you* get to eat that and I can't? All this has to do with **intonation,** the *way* a thing gets said. We make interpretive distinctions by tuning in to **tone of voice,** the particular communicative quality of a person's speech.

"A poem is . . . like a musical score for human speech. . . . You come and you read the poem and you play the voice."

Conversation with Li-Young Lee

In poetry, language works in similar, equally subtle ways. As you're reading a poem, analyzing the intentions of word choice and word order, you will often find a kind of implicit meaning emerges from these lines. In poetry, **tone** is an attitude conveyed toward a poem's subject as suggested by the poet's language. No one element of poetry establishes tone by itself. It is a kind of cumulative effect, resulting from all of poetry's components, including word choice and arrangement, figures of speech, rhythm, and diction and sound.

Tone in poetry is as variable as the different voices you hear every day on the street, capable of humor, seriousness, contemplation, desperation, anger, or any other emotion. A love poem designed to woo its recipient might do so seriously, with soaring language; or it might work just as effectively with comedy, using wordplay. There's no one right tone for a thought or idea, just the prerogative of the author who wishes to best communicate his or her intended meaning.

"Once you get the poem right . . . you sound like yourself talking to yourself. It's that voice that we hear just before we fall asleep, the voice that we start out the day with when everything seems to fall into place." Conversation with Thomas Lynch

The following poems illustrate a range of tones, from the restrained to the emotional to the ambivalent. The first selection describes the internal and external experiences of a World War II aviator operating the gun on the belly of a large bomber.

Randall Jarrell (1914–1965)

Born in Tennessee, Randall Jarrell spent part of his childhood in California before returning to his native state for an education at Vanderbilt University. He published his first collection of poetry, *Blood for a Stranger* (1942), in the same year that he enlisted in the Army Air Corps, in which he served during World War II. After the war, he taught at the Women's College of the University of North Carolina until his death at age fifty-one, when he was hit by a car. Jarrell's poetry is sensitive to the pain of his speakers, whether domestic housewives or soldiers fighting in World War II. In addition to winning the National Book Award for *The Woman at the Washington Zoo* (1960), Jarrell held the position of Poet Laureate. He was also an unusually influential literary critic, championing poetry by Walt Whitman and Robert Frost, and helping to establish the success of such poets as Elizabeth Bishop and William Carlos Williams.

AS YOU READ Think about how the tone of the language (for example, "wet fur froze," "black flak and the nightmare fighters") helps the poem communicate an attitude or particular atmosphere. Notice, also, the bleak efficiency here; it's a poem of only five lines.

The Death of the Ball Turret Gunner (1945)

From my mother's sleep I fell into the State,
And I hunched in its belly till my wet fur froze.
Six miles from earth, loosed from the dream of life,
I woke to black flak and the nightmare fighters.
When I died they washed me out of the turret with a hose.

Writing from Reading

Summarize

1 Describe the fate the flyer imagines for himself.

Analyze Craft

2 Why do you think the word *state* is capitalized?

3 What images are used in this poem?

Analyze Voice

4 How would you characterize the tone of the poem? Does it seem like an unusual or an apt choice for a poem about war?

Synthesize Summary and Analysis

5 How does the description of the flyer's experience show the horror he is imagining?

Interpret the Poem

6 How does the tone of the poem's final line contrast with the image it describes?

7 Is this an anti-war poem or a heroic poem? How do you think the speaker feels about war?

Sometimes a poem's tone is especially subtle or multilayered. Theodore Roethke's "My Papa's Waltz" is one such work. A memory of the poet's father playfully dancing with his son, the poem entertains different attitudes simultaneously. We start with the knowledge that the father is drunk—or at least has been drinking—and that the boy hangs on "like death" because it's hard to follow where the dancing adult leads. The father doesn't fully realize how much he is bending or stretching the bond of love between parent and child. The mother, watching, frowns. By poem's end, however, the dance becomes a kind of elegy, with the speaker "still clinging" to the memories of childhood and the strong if implicit suggestion that the father is dead. These emotions in opposition—fear, delight, disapproval—are bodied forth in a domestic scene, as from kitchen to bedroom "we romped."

Theodore Roethke (1908–1963)

Growing up, Theodore Roethke loved to spend time in the greenhouse his father and uncle owned in Saginaw, Michigan. This was a lifelong fascination; his poems are full of imagery and metaphor that hinge on the natural world. Unsentimental in his portrayal of nature, Roethke was equally unafraid to put his own feelings and experiences into his poems, making him the forerunner of confessional poets like Anne Sexton and Sylvia Plath. His collections were widely acclaimed: *The Waking* (1953) won the Pulitzer Prize, and *Words for the Wind* (1958) won the National Book Award, as did his posthumous *The Far Field* (1964). His mental health was precarious and his mood swings large, but Roethke was a celebrated and devoted teacher; he spent most of his teaching life at the University of Washington.

AS YOU READ Think about how the poet's feelings about memory might have more than one dimension. Consider also how the rhyme of the poem reinforces its meaning and tone using slant rhymes, rather than exact rhymes. In the final two stanzas, however, it's as if the boy gets the hang of his father's waltzing rhythm and can follow along exactly once he gets into the "swing of things" at poem's end.

FOR INTERACTIVE READING . . . Circle the approximate, or slant, rhymes, such as "dizzy" and "easy" or "pans" and "countenance." Note the waltz time and dance step involved.

My Papa's Waltz (1948)

The whiskey on your breath
Could make a small boy dizzy;
But I hung on like death:
Such waltzing was not easy.

We romped until the pans
Slid from the kitchen shelf;
My mother's countenance
Could not unfrown itself.

The hand that held my wrist
Was battered on one knuckle;
At every step you missed
My right ear scraped a buckle.

You beat time on my head
With a palm caked hard by dirt,
Then waltzed me off to bed
Still clinging to your shirt.

Writing from Reading

Summarize

1 What has happened in this poem?

2 How does the mother feel about what has happened? Is it clear how the child feels?

Analyze Craft

3 Pick out phrases and words that indicate the speaker remembers his father's behavior fondly.

4 Pick out phrases and words that indicate the speaker remembers his father's behavior negatively or critically.

Analyze Voice

5 Who is the speaker in this poem?

6 Do you think the poem's variation in tone is purposeful? Discuss why or why not.

Synthesize Summary and Analysis

7 How does the innocence of the child's perspective allow us to draw our own conclusions about what happened here?

Interpret the Poem

8 Discuss the significance of the poem's final line. What if Roethke did not include this image of the boy "still clinging"? Would that change your sense of the poem's tone?

In contrast to the tone and word choice of poets like Stephen Dunn and Theodore Roethke, Wallace Stevens employs a diction that sounds formal and even stately. This is not "conversational" language—a poet talking to himself and us as audience; rather, it is a carefully arranged and presented series of pronouncements, insisting on attentiveness on the reader's part. In this poem—which first appeared in *Poetry* magazine in 1915, although Stevens later revised and enlarged it—he details an aging woman's religious dilemma, a conflict between traditional religious piety and individual, personal spiritual exploration.

Wallace Stevens (1879–1955)

For a brief biography of Wallace Stevens, see chapter 18.

AS YOU READ Consider "Sunday Morning" in the terms that we've been using: as a series of different poetic elements that establish tone. One way of reading this poem is in terms of its ambitious range of referents—to the Holy Land, to Greek gods and "the blood of paradise," etc.; another is to read about an old woman in the sun, drinking a cup of coffee and wondering what happens when she dies.

FOR INTERACTIVE READING . . . Make note of or circle words like "death" or that pertain to death, both obviously (as in "tomb" or "grave") or implicitly where you think Stevens might be making a reference to death. Underline or note words or phrases that are used repeatedly in the poem.

Sunday Morning (1915)

I

Complacencies of the peignoir, and late
Coffee and oranges in a sunny chair,
And the green freedom of a cockatoo
Upon a rug, mingle to dissipate
The holy hush of ancient sacrifice.
She dreams a little, and she feels the dark
Encroachment of that old catastrophe,
As a calm darkens among water-lights.
The pungent oranges and bright, green wings
Seem things in some procession of the dead,
Winding across wide water, without sound.
The day is like wide water, without sound,
Stilled for the passing of her dreaming feet
Over the seas, to silent Palestine,
Dominion of the blood and sepulchre.

II

She hears, upon that water without sound,
A voice that cries, "The tomb in Palestine
Is not the porch of spirits lingering;
It is the grave of Jesus, where he lay."
We live in an old chaos of the sun,
Or old dependency of day and night,
Or island solitude, unsponsored, free,
Of that wide water, inescapable.
Deer walk upon our mountains, and the quail
Whistle about us their spontaneous cries;
Sweet berries ripen in the wilderness;
And, in the isolation of the sky,
At evening, casual flocks of pigeons make
Ambiguous undulations as they sink,
Downward to darkness, on extended wings.

III

She says, "I am content when wakened birds,
Before they fly, test the reality
Of misty fields, by their sweet questionings;
But when the birds are gone, and their warm fields
Return no more, where, then, is paradise?"
There is not any haunt of prophecy,
Nor any old chimera of the grave,
Neither the golden underground, nor isle
Melodious, where spirits gat them home,
Nor visionary South, nor cloudy palm
Remote on heaven's hill, that has endured
As April's green endures; or will endure
Like her remembrance of awakened birds,
Or her desire for June and evening, tipped
By the consummation of the swallow's wings.

IV

She says, "But in contentment I still feel
The need of some imperishable bliss."
Death is the mother of beauty; hence from her,
Alone, shall come fulfillment to our dreams
And our desires. Although she strews the leaves
Of sure obliteration on our paths—
The path sick sorrow took, the many paths
Where triumph rang its brassy phrase, or love
Whispered a little out of tenderness—
She makes the willow shiver in the sun
For maidens who were wont to sit and gaze
Upon the grass, relinquished to their feet.
She causes boys to bring sweet-smelling pears
And plums in ponderous piles. The maidens taste
And stray impassioned in the littering leaves.

V

Supple and turbulent, a ring of men
Shall chant in orgy on a summer morn
Their boisterous devotion to the sun—
Not as a god, but as a god might be,
Naked among them, like a savage source.
Their chant shall be a chant of paradise,
Out of their blood, returning to the sky;
And in their chant shall enter, voice by voice,
The windy lake wherein their lord delights,
The trees, like serafim, and echoing hills,
That choir among themselves long afterward.
They shall know well the heavenly fellowship
Of men that perish and of summer morn—
And whence they came and whither they shall go,
The dew upon their feet shall manifest.

Writing from Reading

Summarize

1 What does the title indicate about the subject of the poem? What activities are typical of a Sunday morning?

2 What information about the situation of the poem—*when* it takes place, *where* it takes place, *what's* at stake or being talked about—do you obtain from the poem's first section?

Analyze Craft

3 In his interview, Stephen Dunn talks about reciting this poem on Sunday mornings with his wife and about Stevens's "exotic" diction. What about the words chosen for this poem might make Dunn describe Stevens's word choices as exotic? Why do you think Stevens chooses to use language like this?

Analyze Voice

4 Look at the opening phrase "Complacencies of the peignoir" or the penultimate one of the second stanza, "Ambiguous undulations as they sink," and consider Stevens's voice. What uses does he make of the language of everyday speech, and how does he alter and heighten it? Note the places where he *does* use everyday language or commonplace objects—such as "coffee and oranges" or "sweet berries ripen in the wilderness." How does this kind of juxtaposition create a voice and tone for this poem?

5 Where in the poem does the speaker hint that the woman is old?

Synthesize Summary and Analysis

6 Each of the stanzas has precisely fifteen lines. How does this formal arrangement serve the poet's purpose, and what does the repetition of such words as "wide water" accomplish?

Interpret the Poem

7 What is the "old catastrophe" mentioned in the first section? Compare stanza 5 here to John Keats's meditation on a Grecian urn (chapter 18). Do he and Stevens have a similar reaction to the past?

Anne Bradstreet was one of the first poets in the American colonies and inarguably our country's first acclaimed female poet. Unbeknownst to Bradstreet, friends of hers saw to the publication of her poems in London in a collection titled *The Tenth Muse, Lately Sprung Up in America,* in 1650. Written in 1678, the following poem introduced a later edition of that volume and voices Bradstreet's mixed feelings about the book's earlier, unauthorized publication.

Anne Bradstreet (1612–1672)

Among the earliest Puritans to settle the American colonies, Anne Bradstreet suffered the hardships of an educated Englishwoman brought to the harsh conditions of a struggling colony. Nevertheless, as her poetry attests, she loved her husband, her home, and her children. It was rare for a Puritan woman to write poetry, and equally rare that she was educated in Latin, Hebrew, Greek, medicine, and theology. The mother of eight children and wife to the governor of Massachusetts, Bradstreet shared most of her poems only with family and friends. However, her brother-in-law took a collection of her poems to England, where they were published as *The Tenth Muse, Lately Sprung Up in America* (1650). Echoing Plato's praise of Sappho, this work by the "tenth muse" was the first book by a New Englander ever to be published.

AS YOU READ Words like "thou" were common in Anne Bradstreet's day; in this poem, they are not examples of elevated poetic diction but, rather, are everyday speech. "Thou" was the informal or diminutive form of "you," and so the very first word of the poem suggests a kind of intimacy with the "offspring" addressed. Notice the ways in which "the author" compares "her book" to a child and the self-effacing claim that her brain is "feeble." She's both proud and apologetic, both serious and tongue-in-cheek, and the mixture of these elements is part of the poem's great charm.

The Author to Her Book

(1678)

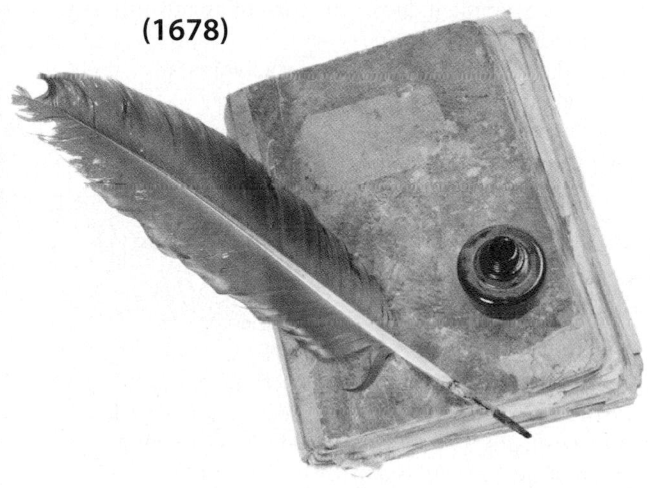

Thou ill-formed offspring of my feeble brain,
Who after birth didst by my side remain,
Till snatched from thence by friends, less wise than true,
Who thee abroad exposed to public view,
Made thee in rags, halting to th' press to trudge,
Where errors were not lessened (all may judge).
At thy return my blushing was not small,
My rambling brat (in print) should mother call.
I cast thee by as one unfit for light,
Thy visage was so irksome in my sight;
Yet being mine own, at length affection would
Thy blemishes amend, if so I could.
I washed thy face, but more defects I saw,
And rubbing off a spot still made a flaw.
I stretched thy joints to make thee even feet,
Yet still thou run'st more hobbling than is meet;
In better dress to trim thee was my mind,
But nought save home-spun cloth, i' th' house I find.
In this array, 'mongst vulgars mayst thou roam.
In critics' hands, beware thou dost not come,
And take thy way where yet thou art not known;
If for thy Father asked, say, thou hadst none;
And for thy Mother, she alas is poor,
Which caused her thus to send thee out of door.

Writing from Reading

Summarize

1 Who or what is the speaker addressing? To what does "ill-formed offspring of my feeble brain" refer?

2 List the complaints the speaker has about her book.

3 Why in the last lines are we told "thy Mother . . . is poor"?

Analyze Craft

4 Discuss how the poet compares a book to a child. How do these lines about the book also reveal her thoughts on motherhood?

Analyze Voice

5 How does the speaker's attitude toward her book change as the poem progresses?

Synthesize Summary and Analysis

6 How does the ambivalence the speaker expresses toward her book contrast with the imagery of motherhood and a mother's attitude toward a child? How do these go together in this poem?

Interpret the Poem

7 What does the line "If for thy Father asked, say, thou hadst none" suggest to you about the author's feelings toward the book?

For Review and Further Study

Charlotte Mew (1869–1928)

I So Liked Spring (1915)

I so liked Spring last year
  Because you were here;—
    The thrushes too—
Because it was these you so liked to hear—
    I so liked you.

  This year's a different thing,—
    I'll not think of you.
But I'll like Spring because it is simply Spring
    As the thrushes do.

Questions for Interactive Reading and Writing

1. Summarize the history of the relationship described.
2. There is an element of surprise in the poem. How does Mew create this surprise?
3. Notice there's only one three-syllable word—"different"—in the poem's nine lines. There's an essential simplicity to the diction throughout, but the situation is a complicated one. Discuss.
4. What word choices create the note of melancholy on which this poem ends?

Gary Soto (b. 1952)

Mexicans Begin Jogging (1981)

At the factory I worked
In the fleck of rubber, under the press
Of an oven yellow with flame,
Until the border patrol opened
Their vans and my boss waved for us to run.
"Over the fence, Soto," he shouted,
And I shouted that I was American.
"No time for lies," he said, and pressed
A dollar in my palm, hurrying me
Through the back door.
Since I was on his time, I ran
And became the wag to a short tail of Mexicans—
Ran past the amazed crowds that lined
The streets and blurred like photographs, in rain.
I ran from that industrial road to the soft
Houses where people paled at the turn of an autumn sky.
What could I do but yell *vivas*
To baseball, milkshakes, and those sociologists
Who would clock me
As I jog into the next century
On the power of a great, silly grin.

Questions for Interactive Reading and Writing

1. What is the action in the poem? What is the misunderstanding?
2. There's good humor here, even in the face of a legal absurdity, and the title word *jogging* suggests a kind of leisure activity of the middle class. What clues does the title reveal about the poem's tone?
3. What does the line "Since I was on his time, I ran" tell us about the speaker?
4. Discuss how Soto frames himself in the group of Mexican workers. Does he feel separate from or unified with them?
5. Note the phrase "great, silly grin" with which the poem closes, and the way the poet likens what he's doing to a kind of *corrida,* or running with the bulls. Why does Soto have a "great, silly grin" for the next century?

William Stafford (1914–1993)

Traveling through the Dark (1962)

Traveling through the dark I found a deer
dead on the edge of the Wilson River road.
It is usually best to roll them into the canyon:
that road is narrow; to swerve might make more dead.

By glow of the tail-light I stumbled back of the car
and stood by the heap, a doe, a recent killing;
she had stiffened already, almost cold.
I dragged her off; she was large in the belly.

My fingers touching her side brought me the reason—
her side was warm; her fawn lay there waiting,
alive, still, never to be born.
Beside that mountain road I hesitated.

The car aimed ahead its lowered parking lights;
under the hood purred the steady engine.
I stood in the glare of the warm exhaust turning red;
around our group I could hear the wilderness listen.

I thought hard for us all—my only swerving—
then pushed her over the edge into the river.

Questions for Interactive Reading and Writing

1. What happens here, and how does the word *usually* establish tone?
2. What does the poet learn when he touches the dead doe? Why does he hesitate? Identify the words that give you clues about the speaker's attitude and why "I hesitated."
3. How does the word *still* do double duty in the phrase "alive, still, never to be born"?
4. Notice the narrative ease of the poem, the uninflected voice. Travel the distance between line 3—"It is usually best to roll them into the canyon"—and what happens at poem's end. Who does the speaker mean by "our group" and how does "the wilderness listen"? What does "my only swerving" suggest, and what do you imagine the speaker thought as he "pushed her over the edge"? How would you describe the tone of the poem, and does it seem appropriate to the scene's subject?
5. Can you detect an implied meaning in the title? Describe the interaction of man and nature here.

William Carlos Williams (1883–1963)

For a brief biography of William Carlos Williams, see chapter 20.

This Is Just to Say (1934)

I have eaten
the plums
that were in
the icebox

and which
you were probably
saving
for breakfast

Forgive me
they were delicious
so sweet
and so cold

Questions for Interactive Reading and Writing

1. What does the word *just* imply—"only" or "fairly" or both? Why is the title a part of the poem that follows? Compare the tone of "This Is Just to Say" to the tone of Samuel Hazo's "Just Words" in the previous chapter.
2. What is the past action narrated and why has the poet narrated it?
3. Does this feel like an actual poem to you? Why or why not?
4. Williams avoids punctuation, but he does capitalize "Forgive." Why? What effect does this produce?
5. Discuss the tone here. Is it sincere? Comic? Apologetic?
6. How much does this simple poem tell the reader about the speaker? Who is the "you" addressed?
7. Think of Wordsworth's definition of a poem as "emotion recollected in tranquility." Would you say Williams agrees?
8. Imagine that you found this note on the icebox door or kitchen table as you come down to breakfast after your guest has left. What would be your reaction?

PERSONA

In some poems, like Anne Bradstreet's, we can be confident that the speaker of a poem is a version of the poet himself or herself. This is equally the case for the poems you've just looked at by Mew, Soto, Stafford, and Williams; most often, when a poet says "I," we can associate that first-person pronoun with the life and mind of the speaker. At other times, a poet "throws" his or her voice—becoming a character other than "I" even when the first-person pronoun is used. Researching a bit of biographical information can help us make an informed decision about this. Knowing, for example, that the poet Ben Jonson lost his eldest son to plague helps us understand that the speaking voice of the following poem is indeed Jonson's.

> "It seems to me that because a poem is a score for the human voice—a voice implies a speaker. So in a way every poem is a portrait of a speaker." Conversation with Li-Young Lee

Ben Jonson (1573–1637)

Born in Westminster, England, Ben Jonson rose to become a well-known and respected playwright, England's poet laureate, and the author of many masques—that is, spectacles that included drama, poetry, and song performed to entertain the court. Jonson's satirical eye led him to create a brand of comedy that consisted of eccentric characters who represent various types of human temperament, as in *Every Man in His Humour* (1598). Though a scholar and a skilled lyrical poet, Jonson was a man of large appetites and volatile temper (he was nearly executed for killing a man in a duel). Among his most famous works are *Volpone* (1606), *The Alchemist* (1610)—both comedies written for the stage—and *The Forest* (1616), a collection of lyrics and epigrams.

AS YOU READ **Note the opposition of the first word "Farewell" and the poem's title. How does this establish tone and serve notice that "joy" has been lost?**

On My First Son

(1616)

Farewell, thou child of my right hand, and joy;
My sin was too much hope of thee, loved boy:
Seven years thou wert lent to me, and I thee pay,
Exacted by the fate, on the just day.
O could I lose all father now! for why
Will man lament the state he should envy,
To have soon 'scaped world's and flesh's rage,
And, if no other misery, yet age?
Rest in soft peace, and asked, say, "Here doth lie
Ben Jonson his best piece of poetry."
For whose sake henceforth all his vows be such
As what he loves may never like too much.

Writing from Reading

Summarize

1 What is the situation revealed in the poem and the poet's attitude?

2 What does he mean by "why / Will man lament the state he should envy," and does the poet truly wish for death?

Analyze Craft

3 Notice the six rhyming couplets of this poem and the two spots where the rhymes are less than exact. What is meant by "Ben Jonson his best piece of poetry"?

4 How old is the child to whom the father says farewell, and what does the poet wish for himself?

Analyze Voice

5 Technically, this poem is an elegy—a lament for a dear dead child. What words and phrases establish that "lament," and what does the poet promise himself in the final two lines?

Synthesize Summary and Analysis

6 "Rest in soft peace" adds a word to "Rest in peace." Who does the poet imagine might ask his "soft" son to identify himself, and where, and when?

Interpret the Poem

7 If age is necessarily linked to misery, can the speaker find comfort in the fact that his son "soon 'scaped world's and flesh's rage"? What is the overall tone of the poem, and does "First Son" in the title suggest that there are or will be more?

While we can say with confidence that Jonson is speaking from his own experience, this is not always necessarily the case. Poets—like novelists and playwrights—often imagine an experience, inventing both speakers and scene. Did Edgar Allan Poe, for instance, really hear a bird crying outside his home, as he asserts in "The Raven"? Did Robert Frost really find himself once, on a walk through the woods, facing two separate roads to choose from, as in "The Road Not Taken" (see chapter 28)? While it's

> "One person, of course, can have 20,000 different kinds of voices." Conversation with Marie Howe

quite possible these poems borrow, perhaps even heavily, from real life, we shouldn't automatically assume they are precise autobiographical accounts. Rather, we think of a poem's speaking voice as a potentially separate entity. This is called a **persona,** a poem's speaker that may or may not use the voice of the poet.

One way to read a poem is, in effect, to measure the distance between the voice of the poet and the voice of the persona delivering the lines. In the **dramatic monologue** "My Last Duchess," for example (see chapter 16), it's perfectly clear that the first-person pronoun of the speaker does not belong to the poet himself; Robert Browning was no duke. He is, in fact, unsympathetic to the man who's showing off his collection of art and arranging a new marriage, and asks us as readers to notice things the character would deny. In the poem "Herbert White" by Frank Bidart (see "For Review and Further Study" on page 127), there's an absolute distance established between writer and speaker; as Bidart observes, he wrote this poem to explore "All that I am not."

A HISTORY OF PERSONA

The Latin word *persona* derives from the ancient Etruscan word for "mask," and it recalls the ancient Greek practice of actors wearing masks to portray different roles. That the voice of a poem may not be in fact the same as that of the poet is an ancient literary distinction. Aristotle writes in *Poetics,* "The poet may imitate by narration—in which case he can either take another personality . . . or speak in his own person, unchanged—or he may present all his characters as living and moving before us." In more recent times, twentieth-century literary scholars sometimes discouraged readers from assuming that even a first-person poem could be autobiographical. Despite these protests from literary critics, many poets readily concede that the speaker using the first person in their poems is, indeed, an autobiographical "I." A group of writers in the 1950s and 1960s, including Robert Lowell, W. D. Snodgrass, Sylvia Plath, and Anne Sexton, were dubbed "confessional poets." This indicated a deeply personal style by poets unafraid to confront painful private history.

"Until the advent of the romantics, the 'I' was very rare in poetry. . . . Poetry was used to memorize . . . to commemorate, to narrate history, to catechize. . . . [Now] . . . this fictitious 'I' . . . pops up in just about 90 percent of contemporary American poetry. . . . To take on different voices and different characterizations is a challenge and a lot more creative." Conversation with Al Young

Sylvia Plath's poem "Daddy" is sometimes called autobiographical. Indeed, the poem is an angry and raw cry of resistance aimed at the poet's father, Otto Plath, who died when she was still a child. Haunted by three decades of grief and memories of her stern father, Plath fashions a poem that voices a bitter response to his lasting psychological grip.

While Plath borrows heavily from real life in her descriptions in the poem, we shouldn't be too quick to call the "I" of this poem a literal version of the poet. Plath uses, among other references, violent Nazi and Holocaust imagery to describe the father figure of this poem. Otto Plath, however, immigrated to America in 1900 and was never affiliated with the Nazi party or known to be physically abusive. Likewise, to accentuate the poem's conflict, Plath's speaker links herself to a Jewish identity whereas

"If we can forget ourselves, we can become someone the poem can speak through." Conversation with Marie Howe

Plath herself was raised primarily in the Unitarian Christian tradition. So, while some descriptions and references in the poem echo authentic aspects of Plath's life, the poem is itself a creative fusion of real-life and fictional elements. Because of this, "Daddy" is a poem that helps us understand why it's important to treat the distinction between poet and persona with care.

Sylvia Plath (1932–1963)

Born in Massachusetts, Sylvia Plath was a successful student and earned her B.A. *summa cum laude* from Smith College. She was awarded a Fulbright scholarship and went to England, where she met and married poet Ted Hughes. Hughes later left Plath and their two young children; Plath responded with a frenzy of creative outpouring, writing her famous *Ariel* poems in the few months leading up to her suicide at age thirty. She had attempted to take her own life between her junior and senior years of college, and her autobiographical novel *The Bell Jar* (1963) focuses on a heroine who attempts suicide. Plath's poetry is marked by violent imagery contained in clear, precise diction; especially in the *Ariel* poems, she invents a poetic self that has a romantic, larger-than-life quality characteristic of poems in the confessional voice.

AS YOU READ This poem uses direct address—from "I" to "you" in the first stanza, and by the second stanza we know that a child addresses a father. As the speaker addresses the father, note if and when her tone changes or shifts.

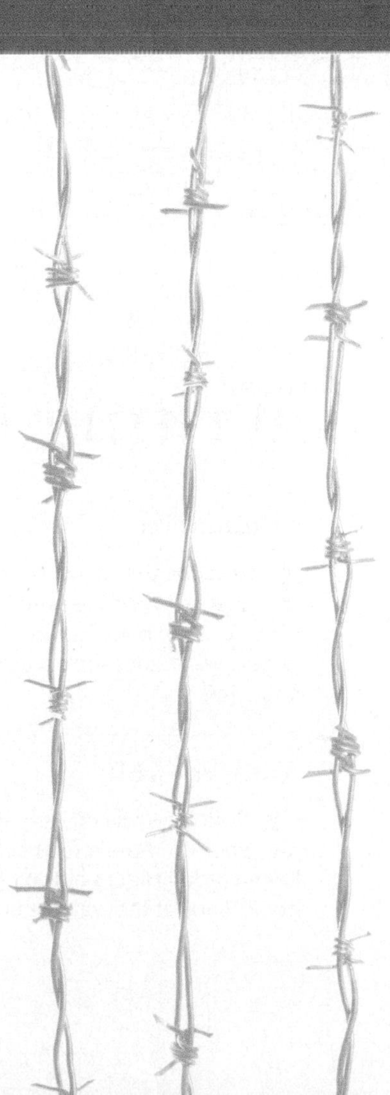

Daddy (1966)

You do not do, you do not do
Any more, black shoe
In which I have lived like a foot
For thirty years, poor and white,
Barely daring to breathe or Achoo.

Daddy, I have had to kill you.
You died before I had time—
Marble-heavy, a bag full of God,
Ghastly statue with one gray toe
Big as a Frisco seal

And a head in the freakish Atlantic
Where it pours bean green over blue
In the waters off beautiful Nauset.
I used to pray to recover you.
Ach, du

In the German tongue, in the Polish town
Scraped flat by the roller
Of wars, wars, wars.
But the name of the town is common.
My Polack friend

Says there are a dozen or two.
So I never could tell where you
Put your foot, your root,
I never could talk to you.
The tongue stuck in my jaw.

It stuck in a barb wire snare.
Ich, ich, ich, ich,
I could hardly speak.
I thought every German was you.
And the language obscene

An engine, an engine
Chuffing me off like a Jew.
A Jew to Dachau, Auschwitz, Belsen.
I began to talk like a Jew.
I think I may well be a Jew.

The snows of the Tyrol, the clear beer
of Vienna
Are not very pure or true.
With my gypsy ancestress and my
weird luck
And my Taroc pack and my Taroc pack
I may be a bit of a Jew.

I have always been scared of *you*,
With your Luftwaffe, your gobbledygoo.
And your neat mustache
And your Aryan eye, bright blue.
Panzer-man, panzer-man, O You—

Not a God but a swastika
So black no sky could squeak through
Every woman adores a Fascist,
The boot in the face, the brute
Brute heart of a brute like you.

You stand at the blackboard daddy,
In the picture I have of you,
A cleft in your chin instead of your foot
But no less a devil for that, no not
Any less the black man who

Bit my pretty red heart in two.
I was ten when they buried you.
At twenty I tried to die
And get back, back, back to you.
I thought even the bones would do.

But they pulled me out of the sack,
And they stuck me together with glue.
And then I knew what to do.
I made a model of you,
A man in black with a Meinkampf look

And a love of the rack and the screw.
And I said I do, I do.
So daddy, I'm finally through.
The black telephone's off at the root,
The voices just can't worm through.

If I've killed one man, I've killed two—
The vampire who said he was you
And drank my blood for a year,
Seven years, if you want to know.
Daddy, you can lie back now.

There's a stake in your fat black heart
And the villagers never liked you.
They are dancing and stamping on you.
They always *knew* it was you.
Daddy, daddy, you bastard, I'm through.

Writing from Reading

Summarize

1 Describe the situation of this poem—who's speaking to whom? How does the poet address her dead father? What does she accuse him of, and why?

Analyze Craft

2 Notice the use of German in this poem and the reference to *Mein Kampf* (Adolf Hitler's autobiographical book). Look at the way the poet compares her father to a vampire ("There's a stake in your fat black heart") and the various references to murder and suicide. What mood does this create?

3 Identify the colloquial language here ("Daddy, daddy, you bastard" or "breathe Achoo"). Why does she choose this language and end the poem with the assertion "I'm through"?

Analyze Voice

4 Give examples of the poet's anger, even rage. Are there any gentle moments in the poem, any suggestions of love or forgiveness? (Consider Theodore Roethke's poem "My Papa's Waltz" by way of contrast.)

5 Notice how often the speaker says "you"—to someone who no longer hears. Look at the rhyme scheme and the insistent repetitive pattern of sound. How would you describe the way repetition contributes to the tone of this poem?

Synthesize Summary and Analysis

6 The Ben Jonson poem has a father speaking to his dead child, and the Sylvia Plath poem consists of a daughter addressing her dead father. How do the tones and attitudes seem similar, how different; which emotions govern which?

Interpret the Poem

7 This monologue is one sided; there's no second point of view or position to be heard. In some sense it's both a *diatribe* and a *polemic* (look up these terms in your dictionary). Does Plath come to terms with her memories at poem's end?

Rita Dove (b. 1952)

Rita Dove was born in Akron, Ohio, and graduated summa cum laude from Miami University in Ohio. She spent a year in Germany on a Fulbright scholarship, then earned an M.F.A. at the University of Iowa before becoming a professor herself. Her ability to render poems that resonate on both a personal and a larger historical level—in addition to her sensitivity toward language and poetic form—has earned her poetry widespread acclaim. Her collection *Thomas and Beulah* (1986) tells the story of her grandparents in short lyrical poems that beautifully render mundane moments; it was awarded the Pulitzer Prize. Less than a decade later, she became the youngest poet to be appointed Poet Laureate, a position she held from 1993 to 1995. She currently teaches at the University of Virginia.

AS YOU READ Think of the resonance of the word *master,* and how it suggests both the history of slavery and a competence at mathematics—in the former case it's used as a noun, in the latter as a verb. These fourteen lines suggest the poem belongs, although loosely, to the traditional sonnet form (see chapter 24); in form therefore it refers to the past but, in tone, it is contemporary.

Flash Cards (1989)

In math I was the whiz kid, keeper
of oranges and apples. *What you don't understand,*
master, my father said; the faster
I answered, the faster they came.

I could see one bud on the teacher's geranium,
one clear bee sputtering at the wet pane.
The tulip trees always dragged after heavy rain
so I tucked my head as my boots slapped home.

My father put up his feet after work
and relaxed with a highball and *The Life of Lincoln.*
After supper we drilled and I climbed the dark

before sleep, before a thin voice hissed
numbers as I spun on a wheel. I had to guess.
Ten, I kept saying, *I'm only ten.*

Writing from Reading

Summarize

1 Describe the place and, perhaps, the time of this poem. How far removed would you say the speaker is at the time of writing?

2 Is it important to know that the poet is African American? What are flash cards? What kind of student is the speaker? Does the term "whiz kid" seem deserved?

Analyze Craft

3 If this poem appears autobiographical to you—if, in other words, the persona feels like the poet herself—what part of the poem suggests this? If not, why not?

4 To be "spun on a wheel" is an ancient Greek form of torture. "After supper we drilled" might be another such torture. Does this poem convey a feeling of triumph or grief?

Analyze Voice

5 What do you think the speaker means by "keeper / of oranges and apples"?

6 In the final line, we're twice given a number—"ten"—as the child's age. Does the tone or attitude seem childlike or adult?

Synthesize Summary and Analysis

7 Describe the relationship the speaker has with the father figure. How would you characterize the two figures in the poem? What changes; what stays the same?

Interpret the Poem

8 What does "the faster / I answered, the faster they came" suggest about life's problems? How does *The Life of Lincoln* connect to the poem's subject, and what is the attitude here?

Sometimes a persona need not even be a *person* in the first place. This may seem strange, but it can produce brilliantly inventive results. In "Golden Retrievals" Mark Doty puts together an engaging combination of persona and Asian spirituality, using his dog for the poem's wise speaker. The practice of Zen Buddhism calls for its adherents to try to live, consciously, in the present moment. Who better to exemplify this attention to the here and now than a golden retriever?

Mark Doty (b. 1953)

Although born in Tennessee, Mark Doty moved frequently when he was young, so he felt, as he puts it, that "I grew up with a sense that home was something one constructed or carried around inside. I grew up loving books because they were reliable company." Doty's poetry, which has won awards including the National Book Critics Circle Award and the T. S. Eliot Prize, was impacted by the death of his partner, Wally, from AIDS. In addition to two collections of poetry that consciously engage with this event, *My Alexandria* (1993) and *Atlantis* (1995), Doty also wrote a memoir on the subject, *Heaven's Coast* (1996). He currently lives in Texas and teaches at the University of Houston.

AS YOU READ Remember Samuel Taylor Coleridge's notion of "the willing suspension of disbelief." Do you believe this poem is spoken by a dog? Look for ways Doty creates the dog as speaker in this poem.

Golden Retrievals

(1998)

Fetch? Balls and sticks capture my attention
seconds at a time. Catch? I don't think so.
Bunny, tumbling leaf, a squirrel who's—oh
joy—actually scared. Sniff the wind, then

I'm off again: muck, pond, ditch, residue
of any thrillingly dead thing. And you?
Either you're sunk in the past, half our walk,
thinking of what you can never bring back,

or else you're off in some fog concerning
—tomorrow, is that what you call it? My work:
to unsnare time's warp (and woof!), retrieving,
my haze-headed friend, you. This shining bark,

a Zen master's bronzy gong, calls you here,
entirely, now: bow-wow, bow-wow, bow-wow.

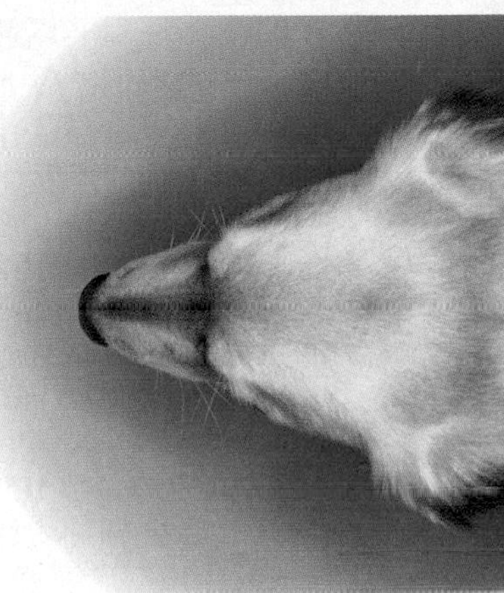

Writing from Reading

Summarize

1 Who is the speaker here, and to whom does he speak?

Analyze Craft

2 "It's a dog's life," as they say. Provide details of that life from the available text. How persuasive is the poet when he writes "bow-wow, bow-wow, bow-wow"?

Analyze Voice

3 What does the dog perceive that his human master fails to? What are his preoccupations, and what concerns the man?

4 Notice the parenthetical joke ("and woof"). How does this help establish tone?

Synthesize Summary and Analysis

5 What does the poet-persona mean by "My work: / to unsnare time's warp . . . retrieving, / my haze-headed friend, you"?

6 If a dog is "man's best friend," what does he teach his companion?

Interpret the Poem

7 Why would the author want to use the dog as a speaker for this poem? Who does the dog represent for the author? For you?

Often a persona entails a shift of gender as opposed to species. The contemporary poet Ai is well known for writing poems using personae separate from herself. While her poems sometimes comment on the African-American experience she herself has witnessed, the speakers of these poems are often characters she wholly creates. In the following poem, she adopts the persona of a man witnessing the 1992 race riots in Los Angeles.

Ai (b. 1947)

"I am the child of a scandalous affair my mother had with a Japanese man she met at a streetcar stop," Ai comments of her own beginnings. (She legally changed her name to Ai, which means "love" in Japanese.) Born in Texas, of Native American, African, Irish, and Japanese descent, Ai grew up in Arizona, San Francisco, and Las Vegas. Her poetry most often takes the form of dramatic monologues, and she explores personalities as diverse as Marilyn Monroe, Leon Trotsky, and J. Edgar Hoover, and dark topics ranging from domestic to public violence. Her collection *Vice* (1999) won the National Book Award, and she received the Lamont Poetry Award from the Academy of American Poets for *Killing Floor* (1979). Ai holds an M.F.A. from the University of California, Irvine, and currently teaches at Oklahoma State University.

AS YOU READ **Consider the "I" of this poem and try to establish its relation to the first-person pronoun of the poet herself. Pay attention to the tense of the narrative—the present tense—and how it reports on what happened on the specific date of the title.**

Riot Act, April 29, 1992 (1993)

I'm going out and get something.
I don't know what.
I don't care.
Whatever's out there, I'm going to get it.
Look in those shop windows at boxes
and boxes of Reeboks and Nikes
to make me fly through the air
like Michael Jordan
like Magic.
While I'm up there, I see Spike Lee.
Looks like he's flying too
straight through the glass
that separates me
from the virtual reality
I watch every day on TV.
I know the difference between
what it is and what it isn't.
Just because I can't touch it
doesn't mean it isn't real.
All I have to do is smash the screen,
reach in and take what I want.
Break out of prison.
South Central homey's newly risen
from the night of living dead,
but this time he lives,
he gets to give the zombies
a taste of their own medicine.
Open wide and let me in,
or else I'll set your world on fire,
but you pretend that you don't hear.

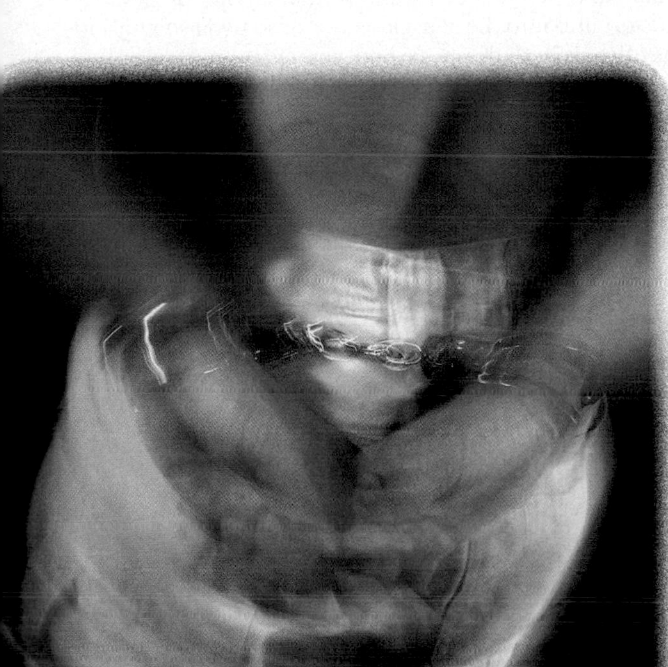

You haven't heard the word is coming down
like the hammer of the gun
of this black son, locked out of the big house,
while massa looks out the window and sees only smoke.
Massa doesn't see anything else,
not because he can't,
but because he won't.
He'd rather hear me talking about mo' money,
mo' honeys and gold chains
and see me carrying my favorite things
from looted stores
than admit that underneath my Raider's cap,
the aftermath is staring back
unblinking through the camera's lens,
courtesy of CNN,
my arms loaded with boxes of shoes
that I will sell at the swap meet
to make a few cents on the declining dollar.
And if I destroy myself
and my neighborhood
"ain't nobody's business, if I do,"
but the police are knocking hard
at my door
and before I can open it,
they break it down
and drag me in the yard.
They take me in to be processed and charged,
to await trial,
while Americans forget
the day wealth finally trickled down
to the rest of us.

Writing from Reading

Summarize

1 Describe the action in the poem. Who is the speaker and the poem's "I"?

Analyze Craft

2 There are many references, here, to contemporary culture—"Raider's cap," "CNN," etc. Michael Jordan, Magic (Johnson), and Spike Lee were three major "players" on the contemporary scene in 1992. How does this help "date" the speaker?

3 Notice the tense shift at poem's end—present to past. Track the activity throughout.

Analyze Voice

4 The phrase "ain't nobody's business, if I do" comes from a Billie Holliday song. How much of this is celebration and how much of this is "the blues"?

Synthesize Summary and Analysis

5 Describe ways in which the poet constructs her speaker's character. If he were standing in a police lineup (as at poem's end), could you pick him out?

Interpret the Poem

6 What is the poet's attitude toward her persona here?

The great Irish poet William Butler Yeats had a notion of "the mask" or "anti-self" and sometimes wrote—as in the "Crazy Jane" sequence—from a woman's point of view. In the poem that follows, he attempts to enter into the consciousness of someone obviously "other" than his own self, and the effect is both dramatic and, somehow, impersonal.

William Butler Yeats (1865–1939)

For a brief biography of William Butler Yeats, see chapter 16.

AS YOU READ Listen for the two separate voices in conversation—the Bishop and Crazy Jane—and decide which of the points of view (either or both) you share.

Crazy Jane Talks with the Bishop (1932)

I met the Bishop on the road
And much said he and I.
"Those breasts are flat and fallen now
Those veins must soon by dry;
Live in a heavenly mansion,
Not in some foul sty."

"Fair and foul are near of kin,
And fair needs foul," I cried.
"My friends are gone, but that's a truth
Nor grave nor bed denied,
Learned in bodily lowliness
And in the heart's pride.

"A woman can be proud and still
When on love intent;
But Love has pitched his mansion in
The place of excrement;
For nothing can be sole or whole
That has not been rent."

Writing from Reading

Summarize

1 Who are the speakers here, and what's the nature of their argument?

2 Assuming that the poet shares the opinion of his title character, what would seem to be Yeats's beliefs as to "fair and foul"?

Analyze Craft

3 Why does "Crazy Jane" have a name and "the Bishop" merely a title?

4 These eighteen lines follow a fixed pattern, and each stanza rhymes in the second, fourth, and final line. What does that do to emphasis, and who has the last word?

Analyze Voice

5 What does the speaker mean by "Love has pitched his mansion in / the place of excrement"? Literally? Metaphorically?

6 Comment on the double meanings in the final stanza: "whole" and "sole" and "rent."

Synthesize Summary and Analysis

7 What ideas about religion—behavior in this life, and the question of the afterlife—are presented here?

8 Discuss the oppositions of body and soul, the church and the fallen woman, faith and physical appearance. Can they be reconciled?

Interpret the Poem

9 Yeats wrote a series of poems from the point of view of an invented character whom he based upon an old woman who lived in a cottage in Gort, a small village near Galway in western Ireland. What does he admire in her, and why would he use *her* language to make what would appear to be *his* point?

For Review and Further Study

Frank Bidart (b. 1939)

Herbert White (1973)

"When I hit her on the head, it was good,

and then I did it to her a couple of times,—
but it was funny,—afterwards,
it was as if somebody else did it . . .

Everything flat, without sharpness, richness or line.

Still, I liked to drive past the woods where she lay,
tell the old lady and the kids I had to take a piss,
hop out and do it to her . . .

The whole buggy of them waiting for me
made me feel good;
but still, just like I knew all along,
she didn't move.

When the body got too discomposed,
I'd just jack off, letting it fall on her . . .

—It sounds crazy, but I tell you
sometimes it was *beautiful*—; I don't know how
to say it, but for a minute, everything was possible—;
and then,
then,—
well, like I said, she didn't move: and I saw,
under me, a little girl was just lying there in the mud:

and I knew I couldn't have done that,—
somebody *else* had to have done that,—
standing above her there,
in those ordinary, shitty leaves. . . .

—One time, I went to see Dad in a motel where he was
staying with a woman; but she was gone;
you could smell the wine in the air; and he started,
real embarrassing, to cry . . .
He was still a little drunk,
and asked me to forgive him for
all he hadn't done—; but, What the shit?
Who would have wanted to stay with Mom? with
bastards
not even his own kids?

I got in the truck, and started to drive,
and saw a little girl—
who I picked up, hit on the head, and
screwed, and screwed, and screwed, and screwed, then

buried,
in the garden of the motel . . .

—You see, ever since I was a kid I wanted
to *feel* things make sense: I remember

looking out the window of my room back home,—
and being almost suffocated by the asphalt;
and grass; and trees; and glass;
just *there*, just *there*, doing nothing!
not saying anything! filling me up—
but also being a wall; dead, and stopping me;
—how I wanted to see beneath it, cut

beneath it, and make it
somehow, come alive . . .

The salt of the earth;
Mom once said, 'Man's spunk is the salt of the earth . . .'

—That night, at that Twenty-nine Palms Motel
I had passed a million times on the road, everything

fit together; was alright;
it seemed like
everything *had* to be there, like I had
spent years
trying, and at last finally finished drawing this
huge circle . . .

—But then, suddenly I knew
somebody *else* did it, some bastard
had hurt a little girl—; the motel
I could see again, it had been
itself all the time, a lousy
pile of bricks, plaster, that didn't seem to
have to be there,—but *was*, just by chance . . .

—Once, on the farm, when I was a kid,
I was screwing a goat; and the rope around his neck
when he tried to get away
pulled tight;—and just when I came,
he *died* . . .
I came back the next day; jacked off over his body;
but it didn't do any good . . .

Mom once said:
'Man's spunk is the salt of the earth, and grows kids.'

I tried so hard to come; more *pain* than anything else;
but didn't do any good . . .

—About six months ago, I heard Dad remarried,
so I drove over to Connecticut to see him and see
if he was happy.
She was twenty-five years younger than him:
she had lots of little kids, and I don't know why,
I felt shaky . . .
I stopped in front of the address; and
snuck up to the window to look in . . .
—There he was, a kid
six months old on his lap, laughing
and bouncing the kid, happy in his old age
to play the papa after years of sleeping around,—
it twisted me up . . .
To think that what he wouldn't give me,
he *wanted* to give them . . .

I could have killed the bastard . . .

—Naturally, I just got right back in the car,
and believe me, was determined, determined,
to head straight for home . . .

but the more I drove,
I kept thinking about getting a girl,
and the more I thought I shouldn't do it,
the more I had to—

I saw her coming out of the movies,
saw she was alone, and
kept circling the blocks as she walked along them,
saying, 'You're going to leave her alone.'
'You're going to leave her alone.'

—The woods were scary!
As the seasons changed, and you saw more and more
of the skull show through, the nights became clearer.
and the buds,—erect like nipples . . .

—But then, one night,
nothing worked . . .
Nothing in the sky
would blur like I wanted it to;
and I couldn't, *couldn't*,
get it to seem to me
that somebody *else* did it . . .

I tried, and tried, but there was just me there,
and her, and the sharp trees
saying, 'That's you standing there.
You're . . .
just you.'

I hope I fry.

—Hell came when I saw
MYSELF . . .
and couldn't stand
What I see . . ."

Questions for Interactive Reading and Writing

1. Who is the speaker here, and whom does he address?
2. As a dramatic monologue, this poem offers a character at war with all our notions of decency—and, in some sense, at war with himself. Note the places in the poem where he comments on and tries to understand his own behavior.
3. Note the usages of dialogue—remembered and overheard speech.
4. How does Bidart make such a heinous character human? Describe the voice of the character, and what he means by "funny. . . ." Note the slang—"did it," "screwed," etc., and discuss how this helps establish the verisimilitude—the seeming truth—of the voice.
5. Dark parts of the human psyche are the subject here, but the speaker does complete his confession by saying, "I hope I fry." Is he sincere?
6. There's a famous line by the French philosopher-playwright Jean-Paul Sartre: "Hell is other people." At the end of this monologue, however, the speaker Herbert White says, "Hell came when I saw / MYSELF." Discuss.
7. This example of a modern-day dramatic monologue explores a son's reaction to his relationship to his father—and the murderous perversity in which the speaker engages. It was considered a tour de force (great achievement) when it was first published and awarded the National Book Critics Good Reads for 2008. How do you reconcile the loathsome character with the art that brought him into being?

Juan Felipe Herrera (b.1948)

Autobiography of a Chicano Teen Poet (1987)

For Rosita, RIP, Alvnita & Chente & Tito &
Julie & Chelita & Yooyee & Beto Jr & Ray G.

I am a downtown boy, handcuffed
when I was eleven
for being accomplice to armed robbery.

I speak shoeshine parlor brown and serve
as the only usher in *Club Sufrimiento 2001.*

You can call me Johnny B. Nice.

Tender hollow-eyed whores and
busted novelists in spiderweb trenchcoats
are partners in the law firm where I live.

Thelonious Monk,
Janis Joplin, sip with me when you can.
I am out here playing my blues,
my autobiography of penny arcade rendezvous.

From here I can see the Mayor.
He just got three years probation for perjury
and now he's working for the "homeless."
Who was he working for in the first place?

I used to go to church, but the wind-up doll got tired
and couldn't speak proper English anymore.
So, God punished it and drove it into the wilderness
where it found a color film of a Wonderkid
selling Language and Infinity to the lost on Inferno
Street.
But, the translation wasn't bilingual, even though
they showed it at the Casino with triple porno movie.

My brother died in the ring,
stabbed 14 times by the King of Desire.
All the electric guitars moaned in the pawnshops
and my mother grew smaller with memory.

Above me,
the phosphor light coughs and sweats.

I can't wait to see the red-striped cellophane
from cigarette packs—whirl
into a fire at the center of the street.

Questions for Interactive Reading and Writing

1. Herrera is known for his interest in spoken word poetry and jazz. Can you imagine this piece as a performance? Why or why not?
2. Herrera was raised in California by parents who were immigrants and farmworkers. He himself was educated at the University of California, Los Angeles, and Stanford University, yet his poetry speaks to his roots. How does this poem appeal to those who may have similar experiences?
3. References abound to musicians such as Thelonius Monk and Janis Joplin, and it helps to know what they stood for and what their music sounds like. Look up these musicians on the internet. Why do you think they are referred to in this poem?

Natasha Trethewey (b. 1966)

Letter Home (2002)

—New Orleans, November 1910

Four weeks have passed since I left, and still
I must write to you of no work. I've worn down
the soles and walked through the tightness
of my new shoes, calling upon the merchants,
their offices bustling. All the while I kept thinking
my plain English and good writing would secure
for me some modest position. Though I dress each day
in my best, hands covered with the lace gloves
you crocheted—no one needs a *girl*. How flat
the word sounds, and heavy. My purse thins.
I spend foolishly to make an appearance of quiet
industry, to mask the desperation that tightens
my throat. I sit watching—

though I pretend not to notice—the dark maids
ambling by with their white charges. Do I deceive
anyone? Were they to see my hands, brown
as your dear face, they'd know I'm not quite
what I pretend to be. I walk these streets
a white woman, or so I think, until I catch the eyes
of some stranger upon me, and I must lower mine,
a *negress* again. There are enough things here
to remind me who I am. Mules lumbering through
the crowded streets send me into reverie, their footfall
the sound of a pointer and chalk hitting the blackboard
at school, only louder. Then there are women, clicking
their tongues in conversation, carrying their loads
on their heads. Their husky voices, the wash pots
and irons of the laundresses call to me. Here,

I thought not to do the work I once did, back-bending
and domestic; my schooling a gift—even those half days
at picking time, listening to Miss J—. How
I'd come to know words, the recitations I practiced
to sound like her, lilting, my sentences curling up
or trailing off at the ends. I read my books until
I nearly broke their spines, and in the cotton field,
I repeated whole sections I'd learned by heart,
spelling each word in my head to make a picture
I could see, as well as a weight I could feel
In my mouth. So now, even as I write this
And think of you at home, Good-bye

is the waving map of your palm, is
a stone on my tongue.

Questions for Interactive Reading and Writing

1. Trethewey's first work focused on prostitutes in New Orleans in the early 1900s. In this poem, she creates a character looking for work and becoming ever more desperate. How does Trethewey present her? Describe the voice of the character here.
2. Why would Trethewey want to create this persona, this voice?
3. What tone does the poem establish? What words show the speaker's unease?

IRONY

In life as well as in writing, we detect tone by careful or instinctive observation. Sometimes, whether we're conscious of it or not, we pick up on a difference between what someone says and what they actually mean. As in other literary genres, in poetry this difference is called **irony,** a discrepancy between what a poem says and what it means.

If you've ever encountered the old story of Robin Hood, you may remember that one of Robin's closest friends is a man called Little John. You may also remember that there's actually nothing little about Little John. He's huge, in fact, burly and fat. Calling him "Little" ultimately draws our attention, playfully, to his considerable size. This nickname is a simple example of **verbal irony,** a statement in which the stated meaning is very different from (or the opposite of) the implied meaning.

> "[The] best ironist is profoundly alert to the world—alert, hears the doubleness of things, works that doubleness. It's a . . . keenness of attention, and rather than keep the world away, it interrogates that world—it tries to measure it."
>
> Conversation with Stephen Dunn

One of the most familiar forms of verbal irony is **sarcasm,** a critical use of spoken approval to express implied disapproval. Who hasn't heard, at some point, a phrase like, "Oh, yeah, you look *great* in that hat," or "This is the best vacation ever," when in fact the hat looks ridiculous and it rains the whole week?

Paul Laurence Dunbar (1872–1906)

Born in Dayton, Ohio, to parents who had been slaves, Paul Laurence Dunbar is remembered chiefly for his poetry, although he also wrote short stories and novels. The only black student in his high school class, Dunbar was class poet and published poems in Dayton newspapers. Although his race at first relegated him to a job as an elevator operator, Dunbar continued to write and soon had a national reputation. While some of his work protests racism, much of it—particularly his poems written in dialect—has been criticized for perpetuating harmful stereotypes of blacks in the Old South. Still, he is recognized as the foremost black poet at the turn of the twentieth century, despite a career cut short by his death from tuberculosis at age thirty-three.

AS YOU READ Irony is double-edged. Look for language that suggests the speaker is seemingly above the battle. Look for words that are insulting. Notice how the poet puts these together in the poem.

To a Captious Critic (1901)

Dear critic, who my lightness so deplores,
Would I might study to be prince of bores,
Right wisely would I rule that dull estate—
But, sir, I may not, till you abdicate.

Writing from Reading

Summarize

1 This is a brief letter to a critic written as a poem. Look up the word *captious,* then speculate on what the critic has done to trigger this response.

Analyze Craft

2 How would you describe the language used in this poem? Formal? Informal? Is poetic diction employed?

3 List the images in the poem. How do these set up the twist in the last line of the poem?

4 Some of the phrasing puts unlikely words together, such as "prince" and "bore." What other phrases like this do you find in this poem?

Analyze Voice

5 How does the speaker feel about the critic? What in the poem reveals his feelings? How would you describe the poem's tone?

6 Although the tone sounds as though it comes directly out of the eighteenth-century satirical poetry of Alexander Pope, what aspects of this brief poem reveal it is written by a more modern voice?

Synthesize Summary and Analysis

7 What does the letter form enable the speaker to accomplish in this poem?

8 Contrast the diction in this poem with the point of the poem.

9 How does the speaker use humor in this poem, and how does he mask insult as respect?

Interpret the Poem

10 Dunbar was praised and criticized for his use of dialect. In writing a poem like this, elevated in language and formal in tone, what point do you think he desires to make?

Because verbal irony can suggest implicit scorn, it's often a good choice for writing that seeks to criticize or attack an idea. **Satire** does this—it's an artistic critique, sometimes quite heated, on some aspect of human immorality or absurdity. In the two poems that follow—one written about World War I, the other about World War II—the poets Wilfred Owen and Kenneth Fearing use both irony and satire to establish attitude—saying, in effect, that far from something to celebrate, war is hell.

Wilfred Owen (1893–1918)

Wilfred Owen, a British poet, is invariably associated with World War I, and with good reason—his best poetry takes the war for its subject, and he himself served and was killed in the war. A poet from a young age, Owen went to France to teach English in 1913, the year before the war broke out. He enlisted in 1917 and was hospitalized for shell shock later that year. In the hospital, Owen met Siegfried Sassoon, whose war poetry inspired Owen to achieve a new level of maturity in his own poems. Owen's carefully structured poems use physical imagery to create a visual record of war horrors, while using pararhyme—that is, words with the same consonants but different vowels—to give an auditory sense of the discord of war. Owen was killed in action one week before the war's end.

AS YOU READ **The poem's Latin title means "It Is Sweet and Proper." As you read, look for contrasting vivid flashes of news about the miseries and dangers of the battlefield.**

Dulce et Decorum Est (1920)

Bent double, like old beggars under sacks,
Knock-kneed, coughing like hags, we cursed through sludge,
Till on the haunting flares we turned our backs
And towards our distant rest began to trudge.
Men marched asleep. Many had lost their boots
But limped on, blood-shod. All went lame; all blind;
Drunk with fatigue; deaf even to the hoots
Of tired, outstripped Five-Nines that dropped behind.

Gas! GAS! Quick, boys!—An ecstasy of fumbling,
Fitting the clumsy helmets just in time;
But someone still was yelling out and stumbling
And floundering like a man in fire or lime . . .
Dim, through the misty panes and thick green light,
As under a green sea, I saw him drowning.

In all my dreams, before my helpless sight,
He plunges at me, guttering, choking, drowning.

If in some smothering dreams you too could pace
Behind the wagon that we flung him in,
And watch the white eyes writing in his face,
His hanging face, like a devil's sick of sin;
If you could hear, at every jolt, the blood
Come gargling from the froth-corrupted lungs,
Obscene as cancer, bitter as the cud
Of vile, incurable sores on innocent tongues,—
My friend, you would not tell with such high zest
To children ardent for some desperate glory,
The old Lie: Dulce et decorum est
Pro patria mori.

Writing from Reading

Summarize

1 Who is "bent double" in this poem?

2 What kind of "gas" is being alluded to in the second stanza? Why is everyone "fumbling" in response? How could gas cause someone to drown?

3 What is happening to the person who is "floundering"?

Analyze Craft

4 The speaker uses numerous images to describe the scene: "like old beggars under sacks," "sludge." List several images from the last stanza. How do these images build suspense in the poem?

5 Wilfred Owen was very young when he composed this poem, but he describes his soldier-comrades in the terms of old age and disease using ordinary, unpoetic words like "coughing." How do these word choices set the scene described in this poem?

Analyze Voice

6 Discuss such phrases as "An ecstasy of fumbling" or "incurable sores on innocent tongues." Why does the speaker use contrasting words like "ecstasy" (a word meaning exquisite delight) and "fumbling," or "incurable" and "innocent"? Given that irony provides a kind of double take on a situation, what do words like these reveal about the author's feelings about war?

Synthesize Summary and Analysis

7 The poem's title says one thing, and the poem describes the opposite experience. The Latin at poem's end means, roughly, "It is sweet and proper to die for one's country." The images would suggest nothing sweet about it. What is "The old Lie"? How does the poet's vivid description of war's horror prepare the reader for the last lines of this poem?

Interpret the Poem

8 World War I erased a generation of young men (including the poet). Is this poem mostly a witness to the poet's own experiences, or is this a social commentary? Would you call the poem propaganda? Could you imagine another poem in which the experiences of the soldiers could be rendered in beautiful language? Is there an argument in this poem, and if so, how convincing is the argument to you?

Published in 1938, when the Nazis began to mobilize throughout Europe, this poem employs satirical verbal irony to criticize not only the brutality of war but also the ways in which potential soldiers are recruited. Fashioned in the form of a newspaper want ad, the poem ironically invites applicants to volunteer to die.

Kenneth Fearing (1902–1961)

Born in Oak Park, Illinois, Kenneth Fearing was raised mostly by an eccentric aunt. After attending the University of Wisconsin, Fearing went to New York where he supported himself in part by writing pulp fiction, much of which bordered on pornography. His first collection of poems, *Angel Arms* (1929), introduced him as a poet of his age with a bitter sense of irony toward the working classes as well as the wealthier. He published poems regularly in *The New Yorker,* although he also went through periods of writing prose. Active in left-wing politics, Fearing was known for his pessimism, cynicism, and misanthropy. A longtime smoker and heavy drinker, Fearing died of cancer while still in his fifties.

AS YOU READ Locate and list the advertising slogans in these lines. Consider who the "we" and the "you" in the poem are.

AD (1938)

Wanted: Men;
Millions of men are *wanted at once* in a big new field;
New, tremendous, thrilling, great.
If you've ever been a figure in the chamber of horrors,
If you've ever escaped from a psychiatric ward,
If you thrill at the thought of throwing poison into wells, have
heavenly visions of people, by the thousands, dying in flames—

You are the very man we want
We mean business and our business is *you*
Wanted: A race of brand-new men.

Apply: Middle Europe;
No skill needed;
No ambition required; no brains wanted and no character allowed;

Take a permanent job in the coming profession
Wages: *Death.*

Writing from Reading

Summarize

1 What is being advertised in this poem?

Analyze Craft

2 "Dulce et decorum est" is a kind of advertising slogan in Latin; this "ad" employs a more modern tone. What advertising slogans are used? How do they build momentum toward the ironic last line?

Analyze Voice

3 How do phrases like "if you've ever escaped from a psychiatric ward" work with the slick, hollow words of marketing to reveal what the speaker feels about World War II? What does his choice of these phrases tell you about his feelings about the war?

Synthesize Summary and Analysis

4 With what ads are you familiar today? Do they use phrases similar to those used in this poem? Compare the kinds of things that are advertised today to what is being advertised in this poem. Why would the speaker use ads as a description of military recruitment?

Interpret the Poem

5 "Dulce et decorum est" is written about World War I, in which gas was a factor in trench warfare; World War II, which has been described as "The Good War," relied more on bombs. Technologies may have changed, but is Fearing making the same case as Owen about war? Why or why not?

Situational irony occurs when a poem portrays a situation in which what happens is the opposite of what's expected to happen. In the following poem, note how our understanding of the gentleman Richard Cory is shaped. Throughout the poem, we hear of his remarkable fortune, manner, and appearance. His fellow townspeople think his life vastly superior to their own. By the end of the poem, however, we realize Richard Cory's life may have been very different from how it appeared on the surface.

Edwin Arlington Robinson (1869–1935)

A native of Maine, Edwin Arlington Robinson devoted his life to poetry, struggling with poverty for many years. He studied at Harvard for two years, and his writing eventually won the admiration of Theodore Roosevelt, who arranged for Robinson to work in a New York customs house. Robinson's poetry gradually became more successful, from his first, self-published collection *The Children of the Night* (1897) to his *Collected Poems* (1921), which won the first Pulitzer Prize for Poetry. With his mastery of traditional forms, his portraits of characters like Miniver Cheevy, and his interest in Arthurian legend, Robinson won two more Pulitzers for *The Man Who Died Twice* (1924) and *Tristram* (1927).

AS YOU READ Notice the rhyming pattern in these quatrains, the way everything's perfectly ordered and in place. The final line therefore doubly reverses expectation that all will be "right" in the end.

Richard Cory (1897)

Whenever Richard Cory went down town,
We people on the pavement looked at him:
He was a gentleman from sole to crown,
Clean favored and imperially slim.

And he was always quietly arrayed,
And he was always human when he talked,
But still he fluttered pulses when he said,
"Good-morning," and he glittered when he walked.

And he was rich—yes, richer than a king—
And admirably schooled in every grace:
In fine, we thought that he was everything
To make us wish that we were in his place.

So on we worked, and waited for the light,
And went without the meat, and cursed the bread;
And Richard Cory, one calm summer night,
Went home and put a bullet through his head.

Writing from Reading

Summarize

1 What happens here, and who tells the story? Who are "we"?

Analyze Craft

2 How do the ballad-like feel of these stanzas and the singsong pattern make the disruption of the final line all the more disturbing and harsh-sounding.

3 What would happen if, instead of "one calm summer night," Robinson had written "one dark and stormy night"?

Analyze Voice

4 This story is told in the past tense, and therefore the speaker knows what has happened. Why does he save the worst for last?

Synthesize Summary and Analysis

5 This poem is presented without verbal irony, but the situation is ironic in the extreme. How does Robinson make you understand Richard Cory's situation without providing all the facts?

Interpret the Poem

6 What would you describe as "the moral" here?

A literary convention familiar to readers of classical drama, **dramatic irony** (sometimes called **tragic irony**) refers to a situation in which the reader knows (or is made aware of) more about a character's circumstances than the character himself knows. **Cosmic irony** occurs when forces beyond the characters' control, like God or fate or the supernatural, foil their plans or expectations. Thomas Hardy's famous poem "The Convergence of the Twain" responds to the sinking of the *Titanic*, which struck an iceberg and sank, killing 1,500 people. Hardy suggests that the vain human "Pride of Life" that conceived of such a glorious ship could not overcome "The Immanent Will," the cosmic forces that formed the iceberg that doomed the ship.

Thomas Hardy (1840–1928)

A British writer proud of his long life span, Thomas Hardy lived at a time when rural England was becoming increasingly industrialized and modern, a fact that figures into his fiction as well as his poetry. Originally trained as an architect, Hardy was drawn to writing and began his career as a novelist, publishing titles that are still well known today, including *Far from the Madding Crowd* (1874), *The Mayor of Casterbridge* (1886), and *Tess of the D'Urbervilles* (1891). But when *Jude the Obscure* (1895) received harsh criticism, Hardy—at the age of fifty-five—gave up novel writing and turned instead to poetry. His poems, like his fiction, are imbued with his bleak, pessimistic outlook, and where his fiction captures characters with strong passions who must nevertheless submit to an unkind and indifferent fate, his poetry equally transmits a passionate sense of loss, as in the poems written following his wife's death, known collectively as *Veteris Vestigiae Flammae* (1914).

AS YOU READ Note the regularity in these eleven stanzas and thirty-three lines—and how it all builds to a shock for which the reader is prepared (as opposed to, say, the shock of "Richard Corey").

The Convergence of the Twain

(1912)

Lines on the loss of the "Titanic"

I
In a solitude of the sea
Deep from human vanity,
And the Pride of Life that planned her, stilly couches she.

II
Steel chambers, late the pyres
Of her salamandrine fires,
Cold currents thrid, and turn to rhythmic tidal lyres.

III
Over the mirrors meant
To glass the opulent
The sea-worm crawls—grotesque, slimed, dumb, indifferent.

IV
Jewels in joy designed
To ravish the sensuous mind
Lie lightless, all their sparkles bleared and black and blind.

V
Dim moon-eyed fishes near
Gaze at the gilded gear
And query: "What does this vaingloriousness down here?"

VI
Well: while was fashioning
This creature of cleaving wing,
The Immanent Will that stirs and urges everything

VII
Prepared a sinister mate
For her—so gaily great—
A Shape of Ice, for the time far and dissociate.

VIII
And as the smart ship grew
In stature, grace, and hue,
In shadowy silent distance grew the Iceberg too.

IX
Alien they seemed to be:
No mortal eye could see
The intimate welding of their later history,

X
Or sign that they were bent
by paths coincident
On being anon twin halves of one august event,

XI
Till the Spinner of the Years
Said "Now!" And each one hears,
And consummation comes, and jars two hemispheres.

Writing from Reading

Summarize

1 What is the story behind the actual *Titanic*?

2 How does Hardy relate the building of the ship to the forming of the iceberg?

3 Who is the "Spinner of the Years"?

Analyze Craft

4 Notice the formal arrangements here and the shock with which the poem ends. How does Hardy use language to create this shock?

5 Note the "intimate welding" of iceberg and ship. How does Hardy make them "twin halves"?

Analyze Voice

6 "Anon" means "soon" in formal poetic diction, and "august" means "important/consequential." How does the word "Now!" make all this more immediate, and what does the poet mean by "consummation comes"?

Synthesize Summary and Analysis

7 Discuss what you think Hardy means by "no mortal eye" when he describes the *Titanic*'s fate.

Interpret the Poem

8 The poet censures "vaingloriousness." Does he suggest that this in some way contributes to the sinking? What is his attitude here?

Stephen Dunn confronts an imagined terrorist in this poem, simultaneously expressing dismay, anger, and fundamental human empathy. While full of feeling, "To a Terrorist" still manages to seem quiet and thoughtful; its voice is somber and far less playful than the voice of "After." Notice how the word "Still" in stanza 4 suggests a kind of conversation; Dunn balances the emotion of the poem with solemn commentary. It's as if the speaker's continuing with a line of inner argument, adding another point to points already made. His poem does more than try to just express emotional reactions. It also tries to *understand* someone unknown and upsetting to the speaker.

Stephen Dunn (b. 1939)

See Dunn's brief biography earlier in this chapter.

AS YOU READ Think about why a writer would ever address a poem to a violent fanatic. Also, consider how Dunn's choice of tone in the poem helps communicate the feelings and experience he seeks to explore, and how another choice of tone (a more severe or enraged attitude, for example) would have affected your reading.

To a Terrorist (1988)

For the historical ache, the ache passed down
which finds its circumstance and becomes
the present ache, I offer this poem

without hope, knowing there's nothing,
not even revenge, which alleviates
a life like yours. I offer it as one

might offer his father's ashes
to the wind, a gesture
when there's nothing else to do.

Still, I must say to you:
I hate your good reasons.
I hate the hatefulness that makes you fall

in love with death, your own included.
Perhaps you're hating me now,
I who own my own house

and live in a country so muscular,
so smug, it thinks its terror is meant
only to mean well, and to protect.

Christ turned his singular cheek,
one man's holiness another's absurdity.
Like you, the rest of us obey the sting,

the surge. I'm just speaking out loud
to cancel my silence. Consider it an old impulse,
doomed to become mere words.

The first poet probably spoke to thunder
and, for a while, believed
thunder had an ear and a choice.

Writing from Reading

Summarize

1 Who is the speaker and who the imagined audience here? What is the conversation's subject, and how does Christ enter in?

Analyze Craft

2 "The first poet probably spoke to thunder" begins the final stanza. How does this comparison relate to the subject of this poem, and does thunder have "an ear and a choice"?

Analyze Voice

3 Do you think this poem's speaker is the poet or a separate persona?

4 How would you describe the speaker's tone in this poem? Why does Dunn choose this kind of voice for the subject matter?

Synthesize Summary and Analysis

5 The poet writes, "I offer this poem / without hope." How does that help situate what poems can and can't do?

Interpret the Poem

6 This poem was written many years before the tragedy of September 11, 2001. Does this affect your reading of the poem? Why or why not?

For Review and Further Study

e. e. cummings (1894–1962)

For a brief biography of e. e. cummings, see chapter 24.

next to of course god america i (1926)

"next to of course god america i
love you land of the pilgrims' and so forth oh
say can you see by the dawn's early my
country 'tis of centuries come and go
and are no more what of it we should worry
in every language even deafanddumb
thy sons acclaim your glorious name by gorry
by jingo by gee by gosh by gum
why talk of beauty what could be more beaut-
iful than these heroic happy dead
who rushed like lions to the roaring slaughter
they did not stop to think they died instead
then shall the voice of liberty be mute?"

He spoke. And drank rapidly a glass of water

Questions for Interactive Reading and Writing

1. There are slogans here, and snippets of formulaic speech; what is e. e. cummings's attitude toward the speaker? Does he share that persona's views?
2. How do the lowercase nouns and lack of punctuation and conjoined words (deafanddumb) help establish tone, and how would you describe the speaker's voice?
3. Like the poem by Dorothy Parker included next in this chapter, this borrows—and bends—the form of a sonnet. How do you read the last line?

Dorothy Parker (1893–1967)

Sonnet for the End of a Sequence (1944)

So take my vows and scatter them to sea;
Who swears the sweetest is no more than human.
And say no kinder words than these of me:
"Ever she longed for peace, but was a woman!
And thus they are, whose silly female dust
Needs little enough to clutter it and bind it,
Who meet a slanted gaze, and ever must
Go build themselves a soul to dwell behind it."

For now I am my own again, my friend!
This scar but points the whiteness of my breast;
This frenzy, like its betters, spins an end,
And now I am my own. And that is best.
Therefore, I am immeasurably grateful
To you, for proving shallow, false, and hateful.

Questions for Interactive Reading and Writing

1. Is this a personal or persona poem, or both? How would you describe the "I"?
2. Would you describe this poem's tone as ironic or sarcastic, and were you surprised by the final couplet?
3. Would you call this a love poem, a "hate" poem, both?

Reading for Voice

When Reading for Voice, Ask Yourself . . .		
What is the speaker's predominant tone in the poem—joyful, mournful, bewildered, or confused—and how does it help convey the poem's meaning?	*Tone:* The vocal quality of a person's speech that helps convey meaning. In a poem, an attitude conveyed toward a poem's subject as suggested by the poet's language.	EXAMPLE: "When I died they washed me out of the turret with a hose."
Who is the speaker in the poem, and why has the poet chosen to use this persona? What does the persona allow the poet to represent more clearly? What is the poet's attitude toward the speaker in the poem?	*Persona:* A poem's speaker that may or may not be the same voice as the poet.	EXAMPLE: "Fetch? Balls and sticks capture my attention / seconds at a time."
Is irony used to help establish the speaker's attitude toward the subject?	*Verbal Irony:* The use of words to express something dissimilar to (or the opposite of) their literal meaning.	EXAMPLE: "Millions of men are *wanted at once* in a big new field; / *New, tremendous, thrilling, great.*"
	Sarcasm: A form of verbal irony using spoken approval to express implied disapproval.	EXAMPLE: "Oh, yeah, you look *great* in that hat."
	Situational Irony: An outcome that turns out to be very different from what was expected.	EXAMPLE: "And Richard Cory, one calm summer night, / Went home and put a bullet through his head."
	Dramatic Irony / Tragic Irony: A discrepancy that is detectable to audience but not to a character or characters.	EXAMPLE: "'next to of course god america i / love you land of the pilgrims' and so forth oh"
	Cosmic Irony: A discrepancy between what characters hope for or expect and what supernatural forces, fate, or God provide.	EXAMPLE: "The Immanent Will that stirs and urges everything"

Writing about Voice

1. Compare the relationships of speaker to father figure in Sylvia Plath's "Daddy," Theodore Roethke's "My Papa's Waltz," and Rita Dove's "Flash Cards."
2. Compare the speakers' attitudes toward war and conflict in "To a Terroist" by Stephen Dunn, "AD" by Kenneth Fearing, "Dulce et Decorum Est," by Wilfred Owen, and "next to of course god america i" by e. e. cummings.
3. Consider the tone of William Stafford's "Traveling through the Dark." How does it reflect the conflict and hesitation the speaker faces, and how does Stafford's tone help convey this hesitation?
4. Analyze the interplay of tone and word choice in Wallace Stevens's "Sunday Morning." How does Stevens's language and attitude toward the subject matter help communicate his character's religious deliberations?
5. Write a short, informal imagined biography for the speaker of one of the following poems: "Riot Act" by Ai; "Golden Retrievals" by Mark Doty; "Herbert White" by Frank Bidart. Use specific material in the poems to help support your invented history.
6. Consider the attitude of Ben Jonson's address to his son and Anne Bradstreet's to her book. Move through the poems and explain, in writing, what we learn. Be specific as to what the poem reveals.
7. What is Thomas Hardy saying about the irony of human existence in "Convergence of the Twain"? Compare it with what Edward Arlington Robinson is saying in "Richard Cory." What do these poems tell us about the way their authors look at life, at death, and how what may seem like an accident is fate?

IT is foolish
to let a young redwood
grow next to a house.

Even in this
one lifetime,
you will have to choose.

—from "Tree" by Jane Hirshfield

JANE Hirshfield tells us in her interview, "Now the tree is real and the house is real. Both actually exist, and as the poem says, the house is cluttered with unique things. It's a real dilemma. Eventually the house and the tree won't be able to occupy the same bit of earth. But a house and a tree are also archetypes and images."

In the case of a tree, you have the image of an object and you also have the larger symbol of what a tree means as archetype: the particular instance that represents the whole. This specific tree, a redwood growing in a specific place, has also come to represent the idea of natural versus man-made things. It embodies—or stands as a symbol for—the ideas of containment and growth.

20 Imagery

"The wider the field of senses a poem draws on, the more fully felt and alive its world is going to be in the mind of the reader."

Conversation with Jane Hirshfield, available on video at http://www.mhhe.com/delbanco1e

"Tree" and its author belong to a tradition of nature writing, of close attention paid to the physical world. In this chapter, we focus on the **image**, the thing seen for and by itself, as well as the **symbol**, what that same thing might stand for or represent. Poetry comes across mainly in terms of an attitude-generating cluster of words, creating vivid sensory (visual, aural, or tactile) impressions through language. Images work in the service of diction and tone; they generate emotion and establish mood. In the case of Hirshfield, the impetus has been provided by the sight of a nearby tree—a "young redwood" that the poet understands will grow much larger over time. Building on that particular sight and specific visual cue, this poem moves out to the general case.

& Symbol

Image is a field where the powers of body and mind can meet.

Poetry is a kind of thinking and feeling done with the whole body, mind, and heart.

Q&A

A Conversation on Writing

Jane Hirshfield

Thinking with the Body

Image is one of the most powerful ways a poem both carries meaning and changes and enlarges it, which is the work that every good poem is trying to do. Image is a field where the powers of body and mind can meet. Everything that we know of the world is constructed on the bedrock of sense experience. . . . Poetry is a kind of thinking and feeling done with the whole body, mind, and heart.

The Meaning of an Image

Every image is also a portrait of a state of soul. Rain in a poem is almost never only rain. In one poem it might be grief; in another it might be renewal after long thirst or after the drought of loneliness. Image in poetry is an enormously flexible, intimate, and powerful tool just because it hands experience from one person's consciousness into another's directly, with the solidity, multiplicity, and subtlety of actual life, which doesn't arrive with interpretations attached. A poem can add some direction to this, but the image itself is sometimes the only thing that's needed.

Meditations on the Ordinary

One of the things that has happened to poetry as it's become more contemporary is more and more things have become the subject of poems, and one of the things which has come into poetry in the twentieth and twenty-first centuries is poems about very ordinary objects, meditations on objects which you wouldn't ordinarily think of as worthy of that important thing we think of as poetry, and yet in fact poetry's work is to see the ordinary world . . . and turn that into something which expounds into larger realms, more resonance, more feeling. It lets you have a bigger life than you would have had if you only saw a button as simply a thing that holds your shirt closed.

Jane Hirshfield lives in a small white cottage in Marin County, California, surrounded by the trees, flowers, and animals that often appear in her poems. Born in New York City in 1953, she was among the first female graduates of Princeton University. Hirshfield has published six books of poetry, including *After* (2006), *Given Sugar, Given Salt* (2001), *The Lives of the Heart* (1997), *The October Palace* (1994), *Of Gravity & Angels* (1988), and *Alaya* (1982); essays about poetry, *Nine Gates: Entering the Mind of Poetry* (1997); and several anthologies of women poets. Early in her career, Hirshfield dedicated three years to the study of Zen practice, and her poetry reflects this lifelong involvement in Buddhism. Many poems focus on the natural world and our human condition within it. Hirshfield has received major honors for her poetry, including, in 2004, the seventieth Academy Fellowship for distinguished poetic achievement by the Academy of American Poets.

To watch this entire interview and hear the author read from her poetry, go to www.mhhe.com/delbanco1e.

RESEARCH ASSIGNMENT In the interview, Hirshfield describes how she uses her own experiences to construct the imagery in her poems. After watching the interview, how would you describe the meaning that Hirshfield herself assigns to her poem "Tree"?

AS YOU READ Monitor any visual images that come to you. Can you picture the poet's description of this scene in your mind's eye?

Two Poems by Jane Hirshfield

Tree (2000)

It is foolish
to let a young redwood
grow next to a house.

Even in this
one lifetime,
you will have to choose.

That great calm being,
this clutter of soup pots and books—

Already the first branch-tips brush at the window.
Softly, calmly, immensity taps at your life.

Writing from Reading

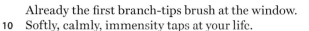

Summarize

1 Describe the physical growth of the redwood tree and how it is impinging on the house.

Analyze Craft

2 What use is the poet making of the literal growth of the tree?

3 Can you picture it? From what literal vantage point does the poet view the tree?

Analyze Voice

4 Is the poet in a panic about the situation? Or does she speak calmly? Is she trying to accept the growth of the tree as part of the progress, or lack of it, in her own life? How does this affect her choice of words?

Synthesize Summary and Analysis

5 How does the poet employ the actual tree in order to speak about something greater than just one single redwood?

Interpret the Poem

6 Do you detect a rhythmic progress in the few stanzas of this poem? If the poet states the problem, wrestles with it, and somehow resolves it, in what particular context does that occur? Would you say the poem speaks to us about a situation in the natural world or in a more abstract philosophical fashion about the situation of our own lives?

CONTINUED FROM PAGE 145

Here's another of her close examinations of an object—in this case a man-made as opposed to a natural thing. As the poem continues, the image of a button becomes "its own story, completed." And once again the poet ("I tell you") speaks directly to her readers, inviting us to enter the world of her scrupulous words.

Button (2000)

It likes both to enter and to leave,
actions it seems to feel as a kind of hide-and-seek.
It knows nothing of what the cloth believes
of its magus-like powers.

If fastening and unfastening are in its nature,
it doesn't care about its nature.

It likes the caress of two fingers
against its slightly thickened edges.
It likes the scent and heat of the proximate body.
The exhilaration of the washing is its wild pleasure.

Amoralist, sensualist, dependent of cotton thread,
its sleep is curled like a cat to a patch of sun,
calico and round.

Its understanding is the understanding
of honey and jasmine, of letting what happens come.

A button envies no neighboring button,
no snap, no knot, no polyester-braided toggle.
It rests on its red-checked shirt in serene disregard.

It is its own story, completed.

Brevity and longevity mean nothing to a button carved
of horn.

Nor do old dreams of passion disturb it,
though once it wandered the ten thousand grasses
with the musk-fragrance caught in its nostrils;
though once it followed—it did, I tell you—that wind
for miles.

Writing from Reading

Summarize

1 The poet speaks of a simple, even humble, object from our everyday lives. How does she describe it, in how many ways, and on how many levels of meaning?

Analyze Craft

2 Is there a specific term we can use to describe the way the poet uses the object in the poem? As what sort of living thing does the poet describe the button?

3 How can a button have a "story"?

4 How does the poet work to make us feel a certain way about the button?

Analyze Voice

5 What attitude does she express toward the object? What central words or phrases alert you to this?

6 What is the effect of the phrase "it did, I tell you," which the poet sets apart from the rest of the last line?

Synthesize Summary and Analysis

7 How does the poet raise a simple everyday object into something greater than itself?

Interpret the Poem

8 Picture the button in all of the states of being or manifestations in which the poet describes it. How important is it that the poet employs the word "horn" to explain the button's origins?

Some of the earliest poetry based almost entirely on image is that of Japanese **haiku.** In haiku (a poetic form containing—in Japanese—seventeen syllables in three lines of five, seven, and five syllables each), two images are juxtaposed in a way that allows a reader to create his or her own understanding of the meaning; the images themselves

> "Every time I heard my parents recite ancient . . . poetry . . . my own experience was that I was hearing language that was manifesting something older and something mysterious and something beautiful that I couldn't account for, and I wanted to be a part of that." Conversation with Li-Young Lee

carry the poem. Haiku also traditionally contain some natural-world reference to a particular season, and so an image from nature is at the heart of each of the following two haiku, one by the eighteenth–nineteenth-century poet Kobayashi Issa (who Hirshfield discusses in her interview) and the other by the seventeenth-century poet Matsuo Bashō, generally considered the first to perfect the haiku form.

Kobayashi Issa (1763–1827)

The Japanese poet used simply the pen name Issa and brought a highly personal voice to the haiku form, using dialect and colloquial language and confessing his personal doubts and loneliness. Issa was born in Kashiwabara, the son of a farmer, and lost his mother at three and his devoted grandmother as a teenager. By age fifteen, Issa had left for Edo (present-day Tokyo), where he entered a school for haiku poets. He spent much of his adult life wandering Japan before settling once again in Kashiwabara, where he married and tried to start a family. All four of his children died in infancy, and his first wife died in childbirth. His poetry, which was influenced by Buddhist themes of sin and compassion, uses simple language to articulate human experiences (as in his collection *The Year of My Life,* 1819, which captures his life events, among them his daughter's death). Despite his hardships, he brings the small pleasures of daily life into the more than 20,000 haiku he wrote in his lifetime.

On a branch (c. 1800)

On a branch
floating downriver
a cricket, singing.

—translated by Jane Hirshfield

Matsuo Bashō (1644–1694)

A Japanese master of the haiku, Matsuo Bashō spent his youth as a servant to a master with whom he had a close friendship. Bashō's first published poetry appeared in 1664, but when his master died two years later, Bashō became a wanderer. He continued to publish poetry, however, and his reputation grew; he soon had a group of twenty students. The students so respected their teacher that they built him a hut, complete with a *bashō*—or banana tree—outside its door, from which he adopted his nickname. Famous in his lifetime, Bashō took four long journeys in Japan during which he visited friends and wrote poetry and travel journals including *The Records of a Weather-Exposed Skeleton* (1684–1688). Bashō's haiku are marked by a precision of imagery—both visual and auditory—that conveys human emotion.

A caterpillar (c. 1680)

A caterpillar,
this deep in fall—
still not a butterfly.

—translated by Robert Hass

Writing from Reading

Summarize

1 Describe the images evoked in both haikus. Note the use of present tense and, in Bashō, the absence of verbs.

Analyze Craft

2 The Japanese original of this form has a precise number of syllables and usually includes at least two varieties of necessary words, one to denote the season and one to end the poem on a certain emotional note; it is written all in one sentence. How does the English form of the haiku differ from the original? What is the role of the image?

Analyze Voice

3 Is there a similarity between the two poets? What makes for this kinship aside from the form of the poems?

4 How does the subject matter affect the voice of the speaker?

Synthesize Summary and Analysis

5 These poems are composed in a specific syllabic form, each focusing on a situation in nature that has meaning for the observer and reader. What limitations does this bring, what freedoms?

Interpret the Poem

6 Each of these situations, tiny in scope, suggests something much larger about nature and about human life. See if you can make the leap between the cricket and the caterpillar and our own problems of living in crisis or living with time.

Like Jane Hirshfield, but nearly a century earlier, Ezra Pound was much impressed by poetry from Asia—particularly Chinese verse and Japanese haiku, with their brief evocations of things closely seen. Living in Paris and taking the metro (the French term for the subway), he made this striking comparison of urban commuters and the petals on a tree. There's no explicit discussion or association, no essay-like analysis of the way light-colored faces cluster in the station's darkness—but the "unnatural" or man-made crowd of commuters seems suddenly to have become a "natural" thing, a part of nature's blooming. What the poet sees is what compels his (and therefore our) attention. No moral here, or conclusion to draw; there is just an image, defined by Pound as "an intellectual and an emotional complex in an instant of time."

Ezra Pound (1885–1972)

Regarded as a crucial modern American poet, Ezra Pound helped foster the careers of important Modernists like James Joyce, T. S. Eliot, and Ernest Hemingway. Pound grew up in Pennsylvania and moved to London in 1908. Later, he would move to Italy and become a supporter of Benito Mussolini, for which in 1945 he was arrested and incarcerated for more than a decade in a Washington, D.C., mental hospital. But before he became a politically controversial figure, Pound forged a bridge between American and European avant-gardes, launching the Imagist movement—which advocated poems pared down to an image without any abstraction—early in his career. He later moved away from Imagism, but elements of its stark, precise quality remained in his poetry. His major works, "Hugh Selwyn Mauberley: Life and Contacts" (1920) and "The Cantos"—written over many years—reflect Modernist techniques such as shifts in time and point of view, an eclectic inclusion of material, and a wide-ranging diction.

AS YOU READ Notice the influence of haiku here—the compression of language and centrality of image all caught "in an instant of time."

In a Station of the Metro (1916)

The apparition of these faces in the crowd;
Petals on a wet, black bough.

Writing from Reading

Summarize

1 What action does this poem describe and what, if anything, goes on?

Analyze Craft

2 How does the word *apparition* color the poem that follows; what emotion does it convey?

Analyze Voice

3 Who is speaking here, and to whom? If the Hirshfield poem yokes the man-made to the natural world, how do these "petals on a wet, black bough" seem similar to or different from her thoughts about a tree?

Synthesize Summary and Analysis

4 We've already used more words in the discussion of this poem than are contained in the poem itself. In what ways does Pound's brevity reinforce his notion of an image as an "intellectual and emotional complex in an instant of time"? In what ways does the image convey an idea or feeling about more time than just a single moment?

Interpret the Poem

5 The title sets the scene, the poem provides the image. Would the feel of the whole be altered if the title read, instead, "At a Football Game" or "On a Bus"?

Pound and several of his fellow poets founded a movement called **Imagism,** which gave the object *seen* in a poem precedence over any other aspect of the poem. The American expatriate Hilda Doolittle, or H.D., as she signed her work, was one of Pound's partners in this "school" or "movement"—also believing in the elemental power of the image. In her poems, as in Pound's, we look at the thing itself, even as the poet attempts to suggest that details of the natural world evoke a meaning beyond their mere physical presence.

H.D. (Hilda Doolittle; 1886–1961)

Born in Bethlehem, Pennsylvania, H.D. became friends with William Carlos Williams and Ezra Pound at the University of Pennsylvania. In 1911, she took a summer trip to London, which turned into a lifelong residency abroad and which launched her poetry career when she reconnected with Pound. Under his influence, she became an Imagist, interested in pared-down verses that portrayed only immediate, real objects. Later, she moved away from Imagism, cultivating her interest in mythology and composing book-length poems about World War II: *The Walls Do Not Fall* (1944), *Tribute to the Angels* (1945), and *The Flowering of the Rod* (1946).

AS YOU READ In "Sea Poppies" what we look at is the thing itself. The image of sea poppies is in sharp focus in this poem. Ask yourself, how does the poet attempt to suggest that details of the natural world evoke a meaning beyond their mere physical nature?

Sea Poppies

(1916)

Amber husk
fluted with gold,
fruit on the sand
marked with a rich grain,

treasure
spilled near the shrub-pines
to bleach on the boulders:

your stalk has caught root
among wet pebbles
and drift flung by the sea
and grated shells
and split conch-shells.

Beautiful, wide-spread,
fire upon leaf,
what meadow yields
so fragrant a leaf
as your bright leaf?

Writing from Reading

Summarize

1 Write your own "snapshot" of this poem.

Analyze Craft

2 List ways in which the poet tries to make the reader *see* sea poppies. What words are most effective here as description and which ones (such as "beautiful") convey value judgments instead?

3 Compare this with Marianne Moore's "The Fish" in chapter 22. Both poems use an image from the natural world; however, the line structure of the Moore poem emphasizes sound over imagery. How does H.D.'s poem keep the image in focus and Moore's poem shift our attention to sound?

Analyze Voice

4 How large a role, if any, does voice play in this poem? How might a more prominent presence alter the tone of this poem?

Synthesize Summary and Analysis

5 Explain how the image takes you to a higher level of understanding of the poem's meaning.

Interpret the Poem

6 Notice how, in the last stanza, H.D. repeats the word *leaf* three times. What effect does this achieve?

The short poems of William Carlos Williams, the physician from Patterson, New Jersey, illustrate a great deal about that modern tendency in poetry defined by Pound as imagism. Here the "thing itself"—an object seen and not discussed or analyzed—becomes the poet's focus and the poem's primary concern. Gertrude Stein's famous pronouncement that "a rose is a rose is a rose" shares much the same aesthetic—or, as Williams puts it (in his 1944 poem "A Sort of Song"), "No ideas but in things."

On first reading, the following brief poem seems to be about almost nothing. There are echoing sounds such as "glazed" and "rain," or "white" and "beside," and the lines have a similar rhythm, but if you recite these words they may well sound like a casual overheard sentence—not a formal arrangement of language in a structured shape. The formality of Williams's work is less than obvious: a thing you have to look closely at in order to notice at all. In fact, there's a nearly haiku-like compression of

"So there's the ordinary shape of the thing and the way that you would say it . . . and if you piece them out on the page, you can convey the feeling by getting this shape absolutely."

Conversation with Robert Hass

and shape to the work. The poet presents us with a couple of objects, a red wheelbarrow glazed with rainwater standing in a yard alongside a bunch of white chickens. Together, the poem's formal elements ingrain in our memory the image of the barrow and the chickens and the rain. The life evoked by objects—in a barnyard or a garden patch, and in particular weather—grows as vivid here as though it were *painted,* and as fixed within our memory as though it had been framed. In this way, a poem that seems at first glance quite casual puts forward an image of eternal order and upholds the importance, in a democratic contemporary fashion (very conversational, very American), of each and every thing and every one of us.

William Carlos Williams (1883–1963)

William Carlos Williams was born in Rutherford, New Jersey, the same town in which he would die eighty years later. This fact is consistent with one of Williams's most fundamental beliefs about poetry: that one ought to write about one's own locale. Williams had many other strong ideas about poetry, among them that the poet should focus only on concrete details and images rather than trying to convey abstract ideas. Although friends with Ezra Pound and T. S. Eliot, Williams in many ways stands in opposition to their complex references and international emphases; unlike his contemporaries, he spent little time abroad. Considered one of the most important of twentieth-century poets, Williams made his living as a doctor with a specialization in pediatrics (he delivered more than 2,000 babies!). His touchstone work, *Paterson,* is an epic in five books—the third of which won the National Book Award in 1950—about Paterson, New Jersey.

AS YOU READ **Notice how Williams divides "wheel" and "barrow" or "rain" and "water" in a line break; others might have written "wheelbarrow" or "rainwater," but the space between the words and lines allows us to consider how those objects separate or fuse.**

The Red Wheelbarrow (1923)

so much depends
upon

a red wheel
barrow

glazed with rain
water

beside the white
chickens.

Writing from Reading

Summarize

1 What images do you see in this poem? How are they connected?

Analyze Craft

2 What does Williams accomplish by beginning each line with a lower-case letter?

3 Why does Williams say "a" red wheelbarrow instead of "the" red wheelbarrow?

Analyze Voice

4 What's *not* said is just as important as what's included here. What has been left out, and how would the poem change if it were included in the poem?

Synthesize Summary and Analysis

5 How does the casual tone combine with the structure to make the poem's point?

Interpret the Poem

6 The only statement in the entire poem that does not describe a physical thing is the opening line—"so much depends." You can read the first line, in effect, as either "very much depends" or "therefore much depends," and the interpretation of the phrase shifts back and forth accordingly. How much of the meaning of this poem depends on the phrasing of this statement?

Another representation of the importance of the image comes in the following poem—again, very plainly presented—by the twentieth-century American poet Wallace Stevens. This self-described **anecdote**—a personal remembrance or brief story—also takes as its topic the *things* of the world, though a jar upon a hill is somehow more surprising than a wheelbarrow in a backyard. A secondary meaning of the word *jar* is "discord" or "disruption," and the imagined "gray and bare" object cleans up what's "slovenly." Perhaps no clearer testimonial to the power of an image (and what poetry can accomplish by "foregrounding" such an image) exists than "Anecdote of the Jar."

Wallace Stevens (1879–1955)

For a brief biography of Wallace Stevens, see chapter 18.

AS YOU READ Notice how the poem's first word is "I," infusing the poet himself with the pride of positioning the important jar. How does this act of shaping—"like nothing else in Tennessee"—organize and change what is around it?

Anecdote of the Jar (1923)

I placed a jar in Tennessee,
And round it was, upon a hill.
It made the slovenly wilderness
Surround that hill.

The wilderness rose up to it,
And sprawled around, no longer wild.
The jar was round upon the ground
And tall and of a port in air.

It took dominion everywhere.
The jar was gray and bare.
It did not give of bird or bush,
Like nothing else in Tennessee.

Writing from Reading

Summarize

1 Describe the jar. Could you draw it?

2 What words does Stevens use to convey the image? Does it represent a Mason jar, a ceramic jug, a particular bowl you have seen?

Analyze Craft

3 Notice how the last word of the first line and the last word of the poem are the same (this is true also of the final word in lines 2 and 4). Then there are three perfect rhymes ("air," "everywhere," "bare"). What does this tell you about the "shaping impulse" on the poet's part?

Analyze Voice

4 Can you read this poem as a companion text to William Carlos Williams's "The Red Wheelbarrow"? In what ways is the voice different, in what ways the same?

Synthesize Summary and Analysis

5 How does the act of *seeing* itself connect to the name of the state repeated twice—at the end of the poem's first and last lines? How different would this anecdote be if the poet had located his jar in Nevada or Rhode Island?

Interpret the Poem

6 How much *depends* on the jar in Tennessee, the jar that "took dominion everywhere"? What if the poet had not "placed a jar in Tennessee"? Would the world—or, even more grandly, the universe—be different?

ALLEGORY AND PARABLE

Allegory and **parable** are related to symbol and are both extended narratives in which people, places, and things function more like conventional symbols directly representing such attributes as good, evil, redemption, hell, or heaven. One of the most famous poetic allegories is Dante's *Divine Comedy.* A parable, like the Fishes and the Loaves from the Gospel of Matthew in the New Testament, is usually an allegory but also a teaching tale with a moral.

Coming up now is another domestic image, another familiar object closely seen: the image of "The Blue Bowl." In this poem, "we" engage in other matters; we work and eat and sleep and attempt to forget what's been buried. The bowl itself—plastic, ceramic, tin, china?—disappears from sight, but the sense of its absent presence remains. In that sense, it stands as a symbol—as well as a literal burial container—of what is cherished and lost.

"Poetry . . . bring[s] image . . . and symbol to bear on unspeakable love or hurt or loss or hate or whatever happens to be." Conversation with Thomas Lynch

Here is a crucial distinction between image and symbol. If, as William Carlos Williams puts it, there are "no ideas but in things," there are certain "things" within our culture that stand—almost inescapably—for "ideas." A jar in Tennessee or a wheelbarrow glazed with rain are specific images, but say such words as "dove" or "cross" or "crown" and it's impossible not to imagine what else they represent. A dove means *peace* as well as bird, a cross means *suffering and sacrifice* as well as arrangement of wood. The connotations of the word *crown* are those of *power, majesty,* but when Christ wears a crown of thorns we know what that headgear signifies instead. The word for this, in pictorial terms, is **iconography**—put a scepter or skull in a painting, and the viewer is supposed to know what those objects represent. In earlier times, these were almost **conventional** associations: *a* stands for one thing, *b* stands for another, and so on and so forth. More modern poets, however, tend to create their own symbols and go against the grain. So when Jane Kenyon makes "the blue bowl" *stand* for something, she's making that object symbolic in a literary way, a way that is specific to its context in the poem, a way it had not been before.

Jane Kenyon (1947–1995)

Born in Ann Arbor, Michigan, Jane Kenyon remained there through her undergraduate and graduate education at the University of Michigan. While at the university, Kenyon met poet Donald Hall, whom she married. The couple settled in the New Hampshire home that had been in Hall's family for generations. There, Kenyon began to take her poetry seriously and published four collections, which met with high praise for their portrayals of New England, the cycles of nature, and the depression with which she struggled. She died at age forty-seven of leukemia.

AS YOU READ Ask yourself who is the "we" of this poem, and notice that the title tells you something—the bowl's color—that the body of the text does not include.

The Blue Bowl (1990)

Like primitives we buried the cat
with his bowl. Bare-handed
we scraped sand and gravel
back into the hole.
They fell with a hiss
and thud on his side,
on his long red fur, the white feathers
between his toes, and his
long, not to say aquiline, nose.

We stood and brushed each other off.
There are sorrows keener than these.

Silent the rest of the day, we worked,
ate, stared, and slept. It stormed
all night; now it clears, and a robin
burbles from a dripping bush
like the neighbor who means well
but always says the wrong thing.

Writing from Reading

Summarize

1 Why does Kenyon give this poem the title she does?

Analyze Craft

2 It would seem that in this poem the image of the bowl takes on itself the emotion of the situation—the death and burial of a beloved pet. Is it a visible presence once dropped into the ground?

Analyze Voice

3 We're told by the poet that "There are sorrows keener than these." What are those sorrows? How does this contribute to the mood of the poem?

Synthesize Summary and Analysis

4 How much of a role does the bowl play in this poem? Is it all-encompassing, like the jar in Tennessee in the Stevens poem?

Interpret the Poem

5 If the burbling robin seems to be saying "the wrong thing," what does the poet suggest here about the possibility of consolation, and does she instead imply that it's better to be "silent the rest of the day"?

POEMS AND PAINTINGS

Put the "blue" from the title of "The Blue Bowl" together with the other two colors mentioned in Kenyon's poem ("long red fur, the white feathers"), and you have the colors of the American flag. This very American poem may not be suggesting anything in particular about the American way of life, but it's hard not to think of red, white, and blue as somehow representative colors—as well as, in and of themselves, vivid particular hues. Our discussion of voice in the previous chapter had largely to do with the sound and the diction of verse, what we *hear* as tone of voice. The "blue bowl" points to what we *see*. Poets have always also had a fascination for the visual, the pictorial representation of things; when William Carlos Williams focuses on a wheelbarrow or chickens, he too insists on telling us that they are red and white. Many poets work with particular paintings in mind, taking verbal cues from the images provided by a work of visual art. Here are three.

W. H. Auden (1907–1973)

For a brief biography of W. H. Auden, see chapter 18.

AS YOU READ Notice that this poem begins, as the title tells us, in a particular place with the poet examining a particular painting. But the opening statement is nonetheless a generality—a blank to be filled in by what he, studying, sees.

Musée des Beaux Arts (1940)

About suffering they were never wrong,
The Old Masters: how well, they understood
Its human position; how it takes place
While someone else is eating or opening a window or just walking dully along;
How, when the aged are reverently, passionately waiting
For the miraculous birth, there always must be
Children who did not specially want it to happen, skating
On a pond at the edge of the wood:
They never forgot

That even the dreadful martyrdom must run its course
Anyhow in a corner, some untidy spot
Where the dogs go on with their doggy life and the torturer's horse
Scratches its innocent behind on a tree.

In Breughel's *Icarus,* for instance: how everything turns away
Quite leisurely from the disaster; the ploughman may
Have heard the splash, the forsaken cry,
But for him it was not an important failure; the sun shone
As it had to on the white legs disappearing into the green
Water; and the expensive delicate ship that must have seen
Something amazing, a boy falling out of the sky,
Had somewhere to get to and sailed calmly on.

Brueghel's *Fall of Icarus*

Pieter Brueghel the Elder. Landscape with the Fall of Icarus, *c. 1554–1555. Oil on panel (transferred to canvas), 2′ 5″ x 3′ 8 1/8″. Musées Royaux des Beaux-Arts de Belgique, Brussels. © akg-images.*

"Beneath their flight / the fisherman while casting his long rod, / or the tired shepherd leaning on his crook, / or the rough plowman as he raised his eyes, / astonished might observe them on the wing, / and worship them as Gods" (Ovid, lines 338–343). In Brueghel's painting, the characters are all in place, but their reactions, as Auden observes in the following poem, demonstrate a resignation far from the astonishment Ovid describes. The plowman turns his head to the ground, the fisherman keeps his eyes on the water, and the boat, with its sails billowed out toward the horizon, keeps sailing. In the bottom right, away from the focus, fallen Icarus drowns, kicking his feet at the sunny sky.

Writing from Reading

Summarize

1 What is happening when suffering "takes place" in this poem? What is the suffering that Auden is referring to? What is the first and final point that Auden makes?

Analyze Craft

2 This is a work of art about a work of art. How does the tone differ from, say, a poem about a button or a tree?

3 Look at the rhyme pattern of the last eight lines. How does what we hear help establish what we see, and why should the poem's last words be "calmly on"?

Analyze Voice

4 Discuss a phrase like "the dogs go on with their doggy life" or "for him it was not an important failure."

Synthesize Summary and Analysis

5 The second stanza of this poem evokes an individual canvas by a particular painter. How much does it help to have a visual image of the image evoked here?

6 How faithful has the poet been to the Brueghel painting described?

Interpret the Poem

7 Why do you think Icarus dies off at the edge of the composition and not stage center? What is the poet saying, by way of this image, about the importance of "great events" and their place in daily life?

Anne Carson (b. 1950)

Growing up in Ontario, Canada, Anne Carson developed a love for the classics when one of her high school teachers taught her ancient Greek during school lunch hours. Carson eventually earned her bachelor's, master's, and doctorate from the University of Toronto, and today is a professor of classics and comparative literature at the University of Michigan. Her interest in the classics is reflected in her work: *Autobiography of Red* (1998), a novel-length poem, is a recasting of a Greek myth in the present day, while *Plainwater* (1996), a collection of poetry and prose, includes a conversation with a seventh-century B.C. poet. She has immersed herself in the world of Greek theatre and translated the work of the poet Sappho. Carson has received awards including a MacArthur Foundation award and a Guggenheim Fellowship.

AS YOU READ Ask yourself how faithful the verbal "tone" here is to the visual mood of the Hopper painting.

Automat

(2000)

Night work
  neon milk
  powdered
  silk
Girl de luxe

Girl work
  plate glass love
  lone
  glove
Night de luxe

Girl work
  smell of black
  down
  the back
Night de luxe

Night work
  clamo
  ad te
  Domine
Girl de luxe

Edward Hopper's *Automat* (1927)

A lone woman sits in an automat sipping a cup of coffee. She is well dressed, not a vagrant, but her missing glove and downcast eyes suggest hurry or distraction. Hopper's intention in the painting is ambiguous. An opaque black window dominates the scene, reflecting only rows of lights from the apparently empty automat. The lone woman's skin is the brightest part of the painting, contrasting sharply with the void of the window, and (for the painting's time) perhaps more than slightly suggesting female sexuality. Consider the coin-operated, Prohibition-era setting: Is the woman trapped, lonely, or waiting? Hopper's work frequently appears to capture a scene immediately before or after the action has occurred; as in *Automat*, it is often difficult to know which is the case.

Edward Hopper (American, 1882–1967). Automat. *1927. Oil on Canvas; 36" x 28$^{1}/_{8}$". Des Moines Art Center Permanent Collections; Purchased with fund from the Edmundson Art Foundation, Inc., 1958.2.*

Writing from Reading

Summarize

1 How would you describe the poet's response to the painting?

Analyze Craft

2 Does the poem seem at all "painterly"? How does it employ visual material?

3 Does the rhyming make clear Carson's response? What effect do the repetitive images have?

Analyze Voice

4 Can you identify the needs and interests of the speaker based on her voice? Is the poet singing the praises of the girl or judging her?

Synthesize Summary and Analysis

5 How would you characterize the effect of the poem compared with the effect of the painting? How does the painting affect your reaction to the poem?

Interpret the Poem

6 Does the quotation in devotional Latin add to the mystery of the poem or make the poem clearer to you? It might help to know that the Latin *clamo ad te Domine* means "I cry out, God, to you."

Cathy Song (b. 1950)

Cathy Song was born in Hawaii of Korean and Chinese descent. She left Hawaii to complete her education—a B.A. from Wellesley College and an M.A. from Boston University—but returned with her husband and children several years later. Her first collection of poetry, *Picture Bride* (1982), was named for the practice of arranged marriages between Asians in America and women in Asia based on exchanged photographs—the practice by which Song's grandmother came to America at the age of twenty-three. The collection won the Yale Series of Younger Poets Prize. Since then, Song has published two more collections of poetry, which have continued her examination of family ties that *Picture Bride* established.

AS YOU READ **Go back and forth to the painting and notice the accuracy or freedom of the poet with respect to the original.**

Girl Powdering Her Neck (1983)

from an ukiyo-e print by Utamaro

The light is the inside
sheen of an oyster shell,
sponged with talc and vapor,
moisture from a bath.
A pair of slippers
are placed outside
the rice-paper doors.
She kneels at a low table
in the room,
her legs folded beneath her
as she sits on a buckwheat pillow.

Her hair is black
with hints of red,
the color of seaweed
spread over rocks.

Morning begins the ritual
wheel of the body,
the application of translucent skins.
She practices pleasure:

Kitigawa Utamaro (1753–1806). c. 1795. Woman Powdering Her Neck. *Musee des Arts Asiatiques–Guimet, Paris, France.*

Kitagawa Utamaro's *Girl Powdering Her Neck* (c. 1750)

Painted as a study of the "floating world" (the translation of "ukiyo-e"), this print depicts a geisha preparing herself in a daily ritual. The Japanese term "ukiyo" connotes the frivolity and passing nature of the nouveau riche way of life that Utamaro depicts. Prints such as this were common in Utamaro's time (mid-1700s) because they could be cheaply mass produced. Common subjects were actors, sumo wrestlers, and groups of women. A distinct aspect of many Utamaro prints is their depiction of women alone, often shown only from the waist up. The personal, individual focus of this print engenders its depth and appeal; note how even the artist's signature becomes part of the composition.

the pressure of three fingertips
applying powder.
Fingerprints of pollen
some other hand will trace.

The peach-dyed kimono
patterned with maple leaves
drifting across the silk,
falls from right to left
in a diagonal, revealing
the nape of her neck
and the curve of a shoulder
like the slope of a hill
set deep in snow in a country
of huge white solemn birds.
Her face appears in the mirror,
a reflection in a winter pond,
rising to meet itself.

She dips a corner of her sleeve
like a brush into water
to wipe the mirror;
she is about to paint herself.
The eyes narrow
in a moment of self-scrutiny.
The mouth parts
as if desiring to disturb
the placid plum face;
break the symmetry of silence.
But the berry-stained lips,
stenciled into the mask of beauty,
do not speak.

Two chrysanthemums
touch in the middle of the lake
and drift apart.

Writing from Reading

Summarize

1 The poet views a print by an eighteenth-century Japanese artist. Do you find that her poem is a description only?

Analyze Craft

2 How does the poet make her attitudes and emotions known even as she seems to describe rather straightforwardly what she sees in the print? How do the metaphors she employs suggest her attitude toward the subject?

Analyze Voice

3 Is there anything in her choice of words that reveals her emotions about the situation or image in the print? Does the vividness of the colors contribute to this effect?

Synthesize Summary and Analysis

4 The poet's reproduction in language of the Utamaro print reveals certain ways of seeing that are as much interpretive as descriptive. Can you describe some of these?

Interpret the Poem

5 The modern American woman of Asian descent looks at the old Japanese print and finds herself in it in many ways, and yet there are differences. Which might these be?

Poems for Review and Further Study

Robert Bly (b. 1926)

Driving to Town Late to Mail a Letter (1962)

It is a cold and snowy night. The main street is deserted.
The only things moving are swirls of snow.
As I lift the mailbox door, I feel its cold iron.
There is a privacy I love in this snowy night.
Driving around, I will waste more time.

Questions for Interactive Reading and Writing

1. This poem is written in the present tense and, in the last line, suggests the future as well. How does that reference enhance the sense of the immediate presence?
2. Why does the speaker emphasize the feel of the iron of the mailbox? How does that contribute to the scene and setting? Is it an image, a symbol—both?
3. A letter is a form of communication, yet the poet seems to value what he calls "privacy." How is this ironic?
4. Contrast the normal sense of urgency in the completion of a task such as this with the poet's apparent desire to "waste" time.

John Dryden (1631–1700)

A Song for St. Cecilia's Day, 1687 (1687)

I

From harmony, from heavenly harmony
  This universal frame began:
  When Nature underneath a heap
    Of jarring atoms lay,
  And could not heave her head,
The tuneful voice was heard from high,
  "Arise, ye more than dead."

Then cold, and hot, and moist, and dry,
In order to their stations leap,
And Music's power obey.
From harmony, from heavenly harmony,
This universal frame began:
From harmony to harmony
Through all the compass of the notes it ran,
The diapason closing full in man.

II

What passion cannot music raise and quell?
When Jubal struck the chorded shell,
His listening brethren stood around,
And, wondering, on their faces fell
To worship that celestial sound.
Less than a god they thought there could not dwell
Within the hollow of that shell,
That spoke so sweetly, and so well.
What passion cannot Music raise and quell!

III

The trumpet's loud clangor
Excites us to arms,
With shrill notes of anger,
And mortal alarms.
The double double double beat
Of the thundering drum
Cries: "Hark! the foes come;
Charge, charge! 'tis too late to retreat."

IV

The soft complaining flute,
In dying notes discovers
The woes of hopeless lovers,
Whose dirge is whispered by the warbling lute.

V

Sharp violins proclaim
Their jealous pangs and desperation,
Fury, frantic indignation,
Depth of pains, and height of passion,
For the fair, disdainful dame.

VI

But O! what art can teach,
What human voice can reach,
The sacred organ's praise?
Notes inspiring holy love,
Notes that wing their heavenly ways
To mend the choirs above.

VII

Orpheus could lead the savage race;
And trees uprooted left their place,
Sequacious of the lyre:
But bright Cecilia raised the wonder higher;
When to her organ vocal breath was given,
An angel heard, and straight appeared,
Mistaking earth for heaven.

Grand Chorus

As from the power of sacred lays
The spheres began to move,
And sung the great Creator's praise
To all the blest above;
So when the last and dreadful hour
This crumbling pageant shall devour,
The trumpet shall be heard on high,
The dead shall live, the living die,
And Music shall untune the sky.

Questions for Interactive Reading and Writing

1. One of the ways to consider this "song" is to look at the length of the stanzas, the beat and rhythm of the lines, the way the separate component parts function as a whole. There's a great deal of music here. How do the rhyme schemes of the stanzas, their regularity and variety, help you hear the music? (In the last nine-line stanza, for example, the last three lines have the same single-word rhyme—"high," "die," "sky"—almost as though the poet made sure "The trumpet shall be heard.")
2. Pick out the solo instruments described. There are trumpets and flutes, violins and drums, lyres and organs—all making music together. How do they blend to make an orchestra, "the compass of the notes"?
3. How does Dryden help us picture "heavenly harmony"? What images do you come away with on first reading of the poem?
4. In the composition of the cosmos, as Dryden and his contemporaries saw it, one string untuned meant the possibility of discord or disharmony, and the possibility of the entire enterprise coming apart. What does Dryden think will happen if the links among instruments come apart in "the last and dreadful hour"?

Paul Laurence Dunbar (1872–1906)

For a brief biography of Paul Laurence Dunbar, see chapter 19.

Farm House by the River (1903)

I know a little country place
  Where still my heart doth linger,
And o'er its fields is every grace
  Lined out by memory's finger.
Back from the lane where poplars grew
  And aspens quake and quiver,
There stands all bath'd in summer's glow
  A farm house by the river.

Its eaves are touched with golden light
  So sweetly, softly shining,
And morning glories full and bright
  About the doors are twining.
And there endowed with every grace
  That nature's hand could give her,
There lived the angel of the place
  In the farm house by the river.

Her eyes were blue, her hair was gold,
  Her face was bright and sunny;
The songs that from her bosom rolled
  Were sweet as summer's honey.
And I loved her well, that maid divine,
  And I prayed the Gracious Giver,
That I some day might call her mine
  In the farm house by the river.

Twas not to be—but God knows best.
  His will for aye be heeded!
Perhaps amid the angels' bliss,
  My little love was needed.
Her spirit from its thralldom torn
  Went singing o'er the river,
And that sweet life my heart shall mourn
  Forever and forever.

She dies one morn at early light
  When all the birds are singing,
And Heaven itself in pure delight
  Its bells of joy seemed ringing.
They laid her dust where soon and late
  The solemn grasses quiver,
And left alone and desolate
  The farm house by the river.

Questions for Interactive Reading and Writing

1. Describe the rhyme scheme. How does the tone of the poem and the rhyme compare to the ballad in chapter 25?
2. The poet speaks of the loss of an Eden-like setting. Where might he be living that the loss of the farmhouse seems so sharp and deep? What else besides the place by the river has the poet lost?
3. List the images and symbols that Dunbar employs to evoke his lost love.

John Keats (1795–1821)

For a brief biography of John Keats, see chapter 18.

Ode to a Nightingale (1819)

I

My heart aches, and a drowsy numbness pains
  My sense, as though of hemlock I had drunk,
Or emptied some dull opiate to the drains
  One minute past, and Lethe-wards had sunk:
'Tis not through envy of thy happy lot,
  But being too happy in thine happiness,—
    That thou, light-wingéd Dryad of the trees,
      In some melodious plot
  Of beechen green and shadows numberless,
    Singest of summer in full-throated ease.

II

O, for a draught of vintage! that hath been
  Cooled a long age in the deep-delvéd earth,
Tasting of Flora and the country green,
  Dance, and Provençal song, and sunburnt mirth!
O for a beaker full of the warm South,
  Full of the true, the blushful Hippocrene,
    With beaded bubbles winking at the brim,
      And purple-stainéd mouth;
  That I might drink, and leave the world unseen,
    And with thee fade away into the forest dim:

III

Fade far away, dissolve, and quite forget
  What thou among the leaves hast never known,
The weariness, the fever, and the fret
  Here, where men sit and hear each other groan;

Where palsy shakes a few, sad, last gray hairs,
Where youth grows pale, and spectre-thin, and dies;
Where but to think is to be full of sorrow
And leaden-eyed despairs,
Where Beauty cannot keep her lustrous eyes,
Or new Love pine at them beyond tomorrow.

IV

Away! away! for I will fly to thee,
Not charioted by Bacchus and his pards,
But on the viewless wings of Poesy,
Though the dull brain perplexes and retards:
Already with thee! tender is the night,
And haply the Queen-Moon is on her throne,
Clustered around by all her starry Fays;
But here there is no light,
Save what from heaven is with the breezes blown
Through verdurous glooms and winding mossy ways.

V

I cannot see what flowers are at my feet,
Nor what soft incense hangs upon the boughs,
But, in embalméd darkness, guess each sweet
Wherewith the seasonable month endows
The grass, the thicket, and the fruit-tree wild;
White hawthorn, and the pastoral eglantine;
Fast fading violets covered up in leaves;
And mid-May's eldest child,
The coming musk-rose, full of dewy wine,
The murmurous haunt of flies on summer eves.

VI

Darkling I listen; and, for many a time
I have been half in love with easeful Death,
Called him soft names in many a muséd rhyme,
To take into the air my quiet breath;
Now more than ever seems it rich to die,
To cease upon the midnight with no pain,
While thou art pouring forth thy soul abroad
In such an ecstasy!
Still wouldst thou sing, and I have ears in vain—
To thy high requiem become a sod.

VII

Thou wast not born for death, immortal Bird!
No hungry generations tread thee down;
The voice I hear this passing night was heard
In ancient days by emperor and clown:
Perhaps the selfsame song that found a path
Through the sad heart of Ruth, when, sick for home,
She stood in tears amid the alien corn;
The same that ofttimes hath
Charmed magic casements, opening on the foam
Of perilous seas, in faery lands forlorn.

VIII

Forlorn! the very word is like a bell
To toll me back from thee to my sole self!
Adieu! the fancy cannot cheat so well
As she is famed to do, deceiving elf.
Adieu! adieu! thy plaintive anthem fades
Past the near meadows, over the still stream,
Up the hill side; and now 'tis buried deep
In the next valley-glades:
Was it a vision, or a waking dream?
Fled is that music:—Do I wake or sleep?

Questions for Interactive Reading and Writing

1. What would "a beaker full of the warm South" look like? Can you drink it? What about "hemlock" or some "dull opiate" instead?
2. The phrase "tender is the night" (stanza 4) was used by F. Scott Fitzgerald as the title of one of his novels. What do the words convey?
3. Track the poet's attitude to the image or symbol of the nightingale through the stanzas. How near is it, how far away?
4. How does the poet, by guessing, describe what "I cannot see"?
5. This poem and Jane Kenyon's "The Blue Bowl" (earlier in this chapter) are both meditations on death. How does Keats's use of the nightingale image compare to Kenyon's use of the cat's blue bowl?

Shirley Geok-Lin Lim (b. 1944)

Scavenging on a Double Bluff (2007)

I

My children call these wish-stones, Anne said,
studying the warm brown quartz
I had picked with its perfect elongated
white circle; when that circle is
unbroken, that's what makes them wishes.
I wished she had not told me this.
All week I thought of getting another
down by Double Bluff Beach.
This afternoon I take the time to bike
and walk. Some of us can pick up unbroken
spindles where others see only fragments

and shell bits; can gather a dozen
in a minute, whole and bleached.
Rocks lie everywhere on mud flats.
Serpentine, granite, sandstone, calcite,
agate: igneous and sedimentary,
names enough to fill my pockets.
I find the colors, lines, and shapes
as I find spindles in the shore litter.
Starving at six makes one grow up sharp
at scavenging, and I have seen
strangers turn dubious at my luck.
My eyes stoop to the search.
I do not stop for the blue herons
or the far islands and inlets. The heron
hunts with me, hour after hour,
although I no longer know what it is
I wish for: love, money, position,
picked up like these shells and stones
that weigh down my backpack.

II

What is the difference between
having nothing and too much?
"You have too much," one complimented,
then asked for my things. But that's beside
the point. It's the work of finding
gives them meaning—work of a mind
honed for surviving. The Chinese,
as I found in Shanghai, at the garden
of the Minor Administrator, prefer
edges of unequally worn stone,
spying buttes, peaks, crags, and scarps
lift up against wear and centuries.
I must have never been Chinese.
I like my rocks smooth and worn
through millennia of water, storm, and tide;
round as the round of loaves; circles
of breasts hurting with milk
on round pillows; as a lunar month finds
an open Oh!, a yellow wheel;
round scrotum swollen at touch.
Complete as unbroken bands
of color, stones that are wishes.
I scavenge dandelion leaves, chicory,
wild onions, beach plums, thimbleberries.
I'm scavenging in case of a famine;
in case I'll have to go hungry,
wishes worn smooth, worn daily,
in my round mouth, my anxious hand.

Questions for Interactive Reading and Writing

1. What is the occasion of the poem? When and where does it take place? What biographical details do we learn about the poet? How do these help us understand what she is doing there on the beach?
2. How does the poet manage to suggest that scavenging for stones on a beach is an action in which we can find some symbolic meaning? What techniques does she use to encourage us to think about the occasion in this fashion?
3. Where does the poet take us in the second part of the poem? To a new location? To a new stage of thinking about the scavenging in part 1?
4. How is the speaker of this poem different in the way she speaks about stones from, say, the friend who collects stones Carolyn Forché speaks of in her poem "The Museum of Stones" (chapter 15)? How does this poet's approach contrast, if it does, with Forché's approach?

Amy Lowell (1874–1925)

Patterns (1914)

I walk down the garden paths,
And all the daffodils
Are blowing, and the bright blue squills.
I walk down the patterned garden-paths
In my stiff, brocaded gown.
With my powdered hair and jeweled fan,
I too am a rare
Pattern. As I wander down
The garden paths.

My dress is richly figured,
And the train
Makes a pink and silver stain
On the gravel, and the thrift
Of the borders.
Just a plate of current fashion,
Tripping by in high-heeled, ribboned shoes.
Not a softness anywhere about me,
Only whalebone and brocade.
And I sink on a seat in the shade
Of a lime tree. For my passion
Wars against the stiff brocade.
The daffodils and squills
Flutter in the breeze

As they please.
And I weep;
For the lime-tree is in blossom
And one small flower has dropped upon my bosom.

And the plashing of waterdrops
In the marble fountain
Comes down the garden-paths.
The dripping never stops.
Underneath my stiffened gown
Is the softness of a woman bathing in a marble basin,
A basin in the midst of hedges grown
So thick, she cannot see her lover hiding,
But she guesses he is near,
And the sliding of the water
Seems the stroking of a dear
Hand upon her.
What is Summer in a fine brocaded gown!
I should like to see it lying in a heap upon the ground.
All the pink and silver crumpled up on the ground.

I would be the pink and silver as I ran along the paths,
And he would stumble after,
Bewildered by my laughter.
I should see the sun flashing from his sword-hilt and the buckles on his shoes.
I would choose
To lead him in a maze along the patterned paths,
A bright and laughing maze for my heavy-booted lover,
Till he caught me in the shade,
And the buttons of his waistcoat bruised my body as he clasped me,
Aching, melting, unafraid.
With the shadows of the leaves and the sundrops,
And the plopping of the waterdrops,
All about us in the open afternoon—
I am very likely to swoon
With the weight of this brocade,
For the sun sifts through the shade.

Underneath the fallen blossom
In my bosom,
Is a letter I have hid.
It was brought to me this morning by a rider from the Duke.
"Madam, we regret to inform you that Lord Hartwell
Died in action Thursday se'nnight."
As I read it in the white, morning sunlight,
The letters squirmed like snakes.
"Any answer, Madam," said my footman.
"No," I told him.
"See that the messenger takes some refreshment.
No, no answer."
And I walked into the garden,
Up and down the patterned paths,
In my stiff, correct brocade.
The blue and yellow flowers stood up proudly in the sun,
Each one.
I stood upright too,
Held rigid to the pattern
By the stiffness of my gown.
Up and down I walked,
Up and down.

In a month he would have been my husband.
In a month, here, underneath this lime,
We would have broken the pattern;
He for me, and I for him,
He as Colonel, I as Lady,
On this shady seat.
He had a whim
That sunlight carried blessing.
And I answered, "It shall be as you have said."
Now he is dead.

In Summer and in Winter I shall walk
Up and down
The patterned garden-paths
In my stiff, brocaded gown.
The squills and daffodils
Will give place to pillared roses, and to asters, and to snow.
I shall go
Up and down,
In my gown.
Gorgeously arrayed,
Boned and stayed.
And the softness of my body will be guarded from embrace
By each button, hook, and lace.
For the man who should loose me is dead,
Fighting with the Duke in Flanders,
In a pattern called a war.
Christ! What are patterns for?

Questions for Interactive Reading and Writing

1. Describe the occasion of the poem. What is the primary emotion felt by the speaker? Does this woman out of history seem remote from the American experience of the poet? Why might Lowell have chosen this particular woman as the speaker?
2. How does "my stiff, brocaded gown . . . each button, hook, and lace" compare with the button in Jane

Hirshfield's poem in this chapter? What image do the words evoke?

3. How does the outer appearance of the woman—her manner, her way of dressing—contrast with her inner state of being? How does the final expressive outburst make that emotion clear?

Cleopatra Mathis (b. 1914)

Lilacs (1983)

They open before we have had a chance
to be unkind to each other.
In the dark the tiny whorls
unfold around the stem, candlelit
against the window; the infrequent dark
where our bodies gather and fill.
The lilacs bloom in their time,
the flowers dry in the billowing tree
which I will cut back
and further back.
What is desire
but a stone to bargain with? a longing
that says *be something else,*
until each holds the other
against change. The year turns,
the tree's frame empties,

empties again. If I could need
only what is given—
the way the limbs protect themselves
in spite of weather. Another dark
conceals the latent buds.
It's true, I am closed
between a past and future winter;
any fear is made bearable when it repeats,
when it's mutable and brief.

Questions for Interactive Reading and Writing

1. Emotion might seem abstract as a subject. How does the poet make it palpable and concrete?
2. The lilacs "bloom in their time." Does the poet's sense of time coincide with or differ from the time of nature?
3. How does the perfection of nature contrast with the poet's sense of needing more than she is given?
4. Compare this poem to Amy Lowell's "Patterns." How might you argue that "Lilacs" is a response to "Patterns"?

Howard Nemerov (1920–1991)

The Blue Swallows (1967)

Across the millstream below the bridge
Seven blue swallows divide the air
In shapes invisible and evanescent,
Kaleidoscopic beyond the mind's
Or memory's power to keep them there.

"History is where tensions were,"
"Form is the diagram of forces."
Thus, helplessly, there on the bridge,
While gazing down upon those birds—
How strange, to be above the birds!—
Thus helplessly the mind in its brain
Weaves up relation's spindrift web,
Seeing the swallows' tails as nibs
Dipped in invisible ink, writing . . .

Poor mind, what would you have them write?
Some cabalistic history
Whose authorship you might ascribe
To God? to Nature? Ah, poor ghost,
You've capitalized your Self enough.
That villainous William of Occam
Cut out the feet from under that dream
Some seven centuries ago.
It's taken that long for the mind
To waken, yawn and stretch, to see
With opened eyes emptied of speech
The real world where the spelling mind
Imposes with its grammar book
Unreal relations on the blue
Swallows. Perhaps when you will have
Fully awakened, I shall show you
A new thing: even the water
Flowing away beneath those birds
Will fail to reflect their flying forms,
And the eyes that see become as stones
Whence never tears shall fall again.

O swallows, swallows, poems are not
The point. Finding again the world,
That is the point, where loveliness
Adorns intelligible things
Because the mind's eye lit the sun.

Questions for Interactive Reading and Writing

1. Where does this poem take place, and who is the "I"?
2. In the final stanza, the poet asserts that "poems are not / The point." Does he mean this, and, if so, what is the point "where loveliness / Adorns intelligible things"?
3. Look up William of Occam and decide why he is "villainous."
4. Would you call these swallows an image or a symbol or both? Why?

Pablo Neruda (1904–1973)

For a biography of Pablo Neruda, see chapter 16.

The Stolen Branch (1952)

In the night we shall go in
to steal
a flowering branch.

We shall climb over the wall
in the darkness of the alien garden,
two shadows in the shadow.

Winter is not yet gone,
and the apple tree appears
suddenly changed
into a cascade of fragrant stars.

In the night we shall go in
up to its trembling firmament,
and your little hands and mine
will steal the stars.

And silently,
to our house,
in the night and the shadow,
with your steps will enter
perfume's silent step
and with starry feet
the clear body of spring.

—translated by Donald D. Walsh

Questions for Interactive Reading and Writing

1. A crime committed in a garden—are there biblical undertones or overtones to this image?
2. Who are the transgressors? "Thieves"? Why does the speaker celebrate their act?
3. In what part of the daily cycle does the act take place? In what season? What does this setting suggest about the motives of the speaker and his companion?
4. If a critic or an instructor were to suggest that Neruda has written a love poem, how would you respond?

Octavio Paz (1914–1998)

Motion (1962)

If you are the amber mare
        I am the road of blood
If you are the first snow
        I am he who lights the hearth of dawn
If you are the tower of night
        I am the spike burning in your mind
If you are the morning tide
        I am the first bird's cry
If you are the basket of oranges
        I am the knife of the sun
If you are the stone altar
        I am the sacrilegious hand
If you are the sleeping land
        I am the green cane
If you are the wind's leap
        I am the buried fire
If you are the water's mouth
        I am the mouth of moss
If you are the forest of the clouds
        I am the axe that parts it
If you are the profaned city
        I am the rain of consecration
If you are the yellow mountain
        I am the red arms of lichen
If you are the rising sun
        I am the road of blood

—translated by Eliot Weinberger

Questions for Interactive Reading and Writing

1. The speaker makes a series of tentative ("if") declarations. Whom is he addressing and why?
2. Do all of the pairings seem to complement each other on first reading? If not, which seem more mysterious or obscure? Which suggest violence? Which suggest peace or pacification? Which, if any, seem to suggest that the poet is Mexican?
3. How is the effect of the chant-like quality of this poem similar to or different from the repetitive list-like structure of Carole Satyamurti's "I Shall Paint My Nails Red," which follows?

Carole Satyamurti (b. 1939)

I Shall Paint My Nails Red (1998)

Because a bit of colour is a public service.

Because I am proud of my hands.

Because it will remind me I'm a woman.

Because I will look like a survivor.

Because I can admire them in traffic jams.

Because my daughter will say ugh.

Because my lover will be surprised.

Because it is quicker than dyeing my hair.

Because it is a ten-minute moratorium.

Because it is reversible.

Questions for Interactive Reading and Writing

1. Contemporary poets are often eclectic in their approach to their work, taking material and form from many different aspects of life and art. Here the poet uses the ordinary form of a list in order to express a less than ordinary emotion. How many areas of life does she mention—besides love and gender—in these ten lines?
2. Make a thumbnail sketch of this woman. Where might she live? What is her current marital status? How old might she be?
3. How would you describe her voice?

Sarah Teasdale (1884–1933)

I Am Not Yours (1915)

I am not yours, not lost in you,
  Not lost, although I long to be
Lost as a candle lit at noon,
  Lost as a snowflake in the sea.

You love me, and I find you still
  A spirit beautiful and bright,
Yet I am I, who long to be
  Lost as a light is lost in light.

Oh plunge me deep in love—put out
  My senses, leave me deaf and blind,
Swept by the tempest of your love,
  A taper in a rushing wind.

Questions for Interactive Reading and Writing

1. The expression of love here seems quite erratic and even close to violence. How does the rhyme scheme contrast with the emotion of the poem?
2. What disturbs the poet about her love? How do the images suggest her state?
3. Compare this poem with those by Amy Lowell and Cleopatra Mathis in this chapter. What are the similarities, what are the differences?

Reading for Images and Symbols

When reading for image, look for language that generates a certain attitude or mental picture using words and language that create vivid visual, aural, and tactile impressions.

Image: the literal representation of any "thing" described—the way it looks.

When reading for image, ask yourself	• What senses (sight, sound, touch, smell, taste) has the poet evoked with an image? • What kinds of words are used to make the image vivid? • What associations (meanings) do you connect with those word choices?	EXAMPLE: "Amber husk / fluted with gold, / fruit on the sand / marked with rich grain"

Symbol: an image that stands for or represents something beyond the thing itself

When reading for symbol, ask yourself	• Is the title a tip-off to a centrally important image, one that is likely to be a symbol? • Does the poem focus on a particular image? • Is an image repeated and returned to in a poem? If so, it is likely to be a symbol. • How is that symbolic image used? The description will point to its deeper meaning.	EXAMPLE: "Button"
Pay attention to common associations	*Conventional association:* An association made so frequently that one thing has come to traditionally represent the other.	EXAMPLE: Dove = peace; shooting star = wish

When reading poetry from earlier times, consider conventional associations from the period. Remember to read in context.	*Iconography:* When one symbol always engenders certain meanings.	EXAMPLE: Skull and crossbones = death
Remember that modern poets may try to create fresh symbols through context.	*Literary symbolism:* Symbolism that is created through the context of a poem.	EXAMPLE: A blue bowl represents death and sorrow *in the context* of Jane Kenyon's poem.

Writing about Images and Symbols

1. Consider the various creatures and landscapes in the poems of this chapter and write a brief essay comparing and contrasting their functions; consider also the attitude of each of the poets to each. Contrast, for example, the chickens described by William Carlos Williams with the nightingale in Keats's poem or Hirshfield's tree with the image in the Pound poem.
2. Take any poem in this chapter and focus on its imagery. At what point does a central image (the jar on the hill in Tennessee, the plums in the refrigerator, etc.) attain the status of symbol?
3. As W. H. Auden suggests of the Old Masters, "About suffering they were never wrong." Find images that evoke "suffering" in five of the poems included here. Compare the way poets such as Paul Laurence Dunbar deal with this emotion, what images they use to portray death and loss.

21 Figures of Speech

THE back, the yoke, the yardage. Lapped seams,
The nearly invisible stitches along the collar
Turned in a sweatshop by Koreans or Malaysians

Gossiping over tea and noodles on their break
Or talking money or politics while one fitted
This armpiece with its overseam to the band

Of cuff I button at my wrist. The presser, the cutter,
The wringer, the mangle. The needle, the union,
The treadle, the bobbin. The code. The infamous blaze

At the Triangle Factory in nineteen-eleven.
One hundred and forty-six died in the flames

—from "Shirt" by Robert Pinsky

"One of the really thrilling things in art is the sense that something may be going too far, or is about to go too far, that there's something shameless about it. . . . You can't do it as . . . special effects in a movie. You can't do it with the immediate emotional impact of music. . . . Poetry has to do it in a different way."

Conversation with Robert Pinsky, available on video at www.mhhe.com/delbanco1e

IN his poem "Shirt," Robert Pinsky gives the reader a great deal of information about the construction of a shirt, the way the fabric gets transformed and shaped for sale and use. This is no technical manual or instruction pamphlet; his intention is to establish a relation between the historical past and the actual shirt-wearing present. When he uses words like "yoke" or "union," he evokes both a literal attribute of fabric and the larger meaning of "yoke" and "union": the language means two things at once. A strategy like this employs **figurative language;** it describes one thing by relating it to something else. People use **figures of speech** every day, and poets use them consciously—nonliteral comparisons that vividly illustrate an idea or theme.

Figures of speech allow writers to make connections and comparisons between seemingly unlike objects and actions. These connections require a particular capacity to perceive relationships between dissimilar things. As Robert Pinsky suggests in his interview, the ability to create metaphor may be a natural gift, an innate talent. "Putting two unlike things together," Pinsky says, "and finding out how they're alike is like being able to jump high or run fast." Very few poets have *no* such gift; indeed, it may be the tell-tale sign of a poet's calling. A person who sees the world only literally is far more likely to be a writer of prose fiction or criticism or drama than a writer who engages in the craft of poetry. One thing suggests another and word leads on to word; image leads to image, sound to sight. The very phrase "figures of speech" makes an implicit linkage, connecting something visual to something spoken and reminding us that language must be both seen and heard.

Q&A

I do like that feeling of information accumulating.

I'm as likely to refer to the Captain Easy comic strip as I am to the Aeneid.

A Conversation on Writing

Robert Pinsky

A New Jersey boy from birth (1940) through his undergraduate years at Rutgers University, Robert Pinsky originally hoped to be a musician. When he changed his focus to poetry in college, however, the change was not wholly unexpected; as a child, he loved the sounds of words, even if he was too young to understand them. This love of language combined with his compelling intellect has made his poetry in collections like *Sadness and Happiness* (1975), *The Figured Wheel: New and Collected Poems 1966–1996* (1996), and *Jersey Rain* (2000) so striking. His translation of the first volume of Dante's *Divine Comedy* (1995) became a best-seller; his work on *The Life of David* (2005) was a close examination of that biblical hero's consequence, and his recent collections of verse include *First Things to Hand* (2006) and *Gulf Music* (2007). In addition to being a Stegner Fellow at Stanford University, Pinsky counts among his honors a Pulitzer Prize nomination, an American Academy of Arts and Letters award, and the position of Poet Laureate of the United States. Pinsky currently teaches in the graduate program at Boston University and edits the poetry for the online journal *Slate.*

The Presence of the Past in Everything

That the past is present in everything is just a deep conviction for me. . . . I grew up in a town where my mother and father went to the same high school as me. My father and I both had Miss Scott for homeroom. . . . Long Branch is a very historical town. . . . Grant, Lincoln, and Mrs. Lincoln visited Long Branch. Diamond Jim Brady went to stay there with Lillian Russell. . . . I grew up with a sense . . . that there's always lore and information behind everything. . . . I want the reader [of my poems] to know that the presence of information is there. . . . I do like that feeling of information accumulating.

Writing As an Amateur Collector of Information

I've never mastered a subject. I've never become a scholarly expert in anything at all. I always make mistakes about dates. Most of the information in my poems is slightly wrong, and frequently made up altogether. . . . I was not a successful student in high school. I was a real failure, a literal failure, in junior high school. In the eighth grade I was in the "dumb class," also called the "bad class." . . . I'm as likely to refer to the Captain Easy comic strip as I am to the *Aeneid.*

The Mystery of Making a Metaphor

Somebody says that the one thing you can't teach or learn is the making of a metaphor—the ability to see resemblances, or to conceive resemblances. Putting two unlike things together and finding how they're alike is like being able to . . . reproduce a tune perfectly the first time you hear it. . . . like the mysterious way one person can hear a tune and play . . . It comes from nowhere. . . . of all the things you do in writing—it's the thing that's most unlike anything you can figure out.

To watch this entire interview and hear the author read from his work, go to www.mhhe.com/delbanco1e.

RESEARCH ASSIGNMENT After you have seen the video, discuss the different ways history informs Robert Pinsky's undertaking in writing "Shirt." List some of the historical references Pinsky mentions in his interview. How does knowing the history of the shirt impact your understanding of the poem? Explain how knowing the history enhanced, detracted from, or was a neutral factor in your enjoyment of "Shirt." Why is history so important to Pinsky?

AS YOU READ Consider the variety of historical connections Pinsky makes. The poem seeks to bridge subjects and elements as diverse as the famous fire at the shirt factory, sweatshops, American slavery, the twentieth-century immigrant experience, and seventeenth-century British poet George Herbert. Alongside these references are words from the world of sewing and tailoring, like "yoke," "mangle," and "bobbin." Pinksy uses this *jargon*, technical language specific to a trade, craft, or profession, to further connect the centuries-old history of garment-making to the culture and events of the poem.

Shirt (1990)

The back, the yoke, the yardage. Lapped seams,
The nearly invisible stitches along the collar
Turned in a sweatshop by Koreans or Malaysians

Gossiping over tea and noodles on their break
Or talking money or politics while one fitted
This armpiece with its overseam to the band

Of cuff I button at my wrist. The presser, the cutter,
The wringer, the mangle. The needle, the union,
The treadle, the bobbin. The code. The infamous blaze

At the Triangle Factory in nineteen-eleven.
One hundred and forty-six died in the flames
On the ninth floor, no hydrants, no fire escapes—

The witness in a building across the street
Who watched how a young man helped a girl to step
Up to the windowsill, then held her out

Away from the masonry wall and let her drop.
And then another. As if he were helping them up
To enter a streetcar, and not eternity.

A third before he dropped her put her arms
Around his neck and kissed him. Then he held
Her into space, and dropped her. Almost at once

He stepped up to the sill himself, his jacket flared
And fluttered up from his shirt as he came down,
Air filling up the legs of his gray trousers—

Like Hart Crane's Bedlamite, "shrill shirt ballooning."
Wonderful how the pattern matches perfectly
Across the placket and over the twin bar-tacked

Corners of both pockets, like a strict rhyme
Or a major chord. Prints, plaids, checks,
Houndstooth, Tattersall, Madras. The clan tartans

Invented by mill-owners inspired by the hoax of Ossian,
To control their savage Scottish workers, tamed
By a fabricated heraldry: MacGregor,

Bailey, MacMartin. The kilt, devised for workers
To wear among the dusty clattering looms.
Weavers, carders, spinners. The loader,

The docker, the navvy. The planter, the picker, the sorter
Sweating at her machine in a litter of cotton
As slaves in calico headrags sweated in fields:

George Herbert, your descendant is a Black
Lady in South Carolina, her name is Irma
And she inspected my shirt. Its color and fit

And feel and its clean smell have satisfied
Both her and me. We have culled its cost and quality
Down to the buttons of simulated bone,

The buttonholes, the sizing, the facing, the characters
Printed in black on neckband and tail. The shape,
The label, the labor, the color, the shade. The shirt.

Writing from Reading

Summarize

1 What connections does the poet make between the people, objects, and events in the poem?

Analyze Craft

2 Why do you think this poem is so full of people and objects?

3 How does the recurring motif of clothing help link historical periods throughout the poem?

Analyze Voice

4 What attitude does the poet express toward the events described here? Would you call this poem a political statement, a social statement, a moral statement—or all of these? Why?

Synthesize Summary and Analysis

5 As Pinsky says, "The associations [in the poem] aren't random. They're historical." What figurative leap does the poet take?

Interpret the Poem

6 Figures of speech enact the same sort of rich connectivity that the poem explores in its diverse historical references. Link the details of shirt making to the larger story here.

FIGURATIVE LANGUAGE

While all genres of writing (and everyday speech) employ figures of speech, poetry—given its especially condensed and vivid discourse—relies crucially and consistently on figurative language. Poets invent nonliteral descriptions like this because figures of speech allow them, in Pound's phrase, to "make it new." They can help amplify a reader's understanding, or they can intensify a reader's imagination. Most importantly, they can also help a writer create a description whose comparisons illustrate a theme or idea in a more purposeful way.

> "Here's what poetry can do. Imagine you're a caterpillar. There's an awful shrug and suddenly you're beautiful for as long as you live."
>
> Conversation with Stephen Dunn

In *Romeo and Juliet,* when the hopelessly infatuated young Romeo looks up to Juliet on her balcony, he whispers, "But, soft! What light through yonder window breaks? It is the east, and Juliet is the sun." Shakespeare has Romeo describe Juliet's radiant, powerful beauty in terms of the radiant, powerful sun. Does Romeo really believe this teenage girl he likes has somehow *become* the sun? Certainly not.

If Shakespeare had instead written, "Who's coming out there by the window? It's that lovely girl I met last night," we would understand his meaning. However, these wholly literal lines would lack the added, richer associations we find in Shakespeare's language—elements like the renewal of the sun rising in the east ending the dark night, and the warmth and sheer beauty of sunlight above us. For Romeo, the sight of Juliet is as beautiful and rejuvenating as a perfect new dawn. It's no accident that Shakespeare adds these figurative associations to his scene—he wants his language to do more for the reader than simply make literal sense.

Understanding how to identify and talk about figures of speech is an important tool for better appreciating poetry. It's one of the ways that the heightened, melodious language of poetry has grown so distinctive. Here are two further examples of figurative speech. In the first instance, the novelist and poet Michael Ondaatje makes a series of rapid comparisons between "your voice" and the series of sounds it evokes; look for the insistent use of "like" in this witty and playful poem. In the second example—again by Robert Pinsky—the poet reimagines television, describing it variously as a container, a showcase for "dreams," and as a means of comfort and escape. Pinsky is more literal and direct, but via the speaker's imagination, a familiar electronic appliance becomes transformed into a series of new images and new ways of thinking about the device itself.

Michael Ondaatje (b. 1943)

Born in Sri Lanka, Michael Ondaatje emigrated to England and then to Canada, where he has made his home since 1962. Although he is perhaps best known for his novel *The English Patient* (1992), which was made into an Academy Award–winning film, Ondaatje began by writing poetry, and today has published more than a dozen collections of poetry. Among his better-known collections are *There's a Trick with a Knife I'm Learning to Do: Poems, 1963–1978* (1978), and *The Cinnamon Peeler: Selected Poems* (1991); both won the Governor General's Award, one of Canada's most prestigious literary prizes. His fiction suggests Ondaatje's poetic sense: in books like *In the Skin of a Lion* (1987) and *Anil's Ghost* (2000), Ondaatje creates image-driven narrative that often reads more like poetry than prose.

AS YOU READ Recite this poem; read it aloud, and listen for its unlikely music—the combination of sounds.

Sweet Like a Crow (1989)

"The Sinhalese are without a doubt one of the least musical people in the world. It would be quite impossible to have less sense of pitch, line, or rhythm."

Paul Bowles

Your voice sounds like a scorpion being pushed
through a glass tube
like someone has just trod on a peacock
like wind howling in a coconut
like a rusty bible, like someone pulling barbed wire
across a stone courtyard, like a pig drowning,
a vattacka being fried
a bone shaking hands
a frog singing at Carnegie Hall.

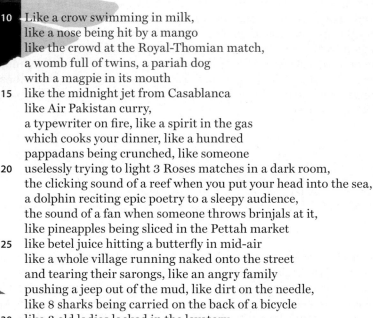

Like a crow swimming in milk,
like a nose being hit by a mango
like the crowd at the Royal-Thomian match,
a womb full of twins, a pariah dog
with a magpie in its mouth
like the midnight jet from Casablanca
like Air Pakistan curry,
a typewriter on fire, like a spirit in the gas
which cooks your dinner, like a hundred
pappadans being crunched, like someone
uselessly trying to light 3 Roses matches in a dark room,
the clicking sound of a reef when you put your head into the sea,
a dolphin reciting epic poetry to a sleepy audience,
the sound of a fan when someone throws brinjals at it,
like pineapples being sliced in the Pettah market
like betel juice hitting a butterfly in mid-air
like a whole village running naked onto the street
and tearing their sarongs, like an angry family
pushing a jeep out of the mud, like dirt on the needle,
like 8 sharks being carried on the back of a bicycle
like 3 old ladies locked in the lavatory
like the sound I heard when having an afternoon sleep
and someone walked through my room in ankle bracelets.

Writing from Reading

Summarize

1 What is the significance of the epigraph by Paul Bowles in this poem? How does the poet respond?

Analyze Craft

2 How does the sequence of comparisons help establish tone?

Analyze Voice

3 Which comparisons here seem serious and which seem lighthearted? Is it difficult to make the distinction?

Synthesize Summary and Analysis

4 The title of this poem suggests something unlikely; we don't tend to think of crows as "sweet." What is the attitude of the speaker to "your voice," and how would you describe the speaker's voice itself?

Interpret the Poem

5 Is this an act of friendship or enmity? How would you—if the poet were making these connections to the sound of *your* voice—respond?

Robert Pinsky (b. 1940)

See the brief biography of Robert Pinsky at the beginning of this chapter.

AS YOU READ "To Television" is an old-fashioned ode to a relatively modern piece of technology. Pinsky contrasts his own way of seeing television with the popular notion that it's a kind of "window." Notice how Pinsky avoids the familiar critique of television as "garbage" or a narcotic and how he uses figurative language to diversify our sense of a familiar object.

To Television (2004)

Not a "window on the world"
But as we call you,
A box a tube

Terrarium of dreams and wonders.
Coffer of shades, ordained
Cotillion of phosphors
Or liquid crystal

Homey miracle, tub
Of acquiescence, vein of defiance.
Your patron in the pantheon would be Hermes

Raster dance,
Quick one, little thief, escort
Of the dying and comfort of the sick,

In a blue glow my father and little sister sat
Snuggled in one chair watching you
Their wife and mother was sick in the head
I scorned you and them as I scorned so much

Now I like you best in a hotel room,
Maybe minutes
Before I have to face an audience: behind
The doors of the armoire, box
Within a box—Tom & Jerry, or also brilliant
And reassuring, Oprah Winfrey.

Thank you, for I watched, I watched
Sid Caesar speaking French and Japanese not
Through knowledge but imagination,
His quickness, and Thank You, I watched live
Jackie Robinson stealing

Home, the image—O strung shell—enduring
Fleeter than light like these words we
Remember in: they too winged
At the helmet and ankles.

Writing from Reading

Summarize

1 How does Pinsky link TV to the ancient Greek god Hermes, the winged messenger who communicated between the human and celestial realms? How does television function as an "escort" and a companion, easing the hardship of the ill?

Analyze Craft

2 Terms like "box," "terrarium," "coffer," "cotillion," "miracle," and "tub" suggest that television does not provide a wide, public panorama so much as a smaller, private experience of perception. How does the poet make his point, and make you read this poem—consider its title—as a traditional "ode," an elevated, formal lyric poem usually written in praise?

Analyze Voice

3 In the terms we've considered before—high, middle, low—describe the poet's tone of voice and the diction here.

Synthesize Summary and Analysis

4 Later in the poem, Pinsky expresses gratitude for the events and people he's viewed on television. How does he reach this conclusion?

Interpret the Poem

5 Is it necessary to identify such cultural references as Sid Caesar and Jackie Robinson in order to follow this poet's intention? How does he link the literal and figurative aspects of our culture?

SIMILE AND METAPHOR

Similes and metaphors, the two most commonly used figures of speech, express resemblances between two unlike things. A **simile** is a direct comparison of two distinct things using the words "like" or "as." If you say that "your friend runs *like* a cheetah" or "your brother's voice is shrill *as* a police siren," your comparisons are similes. By highlighting what two things have in common, poets direct a reader's attention to out-of-the-ordinary, often provocative associations.

You've just read Michael Ondaatje's "Sweet Like a Crow," which uses simile as its foundation. Canadian poet Margaret Atwood shows us, in a brief love lyric, just how radical a departure from ordinary speech a simile can provide.

A BRIEF HISTORY OF FIGURATIVE LANGUAGE

Creating new meanings by comparing unlike objects is an ancient practice, observed in even the earliest preserved oral literatures. Aristotle posited that metaphor helped describe, artistically, that which otherwise couldn't be identified and could likewise amplify the persuasive power of a speaker's language. While classical Western tradition—the literatures of ancient Greece and Rome—handed down traditions of figurative language (simile, metaphor, metonymy, and many more) familiar to modern English speakers, non-Western cultures developed their own subtly special figures of speech. Asian, African, and Middle Eastern literatures, for example, each incorporate complex, culturally informed figurative associations. The fact that any language's figures of speech are sometimes very difficult for foreign speakers to construe attests to their individual, social connotations. It's true in American culture, too. Expressions in American English like "I need to make some dough" or "that was a piece of cake" remind us how individual, even obscure, our own culture's figurative language can be.

Margaret Atwood (b. 1939)

Margaret Atwood, a Canadian writer, is known for both her novels and her poetry, in addition to her short fiction, nonfiction, and children's books. A poet since age sixteen, she has published more than fifteen books of poetry, among them *The Animals in That Country* (1968), *Two-Headed Poems* (1978), and *Morning in the Burned House* (1995), which won the Trillium Award. Her work often engages with ancient mythology and gender relations, and she describes her own poetry as having "a texture of sound which is at least as important to me as the 'argument.'"

AS YOU READ Watch this domestic image from the ordinary world turn on itself and grow harsh.

you fit into me (1971)

you fit into me
like a hook into an eye
a fish hook
an open eye

Writing from Reading

Summarize

1 The poet makes a complex relationship—between two lovers, or partners—into a seemingly simple image. How does the simile of the hook turn dangerous?

Analyze Craft

2 The hook and eye suggest some aspect of clothing or, perhaps, a crocheting instrument and clasp. The "fit" seems painless until the third line and second part of the comparison—a fish hook that snags an eye. Suddenly the image grows painful and bloody and wrenching. How does the snug fit become an open wound?

Analyze Voice

3 Do you detect a certain harshness on the speaker's part? What is her attitude here?

Synthesize Summary and Analysis

4 A simple image transforms itself, using simile, into something much more complex. How does the poet make this happen?

Interpret the Poem

5 Does life often offer such brutal domestic truths as this?

Jane Kenyon (1947–1995)

For a brief biography of Jane Kenyon, see chapter 20.

AS YOU READ **Notice that the title points to the poem's last word. Is this an instance of "back to back"?**

The Suitor (1978)

We lie back to back. Curtains
lift and fall,
like the chest of someone sleeping.
Wind moves the leaves of the box elder;
they show their light undersides,
turning all at once
like a school of fish.
Suddenly I understand that I am happy.
For months this feeling
has been coming closer, stopping
for short visits, like a timid suitor.

Writing from Reading

Summarize

1 Describe, in your own words, the physical images the poem's similes evoke.

Analyze Craft

2 How do the similes help describe the speaker's sudden understanding? Do the two usages of "like" seem natural or forced?

Analyze Voice

3 Do you hear anything complex—in terms of its tonality—in this simple declaration? Does Kenyon's choice of words underline the simplicity of the emotion?

Synthesize Summary and Analysis

4 What role does the natural world play in the poet's turn toward a new understanding of her situation?

Interpret the Poem

5 Who is being courted? Who is the suitor?

A **metaphor** also closely compares two dissimilar things but *without* using words such as "like" or "as." While a simile suggests that X is *like* Y, a metaphor states that X *is* Y. This can make for even bolder, more emphatic turns of phrase. When converted into a metaphor, the simile "My uncle's funny as a clown" becomes "My uncle's a clown." By referring to the person as a clown directly, the metaphor intensifies the sentiment.

Metaphors create an explicit, or specifically stated, connection, as was apparent when Pinsky's "television" morphed into a "terrarium of dreams," among other images. Occasionally, however, a poet's metaphor is implicit—hinted at, but not directly expressed. If, in an argument, a sister tells her brother, "You're such a chicken," she's using an explicit metaphor to compare the boy to a skittish bird. If the brother retorts, "Quit your yapping," he implies that his sister's teasing sounds to him like an obnoxious barking dog. This is called **implied metaphor**—the comparison is only suggested, never stated plainly. Because the brother does not call his sister a "yapping dog" overtly, the metaphor of his sister as dog remains implicit, if still discourteous.

The American poet Sylvia Plath makes delightfully diverse use of the versatility of metaphorical language in the following poem. She piles on image after image at an almost comic rate.

Sylvia Plath (1932–1963)

For a brief biography of Sylvia Plath, see chapter 19.

AS YOU READ Note how many objects and images the speaker figuratively equates herself to, and how they challenge the reader with a sort of poetic brainteaser.

Metaphors (1960)

I'm a riddle in nine syllables,
An elephant, a ponderous house,
A melon strolling on two tendrils.
O red fruit, ivory, fine timbers!
This loaf's big with its yeasty rising.
Money's new-minted in this fat purse.
I'm a means, a stage, a cow in calf.
I've eaten a bag of green apples,
Boarded the train there's no getting off.

Writing from Reading

Summarize

1 How are different metaphors in the poem related to one another?

Analyze Craft

2 Why do you think Plath chooses nine syllables per line? And nine lines?

Analyze Voice

3 Is the speaker here happy or sad, regretting her condition or celebrating it?

Synthesize Summary and Analysis

4 Are these all metaphors for pregnancy? If so, is the "I" of the poem in the early or late stages of pregnancy?

Interpret the Poem

5 Since the poem announces in its title that this will be a sequence of metaphors, does it deliver on its promise?

Sometimes poets will use an **extended metaphor,** or a figurative analogy that's woven through a poem. Poetry provides an emphasis on detailed and focused imagery. Because of this, it's an especially effective medium in which to broaden a comparison and enlarge it through several lines. Once again we can take an example from Shakespeare, whose sonnet in chapter 18 alerts the reader in the opening line that he is deploying an extended metaphor. "Shall I compare thee to a summer's day?" offers a kind

"Charlie Simic says that a poem is like an antique pinball machine with metaphors instead of balls. So everything in the poem, if you think of it this way, knocks against everything else."

Conversation with Carolyn Forché

of hint, a signal from poet to reader to look for the variety of ways he will compare a midsummer day—its best and worst qualities—to the object of his affection. Indeed, virtually every line proceeding from that opening extends the comparison. Here extended metaphor frames the reader's comprehension and offers us a chance, at length, to see Shakespeare's subject the way *he* does.

The following is another "love" poem, in which the poet compares herself and her partner to a pair of automobiles conjoined by jumper cables.

Linda Pastan (b. 1932)

Linda Pastan grew up in a traditional Jewish household in the Bronx. She earned her B.A. from Radcliffe and an M.A. from Brandeis. A married woman with three children, Pastan reflects on domestic life in compressed, lyrical poems. Her later poetry takes up themes of aging and mortality. Collected in books including *A Perfect Circle of Sun* (1971), *The Five Stages of Grief* (1978), and *Queen of a Rainy Country* (2006), Pastan's poetry has won, among other awards, a Pushcart Prize, the Dylan Thomas Award, and the Alice Fay di Castagnola Award from the American Poetry Society. She lives in Maryland with her husband, Ira, a noted molecular biologist.

AS YOU READ **The French would call this a "jeu d'esprit"—a game of wit—and the metaphysical poets such as John Donne and Andrew Marvell would call it an extended "conceit." Notice how it's also a sustained if implicit comparison: woman=car.**

Jump Cabling (1984)

When our cars touched
When you lifted the hood   of mine
To see the intimate workings   underneath,
When we were bound   together
By a pulse of pure   energy,
When my car like the   princess
In the tale woke with   a start,
I thought why not ride the rest of the way together.

Writing from Reading

Summarize

1 What does the "pulse of pure energy" refer to?

Analyze Craft

2 How do metaphors in this poem help illustrate the speaker's thoughts on the person fixing her car?

Analyze Voice

3 Imagine the poet were male and the "princess" a prince. What would change, what stay the same?

Synthesize Summary and Analysis

4 The figurative language describing a "charge" is sustained. In what ways is the image of the poem's title developed here throughout?

5 Compare the relationship described in Pastan's poem to the relationships in Atwood's "you fit into me" and Shakespeare's "Shall I compare thee to a summer's day?" (chapter 18). How does the various use of metaphors differ? How are they similar?

Interpret the Poem

6 What does the space in the layout of the poem represent?

Because extended metaphor is a tempting and sometimes complex means of explaining an impression, writers can lose track of how these figurative creations work. Occasionally an extended comparison will fail because the analogies within it become inconsistent or don't make sense in relation to one another. A **mixed metaphor** results when a writer uses at least two separate, mismatched comparisons in one statement. The effect is usually confusing, and sometimes comic, too. Look at this example: "When you're a big fish in a small pond, you don't want to end up with your tail between your legs." The speaker here mixes an old metaphor about being a fish with another old metaphor about being a dog. The combination of unrelated metaphors ends up baffling us more than clarifying the parts of the comparison.

In "Symposium," Paul Muldoon purposefully strings together a sequence of mixed metaphors. The poet replaces one formulaic phrase with another, and the substitutions make the familiar seem strange. As you read, consider what effect this conscious jumbling has on your interpretation of the poem itself.

Paul Muldoon (b. 1951)

Born in Northern Ireland, Paul Muldoon worked in radio and television for the British Broadcasting Corporation before becoming a professor of poetry at Oxford University. He later accepted a professorship at Princeton University, where he still teaches today. Muldoon's poetry is marked by wit and a propensity for surprising twists, and though much of it is lighthearted in tone, he incorporates serious subject matter and makes frequent use of allusions. His collections include *New Weather* (1973), *The Annals of Chile* (1994), and the Pulitzer Prize–winning *Moy Sand and Gravel* (2002), among others. Recently, he was named poetry editor of *The New Yorker* magazine.

AS YOU READ **Notice the wit here, the intentional use of cliché and the mixture of snippets of speech.**

Symposium

(1995)

You can bring a horse to water but you can't make it hold
its nose to the grindstone and hunt with the hounds.
Every dog has a stitch in time. Two heads? You've been sold
one good turn. One good turn deserves a bird in the hand.

A bird in the hand is better than no bread.
To have your cake is to pay Paul.
Make hay while you can still hit the nail on the head.
For want of a nail the sky might fall.

People in glass houses can't see the wood
for the new broom. Rome wasn't built between two stools.
Empty vessels wait for no man.

A hair of the dog is a friend indeed.
There's no fool like the fool
who's shot his bolt. There's no smoke after the horse is gone.

Writing from Reading

Summarize

1 What is a symposium? Does the title contribute to your reading of the poem?

Analyze Craft

2 Here the figurative language makes unexpected connections between disparate things. Does the use of discontinuity itself become a metaphor for a way of speaking about ordinarily indescribable situations?

Analyze Voice

3 Who's speaking here, and who is the "Paul" that gets paid in the second stanza?

Synthesize Summary and Analysis

4 This poem is full of old metaphorical sayings and advice. What happens to the meaning of these phrases when they're garbled together and mixed?

Interpret the Poem

5 Do you think this poem has an implicit meaning or message, or is it merely wordplay?

HYPERBOLE AND UNDERSTATEMENT

While metaphor and simile are the poet's most often utilized figures of speech, other forms of figurative language help writers achieve vivid description. **Hyperbole,** sometimes called overstatement, is another type of figure of speech that uses verbal exaggeration to make a point. For example, after consuming a large meal, you might say, "I couldn't possibly eat another bite." Unless you're in some kind of medical distress, however, you're likely physically able to eat *something.* This exaggeration simply helps drive home the extent of just how full you feel.

Commemorating the first battle of the American Revolution in his poem "Concord Hymn," Ralph Waldo Emerson describes the first fired rifle round as "the shot heard round the world." Emerson uses hyperbole to tell a truth—that the whole world was ultimately affected by the events in 1775 in the battles of Lexington and Concord.

Metaphor can also help create **understatement,** a purposeful tool in description. This is a kind of opposite to hyperbole. Calling Albert Einstein a "pretty smart guy" actually helps communicate, by downplaying the language, just how brilliant the man was. Such American poets as Robert Frost and William Carlos Williams often rely on understatement to emphasize a point.

SYNECDOCHE AND METONYMY

Synecdoche is a figure of speech that uses a piece or part of a thing to represent the thing in its entirety. At a party, for example, you might ask your host, "Can I have another glass?" Because you're using the word *glass* (part of the thing) not to mean an empty cup, but to instead signify a small container filled with water, ice cubes, and maybe a slice of lemon (the whole thing), the word *glass* is a synecdoche for the entire contents—container, ice, water, lemon, and all. "Was this the face that launched a thousand ships?" writes the British poet Christopher Marlowe, referring to Helen of Troy, the beautiful queen whose abduction leads to the Trojan War in Homer's *Iliad.*

Here "the face" is a synecdoche for the woman in total. In the sentence "After my old Chevy broke down for good, I had to buy some new wheels," the speaker uses "wheels" as a synecdoche to indicate that a whole new vehicle was purchased, not just four new individual wheels. The parts represent a greater whole.

"Poetry gives us an opportunity to do things that prose doesn't."
Conversation with Al Young

Occasionally, synecdoche is also used the other way around—a whole object used to represent a smaller part. "The police had to come and break up the party." We understand in this statement that *individuals* on a police force (part of a whole), and not the entire police force, nor every police force in the world for that matter (a whole), came to subdue the gathering. In this case, "the police" is a synecdoche for those particular, identifiable people wearing the badges.

Czeslaw Milosz (1911–2004)

Poet and translator Czeslaw Milosz was born in Lithuania and grew up closely tied to ancient folk traditions, living in a society that in subsequent decades was destroyed by the Nazis and political turmoil in Eastern Europe. Although raised in a Polish village, he left Poland in 1951 because he opposed the government. He lived in Paris and the United States (he taught Polish literature at the University of California, Berkeley), an exile "in both an outward and inward sense," as an award committee once described him—"a stranger for whom the physical exile is really a reflection of a metaphysical, or even religious, spiritual exile applying to humanity in general." In addition to his poetry, which he wrote in Polish, Milosz wrote a partially autobiographical novel, *The Seizure of Power* (1953), about the Communist regime in Poland. Among his many prestigious awards is the Nobel Prize in Literature, which he received in 1980.

AS YOU READ **Let yourself imagine an anecdote from your own life, some years ago, in which the part can represent the whole.**

Encounter (1936)

We were riding through frozen fields in a wagon at dawn.
A red wing rose in the darkness.

And suddenly a hare ran across the road.
One of us pointed to it with his hand.

That was long ago. Today neither of them is alive,
Not the hare, nor the man who made the gesture.

O my love, where are they, where are they going
The flash of a hand, streak of movement, rustle of pebbles.
I ask not out of sorrow, but in wonder.

—translated by Czeslaw Milosz and Lillian Vallee

Writing from Reading

Summarize

1 The poet uses an anecdote from his life for a larger purpose than just to tell the story. Can you think of an anecdote of your own that might serve the same purpose as this one?

Analyze Craft

2 Where is there an instance of synecdoche in this poem?

Analyze Voice

3 What does the incremental rise in emphasis at the beginning of line 5 and again at the beginning of line 7 bring to the tone of this poem?

Synthesize Summary and Analysis

4 The poet employs an anecdote as an illustration of some higher matter. Is the poem more autobiographical than philosophical, or vice versa?

Interpret the Poem

5 What do you think the speaker means by "wonder"? What is he speculating on?

Synecdoche is considered a form of metonymy, a slightly more general figure of speech. **Metonymy** uses an identifying emblem or closely associated object to represent a thing in its entirety. "Hired gun" is metonymy for an individual paid to shoot people. The gun itself doesn't get hired or paid; it is simply the object associated with the assassin. In the sentence "She really loves reading Harry Potter," the popular books are represented by the name of the main character. People don't, technically, read the *character;* they read the books—the physical objects with pages and words—in which Harry Potter appears.

Diane Wakoski (b. 1937)

A native of California, Diane Wakoski is known for her intensely personal poetry. Often compared to Beat poets, Wakoski dispenses with traditional rhyme and meter, and her poems seem close to prose at times. Still, they are packed with physical imagery, symbol, and allegory as she seeks to create a personal mythology (take, for example, her poem "The Father of My Country," which features George Washington as her adopted father). She has published over forty collections of poetry, among them *Emerald Ice: Selected Poems 1962–1987* (1988) and the four-volume *Archaeology of Movies and Books* (1990–1995), and has taught at Michigan State University since 1976.

AS YOU READ Catalogue the outpouring of seemingly unrelated images.

Inside Out (1988)

I walk the purple carpet into your eye
carrying the silver butter server
but a truck rumbles by,
leaving its black tire prints on my foot
and old images the sound of banging screen doors on hot afternoons and a fly buzzing over the Kool-Aid spilled on the sink
flicker, as reflections on the metal surface.

Come in, you said,
inside your paintings, inside the blood factory, inside the
old songs that line your hands, inside
eyes that change like a snowflake every second,
inside spinach leaves holding that one piece of gravel,
inside the whiskers of a cat,
inside your old hat, and most of all inside your mouth where you
grind the pigments with your teeth, painting
with a broken bottle on the floor, and painting
with an ostrich feather on the moon that rolls out of my mouth.

You cannot let me walk inside you too long inside
the veins where my small feet touch
bottom.
You must reach inside and pull me
like a silver bullet
from your arm.

Writing from Reading

Summarize

1 The poet speaks of intimacy in an outpouring of images. Can you paraphrase the poem?

Analyze Craft

2 Where in the poem does the speaker use metonymy to represent the intended listener?

3 Do the "veins" the speaker mentions represent synecdoche or metonymy?

Analyze Voice

4 Does the intensity of tone match the occasion of the poem?

Synthesize Summary and Analysis

5 How does the outpouring of images express the poet's inner feeling?

Interpret the Poem

6 Nurturing and violent, lyrical, and urgent—to what end do all of these attributes come together in the poem?

PERSONIFICATION AND APOSTROPHE

It's a natural habit to perceive human qualities and emotions in nonhuman things. We see ants moving in a line on the sidewalk and think of marching soldiers. A hurricane might blow "angrily," or a tomato plant wilt "with a sigh." A line of trees swaying in a strong wind momentarily reminds us of dancers. Skyscrapers might look like the hunched shoulders of men and women waiting in a gargantuan line. These are examples of **personification,** figures of speech in which writers ascribe human traits or behavior to something inhuman. In "The Gone Years," contemporary American poet Alice Fulton describes darkness coming at the end of the day: "Night pockets the house / in a blue / muffle . . ." The poet personifies night so it can place a building in its pocket.

Taking in a panoramic morning view of London, William Wordsworth describes the city in the following poem.

William Wordsworth (1770–1850)

For a brief biography of William Wordsworth, see chapter 15.

AS YOU READ Situate yourself in the place and time—the poem's "occasion"—and imagine yourself by Wordsworth's side as he speaks.

Composed upon Westminster Bridge, September 3, 1802 (1807)

Earth has not anything to show more fair:
Dull would he be of soul who could pass by
A sight so touching in its majesty:
This City now doth, like a garment, wear
The beauty of the morning; silent, bare,
Ships, towers, domes, theatres, and temples lie
Open unto the fields, and to the sky;
All bright and glittering in the smokeless air.
Never did sun more beautifully steep
In his first splendor valley, rock, or hill;
Ne'er saw I, never felt, a calm so deep!
The river glideth at his own sweet will:
Dear God! the very houses seem asleep;
And all that mighty heart is lying still!

Writing from Reading

Summarize

1 Paraphrase the first line of the poem in your own words.

Analyze Craft

2 Identify moments of personification in the poem.

Analyze Voice

3 What do the personified comparisons in the poem suggest to you about the speaker's perception of London?

4 Notice how Wordsworth uses both "never" and " ne'er." Is this for the sake of meter only? Why does he write "glideth" instead of "glides"?

Synthesize Summary and Analysis

5 You will notice (see chapter 24) that this poem is a sonnet—a fourteen-line arrangement with a turn at the end of line 8. How does the poet link those seemingly opposite things—an urban view and a pastoral one—within a sonnet's shape?

Interpret the Poem

6 This poem celebrates London and lists its "ships, towers, domes, theatres, and temples." Is there any warning here, or sense of a body at risk?

William Blake (1757–1827)

For a brief biography of William Blake, see the Case Study on Art and Poetry, chapter 26.

AS YOU READ Notice how abstract the "sunflower" is. Could you draw the particular flower, having read the poem?

Ah! Sun-flower (1793)

Ah! sun-flower! weary of time,
Who countest the steps of the Sun,
Seeking after that sweet golden clime
Where the traveler's journey is done;

Where the youth pined away with desire,
And the pale virgin shrouded in snow,
Arise from their graves and aspire,
Where my sun-flower wishes to go.

Writing from Reading

Summarize

1 What metaphorical place does the sunflower "seek"?

Analyze Craft

2 In addition to personification, what other figures of speech can you find in the poem?

Analyze Voice

3 Again, there's a consciously archaic diction—"countest" as opposed to "counts." Why?

Synthesize Summary and Analysis

4 The poet personifies the sunflower both by comparing it to "the youth . . . and the pale virgin" and by suggesting that the flower is "weary of time" and "wishes to go" to the landscape described in the first stanza. What does this suggest about the similarities between the natural and the human world?

Interpret the Poem

5 Why do you think Blake chooses a sunflower for the speaker to address?

Additional figures of speech invoke imagined human elements within poems. **Apostrophe** describes a figure of speech in which a writer calls out to an unseen person, force, or personified idea. Apostrophe derives from an ancient Greek term meaning a "turning away," and it often marks a moment of digression in which a poem's speaker pauses and turns to an invisible presence, often for counsel, in complaint, or for comfort. In "Ode on a Grecian Urn" (chapter 18), John Keats addresses, using apostrophe, a decorative Greek vase:. "Thou still unravished bride of quietness," he writes, speaking symbolically to the urn, "Thou foster-child of silence and slow time."

Gabriella Mistral (1889–1957)

The first Latin American woman to win the Nobel Prize for Literature, Lucila Godoy y Alcayaga was born in Chile. A schoolteacher, she had a passionate love affair with a railroad worker when she was twenty years old. When her lover committed suicide, she began to write poetry and later adopted the pseudonym Gabriella (after the biblical angel) Mistral (a Mediterranean wind and the surname of an author she admired). She was involved in education reform in Mexico and Chile; she served as a delegate to the League of Nations, where she helped found UNICEF; and she worked as consul in Spain, France, Italy, Portugal, and Guatemala. Her poetry, as in the collection *Desolación* (1922), is full of sorrow, but also full of compassion toward children, as in *Ternura* (1924).

AS YOU READ Ask yourself why the poet finds the tree worthy of her attention.

Fugitive Woman (1954)

Festival tree, branches wide,
loose cascade, lively freshness
falling steeply at my back:
Who told you to stop me
and sound out my name?

Under a tree, I was only
washing the journeys from my feet
with my shadow for a road
and dust for a skirt.

How lovely that you throw out your limbs
and that you lower your head,
without grasping that I
don't have ten years to learn
your green cross that has no blood
and the disk of your pedestal!

Examine me, cedar-pine,
with your vertical eyes,
and don't move or uproot
your feet from the living soil:
your new feet can't take it
with scrapes from the cactuses
and bites from the cliffs.

There's a kind of restlessness,
like a hissing that runs
from the simmering zodiac
to the bristling grass.
The whole night is alive
with negations and affirmations,
those of the Angel who commands you
and mine who fights against him;

and a wreck of a woman
wails for her cedar of Lebanon
fallen and covered by night,
who's going to leave at dawn
knowing neither road nor dust
and without ever seeing again
his circle of two thousand pines.

Oh, tree of mine, surrendered
senseless to the blizzard
to dog day and to beast
to the hazard of the tempest.
Pine wandering over the earth!

—translated by Randall Couch

Writing from Reading

Summarize

1 Here the poet talks to a tree (as did William Blake to a sunflower). Is she also talking to herself and others? In what ways?

2 What does "his circle of two thousand pines" suggest? What does the reference to "cedar of Lebanon" mean?

Analyze Craft

3 Discuss figures of speech such as "shadow for a road" and "dust for a skirt." How does the poet achieve her desired effects?

Analyze Voice

4 Does the speaker's voice seem natural? Slightly elevated in tone? Rising to a grand occasion?

Synthesize Summary and Analysis

5 An address to a tree that speaks of higher values and actions—is it possible for you to accept this as a way of speaking about life and the world?

Interpret the Poem

6 What is the larger subject?

PARADOX AND OXYMORON

Poets often deal in **paradox,** seemingly contradictory statements that when closely examined, have a deeper, sometimes complicated, meaning. "Youth," say some stodgy adults, paraphrasing George Bernard Shaw, "is wasted on the young." Though this saying seems to contradict itself by definition, the expression means to explain that the older we get, the more we value the vitality and innocence of our younger years. In

> "Be completely open—innocent, if you will—of the poem. Walk in, just like it's water, and say 'What is this?'"
>
> Conversation with Marie Howe

poetry, paradox attempts to tell a truth of perception or emotion despite an apparent leap in logic. "Love," says the ancient poet Ovid, "is a kind of warfare." A leap like this intends to make the reader think more deeply or subtly about a subject. Consider how Bashō, a seventeenth-century Japanese poet, uses the haiku form to pose a paradox to the listener.

Matsuo Bashō (1644–1694)

For a brief biography of Matsuo Bashō, see chapter 20.

AS YOU READ Notice how the title word is repeated at the end of the first and the third line.

Kyoto (c. 1680)

Even in Kyoto—
Hearing the cuckoo's cry
I long for Kyoto.

—translated by Robert Hass

Writing from Reading

Summarize

1 Why and how do you think the speaker longs for a place and town (Kyoto) he has not left?

2 What do you think is the significance of the birdsong the speaker mentions?

Analyze Craft

3 If you include the title, there are twelve words in this poem—of which three are the same. What does this repetition suggest?

Analyze Voice

4 What's being said here and what, paradoxically, is left unsaid?

Synthesize Summary and Analysis

5 What does this poem suggest about the poet's sense of time and place?

Interpret the Poem

6 Is there a place about which you feel the way Bashō feels and, if so, why?

Oxymoron is a version of paradox that combines contradictory words into a compact, often two-word term. Oxymorons can be amusing, as in "jumbo shrimp" or "definite maybe," but they can also illustrate a writer's particular emotional or spiritual reflection. When Shakespeare calls "parting . . . sweet sorrow," he's making an oxymoronic linkage and saying, in effect, that opposites attract.

The poet William Butler Yeats includes an oxymoronic comparison in the end of his poem "The Fisherman." Yeats was preoccupied throughout his life with the political and spiritual plight of his fellow Irish citizens. Here the speaker imagines an idealized, mythic Irish reader for his poems: "a wise and simple" fisherman who is both "cold and passionate"—terms we commonly believe to be in opposition but that are joined here.

William Butler Yeats (1865–1939)

For a brief biography of William Butler Yeats, see chapter 15.

AS YOU READ Notice how "a man who does not exist" becomes the central figure of the poem.

The Fisherman (1919)

Although I can see him still.
The freckled man who goes
To a grey place on a hill
In grey Connemara clothes
At dawn to cast his flies,
It's long since I began
To call up to the eyes
This wise and simple man.
All day I'd looked in the face
What I had hoped 'twould be
To write for my own race
And the reality;
The living men that I hate,
The dead man that I loved,
The craven man in his seat,
The insolent unreproved,
And no knave brought to book
Who has won a drunken cheer,
The witty man and his joke
Aimed at the commonest ear,
The clever man who cries
The catch-cries of the clown,
The beating down of the wise
And great Art beaten down.

Maybe a twelvemonth since
Suddenly I began,
In scorn of this audience,
Imagining a man,
And his sun-freckled face,
And grey Connemara cloth,
Climbing up to a place
Where stone is dark under froth,
And the down-turn of his wrist
When the flies drop in the stream;
A man who does not exist,
A man who is but a dream;
And cried, 'Before I am old
I shall have written him one
poem maybe as cold
And passionate as the dawn.'

Writing from Reading

Summarize

1 Describe the figure of the fisherman that the speaker imagines. What details do we have?

Analyze Craft

2 Notice that the second stanza begins with the word "Maybe" and repeats that word in the next-to-last line.

3 Look at the rhyme scheme here—the "true" and "near" or approximate rhymes.

Analyze Voice

4 How would you describe the speaker's attitude toward himself?

Synthesize Summary and Analysis

5 What does the poet hope to accomplish, and why? Why does he leave his first imagined audience behind "in scorn," and whose attention does he hope to capture instead?

Interpret the Poem

6 Describe the "one poem" the speaker wants to write for the fisherman. Does the description seem self-contradictory?

PUN

Often lighthearted in nature, a **pun** is a play on words that reveals different meanings in words that are similar or even identical. We generally think of puns as silly and perhaps trivial, as in an old joke like "A bigamist loves not too many, but *two* well." Sometimes, however, writers use puns to capitalize on two separate meanings of a word

> "A poem requires whether consciously or unconsciously some kind of change into a new realization, whether large or small."
>
> Conversation with Jane Hirshfield

and emphasize a point. "Ask for me tomorrow," says the stabbed Mercutio to Romeo in *Romeo and Juliet,* "and you shall find me a grave man." Here, "grave" suggests both a seriousness of manner and the final resting place where Mercutio, who realizes he's dying, is inevitably headed. By exploiting this double meaning, Shakespeare deepens our understanding of the play's action and the character of Mercutio himself.

Sometimes a punned double meaning underscores humor and critique simultaneously, as in the following poem.

A. R. Ammons (1926–2001)

Archie Randolph Ammons was born in North Carolina to a tobacco farmer. While on a Navy destroyer escort in the South Pacific during World War II, Ammons began to write poetry. Published at his own expense, his first collection, *Ommateum* (1955), sold hardly any copies, but his poetry career took off eight years later with his second collection. In all, he published almost thirty collections and won many of the most prestigious awards including the National Book Award for *Garbage* (1993) and again for his *Collected Poems: 1951–1971* (1972), and the National Book Critics Circle Award for *A Coast of Trees* (1981). A professor of creative writing at Cornell University, Ammons was known as a nature poet interested in exploring the poet's consciousness; critic Harold Bloom described him as a transcendentalist in the vein of Ralph Waldo Emerson.

AS YOU READ Consider this poem as an epigram—a short, pithy saying—as well as a pun.

Their Sex Life (1991)

One failure on
Top of another

Writing from Reading

Summarize

1 What scene do these two lines describe, and what's personified?

Analyze Craft

2 Which words in the poem suggest a double meaning?

Analyze Voice

3 Is the poet bitter or sympathetic? Is this poem witty or sad?

Synthesize Summary and Analysis

4 How does the visual look of the poem and its line breaks contribute to meaning and humor?

Interpret the Poem

5 If these lines had no title, how would their meaning change?

HUMOR

Poetry sometimes has a reputation for seriousness and even downright gloominess. And while it's true that poems often explore somber and intensely reflective themes, many poets put the elastic tools of language to comedic use. In this chapter, we have already seen such writers as Paul Muldoon and A. R. Ammons indulge in witty wordplay. Poems like these remind us that humorous use of tools like simile, metaphor, and other figures of speech amplifies our perspective on a topic just as interestingly as the use of serious figurative language.

When people invent witty or even vulgar comparisons to describe a situation, they almost always incorporate figures of speech familiar to readers; the comedy may even depend on it. Think of an expression like "It's cold as a well digger's ass," or "The ice on the road's as slippery as snot on a doorknob." Whether you delight in off-color speech like this or find it repulsive, it's inarguably dependent on vivid figurative language.

A good poem can, in fact, be a lot like a good joke—it can jolt our expectation and open up a new and unexpected way of understanding the human condition. To laugh at a joke is to accept a certain degree of shocked surprise; this holds just as true for a peculiar figure of speech. As a result, writers often find that they can use comic analogies to make a reader simultaneously laugh and think seriously. Both results require the same kind of intelligence.

Look at how a rich combination of metaphors, similes, personification, and other figures heightens both absurdity and credible emotion in the following poem.

Julie Sheehan (b. 1964)

Julie Sheehan, originally from Iowa, won an award for each of her first two poetry collections: the Poetry Out Loud Prize for *Thaw* (2001) and the Barnard Women Poets Prize for *Orient Point* (2006). She earned her degrees from Yale and Columbia, and her poetry has appeared in publications such as *Ploughshares, Kenyon Review,* and *The Best American Poetry 2005.* A new American voice, Sheehan offers a view of the contemporary world in her energetic lines, often with a dose of wry humor. She describes her second collection as "a collage of quilted rhetorics—some more traditional, some experimental, often exploring touchy subjects."

AS YOU READ **Notice how the title and first line—as well as much that follows—play off against the expectation of a love poem; compare to Elizabeth Barrett Browning's "How do I love thee?" (chapter 23).**

Hate Poem (2005)

I hate you. Truly I do.
Everything about me hates everything about you.
The flick of my wrist hates you.
The way I hold my pencil hates you.
The sound made by my tiniest bones were they trapped in the jaws of a moray eel hates you.
Each corpuscle singing in its capillary hates you.

Look out! Fore! I hate you.

The blue-green jewel of sock lint I'm trying to dig from under my third toenail, left foot, hates you.
The history of this keychain hates you.
My sigh in the background as you pick out the cashews hates you.
The goldfish of my genius hates you.
My aorta hates you. Also my ancestors.

A closed window is both a closed window and an obvious symbol of how I hate you.

My voice curt as a hairshirt: hate.
My hesitation when you invite me for a drive: hate.
My pleasant "good morning": hate.
You know how when I'm sleepy I nuzzle my head under your arm? Hate.
The whites of my target-eyes articulate hate. My wit practices it.
My breasts relaxing in their holster from morning to night hate you.
Layers of hate, a parfait.
Hours after our latest row, brandishing the sharp glee of hate,
I dissect you cell by cell, so that I might hate each one individually and at leisure.
My lungs, duplicitous twins, expand with the utter validity of my hate, which can never have enough of you,
Breathlessly, like two idealists in a broken submarine.

Writing from Reading

Summarize

1 We often call a relationship—consider Margaret Atwood's poem "you fit into me"—an example of a "love-hate ambivalence." How does the term apply to these lines?

Analyze Craft

2 How do figurative comparisons underscore humor and emotion in this poem? List examples of hyperbole.

Analyze Voice

3 Is the "I" here a specific first person, and how does it become a representative "I"?

Synthesize Summary and Analysis

4 On the composition of "I Hate You" Julie Sheehan wrote, "It occurred to me, as probably to many, that since hate requires as much passion as love, the two emotions can be described in indistinguishable terms." Note places in the poem where the language used to describe hate seems indistinguishable from or similar to love.

Interpret the Poem

5 Is this poem entirely comic, or does Sheehan explore a "legitimate" theme as well?

For Review and Further Study

John Keats (1795–1821)

For a brief biography of John Keats, see chapter 18.

To Autumn (1819)

I

Season of mists and mellow fruitfulness,
Close bosom-friend of the maturing sun;
Conspiring with him how to load and bless
With fruit the vines that round the thatch-eves run;
To bend with apples the mossed cottage-trees,
And fill all fruit with ripeness to the core;
To swell the gourd, and plump the hazel shells
With a sweet kernel; to set budding more,
And still more, later flowers for the bees,
Until they think warm days will never cease,
For summer has o'er-brimmed their clammy cells.

II

Who hath not seen thee oft amid thy store?
Sometimes whoever seeks abroad may find
Thee sitting careless on a granary floor,
Thy hair soft-lifted by the winnowing wind;
Or on a half-reaped furrow sound asleep,
Drowsed with the fume of poppies, while thy hook
Spares the next swath and all its twinèd flowers:
And sometimes like a gleaner thou dost keep
Steady thy laden head across a brook;
Or by a cider-press, with patient look,
Thou watchest the last oozings hours by hours.

III

Where are the songs of spring? Ay, where are they?
Think not of them, thou hast thy music too—
While barrèd clouds bloom the soft-dying day,
And touch the stubble-plains with rosy hue;
Then in a wailful choir the small gnats mourn
Among the river swallows, borne aloft
Or sinking as the light wind lives or dies;
And full-grown lambs loud bleat from hilly bourn;
Hedge-crickets sing; and now with treble soft
The redbreast whistles from a garden-croft,
And gathering swallows twitter in the skies.

Questions for Interactive Reading and Writing

1. The title of the poem tells you it is a direct address to the season of autumn. What kind of "personality" does Keats create for autumn? How does that personality change over the course of the poem?
2. Determine the rhyme scheme of the three stanzas. Does it ever differ? Discuss the ways the rhyme scheme complements the theme and tone of the poem.
3. Identify instances of personification in this poem besides the overarching personification of autumn.
4. Discuss the significance of the three numbered stanzas in the poem. What changes between them, and what stays the same?

Marge Piercy (b. 1934)

The Secretary Chant (1973)

My hips are a desk.
From my ears hang
chains of paper clips.
Rubber bands form my hair.
My breasts are wells of mimeograph ink.
My feet bear casters.
Buzz. Click.
My head
is a badly organized file.
My head is a switchboard
where crossed lines crackle.
My head is a wastebasket
of worn ideas.
Press my fingers
and in my eyes appear
credit and debit.
Zing. Tinkle.
My navel is a reject button.
From my mouth issue canceled reams.
Swollen, heavy, rectangular
I am about to be delivered
of a baby
Xerox machine.
File me under W
because I wonce
was a woman.

Questions for Interactive Reading and Writing

1. A secretary speaks of herself in a particular fashion. How would you describe it?
2. Discuss how figurative language in this poem portrays ideas of work. Does it help or hurt to know that "secretary" is also the name for a piece of furniture?
3. Why do you think Marge Piercy avoids the words *like* and *as* in the images in her poem?
4. Why does Piercy intentionally spell "once" with a "w" at the end of "The Secretary Chant"?
5. The secretary describes her life in a special voice. Would the opposite—a calm recitation of her duties—affect you in the same way?
6. How does work organize this woman's life? How might it affect our own lives?

Theodore Roethke (1908–1963)

For a brief biography of Theodore Roethke, see chapter 19.

Root Cellar (1948)

Nothing would sleep in that cellar, dank as a ditch,
Bulbs broke out of boxes hunting for chinks in the dark,
Shoots dangled and drooped,
Lolling obscenely from mildewed crates,
Hung down long yellow evil necks, like tropical snakes.
And what a congress of stinks!—
Roots ripe as old bait,
Pulpy stems, rank, silo-rich,
Leaf-mold, manure, lime, piled against slippery planks.
Nothing would give up life:
Even the dirt kept breathing a small breath.

Questions for Interactive Reading and Writing

1. Describe the trip our eyes—and noses—take through this underground world.
2. In what way does word choice here reflect the atmosphere of the cellar the speaker describes?
3. Identify similes and moments of personification in the poem.
4. How do these figures convey a sense of life and vitality among simple inanimate objects that might otherwise appear lifeless?
5. What does the poem's setting suggest about the speaker's perspective on life and death? How would the poem be different if it were set in a vibrant garden?
6. Does the poet sound urgent or matter-of-fact as he describes what he sees and smells?
7. A trip through the root cellar adds up to more than meets the eye—and nose. What makes the rank journey worthwhile?

Walt Whitman (1819–1892)

For a brief biography of Walt Whitman, see chapter 18.

A Noiseless Patient Spider (1891)

A noiseless patient spider,
I mark'd where on a little promontory it stood isolated,
Mark'd how to explore the vacant vast surrounding,
It launch'd forth filament, filament, filament, out of itself,
Ever unreeling them, ever tirelessly speeding them.

And you O my soul where you stand,
Surrounded, detached, in measureless oceans of space,
Ceaselessly musing, venturing, throwing, seeking the
spheres to connect them,
Till the bridge you will need be form'd, till the ductile
anchor hold,
Till the gossamer thread you fling catch somewhere,
O my soul.

Questions for Interactive Reading and Writing

1. Describe the spider's surroundings. How does the speaker align himself with these surroundings?
2. What do you think the speaker wants to "catch" with his soul? How does he connect this desire with the spider's activity?
3. Why do you think Whitman chooses a spider for his comparison? What characteristics of the spider does he explore?
4. Examine the figurative language here, and what the spider stands for.

Nancy Willard (b. 1936)

Saint Pumpkin (1982)

Somebody's in there.
Somebody's sealed himself up
in the round room,
this hassock upholstered in rind,
this padded cell.
He believes if nothing unbinds him
he'll live forever.

Like our first room
it is dark and crowded.
Hunger knows no tongue
to tell it.
Water is glad there.
In this room with two navels
somebody wants to be born again.

So I unlock the pumpkin.
I carve out the lid
from which the stem raises
a dry handle on a damp world.
Lifting, I pull away
wet webs, vines on which hang
the flat tears of the pumpkin,

like fingernails or the currency
of bats. How the seeds shine,
as if water had put out
hundreds of lanterns.
Hundreds of eyes in the windless wood
gaze peacefully past me,
hacking the thickets,
and now a white dew beads the blade.
Has the saint surrendered
himself to his beard?
Has his beard taken root in his cell?

Saint Pumpkin, pray for me,
because when I looked for you, I found nothing,
because unsealed and unkempt, your tomb rots,
because I gave you a false face
and a light of my own making.

Questions for Interactive Reading and Writing

1. The central "figure" of this poem is a person—perhaps someone holy—who has sealed himself inside a pumpkin. Do you find this implausible at poem's start and plausible by poem's end? If so, why, if not, why not?
2. Discuss the various similes—the usages of "like"—and metaphors in this poem.
3. Is there an irony in the tone of the poet's address to this inanimate object?
4. In the final stanza, the poet apostrophizes "Saint Pumpkin" and speaks to it directly. Discuss this poem in terms of the actions described and faith expressed. What sort of worship takes place?
5. Can we find the holy in the ordinary things of this world?

Reading for Figures of Speech

When reading for ***figures of speech,*** identify places where a writer describes one thing in terms of another in order to make a theme or idea feel fresh and new, richer than a literal description would be.

Look for the words *like* or *as* that show a comparison is being used for illustration.	*Simile:* Uses the words *like* or *as* to compare two things. *X* is like *Y*.	EXAMPLE: "you fit into me / like a hook into an eye"
Look for comparisons that merge two unlike objects to create a more vivid association.	*Metaphor:* Compares two things *without using* the words *like* or *as*. *X* is *Y*.	EXAMPLE: "What light through yonder window breaks? It is the east, and Juliet is the sun."
	Does the language suggest a comparison without explicitly naming the thing being compared? *Implied metaphor*	EXAMPLE: "Quit your yapping."
	Is something being described using several direct, parallel comparisons? *Extended metaphor*	EXAMPLE: "When our cars touched / When you lifted the hood of mine / To see the intimate workings underneath, / When we were bound together / By a pulse of pure energy"
Look for objects or ideas used to represent a larger whole.	*Synecdoche: The use of a part or piece of a thing that represents the thing in its entirety.*	EXAMPLE: My best friend just got some new wheels. "Wheels"=a new car
	Metonymy: The use of an identifying emblem or closely associated object to represent a thing in its entirety.	EXAMPLE: The White House released a statement today. "White House"=the President
Consider who (or what) is being described or addressed by the speaker.	*Is it an animal or inanimate object?* *Personification:* Endows a nonhuman thing with human qualities.	EXAMPLE: "This City now doth, like a garment, wear / The beauty of the morning"
	Is someone or something not "present" otherwise in the poem? *Apostrophe:* Addresses an unseen person, thing, or idea.	EXAMPLE: "Where are we going, Walt Whitman?"

Ask yourself if comparisons that seem to contradict each other are used to trigger a fresh understanding, or if they are merely confusing.	*Oxymoron:* Combines two contradictory terms that use contradiction to make a point.	EXAMPLE: "cold / and passionate as the dawn."
	Paradox: States a self-contradictory position to trigger a fresh concept or comprehension.	EXAMPLE: "Youth is wasted on the young."
	Pun: Uses words that are spelled or sound alike to suggest, often humorously, more than one idea.	EXAMPLE: "Writing with a broken pencil is pointless."
	Mixed metaphor: Combines two incompatible metaphors, often resulting in nonsense or confusion.	EXAMPLE: "You can bring a horse to water but you can't make it hold / its nose to the grindstone."
Does the description make a point through exaggeration or restraint?	*Hyperbole:* Describes a thing or experience using purposeful exaggeration.	EXAMPLE: "The shot heard round the world."
	Understatement: Downplays a description to make a point or comparison.	EXAMPLE: "I think I know enough of hate / To know that for destruction ice / Is also great / And would suffice."

Writing about Figures of Speech

1. Compare the different approaches to metaphor that poets take in "Jump Cabling," "The Suitor," and "Hate Poem."
2. Both William Wordsworth and William Butler Yeats have poems in this chapter in which the speaker watches someone or something in admiration. What's literal, what's figurative in the scene observed?
3. Analyze the use of comic similes to make meaning in "Their Sex Life," "Symposium," and "Sweet Like a Crow."
4. Robert Pinsky's "Shirt" uses figurative language sparingly, but vividly. Discuss the purpose of his literal imagery and how it differs from the purpose of his figurative language. Compare the figurative and nonfigurative language in "Shirt" and "To Television."
5. What is the role of the title in "Metaphors," "Fugitive Woman," and "Saint Pumpkin" regarding the addition of implicit or explicit meaning?

22

Sound, Rhyme, & Rhythm

OF all our private parts the heart knows best
that love and grieving share the one body
and keeps a steady iambic tally
of this life's syllables, stressed and unstressed.

—from "Iambs for the Day of Burial" by Thomas Lynch

"The idea that you could play with words is what for me writing poems has always been, sort of a wordplay. It really doesn't matter much to me what the subject is: the subject presents itself after the line presents itself, after the sort of acoustic hook is set in the ear."

Conversation with Thomas Lynch, available on video at www.mhhe.com/delbanco1e

AS you see in "Iambs for the Day of Burial," the way the **sounds** of language work together with **rhyme** and **rhythm** can dramatically affect the way we experience a poem. Here Lynch makes the claim that the beat of the heart—*da-dum, da-dum, da-dum*—is a "steady iambic tally." Referring to one of poetry's most common rhythms, he relates the pulse to "stressed and unstressed" syllables. Poetry, he seems to say, has our very life force within it. The words are simply words, the sounds are sounds we've heard before, and a pattern exists in each sentence. However, a poet chooses particular words in a conscious attempt to shape the meaning of his poems; *sound* and *sense* are, in effect, two sides of one coin.

Although the language of poetry is sometimes difficult to understand, it's important to remember what you already know: all speech is sound. When we worry over the meaning of a poem, as though it were a foreign language or a code to crack, the answer to a poem's puzzle is often its "acoustic hook," the arrangement of sounds that draws us into the poem. When a sound repeats itself, we call that echo *rhyme*. The pattern of such repetition, and the way the poet places the words, even the syllables, in sequence, creates the poem's rhythm. "Iambs for the Day of Burial" aptly makes the claim that rhythm is as natural as breath. The sound of our pulse beating, the way we walk or dance, what our fingers do while tapping on a keyboard are *naturally* rhythmic, and if that word had been, instead, *unnaturally*, it would still have a rhythm though the rhythm would have changed. To understand a poem, as Lynch observes in his interview, it sometimes help to tap it out.

I've always said that writers are readers who go karaoke . . .

Q&A

Language knows you better than yourself.

A Conversation on Writing

Thomas Lynch

The Heartbeat in Poetry

I have this vexing habit—to some people—of sort of tapping things out that are occurring to me acoustically. . . . I've always been drawn to the notion that Wordsworth could work out his poetry—and Shakespeare his own poetry—by keeping an ear to their own metabolic strain, their own breathing and heartbeat, and the notion that there is some connection between language and a natural order: *da-dum, da-dum, da-dum*. It has this appeal to my ear.

Becoming Accountable to Your Own Language

I've always said that writers are readers who go karaoke: They first get up in front of the microphone and sing songs, do cover pieces. Then pretty soon they begin to sound like themselves talking to themselves. I don't know what it was for me. I can remember writing poems that were sort of all borrowings from Yeats and Emily Dickinson, and Edward Arlington Robinson, and Michael Heffernan, and anyone else who I came across. Most of the notions were borrowed from maybe other books that I was reading, not poetry. But at some point you become accountable to the language yourself.

Poetry As Self-Prophecy

I'm aware of this about poetry, and I'm certain musicians must be aware about it with music, and painters with color and image: that it knows you better than yourself. It will make its way into the world, "it" being whatever language wants to do with you. Language knows you better than [you know] yourself. So the poems, when I look back at them now, they were almost prophetic. They knew things about me that came to be true, that I didn't know at the time. But the language did, from whatever part. The words kept pushing themselves onto the page. It knew things. It still does. So I trust it I suppose.

"We need a way to say unspeakable things, and funerals do. So do poems," Thomas Lynch—poet, essayist, and undertaker—once said in an interview. Born in Michigan in 1948, Lynch took over his father's funeral parlor in 1974, and he has been the undertaker for the town of Milford, Michigan, ever since. His poetry—collected in *Skating with Heather Grace* (1986), *Grimalkin* (1994), and *Still Life in Milford* (1998)—explores the intersections of life, death, sex, grief, and other profound aspects of the human experience. Among his books of nonfiction are *The Undertaking—Life Studies from the Dismal Trade*, which won the Heartland Prize for Nonfiction and the American Book Award, and *Bodies in Motion and at Rest*, a collection of essays that won the Great Lakes Book Award. Lynch's written work and commentaries have appeared in prominent venues including *The New York Times*, NPR, *The Washington Post*, and a PBS *Frontline* feature, among many others.

To watch the entire interview and hear the author read from his work, go to www.mhhe.com/delbanco1e.

RESEARCH ASSIGNMENT In his interview, Lynch quotes Yeats as saying about poetry: "It comes by the ear." Lynch weighs the influence of the Catholic church and its liturgy, even childhood prayers, on his understanding of meter and the importance of language. He says "all language has double edges." What does he mean by this, and how is his understanding of double edges in language related to his work, particularly in his poem "Liberty"?

AS YOU READ Consider what the poet means by "life's syllables, stressed and unstressed."

Iambs for the Day of Burial (1998)

Of all our private parts the heart knows best
that love and grieving share the one body
and keeps a steady iambic tally
of this life's syllables, stressed and unstressed.
Our pulse divided by our breathing equals
pleasure measured in pentameters,
pain endured in oddly rhyming pairs:
sadness, gladness, sex and death, nuptials,
funerals. Love made and love forsaken—
each leaves us breathless and beatified,
more than the sum of parts that lived and died
of love or grief. Both leave the heart broken.

Writing from Reading

Summarize

1 Imagine these twelve lines are spoken at a grave, linking love and grief. How does the poet develop that linkage and establish the connection?

Analyze Craft

2 This is a poem about its own making and structure. Give examples of "pentameters . . . and oddly rhyming pairs." Does the strategy work?

Analyze Voice

3 Lynch is a professional undertaker as well as a poet; his family has operated Lynch & Sons Funeral Home in Milford, Michigan, for decades. How is Lynch's profession reflected by any of his word choices or the tone of the poem? What about the poem is surprising, considering the poet's frequent interaction with the dead?

Synthesize Summary and Analysis

4 What connections are there between the rhythm of this poem and its subject matter? Why is this particular rhythm appropriate? Identify places where there is deviation in the rhythm. How do these deviations contribute to the overarching gravity of the poem?

Interpret the Poem

5 Discuss the idea that love and grief "both leave the heart broken." Do you agree?

SOUND

From its earliest presence in religious ritual and public entertainment, poetry has been written to accompany music; no form of writing is more closely associated with song and sound. "Musical thought" is how the Scottish writer Thomas Carlyle defined the genre. "[Poetry is] a sonorous molded shape of form," said the Russian poet Osip Mandelstam.

Poets have always paid special attention to the musical elements of their own language. This attention differentiates poetry from language used only to communicate information. Poetry's special sound effects of stresses, rhymes, and repetitions invite a reader to inspect, carefully, the texture and sound of words. A poet chooses language based on sound as well as on meaning. We read, for example, the word *glassy* and can perceive smooth surfaces beneath the double "s" sound. We say the word *trickle* and

"'Meter' comes from the word for 'measure,' so the meters are measures of language in a line. . . . It is very different from music. It has to do with the pace of the language and how everything in the poem is about patterns of vowels, patterns of consonants, patterns of sounds, patterns of stresses . . . even if you can't quite hear the words or make them out . . . you hear a kind of beautiful . . . patterning of meaning." Conversation with Carolyn Forché

hear the light, small splashes of water from a kitchen sink faucet. When a writer uses a variety of active verbs, we feel velocity and action evoked in a poem. When a writer fills a line with **monosyllabic** (one-syllable) words, we perceive important emphasis and purpose. Think, for instance, of that memorable catchphrase for insecticide: "Raid kills bugs dead." Or, as in the last two words from the poem by Gerard Manley Hopkins near the end of this chapter, the simple finality of "Praise him."

When poets arrange the sounds of words together, either purposefully or by sheer instinct, to produce a pleasing effect, they create **euphony,** musically pleasing poetic language. An opening like this from one of Lord Byron's love poems helps illustrate how euphonious language can mirror a poem's emotions:

She walks in beauty, like the night
Of cloudless climes and starry skies;
And all that's best of dark and bright
Meet in her aspect and her eyes. . . .

The agreeable flow of the language itself (notice, for instance, how often the "i" gets repeated) helps reinforce Byron's loving description. "Like/night/climes/skies/ bright/ eyes" all sound out a chorus of praise.

In contrast, when poets describe something unpleasant or dissonant, they often employ **cacophony,** harsh-sounding, grating, or even hard-to-pronounce syllables. Listen to these cacophonous lines by Jonathan Swift, who wanted to make fun of the pretty language of nature poetry of his day in this description of a rainstorm flooding London. If you read these lines aloud—and even though their last words rhyme—you'll likely feel your mouth squeezing the sounds out with difficulty:

Sweeping from butchers stalls, dung, guts, and blood,
Drowned puppies, stinking sprats, all drenched in mud,
Dead cats and turnip-tops, come tumbling down the flood.

Not exactly the subject matter we associate with English verse!

You don't have to know all of the following terms to read and enjoy a poem. By learning, however, to recognize the musical effects of sound, you will strengthen your understanding of a poem's meaning and dimensions.

"The poem is made out of the sounds." Conversation with Robert Pinsky

Safe and sound. Drunk and disorderly. Back to basics. Our language is full of catchy phrases like these that repeat their opening sounds. The effect is both memorable and musical. **Alliteration** describes this technique—the repetition of the initial consonant sounds of a sequence of words. Like many forms of repetition, this technique links sound and sense together and intensifies their combined power. As the sounds echo each other, they pull together the meanings of words. Alliterative linkage flourished in our language long before the habit of connecting lines by end-rhyme: It was with us from the start of English verse.

Also demonstrating a kind of kinship between sounds is **consonance,** a repetition of *consonant* sounds or similar patterns in neighboring words. The words

taken and token
whole and whale

employ consonance in its most familiar definition, within words that are identical except for differing vowels. Consonance also refers, moreover, to a sentence like,

*Calm**l**y, he ca**ll**ed to the mu**l**e in the o**l**d fie**l**d*

with its repeated rolling "l."

OLD ENGLISH ALLITERATIVE VERSE

One of the primary sources of our contemporary lexicon, Old English is the language of the oldest surviving poetry born in Britain. Alliteration is closely associated with this early verse and was used—more often than rhyme—to establish the structure of the Old English poetic line. In this tradition, two short half-lines are divided by a break but unified by alliterated, stressed syllables. These repeated consonants give Old English alliterative verse a distinctive and robust sound, ideal for the dramatic public performances in which these poems might have been heard.

Assonance is a kind of flip side to consonance. It's the repetition of the same *vowel* sound in neighboring words. Used for musical effect and for poetic emphasis, assonance can tie ideas together in a poem over the course of different phrases and lines.

Robert Herrick's "Delight in Disorder" (for the whole poem, see the Anthology of Poems for Further Reading, chapter 29) employs assonance in the second and third lines of this opening stanza. Note how the shared "o" vowel sound helps join the images of the clothing together:

*A sweet dis**o**rder in the dress*
*Kindles in cl**o**thes a **wa**nt**o**nness.*
*A l**aw**n about the sh**ou**lders thr**ow**n*
*Int**o** a fine distracti**o**n . . .*

Sometimes the various sound elements of poetry combine to evoke the very thing their language describes. **Onomatopoeia** is a use of words that imitate the sounds they refer to. Think of words like *buzz* or *pop* or *sizzle.* We hear what they portray in the very sounds they make. When they appear in poetry or song ("clickety-clack along the track"), they further unify sound and meaning.

Listen to these lines describing the natural landscape by Alfred Lord Tennyson:

The moan of doves in immemorial elms,
And murmuring of innumerable bees.

Can you associate the doves' cry with the words *moan* and *immemorial*? Can you, in a sense, "hear" the low buzz of the bees in *murmuring* and *innumerable*?

The words *immemorial, murmuring,* and *innumerable* are **polysyllabic,** meaning they have many syllables, as opposed to the monosyllabic, or single syllable—"The moan of doves in . . . elms." In this regard, one of the glories of English is its ability to marry monosyllabic Anglo-Saxon directness with polysyllabic Latin and medieval French, a discourse brought to England when William the Conqueror, in 1066, declared that *his* would be the language of the court. English poets ever since the Norman Conquest have had a grab bag of **sonorities** to choose from, and the word *sonority* itself is just a fancy Latinate way of saying *sound.*

Think of English as a mighty river with several tributaries. By now the waters are thoroughly mixed (a process that continues yearly), and it takes analysis to separate them out. You don't have to be a linguist and fluent in foreign languages to get a sense of which words are simple, which complex—or, by extension, which language they might have derived from and what their root meaning might be.

Here the poet Seamus Heaney stresses Anglo-Saxon, making a kind of onomatopoetic statement about the way his ancestors worked. In the 218 words of "Digging," there are only six that have three syllables and none that have more. The six polysyllabic words (gravelly, flowerbeds, potatoes, grandfather, sloppily, awaken) all refer to matters of the earth or family or physical behavior. For in the end the poet claims that working with a pen is just as hard as working in a garden or bog. Note how the poem's final words are each monosyllabic, stressed, and equally a kind of "digging"; the two skills seem akin.

Seamus Heaney (b. 1939)

Described as "the best Irish poet since W. B. Yeats," Seamus Heaney is—like Yeats—both Irish and a Nobel Prize laureate. Since he was born to a Roman Catholic family in a Protestant area of Ireland, it is perhaps not surprising that Heaney's poetry portrays Ireland's political problems. However, this is only one aspect of Heaney's poetry; his poems convey a deep sense of history, both personal and collective, in verses marked by quiet compression. In addition to the poetry collected in books like *Death of a Naturalist* (1966) and *Opened Ground* (1999), Heaney is known for his translations, most notably *Beowulf,* and his criticism. He has taught at Harvard for part of each year since 1981 but otherwise lives in Dublin.

AS YOU READ **Consider how sound works to mimic the meaning of words, or to intensify their overall effect.**

Digging (1966)

Between my finger and my thumb
The squat pen rests; snug as a gun.

Under my window, a clean rasping sound
When the spade sinks into gravelly ground:
My father, digging. I look down

Till his straining rump among the flowerbeds
Bends low, comes up twenty years away
Stooping in rhythm through potato drills
Where he was digging.

The coarse boot nestled on the lug, the shaft
Against the inside knee was levered firmly.
He rooted out tall tops, buried the bright edge deep
To scatter new potatoes that we picked
Loving their cool hardness in our hands.

By God, the old man could handle a spade
Just like his old man.

My grandfather cut more turf in a day
Than any other man on Toner's bog.
Once I carried him milk in a bottle
Corked sloppily with paper. He straightened up
To drink it, then fell to right away
Nicking and slicing neatly, heaving sods
Over his shoulder, digging down and down
For the good turf. Digging.

The cold smell of potato mould, the squelch and slap
Of soggy peat, the curt cuts of an edge
Through living roots awaken in my head.
But I've no spade to follow men like them.

Between my finger and my thumb
The squat pen rests.
I'll dig with it.

Writing from Reading

Summarize

1 Why do you think the speaker repeats the title word often in the poem? What other "-ing" (participial) words does he use? Are they related to one another? How does their sound echo their meaning?

Analyze Craft

2 Find instances of consonance and assonance in the poem. How do they work to connect or unify the language?

3 Read this poem aloud. How would you describe the sound of the language? How does this description seem to fit or contrast with the poem's subject?

Analyze Voice

4 Can you make an analogy between the work the poet describes and his own way of making lines?

Synthesize Summary and Analysis

5 Making a poem about work in his family, the poet discovers a link to his own present labors. Do you find that physical labor and creative labor are equivalent?

Interpret the Poem

6 Is this a poem of justification or celebration?

For Review and Further Study

John Keats (1795–1821)

For a brief biography of John Keats, see chapter 18.

Bright star, would I were as steadfast as thou art (1838)

Bright star, would I were steadfast as thou art—
Not in lone splendour hung aloft the night
And watching, with eternal lids apart,
Like nature's patient, sleepless Eremite,
The moving waters at their priestlike task
Of pure ablution round earth's human shores,
Or gazing on the new soft-fallen mask
Of snow upon the mountains and the moors—
No—yet still steadfast, still unchangeable,
Pillow'd upon my fair love's ripening breast,
To feel for ever its soft fall and swell,
Awake for ever in a sweet unrest,
Still, still to hear her tender-taken breath,
And so live ever—or else swoon to death.

Questions for Interactive Reading and Writing

1. This is an **apostrophe** (see chapter 21)—a poem in which the speaker speaks, improbably enough, to a personified object, a star—addressing it in the informal second person "thou." How does this establish tone?
2. As with Kelly Cherry's "The Raiment We Put On" (later in this chapter), this is a perfect Shakespearean sonnet with an occasional near rhyme. Why is this particular poem suited to the sonnet form?
3. Look up "Eremite," "ablution," and any other words that may confuse you here. "Splendour" is the British spelling, and natural enough for Keats, but why would he have put an apostrophe in "Pillow'd"? And why does he—remember Keats died of tuberculosis at twenty-five—conclude with "swoon to death"?
4. The word *steadfast* is used twice and the word *still* appears four times, the word *ever* three. How does this affect the poem's music, and how would you describe such a line as "To feel for ever its soft fall and swell"?

Edna St. Vincent Millay (1892–1950)

Only until this cigarette is ended (1921)

Only until this cigarette is ended,
A little moment at the end of all,
While on the floor the quiet ashes fall,
And in the firelight to a lance extended,
Bizarrely with the jazzing music blended,
The broken shadow dances on the wall,
I will permit my memory to recall
The vision of you, by all my dreams attended.
And then adieu,—farewell!—the dream is done.
Yours is a face of which I can forget
The color and the features, every one,
The words not ever, and the smiles not yet;
But in your day this moment is the sun
Upon a hill, after the sun has set.

Questions for Interactive Reading and Writing

1. Paraphrase this sonnet and compare it to Kelly Cherry's use of "I" and "you" in her sonnet, "The Raiment We Put On" (later in this chapter).
2. How much time elapses in the poem? What does this suggest about the speaker's mood and thoughts? How much actual control do you believe she has over her thoughts?
3. Can you explain the paradox (seemingly contradictory statement) of the final two lines?
4. From Sappho to Shakespeare to Millay and beyond, poets have written about love and its pains and losses. How close to despair do you find Millay in this poem compared to other love poems you have read? How close to joy?

Christina Rossetti (1830–1894)

A Birthday (1861)

My heart is like a singing bird
  Whose nest is in a watered shoot;
My heart is like an apple-tree
  Whose boughs are bent with thick-set fruit;
My heart is like a rainbow shell
  That paddles in a halcyon sea;
My heart is gladder than all these,
  Because my love is come to me.

Raise me a dais of silk and down;
  Hang it with vair and purple dyes;
Carve it in doves and pomegranates,
  And peacocks with a hundred eyes;
Work it in gold and silver grapes,
  In leaves and silver fleur-de-lys;
Because the birthday of my life
  Is come, my love is come to me.

Questions for Interactive Reading and Writing

1. Discuss the repetitions here, as well as variation. Lines 1, 3, 5, and 7 make a kind of chorus, and the last lines of the two stanzas are similar. How does this compare to the ballad form?
2. Although this poem was written roughly 150 years ago, it uses a consciously "archaic" diction—perhaps medieval, perhaps even biblical in tone. How do words like "halcyon" and "vair" and "fleurs-de-lys" contribute to this effect?
3. "A singing bird" appears in the first line, and there are other birds throughout. Does the speaker compare herself to these creatures; if so, why?
4. The second stanza is couched in the imperative mode—as a series of orders to be obeyed. This is a poem of celebration, edging up to excess; list the similes.
5. What does Rosetti mean by "the birthday of my life"?

RHYME

The sound component most often associated with poetry is called rhyme. **Rhyme** (**rime**) consists of the echoing repetition of sounds in end syllables of words, often (though not always) at the end of a line of poetry. Rhyme offers one of the primary pleasures of verse; all children are alert to it, and a sound repeated is a sound remembered. "Jack Sprat could eat no fat" and "Old Mother Hubbard went to the cupboard" remain alive as nursery rhymes because of their emphatic repetition.

> "Nursery rhymes [with] those really adorable rhythms that just stay in the head—that was my first sense of the pleasure of language." Conversation with Robert Hass

That said, it's a misconception to think all poetry *has* to rhyme. This mistaken notion has resulted in a lot of bad poetry and greeting cards with awkward or forced rhyming language. Of course you've already seen in this book many successful poems that don't rely on the device, and—as our brief discussion of Anglo-Saxon poetry suggests—the technique of end-rhyme consonance was not always part of the genre. Elegant rhyme, however, can make a poem feel connected and whole, and it often surprises the reader with an unexpected or evocative connection. The linkage between words like "solitaire" and "easy chair" or "greenery" and "scenery" makes for a kind of equation—one word equals another in the mind's ear, and the echo enhances effect.

In the first such pairing, the rhyme comes in the final syllable: *aire* and *air,* in the second there's also **internal rhyme;** *green* and *scene* are rhyming words, and *greenery* and *scenery* sound therefore entirely alike. Had the words been *greenish* and *scenario,* there still would be internal rhyme but the sound of the whole would be changed. Poets have at their disposal many different variations of rhyme, and part of the pleasure of writing a poem derives from this choice of technique. So, too, should we as readers *notice* the use that has been made of rhyme.

"Rhyme . . . is a form of relationship and connection, of encounter and metamorphosis. . . . There is something charged and magnetic about a good rhyme, something unsuspected and inevitable, utterly surprising and unforeseen and yet also binding and necessary. It is as if the poet called up the inner yearning for words to find each other." Conversation with Edward Hirsch

Take these lines in Robert Frost's poem (for the whole poem, see chapter 18):

The woods are lovely, dark and deep,
But I have promises to keep,
And miles to go before I sleep,
And miles to go before I sleep.

These are **end rhymes,** rhyming sounds that conclude the four lines of the stanza. Frost chose to repeat the end rhyme for each of his quatrain's four lines and repeat the third line verbatim; this act of willed repetition has much to do with the action described, and how the speaker here will keep on moving through the dark.

If, however, Frost had written "The woods are lovely, dark and deep, / But I have promises I've made, / And miles to go before I'm home, / And miles to go before I rest," our response would be quite different. We might acquire *some* sense of the poem's famous meditation, and its meaning would not change. The substance stays the same. On the whole, however, these modified phrases lose their mournful, musical connectivity; the *sound* is an important—even a crucial—part of *sense.* It's not an accident that one of the synonyms for *language* is *tongue;* we sound out what we see.

While we usually think of rhyme as solely a sound device, **eye rhyme** (also called **sight rhyme**) refers to words that share similar spellings but—when spoken—have different sounds. Words like "lint" and "pint" or "full" and "lull" exemplify eye rhyme, as does the final, sometimes confounding couplet of this old children's song:

The itsy bitsy spider climbed up the water spout
Down came the rain and washed the spider out
Out came the sun and dried up all the rain
And the itsy bitsy spider climbed up the spout again.

In contemporary English, *again* does not rhyme with *rain,* and so these lines may introduce kids to their first example of eye rhyme; in its original usage, however, the two words were likely true rhymes. In the seventeenth-century English speech of William Shakespeare's time, it seems probable that the "o" in "love" and "move" was pronounced in the same way, so when Prince Hamlet says "doubt that the sun doth move / but never doubt I love" he's using consonance, not dissonance, to make his point; how words look and how they sound are not always one and the same.

"One of the beauties of formal verse is that it's . . . very memorable. You have a rhyme scheme perhaps to guide your memory. I think the reason that rhyme patterns were established in the first place was as a mnemonic so that we would be able to memorize."

Conversation with Carolyn Forché

In **exact rhyme** (also **pure, perfect,** or **true rhyme**), the final vowel and consonant sounds are identical, regardless of spelling. For most readers, it's the most familiar form. Think of "heard" and "word" or "simple," "pimple," and "dimple." Rhymes like these offer a clear, bright connectivity of sound.

In eighteenth-century England, Alexander Pope composed the following piece in **heroic couplets,** two successive rhyming lines in iambic pentameter (the most commonly used metric pattern in English literature). In addition to the musical pleasure that rhythm can bring to a poem, rhyme schemes can organize a poem in central ways. The heroic couplet scheme of *AA/BB*, for example, is very different from *AB/AB* or *AB/BA*, and one of the most useful ways to look at the craft of poetry is to look for the rhyme scheme involved. Heroic couplets stress the connection between each of the paired lines.

Alexander Pope (1688–1744)

Born in London, Alexander Pope suffered from a bone disease as a child, and consequently never grew taller than four and a half feet. What he lacked in stature, he more than made up for in literary genius. Largely self-educated and self-sufficient—his translations of the *Iliad* and the *Odyssey* earned him enough money to buy an estate and live solely as a man of letters—Pope became the leading poet of his day, thanks to his mastery of style, the heroic couplet, and satirical writing. His sparkling wit attacked not only his contemporaries, in works like *The Dunciad* (1728), but also great works of literature, like *Paradise Lost* in his famous mock-epic *The Rape of the Lock* (1714). Pope also composed verse that showed his appreciation of beauty, including *Pastorals* (1709) and *Windsor Forest* (1713).

AS YOU READ Note how the rhyme scheme helps notate the repetitions of sound and puts a kind of emphasis on the meaning here.

[True ease in writing comes from art, not chance]

—from "An Essay on Criticism" (1711)

True ease in writing comes from art, not chance, a
As those move easiest who have learned to dance. a
'Tis not enough no harshness gives offense, b
The sound must seem an echo to the sense: b
Soft is the strain when Zephyr gently blows, c
And the smooth stream in smoother numbers flows; c
But when loud surges lash the sounding shore, d
The hoarse, rough verse should like the torrent roar; d
When Ajax strives some rock's vast weight to throw, e
The line too labors, and the words move slow; e
Not so, when swift Camilla scours the plain, f
Flies o'er the unbending corn, and skims along the main. f
Hear how Timotheus' varied lays surprise, g
And bid alternate passions fall and rise! g

Writing from Reading

Summarize

1 The poet offers a disquisition (formal explanation, discussion of a subject) on the relation of sound and sense in poetry. Why might he be taking this up as a subject? Have you seen any poets before Pope working on this idea?

Analyze Craft

2 Describe the paradox in comparing "ease" to "art." What is the effect of this comparison?

3 What is the meaning of the phrase "smoother numbers"?

4 Look up the classical references: Ajax, Camilla, etc. What is the function of these allusions?

Analyze Voice

5 What, if anything, distinguishes the poet's rhyming couplets from that of songs or poems presented as songs in verse?

Synthesize Summary and Analysis

6 These rhyming couplets provide some lessons on the relation of craft and voice. Which rhymes do you consider the smoothest, and which rhymes here trouble you?

Interpret the Poem

7 Does a poem such as this veer too much toward didactism—overexplicit instruction—or philosophy?

There are many variations of patterns available as rhyme—some that the ear can respond to, such as those of nursery rhymes or those of rhyming couplets. Most of us can also *hear* the echo in the first four lines *(AB/AB)* of Lord Byron's "She walks in beauty . . ." (night/skies/bright/eyes) or the *AB/AB* in the first stanza of "Leda and the Swan" by William Butler Yeats (for the whole poem, see chapter 16). In this poem, the god Zeus assumes the form of a swan and rapes the girl Leda, in the process fathering the famously beautiful Helen of Troy. Note the rhyme scheme is less obvious than that of Byron, and think of how the rhyming words differ (*still/bill* versus *caressed/breast*).

A sudden blow: the great wings beating still *a*
Above the staggering girl, her thighs caressed *b*
By the dark webs, her nape caught in his bill, *a*
He holds her helpless breast upon his breast. *b*

Some rhyme schemes are more elaborate, such as the first lines of "Pied Beauty" (by Gerard Manley Hopkins, later in this chapter): *ABC/ABC*. In other cases—if a rhyme is eight or twelve lines distant—the ear will likely fail to retain the sound as echo, though the eye might perhaps notice a repeated word. If, for instance, we write "many" again, you might remember that we used that word in the first sentence of the previous paragraph, but it likely won't function as an echoing *sound* (as would the words *found* or *ground*). The presence or absence of patterned repetition is a crucial factor in how a poem works.

Slant rhyme (also called **near, imperfect,** or **off rhyme**) refers to a case in which vowel or consonant sounds are similar but not exactly the same. Examples include word combinations like

heap, rap, tape
aluminum, linoleum

"Sometimes . . . rhymes clink. The sound is too aggressive. I mean, if I ever have to read *breath* and *death* again, I think it will kill me. . . . Maybe because I'm a modern person, half rhymes often sound more beautiful to me than full rhymes. They . . . de-emphasize the rhyming and emphasize more the sound patterning and make it sound more natural." Conversation with Edward Hirsch

In contrast to the vivid precision of exact rhymes, slant rhyme provides a subtler, sometimes natural-sounding correlation of sound. Yeats uses both exact (*still, bill*) and slant rhyme (*caressed, breast*) in "Leda and the Swan," and unlike Pope, Yeats does not use the end rhyme to create a hard stop at the close of each line but allows the sentence to spill over for a more natural sound. The use of exact, slant, or no rhyme contributes to the poem's voice, as does the way the rhyme fits into the sentence structure of the poem's individual lines.

Thomas Lynch also incorporates both exact and slant rhyme in "Iambs for the Day of Burial." Look at the first four lines of that poem, with the precise rhyming pattern of "best" and "stressed" and the slant rhyme of "body" and "tally." Then see how he repeats yet varies that pattern—ending with "forsaken" and "broken" as slant rhymes and "beatified" and "died" as perfect rhymes.

In chapter 18, for example, we included Elizabeth Bishop's poem "The Fish" as a way of showing the use and value of clear, simple, direct American English. Marianne Moore uses a similar diction in her poem of the same title, "The Fish." Moore introduces rhyme into the poem in a way that plays with echoing: the ear hears *and-stand* or *green-submarine* as exact rhymes.

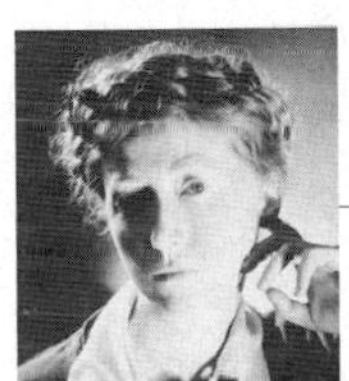

Marianne Moore (1887–1972)

Born near Saint Louis, Missouri, Marianne Moore was educated at Bryn Mawr. She lived her adult life with her mother in New York City, where she was an ardent fan of the Dodgers (then located in the New York borough of Brooklyn). Although a modernist and contemporary of Ezra Pound, William Carlos Williams, and H.D., Moore refused to conform to any standard but her own. Her stanzas are unique, composed of lines that count syllables, rather than stresses, and that often hide their rhyme internally. A lover of animals, Moore often uses them or other everyday objects as a springboard for deeper exploration in her poems. In addition to actively publishing her poetry, Moore was an astute literary critic. Poets including Elizabeth Bishop, Richard Wilbur, and Randall Jarrell cite Moore as influential to their poetry.

AS YOU READ Watch for the way these lines mirror the motion of a swimming fish.

The Fish

(1921)

wade
through black jade.
Of the crow-blue mussel-shells, one keeps
adjusting the ash-heaps;
opening and shutting itself like

an
injured fan.
The barnacles which encrust the side
of the wave, cannot hide
there for the submerged shafts of the

sun,
split like spun
glass, move themselves with spotlight swiftness
into the crevices—
in and out, illuminating

the
turquoise sea
of bodies. The water drives a wedge
of iron through the iron edge
of the cliff; whereupon the stars,

pink
rice-grains, ink-
bespattered jelly-fish, crabs like green
lilies, and submarine
toadstools, slide each on the other.

All
external
marks of abuse are present on this
defiant edifice—
all the physical features of

ac-
cident—lack
of cornice, dynamite grooves, burns, and
hatchet strokes, these things stand
out on it; the chasm-side is

dead.
Repeated
evidence has proved that it can live
on what can not revive
its youth. The sea grows old in it.

Writing from Reading

Summarize

1 Go through each stanza and indicate what is being described.

Analyze Craft

2 Discuss the use of exact rhyme in the poem with respect to the poem's shape. What contrast do you find between the traditional style of the rhyme scheme and the structure of the poem?

3 Are all the rhymes exact? What other varieties of rhyme do you see in the poem?

4 How does the hyphen in the word *accident* affect our usual expectations for that word? How does it set up the rhyme with *lack*?

Analyze Voice

5 "All the physical features"—as the poet puts it—announce themselves here; from the very first word and its immediate rhyme ("wade," then three words later, "jade") to the strange shape of the lines and stanzas, we are introduced to a particular way of seeing/saying, an individual use of language.

Synthesize Summary and Analysis

6 Go through the poem and "read" its rhyme scheme. Which rhymes seem surprising? Which seem to link words together as concepts?

Interpret the Poem

7 The *arrangement* of the poem—its rhythm, rhyme, and line lengths—takes center stage here. Based on the images and sounds with which Moore composes the poem, what "fishy" point is the poet trying to make?

Perhaps the leading exponent of slant rhyme in our literature is "the belle of Amherst," Emily Dickinson. The words *despair* and *fear* in the brief poem that follows are somehow enlarged and given a kind of kinship—though the poem considers their "difference"—by their associated sounds.

> "When I started to realize that there were words that rhymed in English, it felt like magic to me. . . . I thought, *wren* and *yarn* must share something other than just words. So forever in my mind those tiny little birds and yarn were conflated: they shared not just names." Conversation with Li-Young Lee

Emily Dickinson (1830–1886)

For a brief biography of Emily Dickinson, see the Case Study on American Plain Style, chapter 28.

AS YOU READ Try reading this poem aloud several times, allowing the meaning to emerge not just from the statements but also from the way they follow along in brief lines.

The difference between Despair (c. 1862)

The difference between Despair
And Fear—is like the One
Between the instant of a Wreck
And when the Wreck has been—

The Mind is smooth—no Motion—
Contented as the Eye
Upon the Forehead of a Bust—
That knows—it cannot see—

Writing from Reading

Summarize

1 How would you describe the difference between despair and fear?

Analyze Craft

2 What constitutes a "statement" in poetry as opposed to a message or statement in a document or newspaper story?

3 Find instances of consonance and assonance in the poem. How do they work to connect or unify the language in the poem?

Analyze Voice

4 Read this poem aloud. How would you describe the language? How does this description seem to fit or contrast with the poem's subject?

5 Notice the shift between the first stanza, in which the poet presents a thought or idea, and the second, in which she focuses on the organ of thought. Can you explain the shift?

Synthesize Summary and Analysis

6 What kind of a wreck would the poet in her time be thinking of?

Interpret the Poem

7 How can "the Eye / Upon the Forehead of a Bust" know it cannot see?

Masculine rhyme (also **rising rhyme**) refers to end rhymes of polysyllabic words with a stressed final syllable, as in "remove" and "approve," and rhymes of monosyllabic words, like "good" and "wood." In contrast, **feminine rhyme** refers to rhymes between polysyllabic words in which the final syllable is unstressed. Examples include "bother" and "father" or "monkey" and "funky." A good poet is conscious of the distinction between masculine and feminine rhymes and the effects they produce. A **rhyme scheme** refers to the pattern of rhyme throughout a particular poem. To notate a rhyme scheme, we represent each new end rhyme with a lowercase letter following its line (as you saw with the poems by Pope and Yeats). When a sound recurs, we use the same letter to mark the repeated rhyme.

For Review and Further Study

Julia Alvarez (b. 1950)

Woman's Work (1994)

Who says a woman's work isn't high art?
She'd challenge as she scrubbed the bathroom tiles.
Keep house as if the address were your heart.

We'd clean the whole upstairs before we'd start
downstairs. I'd sigh, hearing my friends outside.
Doing her woman's work was a hard art

to practice when the summer sun would bar
the floor I swept till she was satisfied.
She kept me prisoner in her housebound heart.

She'd shine the tines of forks, the wheels of carts,
cut lacy lattices for all her pies.
Her woman's work was nothing less than art.

And, I, her masterpiece since I was smart,
was primed, praised, polished, scolded and advised
to keep a house much better than my heart.

I did not want to be her counterpart!
I struck out . . . but became my mother's child:
a woman working at home on her art,
housekeeping paper as if it were her heart.

Questions for Interactive Reading and Writing

1. Look at the rhyme scheme here—the exact and slant rhymes. Notate the rhyme scheme. What impact does the rhyme scheme have on your understanding of the poem?
2. In the next chapter (Fixed Poetic Forms), we discuss the villanelle. How does this poem follow and then diverge from that form?
3. The speaker remembers her mother and her mother's domestic behavior. What does she herself practice as a "woman's work"? And how does this connect to the work of Seamus Heaney in "Digging"?
4. Is there a linkage here, or opposition, between the tasks of housekeeping and "her art"?
5. What is the significance of the line "And, I, her masterpiece since I was smart"?

Kelly Cherry (b. 1940)

The Raiment We Put On (1994)

Do you remember? We were in a room
with walls as warm as anybody's breath,
and music wove us on its patterning loom,
the complicated loom of life and death.
Your hands moved over my face like small clouds.
(Rain fell into a river and sank, somewhere.)
I moved among your fingers, brushed by the small crowds
of them, feeling myself known, everywhere,
and in that desperate country so far from here,
I heard you say my name over and over,
your voice threading its way into my ear.
I will spend my days working to discover
the pattern and its meaning, what you meant,
what has been raveled and what has been rent.

Questions for Interactive Reading and Writing

1. What does the title have to do with the text as such?
2. What effect do the vowel sounds in words such as *loom* and *over* have on your understanding of the poem?
3. What does the poet mean by "raveled" and "rent" in the last line?
4. The poem is told in first person and directed at a second-person "you." The first-person plural "We" suggests that it's a shared memory. However, we don't know the name of "you" or "I"—even though "I heard you say my name over and over." Look at the use of pronouns here. What impression is created by the use of pronouns without actual names?

Marilyn Nelson (b. 1946)

Chopin (1989)

It's Sunday evening. Pomp holds the receipts
of all the colored families on the Hill
in his wide lap, and shows which white store cheats
these patrons, who can't read a weekly bill.
His parlor's full of men holding their hats
and women who admire his girls' good hair.
Pomp warns them not to vote for Democrats,
controlling half of Hickman from his chair.
The varying degrees of cheating seen,
he nods toward the piano. Slender, tall,
a Fisk girl passing-white, almost nineteen,
his Blanche folds the piano's paisley shawl
and plays Chopin. And blessed are the meek
who have to buy in white men's stores next week.

Questions for Interactive Reading and Writing

1. Beyond the physical setting, there is the social and political situation. Based on the information in the poem, describe the place, the time, the social and political relations. Why, for example, is the rich man who "holds the receipts" called "Pomp"?
2. The rhyme scheme seems calm and yet appealing. Can we assume a similarity between the rhyme scheme and the piano piece referred to in the poem? Why is this possible?
3. What is the effect on the ironic tone of the poem of the use of the conjunctions—"and. . . . And . . ."—in the next-to-last line?
4. The sonnet form, invented by an Italian poet and perfected by an English genius—Shakespeare—gives us here a portrait of a moment in modern black American life. What seems universal about this poetic form? What seems particular to the time?

RHYTHM

As much as it depends on patterns and repetition of sound, poetry also relies on patterns and repetition of rhythm. The classic phrase *rhythm and meter* may sound intimidating with its old-fashioned, mathematical connotation, but the rhythm in our language is actually very natural. Human beings are instinctively tuned to rhythm. It's tied to our heartbeat, our breathing, our walking, the passage of our days and weather, the way we learn to shoot a basketball or dance. The word itself comes from an ancient Greek term meaning "flow," which may after all these centuries still be the simplest way of defining the concept.

"The first way to study [a poem] is to say a poem out loud. . . . If you say those words out loud . . . your breath pattern is flowing through your body in exactly the way it flowed through [the poet's body] when he said those words. . . . Poetry is [a] kind of existential breath sculpture." Conversation with Robert Hass

Stresses and Pauses

The English language depends on rhythmical variation to create meaning even on a basic level. Whether conscious of it or not, we all tend to process the meaning of language through its patterns of sound emphasis. In other words, we don't ask a question like "HEY CAN I BORROW YOUR CAR TONIGHT?" with the same emphasis on each sound in the sentence. If we spoke like that, we'd sound like a robot from an old science fiction movie. Instead, the sentence becomes a collection of subtly contrasting emphases, perhaps, "HEY, can I BORrow your CAR toNIGHT?" These changes are

> "There are different kinds of silences. There's a silence of mystery, then there's the silence of secrets—like 'I know something but I'm not telling.' Or there's the silence of 'I know something but I forgot what it is.' So there are all kinds of different silences, and they have different colors, and different ranges, and different depths, and different widths. I think in poetry we're using language a lot of times to inflect those different silences." Conversation with Li-Young Lee

called **stresses** (or **accents**), the emphasis or "push" we put on the pitch (the musical quality), duration, or volume of a syllable.

The same holds just as true for a line or sentence as for a single word. Heroic couplets, for example, tend to be **end-stopped**—meaning they insist upon their rhyming emphasis and don't encourage the reader to continue without pause. **Enjambment** (from a French word meaning "stride" or "encroach") consists of the running-over of a phrase from one line into another, so that closely related words belong to different lines. This makes the rhythm of the sentence seem more closely akin to natural speech, and it's very often used in *open* or *free* verse (see chapter 24.) A **caesura** is a pause, usually in the middle of a line, that marks a kind of rhythmic division—a place to catch your breath. All these are ways of organizing the sound and sense of poetry, *craft* in the service of *voice.*

We stress the *first* syllables of words like

> ***BA****lance*
> ***STITCH****ing*
> ***TEEN****age*

The second syllable of each word receives a stress in words like

> *be****CAUSE***
> *gui****TAR***
> *a****ROUND***

In combination, all these words in our language create diverse rhythmic sounds. Hence, **rhythm** refers to this sequence of stressed and unstressed sounds in a poem. There's an inescapable music in the five brief stanzas in "Sadie and Maud," by Gwendolyn Brooks, with their perfect *B* rhymes in lines 2 and 4:

Gwendolyn Brooks (1917–2000)

For a brief biography of Gwendolyn Brooks, see chapter 18.

AS YOU READ Notice the rhyme scheme, and how it contributes to the singsong effect.

Sadie and Maud (1945)

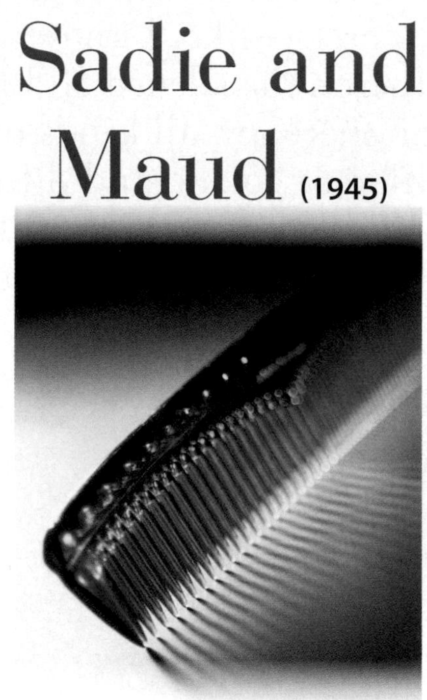

Maud went to college.
Sadie stayed at home.
Sadie scraped life
With a fine-tooth comb.

She didn't leave a tangle in.
Her comb found every strand.
Sadie was one of the livingest chits
In all the land.

Sadie bore two babies
Under her maiden name.
Maud and Ma and Papa
Nearly died of shame.

When Sadie said her last so-long
Her girls struck out from home.
(Sadie had left as heritage
Her fine-tooth comb.)

Maud, who went to college,
Is a thin brown mouse.
She is living all alone
In this old house.

Writing from Reading

Summarize

1 List the way these two histories are similar or different. What is Sadie's "last so-long," and how does the poet feel about the way Maud lives?

Analyze Craft

2 Describe the poem's rhythm. Is it in a tightly controlled metrical form, or does it sound more like natural speech? Why do you think this is?

3 Discuss sound in the final line of the poem. Why do you think Brooks chooses monosyllabic words here?

Analyze Voice

4 "Ma and Papa" are referred to the way that Sadie might say it, and not as "mother and father." How does this contribute to the tone of the whole, and what does "livingest chits" suggest?

Synthesize Summary and Analysis

5 This poem tells a story of hardship as well as a kind of pleasure. How does the rhyme scheme affect your reading of the poem's subject matter?

Interpret the Poem

6 Fairy tales and nursery rhymes often deal in opposition—think, for example, of the story of the city mouse and the country mouse or the tortoise and the hare. What moral here—if any—does Brooks suggest we draw?

METER

Meter refers to a sequence of stressed and unstressed syllables that forms an essentially regular pattern in lines of poetry. A poem's meter functions like the bass line or drumbeat to a piece of music, keeping time and arranging a poem's sounds. One unique feature of poetry (as compared, for example, to fiction) is that these rhythmic stresses are often arranged in specific intervals. We measure these patterns of stresses to understand how poets shape, simultaneously, their sound and the reader's understanding. The unit of measurement with which we examine meter is called a **foot,** usually a group of two or three syllables containing a single stress. This study is a component of **prosody,** the analysis of a poem's rhythm and metrical structures.

Scansion

Scansion is the process of determining the metrical pattern of a **line** of poetry by marking its stresses and feet. We most often use a / symbol to mark a stressed syllable and a ~ to indicate an unstressed syllable. Also, we use a vertical line | (sometimes through a word, when needed) to mark divisions between feet. The most common foot in English and American poetry is the **iambic foot,** an unstressed syllable followed by a stressed syllable, as in the word *subLIME.*

> "The only reason we scan is so that we can learn to hear it, learn to hear that music when we read, and learn to hear what poetry's music is." Conversation with Carolyn Forché

The following chart notes the four chief metrical feet in poetry in English:

COMMON METRIC FEET

FOOT/VERSE FORM	STRESSES	EXAMPLE
iamb/iambic	~ /	because, and then
trochee/trochaic	/ ~	evil, pizza
anapest/anapestic	~ ~ /	understand, in the east
dactyl/dactyllic	/ ~ ~	merrily, happening

Other, less common syllable patterns include **spondees** (two stressed syllables), **pyrrhics** (two unstressed syllables), **amphibrachs** (three syllables: unstressed, stressed, unstressed), and **cretic/amphimacer** (three syllables: stressed, unstressed, stressed).

We also measure meter by the number of feet a line of poetry contains. The name of the foot combines with the number of feet; this constitutes the overall metrical form of a poem.

Number of Feet Per Line

monometer:	one foot	**pentameter:**	five feet
dimeter:	two feet	**hexameter:**	six feet
trimeter:	three feet	**heptameter:**	seven feet
tetrameter:	four feet	**octameter:**	eight feet

When discussing the meter of a poem, we combine the type of metrical foot used in a poem with the number of feet in a line. So, for example, we use the term **iambic pentameter** to refer to a line of poetry with five iambs.

COMMON METRIC PATTERNS

Iambic pentameter: five iambs, as in these lines: "When I have fears that I may cease to be . . ." —John Keats

Blank verse refers to lines of unrhymed iambic pentameter. Used in dramatic Renaissance poetry, it has lasted through the centuries and found its way into the work of modernists like Robert Frost, Wallace Stevens, and Elizabeth Bishop.

Iambic tetrameter is a line containing four iambs: "Because I could not stop for death . . ." —Emily Dickinson

Trochaic tetrameter is a line containing four trochees. Here are two lines from the poem "The Song of Hiawatha": "Heavy with the heat and silence / Grew the afternoon of Summer . . ." —Henry Wadsworth Longfellow

Anapestic trimeter is a line that contain three anapests, as in these lines: "From the center all round to the sea / I am lord of the fowl and the brute . . ." —William Cowper

Dactylic tetrameter is a line that contains four dactyls, as in these flowing lines: "Just for a handful of silver he left us, / Just for a riband to stick in his coat. . . ." —Robert Browning

"Poetry comes from a time when we didn't have all this electronic gear and screens and so forth. You had the human body and the human voice. . . . You know, the word 'foot' in poetry comes from the days when people would actually dance so that you measured what was said by bodily movements. I think it will always be that way for . . . people who really cut past all the intellectual trappings of poetry and get back to the emotions." Conversation with Al Young

The following light poem by Samuel Taylor Coleridge demonstrates, in sound, the various kinds of metrical feet while it simultaneously explains them. Coleridge may seem pedantic in his definitions, but in his time he could take words like "Amphibrachys" and "Amphimacer" for granted, and he's being playful here.

Samuel Taylor Coleridge (1772–1834)

One of the leading poets of the Romantic period in England, Samuel Taylor Coleridge first planned with Robert Southey—future Poet Laureate—to begin a utopian society in Pennsylvania. When their plans fell through, Coleridge turned to a writing career. In 1797 he forged a close friendship with William Wordsworth. The two published *Lyrical Ballads,* the seminal work of the Romantic period in which Coleridge's famous "The Rime of the Ancient Mariner" first appeared. Coleridge is also known for pioneering the form of "conversation poems"—poems that begin with a speaker addressing somebody in the present, then follow the mind as it travels in meditation before returning to the present; "The Eolian Harp" and "This Lime-Tree Bower My Prison" are prime examples. Coleridge gave lectures and drew a small following as a talented conversationalist until his death in 1834.

AS YOU READ See if you can scan this poem with a pencil to find the stresses and feet.

Trochee trips from long to short (1806)

Trochee trips from long to short;
From long to long in solemn sort
Slow Spondee stalks; strong foot! yet ill able
Ever to come up with Dactyl's trisyllable.
Iambics march from short to long;—
With a leap and a bound the swift Anapests throng;
One syllable long, with one short at each side,
Amphibrachys hastes with a stately stride;—
First and last being long, middle short, Amphimacer
Strikes his thundering hoofs like a proud high-bred Racer.

If Derwent be innocent, steady, and wise,
And delight in the things of earth, water, and skies;
Tender warmth at his heart, with these metres to show it,
With sound sense in his brains, may make Derwent a poet,—
May crown him with fame, and must win him the love
Of his father on earth and his Father above.
  My dear, dear child!
Could you stand upon Skiddaw, you would not from its whole ridge
See a man who so loves you as your fond S. T. Coleridge.

Writing from Reading

Summarize

1 What might have prompted the poet to write this playful but instructive treatment of rhyme schemes?

Analyze Craft

2 Define each of the rhymes as Coleridge outlines them.

Analyze Voice

3 Who is the person—the poet—behind these lines?

Synthesize Summary and Analysis

4 The poet reenacts the basic meters of poetry. Does he follow Pope (see the excerpt from "An Essay on Criticism" earlier in this chapter) in this?

Interpret the Poem

5 What is the meaning of this poem beyond the instructional purpose?

METRICAL VARIATION

After all this discussion about the balancing act between rhythm and meter, it may sound strange (or even frustrating) to hear that poets writing in formal structures are often liable to break free occasionally of their own chosen metrical form. As the poet Paul Muldoon once wrote, "Form is a straitjacket the way that a straitjacket was a straitjacket for Houdini." In comparing rhythm, rhyme, and meter to a famous magician's escape act, Muldoon suggests that the traditional formal constraints can be used purposefully and then evaded; *too* regular a use of rhythm and meter can be dull. **Doggerel,** an obviously patterned piece of rhyme, can sometimes seem almost childish and, when extensive, boring; these are rules that can be broken once they have been learned.

Sound can speed a poem's language up ("reeling round and round") or slow it down ("steadfast, he stood up straight"). In the poem by Gerard Manley Hopkins that follows, note the repeated consonants. "Swift" and "slow," "sweet" and "sour" might seem to have opposite meanings, but they are connected by sound; alliteration yokes together the variety of images Hopkins celebrates in the natural world. In the first stanza, "glory" links in sound to "God" and "couple-color" achieves its comparison to "cow" both through sound and sight. So, alliteration not only increases the musicality of the poem but also helps unify the language of a poem that is, itself, *about* unity. The metrical variation of Hopkins's poem—and his work in general—is what he called **sprung verse,** and it's a perfect example of change within consistency.

Gerard Manley Hopkins (1844–1889)

An English poet of the Victorian era, Gerard Manley Hopkins is often grouped with the Modernist poets because of his innovative poetic form. Hopkins was educated at Oxford and began writing verse there. Three years into his education, he converted to Roman Catholicism and burned his poetry, fearing it interfered with his devotion to God. Seven years later, when a shipwreck killed five nuns, Hopkins asked permission from the church to write a poem commemorating the occurrence. From 1876 onward, Hopkins wrote poems that show God's presence and design in every earthly thing, in verses of sprung meter—lines with a set amount of stresses but with a liberality of unstressed syllables. Hopkins's poetic ear is almost unparalleled, but rather than court literary celebrity, he spent his life as a priest and a teacher. His poetry was not published until thirty years after his premature death from typhoid fever.

AS YOU READ Think about the effects of sound on your understanding of a poem's descriptions and overall meaning. Read the poem silently, then aloud. Consider how your perceptions change.

Pied Beauty (1877)

Glory be to God for dappled things—
For skies of couple-color as a brinded cow;
For rose-moles all in stipple upon trout that swim;
Fresh-firecoal chestnut-falls; finches' wings;
Landscape plotted and pieced—fold, fallow, and plough;
And all trades, their gear and tackle and trim.

All things counter, original, spare, strange;
Whatever is fickle, freckled (who knows how?)
With swift, slow; sweet, sour; adazzle, dim;
He fathers-forth whose beauty is past change:
Praise him.

Writing from Reading

Summarize

1 Think of this poem as a kind of sermon delivered by Father Hopkins. What does he urge his readership or congregation to do? What does the word *Pied* mean?

Analyze Craft

2 Note the repeated consonants. "Swift" and "slow," "sweet" and "sour" might seem to have opposite meanings, but they are connected by sound. How does alliteration yoke together the variety of images Hopkins celebrates in the natural world?

Analyze Voice

3 In the first stanza "glory" links in sound to "God" and "couple-color" achieves its comparison to "cow" both sonically and visually. Locate other examples of this technique. How does this sonorous connection emphasize the speaker's praise in this poem?

Synthesize Summary and Analysis

4 The last two words here are simple—monosyllabic—and solemn. If you were to recite this poem, would the last line be quiet or loud?

Interpret the Poem

5 How does alliteration not only increase the musicality of the poem but also help demonstrate that "Pied Beauty" is, itself, *about* unity?

For Review and Further Study

Anonymous Scottish Ballad

Bonnie Barbara Allan (date unknown)

It was in and about the Martinmas time,
When the green leaves were afalling,
That Sir John Graeme, in the West Country,
Fell in love with Barbara Allan.

He sent his men down through the town,
To the place where she was dwelling:
"Oh haste and come to my master dear,
Gin ye be Barbara Allan."

O hooly, hooly rose she up,
To the place where he was lying,
And when she drew the curtain by:
"Young man, I think you're dying."

"O it's I'm sick, and very, very sick,
And 'tis a' for Bonnie Allan."—
"O the better for me ye's never be,
Tho your heart's blood were aspilling."

"O dinna ye mind, young man," she said,
"When ye was in the tavern adrinking,
That ye made the health gae round and round,
And slighted Barbara Allan?"

He turned his face unto the wall,
And death was with him dealing:
"Adieu, adieu, my dear friends all,
And be kind to Barbara Allan."

And slowly, slowly raise her up,
And slowly, slowly left him,
And sighing said she could not stay,
Since death of life had reft him.

She had not gane a mile but twa,
When she heard the dead-bell ringing,
And every jow that the dead-bell geid,
It cried, "Woe to Barbara Allan!"

"O mother, mother, make my bed!
O make it saft and narrow!
Since my love died for me today,
I'll die for him tomorrow."

Questions for Interactive Reading and Writing

1. This poem has often been set to music and performed—what in its *sound* feels like *song?*
2. Do the repetitions here enhance or undermine tone?
3. Paraphrase this story in prose. What, if anything, is gained, and what gets lost?

Amy Clampitt (1920–1994)

John Donne in California (1990)

Is the Pacific Sea my home? Or is
Jerusalem? pondered John Donne,
who never stood among these strenuous,
huge, wind-curried hills, their green
gobleted just now with native poppies'
opulent red-gold, where New World lizards run
among strange bells, thistles wear the guise
of lizards, and one shining oak is poison;

or cast an eye on lofted strong-arm
redwoods' fog-fondled silhouette,
their sapling wisps among the ferns in time
more his (perhaps) than our compeer: here at
the round earth's numbly imagined rim,
its ridges drowned in the irradiating vat
of evening, the land ends; the magnesium
glare whose unbridged nakedness is bright
beyond imaging, begins. John Donne,
I think, would have been more at home
than the frail wick of metaphor I've brought
to see by, and cannot, for the conflagration
of this nightfall's utter strangeness.

Questions for Interactive Reading and Writing

1. What is it about California—and perhaps life itself—that the poet finds so confounding?
2. Do the rhythms of the poem, with their slant rhymes and somewhat obscure metaphors—"irradiating vat of evening," for example—dramatize a sense of the poet's confusions?

3. Read the following poem by John Donne to which this poem refers. Clampitt's line "Is the Pacific sea my home?" is a direct quotation from Donne's "Hymn to God, My God, In My Sickness." What is it about home in the Donne poem that Clampitt presumes is suitable for this occasion?

John Donne (1572–1631)

For a brief biography of John Donne, see chapter 25.

Hymn to God, My God, In My Sickness (1633)

Since I am coming to that Holy room,
Where, with Thy choir of saints for evermore,
I shall be made Thy music; as I come
I tune the instrument here at the door,
And what I must do then, think here before;

Whilst my physicians by their love are grown
Cosmographers, and I their map, who lie
Flat on this bed, that by them may be shown
That this is my south-west discovery,
Per fretum febris, by these straits to die;

I joy, that in these straits I see my west;
For, though those currents yield return to none,
What shall my west hurt me? As west and east
In all flat maps—and I am one—are one,
So death doth touch the resurrection.

Is the Pacific sea my home? Or are
The eastern riches? Is Jerusalem?
Anyan, and Magellan, and Gibraltar?
All straits, and none but straits, are ways to them
Whether where Japhet dwelt, or Cham, or Shem.

We think that Paradise and Calvary,
Christ's cross and Adam's tree, stood in one place;
Look, Lord, and find both Adams met in me;
As the first Adam's sweat surrounds my face,
May the last Adam's blood my soul embrace.

So, in His purple wrapp'd, receive me, Lord;
By these His thorns, give me His other crown;
And as to others' souls I preach'd Thy word,
Be this my text, my sermon to mine own,
"Therefore that He may raise, the Lord throws down."

Questions for Interactive Reading and Writing

1. What is the occasion for the poem?
2. What overarching metaphors does Donne employ? Do they work together or seem contradictory?
3. What pun does he make on the word *straits*? What does he mean by "first Adam" and "last Adam"?
4. Is "death doth touch" in line 15 an example of assonance?
5. Where does the "turn" of the poem occur? What does the poet mean by "my sermon to mine own"?
6. How does the speaker's sickness and impending death become, for him, a triumph?

Sonia Sanchez (b. 1934)

Poem at Thirty (1966)

it is midnight
no magical bewitching
hour for me
i know only that
i am here waiting
remembering that
once as a child
i walked two
miles in my sleep.
did i know
then where i
was going?
traveling. i'm
always traveling.
i want to tell
you about me
about nights on a
brown couch when
i wrapped my
bones in lint and
refused to move.
no one touches
me anymore.
father do not
send me out
among strangers.
you you black man
stretching scraping
the mold from your body.
here is my hand.
i am not afraid
of the night.

Questions for Interactive Reading and Writing

1. Christina Rosetti was thirty-one when she composed "A Birthday." How is it similar to "Poem at Thirty"? How is it dissimilar?
2. How is sleepwalking, the poem's central metaphor, related to what the poet calls "traveling"?
3. Does the situation in the last few lines seem obscure? How might you describe it?
4. How would you describe the way the poem sounds in your ear? In his interview, Thomas Lynch talks about a poet beginning to sound like himself or herself. Can you detect such growth in this poem?
5. Discuss the diction/tone of "Poem at Thirty." Why do you think the poet uses a lowercase "i"?

Kevin Young (b. 1970)

Jook (2003)

You have me
to you quite addicted

dear, my hands
in your mouth,

my wet-
nurse, succor,

cure. That old
booze

of you's
what I want,

dry gin, new
world, Old Crow.

Questions for Interactive Reading and Writing

1. Find a dictionary definition of "jook." How do the meanings help you understand the plight of the speaker? To whom is he speaking? Why does he use this central metaphor?
2. Why does he start with an inversion—not writing "You have me quite addicted to you" instead? Why does he end with the name of a whiskey, "Old Crow"?
3. The poet uses pun—"succor"—and melds rhythms and sounds—"booze of you's"—to create a certain effect. How would you describe that effect?
4. How does the theme of addiction and drinking add to the understanding of the speaker's situation?
5. Some of the earliest poems we know, such as Sappho's work, present love as an illness or an addiction. What changes if you read Young's poem in this context?

Reading for Sound, Rhyme, and Rhythm

When reading for *sound, rhyme,* and *rhythm,* examine how the sounds of the words work together with rhyme and rhythm to draw the reader into the poem and shape its meaning.

What kinds of words has the poet chosen (monosyllabic, polysyllabic, harsh, or melodious)?	*Euphony:* Musically pleasing poetic language.	EXAMPLE: "She walks in beauty, like the night / Of cloudless climes and starry skies / And all that's best of dark and bright / Meet in her aspect and her eyes."
	Cacophony: Harsh-sounding poetic language.	EXAMPLE: "Sweeping from butchers stalls, dung, guts, and blood, / Drowned puppies, stinking sprats, all drenched in mud / Dead cats and turnip-tops, come tumbling down the flood."

Has the poet used the repetition of consonant or vowel sounds in the poem?	*Alliteration:* The repetition of the initial consonant sounds of nearby words. *Consonance:* A repetition of consonants or consonant patterns in neighboring words. *Assonance:* The repetition of vowel sounds or vowel patterns in neighboring words.	EXAMPLE: I'm *r*ight as *r*ain, *r*eading in my *r*oom. EXAMPLE: Ca*l*m*l*y he ca*ll*ed to the mu*l*e in the o*l*d fie*l*d. EXAMPLE: The r*ai*n c*a*me ag*ai*n, s*a*me as yesterd*ay*.
Do words in the poem sound like what they represent?	*Onomatopoiea:* The use of words that imitate the sounds they refer to.	EXAMPLE: *Snap, crackle, pop*
Is rhyme used in the poem?	*Is there rhyme within the lines?* *Internal rhyme:* Rhyming between words in the same line, or words in the middle of two different phrases. *Does the rhyme come at the end of the lines?* *End rhyme:* Rhyming sounds that conclude lines of poetry. *Which syllable of the end word is stressed?* *Masculine rhyme:* End rhyme between polysyllabic words with a stressed final syllable, or between monosyllabic words. *Feminine rhyme:* End rhyme between polysyllabic words with unstressed final syllables. *Are the sounds in the rhyme identical?* **Identical:** *Exact rhyme:* Rhyme in which the end sounds of words are identical. **Not identical:** *Slant rhyme:* Rhyme in which the sounds are similar but do not rhyme. *Eye rhyme:* Words that are spelled similarly but do not rhyme.	EXAMPLE: "the *grains* beyond *age*, the dark *veins* of her mother" EXAMPLE: "The itsy bitsy spider climbed up the water *spout* / Down came the rains and washed the spider *out*" EXAMPLE: "I showed admirable re*move* / but mom did not ap*prove*." EXAMPLE: "Making money's a *bo*ther / so I just ask *fa*ther." EXAMPLE: "bat" and "cat" EXAMPLE: "cat" and "barette" EXAMPLE: "lint" and "pint"

Where do the lines break, where does the poem speed up, and where does it slow down?	*End-stopped lines:* Lines that don't encourage the reader to continue without pause.	EXAMPLE: "Trochee trips from long to short; / From long to long in solemn sort"
	Enjambment: The running-over of a phrase from one line into another, so that closely related words belong to different lines.	EXAMPLE: "Is the Pacific Sea my home? Or is / Jerusalem? pondered John Donne"
How do sounds work together in a line to create a rhythm of stressed and unstressed syllables?	*What pattern of stresses has the poet used to shape the sound of the lines in a poem?* ~ / ~ / ~ / ~ / ~ / "Of all our private parts the heart knows best"	
How are the stressed and unstressed syllables grouped together in a line?	**Foot** — **Marks** — **Example** *Iamb* — ~ / — be'*cause*, and' *then* *Trochee* — / ~ — *e*'vil, *pi*'zza *Anapest* — ~ ~ / — un'der'*stand*, in' the' *east* *Dactyl* — / ~ ~ — *mer*'ri'ly, *hap*'pen'ing	
What is the meter of the line?	*Count the number of feet in a line to determine the meter.* Common meters include: *Monometer:* One foot — *Dimeter:* Two feet *Trimeter:* Three feet — *Tetrameter:* Four feet *Pentameter:* Five feet — *Hexameter:* Six feet *Heptameter:* Seven feet — *Octameter:* Eight feet EXAMPLE: ""Of all our private parts the heart knows best" is five iambic feet; five feet = *pentameter.*	
Is there inconsistent meter (metrical variation) in the poem?	*Sprung verse:* A rhythm that imitates ordinary speech by putting stresses on words that would not be stressed in consistent metrical patterns.	EXAMPLE: ""Whatever is fickle, freckled (who knows how?)"

Writing about Sound, Rhyme, and Rhythm

1. Compare the sounds of the language in Thomas Lynch's "Iambs for the Day of Burial" and Seamus Heaney's "Digging."
2. Consider how sound underscores the subject and themes of Kelly Cherry's "The Raiment We Put On" and Gwendolyn Brooks's "Sadie and Maud"; both use plainspoken language. This is true of the work of Julia Alvarez and Sonia Sanchez as well. Examine how the rhythm of each poem affects (or changes) the reader's understanding of this plainspoken tone.
3. Examine the use of sonic effects like alliteration, assonance, consonance, onomatopoeia, and/or other effects in John Keats's "Bright Star. . . ." and Gerard Manley Hopkins's "Pied Beauty."
4. Look at the poems in this chapter by Marianne Moore, Alexander Pope, and Samuel Taylor Coleridge. Discuss the ways their subject is self-reflexive (a poem about poetry itself).
5. Find a metered poem in this chapter (or another in the book) and identify moments where the poet varies the rhythm. Comment on the purpose and the effect of this variation.

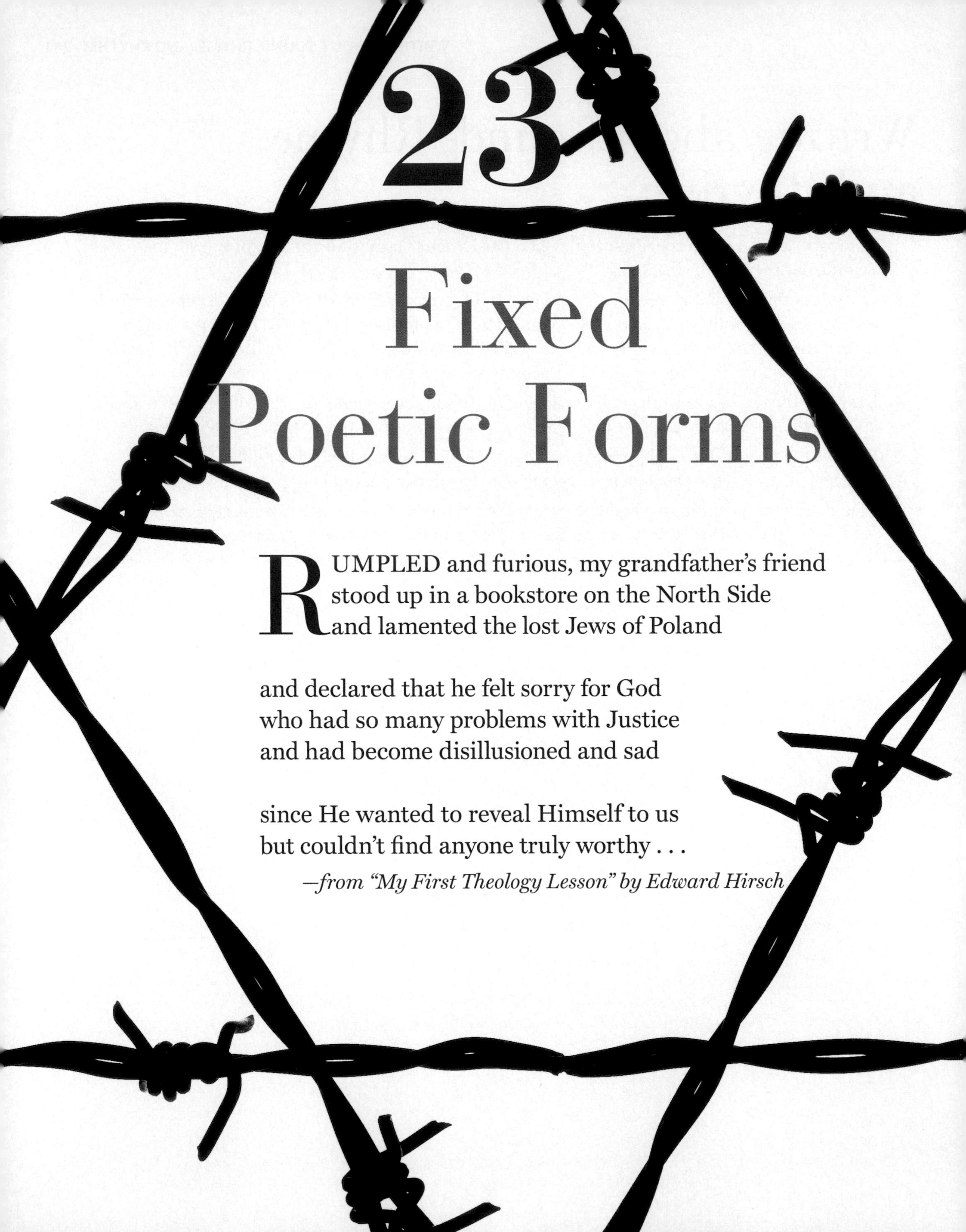

23 Fixed Poetic Forms

RUMPLED and furious, my grandfather's friend
stood up in a bookstore on the North Side
and lamented the lost Jews of Poland

and declared that he felt sorry for God
who had so many problems with Justice
and had become disillusioned and sad

since He wanted to reveal Himself to us
but couldn't find anyone truly worthy . . .

—*from "My First Theology Lesson" by Edward Hirsch*

"The only way you can write a good formal poem is if you can control the form. . . . The form becomes the way in which you can express what you need to say. . . . And if you can use the form as a vehicle in that way, then you can . . . write a good poem. Otherwise, the form will control you."

Conversation with Edward Hirsch, available on video at www.mhhe.com/delbanco1e

COMPOSING in a poetic form that's been a fixture in literature for more than 700 years, Edward Hirsch shapes this episode from his childhood on the North Side of Chicago.

Gathered for conversation in a bookstore, a group of Jewish men (including the poet's grandfather) listen as a colleague angrily laments the apparent retreat of God from the modern world. In the wake of the twentieth century's violence and the savagery of the Holocaust, God has seemingly withdrawn, unable to find "anyone truly worthy" to receive Him on the earth. This is the position maintained by the grandfather's "furious . . . friend." For the poem's speaker, recollecting the argument many years later, this lament constitutes an early lesson on the nature of religion.

Before committing any idea or memory to verse, poets begin, literally, with an infinite number of possibilities for framing their ideas on the page. In this case, Hirsch weds his poetic intention to the shape and form of the sonnet, a fourteen-line poem traditionally associated with argumentation and persuasion. As he points out in the interview, "The thing that seems to identify [a sonnet] as a sonnet is a structural principle. Some kind of argument is set up and resolved or refuted or avoided."

In trying to re-create a passionate discussion about the nature of God, Hirsch uses a form that matches his purposes ideally. "So here I have," he says, "a . . . kind of furious argument, and here I've got to try and tame it. . . . I've got to find a way to formalize it so that someone else can experience what I experienced. And here the sonnet form helped me."

For much of poetry's millennia-old lifetime, poets have been attracted to set patterns in which to arrange their work. Historically these patterns have served different purposes. To begin with, poets echoed formal designs observable by artists in nature. In turn, the patterns followed the music of religious rituals that celebrate natural cycles; these ritual observances were often expressed as poetry. Also, the means for writing language down and reading it aloud haven't previously been as accessible as is today's familiar word-processing technology. Thus, on a more practical level, formal structures served as early mnemonic devices—mental tools for storing and remembering the hundreds of lines a poet might need to recall in a public performance.

The word *poem* comes from an ancient Greek expression meaning "something made"; the different ways poets *construct* their poems are therefore fundamental to our understanding of the genre. As you'll see, the meaning of a poem and the arrangement of its language combine in a kind of marriage of structure and purpose.

Poems take place in our lives . . .

Q&A

Sometimes you want to capture something that's more complicated.

A Conversation on Writing

Edward Hirsch

How to Think about Form: The Sonnet

A form like the sonnet . . . exists in poetry not just because some people like me like to write them. . . . It must be serving some kind of function. . . . Otherwise it would die out. They're just too hard, these forms. They're too hard to write. They take too much thinking. There must be a reason for them; otherwise they'd just collapse. . . . And . . . the thing that seems to identify [a sonnet] as a sonnet is a structural principle. Some kind of argument is set up and resolved or refuted or avoided.

The Poetry in Our Lives

Poems take place in our lives . . . because we're human and we're trying to explain and understand what it means to be alive. They're not there so teachers can get you to memorize what the nature of a poetic form is. They're not there for medicinal purposes, to cure you of something. . . . They're there . . . to help you think about what it means to love someone, and what it means to be dying, and what it means to have someone dying on you, and what it means to dislike someone, and what it means to be enraged . . . complicated and multiple [feelings that] have all kinds of nuances.

Why Can't You Just Say What You Mean?

Why can't you just say what you mean? . . . Well, there are a lot of reasons. . . . Sometimes you want to capture something that's more complicated. You don't just love your father; you love your father, but you also hate him. You love him and you hate him at the same time. . . . If you just tell them, it doesn't mean anything. . . . But in a poem you can capture that combination of feelings.

As Chicago-born (b. 1950) Edward Hirsch says in his interview for this book, "I began writing poetry in high school the way almost everyone begins writing poetry. It was really emotional desperation." Although he has advanced and refined his poetry—as evidenced by awards that include the National Book Critics Circle Award and the American Academy of Arts & Letters Award for Literature—emotion still lies at its heart. Equally able to portray the emptiness of a world without God at its center and the sense of hope we might gain from art, Hirsch's verse often uses formal structures or the shape of elegies, though his more recent poetry departs into free verse. In addition to award-winning collections like *For the Sleepwalkers* (1981) and *Wild Gratitude* (1986), Hirsch has written essays that have appeared in *The New Yorker* and a best-selling book, *How to Read a Poem: And Fall in Love with Poetry* (1999), as well as a regular poetry column for *The Washington Post*. After teaching at the University of Houston for nearly two decades, Hirsch now serves as the president of the J. S. Guggenheim Memorial Foundation.

To watch this entire interview and hear the author read from his work, go to www.mhhe.com/delbanco1e.

RESEARCH ASSIGNMENT Discuss how Hirsch describes choosing the sonnet form for the event he wants to describe. Why did he think it an apt choice?

AS YOU READ Consider how the subject matter suits the sonnet form Hirsch has chosen. Examine how his use of a fixed form helps organize and deliver the anger and dismay the "grandfather's friend" feels about the world.

My First Theology Lesson (2003)

Rumpled and furious, my grandfather's friend
stood up in a bookstore on the North Side
and lamented the lost Jews of Poland

and declared that he felt sorry for God
who had so many problems with Justice
and had become disillusioned and sad

since He wanted to reveal Himself to us
but couldn't find anyone truly worthy
(it was always the wrong time or place

in our deranged and barbaric century)
and so withdrew into His own radiance
and left us a limited mind and body

to contemplate the ghostly absence,
ourselves alone in a divine wilderness.

Writing from Reading

Summarize

1 Describe the situation here. Why does the speaker feel "sorry for God," and is that an expression of blasphemy or faith?

Analyze Craft

2 Discuss the formal features of this sonnet. What kind of rhymes does Hirsch use? Is the poem composed in strict meter?

Analyze Voice

3 What language suggests that the poem is a kind of argument, a laying out of rhetorical positions? What is present, for example, in "the ghostly absence"?

Synthesize Summary and Analysis

4 The title "My First Theology Lesson" suggests there have been others. Would you say the poet now agrees with the position voiced here, or does he seem opposed to it?

Interpret the Poem

5 Why does the poet refer to this episode as a "theology lesson"? If "a divine wilderness" suggests the Garden of Eden, what has happened to that wilderness today?

FORM, FIXED FORM, OPEN FORM

All literature has shape. Like architects designing a building, poets must consider how they wish to arrange and enclose their language, how to best give it foundation and structure. Sometimes these designs follow patterns that have existed for centuries, and sometimes they are wholly new creations. In some cases, a poet knows in advance exactly how a poem's language will be arranged; at other times, he or she makes this decision during the process of composition itself. Regardless of these creative choices on the part of the writer, every poem possesses **form,** an overall shape and structure; if that structure has been long established, its shape will have a name.

"Metrical poetry in English mean[s] balancing unstressed and stressed syllables . . . as a kind of . . . building block. . . . You could make a little waltz form of that rhythm [and] . . . do it forever and ever." Conversation with Robert Hass

Though our contemporary language is extensive in vocabulary and intonation, each word edges up against the next and becomes part of the whole. We use the term **fixed form** (or **closed form**) to describe an arrangement of text that requires a poet to obey set written combinations. These will include line length, meter, stanza structure, and rhyme scheme. Over centuries, poets have invented fixed forms and borrowed forms from other languages to suit their needs. These combinations help poets give shape and order to the emotion or experience they wish to convey. By understanding the patterns and overall trajectory of a fixed form, you'll learn what to expect from the genres (how a sonnet, for example, takes on a different subject from a villanelle) and how poets both innovate and imitate previous traditions.

Keep in mind that poets working in a fixed form don't necessarily feel that they must conform to *every* part of a formal design. Think of it this way: As a child, you may have played a game with your friends and changed the rules a little to make the contest more exciting or interesting. Writers share this affection for flexibility. They may vary their work to better fit their intentions, or purposefully stray from formal expectations in hopes of changing a poem's design.

"We've all heard poems [where] the rhymes seemed just there to fill out the forms. . . . The form is dead in that way. It is not alive. The form is controlling you." Conversation with Edward Hirsch

Open form (or **free verse**) refers to poetry ungoverned by metrical or rhyme schemes. Although it became fashionable in the twentieth century, the tradition of writing without strict adherence to formal constraints dates to the Psalms of the Bible and probably even further back. Using meaning to guide a poem's overall shape, poets writing in open form do not so much abandon form as use formal elements like rhyme, rhythm, and line length to individually embody their intentions. Because the blank page provides a kind of silent canvas on which to inscribe sound in language, poets can use the combination of white space and interesting syntax to create their own form and structure. Look, for example, at the poems in this book by e. e. cummings and you'll get a sense of open form's ability to devise its own particular meaning and order.

Some people think that open form poetry goes so far as to invite the reader into the creative process itself. By personally considering and then connecting a poem's form and substance, readers can participate in the creation of a poem's meaning. We'll talk about open form poetry in more detail in the next chapter; what follows is a close examination of forms that have long been—by contrast—closed and fixed.

THE BUILDING BLOCKS OF FORM

To best understand how poets conceive and construct fixed forms, it's important to recognize some of the components that contribute to a poem's particular shape. Becoming familiar with the architecture of verse is useful—even crucial—in this context. Here are a few examples.

The most basic unit of poetry is, of course, the **line,** a row of words containing phrases and/or sentences. Like the paragraphs in a work of prose, poetry is governed by groupings of lines. A **stanza** is a unit of two or more lines, set off by an extra line space, often sharing the same rhythm and meter. (**Blank verse** is a form of such grouping in which the line, as opposed to the stanza, provides the central organizational arrangement.)

In a fixed form poem, a stanza will contain or develop a consistent idea and demonstrate a regular rhyme scheme (as discussed in more depth later in this chapter). The term originates from an old Italian word meaning "stopping place" or "room";

> "Poetry is like architecture in that we're using the materiality of language, but we're also using silence, interspaciousness, as part of the medium in poetry. So a lot of times it's like the use of space in architecture; we're using silence—that's the real habitation." Conversation with Li-Young Lee

if you think of a poem as a work of architecture, you can imagine a stanza as a kind of chamber of language that contains a thought. In addition to arranging lines into stanzas, poets also arrange stanzas into defined groupings. Though there are no rules about how a poet should or shouldn't create stanzas, tradition has generated a handful of set stanza patterns.

Here are a pair of stanzas in the *abab* rhyme pattern. Such patterns make up a poem's **rhyme scheme** (for more information, see Rhyme in chapter 22). These stanzas come from a poem itself called "Stanzas," written in 1838 by Mary Shelley—best known as the author of *Frankenstein* (1818). Try to picture this "room" as a rectangle or square in which the walls are perfectly proportioned and the lines are parallel:

But gentle sleep shall veil my sight,
And Psyche's lamp shall darkling be,
When, in the visions of the night,
Thou dost renew thy vows to me.

Then come to me in dreams, my love,
I will not ask a dearer bliss;
Come with the starry beams, my love,
And press mine eyelids with thy kiss.

"Think of the stanza—'stanza' comes from the word for a room. So in the poem, each stanza is like a room in a house. And something happens in that room. Often the first stanza is like the entryway of the house. It brings you into the poem, it is [the] foyer. Then you . . . are in the more public rooms, and the poem eventually lets you into its private rooms." Conversation with Carolyn Forché

In its strictest sense, a **couplet** (also discussed in chapter 22) is two lines of poetry forming a unit of meaning. Often couplets are rhymed, strung together without a break, and share the same meter. One such form is the **heroic couplet,** two lines of rhymed iambic pentameter. Organized in small double steps, heroic couplets create a sort of chain that helps a long poem flow forward. Along with John Dryden, Alexander Pope is credited with perfecting heroic couplets in English poetry. Here's a brief excerpt from his "Essay on Man" (1733) featuring this particular fixed form:

Know then thyself, presume not God to scan; *a*
The proper study of mankind is Man. *a*
Placed on this isthmus of a middle state, *b*
A being darkly wise, and rudely great. *b*

Less common than the couplet, a **tercet** is a group of three lines of poetry. Sometimes the term **triplet** is specifically substituted, meaning a three-line stanza in which all the lines rhyme.

Probably the best-known fixed form using tercets is **terza rima,** a fixed form featuring the interlocking rhyme scheme *aba, bcb, cdc, ded,* etc. Invented and then popularized by the medieval Italian poet Dante Alighieri, terza rima is the exclusive fixed form of his epic *Divine Comedy,* which includes the sections "Inferno," "Purgatorio," and "Paradiso."

Echoing Dante, Percy Bysshe Shelley employs terza rima in his "Ode to the West Wind" (1820), which appears in its entirety later in the chapter. Here are the first three tercets:

O wild West Wind, thou breath of Autumn's being, *a*
Thou, from whose unseen presence the leaves dead *b*
Are driven, like ghosts from an enchanter fleeing, *a*

Yellow, and black, and pale, and hectic red, *b*
Pestilence-stricken multitudes: O thou, *c*
Who chariotest to their dark wintry bed *b*

The winged seeds, where they lie cold and low, *c*
Each like a corpse within its grave, until *d*
Thine azure sister of the Spring shall blow . . . *c*

Quatrains, four-line stanzas, are the most popular stanzaic form in English poetry. Easily varied in meter, line length, and rhyme scheme, the quatrain is highly

"I think part of the pleasure of reading poetry is to know the intricacy of its prosody because you see content and form are completely intertwined. They emerge out of each other. Often the content is discovered because of the form." Conversation with Carolyn Forché

adaptable. You'll find dozens of poems in this book employing it, in both fixed and open form poetry. Worth noting here in particular is the traditional **ballad stanza,** a quatrain in which the first and third lines possess four stresses, while the second and fourth have three stresses. You can still find this arrangement, popular as a song form since the Middle Ages, in works that span the past several hundred years, including modern poetry and contemporary music lyrics. For example, such contemporary composers as Bob Dylan often use the traditional ballad stanzaic form. Here is an example of an English ballad, "Lament of the Border Widow," from centuries ago.

My love he built me a bonny bower,
And clad it a' wi' lilye flour,
A brawer bower ye ne'er did see,
Than my true love he built for me.

A variation on ballad meter, **common measure** uses iambic quatrains with the same alternating four-stress/three-stress meter but sometimes with an *abab* rhyme scheme.

THE SONNET

Easily the most recognizable fixed form in poetry, the **sonnet** (*sonneto,* "little sound" or "little song," in Italian) is a fourteen-line poem in a recognizable pattern of rhyme, often metered in iambic pentameter.

The fourteenth-century Italian poet Francesco Petrarch (1304–1374) is credited as the first master of this form, in which he wrote about his unrequited love, Laura.

"I . . . remember . . . writing sonnets. . . . I think it was some point in the mid-1980s . . . you could put fourteen lines on a postcard and mail it for fourteen cents. We thought, well, this was the postal service imitating art. And so we [sent] . . . fourteeners just back and forth and back. . . . As postage rates went up, we started writing more epic poems and putting them in envelopes." Conversation with Thomas Lynch

The form he perfected came to be known as the **Petrarchan** (or **Italian**) **sonnet** and is the most frequently used sonnet form. The Petrarchan sonnet consists of an **octave** (eight lines) and then a **sestet** (six lines).

PETRARCHAN SONNET

Fourteen lines
Two stanzas, eight lines/six lines

abbaabba

cdecde or *cdcdcd*

Since its inception, generations upon generations of poets have tried their hands at the Petrarchan sonnet, often choosing love as a subject matter for the tightly controlled form. A celebrated example by Elizabeth Barrett Browning follows.

Elizabeth Barrett Browning (1806–1861)

England's most respected female poet in her lifetime, Elizabeth Barrett Browning showed by her own example that women could be educated and important artists. Her education took place at home, and she learned Greek by sitting in on her brother's tutoring sessions. This traditionally male knowledge enabled her to engage with literary and scholarly culture in a serious way. Although she was an invalid confined to her father's house, her elopement with Robert Browning when she was thirty-nine restored her health. In addition to *Sonnets from the Portuguese* (1850), a sequence of love sonnets that contains her much-quoted "How do I love thee?", one of her most famous works is *Aurora Leigh* (1857), a "novel-poem," as she described it. The book follows a young woman's rise to become a great poet and champions the current day as a time worth writing about. Barrett Browning's poetry engages with social issues, and true to Victorian fashion, she used her pen to impart moral instruction.

AS YOU READ Look for the shape of the whole—the way a question gets answered in a very different kind of "argument" than is the case with Hirsch.

How do I love thee? Let me count the ways (1850)

How do I love thee? Let me count the ways.
I love thee to the depth and breadth and height
My soul can reach, when feeling out of sight
For the ends of being and ideal grace.
I love thee to the level of every day's
Most quiet need, by sun and candle-light.
I love thee freely, as men strive for right.
I love thee purely, as they turn from praise.
I love thee with the passion put to use
In my old griefs, and with my childhood's faith.
I love thee with a love I seemed to lose
With my lost saints. I love thee with the breath,
Smiles, tears, of all my life; and, if God choose,
I shall but love thee better after death.

Writing from Reading

Summarize

1 Writing to her husband, Robert, how does Elizabeth Barrett Browning record her love?

Analyze Craft

2 Employing the sonnet form, with its careful rhyme scheme and meter, gives the poem a discipline that subtly increases its seriousness. Identify the rhyme scheme and the repetitions here.

Analyze Voice

3 The poem is emphatic in its devotion and phrased with intensity. This is not a whimsical little love lyric. It's a serious dedication, an essential catalog of the speaker's affection. How does the last line emphasize that seriousness, and what does the promise tell you about the speaker?

Synthesize Summary and Analysis

4 What better form to "count" these measures of her love than a sonnet with its carefully measured formal patterns? What aspects of meaning would the poem lose if you translated it into lines of prose?

Interpret the Poem

5 "I love thee with the breath, / Smiles, tears, of all my life." What does this mean, and how is its meaning affected by the line that follows?

Not all sonnets, however, make romantic love their concern, as we saw with this chapter's opening poem, "My First Theology Lesson." Indeed, the form is often used for a speaker to muse analytically on a thought, idea, or sentiment. Traditionally, after a sonnet's first octave introduces its subject, the remaining sestet begins with a turn that

> "I think part of the pleasure of reading poetry is to know the intricacies of its prosody because, you see, content and form are completely intertwined, they emerge out of each other. Often the content is discovered because of the form."
>
> Conversation with Carolyn Forché

proposes some kind of answer or resolution to the subject at hand. Many poets have maintained this essential notion of an argument and counterargument, eight lines of "call" and six of "response." John Keats demonstrates this structure in the following sonnet. Here the poet analyzes the transformative power of reading the Greek poet Homer in a noted translation by George Chapman.

John Keats (1795–1821)

For a brief biography of John Keats, see chapter 18.

AS YOU READ Note the rhyme scheme and repeating sounds (fourteen lines with four rhymes), the thoroughly formal arrangement that looks at something new.

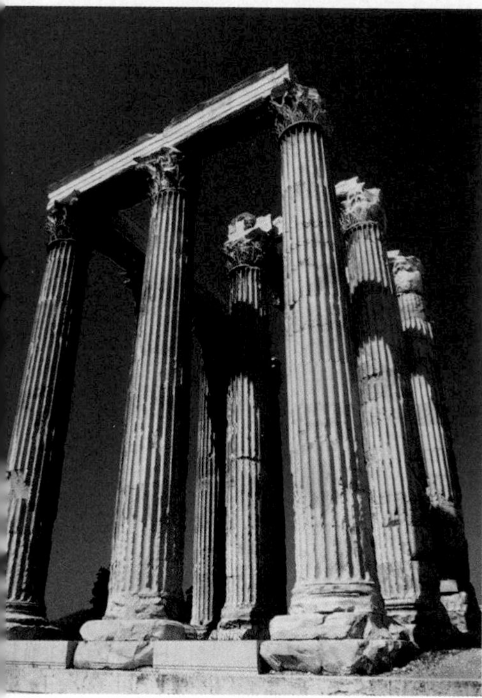

On First Looking into Chapman's Homer (1816)

Much have I traveled in the realms of gold,
 And many goodly states and kingdoms seen;
 Round many western islands have I been
Which bards in fealty to Apollo hold.
Oft of one wide expanse had I been told
 That deep-browed Homer rules as his demesne;
 Yet did I never breathe its pure serene
Till I heard Chapman speak out loud and bold:
Then felt I like some watcher of the skies
 When a new planet swims into his ken;
Or like stout Cortez when with eagle eyes
 He stared at the Pacific—and all his men
Looked at each other with a wild surmise—
 Silent, upon a peak in Darien.

Writing from Reading

Summarize

1 Does this poem present a particular idea or case? What does the speaker want to explain?

Analyze Craft

2 Do you notice a turn in this poem? What language signals the shift from octave to sestet?

Analyze Voice

3 What are the "realms of gold" and what is the "wild surmise"? Is the speaker in the poem talking to himself here or making a point to his readership that they should also read Chapman's Homer? What does he mean by "bards in fealty to Apollo"?

Synthesize Summary and Analysis

4 This sonnet is, as we have seen, a traditional form—but the poem reports on "first" discovery. How does it marry the ancient and new, the "new planet" and old ocean?

Interpret the Poem

5 Though Keats accidentally confuses the explorer Cortez with Balboa (the first European to see the Pacific Ocean from a peak in Panama), why do you think he compares reading Homer to the life of a famous explorer?

Here Keats follows the traditional shape of the Petrarchan or Italian sonnet—but there are others as well. Readers familiar with Shakespeare's love poetry will likely recognize a different fourteen-line pattern from the octet/sestet form. English poets, faced with a language less conducive to natural rhyming than Italian, found a slightly reduced rhyme scheme a bit easier to work with. Known as the **Shakespearean** (also **English** or **Elizabethan**) **sonnet,** this fixed form is composed of three quatrains and a terminal (final) couplet, all in iambic pentameter and rhymed *abab cdcd efef gg.*

SHAKESPEAREAN SONNET

Fourteen lines
Three quatrains and a final couplet

abab cdcd efef gg

You'll see sonnets in this form often, and no small number in this very book (see, for example, Shakespeare's "Shall I compare thee to a summer's day?", chapter 18).

"Now . . . Italian is very, very rich in rhymes. The Russian poet Osip Mandelstam said—writing about Dante—that Italian is like baby talk because everything rhymes with everything else. Rhyming is much more difficult in English. . . . The Shakespearean model . . . rhymes but uses different rhymes in each of the four-line stanzas. . . . It gives you more room to move in." Conversation with Edward Hirsch

Though the Elizabethan sonnet took new liberties with rhyme, many of these "newer" sonnets preserved the Petrarchan sonnet's argumentative eight-line "call" and six-line "response." See how Shakespeare uses the sonnet's tight rhetorical structure first to worry through his troubled emotions and then to find some comfort.

William Shakespeare (1565–1616)

For a brief biography of William Shakespeare, see chapter 33.

AS YOU READ Look for evidence of what Hirsch called an "argument" here. What are the opposing positions, and do they become reconciled?

When, in disgrace with Fortune and men's eyes (1609)

When, in disgrace with Fortune and men's eyes
I all alone beweep my outcast state,
And trouble deaf heaven with my bootless cries,
And look upon myself and curse my fate,
Wishing me like to one more rich in hope,
Featured like him, like him with friends possessed,
Desiring this man's art, and that man's scope,
With what I most enjoy contented least,
Yet in these thoughts myself almost despising,
Haply I think on thee, and then my state,
Like to the lark at break of day arising
From sullen earth, sings hymns at heaven's gate;
For thy sweet love remembered such wealth brings
That then I scorn to change my state with kings.

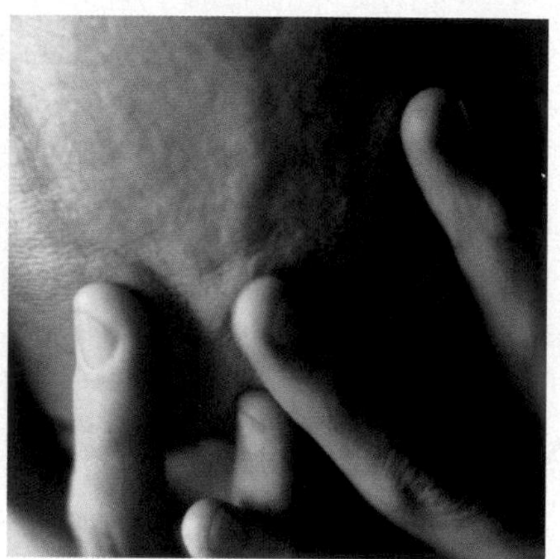

Writing from Reading

Summarize

1 This poem deals with the opposition between public and private life, the outer trappings of success and the inner sense of satisfaction or reward. If the speaker feels "outcast" and "in disgrace," why should he "scorn to change my state with kings"?

Analyze Craft

2 Discuss how this poem is structured. Where do you detect changes in thought or tone?

3 How many sections do you perceive in the poem? How does the rhyme scheme signal section breaks?

Analyze Voice

4 Notice the implicit pun between "haply"—which means "by accident"—and "happily." Look also at the distinction between "deaf heaven" and "at heaven's gate." How do we get from the one to the other, and how does the voice manage both?

Synthesize Summary and Analysis

5 If this poem contained no metrical pattern or rhyme scheme, do you think it would illustrate its ideas as effectively? Why or why not?

Interpret the Poem

6 Less directly a love poem than Elizabeth Barrett Browning's, this sonnet is nonetheless devoted to "thy sweet love remembered." How does the final couplet, with its emphatic *gg* rhyme, help make that point?

Fairly or unfairly, the sonnet is nowadays viewed as an antique form. The poet Robert Bly has been quoted as saying that when he edited a literary magazine in the 1960s, "We sent rejection slips saying things like, 'The sonnet is the place where old professors go to die,' and then [writers would] write us insulting letters. . . ." Nevertheless, sonnet practitioners have continued to work, and brilliantly, within the poem's boundaries. Sometimes contemporary writers follow only very loosely the formal obligations of the sonnet, composing fourteen lines and rhyming them freely and in no regular pattern. Here's one witty contemporary example that takes four versions of the sonnet form (with the third one only approximating it) and strings them together as a story or "saga" in the conversational mode.

> "If you come away from school, and you know what a sonnet is, but you never want to read one again, then your education has failed you." Conversation with Edward Hirsch

Maxine Kumin (b. 1925)

Maxine Kumin was born in Philadelphia and educated at Radcliffe. Her career as a poet has spanned more than forty-five years, from her first collection *Halfway* (1961) to her recent *Still to Mow* (2007), and she has garnered honors including the Pulitzer Prize and the position of Poet Laureate in the state of New Hampshire. Her poetry leans toward formal verse, but she is often read and written of in conjunction with confessional poets such as Sylvia Plath and Anne Sexton. Kumin and Sexton shared a close friendship and were, at times, collaborators. A fondness for and knowledge of the rural life—Kumin gardens and raises horses in New Hampshire—has characterized her memoirs and essays as well.

AS YOU READ **Notice the formality of the opening line in "1. Lifestyle"—"begetters" is no doubt a conscious echo of Shakespeare's language (he dedicated his collection of sonnets to their "onlie begetter")—and the slang use of "hereabouts" in line 2.**

Saga (1991)

I. Lifestyle

Invincible begetters, assorted Scutzes
have always lived hereabouts in the woods
trapping beaver or fox, poaching enough
deer to get by on. Winters, they barricade
their groundsills with spoiled hay, which can ignite
from a careless cigarette or chimney spark.
In the fifties, one family barely got out
when the place lit up like the Fair midway at dark.

The singular name of Scutz, it is thought, derives
from *skuft,* Middle Dutch for the nape one is strung up by.
Hangmen or hanged, they led the same snug lives
in an Old World loft adjoining the pigsty
as now, three generations tucked in two
rooms with color tv, in the New.

II. Leisure

The seldom-traveled dirt road by their door
is where, good days, the Scutzes take their ease.
It serves as living room, garage, *pissoir*
as well as barnyard. Hens scratch and rabbits doze
under cars jacked up on stumps of trees.
Someone produces a dozen bottles of beer.
Someone tacks a target to a tire
across the road and hoists it seductively
human-high. The Scutzes love to shoot.
Later, they line the empty bottles up.

The music of glassbreak gladdens them. The brute
sound of a bullet widening a rip
in rubber, the rifle kick, the powder smell
pure bliss. Deadeyes, the Scutzes lightly kill.

III. Shelter

Old doors slanted over packing crates
shelter the Scutzes' several frantic dogs
pinioned on six-foot chains they haven't been
loosed from since January of '91
when someone on skis crept up in snow fog
and undid all of their catches in the night.
Each of the Scutzes' dogs has a dish or plate
to eat from, usually overturned in the dirt.
What do they do for water? Pray for rain.
What do they do for warmth? Remember when
they lay in the litter together, a sweet
jumble of laundry, spotted and stained.

O we are smug in the face of the Scutzes, we
who stroll past their domain, its aromas of ripe decay,
its casual discards mottled with smut and pee.
What do we neighbors do? Look the other way.

IV. Self-fulfilled Prophecy

If Lonnie Scutz comes back, he's guaranteed
free room and board in the State's crowbar hotel.
His girlfriend Grace, a toddler at her heels
and in her arms a grubby ten-month jewel,
looks to be pregnant again, but not his seed.
It's rumored this one was sired by his dad.

Towheads with skyblue eyes, they'll go to school
now and then, struggle to learn to read
and write, forget to carry when they add,
be mocked, kept back or made to play the fool
and soon enough drop out. Their nimble code,
hit first or get hit, supplants the Golden Rule.

It all works out the way we knew it would.
They'll come to no good end, the Scutzes' kids.

Writing from Reading

Summarize

1 Who's speaking here, and to whom; why does the speaker say "we"? What is the story told?

Analyze Craft

2 Diagram the various versions of the sonnet form in these sections. Why, do you think, is the third such sonnet ("Shelter"), as a form, inexact?

Analyze Voice

3 In terms we've used before—high diction, middle diction—discuss the narrative tone and the narrator's "speaking" voice.

Synthesize Summary and Analysis

4 Consider William Faulkner's "A Rose for Emily" (chapter 12) and discuss the way the narrator there also employs a collective townsperson's voice. What's different; what's the same?

5 "What do we neighbors do? Look the other way." How do you reconcile this with the close attention paid by the poet to the story of the Scutzes, and does the poet endorse "non-intervention" or wish that behavior might change?

Interpret the Poem

6 This poem about the rural poor refers to Middle Dutch, the Old World, the Golden Rule and uses French words such as *pissoir* while describing a family whose code is *"hit first or get hit."* How does the series of sonnets help fuse the old and the new?

THE SONNET'S WORLD TOUR

When Francesco Petrarch published his *Canzoniere* (Song-book) in the fourteenth century in Italy, he could not have imagined the immense impact his collection would have on future readers of world literature. A sequence of 366 poems including 317 sonnets, the volume was widely successful in its own time, and it directly influenced the poetry, within his own lifetime, of his noted poet-contemporaries Boccacio and Geoffrey Chaucer. By the mid-sixteenth century, Petrarch's sonnets had reached scholars throughout western Europe, and the form had already become a fixture of poetic genres in a plentiful number of European languages. In England in particular during this time, Sir Thomas Wyatt (1503–1542) imported the Italian sonnet to English poetry and helped introduce its now trademark closing couplet. Henry Howard, the Earl of Surrey (1517–1547), is credited with first employing the English rhyme scheme of *abab cdcd efef gg*. It's not too much to say that these two men, taking their inspiration from Petrarch, helped inaugurate modern English poetry. From Edmund Spenser and Shakespeare, who each added his own characteristic flourishes to the sonnet form, to Keats and Elizabeth Barrett Browning, to W. B. Yeats and T. S. Eliot, to living poets who are even at this moment trying their hand at the form in any number of countries, the sonnet's hold on the Western poetic imagination is extraordinary and unmatched.

THE VILLANELLE

The sonnet is just one of the dozens of fixed forms that came "across channel" to England from a foreign language. Another is the **villanelle,** from France, a much more rigorous formal exercise than the sonnet, consisting of nineteen lines and only two rhymes, all in iambic pentameter.

The villanelle, with its Italian root word *villano* meaning "peasant," is a "rural" or "rustic" form with a full refrain or repetition of the first and third lines in song-like fashion. Though its word origin is in Italy, French troubadours are responsible for the form of villanelle we recognize today. In medieval Europe, wandering poets or troubadours plied their trade by demonstrating technical proficiency; their subject matter was limited and their dexterity limitless—as these forms suggest.

The technical arrangement of the villanelle requires five three-line stanzas, or tercets, and a final quatrain. The first and third lines of the first tercet recur alternately in the following stanzas as a refrain and form a final couplet. Why this nineteen-line poem proved popular and an eighteen- or twenty-line version of the same variety has no name is one of the mysteries of tradition, but it has something to do with the power of repetition: the repeated lines add up to more than mere parts of the whole. One of the best-known villanelles in English comes from the twentieth-century Welsh poet Dylan Thomas.

VILLANELLE

Nineteen lines
Five tercets/final quatrain

aba aba aba aba aba abab

The first and third lines of the tercets recur (the poem's opening line is the final line of the second and fourth stanzas, and the last line of the first stanza is the final line of the third and fifth stanzas) and form a final couplet.

Dylan Thomas (1914–1953)

Born in Wales, Dylan Thomas decided not to go to college so that he could focus immediately on writing. His *18 Poems* (1934), published when he was twenty, brought him instant critical acclaim for the bold diction and imagery contained in formal structures. In addition to other collections of poetry like *Deaths and Entrances* (1946) and *In Country Sleep* (1951), Thomas also wrote prose—as in his autobiographical sketches *Portrait of the Artist As a Young Dog* (1940)—and plays, as in his successful radio script *Under Milk Wood* (1954). Most of his poetry takes for its theme the unity of the life-and-death cycle, capturing the paradox of living because of death and dying because of life. Although he married in his early twenties and had three children, Thomas lived a bohemian lifestyle, giving boisterous readings in the United States and drinking heavily toward the end of his life. He died suddenly, at thirty-nine, from the effects of alcoholism.

AS YOU READ Almost an incantation, this poem gains strength from its lack of variety; listen for the "chorus" and repeated sounds and lines as you read this poem aloud.

Do not go gentle into that good night (1952)

Do not go gentle into that good night,
Old age should burn and rave at close of day;
Rage, rage against the dying of the light.

Though wise men at their end know dark is right,
Because their words had forked no lightning they
Do not go gentle into that good night.

Good men, the last wave by, crying how bright
Their frail deeds might have danced in a green bay,
Rage, rage against the dying of the light.

Wild men who caught and sang the sun in flight,
And learn, too late, they grieved it on its way,
Do not go gentle into that good night.

Grave men, near death, who see with blinding sight
Blind eyes could blaze like meteors and be gay,
Rage, rage against the dying of the light.

And you, my father, there on the sad height,
Curse, bless me now with your fierce tears, I pray.
Do not go gentle into that good night.
Rage, rage against the dying of the light.

Writing from Reading

Summarize

1 Who's speaking, and to whom? What does "good night" here signify, or "the dying of the light"?

Analyze Craft

2 This poem, a desperate plea from the speaker to his declining father to "rage against" death, becomes especially dramatic and poignant in its choral lines. What effect do the repetitions create?

Analyze Voice

3 As the American poet Robert Hass has said of the form's repetition, "The effect is mesmerizing; it makes of the music of the poem a kind of haunted waltz." Why is this form appropriate for this speaker and his audience?

Synthesize Summary and Analysis

4 Notice that it takes until the final stanza for the poet to address his father directly—making a particular instance out of the general case. How does this heighten the tone and deepen the emotion expressed here?

Interpret the Poem

5 The mode of this syntax is imperative, a series of commands. Yet it is also a kind of prayer ("Curse, bless me now with your fierce tears, I pray."). What does that juxtaposition—a blessing, a curse—signify?

Here's another of the best-known villanelles in the language—though a little less formally strict than Thomas's. As Elizabeth Bishop's poem proceeds, the repetition causes the lines to sound as though they're actually trying, deliberately, to convince the speaker (and reader) of a difficult premise. As the poet-critic J. D. McClatchy writes of the final quatrain: "The whole stanza is in danger of breaking apart, and breaking down. In this last line the poet's voice literally cracks. The villanelle—that strictest and most intractable of verse forms—can barely control the grief, yet helps the poet keep her balance."

Elizabeth Bishop (1911–1979)

For a brief biography of Elizabeth Bishop, see chapter 18.

AS YOU READ Note how the repeated refrains of the poem change slightly, both in form and in context. How do the emotions generated by loss and losing enlarge in repetition?

One Art (1976)

The art of losing isn't hard to master;
so many things seem filled with the intent
to be lost that their loss is no disaster.

Lose something everyday. Accept the fluster
of lost door keys, the hour badly spent.
The art of losing isn't hard to master.

Then practice losing further, losing faster:
places, and names, and where it was you meant
to travel. None of these will bring disaster.

I lost my mother's watch. And look! my last, or
next-to-last, of three loved houses went.
The art of losing isn't hard to master.

I lost two cities, lovely ones. And, vaster,
some realms I owned, two rivers, a continent.
I miss them, but it wasn't a disaster.

—Even losing you (the joking voice, a gesture
I love) I shan't have lied. It's evident
the art of losing's not too hard to master
though it may look like (*Write* it!) like disaster.

Writing from Reading

Summarize

1 Since it's so often repeated, the opening line (or "topic sentence") of a villanelle must be worth hearing more than once. What do you think the poet means by "the art of losing," and which examples does she use?

Analyze Craft

2 Determine the poem's rhyme scheme. Where do you notice Bishop using slant rhymes?

Analyze Voice

3 What does J. D. McClatchy mean when he says the poet's voice "cracks" in the final stanza? How does the final stanza seem to "break down"?

Synthesize Summary and Analysis

4 Does the significance of the repeated lines seem to change as the poem reflects on increasingly serious losses? Why or why not?

5 How would you compare this to Keats's "On First Looking into Chapman's Homer"?

Interpret the Poem

6 What do you think the speaker means by losing "two cities"? And "some realms I owned"? Does this remind you of Keats' "On First Looking into Chapman's Homer"?

THE SESTINA

Another form that derives from the French is the sestina. An even more elaborately constructed poem than the villanelle, a **sestina** consists of six stanzas composed of six lines each. Featuring word repetition rather than rhyme, the final word of each line in the first stanza is repeated in a different order in the following five stanzas.

SESTINA

Six stanzas, six lines each

The final word of each line in the first stanza is repeated in a different order in the following five stanzas.

The concluding stanza, the envoi ("farewell"), summarizes the main idea.

Again it's difficult to know why this *particular* technical form has come down through the centuries, but the challenge of the sestina continues to engage modern poets; Ezra Pound, T. S. Eliot, and other twentieth-century poets have tried it on for size. As another poem by Elizabeth Bishop demonstrates, the sestina concludes with a three-line **envoi,** or "farewell." The final words of the first stanza are repeated in a different order in the second stanza, and the third, and so on, until the envoi (in which the same six words appear) has gathered force and meaning.

AS YOU READ Put yourself in the scene, in the house, in the season, as the poet does as she imagines this moment out of childhood.

Sestina (1956)

September rain falls on the house.
In the failing light, the old grandmother
sits in the kitchen with the child
beside the Little Marvel Stove,
reading the jokes from the almanac,
laughing and talking to hide her tears.

She thinks that her equinoctial tears
and the rain that beats on the roof of the house
were both foretold by the almanac,
but only known to a grandmother.
The iron kettle sings on the stove.
She cuts some bread and says to the child,

It's time for tea now; but the child
is watching the teakettle's small hard tears
dance like mad on the hot black stove,
the way the rain must dance on the house.
Tidying up, the old grandmother
hangs up the clever almanac

on its string. Birdlike, the almanac
hovers half open above the child,
hovers above the old grandmother
and her teacup full of dark brown tears.
She shivers and says she thinks the house
feels chilly, and puts more wood in the stove.

It was to be, says the Marvel Stove.
I know what I know, says the almanac.
With crayons the child draws a rigid house
and a winding pathway. Then the child
puts in a man with buttons like tears
and shows it proudly to the grandmother.

But secretly, while the grandmother
busies herself about the stove,
the little moons fall down like tears
from between the pages of the almanac
into the flower bed the child
has carefully placed in the front of the house.

Time to plant tears, says the almanac.
The grandmother sings to the marvelous stove
and the child draws another inscrutable house.

Writing from Reading

Summarize

1 Write down the story the poem tells.

Analyze Craft

2 The poem, as many do, has a turn, this one coming at the beginning of the sixth stanza, announced by the word *but*. What seems different here from the first five stanzas?

Analyze Voice

3 How would you describe the poet's tone? Be specific about the word *tears*.

Synthesize Summary and Analysis

4 How does the rhyme scheme help the story unfold? How might the story seem different in a different rhyme scheme?

Interpret the Poem

5 How does the repetition enforce or not enforce the sense of the timelessness of childhood? Is the sestina form particularly suited for this kind of mood, or is it merely a variation on ways to create the mood?

THE PANTOUM

Another formal arrangement in verse—which comes to our language also from the French, by way of Malaysia—is the pantoum. A kind of variation on the villanelle, its lines are grouped into quatrains, and there can be as many or as few of them as the poet chooses. Its music, however, is even more demanding than that of the sestina or the villanelle. (The composer Maurice Ravel called the second movement of his Piano Trio in A minor a "Pantoum." It's likely not an accident that the poet Donald Justice, whose pantoum follows, was trained as a composer and first hoped to be a musician.) The "fixed form" pantoum consists of quatrains with a rhyme scheme of *abab,* and it says everything twice; the lines of the poem may vary in length. For all quatrains except the first, the first line of the current quatrain repeats the second line of the preceding quatrain; the third line of the current stanza repeats the fourth of the preceding quatrain—though in the following pantoum the rhyme scheme has been abandoned and the repetition is inexact.

PANTOUM

Quatrains

Rhyme scheme for each quatrain: *abab*

The first line repeats the second line of the preceding quatrain, except for the first quatrain.
The third line repeats the final line of the preceding quatrain.
The second line of the final quatrain repeats the third line of the first quatrain.
The last line repeats the first line of the first quatrain.

Donald Justice (1925–2004)

A native of Miami, Florida, Donald Justice had an illustrious career as both poet and professor. Among his more than ten books of verse—some of which combine poetry and prose—is the Pulitzer Prize–winning *Selected Poems* (1979). Justice's poetry reflects the sadness and isolation of twentieth-century life, first in formal verse early in his career, then in more experimental verse mid-career, and finally in a return to formal verse. He taught at a number of American universities, both public and private, including the University of Missouri, Syracuse, the University of California, Princeton, the University of Virginia, and the University of Iowa. In 2003, he was offered the post of Poet Laureate but declined because of his failing health.

AS YOU READ Consider how "the usual sorrows" get changed by repetition, and how the poem's slow progression differs from the repetitions of a villanelle.

Pantoum of the Great Depression (1994)

Our lives avoided tragedy
Simply by going on and on,
Without end and with little apparent meaning.
Oh, there were storms and small catastrophes.

Simply by going on and on
We managed. No need for the heroic.
Oh, there were storms and small catastrophes.
I don't remember all the particulars.

We managed. No need for the heroic.
There were the usual celebrations, the usual sorrows.
I don't remember all the particulars.
Across the fence, the neighbors were our chorus.

There were the usual celebrations, the usual sorrows
Thank God no one said anything in verse.
The neighbors were our only chorus,
And if we suffered we kept quiet about it.

At no time did anyone say anything in verse.
It was the ordinary pities and fears consumed us,
And if we suffered we kept quiet about it.
No audience would ever know our story.

It was the ordinary pities and fears consumed us.
We gathered on porches; the moon rose; we were poor.
What audience would ever know our story?
Beyond our windows shone the actual world.

We gathered on porches; the moon rose; we were poor.
And time went by, drawn by slow horses.
Somewhere beyond our windows shone the world;
But the Great Depression had entered our souls like fog.

And time went by, drawn by slow horses.
We did not ourselves know what the end was.
The Great Depression had entered our souls like fog.
We had our flaws, perhaps a few private virtues.

But we did not ourselves know what the end was.
People like us simply go on.
We have our flaws, perhaps a few private virtues,
But it is by blind chance only that we escape tragedy.

And there is no plot in that; it is devoid of poetry

Writing from Reading

Summarize

1 How far distant is this memory; is it personal, and how can you tell? Track the usage of "I" and "we."

Analyze Craft

2 Make a diagram of the formal elements here, the repeated rhymes and lines.

Analyze Voice

3 When the poet writes "At no time did anyone say anything in verse," how far do you think his tongue is in his cheek? When he writes "No audience would ever know our story," how does he prove that untrue?

Synthesize Summary and Analysis

4 This is, in part, a poem about the making of poetry. But when Justice writes "there is no plot in that," he seems to be also referring to prose. How close does the poem come to being a story?

Interpret the Poem

5 "The Great Depression" refers to a specific moment in our nation's history, but it can signify, as well, a mood of melancholy and inertia. How do the public and private meanings of the phrase connect?

Erica Funkhouser (b. 1949)

Erica Funkhouser teaches writing at the Massachusetts Institute of Technology. She has published five collections of poetry: *Earthly* (2008), *The Actual World* (1997), *Pursuit* (2002), *Sure Shot and Other Poems* (1992), and *Natural Affinities* (1983). Her poems are inspired by everyday objects and nature and have appeared in prestigious venues including *The Paris Review, Ploughshares, The Atlantic Monthly,* and *The New Yorker.* She also has an interest in the Lewis and Clark Expedition and was a contributor to the PBS *Lewis and Clark* series, directed by Ken Burns. She lives in Essex, Massachusetts.

AS YOU READ If Donald Justice's pantoum is about "depression," look for the tone and emotional register in this exact example of the fixed form.

First Pantoum of Summer (2003)

One sleep depletes, another fills the well.
Our night's companion shapes the coming day.
My bed, half empty, rattled like a cell
when you took off for town. I couldn't stay.

Our night's companion shapes the coming day,
and where we make our bed can make us weep.
When you took off for town, I couldn't stay.
I fell into these words—a second sleep.

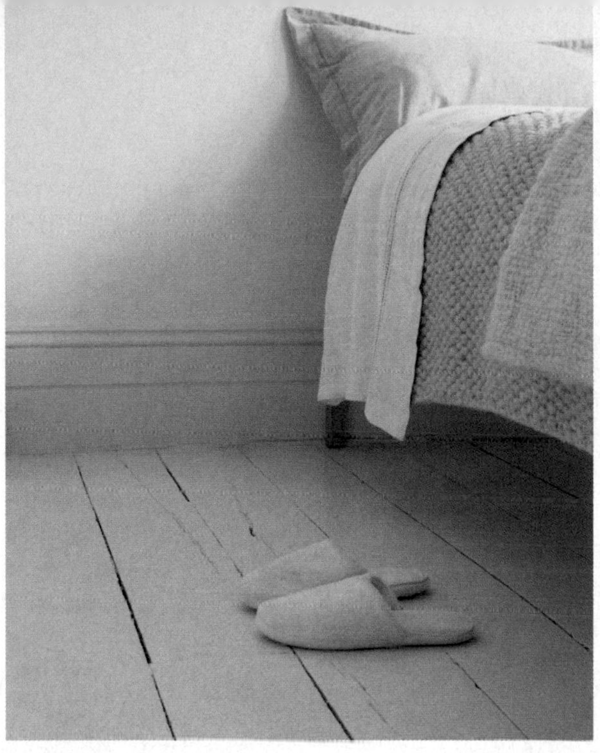

Where we make our bed can make us weep
or leave us clean and clear and ravenous.
I fell into these words—a second sleep,
a summer sleep, the windows generous.

You left me clean and clear and ravenous.
I drank new air, a warm and welcome stream
of summer sleep, the windows generous.
Here or away, you lead me out of dream.

I drank new air, a warm and welcome stream.
My bed, half empty, rattled like a cell.
Here or away, you lead me out of dream.
One sleep depletes, another fills the well.

Writing from Reading

Summarize

1 If this is a love poem, to whom is it addressed and why? Why does the speaker focus on a particular season?

Analyze Craft

2 How does the speaker create what she calls a "second sleep"? And if this is the "first pantoum of summer," can you find evidence there will be a second or a third?

Analyze Voice

3 Describe the speaker's tone. Is it affectionate, disappointed, or angry? Or a mixture of emotions?

Synthesize Summary and Analysis

4 Does the poet describe—or lament the variations of sleep when with a loved one? Can you make a sketch of the absent lover based on details in the poem?

Interpret the Poem

5 How do repetition and variation bring the deep expression of the poet's situation to our attention?

HAIKU

Poets since Homer have worked in several other shorter poetic forms that demand attention. One of these is the distinctive Eastern variety of short poem, the **haiku,** put forward first by Japanese poets in the sixteenth century. The original verse form calls for seventeen syllables and three lines: five/seven/five. In part because of its succinctness and brevity, the form presents a single idea, image, or feeling: Its focus is like that of a photographic snapshot. In chapter 20, Jane Hirshfield discussed the influence of haiku on her work, and there we also saw Ezra Pound's Imagist description of passengers in the Paris metro; his definition of the image as the connection of idea and emotion in an instant of time is wholly captured here. Translators who put these poems into English try to approximate the original verse faithfully, which sometimes means breaking out of the original five/seven/five metrical pattern.

HAIKU

Translators try to approximate the Japanese seventeen syllables and three-line (five/seven/five) structure.

You'll see in these poems by three of Japan's most revered haiku masters (translated by Robert Hass, another modern-day poet who has been inspired by haiku) an elegant attention to quiet, meditative, sometimes humorous moments—it's as if they're translating little bits of time itself onto the page.

AS YOU READ Try reading the three haikus one after another, for the fleeting pleasure and lingering emotion that each one generates.

Matsuo Bashō (1644–1694)

For a brief biography of Matsuo Bashō, see chapter 20.

Deep autumn

(c. 1600)

Deep autumn—
my neighbor,
how does he live, I wonder?

—translated by Robert Hass

Yosa Buson (1716–1784)

Yosa Buson was born near modern-day Osaka, Japan. He modeled his poetry as well as his life after those of the great haiku master Matsuo Bashō; like Bashō, he spent a period traveling in northern Japan. Buson himself became a master poet known for his ability to blend older, elegant forms with pieces of contemporary life. Buson eventually settled in Kyoto and perfected his artistry not just in poetry but in painting, calligraphy, and in the practice of the meditative tea ceremony as well.

Tethered horse (c. 1700)

Tethered horse;
snow
in both stirrups.

—translated by Robert Hass

Kobayashi Issa (1763–1828)

For a brief biography of Issa, see chapter 20.

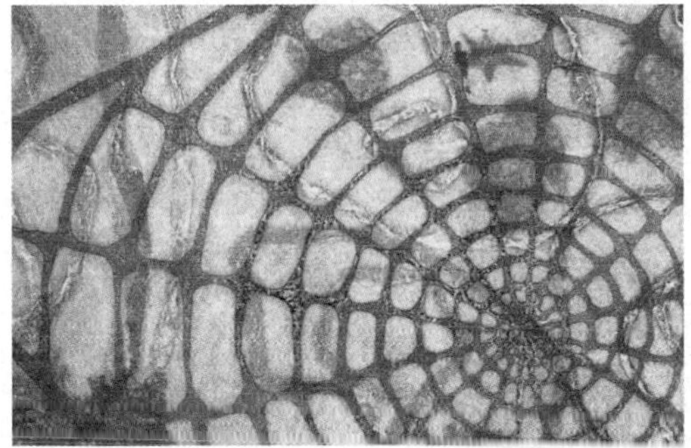

Don't worry, spiders (c. 1800)

Don't worry, spiders,
I keep house
casually.

—translated by Robert Hass

Writing from Reading

Summarize

1 How do each of these haiku touch on the cycles of the seasons?

Analyze Craft

2 These poems have been "Englished" and do not have the precise number of syllables contained in the original. Does that make a difference, and, if not, why not?

Analyze Voice

3 In two of these three haiku, the first-person pronoun has been used. How personal or impersonal is "I"?

4 The form tends to make the poet speak about the smallest details of everyday life. What kind of tone does that create?

Synthesize Summary and Analysis

5 How do the separate lines affect your perception of these images?

How would your perception differ if all three lines of a haiku were strung together on one line?

Interpret the Poem

6 Imagine the moments in which each of these haiku were triggered. How do you envision what's going on? Where are the poets in relation to what they're observing? Which of these moments of observation do you relate to?

EPIGRAM

Epigrams are very short, often satirical poems on a single subject. Their primary function, besides deploying wit, is to make a pointed commentary of some kind. Shakespeare said that brevity is the soul of wit, and Samuel Taylor Coleridge puts both soul and wit into play.

AS YOU READ Poetry, as we have seen, is a condensed form and an intensive use of language; the epigram is an extreme example of poetic form since it reduces matters to their very briefest expression. Note the way, however, that these condensed meanings expand and enlarge with each rereading in these five epigrams.

Samuel Taylor Coleridge (1772–1834)

For a brief biography of Samuel Taylor Coleridge, see chapter 22.

What Is an Epigram? (1802)

What is an epigram? A dwarfish whole;
Its body brevity, and wit its soul.

Langston Hughes (1902–1967)

For a brief biography of Langston Hughes, see the Case Study on Langston Hughes and His Contemporaries, chapter 26.

Prayer (1955)

Oh, God of dust and rainbows, help us see
That without dust the rainbow would not be.

J. V. Cunningham (1911–1985)

James Vincent Cunningham was born in Maryland but considered Montana his home state, as his family moved there when he was three years old. Cunningham is most identified with the epigram, and although his short, witty poems were well appreciated by his colleagues, he never gained much recognition in his lifetime. A successful high school student, Cunningham was unable to attend college following his graduation because his father's death made it necessary for him to get a job. When he lost that job because of the stock market crash in 1929, Cunningham became a poor wanderer, working odd jobs until poet Yvor Winters invited him to come to Stanford University, where Winters taught. Cunningham earned his bachelor's degree and doctorate at Stanford, which enabled him to launch a career in the academy. Although he taught at several universities, he spent the majority of his time at Brandeis University.

Two Epigrams (1942)

53
On a cold night I came through the cold rain
And false snow to the wind shrill on your pane
With no hope and no anger and no fear.
Who are you? and with whom do you sleep here?

76
Good Fortune, when I hailed her recently,
Passed by me with the intimacy of shame
As one that in the dark had handled me
And could no longer recollect my name.

A. R. Ammons (1926–2001)

For a brief biography of A. R. Ammons, see chapter 21.

Small Song (1970)

The reeds give
way to the

wind and give
the wind away.

Writing from Reading

Summarize

1 What actually occurs in each of the preceding epigrams?

Analyze Craft

2 Wit would seem to be a crucial component of these poems, as Coleridge suggests. But there is melancholy here as well. How would you describe the tone of "Small Songs" for example? What about its meaning is suggested by its shape?

Analyze Voice

3 How does the statement made by an epigram, which makes a single point and not a counterargument, differ from the statement made by a sonnet?

Synthesize Summary and Analysis

4 Paraphrase these epigrams and compare the points they make. What makes the form appropriate for this type of statement?

Interpret the Poems

5 If the haiku is an Eastern form and the epigram Western, what similarities do you see in both forms and what seems different? How do these forms effect a different way of seeing everyday life?

LIMERICK

Unlike the other fixed forms we've examined, the **limerick** originates in the English language. It's a light, often humorous verse form consisting of five anapestic (two short syllables followed by one long one) lines, with a rhyme scheme of *aabba*. The first, second, and fifth lines consist of three feet, while the third and fourth lines consist of two feet.

Though the limerick is considered light and unserious (sometimes downright vulgar), in the hands of a skillful poet it can be quite an impressive display of technique.

AS YOU READ Read these three poems aloud, and with emphasis; see how they depend on rhyme.

Edward Lear (1812–1888)

Edward Lear was born in 1812 outside of London, the twentieth child of stockbroker Jeremiah Lear and his wife Ann. Following poor investments in the market, the Lears fell on hard times, and Edward's upbringing was entrusted to his sister Ann, twenty-one years his senior. At age six, Edward became prone to epileptic seizures, a condition that at the time was often associated with demonic possession. Nevertheless, despite his poor health, Lear began to sell poetry and illustrations at age fifteen; and by age nineteen he earned his living illustrating birds for the scientific book *Illustrations of the Family of Psittacidae, or Parrots* (1830). His first book of poetry, *A Book of Nonsense,* was published in 1846 and contributed greatly to the popularity of the limerick form. He published *The History of the Seven Families of the Lake Pipple-Popple* in 1865, and his most famous work, *The Owl and the Pussycat,* in 1867. Lear spent most of his life traveling abroad in the Mediterranean, and he published several more volumes of illustrated poetry before his death in San Remo, Italy, in 1888.

There was an Old Man with a gong (1846)

There was an Old Man with a gong,
Who bumped at it all the day long;
But they called out, "Oh, law!
you're a horrid old bore!"
So they smashed that Old Man with a gong.

Most limericks, whether proper or vulgar, include a place-name at poem's start. Their lilting singsong rhyme pattern can also make them appropriate for children's rhymes, as in the following.

J. D. Landis (b. 1942)

James David Landis was born in Springfield, Massachusetts, attended Yale University, and spent much of his career as a publishing executive in New York. The author of such novels as *Longing* (2000) and *Artist of the Beautiful* (2005), he has written many books for young adults, such as *The Sisters Impossible* (1979), *Daddy's Girl* (1984), and *The Band Never Dances* (1989). His collection of poems for children, *Cars on Mars, and 49 Other Poems for Kids on Earth,* appeared in 2008.

Starvation Diet (2008)

There was once a fat man from Madrid
Who was told to eat nothing but squid.
He chewed and he chewed.
He chewed and he chewed.
But of squid he could never get rid.

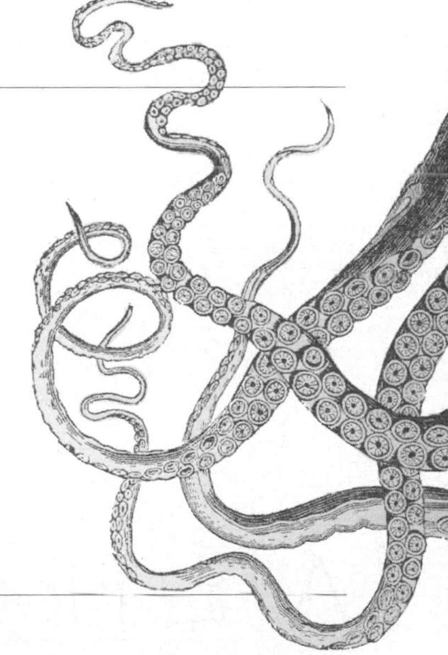

Laurence Perrine (b. 1915)

Laurence Perrine has published numerous collections of poetry, among them *Sound and Nonsense: Original Limericks* (1994), as well as several influential textbooks, including the poetry anthology *Sound and Sense.* With a B.A. from Oberlin College and a Ph.D. from Yale, Perrine began his teaching career in 1946 at Southern Methodist University, where he taught until his retirement in 1980. Perrine also served as president of the National Council of Teachers of English.

The limerick's never averse (1982)

The limerick's never averse
To expressing itself in a terse
Economical style,
And yet, all the while,
The limerick's *always* a verse.

Writing from Reading

Summarize

1 What is constant in this form, and what—if anything—varies?

Analyze Craft

2 Think of a limerick as a puzzle to be solved—five lines that are "*always* a verse." How does the poet move from "never" to "always," and how does the rhyme scheme here support the poet's point?

Analyze Voice

3 If epigrams depend on wit, a limerick can't exist without it—or, at least, without good (and sometimes bawdy) humor. Based on the examples in this chapter, what distinction do you draw between humor and wit?

Synthesize Summary and Analysis

4 The third of these three limericks is both an example of the form and a definition of it; it leaves out the place-name, however. Of these three examples, therefore, only the second is fully "fixed" as a traditional limerick. What are the ways in which such a form can be both rigid and supple?

Interpret the Poem

5 Poets love wordplay and engage in it often. How serious can this form be?

ELEGY

On a more somber note, an **elegy** is a poem of lamentation memorializing the dead or contemplating some nuance of life's melancholy. In its original incarnation in ancient Greece, it employed a fixed form of dactylic hexameter and iambic pentameter couplets. Over the centuries, the form has evolved and expanded beyond its early metrical features. A contemporary elegy need not conform to its original classical structure, but it will still reflect a speaker's solemn attention to aspects of grief and mortality.

A. E. Housman (1859–1936)

A British poet with a bleak outlook, Alfred Edward Housman published only two small volumes of poetry in his lifetime, *A Shropshire Lad* (1896) and *Last Poems* (1922); a third, arguably inferior collection was published posthumously. Despite this limited output, Housman said a lot in a little; his stanzas are compressed yet achieve a sense of poignancy over the fleeting nature of youth and life. Housman also had a reputation as a Latin literature scholar and critic and taught Latin at Cambridge University despite having failed his final exams as an undergraduate at Oxford.

AS YOU READ Picture a ceremony, a formal event, at which the poet might read this poem as a tribute.

To an Athlete Dying Young (1896)

The time you won your town the race
We chaired you through the market-place;
Man and boy stood cheering by,
And home we brought you shoulder-high.

Today, the road all runners come,
Shoulder-high we bring you home,
And set you at your threshold down,
Townsman of a stiller town.

Smart lad, to slip betimes away
From fields where glory does not stay,
And early though the laurel grows
It withers quicker than the rose.

Eyes the shady night has shut
Cannot see the record cut,
And silence sounds no worse than cheers
After earth has stopped the ears:

Now you will not swell the rout
Of lads that wore their honors out,
Runners whom renown outran
And the name died before the man.

So set, before its echoes fade,
The fleet foot on the sill of shade,
And hold to the low lintel up
The still-defended challenge-cup.

And round that early-laureled head
Will flock to gaze the strengthless dead,
And find unwithered on its curls
The garland briefer than a girl's.

Writing from Reading

Summarize

1 What does Housman accomplish in his description of the athlete as a "Smart lad, to slip betimes away"?

Analyze Craft

2 How does the poet use details from the world of sports to move the poem along?

3 Why do you think the poet chooses formal-sounding couplets for his elegy?

Analyze Voice

4 Does the diction—the word choice elected—sound as formal as the rhyme scheme? What is the speaker's relationship to the athlete?

Synthesize Summary and Analysis

5 The rhyme and the diction together create a certain effect, and the speaker offers comfort. Does the attitude lend distance to the poem or make it seem more sympathetic, and in what ways?

Interpret the Poem

6 Compare this to Ben Jonson's "envy" in his elegy "On My First Son" in chapter 19. In what ways are they similar? In what ways different? How would you describe the feelings in each poem about youth?

While the contemporary everyday reader may not know for whom Housman's elegy is composed, W. H. Auden's elegy for the Irish poet William Butler Yeats addresses the death of a literary giant. Living poets often feel a kinship with the great poets of the past. In the case of Auden and Yeats, the sense of kinship was fresh and vital, so that Auden mourned Yeats's death as he might have mourned that of a close relative. Note how Auden remarks on the scope of Yeats's death, how the event is simultaneously momentous and anonymous.

W. H. Auden (1907–1973)

For a brief biography of W. H. Auden, see chapter 18.

AS YOU READ **Consider the logic of associating death with the coldest season of the year.**

In Memory of W. B. Yeats (1940)

[D. January 1939]

I

He disappeared in the dead of winter:
The brooks were frozen, the air-ports almost deserted,
And snow disfigured the public statues;
The mercury sank in the mouth of the dying day.
O all the instruments agree
The day of his death was a dark cold day.

Far from his illness
The wolves ran on through the evergreen forests,
The peasant river was untempted by the fashionable quays;
By mourning tongues
The death of the poet was kept from his poems.

But for him it was his last afternoon as himself,
An afternoon of nurses and rumours;
The provinces of his body revolted,
The squares of his mind were empty,
Silence invaded the suburbs,
The current of his feeling failed; he became his admirers.

Now he is scattered among a hundred cities
And wholly given over to unfamiliar affections;
To find his happiness in another kind of wood
And be punished under a foreign code of conscience.
The words of a dead man
Are modified in the guts of the living.

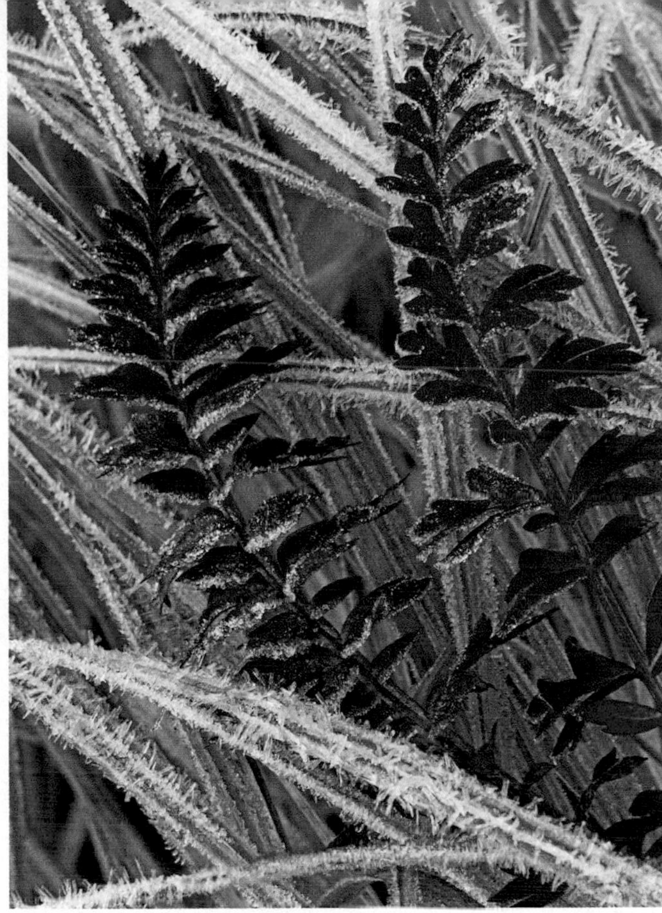

But in the importance and noise of to-morrow
When the brokers are roaring like beasts on the floor of the Bourse,
And the poor have the sufferings to which they are fairly accustomed,
And each in the cell of himself is almost convinced of his freedom;
A few thousand will think of this day
As one thinks of a day when one did something slightly unusual.
O all the instruments agree
The day of his death was a dark cold day.

II

You were silly like us: your gift survived it all;
The parish of rich women, physical decay,
Yourself; mad Ireland hurt you into poetry.
Now Ireland has her madness and her weather still,
For poetry makes nothing happen: it survives
In the valley of its saying where executives
Would never want to tamper; it flows south
From ranches of isolation and the busy griefs,
Raw towns that we believe and die in; it survives,
A way of happening, a mouth.

III

Earth, receive an honoured guest;
William Yeats is laid to rest:
Let the Irish vessel lie
Emptied of its poetry.

Time that is intolerant
Of the brave and innocent,
And indifferent in a week
To a beautiful physique,

Worships language and forgives
Everyone by whom it lives;
Pardons cowardice, conceit,
Lays its honours at their feet.

Time that with this strange excuse
Pardoned Kipling and his views,
And will pardon Paul Claudel,
Pardons him for writing well.

In the nightmare of the dark
All the dogs of Europe bark,
And the living nations wait,
Each sequestered in its hate;

Intellectual disgrace
Stares from every human face,
And the seas of pity lie
Locked and frozen in each eye.

Follow, poet, follow right
To the bottom of the night,
With your unconstraining Voice
Still persuade us to rejoice;

With the farming of a verse
Make a vineyard of the curse,
Sing of human unsuccess
In a rapture of distress;

In the deserts of the heart
Let the healing fountain start,
In the prison of his days
Teach the free man how to praise.

Writing from Reading

Summarize

1 The death of the Irish poet is a day to remember for Auden. Why do you think he honors Yeats in such a formal way?

Analyze Craft

2 Nature itself seems to be dying, or at least in mourning. With what images and metaphors does Auden achieve this effect? Why does Auden compare the dying poet to a country or city, with "provinces," "squares," "suburbs"?

Analyze Voice

3 Do you hear a personal or public voice when you listen to this speaker, a private or collective grief? What language from the poem supports your answer?

Synthesize Summary and Analysis

4 An elegy, elaborate or simple, speaks of life as well as death. Does this statement seem accurate to you? How does Auden's lament refer to what continues as well as to what has stopped?

Interpret the Poem

5 Discuss the meaning of the lines "The death of the poet was kept from his poems" and ". . . he became his admirers." What does Auden suggest here about the relationship of the poet to his own poetry?

Theodore Roethke (1907–1973)

For a brief biography of Theodore Roethke, see chapter 19.

AS YOU READ **Try to put yourself in the mind of the speaker of the poem, the teacher lamenting the death of his student.**

Elegy for Jane (1953)

My Student Thrown by a Horse

I remember the neckcurls, limp and damp as tendrils;
And her quick look, a sidelong pickerel smile;
And how, once startled into talk, the light syllables leaped for her,
And she balanced in the delight of her thought,
A wren, happy, tail into the wind,
Her song trembling the twigs and small branches.
The shade sang with her;
The leaves, their whispers turned to kissing;
And the mold sang in the bleached valleys under the rose.

Oh, when she was sad, she cast herself down into such a pure depth,
Even a father could not find her:
Scraping her cheek against straw;
Stirring the clearest water.

My sparrow, you are not here,
Waiting like a fern, making a spiny shadow.
The sides of wet stones cannot console me,
Nor the moss, wound with the last light.

If only I could nudge you from this sleep,
My maimed darling, my skittery pigeon.
Over this damp grave I speak the words of my love:
I, with no rights in this matter,
Neither father nor lover.

Writing from Reading

Summarize

1 The poem presents a sorrowful occasion, in which the poet tries to speak through his pain. Can you paraphrase his speech?

Analyze Craft

2 What metaphors does the poet employ to achieve his end? Do they all come from nature, and in what ways, if any, do they appear "artificial"?

Analyze Voice

3 What new and unexpected textures does this poet add to the generic voice of the poet mourning for the beloved dead?

Synthesize Summary and Analysis

4 Do you think the poet has found the proper metaphors, images, and tone in order to make his grief memorable for a reader? What makes them memorable to you?

Interpret the Poem

5 How do we express great sorrow at the loss of those we love but who are not our kin? Is there a sorrow we feel beyond that which comes from knowing of an individual death, and how would you describe it?

ODE

Like the elegy, the **ode** no longer obliges the poet to a specific rhyme scheme or stanza length. It does, however, take a recognizable shape in its celebration of a quality or condition or situation. The main features of this variety of lyric are an elaborate stanzaic structure, a certain ceremonial feel in tone and style, and a sense of address—whether to a private or a public issue. By the nineteenth century, the ode form was more frequently dedicated to abstract subjects than to specific public figures or events.

Despite numerous variations on the ode form over time, the essential nature of the form has remained the same: a poem that declares its topic in the title, and then considers an idea or object or mood at length.

In Shelley's "Ode to the West Wind," the speaker calls to the coming autumn wind and asks it to "make me thy lyre," to project his words beyond the boundaries of both his physical location and his physical body.

Percy Bysshe Shelley (1792–1822)

The life of Percy Bysshe Shelley, a British Romantic poet, was marked by nonconformity. He was expelled from Oxford University because he had coauthored a pamphlet called *The Necessity of Atheism;* shortly thereafter, he married the daughter of a tavern owner when both he and his wife were still teenagers. He eventually grew estranged from his wife and fell in love with Mary Wollstonecraft Godwin (daughter of Mary Wollstonecraft and future author of *Frankenstein*); he then invited his wife to live with him and Mary as a sister. After his wife's apparent suicide, Shelley married Mary and the couple moved to Italy, where over the course of four years, Shelley wrote his most important works: *Prometheus Unbound, Adonais,* and his famous poems "Hymn to Intellectual Beauty," "Ode to the West Wind," and "Ozymandias." An idealist who believed in intellectual beauty rather than God, Shelley's poetry champions hope and imagination. He drowned, surprised by a storm while sailing, before his thirtieth birthday.

AS YOU READ **Consider the language and the situation here: the poet speaking to the wind itself.**

Ode to the West Wind (1820)

I

O wild West Wind, thou breath of Autumn's being,
Thou, from whose unseen presence the leaves dead
Are driven, like ghosts from an enchanter fleeing,

Yellow, and black, and pale, and hectic red,
Pestilence-stricken multitudes: O thou,
Who chariotest to their dark wintry bed

The wingèd seeds, where they lie cold and low,
Each like a corpse within its grave, until
Thine azure sister of the Spring shall blow

Her clarion o'er the dreaming earth, and fill
(Driving sweet buds like flocks to feed in air)
With living hues and odors plain and hill:

Wild Spirit, which art moving everywhere;
Destroyer and preserver; hear, oh, hear!

II

Thou on whose stream, mid the steep sky's commotion,
Loose clouds like earth's decaying leaves are shed,
Shook from the tangled boughs of Heaven and Ocean,

Angels of rain and lightning: there are spread
On the blue surface of thine airy surge,
Like the bright hair uplifted from the head

Of some fierce Maenad, even from the dim verge
Of the horizon to the zenith's height,
The locks of the approaching storm. Thou dirge

Of the dying year, to which this closing night
Will be the dome of a vast sepulcher,
Vaulted with all thy congregated might

Of vapors, from whose solid atmosphere
Black rain, and fire, and hail will burst: oh, hear!

III

Thou who didst waken from his summer dreams
The blue Mediterranean, where he lay,
Lulled by the coil of his crystàlline streams,

Beside a pumice isle in Baiae's bay,
And saw in sleep old palaces and towers
Quivering within the wave's intenser day,

All overgrown with azure moss and flowers
So sweet, the sense faints picturing them! Thou
For whose path the Atlantic's level powers

Cleave themselves into chasms, while far below
The sea-blooms and the oozy woods which wear
The sapless foliage of the ocean, know

Thy voice, and suddenly grow gray with fear,
And tremble and despoil themselves: oh, hear!

IV

If I were a dead leaf thou mightest bear;
If I were a swift cloud to fly with thee;
A wave to pant beneath thy power, and share
The impulse of thy strength, only less free
Than thou, O uncontrollable! If even
I were as in my boyhood, and could be

The comrade of thy wanderings over Heaven,
As then, when to outstrip thy skyey speed
Scarce seemed a vision; I would ne'er have striven

As thus with thee in prayer in my sore need.
Oh, lift me as a wave, a leaf, a cloud!
I fall upon the thorns of life! I bleed!

A heavy weight of hours has chained and bowed
One too like thee: tameless, and swift, and proud.

V

Make me thy lyre, even as the forest is:
What if my leaves are falling like its own!
The tumult of thy mighty harmonies

Will take from both a deep, autumnal tone,
Sweet though in sadness. Be thou, Spirit fierce,
My spirit! Be thou me, impetuous one!

Drive my dead thoughts over the universe
Like withered leaves to quicken a new birth!
And, by the incantation of this verse,

Scatter, as from an unextinguished hearth
Ashes and sparks, my words among mankind!
Be through my lips to unawakened earth

The trumpet of a prophecy! O Wind,
If Winter comes, can Spring be far behind?

Writing from Reading

Summarize

1 The speaker describes the wind in various ways throughout the poem, for example, as "the trumpet of a prophecy" at the poem's end. Identify these descriptions of the wind. What do they tell you about how the speaker sees the wind?

Analyze Craft

2 How does this poem reflect the definition of an ode, as a formal, elevated celebration and reflection? What about the "west wind" is the speaker praising?

Analyze Voice

3 How do the poem's sections govern the speaker's emotions and thinking? How do the poem's attention and focus change over the trajectory of the different sections?

Synthesize Summary and Analysis

4 What is the importance of nature as it's described over the course of the poem? How would you characterize nature's power, according to Shelley's speaker?

Interpret the Poem

5 What does the spirit embodied by the wind represent?

For Review and Further Study

Louise Bogan (1897–1970)

The Changed Woman (1923)

The light flower leaves its little core
Begun upon the waiting bough.
Again she bears what she once bore
And what she knew she re-learns now.

The cracked glass fuses at a touch,
The wound heals over, and is set
In the whole flesh, and is not much
Quite to remember or forget.

Rocket and tree, and dome and bubble
Again behind her freshened eyes
Are treacherous. She need not trouble.
Her lids will know them when she dies.

And while she lives, the unwise, heady
Dream, ever denied and driven,
Will one day find her bosom ready—
That never thought to be forgiven.

Questions for Interactive Reading

1. Can you imagine one specific occasion for this poem, or does it speak of many similar events? "Flower" and "bough" connect the "she" in the woman of the title to the natural world. "Cracked glass" and "wound" suggest trouble and pain. How might such images contribute to the overall person suggested in the title?
2. What "change," if any, occurs in the poem? What does this suggest about the change in the woman of whom the poem speaks?
3. Does the formal presentation of deep pain and sorrow remind you of other poems about women with lives in turmoil?

Nikki Giovanni (b. 1943)

Knoxville, Tennessee (1968)

I always like summer
best
you can eat fresh corn
from daddy's garden
and okra
and greens
and cabbage
and lots of
barbecue
and buttermilk
and homemade ice-cream
at the church picnic
and listen to
gospel music
outside
at the church
homecoming
and go to the mountains with
your grandmother
and go barefooted
and be warm
all the time
not only when you go to bed
and sleep

Questions for Interactive Reading

1. The poet depicts this world as a place of distinct seasons. What effect does the list of a Southern summer's pleasures create for you?
2. Implicit in the poem is a waking world and a world of night, and also an inside world and an outside world. Why does the poet focus on the waking part and the outside part in this poem?
3. Does the reference to "daddy's garden" call to mind an image beyond the seemingly ordinary setting of the poem?
4. Does the plain, straightforward natural voice of the poem mask anything more complex and difficult? Or should we take the poem at face value and accept the speaker's simple delight in summer?

Marilyn Hacker (b. 1942)

Elektra on Third Avenue (1974)

At six, when April chills our hands and feet
walking downtown, we stop at Clancy's Bar
or Bickford's, where the part-time hustlers are,
scoffing between the mailroom and the street.
Old pensioners appraise them while they eat,

and so do we, debating half in jest
which piece of hasty pudding we'd like best.
I know you know I think your mouth is sweet
as anything exhibited for sale,
fresh coffee cake or boys fresh out of jail,
which tender hint of incest brings me near
to ordering more coffee or more beer.
The homebound crowd provides more youth to cruise.
We nurse our cups, nudge knees, and pick and choose.

Questions for Interactive Reading

1. A traditional form and an old myth, the story of Electra, have been brought together to create a New York street scene. Why might the poet have chosen this way to present the emotion—and story—of this poem?
2. Do some of the juxtapositions of phrases—"fresh coffee cake or boys fresh out of jail"—seem shocking? Do any others seem as strong?
3. Can you detect a playful quality to the poem overall? In what way does this reflect the possibility that the poet has described a game she plays with her lover?

Seamus Heaney (b. 1939)

For a brief biography of Seamus Heaney, see chapter 22.

Mid-Term Break (1966)

I sat all morning in the college sick bay
Counting bells knelling classes to a close,
At two o'clock our neighbors drove me home.

In the porch I met my father crying—
He had always taken funerals in his stride—
And Big Jim Evans saying it was a hard blow.

The baby cooed and laughed and rocked the pram
When I came in, and I was embarrassed
By old men standing up to shake my hand

And tell me they were "sorry for my trouble,"
Whispers informed strangers I was the eldest,
Away at school, as my mother held my hand

In hers and coughed out angry tearless sighs.
At ten o'clock the ambulance arrived
With the corpse, stanched and bandaged by the nurses.

Next morning I went up into the room. Snowdrops
And candles soothed the bedside; I saw him
For the first time in six weeks. Paler now,

Wearing a poppy bruise on the left temple,
He lay in the four foot box as in a cot.
No gaudy scars, the bumper knocked him clear.

A four foot box, a foot for every year.

Questions for Interactive Reading

1. How much do we learn about the speaker's life in this poem?
2. Why do you think Heaney employs such a thorough amount of narrative detail in this elegy?
3. How does the final line of the poem contrast with the detail of the preceding lines?

Andrew Hudgins (b.1951)

Elegy for My Father, Who Is Not Dead (1991)

One day I'll lift the telephone
and be told my father's dead. He's ready.
In the sureness of his faith, he talks
about the world beyond this world
as though his reservations have
been made. I think he wants to go,
a little bit—a new desire
to travel building up, an itch
to see fresh worlds. Or older ones.
He thinks that when I follow him
he'll wrap me in his arms and laugh,
the way he did when I arrived
on earth. I do not think he's right.
He's ready. I am not. I can't
just say good-bye as cheerfully
as if he were embarking on a trip
to make my later trip go well.
I see myself on deck, convinced
his ship's gone down, while he's convinced
I'll see him standing on the dock
and waving, shouting, Welcome back.

Questions for Interactive Reading

1. Usually the poet speaks in an elegy of someone already dead. What makes this poem distinct from other elegies?
2. How does the father-son theme enhance the traditional form? The father has his "faith." Does the son have values he holds to?

3. What effect does the poet create by including an image of his own birth? Do the images of travel and a voyage seem appropriate for an elegy?
4. With what line does the poem seem to turn back against its original statement?

Dorianne Laux (b. 1952)

The Shipfitter's Wife (1999)

I loved him most
when he came home from work,
his fingers still curled from fitting pipe,
his denim shirt ringed with sweat,
and smelling of salt, the drying weeds
of the ocean. I'd go to where he sat
on the edge of the bed, his forehead
anointed with grease, his cracked hands
jammed between his thighs, and unlace
the steel-toed boots, stroke his ankles,
and calves, the pads and bones of his feet.
Then I'd open his clothes and take
the whole day inside me—the ship's
gray sides, the miles of copper pipe,
the voice of the first man clanging
off the hull's silver ribs. Spark of lead
kissing metal. The clamp, the winch,
the white fire of the torch, the whistle
and the long drive home.

Questions for Interactive Reading

1. How does the woman describe her husband? Since this is a past-tense set of memories, and if she loved him "most" when he came home from work, how far removed is the remembered past?
2. Why do you think the speaker floods this poem with specific, concrete images?
3. Would you call this poem an elegy? Why or why not?

Jacqueline Osherow (b. 1956)

Song for the Music in the Warsaw Ghetto (1996)

Pity the tune bereft of singers
Pity the tone bereft of chords
Where shall we weep? By which waters?
Pity the song bereft of words
Pity the harps hung on rifles
The unsuspected cunning in each hand
Pity the shrill, bewildered nightingales
How could they sing in that strange land?

Pity the string that has no bow
Pity the flute that has no breath
Pity the rifle's muted solo
Pity its soundless aftermath

Questions for Interactive Reading

1. List some of the paradoxes in the poem—as in tune without singers, tone without chords, and so on.
2. How many times does the poet repeat the word *pity*? What effect does this create?
3. "Where shall we weep? By which waters?" From where in the Bible is the poet quoting? Does her use of this allusion broaden or narrow the context of the poem?
4. The destruction of the Warsaw Ghetto leaves, as the poet puts it in the image of the rifle's "solo," a "soundless aftermath." Do you find this paradoxical? Why?
5. Does the poem have an "aftermath" in your mind? Reread the poem, then give examples of the language you remember, and explain why.

Robert Pinsky (b. 1940)

For a brief biography of Robert Pinsky, see chapter 21.

Sonnet (1983)

Afternoon sun on her back,
calm irregular slap
of water against a dock.

Thin pines clamber
over the hill's top—
nothing to remember,

only the same lake
that keeps making the same
sounds under her cheek

and flashing the same color.
No one to say her name,
no need, no one to praise her,

only the lake's voice—over
and over, to keep it before her.

Questions for Interactive Reading and Writing

1. Contrast the regular rhythms of the form with the apparent calm and relaxed nature of the subject of the poem. Do the half rhymes—"lake . . . cheek," "color . . . her"—suggest anything about the essence of the subject? Why do you think the poet chose the sonnet form and not a less fixed form for this particular poem?
2. How old might the woman be? Can you make an argument that the "her" of the poem might be a young girl? What evidence—one way or the other—does the poet provide?
3. If you were going to make a painting of the same subject as the poem—a portrait of a woman on a dock at lakeside on a summer afternoon—what colors might you use? Would you, in the spirit of the poem, make a realistic portrait? Or would it be more abstract, less distinct? Explain why you would make these choices.

Mary Jo Salter (b. 1954)

Video Blues (1999)

My husband has a crush on Myrna Loy,
and likes to rent her movies, for a treat.
It makes some evenings harder to enjoy.

The list of actresses who might employ
him as their slave is too long to repeat.
(My husband has a crush on Myrna Loy,

Carole Lombard, Paulette Goddard, coy
Jean Arthur with that voice as dry as wheat . . .)
It makes some evenings harder to enjoy.

Does he confess all this just to annoy
a loyal spouse? I know I can't compete.
My husband has a crush on Myrna Loy.

And can't a woman have her dreamboats? Boy,
I wouldn't say my life is incomplete,
but some evening I could certainly enjoy

two hours with Cary Grant as *my* own toy.
I guess, though, we were destined not to meet.
My husband has a crush on Myrna Loy
which makes some evenings harder to enjoy.

Questions for Interactive Reading and Writing

1. How would you describe the mood of this poem. Sad? Wistful? Dejected? Disappointed? Resigned? Confused? Or a comic combination of all these?
2. Why do you think the poet chose this particular form, the villanelle, over, say, the sonnet form or free verse? Is there something special about the subject that suits this form?
3. Does the distracted video-watching husband of the poem have any counterpart in spouses from earlier times? Or is he a particularly contemporary individual?

Gjertrud Schnackenberg (b. 1953)

Snow Melting (1982)

Snow melting when I left you, and I took
This fragile bone we'd found in melting snow
Before I left, exposed beside a brook
Where raccoons washed their hands. And this, I know,

Is that raccoon we'd watched for every day.
Though at the time her wild human hand
Had gestured inexplicably, I say
Her meaning now is more than I can stand.

We've reasons, we have reasons, so we say,
For giving love, and for withholding it.
I who would love must marvel at the way
I know aloneness when I'm holding it,

Know near and far as words for live and die,
Know distance, as I'm trying to draw near,
Growing immense, and know, but don't know why,
Things seen up close enlarge, then disappear.

Tonight this small room seems too huge to cross.
And my life is that looming kind of place.
Here, left with this alone, and at a loss
I hold an alien and vacant face

Which shrinks away, and yet is magnified—
More so than I seem able to explain.
Tonight the giant galaxies outside
Are tiny, tiny on my windowpane.

Questions for Interactive Reading and Writing

1. Write down the pattern of the rhymes. Had you noticed them when you first read the poem, or did the subject catch you up in its intensity? How would you describe the subject of the poem?
2. Does the image of melting snow contrast in fruitful ways with the pain and sorrow felt by the speaker? Does it represent any part of the way she feels, and what does the word "melting" convey?
3. How long ago did the speaker depart? How many seasons of thaw away from that event does she appear to be?
4. What might be the "meaning" of the long-dead raccoon's gesture?
5. In what way are the galaxies outside the window "tiny, tiny"?

David Wojahn (b. 1953)

The Assassination of John Lennon As Depicted by the Madame Tussaud Wax Museum, Niagara Falls, Ontario, 1987 (1990)

Smuggled human hair from Mexico
Falls radiant upon the waxy O

Of her scream. Shades on, leather coat and pants, Yoko
On her knees—like the famous Kent State photo

Where the girl can't shriek her boyfriend alive, her arms
Windmilling Ohio sky.
A pump in John's chest heaves

To mimic death throes. The blood is made of latex.
His glasses: broken on the plastic sidewalk.

A scowling David Chapman, his arms outstretched,
His pistol barrel spiraling fake smoke

In a siren's red wash, completes the composition,
And somewhere background music plays "Imagine"

Before the tableau darkens. We push a button
To renew the scream.
The chest starts up again.

Questions for Interactive Reading and Writing

1. How does this poem echo the conventions of the sonnet, in terms of meter and/or rhyme? How does it diverge from them?
2. Does this sonnet seem to deliberate on an idea or message? Why do you think the "we" speaker wants to start the chest up again?
3. Does it seem strange to write about a rock and roll singer in this centuries-old form? Why or why not?
4. What is the nature of this singular event in the pop culture world that allows the poet to elevate it nearly to the level of modern myth?

Reading for Fixed Forms

When reading for fixed forms, note patterns in line length, meter, stanza structure, and rhyme scheme, and consider how the poem uses these preestablished schemes.

How is the poem broken up visually?	*Stanza:* Unit of two or more lines, set off by a space, and often sharing the same rhythm and meter. *Notice lines grouped by rhyme, meter, or purpose.* **Two lines:** *Couplet:* Two lines of poetry that form a unit of meaning. *Heroic couplet:* Two lines of rhymed, iambic pentameter. **Three lines:** *Tercet:* A three-line stanza. *Triplet:* A tercet in which all three lines rhyme. *Terza rima:* Tercets of interlocking rhymes with the middle line rhyming with the first and third lines of the preceding tercet: *aba, bcb, cdc, ded,* etc. **Four lines:** *Quatrain:* A four-line stanza. *Ballad stanza:* Quatrain consisting of alternating four-stress and three-stress lines, usually rhymed *abcb.* *Common measure:* A ballad stanza popular to hymns, consistently iambic, and usually featuring an *abcb* or *abab* rhyme scheme.
Are there fourteen lines in the poem?	*Sonnet:* Fourteen line poem, usually in iambic pentameter, with a varied rhyme scheme that employs a call-and-response structure with an answer in the final two lines. *Petrarchan (Italian) sonnet:* A sonnet consisting of an octave rhyming *abbaabba* and of a sestet using any arrangement of two or three additional rhymes, such as *cdcdcd* or *cdecde.* *Shakespearean (English, Elizabethan) sonnet:* A sonnet comprising three quatrains and a final couplet in iambic pentameter with the rhyme scheme *abab cdcd efef gg.*
Is the poem only a few lines?	*Haiku:* An unrhymed Japanese poem, often featuring observations on nature, generally written in three lines of five, seven, and five syllables. *Epigram:* A short poem highlighting a witty idea, satirical thought, or condensed comment. *Limerick:* A humorous poem of five usually anapestic lines with the rhyme scheme of *aabba.*

Are lines repeated?	*Villanelle:* A poem consisting of five tercets and a concluding quatrain. Each tercet rhymes *aba* and the final quatrain rhymes *abaa*. The poem's opening line repeats as the final line of the second and fourth stanzas and in the second-to-last line of the poem. The last line of the first stanza repeats as the final line of the third and fifth stanzas and is also the final line of the poem overall. *Sestina:* A poem of six six-line stanzas and a three-line envoi, usually unrhymed, in which each stanza repeats the end words of the lines of the first stanza, but in different order, the envoi using the six words again, three in the middle of the lines and three at the end. *Envoi:* A short closing stanza in certain verse forms, such as the ballade or sestina, summarizing its main ideas. *Pantoum:* A variation on the villanelle, consisting of an unspecified number of quatrains with the rhyme scheme *abab*. The first line of each quatrain repeats the second line of the preceding quatrain, and the third line repeats the final line of the preceding quatrain. In the final quatrain, the second line repeats the third line of the first quatrain, and the last line of the poem repeats the first line of the poem.
What is the tone of the poem?	*Elegy:* A mournful poem lamenting the dead or reflecting somberly on life's hardship. *Ode:* An elevated, formal lyric poem often written in commemoration of someone or an abstract subject.

Writing about Fixed Forms

1. Analyze the argumentative/rhetorical purposes of Hirsch's "My First Theology Lesson" and Kumin's "Saga."
2. Compare and contrast Shakespeare's attitude toward love in two different sonnets (see chapter 15 and chapter 18, for example). Pay special attention to how he uses the sonnet's architecture to build his meaning.
3. Compare the form of one haiku and one epigram from the chapter. Can a haiku be an epigram?
4. Compare the speaker's relationship to his subject matter in Shelley's "Ode to the West Wind" and Keats's "Ode on a Grecian Urn" (chapter 18).
5. How does the tone and approach to meditating on death and mortality differ in "In Memory of W. B. Yeats," "To an Athlete Dying Young," and "The Shipfitter's Wife"?
6. How does the form support the poets' reflections on time and familial structure in Thomas's "Do not go gentle into that good night" and Bishop's "One Art"?

24 Open Form

ALL the new thinking is about loss.
In this it resembles all the old thinking.
The idea, for example, that each particular erases
the luminous clarity of a general idea. That the clown-
faced woodpecker probing the dead sculpted trunk
of that black birch is, by his presence,
some tragic falling off from a first world
of undivided light. Or the other notion that,
because there is in this world no one thing
to which the bramble of *blackberry* corresponds,
a word is elegy to what it signifies.

—from "Meditation at Lagunitas" by Robert Hass

"Starting with Walt Whitman, people began to experiment with not having a set number of lines or preconditions for the writing, of just letting it flow out and see what happens, and that got to be called free verse, open form. There's nothing particularly complicated about understanding it. You just say it out loud. If you say words . . . in a certain pattern, if you start just saying, as I'm saying to you now, [words] in sentences with pauses . . . , if you reflect in the way you put those down on the page, those rhythms, you'll get this thing I was saying, which is the emotion of the rhythm of the truth of the experience that the piece of writing is talking about."

Conversation with Robert Hass, available on video at www.mhhe.com/delbanco1e

ROBERT Hass's poem "Meditation at Lagunitas" is an intimate reflection on words—their purpose and power, their often profound connections to memory. "All the new thinking is about loss," says the poem's speaker, and, "a word is elegy to what it signifies." By poem's end, the repetition of the word *blackberry* has become a vocal testament to the sensual potential of language; you can see and hear and touch and feel it, *taste* the word. The poet reacts critically to the academic idea that language may be unable to capture the individual essence of a "particular" thing or object, and that language itself may misrepresent the physical specifics we wordlessly see and feel. Hass's poem asserts the reverse. Words, he writes, really do make manifest by naming our memories and sensations. Words can serve us as powerfully and immediately as memories from childhood or of love.

To best embody the ideas and images he sets out to express, Hass has chosen **open form.** The term describes poetry that employs the sounds and rhythms of natural speech, repetition, grammatical variation, and organized patterns of imagery rather than formal rhyming structures. And instead of metrical feet, the line itself is the chief rhythmical unit we use to examine the individual components of an open form poem. So, how a line is arranged, and where it breaks, can be absolutely crucial to understanding a poem of this kind. "Meditation at Lagunitas" delves into complicated issues of language and memory yet is grounded in candid, vivid images and memories. As you listen to Hass read and discuss the poem in his interview, think about why he chose this particular form and about how different the poem would feel in formal fixed meter and rhyme.

When I first heard poems, I felt like somebody was telling me the truth.

Q&A

. . . Our consciousness is huge and mostly unexplored . . .

A Conversation on Writing

Robert Hass

Poetry Goes with Equality in America

The country was founded by people who believe that, in order to save your soul, you had to learn to read. . . . So women were taught to read as well as men . . . , and the first book of poetry published in the United States was published by a woman. The first book of poems published by a black person, an African in the United States, was published by a woman. . . . So our country has been, from the start, one in which the attainment of literacy was a very powerful tool. . . . From the beginning, the core of it in some way had been the ability to read and figure out poetry.

Sound and the Size of Our Inner World

There's a way in which a poem or a story or something opens the size of the inner world to you, one's own inner world. You know, our consciousness is huge and mostly unexplored, and sometimes, something will, like throwing a stone into a well, give you a sense of those depths. For me, if I remember rightly, it was a poem in a school textbook by Tennyson. The lines I remember are "Blow, bugles, blow, set the wild echoes flying, / And answer, echoes, answer, dying, dying, dying." It seems corny to me now, but at the time, something opened in me to that sound that I now think had to do with the sense of the size of our inner life, the vastness of our capacity for loneliness, for happiness, for wonder.

The Emotional Truthfulness of Poems

I grew up in a house where there were drinking problems. In families that are troubled, there's a lot of denial. Nobody tells the truth much about anything. . . . A lot of it is kindness; it's short of hypocrisy. In some families, in some parts of the world, in dysfunctional institutions of all kinds, nobody ever tells the truth about anything, you know. When I first heard poems, I felt like somebody was telling me the truth.

Native to California—where he continues to live and teach—Robert Hass (b. 1941) has shaped his poetry through the lush landscape that frequently enters into his poems. His first book of poetry, *Field Guide* (1973), the name of which signals Hass's environmental interest, won the Yale Series of Younger Poets Prize. His subsequent collections, along with his work as translator—from Polish and Japanese, among other languages—compose Hass's body of creative work, which is known for its meditative quality and haiku-like clarity. In addition to winning the National Book Award and the Pulitzer Prize for his collection *Time and Materials* (2007), Hass held the position of Poet Laureate from 1995 to 1997. He used his term to bring poetry into areas he deemed devoid of imagination, such as the corporate world.

To watch this entire interview and hear the author read from his work, go to www.mhhe.com/delbanco1e.

RESEARCH ASSIGNMENT In his interview, Hass talks about trying to translate Czeslaw Milosz, a poet exiled from Poland and teaching with him at the University of California, Berkeley. What was his experience? What did it teach him about translation? Contrast his experience with that of Ezra Pound, whom he discusses as the translator of a Chinese poem, "A River-Merchant's Wife." Why does Hass say that translation makes the world accessible to us but at the same time is impossible?

AS YOU READ Listen for what seems conversational here, even prosaic, and for what makes this "meditation" inescapably a poem.

Meditation at Lagunitas

(1979)

All the new thinking is about loss.
In this it resembles all the old thinking.
The idea, for example, that each particular erases
the luminous clarity of a general idea. That the clown-
faced woodpecker probing the dead sculpted trunk
of that black birch is, by his presence,
some tragic falling off from a first world
of undivided light. Or the other notion that,
because there is in this world no one thing
to which the bramble of *blackberry* corresponds,
a word is elegy to what it signifies.
We talked about it late last night and in the voice
of my friend, there was a thin wire of grief, a tone
almost querulous. After a while I understood that,
talking this way, everything dissolves: *justice,*
pine, hair, woman, you and *I*. There was a woman
I made love to and I remembered how, holding
her small shoulders in my hands sometimes,
I felt a violent wonder at her presence
like a thirst for salt, for my childhood river
with its island willows, silly music from the pleasure boat,
muddy places where we caught the little orange-silver fish
called *pumpkinseed*. It hardly had to do with her.
Longing, we say, because desire is full
of endless distances. I must have been the same to her.
But I remember so much, the way her hands dismantled bread,
the thing her father said that hurt her, what
she dreamed. There are moments when the body is as numinous
as words, days that are the good flesh continuing.
Such tenderness, those afternoons and evenings,
saying *blackberry, blackberry, blackberry.*

Writing from Reading

Summarize

1 Try to describe the situation here—the setting, the speaker, the intended audience. Where is "Lagunitas," for example, and what does it have to do with the text that follows?

2 In a dictionary, look up the word *numinous* and relate it to the experience described here.

Analyze Craft

3 Do you think these choices of setting, speaker, and audience were conscious and premeditated or sheer instinct on the part of the poet, or perhaps a combination of all these?

Analyze Voice

4 Do the speaker's memories of a past love remind you of vivid memories in your own life? What language in the poem reminds you of these memories?

5 Why do you think the details remain in the speaker's mind?

Synthesize Summary and Analysis

6 What does the poet mean by "a word is elegy to what it signifies"? And what does he mean by "the body is numinous as words"?

Interpret the Poem

7 Discuss the "tenderness" of the repeated final word. Is this finally a poem about loss—as in the opening assertion—or gain?

OPEN FORM POETRY

The presence of formal meter in a poem gives us rhythmic intervals we perceive much like a steady musical beat. While this meter may sometimes vary (allowing a poet flexibility of diction, voice, and meaning), it stays generally consistent over the course of a poem. Closed, metrical forms like this dominated poetry in English for hundreds of years. However, such formality was never the whole story; there have always been what we call "open forms" as well. While we may associate open form poetry with contemporary poets, we can see it as early as the King James Bible's Psalms and "Song of Songs," in which English translators attempted to evoke the text's original Hebrew cadences. The "Song of Songs" is often regarded as an allegorical series of love poems between humanity and God, as in these joyful lines depicting the beginning of spring (the "turtle" described in the last line is a translation of "turtle dove"):

My beloved spake, and said unto me, Rise up, my love,
my fair one, and come away.
For, lo, the winter is past, the rain is over and gone;
The flowers appear on the earth; the time of the singing
of birds is come,
and the voice of the turtle is heard in our land. . . .

In open form poetry, meter, stanza arrangement, and set rhyme schemes are never completely abandoned, but the poet feels less obligated to employ those techniques as if they were strict rules. Instead, the practitioner takes sounds and shape not from a preset formal pattern of meter and rhyme, but from the writer's own individual preference—a preference that might well vary from day to day and subject to subject, as well as line by line. Between the late nineteenth and early twentieth centuries, many poets began to reject the formal obligations that had long been a part of the genre. By this design, they allowed the poetic line (its extent, internal sounds, images, pauses, and breaks) to help shape the form.

> "It's no accident that all the great books—the great religious books, the Bible, the Koran, the Sutras—are composed in poetry. So, poetry I think is our original primal language, and I think that when we find ourselves in situations of distress or novelty, we automatically start thinking that way and expressing ourselves that way."
>
> Conversation with Al Young

VERS LIBRE, FREE VERSE, AND OPEN FORM

The term *open form* was coined to avoid the misleading connotations of the other commonly used term for unmetered poetry, "free verse." "Free verse" is derived from the designation *vers libre,* a school of seventeenth-century French poetry (*vers libre* means "free verse" in French). "Open form" avoids the conclusion that poetry of this kind is completely ungoverned or unconcerned with craft. While skilled free verse poets may not always strictly observe rules of rhythm and rhyme, they are careful to fashion their lines with conscious attention to form, sound, and shape.

The New York–born poet Walt Whitman is often credited with inaugurating the widespread use of free verse in modern and contemporary poetry. His volume of poems *Leaves of Grass,* first published in 1855, took imaginative liberties with line length, rhyme, repetition, and word choice. No one had ever heard poems quite like Whitman's before. In this brief opening section from "Song of Myself," one of the poems in *Leaves of Grass,* note the surprising liberties Whitman takes with his language, his line length, his direct address to "you" the reader, and the fresh sound of his voice.

Walt Whitman (1819–1892)

For a brief biography of Walt Whitman, see chapter 18.

AS YOU READ Imagine yourself in a shared space with Whitman—the "you" to whom the "I" speaks. He's embarked on a long monologue. What might be your response?

Song of Myself (1855)

I Celebrate myself, and sing myself,
And what I assume you shall assume,
For every atom belonging to me as good belongs to you.

I loafe and invite my soul,
I lean and loafe at my ease observing a spear of summer grass.

My tongue, every atom of my blood, form'd from this soil, this air,
Born here of parents born here from parents the same, and their parents the same,
I, now thirty-seven years old in perfect health begin,
Hoping to cease not till death.

Creeds and schools in abeyance,
Retiring back a while sufficed at what they are, but never forgotten,
I harbor for good or bad, I permit to speak at every hazard,
Nature without check with original energy.

Writing from Reading

Summarize

1 It's hard to summarize these lines, because they begin a very long poem indeed. How do they set the stage?

Analyze Craft

2 What do you notice about the line length here—its random nature as opposed to patterns? What does that tell you about freedom and "original energy"?

Analyze Voice

3 As it happens, Whitman's hope—that we would "cease not till death"—was realized; he worked at this poem for all his long life. What is modest or boastful about a phrase like "Born here of parents born here from parents the same, and their parents the same . . ."?

Synthesize Summary and Analysis

4 What sort of claims for art and life does the poet make here, and how do they seem "revolutionary"?

Interpret the Poem

5 Why does the poet claim that he will let "Nature without check" do the speaking?

Walt Whitman is, as suggested above, a major presence in the world of American letters. Poets often tip their caps to the work of other poets—as in Anthony Hecht's response to Matthew Arnold's "Dover Beach" (see chapter 18). In the For Review and Further Study section of this chapter, the poet Allen Ginsberg remembers his great predecessor while shopping in California, a state Whitman never visited.

Here a contemporary American Indian author responds to the white-bearded ghost of an artist he, too, can treasure as an ancestor, even though there's something almost comic in the juxtaposition of basketball to Whitman's Civil War. In "Defending Walt Whitman," Sherman Alexie employs a number of formal techniques to tell a brief allegorical story about poetry and sport. Alexie writes with a design dictated by image and the emotions generated by the occasion of the poem: basketball and the life of young American Indian boys. Yet the nation's first major "free" poet takes center stage in his title. There is, with Whitman's "presence" in the poem, an awareness of tradition even while the artist struggles to report on change. When Alexie claims, about Whitman, that "this game belongs to him," he's celebrating poetry as well.

Sherman Alexie (b. 1966)

Sherman Alexie grew up on the Spokane Indian Reservation in Washington (he is of Spokane/Coeur d'Alene descent). He attended college with the goal of becoming a doctor. His career as a poet took off shortly after graduation; by 1993, he had received two major fellowships and published two books of poetry. Next, he turned to short stories with *The Lone Ranger and Tonto Fistfight in Heaven* (1993) and then produced a novel, *Reservation Blues* (1995). He also wrote the screenplay for the award-winning, independently produced film *Smoke Signals* (1998). His signature blend of irony, humor, cynicism, and critique of modern Native American life has won him many honors including the PEN/Hemingway award, the PEN/Malamud award, and the Pushcart Prize. In 2007, he received the National Book Award for Young People's Literature with *The Absolutely True Diary of a Part-Time Indian*. He calls Seattle home.

AS YOU READ Think of this as a kind of conversation between the contemporary and the ancestral, the living and the dead.

Defending Walt Whitman (1996)

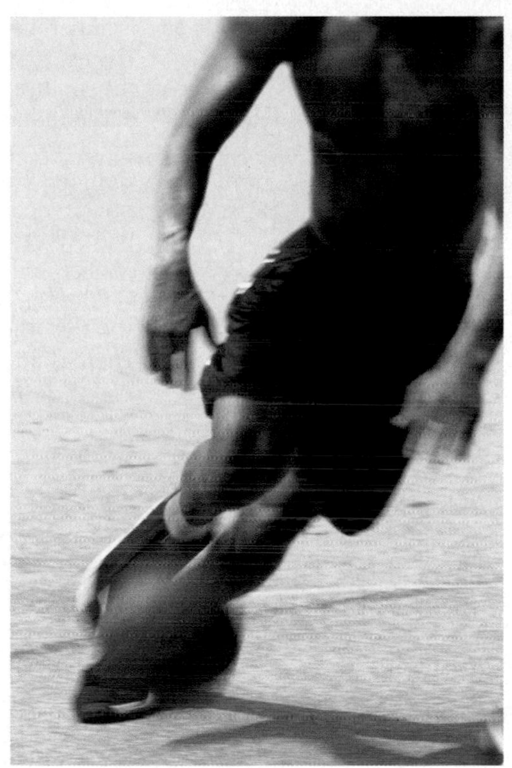

Basketball is like this for young Indian boys, all arms and legs
and serious stomach muscles. Every body is brown!
These are the twentieth-century warriors who will never kill,
although a few sat quietly in the deserts of Kuwait,
waiting for orders to do something, do something.

God, there is nothing as beautiful as a jump shot
on a reservation summer basketball court
where the ball is moist with sweat
and makes a sound when it swishes through the net
that causes Walt Whitman to weep because it is so perfect.

There are veterans of foreign wars here,
whose bodies are still dominated
by collarbones and knees, whose bodies still respond
in the ways that bodies are supposed to respond when we are young.
Every body is brown! Look there, that boy can run
up and down this court forever. He can leap for a rebound
with his back arched like a salmon, all meat and bone
synchronized, magnetic, as if the court were a river,
as if the rim were a dam, as if the air were a ladder
leading the Indian boy toward home.

Some of the Indian boys still wear their military haircuts
while a few have let their hair grow back.
It will never be the same as it was before!
One Indian boy has never cut his hair, not once, and he braids it
into wild patterns that do not measure anything.
He is just a boy with too much time on his hands.
Look at him. He wants to play this game in bare feet.

God, the sun is so bright! There is no place like this.
Walt Whitman stretches his calf muscles
on the sidelines. He has the next game.
His huge beard is ridiculous on the reservation.
Some body throws a crazy pass and Walt Whitman catches it with quick hands.
He brings the ball close to his nose
and breathes in all of its smells: leather, brown skin, sweat, black hair,
burning oil, twisted ankle, long drink of warm water,
gunpowder, pine tree. Walt Whitman squeezes the ball tightly.
He wants to run. He hardly has the patience to wait for his turn.
"What's the score?" he asks. He asks, "What's the score?"

Basketball is like this for Walt Whitman. He watches these Indian boys
as if they were the last bodies on earth. Every body is brown!
Walt Whitman shakes because he believes in God.
Walt Whitman dreams of the Indian boy who will defend him,
trapping him in the corner, all flailing arms and legs
and legendary stomach muscles. Walt Whitman shakes
because he believes in God. Walt Whitman dreams
of the first jump shot he will take, the ball arcing clumsily
from his fingers, striking the rim so hard that it sparks.
Walt Whitman shakes because he believes in God.
Walt Whitman closes his eyes. He is a small man and his beard
is ludicrous on the reservation, absolutely insane.
His beard makes the Indian boys righteously laugh. His beard frightens
the smallest Indian boys. His beard tickles the skin
of the Indian boys who dribble past him. His beard, his beard!

God, there is beauty in every body. Walt Whitman stands
at center court while the Indian boys run from basket to basket.
Walt Whitman cannot tell the difference between
offense and defense. He does not care if he touches the ball.
Half of the Indian boys wear T-shirts damp with sweat
and the other half are bareback, skin slick and shiny.
There is no place like this. Walt Whitman smiles.
Walt Whitman shakes. This game belongs to him.

Writing from Reading

Summarize

1 Think of this poem as a discussion of the impact of the past. What has changed; what stays the same?

Analyze Craft

2 Why do you think Alexie repeats certain phrases and words?

Analyze Voice

3 How does the language of this poem compare to language in poems in this book by Walt Whitman himself? "Defending" is something a basketball player must do, and it means "standing up for" or "taking the side of" as well. How would you describe the diction and the poet's tone?

Synthesize Summary and Analysis

4 Whitman wrote at length about the Civil War; Alexie here refers to "the deserts of Kuwait" and the first Gulf War. How does he treat his "warriors," and what does he respect?

Interpret the Poem

5 Discuss the imaginary presence in this poem of Walt Whitman attending a pickup basketball game on an American Indian reservation. What connections do you think Alexie wants to make here among Whitman, Native Americans, basketball, and war?

Modern writers have disagreed on the place of open form poetry in the wider arena of English and American literature. Many believe open form poetry reflects a democratic spirit, an opportunity to use the musical potential of the poetic line with greater fulfillment and flexibility. Others think that poetry unconcerned with rhythmic structure is simply amateurish. Robert Frost famously compared the writing of free verse poetry to a game of tennis with no net.

It is hard to disagree that the prevalence of open form poetry has helped facilitate a lot of bland, lightweight poems and that it even perpetuates the misconception that "anything can be a poem." As British novelist A. S. Byatt writes, "Free verse has come to represent democracy, equal opportunity, and self-expression. But in bulk and unaware of the forms from which it has been freed . . . it can be extremely depressing."

Practitioners of open form poetry insist that a successful poem "finds" a form using the poet's instinct and intent, and that the absence of iambic pentameter or end rhyme (or other traditional devices) does not condemn a poem to pointlessness. In other words, when you write a poem you have definitely created a form of some kind, and that form in turn creates impressions in the reader. Of this aspect of composition, poet C. D. Wright says, "Poetry without form is a fiction. But that there is a freedom in words is the larger fact, and in poetry, where formal restrictions can bear down heavily, it is important to remember the cage is never locked."

> "You know, free verse to me . . . is nothing less than . . . a discovery, and we haven't even got to the bottom of it yet. We're only scratching the surface because ultimately free verse is a form of writing in which the poem is completely organized by instances of coincidence . . . stanzas are units of coincidence and lines become units of coincidence, and the whole poem becomes organized with that in mind. . . . It sounds simple, but it's a lot harder to do than one would think." Conversation with Li-Young Lee

Next a pair of open form poems by a pair of American masters—one dead, one still at work—demonstrate how supple the technique can be, and how personal. When e. e. cummings argues for the primacy of feeling and writes "who pays any attention / to the syntax of things," he's arguing, in effect, for the value of open form verse—breaking the rules of syntax in the subsequent phrase by leaving out the first-person pronoun that should "properly" be there before "will never wholly kiss you." And in this poem, certainly, "feeling is first."

e. e. cummings (1894–1962)

Born in Cambridge, Massachusetts, Edward Estlin Cummings earned both his undergraduate and graduate degrees from Harvard. Although at first he wrote poetry modeled after the pre-Raphaelites and other classical forms, he soon developed his own innovative style that focused on the poem's appearance on the page, a lack of capitalization, and a free, liberal use of words (he often turned verbs into nouns and vice versa). His poems appear complex and are pleasing orally, yet the ideas behind them are often simple messages against conformity and in favor of love. Consistent with his bohemian spirit, e. e. cummings made a career of being an artist, both in poetry and in drawing/painting. In addition to his poetry collections, such as *Tulips and Chimneys* (1923), e. e. cummings wrote a series of lectures that he delivered at Harvard, though by his request they were called "nonlectures" and later published as *Six Nonlectures* (1953).

AS YOU READ **Place the poem somewhere between the loosest of sonnets and the most restricted free verse.**

since feeling is first (1926)

since feeling is first
who pays any attention
to the syntax of things
will never wholly kiss you;

wholly to be a fool
while Spring is in the world

my blood approves,
and kisses are a far better fate
than wisdom
lady i swear by all flowers. Don't cry
—the best gesture of my brain is less than
your eyelids' flutter which says

we are for each other:then
laugh,leaning back in my arms
for life's not a paragraph

And death i think is no parenthesis

Writing from Reading

Summarize

1 Do you agree or disagree with the assessment that this is a love poem, said in modern language, by an old-fashioned soul? Why?

Analyze Craft

2 What controls the progress of the poem? Is it the unfolding of the anecdote of the kiss or the deeply ingrained sense of form that the poet never really wholly disregards?

Analyze Voice

3 The pun-making poet—wholly= holy—is also a fun-making poet. What is the link between free verse in this instance and the freeing of the poet's sense of humor?

Synthesize Summary and Analysis

4 The poet attempts to create an order (syntax) based on feelings, and the result is either delightful or frivolous. Which do you find it to be?

Interpret the Poem

5 What is the role in this poem of instinct versus intellect?

Galway Kinnell (b. 1927)

Born in Providence, Rhode Island, Galway Kinnell was educated at Princeton and the University of Rochester. In addition to serving in the U.S. Navy, Kinnell also worked for the Congress of Racial Equality during the civil rights movement. His poetry, including his book length poem on the Vietnam War, *The Book of Nightmares* (1971), demonstrates a deep awareness of the nation's life. More often, however, Kinnell's poetry shows a consciousness of the natural world and of death, but in such a way that it is energetic rather than filled with despair. Kinnell has taught at many universities, and his *Selected Poems* (1980) won both the Pulitzer Prize and the National Book Award.

AS YOU READ **Think about how individual choices of rhythm, language, sound, pauses, line length, and endings help this piece become more than sentences of prose cut into shorter lines.**

FOR INTERACTIVE READING . . . Look for repetitions of words and make note of them.

After Making Love We Hear Footsteps (1980)

For I can snore like a bullhorn
or play loud music
or sit up talking with any reasonably sober Irishman
and Fergus will only sink deeper
into his dreamless sleep, which goes by all in one flash,
but let there be that heavy breathing
or a stifled come-cry anywhere in the house
and he will wrench himself awake
and make for it on the run—as now, we lie together,
after making love, quiet, touching along the length of our bodies,
familiar touch of the long-married,
and he appears—in his baseball pajamas, it happens,
the neck opening so small he has to screw them on—
and flops down between us and hugs us and snuggles himself to sleep,
his face gleaming with satisfaction at being this very child.

In the half darkness we look at each other
and smile
and touch arms across this little, startlingly muscled body—
this one whom habit of memory propels to the ground of his making,
sleeper only the mortal sounds can sing awake,
this blessing love gives again into our arms.

Writing from Reading

Summarize

1 Why is this poem in two stanzas? How does the second respond to the first?

Analyze Craft

2 Are there rhymes in this poem? Do they help connect the elements contained?

3 How many sentences make up this poem? Why do you think Kinnell chooses to write so few separate sentences in a poem with so many lines?

Analyze Voice

4 How would you describe the speaker's attitude toward his child?

Synthesize Summary and Analysis

5 Open form poets often consider the line the principal unit of sense and meaning. How do individual lines in the poem help create a sense of order or form?

Interpret the Poem

6 What does the poet mean by "this one whom habit of memory propels to the ground of his making," and can you read this poem as a text about the making of poetry itself?

In the spirit of the "free" and "open" possibilities of contemporary poetry, C. K. Williams creates a narrative with lines much longer than those of most unmetered verse. "Tar" conveys deep emotion by means of a story line or set of anecdotes (incidents) composed in very long lines. "Three Mile Island" refers to the location of a nuclear plant in Pennsylvania and a meltdown there in 1979.

C. K. Williams (b. 1936)

Born in Newark, New Jersey, Charles Kenneth Williams turned to poetry at age nineteen, after he had finished his required English courses at the University of Pennsylvania, where he earned his degree. Williams's ten books of poetry—including the Pulitzer Prize–winning *Repair* (1999) and the National Book Award–winning *The Singing* (2003)—emphasize the pain of human existence in lines that are unconventionally long. The length of his lines is reminiscent of Whitman, though he wholly lacks Whitman's optimism. Williams was a group therapist for troubled adolescents in Philadelphia, edited materials in psychiatry and architecture, and is currently at Princeton University, continuing an academic career that has included Columbia, George Mason, and Drexel Universities.

AS YOU READ Pay attention to the line breaks. They depend on a visual cue. It would have been simple enough to keep words like "atmosphere" or "Susquehanna" or "clinging" as single words, not hyphenated ones, but Williams calls our attention to the way lines fuse or break apart. That hurtling description of risk and wreckage enters the narrative at least in part by way of its line length; there's no chance to pause for breath.

FOR INTERACTIVE READING . . . Look up the word *tar* in a dictionary and think about how this word connects the national event in the poem with the personal housework that is going on.

Tar (1983)

The first morning of Three Mile Island: those first disquieting, uncertain, mystifying hours.
All morning a crew of workmen have been tearing the old decrepit roof off our building,
and all morning, trying to distract myself, I've been wandering out to watch them
as they hack away the leaden layers of asbestos paper and disassemble the disintegrating drains.
After half a night of listening to the news, wondering how to know a hundred miles downwind
if and when to make a run for it and where, then a coming bolt awake at seven
when the roofers we've been waiting for since winter sent their ladders shrieking up our wall,
we still know less than nothing: the utility company continues making little of the accident,
the slick federal spokesmen still have their evasions in some semblance of order.
Surely we suspect now we're being lied to, but in the meantime, there are the roofers,
setting winch-frames, sledging rounds of tar apart, and there I am, on the curb across, gawking.

I never realized what brutal work it is, how matter-of-factly and harrowingly dangerous.
The ladders flex and quiver, things skid from the edge, the materials are bulky and recalcitrant.
When the rusty, antique nails are levered out, their heads pull off; the under-roofing crumbles.
Even the battered little furnace, roaring along as patient as a donkey, chokes and clogs,
a dense, malignant smoke shoots up, someone has to fiddle with a cock, then hammer it,
before the gush and stench will deintensify, the dark, Dantean broth wearily subside.
In its crucible, the stuff looks bland, like licorice, spill it, though, on your boots or coveralls,
it sears, and everything is permeated with it, the furnace gunked with burst and half-burst bubbles,
the men themselves so completely slashed and mucked they seem almost from another realm, like trolls.
When they take their break, they leave their brooms standing at attention in the asphalt pails,
work gloves clinging like Brer Rabbit to the bitten shafts, and they slouch along the precipitous lip,
the enormous sky behind them, the heavy noontime air alive with shimmers and mirages.

Sometime in the afternoon I had to go inside: the advent of our vigil was upon us.
However much we didn't want to, however little we would do about it, we'd understood:
we were going to perish of all this, if not now, then soon, if not soon, then someday.
Someday, some final generation, hysterically aswarm beneath an atmosphere as unrelenting as rock,
would rue us all, anathematize our earthly comforts, curse our surfeits and submissions.
I think I know, though I might rather not, why my roofers stay so clear to me and why the rest,
the terror of that time, the reflexive disbelief and distancing, all we should hold on to, dims so.
I remember the president in his absurd protective booties, looking absolutely unafraid, the fool.
I remember a woman on the front page glaring across the misty Susquehanna at those looming stacks.
But, more vividly, the men, silvered with glitter from the shingles, clinging like starlings beneath the eaves.
Even the leftover carats of tar in the gutter, so black they seemed to suck the light out of the air.
By nightfall kids had come across them: every sidewalk on the block was scribbled with obscenities and hearts.

Writing from Reading

Summarize

1 An "occasional" poem takes a specific event or date as its subject. What is the occasion for this poem?

Analyze Craft

2 Compare the line length here with the lines in Walt Whitman's "Song of Myself." This poem is not, of course, a celebration, but what effect does choosing long lines have in this poem?

3 Sometimes the language in "Tar" feels very plainspoken and co nversational; at other times it sounds elevated and more traditionally poetic. Where do these changes happen? What kind of events or images do they describe? What is their significance?

Analyze Voice

4 What do you think the poet means by "I think I know, though I might rather not" or "I remember"? Do these lines set a tone for this poem? What other lines can you point to that create the poem's tone?

Synthesize Summary and Analysis

5 The poem takes place amid a real-life national crisis. What is the relationship of the event at Three Mile Island and Williams's description of the housework going on in his building?

Interpret the Poem

6 As this is a poem of political and social commentary, is it surprising that these lines should end as they do, and in what ways does "the terror of that time" transform itself into graffiti—as in "obscenities and hearts"?

The poet Sharon Olds describes internal wreckage, though she, too, deals with "obscenities and hearts." Here, too, the language is that of everyday discourse, the experience described a common one—but shot through with the power of erotic and psychological encounter.

Sharon Olds (b. 1942)

Born in California, Sharon Olds received a B.A. from Stanford University and a Ph.D. from Columbia University. Her award-winning poetry collections include *The Dead and the Living* (1983), which won the National Book Critics Circle Award, and *The Father* (1992), which was shortlisted for the T. S. Eliot Prize. A poet in the confessional tradition of poets such as Anne Sexton and Sylvia Plath—that is, poetry that takes the poet's personal life as its subject—Olds writes on themes of the body, family life, sex, and violence. She currently teaches at New York University and has been involved as a founder and teacher of the creative writing program for the physically disabled at Goldwater Hospital in New York City.

AS YOU READ Ask yourself if this is a poem about morality or whether it has another subject.

Sex without Love (1984)

How do they do it, the ones who make love
without love? Beautiful as dancers,
gliding over each other like ice-skaters
over the ice, fingers hooked
inside each other's bodies, faces
red as steak, wine, wet as the
children at birth whose mothers are going to
give them away. How do they come to the
come to the   come to the   God   come to the
still waters, and not love
the one who came there with them, light
rising slowly as steam off their joined
skin? These are the true religious,
the purists, the pros, the ones who will not
accept a false Messiah, love the
priest instead of the God. They do not
mistake the lover for their own pleasure,
they are like great runners: they know they are alone
with the road surface, the cold, the wind,
the fit of their shoes, their over-all cardio-
vascular health—just factors, like the partner
in the bed, and not the truth, which is the
single body alone in the universe
against its own best time.

Writing from Reading

Summarize

1 The poet meditates on the question of sex and love. What conclusion does the speaker in the poem draw about this realationship?

Analyze Craft

2 Discuss the poem's lineation and lack of stanza breaks. Why do you think Olds makes these choices?

3 What other poetic techniques suggest this poem's open form style has specific intentions?

Analyze Voice

4 The poem incorporates many similes. How do they help express the speaker's attitude toward the subject matter?

Synthesize Summary and Analysis

5 The poet takes up a question important to moralists and romantics alike. With whom does she seem to stand?

Interpret the Poem

6 What does the poem imply about the relation of love and sex in the context of our lives? Can we ever feel as though we are together with someone and not terribly alone?

Robert Hass (b. 1941)

For a brief biography of Robert Hass, see the beginning of this chapter.

Dragonflies Mating (1996)

I

The people who lived here before us
also loved these high mountain meadows on summer mornings.
They made their way up here in easy stages
when heat began to dry the valleys out,
following the berry harvest probably and the pine buds:
climbing and making camp and gathering,
then breaking camp and climbing and making camp and gathering.
A few miles a day. They sent out the children
to dig up bulbs of the mariposa lilies that they liked to roast
at night by the fire where they sat talking about how this year
was different from last year. Told stories,
knew where they were on earth from the names,
owl moon, bear moon, gooseberry moon.

II

Jaime de Angulo (1934) was talking to a Channel Island Indian
in a Santa Barbara bar. You tell me how your people said
the world was made. Well, the guy said, Coyote was on the mountain
and he had to pee. Wait a minute, Jaime said,
I was talking to a Pomo the other day and he said
Red Fox made the world. They say Red Fox, the guy shrugged,
we say Coyote. So, he had to pee
and he didn't want to drown anybody, so he turned toward the place
where the ocean would be. Wait a minute, Jaime said,
if there were no people yet, how could he drown anybody?
The Channelleño got a funny look on his face. You know,
he said, when I was a kid, I wondered about that,
and I asked my father. We were living up toward Santa Ynez.
He was sitting on a bench in the yard shaving down fence posts
with an ax, and I said, how come Coyote was worried about people
when he had to pee and there were no people? The guy laughed.
And my old man looked up at me with this funny smile
and said, You know, when I was a kid, I wondered about that.

III

Thinking about that story just now, early morning heat,
first day in the mountains, I remembered stories about sick Indians
and—in the same thought—standing on the free throw line.

St. Raphael's parish, where the northern-most of the missions
had been, was founded as a hospital, was named for the angel
in the scriptures who healed the blind man with a fish

he laid across his eyes—I wouldn't mind being that age again,
hearing those stories, eyes turned upward toward the young nun
in her white, fresh-smelling, immaculately laundered robes.—

The Franciscan priests who brought their faith in God
across the Atlantic, brought with the baroque statues and metalwork
  crosses
and elaborately embroidered cloaks, influenza and syphilis and the
  coughing disease.

Which is why we settled an almost empty California.
There were drawings in the mission museum of the long, dark wards
full of small brown people, wasted, coughing into blankets,

the saintly Franciscan fathers moving patiently among them.
It would, Sister Marietta said, have broken your hearts to see it.
They meant so well, she said, and such a terrible thing

came here with their love. And I remembered how I hated it
after school—because I loved basketball practice more than anything
on earth—that I never knew if my mother was going to show up

well into one of those weeks of drinking she disappeared into,
and humiliate me in front of my classmates with her bright, confident
  eyes,
and slurred, though carefully pronounced words, and the appalling

impromptu sets of mismatched clothes she was given to
when she had the dim idea of making a good impression in that state.
Sometimes from the gym floor with its sweet, heady smell of varnish

I'd see her in the entryway looking for me, and I'd bounce
the ball two or three times, study the orange rim as if it were,
which it was, the true level of the world, the one sure thing

the power in my hands could summon. I'd bounce the ball
once more, feel the grain of the leather in my fingertips and shoot.
It was a perfect thing; it was almost like killing her.

IV

When we say "mother" in poems,
we usually mean some woman in her late twenties
or early thirties trying to raise a child.

We use this particular noun
to secure the pathos of the child's point of view
and to hold her responsible.

V

If you're afraid now?
Fear is a teacher.
Sometimes you thought that
Nothing could reach her,
Nothing can reach you.
Wouldn't you rather
sit by the river, sit
On the dead bank,
Deader than winter,
Where all the roots gape?

VI

This morning in the early sun,
steam rising from the pond the color of smoky topaz,
a pair of delicate, copper-red, needle-fine insects
are mating in the unopened crown of a Shasta daisy
just outside your door. The green flowerheads look like wombs
or the upright, supplicant bulbs of a vegetal pre-erection.
The insect lovers seem to be transferring the cosmos into each other
by attaching at the tail, holding utterly still, and quivering intently.

I think (on what evidence?) that they are different from us.
That they mate and are done with mating.
They don't carry all this half-mated longing up out of childhood
and then go looking for it everywhere.
And so, I think, they can't wound each other the way we do.
They don't go through life dizzy or groggy with their hunger,
kill with it, smear it on everything, though it is perhaps also true
that nothing happens to them quite like what happens to us
when the blue-backed swallow dips swiftly toward the green pond
and the pond's green-and-blue reflected swallow marries it a moment
in the reflected sky and the heart goes out to the end of the rope
it has been throwing into abyss after abyss, and a singing shimmers
from every color the morning has risen into.

My insect instructors have stilled, they are probably stuck together
in some bliss and minute pulse of after-longing
evolution worked out to suck the last juice of the world
into the receiver body. They can't separate probably
until it is done.

Writing from Reading

Summarize

1 The poet arrives at a certain location and catches sight of the dragonflies. What happens next? Where do his thoughts take him? Break down each subsequent numbered part and paraphrase it.

Analyze Craft

2 The poet employs a number of techniques, including several from prose narrative, to move his poem along. What effect does he create using anecdote and dialogue?

3 As we have seen elsewhere, Robert Hass is very interested in—and a translator of—the brief Japanese form of haiku. Yet this is a long and nontraditional poem, quite different in form and content from a poem of only seventeen syllables. What similarities do you find between the attitudes Hass and the haiku poets express?

Analyze Voice

4 "Fear is a teacher." What other emotion, besides fear, does the poet feel along with the calm he conveys?

Synthesize Summary and Analysis

5 The poet observes the natural world and looks into himself as well, touching on local and personal history. Have you encountered other poets who do this? Who? Is there a tradition into which Hass's poem seems to fall?

Interpret the Poem

6 What wisdom for human behavior and life does the poet find in the mating habits of these insects?

VISUAL POETRY

Poets writing outside of fixed forms occasionally decide to shape their lines into a recognizable picture. **Visual** (or **concrete**) **poetry** is poetry written in the shape of something it describes. In his poem "Easter Wings," George Herbert works within a noticeable rhyme scheme (*ababacdcdc*) and metric regularity, but he arranges the lines in an unconventional form. His verse is not "free," but neither is it organized by a previous tradition; no series of earlier poems has this particular *shape.*

George Herbert (1593–1633)

Born into a prominent Welsh family, George Herbert was one of ten children, all of whom his mother raised alone after their father's early death. Educated at Trinity College, Cambridge, Herbert held the post of public orator, or spokesman, for the university. Although his election to Parliament suggested a political career, he became a minister to a rural parish in 1630, where he served until his death from consumption. Herbert's reputation as a poet rests solely on one volume, *The Temple* (1633), published posthumously; the rest of his poetry has been lost. *The Temple,* however, shows a great range, not only in poetic style—from lengthy poems to short lyrics, shape poems, acrostics, and sonnets—but also in feeling, as Herbert concerned himself with his relationship to God.

AS YOU READ Go back and forth between the lines and a glance at the shape.

Easter Wings (1633)

Lord, who createdst man in wealth and store,
Though foolishly he lost the same,
Decaying more and more,
Till he became
Most poor:
With thee
O let me rise
As larks, harmoniously,
And sing this day thy victories:
Then shall the fall further the flight in me.
My tender age in sorrow did begin:
And still with sicknesses and shame
Thou didst so punish sin,
That I became
Most thin.
With thee
Let me combine
And feel this day thy victory
For, if I imp my wing on thine,
Affliction shall advance the flight in me.

Writing from Reading

Summarize

1 This poem celebrates the resurrection of Jesus Christ on Easter, as described in the New Testament. In what ways is this poem a prayer?

Analyze Craft

2 How does the shape reflect the subject of the poem?

3 Which places here in the poem's winged form reflect or combine with specific syntax or diction choices? What is the effect?

Analyze Voice

4 Does the form of prayerful speech give the sound of the poem a shape?

Synthesize Summary and Analysis

5 The poet seeks to give physical as well as aural shape to his words. Does this seem appropriate—or a playful trick?

Interpret the Poem

6 Why might Herbert have viewed poetry and prayer as similar activities? How do you distinguish between this poem and a prayer?

"Easter Wings" is quite a different entity when read aloud than when looked at in silence. And because he knew his work would be physically published, Herbert wrote with the assumption that the poem would be viewed. This is an assumption that the ancient Greek poet Homer or the *Beowulf* poet, for example, could not have made. The later poet's audience would *view* as well as *listen to* the verse, and the visual component matters at least as much as how the poem sounds.

John Hollander (b. 1929)

Scholar and poet John Hollander was born in New York City, educated at Columbia University and Indiana University, and taught for decades at Yale. His first collection of poetry, *A Crackling of Thorns* (1958), won the Yale Series of Younger Poets Award, launching a career that would yield seventeen books of poetry, eight well-respected books of literary criticism, and more than twenty edited works. Hollander's love of music, which led him to write liner notes for albums to support himself between his master's degree and Ph.D., resulted in his writing opera librettos and lyrics for composers including Milton Babbitt and George Perle.

AS YOU READ Follow the shape, but also ponder the meaning below the surface of the shape.

Swan and Shadow

(1969)

Dusk
Above the
water hang the
loud
flies
Here
O so
gray
then
What A pale signal will appear
When Soon before its shadow fades
Where Here in this pool of opened eye
In us No Upon us As at the very edges
of where we take shape in the dark air
this object bares its image awakening
ripples of recognition that will
brush darkness up into light
even after this bird this hour both drift by atop the perfect sad instant now
already passing out of sight
toward yet-untroubled reflection
this image bears its object darkening
into memorial shades Scattered bits of
light No of water Or something across
water Breaking up No Being regathered
soon Yet by then a swan will have
gone Yes out of mind into what
vast
pale
hush
of a
place
past
sudden dark as
if a swan
sang

Writing from Reading

Summarize

1 How is what happens in the image of the top swan reflected in the image of the bottom swan?

Analyze Craft

2 Discuss how the poem's capitalization, lack of punctuation, and syntax relate to (or contrast with) the clear shape of the poem visually. Do these elements emerge out of the necessity of rendering a clear image, or do they serve other purposes?

3 Why the image of a swan? Where else have you seen it in myth and poetry?

Analyze Voice

4 Is there anything in the way the poet shapes the poem that might make for confusion if it were read aloud?

Synthesize Summary and Analysis

5 Discuss Hollander's combination of visual representation and language. What aspects of the poem strike you as particularly interesting or important? Does it hold together on its own as an interesting poem or require the visual form to complete it?

6 Compare the language and tone in the "swan" section of the poem versus the "shadow" section of the poem. Does the poem acknowledge a shift between the image and the image's shadow?

Interpret the Poem

7 Our lives in time, our own ephemeral images—how does the poem speak to such questions?

Chen Li (b. 1954)

A Taiwanese poet, Chen Li has contributed to Taiwan's letters both his original work and his translations—in collaboration with his wife Chan Fen-ling—of poets including Pablo Neruda and Seamus Heaney. Li has gone through several stages in his own poetry, first taking up Modernist technique, then demonstrating political and social consciousness, and finally broadening to an eclectic mix of subject matter. Li has presented his poetry at the Rotterdam International Poetry Festival. His work has further reached a wide audience with its English, French, Dutch, and Japanese translations. He teaches at the Hualien Girls Middle School and National Dong Hwa University.

AS YOU READ The translator of this poem noted the following about this untranslatable poem: The Chinese character 兵 (pronounced "bing") means "soldier." 乒 and 乓 (pronounced "ping" and "pong"), which look like one-legged soldiers, are two onomatopoeic words imitating sounds of collision or gunshots. The character 丘 (pronounced "chiou") means "hill."

War Symphony (1995)

兵兵兵兵兵兵兵兵兵兵兵兵兵兵兵兵兵兵兵兵兵兵兵兵
兵兵兵兵兵兵兵兵兵兵兵兵兵兵兵兵兵兵兵兵兵兵兵兵
兵兵兵兵兵兵兵兵兵兵兵兵兵兵兵兵兵兵兵兵兵兵兵兵
兵兵兵兵兵兵兵兵兵兵兵兵兵兵兵兵兵兵兵兵兵兵兵兵
兵兵兵兵兵兵兵兵兵兵兵兵兵兵兵兵兵兵兵兵兵兵兵兵
兵兵兵兵兵兵兵兵兵兵兵兵兵兵兵兵兵兵兵兵兵兵兵兵
兵兵兵兵兵兵兵兵兵兵兵兵兵兵兵兵兵兵兵兵兵兵兵兵
兵兵兵兵兵兵兵兵兵兵兵兵兵兵兵兵兵兵兵兵兵兵兵兵
兵兵兵兵兵兵兵兵兵兵兵兵兵兵兵兵兵兵兵兵兵兵兵兵
兵兵兵兵兵兵兵兵兵兵兵兵兵兵兵兵兵兵兵兵兵兵兵兵
兵兵兵兵兵兵兵兵兵兵兵兵兵兵兵兵兵兵兵兵兵兵兵兵
兵兵兵兵兵兵兵兵兵兵兵兵兵兵兵兵兵兵兵兵兵兵兵兵
兵兵兵兵兵兵兵兵兵兵兵兵兵兵兵兵兵兵兵兵兵兵兵兵
兵兵兵兵兵兵兵兵兵兵兵兵兵兵兵兵兵兵兵兵兵兵兵兵
兵兵兵兵兵兵兵兵兵兵兵兵兵兵兵兵兵兵兵兵兵兵兵兵
兵兵兵兵兵兵兵兵兵兵兵兵兵兵兵兵兵兵兵兵兵兵兵兵

兵兵兵兵兵兵兵乒兵兵兵兵兵兵兵乓兵兵兵兵兵兵兵乒
兵兵兵乓兵兵乒兵兵兵乒乒兵兵乒乓兵兵乒乓兵兵乓乓
乒乒兵兵兵兵乓乓乓乓兵兵乒乒乓乓乒乓兵乓兵兵乓乓
兵乒兵乒乒乒乓乓兵兵乒乒乓乓乓乓乒乒乓乓乒兵乓乓
乒兵乓乓乒兵乓乓乒乒乓乓乒乒乓乓乒乒乓乓乒乒乓乓
乒乒乓乓乒乒乓乓乒乒乓乓乒乒乓乓乒乒乓乓乒乒乓乓
乒乒乓乓乒乒乓乓乒乒乓乓乒乒乓乓乒乒乓乓乒乒乓乓
乒乓乒乓乒乓乒乓乒乓乒乓乒乓乒乓乒乓乒乓乒乓乒乓
乒乓乒乓乒乒乓乓乒乓乒乓乒乒乓乓乒乓乒乓乒乒乓乓
乒乒乒乒乒乒乒乒乓乓乓乓乓乓乓乓乒乒　乒乒乒　乓
乓乓　乒乓乒乒　乒　乓　　乒乒　　　乒乒　　乓乓
 乒乒　　乓乒　乒　乓　　乒　乓　乒乒乒　　乓　乒
  乒乒　乓　乓乓　乒　　乒　　乓　　乒　乓　　乒
乒　　　　　　　乓乓　　　　　　　乓　　　乒　乓
　乒　　　乓　　　　　乒　　　　　乓　　　　乓
　　　乒　　　　　　　　　　　　　　　　　乓

丘丘丘丘丘丘丘丘丘丘丘丘丘丘丘丘丘丘丘丘丘丘丘丘
丘丘丘丘丘丘丘丘丘丘丘丘丘丘丘丘丘丘丘丘丘丘丘丘
丘丘丘丘丘丘丘丘丘丘丘丘丘丘丘丘丘丘丘丘丘丘丘丘
丘丘丘丘丘丘丘丘丘丘丘丘丘丘丘丘丘丘丘丘丘丘丘丘
丘丘丘丘丘丘丘丘丘丘丘丘丘丘丘丘丘丘丘丘丘丘丘丘
丘丘丘丘丘丘丘丘丘丘丘丘丘丘丘丘丘丘丘丘丘丘丘丘
丘丘丘丘丘丘丘丘丘丘丘丘丘丘丘丘丘丘丘丘丘丘丘丘
丘丘丘丘丘丘丘丘丘丘丘丘丘丘丘丘丘丘丘丘丘丘丘丘
丘丘丘丘丘丘丘丘丘丘丘丘丘丘丘丘丘丘丘丘丘丘丘丘
丘丘丘丘丘丘丘丘丘丘丘丘丘丘丘丘丘丘丘丘丘丘丘丘
丘丘丘丘丘丘丘丘丘丘丘丘丘丘丘丘丘丘丘丘丘丘丘丘
丘丘丘丘丘丘丘丘丘丘丘丘丘丘丘丘丘丘丘丘丘丘丘丘
丘丘丘丘丘丘丘丘丘丘丘丘丘丘丘丘丘丘丘丘丘丘丘丘
丘丘丘丘丘丘丘丘丘丘丘丘丘丘丘丘丘丘丘丘丘丘丘丘
丘丘丘丘丘丘丘丘丘丘丘丘丘丘丘丘丘丘丘丘丘丘丘丘
丘丘丘丘丘丘丘丘丘丘丘丘丘丘丘丘丘丘丘丘丘丘丘丘

Writing from Reading

Summarize

1 Given the pictorial nature of the Chinese characters, the poem is telling a story as much through images as it is through sounds. What picture do you see here?

Analyze Craft

2 Can you get the sense of this "sound" poem about battle without saying it out loud? What does it sound like when you read it aloud?

3 How does the noise of the back and forth—"ping . . . pong"—of saying the Chinese characters create a verbal dramatization of a scene of war?

4 Does the sound of "chiou" resolve the previous back and forth of sounds?

Analyze Voice

5 Chinese is a highly musical language with the meaning of words often tied to the pitch at which the word is spoken. Given the differences between the tonal nature of the Chinese language and that of European languages, why might you find it difficult to hear the poet's voice without adding the sound of your own voice?

Synthesize Summary and Analysis

6 The sound of the poem works to become the meaning of the poem. Where have you encountered this concept in your reading of other poems?

Interpret the Poem

7 Would it be possible to make a poem such as this in English? Explain.

Dylan Thomas (1914–1953)

For a brief biography of Dylan Thomas, see chapter 23.

AS YOU READ **Allow your eye to guide you to meanings in the shape. Why does the "I" link the two parts?**

Vision and Prayer (1945)

Who
Are you
Who is born
In the next room
So loud to my own
That I can hear the womb
Opening and the dark run
Over the ghost and the dropped son
Behind the wall thin as a wren's bone?
In the birth bloody room unknown
To the burn and turn of time
And the heart print of man
Bows no baptism
But dark alone
Blessing on
The wild
Child.
I
Must lie
Still as stone
By the wren bone
Wall hearing the moan
Of the mother hidden
And the shadowed head of pain
Casting tomorrow like a thorn
And the midwives of miracle sing
Until the turbulent new born
Burns me his name and his flame
And the winged wall is torn
By his torrid crown
And the dark thrown
From his loin
To bright
Light.

Writing from Reading

Summarize

1 The poet hears the sounds of his son's birth. How does he focus his attentiveness?

Analyze Craft

2 Why does the poet choose to give this particular shape to his lines? Does it enhance their meaning? Does it intensify emotion? What metaphors does he employ also to this end?

Analyze Voice

3 However odd the shape of the poem, does the voice seem normal for the occasion? Where does it veer toward a prayerful tone?

Synthesize Summary and Analysis

4 The particular shape works together with the feeling about the situation to create a particular effect. How is this related to the larger question of how form guides emotion in all poems?

Interpret the Poem

5 How does this event fit into the larger questions of life and death? What is the significance of the "I" on its own central line?

PROSE POEMS

We may be accustomed to think that line breaks are required of poetry. Some writers, however, compose poems in dense, compact units of unbroken lines. **Prose poems** use the devices and imagery characteristic of traditionally lined poetry, but in compact units. French poets of the nineteenth century inaugurated the modern use of the form, and it has seen consistent usage in twentieth-century poetry in English as well. There's no clearly defined line separating the prose poem from the short short story. The mere fact that a poet intends a piece to be read and heard as a prose poem is reason enough to consider it so, as in this example from Carolyn Forché.

Carolyn Forché (b. 1950)

For a brief biography of Carolyn Forché, see chapter 15.

AS YOU READ Picture the scene, as you would for a short story or a movie. Night, a Central American nation, a family dinner. An American poet and her companion are guests of the military man.

The Colonel (1982)

What you have heard is true. I was in his house. His wife carried a tray of coffee and sugar. His daughter filed her nails, his son went out for the night. There were daily papers, pet dogs, a pistol on the cushion beside him. The moon swung bare on its black cord over the house. On the television was a cop show. It was in English. Broken bottles were embedded in the walls around the house to scoop the kneecaps from a man's legs or cut his hands to lace. On the windows there were gratings like those in liquor stores. We had dinner, rack of lamb, good wine, a gold bell was on the table for calling the maid. The maid brought green mangoes, salt, a type of bread. I was asked how I enjoyed the country. There was a brief commercial in Spanish. His wife took everything away. There was some talk then of how difficult it had become to govern. The parrot said hello on the terrace. The colonel told it to shut up, and pushed himself from the table. My friend said to me with his eyes: say nothing. The colonel returned with a sack used to bring groceries home. He spilled many human ears on the table. They were like dried peach halves. There is no other way to say this. He took one of them in his hands, shook it in our faces, dropped it into a water glass. It came alive there. I am tired of fooling around he said. As for the rights of anyone, tell your people they can go fuck themselves. He swept the ears to the floor with his arm and held the last of the wine in the air. Something for your poetry, no? he said. Some of the ears on the floor caught this scrap of his voice. Some of the ears on the floor were pressed to the ground.

Writing from Reading

Summarize

1 Carolyn Forché has said that this event in fact took place—and announces "I [she herself] was in his house" at poem's start. What kind of truth is she telling, and how does she seem to respond?

Analyze Craft

2 What symbolism is evoked by the poem's final disturbing image of ears catching "this scrap of his voice" and ears "pressed to the ground"?

Analyze Voice

3 How does the language here feel more like a story than a poem? How does the plain language intensify the speaker's story?

Synthesize Summary and Analysis

4 With unbroken lines, this prose poem forms a thick block of text. How does this form reflect the poem's subject and title character?

Interpret the Poem

5 Who is the "you" the speaker mentions in the opening line? Does she intend someone specific? And how does the "I am tired of fooling around . . ." get differentiated from the speaker's "I"?

Louis Jenkins (b. 1942)

Although born in Enid, Oklahoma, and raised for some time in Kansas, Louis Jenkins is a thirty-year resident of Duluth, Minnesota, and has been called by Garrison Keillor the "great wit of the North." A master of prose poetry, Jenkins is the author of eleven books of poetry, including most recently *North of the Cities* (2007), *Four Places on Lake Superior's North Shore* (2005), and *Distance from the Sun* (2004). His book of prose poetry, *Nice Fish* (1995), won the Minnesota Book Award in 1995. Says Jenkins, "I write some poems that are lines, but to me prose poems seem to be comfortable. It has a casual quality to it that other verse does not."

AS YOU READ Think about where you would break the lines if this were a traditionally lineated poem. Consider the effect the prose form has on the language and the tone overall.

Football

(1995)

I take the snap from center, fake to the right, fade back . . . I've got protection. I've got a receiver open downfield. . . . What the hell is this? This isn't a football, it's a shoe, a man's brown leather oxford. A cousin to a football maybe, the same skin, but not the same, a thing made for the earth, not the air. I realize that this is a world where anything is possible and I understand, also, that one often has to make do with what one has. I have eaten pancakes, for instance, with that clear corn syrup on them because there was no maple syrup and they weren't very good. Well, anyway, this is different. (My man downfield is waving his arms.) One has certain responsibilities, one has to make choices. This isn't right and I'm not going to throw it.

Writing from Reading

Summarize

1 Why do you think the poet chooses the prose poem to describe this comic, imaginary event?

Analyze Craft

2 What elements from traditionally lineated poetry can you find in this poem?

Analyze Voice

3 How does the statement "I realize that this is a world where anything is possible" prefigure the last sentence, and what does refusal entail?

Synthesize Summary and Analysis

4 At what point in the poem do you come to recognize that this is an imagined event and not an actual game?

Interpret the Poem

5 Can there be any connection between the strange substitution of the shoe for a football and corn syrup on pancakes? Why do you think the speaker is reminded of the breakfast?

Ray Gonzalez (1952)

Ray Gonzalez is the author of sixteen books of poetry, nonfiction, and fiction. Recent titles include *Renaming the Earth: Personal Essays* (2008) and *Consideration of the Guitar* (2005). Gonzalez's 1996 collection, *Heat Arrivals,* won the PEN/Josephine Miles Book Award. He is also an author of short stories and the editor of twelve poetry anthologies. Gonzalez is the poetry editor of *The Bloomsbury Review* and publisher of *Luna,* a journal of poetry. He is a full Professor of English and teaches in the MFA program at the University of Minnesota in Minneapolis.

AS YOU READ **Keep track of the story of the ritual and the chain of images.**

Corn Face Mesilla[1] (2002)

Someone dissolves into yesterday's climber who made it to the top of the night walk, the massive snow capped mountain in his dream waiting for him to select certain animals to play with. Someone plants a grain of sand in one of those closed eyes and the pain is positioned to show him how the harvest will be. Someone doesn't understand and decides to stand in front of the rock wall and look up forever, condemned and called as a corn follower who made it this far without dropping the bundle of husks

[1]Mesilla, New Mexico, is a small town between Las Cruces, New Mexico, and El Paso, Texas.

on his back. Someone doesn't want to be identified, so the fields are never cleared of rocks, the galleries never illuminated with bloody portraits, the meeting at the lake never held, the ceremony never disrupted by the enemies of the magnolia trees. Someone survives the picking of the corn and becomes an unknown woman standing on a great block of ice, her ability to be worshipped reinforced by the autumn return of a thousand birds flying out of a sun that blinds everything first before rising in the sky to look beyond the fields.

Writing from Reading

Summarize

1 The poet observes and describes a participant—"someone"—in an Indian corn harvest ritual. Make a description of the ritual with the clues given in the poem.

Analyze Craft

2 What effect does the poet create by the repetition of "someone"? If you separated each line with a space, how would the effect change, or would it remain the same?

Analyze Voice

3 The poet creates a chant-like effect by using repetition. Why is repetition so important to this poem?

Synthesize Summary and Analysis

4 The poet employs chant-like lines in a prose-like block of language to tell the story of what may possibly be a ritual he sees in a dream. Does it seem possible that a series of simple lines of prose can create such an effect? What does it suggest to you about the line between poetry and prose?

Interpret the Poem

5 Who is the subject of the dream? Who is the dreamer?

For Review and Further Study

Marilyn Chin (b. 1955)

Turtle Soup (1987)

You go home one evening tired from work,
and your mother boils you turtle soup.
Twelve hours hunched over the hearth
(who knows what else is in that cauldron).

You say, "Ma, you've poached the symbol of long life;
that turtle lived four thousand years, swam
the Wei, up the Yellow, over the Yangtze.
Witnessed the Bronze Age, the High Tang,
grazed on splendid sericulture."
(So, she boils the life out of him.)

"All our ancestors have been fools.
Remember Uncle Wu who rode ten thousand miles
to kill a famous Manchu and ended up
with his head on a pole? Eat, child,
its liver will make you strong."

"Sometimes you're the life, sometimes the sacrifice."
Her sobbing is inconsolable.
So, you spread that gentle napkin
over your lap in decorous Pasadena.

Baby, some high priestess has got it wrong.
The golden decal on the green underbelly
says "Made in Hong Kong."

Is there nothing left but the shell
and humanity's strange inscriptions,
the songs, the rites, the oracles?

—for Ben Huang

Questions for Interactive Reading and Writing

1. This poem reports on a domestic scene. How would you describe it, including location?
2. How "free" do you find the form of this poem? How "free" do you find the lines? Do you notice any near rhymes?
3. What evidence of a clash of cultures or generations do you see in the poem?
4. What is the poem's tone?
5. What does the poet mean by "humanity's strange inscriptions"?

Sandra Cisneros (b. 1954)

Pumpkin Eater (1994)

I'm no trouble.
Honest to God I'm not.
I'm not

the kind of woman
who telephones in the middle of the night,
—who told you that?—
splitting the night like machete.
Before and after.   After.   Before.
No, no, not me.
I'm not

the she who slings words bigger than rocks,
sharper than Houdini knives,
verbal Molotovs.
The one who did that—*yo no fuí*—
that wasn't me.

I'm no hysteric,
terrorist,
emotional anarchist.

I keep inside a pumpkin shell.
There I do very well.
Shut a blind eye to where
my pumpkin-eater roams.
I keep like fruitcake.
Subsist on air.
Not a worry nor care.
Please.
I'm as free for the taking
as the eyes of Saint Lucy.
No trouble at all.

I swear, I swear, I swear . . .

Questions for Interactive Reading and Writing

1. How does the buildup of emotion influence the form of this poem?
2. What does the speaker's emphatic and repeated denials suggest about her situation and possibly even her character?
3. What effect on your understanding of her, and the poem itself, does the invocation of the nursery rhyme have?
4. Look up the reference to "the eyes of Saint Lucy." What impact does that reference have on the meaning of the poem?

Mari Evans (b. 1923)

Spectrum (1968)

Petulance is purple
happiness pink
ennui chartreuse
and love
—I think
is blue
like midnight sometimes
or a robin's egg
sometimes

Questions for Interactive Reading and Writing

1. Describe the moods or emotional states the poet lists. Why does she attach a color to each of them? Do you find an order in the list?
2. Love is two shades of blue. How would you distinguish between them?
3. Is the poet speaking of love in a general sense or about a particular instance? Explain.

4. How does the conjunction "and" shift the poem toward its main subject? How does the last word—the repetition of "sometimes"—change the meaning of the poem?

Allen Ginsberg (1926–1997)

A Supermarket in California (1955)

What thoughts I have of you tonight, Walt Whitman, for I walked down the sidestreets under the trees with a headache self-conscious looking at the full moon.

In my hungry fatigue, and shopping for images, I went into the neon fruit supermarket, dreaming of your enumerations!

What peaches and what penumbras! Whole families shopping at night! Aisles full of husbands! Wives in the avocados, babies in the tomatoes!—and you, García Lorca, what were you doing down by the watermelons?

I saw you, Walt Whitman, childless, lonely old grubber, poking among the meats in the refrigerator and eyeing the grocery boys.

I heard you asking questions of each: Who killed the pork chops? What price bananas? Are you my Angel?

I wandered in and out of the brilliant stacks of cans following you, and followed in my imagination by the store detective.

We strode down the open corridors together in our solitary fancy tasting artichokes, possessing every frozen delicacy, and never passing the cashier.

Where are we going, Walt Whitman? The doors close in an hour. Which way does your beard point tonight?

(I touch your book and dream of our odyssey in the supermarket and feel absurd.)

Will we walk all night through solitary streets? The trees add shade to shade, lights out in the houses, we'll both be lonely.

Will we stroll dreaming of the lost America of love past blue automobiles in driveways, home to our silent cottage?

Ah, dear father, graybeard, lonely old courage-teacher, what America did you have when Charon quit poling his ferry and you got out on a smoking bank and stood watching the boat disappear on the black waters of Lethe?

Questions for Interactive Reading and Writing

1. An American poet on the West Coast speaks to an American East Coast poet of an earlier day. What kinship does the modern poet feel for the older writer?
2. Why does the poet choose a California supermarket for the setting of this poem?
3. Where is the "poetry" in this freely told story?
4. How would you describe the leap the poet makes from the line "Aisles full of husbands . . ." to "wives in the avocados, babies in the tomatoes . . .?"
5. Who is García Lorca? Why is it fitting that he should appear to the poet also?
6. What is the technical device the poet uses when he addresses Whitman by means of carrying his book of poems?

Lorna Goodison (b. 1947)

On Becoming a Tiger (2000)

The day that they stole her tiger's-eye ring
was the day that she became a tiger.
She was inspired by advice received from Rilke

who recommended that, if the business of drinking
should become too bitter,
that one should change oneself into wine.

The tiger was actually always asleep
inside her, she had seen it
stretched out, drowsing and inert

when she lay upon her side and stared
for seven consecutive days into a tall mirror
that she had turned on its side.

Her focus had penetrated all exterior
till at last she could see within her
a red glowing landscape of memory and poems,

a heart within her heart
and lying there big, bright, and golden
was the tiger, wildly darkly striped.

At night she dreams that her mother
undresses her and discovers that, under
her outerwear, her bare limbs are marked
of the huge and fierce cat of Asia
with the stunning golden quartz eyes.

She has taken to wearing long dresses
to cover the rounded tail coiling behind her.
She has filled her vases with tiger lilies

and replaced her domestic cat
with a smaller relative of hers, the ocelot.
At four in the morning she practices stalking

up and down the long expanse of the hall.
What are the ingredients in tiger's milk?
Do tigers ever mate for life?

Can she rewrite the story of Little Black Sambo?
Can a non-tiger take a tiger for a wife?
To these and other questions,

she is seeking urgent answers
now that she is living an openly
tigerly life.

Questions for Interactive Reading and Writing

1. How do the three line stanzas serve to control the movement of the poem?
2. The poet refers to the German poet Rainer Maria Rilke and a metaphor about transformation. Rilke's sonnet 29 (in *Sonnets to Orpheus*) contains the lines, "What is your most painful experience? / If your drink is bitter, turn into wine." How does the Goodison poem reflect that advice?
3. How does the kinship the speaker feels with the imaginary tiger affect her everyday activities?
4. What part, if any, does race play in the poem?

D. H. Lawrence (1885–1930)

For a brief biography of D. H. Lawrence, see chapter 9.

Snake (1921)

A snake came to my water-trough
On a hot, hot day, and I in pajamas for the heat,
To drink there.

In the deep, strange-scented shade of the great dark carob-tree
I came down the steps with my pitcher
And must wait, must stand and wait, for there he was at the trough before me.

He reached down from a fissure in the earth-wall in the gloom
And trailed his yellow-brown slackness soft-bellied down, over the edge of the stone trough
And rested his throat upon the stone bottom,
And where the water had dripped from the tap, in a small clearness,
He sipped with his straight mouth,
Softly drank through his straight gums, into his slack long body,
Silently.
Someone was before me at my water-trough,
And I, like a second comer, waiting.
He lifted his head from his drinking, as cattle do,
And looked at me vaguely, as drinking cattle do,
And flickered his two-forked tongue from his lips, and mused a moment,
And stooped and drank a little more,
Being earth-brown, earth-golden from the burning bowels of the earth
On the day of Sicilian July, with Etna smoking.

The voice of my education said to me
He must be killed,
For in Sicily the black, black snakes are innocent, the gold are venomous.

And voices in me said, If you were a man
You would take a stick and break him now, and finish him off.

But must I confess how I liked him,
How glad I was he had come like a guest in quiet, to drink at my water-trough

And depart peaceful, pacified, and thankless,
Into the burning bowels of this earth?

Was it cowardice, that I dared not kill him?
Was it perversity, that I longed to talk to him? Was it humility, to feel so honored?
I felt so honored.

And yet those voices:
If you were not afraid, you would kill him!

And truly I was afraid, I was most afraid,
But even so, honored still more
That he should seek my hospitality
From out the dark door of the secret earth.

He drank enough
And lifted his head, dreamily, as one who has drunken,
And flickered his tongue like a forked night on the air, so black,
Seeming to lick his lips,
And looked around like a god, unseeing, into the air,
And slowly turned his head,
And slowly, very slowly, as if thrice adream,
Proceeded to draw his slow length curving round
And climb again the broken bank of my wall-face.

And as he put his head into that dreadful hole,
And as he slowly drew up, snake-easing his shoulders, and entered farther,
A sort of horror, a sort of protest against his withdrawing into that horrid black hole,
Deliberately going into the blackness, and slowly drawing himself after,
Overcame me now his back was turned.

I looked round, I put down my pitcher,
I picked up a clumsy log
And threw it at the water-trough with a clatter.

I think it did not hit him,
But suddenly that part of him that was left behind convulsed in undignified haste.
Writhed like lightning, and was gone
Into the black hole, the earth-lipped fissure in the wall-front,
At which, in the intense still noon, I stared with fascination.

And immediately I regretted it.
I thought how paltry, how vulgar, what a mean act!
I despised myself and the voices of my accursed human education.

And I thought of the albatross
And I wished he would come back, my snake.

For he seemed to me again like a king,
Like a king in exile, uncrowned in the underworld,
Now due to be crowned again.

And so, I missed my chance with one of the lords
Of life.
And I have something to expiate:
A pettiness.

Questions for Interactive Reading and Writing

1. Why should we consider this description of an encounter between man and snake a poem and not prose? Can you read it as if it were a letter? What separates this text from plain prose?
2. In what ways does the poet-speaker find the meeting with the snake a test of his modern beliefs and values? What biblical symbol stands behind the image of this particular snake? What biblical test of beliefs and values?
3. What in particular surprises the man about his own behavior?
4. Why does the image of the "earth-lipped fissure in the wall-front" frighten him?
5. Why does he call his education "accursed"?
6. What is the overall outcome of the encounter, and how does the poet characterize it?

Denise Levertov (1923–1997)

The Ache of Marriage (1964)

The ache of marriage:

thigh and tongue, beloved,
are heavy with it,
it throbs in the teeth

We look for communion
and are turned away, beloved,
each and each

It is leviathan and we
in its belly
looking for joy, some joy
not to be known outside it

two by two in the ark of
the ache of it.

Questions for Interactive Reading and Writing

1. Is this poem a celebration or a complaint or lament? Whom is the poet addressing?
2. What are the central metaphors the poet uses for marriage?

3. How do the sounds of the poem—the arrangement of the consonants and vowels—reflect the argument of the poem?
4. Does the poet find any relief from the "ache"?

Alberto Alvaro Rios (b. 1952)

Nani (1982)

Sitting at her table, she serves
the sopa de arroz to me
instinctively, and I watch her,
the absolute mamá, and eat words
I might have had to say more
out of embarrassment. To speak,
now-foreign words I used to speak,
too, dribble down her mouth as she serves
me albóndigas. No more
than a third are easy to me.
by the stove she does something with words
and looks at me only with her
back. I am full. I tell her
I taste the mint, and watch her speak
smiles at the stove. All my words
make her smile. Nani never serves
herself, she only watches me
with her skin, her hair. I ask for more.

I watch the mamá warming more
tortillas for me. I watch her
fingers in the flame for me.
Near her mouth, I see a wrinkle speak
of a man whose body serves
the ants like she serves me, then more words
from more wrinkles about children, words
about this and that, flowing more
easily from these other mouths. Each serves
as a tremendous string around her,
holding her together. They speak
Nani was this and that to me
and I wonder just how much of me
will die with her, what were the words
I could have been, was. Her insides speak
through a hundred wrinkles, now, more
than she can bear, steel around her,
shouting, then, What is this thing she serves?

She asks me if I want more.
I own no words to stop her.
Even before I speak, she serves.

Questions for Interactive Reading and Writing

1. What is the relation between the speaker and Nani?
2. Do you need to know the English names of the dishes Nani serves in order to understand the poem?
3. What is the connection between food and words? How does the poet establish this as a metaphor?
4. Why does the poet emphasize Nani's "wrinkles"?
5. How would the effect of the poem change if it were written in rhyming couplets?

Robert Sward (b. 1933)

God Is in the Cracks (2006)

"Just a tiny crack separates this world
from the next, and you step over it
every day,
God is in the cracks."
Foot propped up, nurse hovering, phone ringing.
"Relax and breathe from your heels.
Now, that's breathing.
So, tell me, have you enrolled yet?"

"Enrolled?"

"In the Illinois College of Podiatry."

"Dad, I have a job. I teach."

"Ha! Well, I'm a man of the lower extremities."

"Dad, I'm fifty-three."

"So what? I'm eighty. I knew you
before you began wearing shoes.
Too good for feet?" he asks.
"*I. Me. Mind:*
That's all I get from your poetry.
Your words lack feet. Forget the mind.
Mind is all over the place. There's no support.
You want me to be proud of you? Be a foot man.
Here, son," he says, handing me back my shoes,
"try walking in these.
Arch supports. Now there's a subject.
Some day you'll write about arch supports."

Questions for Interactive Reading and Writing

1. The poem contains informal dialogue reminiscent of a scene in a contemporary short story. Why doesn't the poet give us the setting? Can you imagine a setting to go along with it?
2. What does the father mean by "God is in the cracks," and is he possibly referring to that well-known phrase, "The Devil's in the details"? Does the poet offer a similar opinion in the poem itself?
3. What might the father mean when he says that his son's words, and, presumably, his poetry, lack feet?
4. How many references are there in this short poem to shoes and feet? What effect do these create? How would you describe the overall effect of the poem—is it humorous? bittersweet? pathetic? sorrowful? Or is there another way entirely to describe it?

James Wright (1927–1980)

For a brief biography of James Wright, see chapter 18.

Autumn Begins in Martins Ferry, Ohio (1959)

In the Shreve High football stadium,
I think of Polacks nursing long beers in Tiltonsville,
And gray faces of Negroes in the blast furnace at
  Benwood,
And the ruptured night watchman of Wheeling Steel,
Dreaming of heroes.

All the proud fathers are ashamed to go home.
Their women cluck like starved pullets,
Dying for love.

Therefore,
Their sons grow suicidally beautiful
At the beginning of October,
And gallop terribly against each other's bodies.

Questions for Interactive Reading and Writing

1. Try a paraphrase of the poem. The setting should give you the meaning of the line about the sons who "gallop terribly against each other's bodies."
2. Describe the social structure of life in Martin's Ferry, Ohio, based on statements in the poem.
3. How do the lives people lead here stand against the way they dream of "heroes"? Why might the "proud fathers" be "ashamed to go home"?
4. Where does the poem turn?
5. Does the contrast between the women—the wives—who are "dying for love" and the sons who "grow suicidally beautiful" make sense?
6. How essentially American is this poem? Can you imagine a French version? A Mexican version? An Iraqi version?

Reading for Open Form

When reading for open form, look for poetry that employs a structure determined by its own purpose and uses its own line lengths, line breaks, and rhythm (especially the rhythms of natural speech) instead of traditional patterns of meter, stanza structure, and rhyme.

Is there repetition in the poem?	EXAMPLE: "because there is in this world no one thing / to which the bramble of *blackberry* corresponds, / . . . saying *blackberry, blackberry, blackberry.*"

Is there grammatical variation in the poem?	EXAMPLE: "since feeling is first / who pays any attention / to the syntax of things / will never wholly kiss you // wholly to be a fool / while Spring is in the world"
Are there organized patterns of imagery?	EXAMPLE: "Even the battered little furnace, roaring along as patient as a donkey, chokes and clogs, / a dense, malignant smoke shoots up, someone has to fiddle with a cock, then hammer it, / before the gush and stench will deintensify, the dark, Dantean broth wearily subside."
How does the line itself create a rhythmical unit?	EXAMPLE: "I Celebrate myself, and sing myself" EXAMPLE: "Someone dissolves into yesterday's climber who made it to the top of the night walk"
How is a line arranged? Where does it break to create its own visual effect?	EXAMPLE: "And so, I missed my chance with one of the lords Of life. And I have something to expiate: A pettiness." EXAMPLE: "Easter Wings"—shaped in triangles like angel wings

Writing about Open Form

1. Using Wright's "Autumn Begins in Martins Ferry, Ohio," analyze the poem's use of open form elements (including line length, sound, and stanza structure).
2. Divide one of the three prose poems included in this chapter into a lined poem with separate stanzas. Then, write an informal explanation of your line breaks and stanza breaks. Include observations on how your reading of the poem transforms with your formal changes.
3. Begin with Whitman's "Song of Myself" and then read through the two subsequent poems in this chapter that invoke Whitman (by Alexie and Ginsberg). Discuss how these two more contemporary poets both imitate and break from Whitman's form and subject matter.
4. Using "Easter Wings" or "Swan and Shadow," examine the linkage between a poem's subject and its shape. Consider how different the poem would be if it did not visually depict an object.

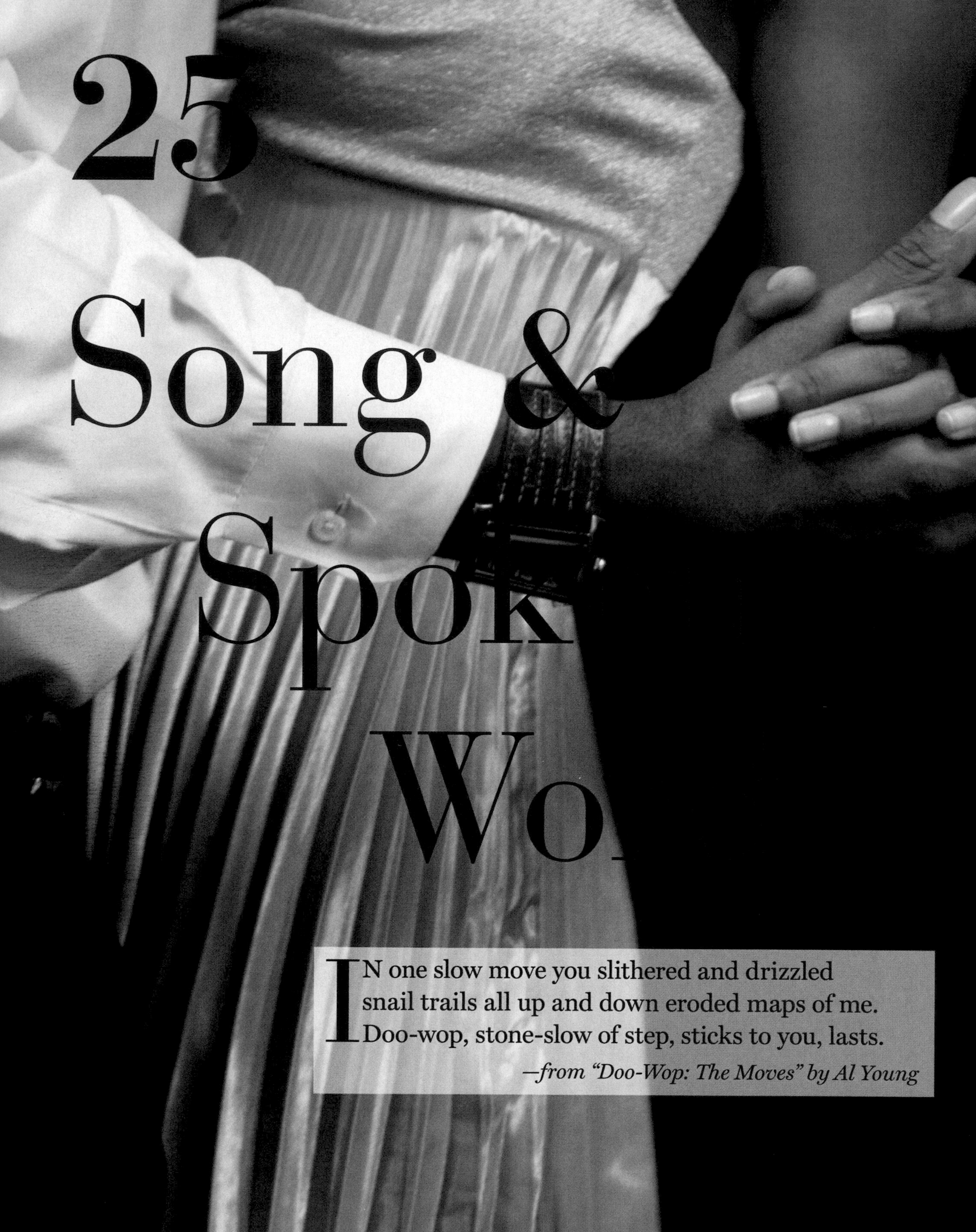

25 Song & Spok Wo

IN one slow move you slithered and drizzled
snail trails all up and down eroded maps of me.
Doo-wop, stone-slow of step, sticks to you, lasts.

—from "Doo-Wop: The Moves" by Al Young

"A lot of people are mystified by the relationship . . . between poetry and song, and I've always been surprised that people can't hear how obvious that relationship is. . . . Put your hand to your heart and hear that iambic beat. Everything around us is in tempo and works through rhythm and works through a kind of musicality."

Conversation with Al Young, available on video at www.mhhe.com/delbanco1e

VERSE and song are kissing cousins. In chapter 15, we included a lyric likely set to music by Sappho and a song by Robert Burns; in chapter 16, we talked about the origins of poetry as song, with sacred verses such as the Song of Solomon. In fact, each of our previous chapters on poetry has—to a greater or lesser degree—linked the *craft* of poetry to attributes of *voice*. What could be more musical than rhythm? When a poet chooses words, they are selected for pitch and tone. The word *sonnet* itself means "little song." Words such as *rhythm, pitch,* and *tone* belong to the vocabulary of music and musicians; the word *lyric* attests to this connection. You can almost hear the sliding on the dance floor in "Doo-Wop: The Moves" with "in one slow move you slithered." There are, of course, certain kinds of poetry that focus on the eye, not ear, but by and large poetry is intended to be heard as well as seen.

Poetry began as recitation; it's in the genre's DNA. It goes all the way back to the origins of the Greek epic, when the Greek *rhapsodes,* festival poetry performers, chanted the lines of the long poems of war and peace. Sappho supposedly said her poems out loud for the delectation of a small group of devotees. The bardic tradition *requires* speech and even a kind of rhythmic song in order to reach its audience; there were no books, but there were lyres and harps. The blind bard Homer invokes the Muse, so that she may "sing" in and through him, telling the tale of the wrath of Achilles. Centuries later, the great Latin epic *The Aeneid* does much the same; Virgil begins his account of the escape from Troy and founding of Rome with the invocation of "Arms and the man I *sing*. . . ." In this way, poetry reaches beyond the page, relying on verbal performance and aspiring to song.

The following lines from the former Poet Laureate of the state of California make clear this poet's love of music and musicality in language. Al Young has written album liner notes for Motown records and two volumes of memoirs based on his life with popular music, jazz, and hip-hop. He is also an outspoken proponent of spoken word poetry and poetry as a public forum. As it was for ancient bards, for Young poetry is something resembling pure song.

The poem is there for the human body to sound or to act out.

Q&A

. . . all of poetry is yet to be created . . .

A Conversation on Writing

Al Young

Music and Language

Music is just naturally related to language and language to music. . . . When you're looking at a poem on a page, that is not the poem. The poem is there for the human body to sound or to act out. And each of us reciting the same Emily Dickinson poem or Langston Hughes poem will in fact bring a new poem into being. In the same way that you have Yo-Yo Ma playing a Bach cello concerto and you have . . . a cellist with the Kronos Quartet—they'll play it completely differently. The same notes, but they don't mean anything until someone brings feeling to it, brings a personal voice to it.

Poetry, Hip-Hop, and Spoken Word

With most kids who get into poetry now, they have no problem relating it to music because a lot of them started as hip-hop or rap or spoken word aficionados or performers. And when you go to the poetry clubs, you see how excited they are to be actually saying something using those rhythms and inflections. And I've noticed that a student . . . who will not write a paper on a social situation or a political situation now, will get up at a poetry club or a rap performance and will say all kinds of things, many of them insightful and nuanced.

Poetry and Live Audiences

Poetry becomes a joy when you're doing it to a live audience. . . . People are moving with your rhythms and your inflections and you're not alone. . . . You're just talking to each other and using poetry to do it. So, I think that—to paraphrase Ralph Waldo Emerson, who said somewhere—all of American literature is yet to be written. Well, all of poetry is yet to be created, and I think the future of poetry is quite healthy.

Al Young was born (1939) in Biloxi, Mississippi, raised in the rural South and Detroit, and eventually made his way to California, where he was named state Poet Laureate in 2005. Young's career has ranged from poet and novelist to screenwriter for Sidney Poitier and Bill Cosby. He has also taught creative writing at a number of universities, including Stanford and several campuses of the University of California. Young has an interest in jazz and blues and performs stories and poems to musical accompaniment. A recipient of Guggenheim, Fulbright, and National Endowment for the Arts Fellowships, Young currently lives in Berkeley, California.

To watch this entire interview and hear the author read "Doo-Wop: The Moves" and other poems, go to www.mhhe.com/delbanco1e.

RESEARCH ASSIGNMENT After watching the interview with Al Young, describe his view of traditional forms of poetry, such as the sonnet, and the music of poetry. Playing devil's advocate, disagree with Young's view and then turn around and support his view. Explore your own views on what makes music in poetry.

AS YOU READ Say the poem out loud and give yourself over to the pleasurable relation of word and rhythm, just as you would to a piece of music or a popular song.

Doo-Wop: The Moves (2006)

Let's make no bones about it—whatever
this means or ever meant to you. Darling,
you know your way through what I'm about
to say. Doo-wop still steals the moment,
this sizzling thrill of closeness; the slowness
of our touch too much, too messy to process.

Back when dawn rose off the river, we'd feel it.
Feel felt like enough when flowering was new
and not easy to handle. Neither was breathing.
All that light funneling in from Canada, ferried
over the river while you put a move on my heart.

Heart and soul, flesh and bone—doo-wop
was known to sabotage. All across the land
White Citizens Councils shouted and warned:
Negro music is corrupting White youth. Boycott
Negro Music. We were young, too. You pressed
your hand behind my neck, you kissed my mouth.

Wham! So who'd kissed whom? You still wonder?
In one slow move you slithered and drizzled
snail trails all up and down eroded maps of me.
Doo-wop, stone-slow of step, sticks to you, lasts.

The doo-wop mind cries: O baby you know
I love you, always thinking of you, I place no one
above you, and you know I'll never snub you.
Under doo-wop's spell, you make no bones.
You shake your perfumed boodie. You go for keeps.

Writing from Reading

Summarize

1 What has the speaker remembered here? What happened between him and his "darling"?

Analyze Craft

2 This poem announces, in its title, that it's a "Doo-Wop" musical tribute. In the poem, how do the doo-wop lyrics and the sound of doo-wop music get replicated in the lines of the poem?

3 How much of the poem's success depends on saying it, or trying to sing it, out loud?

4 Which phrases or lines distinguish the poem from a popular song?

Analyze Voice

5 How would you describe the tone of this poem?

6 What is the poet's attitude toward this particular variety of song? Toward music in general?

7 Do you find that the allusions to politics and history enhance the poem or weigh too heavily on it?

Synthesize Summary and Analysis

8 How does the speaker's love of music increase the power of his emotion toward the person he loves?

9 Why does he turn to music to express his emotions?

Interpret the Poem

10 How do love, music, politics, race all come together in this poem?

"Is poetry an aural or written art? For me, it's both. As time goes on, the way the poem looks is really important to me. But also the way it sounds. And I'm trying to find the perfect coincidence of the way the poem looks, the way it sounds, the way it means, the silence and the speech in the poem" Conversation with Li-Young Lee

RHYTHM AND SOUND

From Homer onward, poets have used rhythmical patterns and sounds. These rise from the page to emulate something chanted, attesting to the radically musical nature of Western poetry. Rhythm is one of the elemental qualities that separates poetry from ordinary speech and is the central technique in poetic song. (See chapter 22 for a fuller discussion of rhythm.) The most popular hits on the radio engage you with their "beat"; you can dance (or at least tap your foot) to them. Poet and classical scholar Laura Fargas writes about the overwhelming power of the three-syllable clusters (/ ~ ~) of dactylic hexameter, the traditional meter of ancient Greek poetry: "You couldn't vary from its rhythm if you wanted to. Think of griot chanting, or prayer chanting in Hebrew, Arabic, or Hindi, to get a sense of the basic sound, and then allow for variations for emphasis that a really good performer could use to make the story more vivid at appropriate moments—hesitations, hastenings, variations in tone of voice."

"Twenty-five hundred years ago, Homer, some guy stood up and chanted this poem about a war on the Turkish coast that has become a founding epic of western civilization. You can say out those rhythms. . . . Rhythms, they say, that in Greek sound like the surge of the sea that ships sailed across to fight that war."

Conversation with Robert Hass

Voice is also an integral part of any song—the human voice it is written for and the poet's voice that embodies and produces it. We can never fully *define* it, but we can try to *describe* it. What should we pay attention to in voice? We note, for example, the poet's use of sounds (see chapter 22) such as *alliteration* (when the first letter of a word is repeated, as in *Five **m**iles **m**eandering with a **m**azy **m**otion*), *assonance* (when vowels within words are repeated, as in *Where **A**lph, the sacred river r**a**n / through c**a**verns measureless to m**a**n),* consonance (when consonants within words are repeated, as in *for the whole / Of the sea is hilly with whales*), and *rhyme* (ran—man). Rhythmical patterns are important, but voice connects its author to an audience, and often the voice is more important than individual authorship in creating a song's or poem's context.

Anonymous

AS YOU READ Try to imagine what circumstances might have prompted the unknown poet to compose these lines.

Western Wind (c. 1500)

Western wind, when will thou blow
The small rain down can rain?
Christ, if my love were in my arms
And I in my bed again!

Writing from Reading

Summarize

1 In what circumstance does the anonymous poet find himself? Herself?

Analyze Craft

2 For you, what is the most compelling line or image in the poem, and why does it strike you?

3 What effect does the word *Christ* have on the poem? If it were omitted, how would the poem change?

4 How do sounds—rhyme, rhythm, repetition, alliteration, and so on—make this poem song-like?

Analyze Voice

5 "Western Wind" accomplishes much in a small space; list everything that you know about the speaker's situation and feelings.

6 This poem is a lament and outcry in a difficult time by an anonymous speaker. Does the anonymity of the speaker make the poem more or less effective? Or does it not matter?

Synthesize Summary and Analysis

7 Most lyric poetry laments loss and absence. What distinguishes this anonymous lyric from others of its kind (such as the fragment by Sappho in chapter 15 or Leonard Cohen's "For Anne" in chapter 16)?

Interpret the Poem

8 What does the last line suggest in coming after the previous three?

BALLAD

In twenty-first-century popular music, the word *ballad* is used to describe slow, often confessional songs. Traditionally, a **ballad** is a song or poem that tells a lively or tragic story in simple language, using rhyming four-line stanzas and a set meter (see chapter 22 for more on meter). Whoever first composed the following ballad was, in the artistic sense, detached; the maker does not criticize the king's malevolent decision to send his noble warriors to their deaths at sea. This historical ballad—its hero was a fighter-sailor of the thirteenth century—would have been the work of many hands, and we have no way of knowing who first "wrote" it.

> "The well that I always go back to is actually folk material. I was listening to Leadbelly the other day and just was amazed at what he was singing. Each line takes a remarkable leap into another reality and we accept it because it's sung, and so it sort of disarms our intellectual acumen, and we accept all these fantastic leaps."
>
> Conversation with Al Young

Anonymous

AS YOU READ Focus on the story, but also notice that the rhyming and its effects enhance the story itself.

Sir Patrick Spence (1765)

The King sits in Dumferling toune,
  Drinking the blude-reid wine:
"O whar will I get guid sailor,
  To sail this schip of mine?"

Up and spak an eldern knicht,
  Sat at the kings richt kne:
"Sir Patrick Spence is the best sailor
  That sails upon the se."

The king has written a braid letter,
  And signed it wi' his hand,
And sent it to Sir Patrick Spence,
  Was walking on the sand.

The first line that Sir Patrick red,
  A loud lauch lauchèd he;
The next line that Sir Patrick red,
  The teir blinded his ee.

"O wha is this has don this deid,
  This ill deid don to me,
To send me out this time o' the yeir,
  To sail upon the se!

"Mak haste, mak haste, my mirry men all,
  Our guid schip sails the morne."
"O say na sae, my master deir,
  For I feir a deadlie storme.

"Late late yestreen I saw the new moone,
Wi' the auld moone in hir arme,
And I feir, I feir, my deir master,
That we will cum to harme."

O our Scots nobles wer richt laith
To weet their cork-heild schoone,
Bot lang owre a' the play wer play'd,
Thair hats they swam aboone.

O lang, lang may their ladies sit,
Wi' thair fans into their hand,
Or ere they se Sir Patrick Spence
Cum sailing to the land.

O lang, lang may the ladies stand,
Wi' their gold kems in their hair,
Waiting for thair ain deir lords,
For they'll se thame na mair.

Haf owre, half owre to Aberdour,
It's fiftie fadom deip,
And thair lies guid Sir Patrick Spence,
Wi' the Scots lords at his feit.

Writing from Reading

Summarize

1 Read (or chant) this poem out loud. Did you find that the old-fashioned spellings and words were easier to understand this way? Paraphrase each stanza. What is the plot of the poem?

Analyze Craft

2 How does the rhythmical pattern, the use of language, or the use of rhyme contribute to the poem's song-like quality?

Analyze Voice

3 How would you describe the tone of this ballad?

4 We do not know who the original author of "Sir Patrick Spence" is—but the poem does have a voice that distinguishes it from other songs. How would you describe the voice of this particular work *or* the voice of a folk ballad (using specific examples from this poem as evidence)?

5 Look up any unfamiliar words and replace them with modern-day approximations. How does this change the poem's voice?

Synthesize Summary and Analysis

6 The technical components of the poem, and its musical qualities, create a moving story about loyalty, love, and history. Can you name some contemporary ballads that work in similar fashion?

7 Compare this traditional Scottish ballad with another, "Bonnie Barbara Allen" in chapter 22. How is the rhythm similar? What other similarities do you find?

Interpret the Poem

8 What lessons does the anonymous poet put forward about life?

SONGS OF THE COUNTRYSIDE: PASTORAL POETRY

As a poetic form, song itself emerges out of the conventions of peasant life in small towns and in the countryside, in the so-called **pastoral** (as in "countryside") **poetry** of the Roman poets. Anonymous lyrics from the thirteenth through early sixteenth centuries in England continue the tradition. As with "Western Wind" and the early

> "Poems come from poems, songs come from songs. They come from experience. You bring your own experience to everything that flows through you." Conversation with Robert Hass

ballads, we cannot name the author or do much more than approximate the date and place of composition; although we do not know their tunes, these early poems have the feel of something sung. By the sixteenth century, we do know the names of the authors, and at least something about them as individuals. Here English poet Christopher Marlowe gives us his version of a country boy's plea to his pastoral love. No shepherd is likely to have engaged in courtship in this way, but Marlowe imagines what it might be like to sing in rhyming couplets about these shared "delights."

Christopher Marlowe (1564–1593)

Born in Canterbury, Christopher Marlowe was to become the playwright and poet who paved the way for Elizabethan drama, including Shakespeare's work. While on scholarship at Corpus Christi College in Cambridge, Marlowe also served as a spy in the queen's secret service, which kept the Protestant queen safe from Catholic plots. Meanwhile, he cultivated a brilliant literary career with five dramas, among them *Tamburlaine* and *Doctor Faustus,* in which he perfected the blank verse form that Shakespeare would use in his plays. Marlowe also wrote poetry, though much of it is lost. The circumstances of his death at age twenty-nine are unclear; a widespread version holds that he was stabbed in a tavern fight, reportedly in an argument over the bill. Modern research suggests that his death may have been linked to his espionage activity.

AS YOU READ Think of a song in a musical in which the singer dressed in a shepherd's costume calls out to the object of his affections.

The Passionate Shepherd to His Love (c. 1599)

Come live with me and be my love,
And we will all the pleasures prove
That valleys, groves, hills, and fields,
Woods, or steepy mountain yields.

And we will sit upon rocks,
Seeing the shepherds feed their flocks,
By shallow rivers to whose falls
Melodious birds sing madrigals.

And I will make thee beds of roses
And a thousand fragrant posies,
A cap of flowers, and a kirtle
Embroidered all with leaves of myrtle;

A gown made of the finest wool
Which from our pretty lambs we pull;
Fair lined slippers for the cold,
With buckles of the purest gold;

A belt of straw and ivy buds,
With coral clasps and amber studs:
And if these pleasures may thee move,
Come live with me and be my love.

The shepherds' swains shall dance and sing
For thy delight each May morning.
If these delights thy mind may move,
Then live with me and be my love.

Writing from Reading

Summarize

1 What exactly is the shepherd promising?

2 How might a city dweller serenade his or her love interest? Write "The Passionate Lawyer to Her Love," "The Passionate Waiter to His Love" (or something similar).

Analyze Craft

3 What are some of the pastoral, or supposedly natural, images in this poem?

4 In what ways is this poem like many contemporary love songs, and how is it different? Consider tone, style, and various aspects of language and word choice as well as content in your response.

Analyze Voice

5 As suggested, it's unlikely that a shepherd *in reality* would speak to his lover in rhyming couplets. Why can he speak this way in a poem?

Synthesize Summary and Analysis

6 The poet constructs a rarefied variety of a song in order to express certain otherwise inexpressible emotions. Why does he choose a song to express his emotions?

Interpret the Poem

7 Why does this poem idealize life in this fashion? Look at three very different love poems in this chapter—"Doo-Wop: The Moves," "Western Wind," and "A Song." What is the place of idealization in love poetry?

SHAKESPEARE IN SONG

William Shakespeare incorporates song in certain plays, mainly the comedies or those late plays that contain both dark and light situations. Many of his dances performed onstage in verbal silence had musical accompaniment—and when (*Henry IV* 1.3.1) the stage directions say *"Here the lady sings a Welsh song,"* it's not necessarily the case that Shakespeare wrote what she performed. Some scholars argue that some of his songs are in fact folk tunes or ditties not of his own composition; others bear the particular stamp of the playwright's particular language. The following **dirge,** or funeral song, from *Cymbeline* is sung for a character the speakers believe to be dead (but who is really in disguise).

William Shakespeare (1564–1616)

For a brief biography of William Shakespeare, see chapter 18.

AS YOU READ Consider how the song helps give the audience some breathing room in the middle of the dramatic action.

Fear no more the heat o' the sun

—*from* Cymbeline (c. 1608–1610)

Fear no more the heat o' the sun,
  Nor the furious winter's rages;
Thou thy worldly task hast done,
  Home art gone, and ta'en thy wages:
Golden lads and girls all must,
As chimney-sweepers, come to dust.

Fear no more the frown o' the great;
  Thou art past the tyrant's stroke:
Care no more to clothe and eat;
  To thee the reed is as the oak:
The scepter, learning, physic, must
All follow this, and come to dust.

Fear no more the lightning flash,
  Nor the all-dreaded thunder stone;
Fear not slander, censure rash;
  Thou hast finished joy and moan:
All lovers young, all lovers must
Consign to thee, and come to dust.

No exorciser harm thee!
  Nor no witchcraft charm thee!
Ghost unlaid forbear thee!
  Nothing ill come near thee!
Quiet consummation have;
And renownéd be thy grave!

Writing from Reading

Summarize

1 Paraphrase this song into straightforward language. What is being expressed?

Analyze Craft

2 What is particularly musical about the punctuation of this dirge? In your response, consider the repetition of exclamation points in the final stanza.

3 In the last stanza, the meter and rhythm of the poem change. How does it change—and why? See chapter 22 for more on meter.

Analyze Voice

4 Why does the voice seem impersonal? Who is speaking here?

Synthesize Summary and Analysis

5 How does the tone in this funeral song include great wit and irony and remain true to its funereal purpose?

Interpret the Poem

6 How does the pun that ends the first stanza—"chimney-sweepers, come to dust"—affect the meaning of the poem?

7 If you were directing a production of *Cymbeline,* what kind of music (and/or sound effects) would you use to accompany or help voice this funeral song?

LANGUAGE AS MELODY

Sometimes the poet drops the pretense of having a character perform, as in Marlowe's shepherd's serenade to his love, and creates his or her own song. Consider the usually more somber John Donne's playful outburst on the subject of love, and constancy or lack of it. Donne's rhyming poem seems to aspire to the condition of music. The lyrical line is **melodious** (tuneful, like a melody), but it is not by itself a **melody** (the linear succession of various musical pitches recognized as a unit).

John Donne (1572–1631)

John Donne (pronounced *Dunn*) was born into a Catholic family in London, England, at a time when Catholics were persecuted under the Protestant crown. He converted to the Church of England while in his twenties, the decade in which he wrote his famous *Satires* and *Songs and Sonnets.* In 1601, Donne secretly married his employer's niece, Ann More, which so angered his employer that he fired Donne and had him imprisoned for a short period. Donne then struggled with poverty, especially since he and Ann had twelve children. Eventually, under pressure from the king, Donne became a clergyman and was famous for his intelligent and riveting sermons. He imbued his poetry with his wit as well as his passionate disposition—interested in sex and love, yet with a faith in God and an acute awareness of his own mortality. His poems are known for both his use of conceit (or extended metaphor) and his ability to capture and articulate the paradoxes of human existence.

AS YOU READ Enjoy the rhymes and the striking images of meteors, of the Devil's foot, and of mermaids, all in the service of a lament.

Song (1633)

Go and catch a falling star,
Get with child a mandrake root,
Tell me where all past years are,
Or who cleft the Devil's foot;
Teach me to hear mermaids singing,
Or to keep off envy's stinging,
And find
What wind
Serves to advance an honest mind.

If thou be'st born to strange sights,
Things invisible to see,
Ride ten thousand days and nights,
Till Age snow white hairs on thee,
Thou, when thou return'st, wilt tell me
All strange wonders that befell thee,
And swear
Nowhere
Lives a woman true, and fair.

If thou find'st one, let me know,
Such a pilgrimage were sweet—
Yet do not, I would not go,
Though at next door we might meet;
Though she were true, when you met her,
And last, till you write your letter,
Yet she
Will be
False, ere I come, to two or three.

Writing from Reading

Summarize

1 Why do you think this poem is titled "Song"?

Analyze Craft

2 How do the rhythmical patterns in this poem suggest music, and/or how would they lend themselves well to accompaniment? Use specific examples in your response.

3 What is the effect of the pair of two-word lines near the end of each stanza? Consider how these lines affect the poem visually and aurally.

Analyze Voice

4 Who is the speaker addressing, and for what purpose?

Synthesize Summary and Analysis

5 Does this poem seem to be a lament in the form of a song about one of life's apparent—to the poet at least—inconstancies, or is it just a bit of inspired fun? What language do you see that suggests it might be both?

Interpret the Poem

6 If this poem were set to music, how might such music sound? Describe what you think it should sound like—and how it might change in tone or timbre as the song progresses.

7 What are the particular aspects of life and love that this poet laments? How would you defend or disagree with his lament?

NATIVE AMERICAN POETRY

On our own continent, the earliest songs were, of course, Indian worship chants. For example, the "Night Chant" was part of a nine-day healing ritual that also included the creation of sand paintings and the performance of sacred dances. The aim was to restore a patient (often someone who had become blind, deaf, or paralyzed) to a state of health and harmony. A medicine man would lead the guests in a call-and response of chanting and singing. The "Night Chant" was passed down orally through generations. The chant involves an invocation of nature, characterized by repetition, and is ultimately a song of comfort, with repeated lines like "The Rainbow returned with me," and a long sequence of restoration based on a slightly varied line:

Beautifully my children to me are restored
Beautifully my wife is to me restored . . .

Two lines near the conclusion of the chant declare,

In beauty may I walk
All day long may I walk.

Compare these lines to the final lines of Joy Harjo's song below.

Joy Harjo (b. 1951)

Some poets, such as American Indian poet and composer Joy Harjo, set their own work to music. A member of the Muscogee (Creek) Indian tribe, Harjo was born in Tulsa, Oklahoma. She changed her major from art to poetry before completing her B.A. at the University of New Mexico. From there, she earned an M.F.A. at the Iowa Writers Workshop. In addition to producing eight collections of poems, Harjo is a musician. She performed on saxophone with her band, Poetic Justice before going solo. Her CDs feature both her playing and her poetry. She currently teaches at the University of New Mexico.

AS YOU READ See if you think that the text is complete without the voice of the singer and the music.

Morning Song (2001)

The red dawn is now rearranging the earth
Thought by thought
Beauty by beauty
Each sunrise a link on the ladder
Thought by thought
Beauty by beauty
The ladder the backbone
Of shimmering deity
Thought by thought
Beauty by beauty
Child stirring in the web of your mother
Don't be afraid
Old man turning to walk through the door
Do not be afraid

Writing from Reading

Summarize

1 Rewrite this poem in complete sentences.

Analyze Craft

2 Why does it serve so many poems and songs well to break traditional rules of syntax? How do songs create their own rules? What are the "rules" in Harjo's poem?

3 What is the relationship between the images in the poem? Consider especially: "Child stirring in the web of your mother" and "Old man turning to walk through the door."

4 How does Harjo use long and short lines to achieve musical effects?

Analyze Voice

5 What is the purpose of this song? How does the voice sound to you?

Synthesize Summary and Analysis

6 Why does it seem appropriate for this to be a "morning" song rather than a poem associated with another part of the day?

Interpret the Poem

7 What does the refrain "Thought by thought / Beauty by beauty" mean or suggest? How does it work in the context of the larger song? Why is the line "Don't be afraid" repeated as "Do not be afraid"?

SPOKEN WORD PIONEERS

Poetry, from earliest times, has not lacked for performance. In the United States, the recitation of poetry was a standard educational experience until recently, but poetry from the 1950s and '60s written by the so-called **Beat** generation was recited, chanted, and sometimes even sung. *Beat*—the very word suggests the rhythmic *beating* out of emphases, repeated sound, and public as opposed to private aspects of delivery. (One of the leading Beat poets was Allen Ginsberg, whose "Supermarket in California" appears in chapter 24.) With the Beats, as with what we're calling **spoken word** poetry today, the written form of a poem seems secondary to the performance of it; the *scene* was not a silent one—much more akin to theater than what Dylan Thomas called "my craft or sullen art."

> "The poetry reading was beginning to be a kind of public event that people went to . . . because of the Beat scene. It seemed really cool to go to the Anxious Asp or the Green Street Cafe or the Coexistence Bagel Shop . . . and hear spoken poetry read. It made it seem alive and accessible and not something in books."
>
> Conversation with Robert Hass

Although the evolution of spoken word poetry can be traced as far back as the Beats, it may be best to begin with the precursors to rap, from the late sixties, and then go on to look at how rap songs influenced spoken word. What we know as **rap** is also oral in its presentation, but the performers are as much singers and musicians as poets. Improvisation plays its part, as does choral response or repetition; these artists are most often young, and their diction is colloquial, street-smart. They gather together in back rooms or ballrooms, chanting their work out loud as part of a competition; sometimes the audience appoints itself as arbiter, ranking with applause; more formally there are actual judges to rate the "show." Rap has also led to the syncopated fusion of one of today's most popular music forms, **hip-hop.**

The Last Poets (1968)

"Born" on May 19, 1968, for a Malcolm X birthday celebration, The Last Poets have been called the grandfathers of rap. Although the combination of members shifted over the years, the group's mission was always clear: to express the feelings behind the Black Arts Movement of the 1960s and the overall experience of being black in America. Their angry, revolutionary poetry set to music appeared on albums including *The Last Poets* (1970) and *This Is Madness* (1971). The group—consisting of Gylan Kain, Abiodun Oyewole, David Nelson, Felipe Luciano, Umar Bin Hassan, Jalal Nurdidin, and Suliaman El-Hadi—took its name from a poem by South African poet Keorapetse Kgositsile, who wrote that he lived in the last generation that knew poetry because guns were replacing it.

AS YOU READ Ask yourself how much or how little you can associate yourself with the emotion called up in the poem.

My people (1984)

My people are Black, beige, yellow
Brown and beautiful
A garden of life
with a love as sweet as scuppernong wine
growing in muddy waters
making brown babies with
pink feet and quick minds
My people warm sometimes hot
always cool always together
My people let's be together
understand that we've lived together
understand that we've died together
understand My brother that I've
smelled your piss in my hallway
and it smell just like mine
understand that I love your woman
my sister and her rare beauty
is reason enough for a revolution
yes sister my honest sister

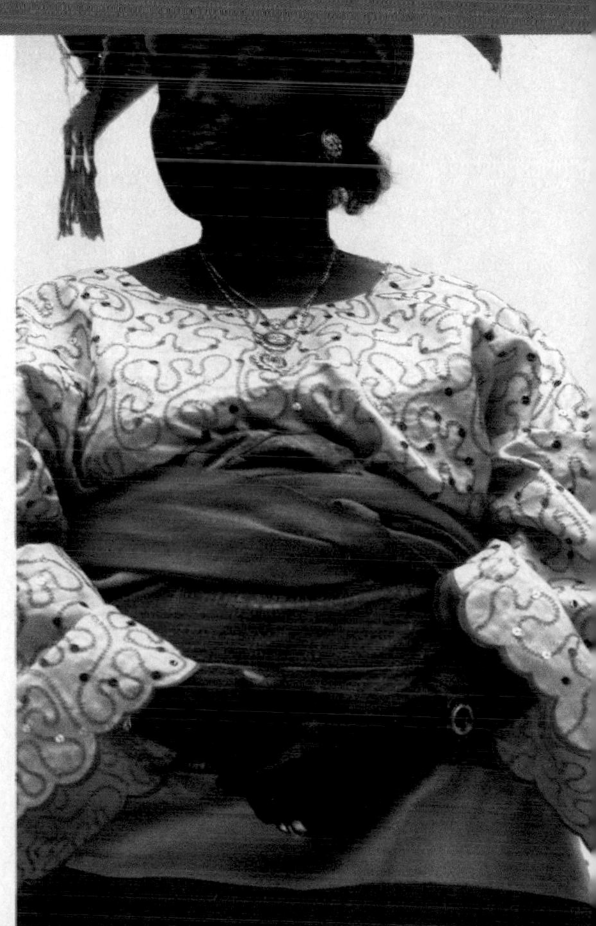

I have had ugly moments with you
but you are the only beauty I've ever known
Yes sister my honest sister
you are the joy in my smile
you are the reality of my dreams
you are the only sister I have
and I need you
I need you to feed the children
of our race
I need you to feed the lovers of our race
I need you to be the summer of my winters
I need you because
you are the natural life in the living
at night there is a moon
to make the Blackness be felt
I am that Blackness
filling up the world
with My soul
and the world knows me
You are that moon
my moon Goddess shining down light
on my Black face
that fills the universe
My moon I am your sun
and I shall take this peace
of light and build a world
for you my sister
Sometimes the waters are rough
and the hungry tide swallows the shore
washing away all memories
of children's footsteps
playing in the sand
where is the world I promised my son?
must he push back the tide
and build the world
that I have rapped about
Am I so godly until I forget
what a man is?
Am I so right until
there is no room for patience
My brother Oh in brother
father of a son
father of a warrior
My brother the sun
My brother the warrior
Be the beginning and the end
for my sister
Be the revolution for our world
turn yourself into yourself
and then onto this disordered world
and arrange the laughter for joy
the tears for sorrow
Turn purple pants, alligator shoes
leather jackets, brown boots
polka dot ties, silk suits,
Turn miniskirts, false eyelashes,
red wigs, afro wigs, Easter bonnets,
bellbottoms turn this confusion
into Unity Unity
so that the sun will follow
our foot steps in the day
so that the moon will glow
in our living rooms at night
so that food, clothing, and shelter
will be free
because we are born free
to have the world as our playground
My people.

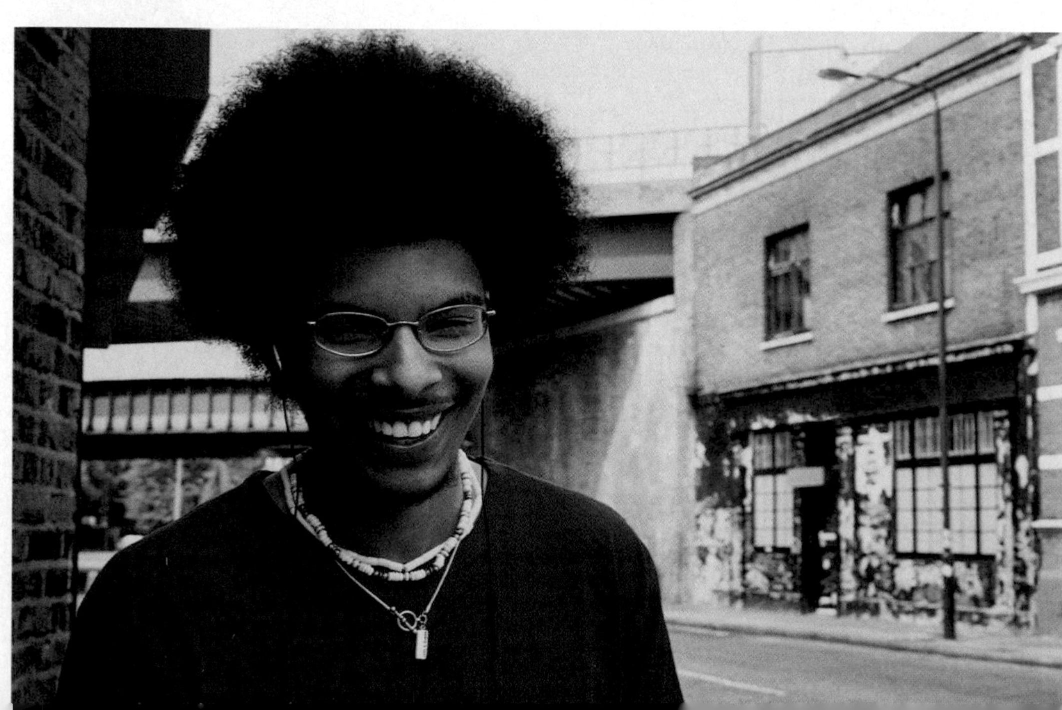

Writing from Reading

Summarize

1 The poets celebrate their identity as a social and racial group. What aspects are celebrated?

Analyze Craft

2 What techniques do you discern at work in the poem? Does the addressee of the poem change or remain the same?

Analyze Voice

3 What role does pride play in the establishment of the voice?

4 How would you describe the importance of the voice to the success of the poem?

Synthesize Summary and Analysis

5 Which basic techniques and emphasis in voice make the poem work?

Interpret the Poem

6 Is the audience for the poem exclusive to the group lauded in the poem or does "My people" have a broader appeal?

What we describe as **slam** includes all varieties of poetry and poets, from local café poets to Poets Laureate of the United States. Spoken word advocate Nancy Schwalb credits Marc Smith with inventing the poetry slam in Chicago in 1979 or '80, as a way to bring poetry down from the ivory tower and into the streets. It has done so—to an increasing, and increasingly devoted audience—all across America (and with no signs of slowing) ever since. Issues of race and gender appear in much of this work, as do politics and personal relations, love, hate, envy, worry about life, and death. In other words, spoken word poetry is much like all poetry down through the ages. It just swings a little more.

Marc Smith (b. 1950)

The founder of the poetry slam, Marc Smith was born in southeast Chicago. He organized the first poetry slam at Chicago's Green Mill Tavern in 1987, where the weekly slam has continued for more than twenty years. He brings a sense of rhythm and drama to his performance of spoken word poetry, which has pleased audiences at venues including Lincoln Center, the Kennedy Center, the Art Institute of Chicago, and the Queensland Poetry Fest in Australia. Smith has contributed to the anthologies *The Spoken Word Revolution* (2003) and *The Spoken Word Revolution Redux* (2007); he has also written and produced two plays, *Flea Market, a night of monologues* and *A House Party for Henry.*

AS YOU READ Envision the various settings of each stanza. Consider how the voice of the speaker changes in each different place.

Dusty Blues (1996)

The moon, when swinging trumpets blow,
Goes blue as red the rhythm cuts
The rain with saucy cinder-beats;
And blackbirds hop the high hot lines.

(It's a scats madder scene.)

In cellar grays where notes collide
The bulb's half eclipse cleaves a brain;
And "Death," the wailing madman cries,
"Leaves me half breaths, baby."

Oh the wind that crosses elms at night
Flows through the tubes of tacit life
Proclaiming in its haunting moan,
"All is senseless, Pops."

But the brew within the brassy stove
Cooks clean to alabaster bones;
And "Fame" the jiving jazzman's told,
"Hangs with the blackbirds
Up on those high hot lines!"

It's a blue-back crooked dream.

Writing from Reading

Summarize

1 Describe in plain speech the various settings the poem travels through.

Analyze Craft

2 How does Smith transition from one setting to the next, and how does he bring the poem full circle at the end?

Analyze Voice

3 Consider whether the speaker of dialogue in the poem is one person or many different people. What clues in the language make you think so?

Synthesize Summary and Analysis

4 Describe the speaker of this poem. Based on your answer, who do you think is speaking back?

Interpret the Poem

5 Does the poem speak to a particular generation in a particular time and place, or does it have a more universal appeal?

THE SECOND WAVE

Today, slams are one of the most popular public forums for poetry. Surrounded by new technology, we live in a time of multiple sounds and modes of presentation, creating multimedia performance poems, along with the traditional public theater of the slams. It's been possible to read Wallace Stevens, Percy Bysshe Shelley, or William Butler Yeats and the rest in silence; what follows are a set of texts that need to be *performed*.

Three Spoken Word Poems

AS YOU READ Read these poems out loud and compare them to your favorite rap or hip-hop tunes.

Kenneth Carroll (b. 1959)

Kenneth Carroll has been integral to poetry in Washington, D.C., where he was born and continues to live. He has served as D.C. site coordinator for WritersCorps, as president of the African American Writers Guild, and as a board member of the Poetry Committee of Greater Washington. He also taught high school English in Washington for a number of years and has performed his poetry at the Kennedy Center and the Library of Congress. His work (including his poetry, essays, short stories, and plays) has appeared in numerous journals and magazines. His collection *So What! For the White Dude Who Said This Ain't Poetry* was published in 1997.

So What! (for the white dude who said dis ain't poetry) (1997)

a faucet dripping arrogance in sycophantic half steps
a literary tarzan trying to save the natives from they own ignorance
short on knowledge, long on knowing he instructs without reference,
ain't poetry?

"no dialectics needed sambo, your thing just is not poetry,"
said the gold coast representative
never been in the mines
never sweated riches but 'bwana knows best'

a minute man wit a culture 30 seconds old
ain't poetry? mmmm . . .
maybe if i throwed soup cans in it
or something obscure dark & cryptic
alluded to hackneyed over hyped dead writers
& avoided references to the dark continent of
my origin this work could be saved

ain't poetry?
minute rice analysis
cracker instant oats
pour in europe and stir: a cold water recipe
. . . meanwhile my village dances to simmering rhythms
spiced by intellectual development measured in tens
of thousands of years

homer, his lips stuck to the chilly nipple
of his mother's frozen breast,
could only dream civilizations
as dark men & women built pyramids
& shaped words to fit eternity
poets retired & came back as ancestor spirits
while greece contemplated a working alphabet & gods
but this shit ain't poetry cause johnny come lately say so
. . . and he should know

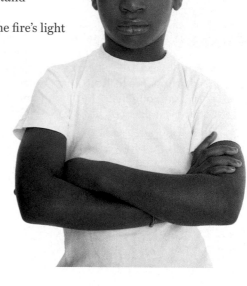

ain't poetry?
our systems were a mystery
alexander burned all that he & aristotle couldn't understand
the ensuing blaze warmed the icecapade continent
as the pillaging plagiarizers worked their un magic in the fire's light

ain't poetry?
the sails on your scholar ship are bloody
you scribble death upon the pages on the world
persecuting your brightest stars, preferring
whoring scribes who search for insignificance
to entertain the inane
. . . so dis ain't poetry . . . so you dis'n me?

ain't poetry, huh?   ain't india either sucka!
what is round, rotating and will never
fit into a box marked trite poetic conventions:
the world and its inhabitants
you are trying to fold the world in half
to place it neatly into your square mind

ain't poetry?
ain't dat a bitch!
a new jack dis
half empty memory banks
culture validated by gun powder
your qualifications are shaky
like a bamboo bridge stretched across
the white supremacist waters of your existence
you are still preaching the missionary position
as the natives re-read the karma sutra

a day late, a dollar short
always missing the bus
you are peeing in the snow
while we design a papyrus for the living
a patronizing peeping tom
seeing in but unable to decipher
without an oxford interpreter

we are a black fire
burning across the pages of your random house guide
to modern american poetry
where you cannot find references to shine or even signifying monkeys
we have left your meter in shambles
as we laugh at you tripping over lemons piled on the steps

the drumming you hear coming from the hills ain't poetry either
(but of course it is!)
it is the maroons planning your demise
it is ritual music and david walker's appeal
it is brown hips dancing verses
it is what it feels like to be kissed by full lips

it is natural
like sun ra returning in a charlie parker space ship
from galaxies wit' no names
while europe sails the wrong way
in search of a short cut to imperialism

damn columbus, you are lost and desperate
and denying the only music you really hear
you riffin' with a trumpet that plays one note
while the planet be's and bops
like coltrane star hopping through
the theloniosphere as a white boy
from downbeat points to the heavens & screams,
"that ain't music, that ain't music!"

we are like miles,
a black whirlwind
wit a red trumpet,
blowing blue stanzas
saying, so what!
yeah goddamn it
SO WHAT!**

Lawson Fusao Inada (b. 1938)

When Lawson Inada's grandparents immigrated from Japan to California, they might not have imagined their grandson would be a poet important to the beginning of Asian American literature. Inada was born in Fresno, California, and interned in one of the many camps in which Japanese Americans were confined during World War II. As a teenager, Inada fell in love with jazz music, and although he abandoned his aspirations to become a jazz musician, he cites jazz as the biggest influence on his poetry. In addition to his collections—which were published by major publishing houses, a first for Asian American poetry—Inada enjoyed performing his poems to music. He is a professor emeritus of Southern Oregon University and the state of Oregon's Poet Laureate.

Grandmother

(1997)

for Grandmother Miju Inada and Yoshiko Saito

Except for the fact that Grandmother taught me
chopsticks and Japanese before forks and English,
my relationship with Her wasn't all that much.

As a matter of fact, Grandmother, with Her old-
fashioned ways, was actually somewhat of an extra-
vagant source of confusion and distraction.

For example, just to waste time on a rainy day
in a boring barrack room in our ordinary
concentration camp in Arkansas, She'd say:

"The Great God Thunder is very powerful.
Listen to Him. When He storms, be careful.
Or He will send Lightning to take your navel!"

Or, on just another quiet night in Colorado,
on the way to the shower house, She may pause
in the warm desert sand to simply say:

"Ah, the Full Moon! Look closely, Grandson.
It's the same Moon, and the same Story.
'Two Rabbits with Mallets Pounding Rice.'"

Time passes. Grandmother passes. I've learned
the facts since. Still, in some storms I feel
a twitch, and in the still of certain nights,

with the right chopsticks, I can eat with
the Rabbits who have scattered all the Rice.

Emily XYZ (c. 1958)

Emily XYZ is a spoken word poet who has been active on the poetry scene in New York City since the early 1980s. She is best known for her two-voice arrangements of her poetry, which she performs with Myers Bartlett. Before hitting her stride with the two-voice arrangement, Emily XYZ staged poetry for up to eight voices. She has released a book, *The Emily XYZ Songbook* (2005), complete with a CD on which she and Bartlett perform to electronic music composed by Virgil Moorefield. Some of her poems have been successful recordings, such as "Who Shot Sadat?" and "Slot Machine," which was featured on the PBS TV series *The United States of Poetry*.

Ship of State of Fools (2002)

It's October and a big battle is shaping up
not with the Diamondbacks
not with the Democrats
but between our fundamentalists
and their fundamentalists.

Our fundamentalists say
it's time for them to pay the price in blood
for all the trouble they've caused in the world
by being such violent wackos all the time
and having no respect whatsoever
for human life.

Their fundamentalists say
it's time for you to pay the price in blood
for all the trouble you've caused in the world
by being such fucking assholes all the time
and having no respect whatsoever
for human life.

One thing is for sure:

The driver of this car will not be killed
The second in command will not be killed
The loan will remain in effect
and even if it's hit,
the car will not roll over
But the passengers
had better look out
and the pedestrians
had better look out
and the people who live by the road
thinking they're safe
thinking, This is what we voted for
should be ready:

Red lights will be run
All directions will be right
Hatred will come in for the kill
History will do its thing again.

Writing from Reading

Summarize

1 Envision these poems in competition with one another at a poetry slam. Give your vote, from 1 to 10, to each poem and explain your judgment.

Analyze Craft

2 Compare the rhythm in each of these poems.

3 How is rhyme used to create a rhythmic beat?

Analyze Voice

4 What's gained by oral presentation of the poems, and what—while reading them in silence—is lost?

Synthesize Summary and Analysis

5 Each of these poems seems to depend on a publicly displayed relation among sound, rhythm, and meaning. Is this traditional in poetry or some new shift of emphasis?

Interpret the Poems

6 "There appears to be a relation between political awareness of individual lives in the contemporary United States and the rise of spoken word and its variations," writes the probably pseudonymous Prof. I.M. Hipp. Test out this critic's idea about spoken word poetry. Do you agree or disagree with him, and why?

For Review and Further Study

Miguel Algarin (b. 1941)

HIV (1997)

I. *Revelation*
Revel at ion,
Rebel at I on a course
To regret erections,
To whip the cream in my scrotum
Till it hardens into unsweetened,
Unsafe revved elations
Of milk turned sour
By the human body,
Of propagation of destruction.
The epiphany: I am unsafe,
You who want me
Know that I who want you,
Harbor the bitter balm of defeat.

II. *Salvation*
If I were to show you
How to continue holding on,
I would not kiss you,
I would not mix my fluids with yours,
For your salvation
Cannot bear the live weight
Of your sharing liquids with me.

III. *Language*
To tell,
To talk,
To tongue into sounds
How I would cleanse you with urine,
How my tasting tongue would wash your body,
How my saliva and sperm would bloat you,
To touch you in our lovemaking
And not tell you
Would amount to murder.
To talk about how to language this
So that you would still languish
In my unsafe arms and die,
Seems beyond me,
I would almost rather lie
But my tongue muscle moves involuntarily
To tell of the danger in me.

IV. *Of Health*
To use my full and willing
Body to reveal and speak
The strength that I impart
Without fear,
Without killing,
Without taking away what I would give,
To use my man's tongue
To share,
To give,
To lend,
To exact nothing,
To receive all things,
To expand my macho
And let the whole world
Into the safety of my mature masculinity.

V. *Quarantine*
Sometimes I fear touching your plump ear lobes,
I might contaminate you.
Sometimes I refuse odors that would
Drive my hands to spread your thick thighs.
Sometimes closing my ears to your voice
Wrenches my stomach and I vomit to calm wanting.
Can it be that I am the bearer of plagues?
Am I poison to desire?
Do I have to deny yearning for firm full flesh
So that I'll not kill what I love?
No juices can flow 'tween you and me.
Quicksand will suck me in.

Questions for Interactive Reading and Writing

1. What is the occasion for the poem? To whom is the poet speaking?
2. Describe the emotions felt and expressed by the poet.
3. Why does the poet break the poem into numbered parts?
4. What is the effect of the explicit language and imagery?

Jimmy Santiago Baca (b. 1952)

Choices (1986)

An acquaintance at Los Alamos Labs
who engineers weapons
black x'd a mark where I live
on his office map.
Star-wars humor. . . .
He exchanged muddy boots
and patched jeans
for a white intern's coat
and black polished shoes.
A month ago, after butchering a gouged bull,
we stood on a pasture hill,
and he wondered with pained features
where money would come from
to finish his shed, plant alfalfa,
and fix his tractor.
Now his fingers
yank horsetail grass,
he crimps herringbone tail-seed
between teeth, and grits out words,
"Om gonna buy another tractor
next week. More land too."
Silence between us is gray water
let down in a tin pail
in a deep, deep well,
a silence
milled in continental grindings
millions of years ago.
I throw my heart
into the well, and it falls
a shimmering pebble to the bottom.
Words are hard
to come by, "Would have lost everything
I've worked for, not takin' the job."
His words try to
retrieve
my heart
from the deep well.
We walk on in silence,
our friendship
rippling away.

Questions for Interactive Reading and Writing

1. Describe the setting. What is the relationship between the speaker and the other man?
2. How would you make a short story out of this material?
3. What is the tone, the feel of the poem?
4. What effect does the poet create by employing the image of the "tin pail / in a deep, deep well"?
5. The poet first speaks of his "acquaintance" but then ends the poem by talking about his "friendship" for the man. What, if anything, has changed over the course of the poem that would justify the two different ways of speaking about the other man?

Lewis Carroll (1832–1898)

Jabberwocky (1871)

'Twas brillig, and the slithy toves
  Did gyre and gimble in the wabe:
All mimsy were the borogoves,
  And the mome raths outgrabe.

"Beware the Jabberwock, my son!
  The jaws that bite, the claws that catch!
Beware the Jubjub bird, and shun
  The frumious Bandersnatch!"

He took his vorpal sword in hand:
  Long time the manxome foe he sought—
So rested he by the Tumtum tree,
  And stood awhile in thought.

And, as in uffish thought he stood,
  The Jabberwock, with eyes of flame,
Came whiffling through the tulgey wood,
  And burbled as it came!

One, two! One, two! And through and through
  The vorpal blade went snicker-snack!
He left it dead, and with its head
  He went galumphing back.

"And, hast thou slain the Jabberwock?
Come to my arms, my beamish boy!
O frabjous day! Callooh, Callay!"
He chortled in his joy.

'Twas brillig, and the slithy toves
Did gyre and gimble in the wabe;
All mimsy were the borogoves,
And the mome raths outgrabe.

Questions for Interactive Reading and Writing

1. For all of its nonsense, do you hear a pattern as you recite the poem? What is the "sense" in such "nonsense," and how does Carroll invent his words or reinvigorate his language? Describe the pattern.
2. Compare the language of "Jabberwocky" to the ballad of "Sir Patrick Spence" earlier in this chapter. How does Carroll's use of sounds create a more dreamlike—or nightmarish—story than the jaunty narrative of "Sir Patrick Spence"?
3. Why might you find pleasure in the saying of this poem? Why not? What is your reaction to the nonsense words?

Gil Scott-Heron (b. 1949)

The Revolution Will Not Be Televised (1970)

You will not be able to stay home, brother.
You will not be able to plug in, turn on and cop out.
You will not be able to lose yourself on scag and
skip out for beer during commercials because
The revolution will not be televised.

The revolution will not be televised.
The revolution will not be brought to you by Xerox in
four parts without commercial interruption.
The revolution will not show you pictures of Nixon
blowing a bugle and leading a charge by John Mitchell,
General Abramson and Spiro Agnew to eat hog maws
confiscated from a Harlem sanctuary.
The revolution will not be televised.

The revolution will not be brought to you by
The Schaeffer Award Theatre and will not star
Natalie Wood and Steve McQueen or Bullwinkle
and Julia.
The revolution will not give your mouth sex appeal.
The revolution will not get rid of the nubs.
The revolution will not make you look five pounds
thinner.
The revolution will not be televised, brother.

There will be no pictures of you and Willie Mae
pushing that shopping cart down the block on the
dead run
or trying to slide that color tv in a stolen ambulance.
NBC will not be able to predict the winner at 8:32 on
reports from twenty-nine districts.
The revolution will not be televised.

There will be no pictures of pigs shooting down brothers
on the instant replay.
There will be no pictures of pigs shooting down brothers
on the instant replay.
There will be no slow motion or still lifes of Roy
Wilkins strolling through Watts in a red, black
and green liberation jumpsuit that he had been
saving for just the proper occasion.

Green Acres, Beverly Hillbillies and Hooterville Junction
will no longer be so damned relevant
and women will not care if Dick finally got down with
Jane
on *Search for Tomorrow*
because black people will be in the streets looking for
A Brighter Day.
The revolution will not be televised.

There will be no highlights on the *Eleven O'Clock News*
and no pictures of hairy armed women liberationists
and Jackie Onassis blowing her nose.
The theme song will not be written by Jim Webb or
Francis Scott Key
nor sung by Glen Campbell, Tom Jones, Johnny Cash,
Englebert Humperdink or Rare Earth.
The revolution will not be televised.

The revolution will not be right back after a
message about a white tornado, white lightning or white
people.
You will not have to worry about a dove in your bedroom,
the tiger in your tank or the giant in your toilet bowl.
The revolution will not go better with Coke.
The revolution will not fight germs that may cause bad
breath.
The revolution *will* put you in the driver's seat.
The revolution will not be televised
will not be televised
not be televised
be televised
The revolution will be no re-run, brothers.
The revolution will be LIVE.

Questions for Interactive Reading and Writing

1. What role does politics play in the beginning of the poem?
2. How does rhythm play a role in the development of meaning?
3. Is there in the poem a social critique of modern American society that you can appreciate without accepting the idea of political revolution?
4. How does spoken word poetry invite a political perspective?

Langston Hughes (1902–1967)

For a brief biography of Langston Hughes, see chapter 26, the Case Study on Langston Hughes and His Contemporaries.

The Blues (1958)

When the shoe strings break
On *both* your shoes
And you're in a hurry—
That's the blues.

When you go to buy a candy bar
And you've lost the dime you had—
Slipped through a hole in your pocket somewhere—
That's the blues, too, *and bad!*

Questions for Interactive Reading and Writing

1. What attracts a poet like Hughes to the blues form? (See the casebook on Langston Hughes, chapter 26.)
2. Can you imagine someone singing this to the accompaniment of a piano and bass?

Audre Lorde (1934–1992)

The Electric Slide Boogie (1993)

New Year's Day 1:16 AM
and my body is weary beyond
time to withdraw and rest
ample room allowed me in everyone's head
but community calls
right over the threshold
drums beating through the walls
children playing their truck dramas
under the collapsible coatrack
in the narrow hallway outside my room

The TV lounge next door is wide open
it is midnight in Idaho
and the throb easy subtle spin
of the electric slide boogie
step-stepping
around the corner of the parlor
past the sweet clink
of dining room glasses
and the edged aroma of slightly overdone
dutch-apple pie
all laced together
with the rich dark laughter
of Gloria
and her higher-octave sisters

How hard it is to sleep
in the middle of life.

Questions for Interactive Reading and Writing

1. How would you describe the holiday spirit of the poem, given the time the poet reveals in it?
2. What elements does the poet use to capture "the throb easy subtle spin" of the dance?
3. What are the greatest contrasting images of the poem?
4. Are the last two lines a complaint or a celebration?

Willie Perdomo (b. 1967)

Postcards of El Barrio (1996)

are rarely ever
sent to me

hanging off a broken stick
a dull red, white and blue flag
one star instead of fifty
blows a hot breeze
of bullet beans

congas y timbales bingbangbongboom
down the block and back,
our blood stands on its toes
and we start to dance

winos lean over their canes and begin
a different story with the same ending:
"Geronimo wasn't shit compared to Papo"

chickens, rats, rabbits and cats are
tired of walking on broken glass gardens
they wait for the city to come
and knock all the gates down

once in a full blue moon
rising above crumbling gray rooftops
I see a morenito sitting on a stoop
licking the melting pineapple
ice off his palms

the violent revolutions
of red and white police sirens upset the sky blue peace
of neon crucifixions slow orange and yellow bulbs
race around the rims of stained bodega canopies
hiding from the rain
Old Man Jimmy
sings the blues

postcards of El Barrio
are rarely ever sent to me.

Questions for Interactive Reading and Writing

1. Read the poem aloud. How do the rhythms make your voice sound?
2. What does the poet mean by "our blood stands on its toes"?
3. Why is the poem itself in a sense a postcard of El Barrio?

Quincy Troupe (b. 1943)

Poem Reaching towards Something (1997)

we walk through a calligraphy of hats slicing off
  foreheads
ace-deuce cocked, they slant, razor sharp, clean
through imagination, our spirits knee-deep in what we
  have forgotten
entrancing our bodies now to dance, like enraptured
  water lilies—
my memory & me—the rhythm in liquid stride of a
  certain look—
rippling eyeballs through breezes—
riffling choirs of trees where a trillion slivers of sunlight
  prance

across filigreeing leaves, a zillion voices of bamboo reeds
green with summer's saxophone burst
wrap themselves, like transparent prisms of dew—
drops around images, laced with pearls & rhinestones
perhaps it is through this, or the decoding of syllables
that we learn speech, that sonorous river of broken mirrors
carrying our dreams, assaulted by pellets of rain-
drops, the prisons of words entrapping us between parentheses—
two bat wings curving into cynical smiles

still, there is something here that needs explaining beyond
the hopelessness of miles, the light at the end of the midnight tunnel—
some say it is a train coming right at us—
where do the tumbling words spend themselves after they have spent
all meaning residing in the warehouse of language
after they have slipped like smoke
from our lips, where do the symbols they carry stop everything
put down roots, cleanse themselves of everything but clarity—
though here eye might be asking a little too much of any poet's head
full as it is with double-entendres
still, there are these hats slicing foreheads off in the middle
of crowds, the calligraphy of this penumbra slanting
ace-deuce cocked, carrying the perforated legacy of bebop, these bold
peccadillo, pirouetting pellagras, razor-sharp-clean, they cut
into our rip-tiding dreams carrying their whirlpooling imaginations
their rivers of schemes assaulted by pellets of rain-
drops, these broken mirrors reflecting sonorous
words entrapping us between parentheses—
two hat wings curved, imprisoning the world

Questions for Interactive Reading and Writing

1. Who is the "we" throughout this poem? Using plain language, describe the situation.
2. Is there a physical setting in this poem? Describe it using details from the poem.
3. How does Troupe's use of "eye" in place of the pronoun "I" in line 25 affect the poem?

26

Langston Hughes

I, TOO, sing America.
I am the darker brother.

—from "I, Too" by Langston Hughes

"In the last decade something beyond the watch and guard of statistics has happened in the life of the American Negro. . . . The Sociologist, the Philanthropist, the Race-leader are not unaware of the New Negro, but they are at a loss to account for him. He simply cannot be swathed in their formula. For the younger generation is vibrant with a new psychology; the new spirit is awake in the masses, and under the very eyes of the professional observers is transforming what has been a perennial problem into the progressive phases of contemporary Negro life."

—from "The New Negro" by Alain Locke

A Case Study on *Langston Hughes and His Contemporaries*

Langston Hughes

Hughes's Contemporaries

The Harlem Renaissance

The historical moment in which Langston Hughes and his contemporaries lived was crucial to launching their careers. All came of age during the Harlem Renaissance, a movement that took place in the 1920s and early 1930s, a time of cultural awakening for African Americans in terms of literature, music, art, theater, and political thinking.

The Cotton Club, a famous night club in Harlem where Duke Ellington, Cab Calloway, and other gifted black musicians played for an exclusively white clientele.

Josephine Baker (1906–1975), although also known for appearing in men's clothing, was more popular for her tendency to perform onstage in the nude.

The New Culture of Harlem

The Harlem Renaissance is named after the cultural activity—the fiction, poetry, and essays about black life in America—that flourished mainly in a two-mile section of Manhattan in New York City in which many African Americans settled—200,000 blacks lived there by 1928—in the great migration of blacks to find employment and education in the North. Harlem served as the epicenter of the Harlem Renaissance, as it boasted clubs where musicians including Duke Ellington, Louis Armstrong, and Bessie Smith performed; theaters such as the Apollo for black entertainers; and a common neighborhood in which important writers lived, among them Jean Toomer, Claude McKay, and Zora Neale Hurston (see chapter 14, Stories for Further Reading, for Hurston's "Gilded Six-Bits").

Fats Waller (1904–1943) and his hot jazz epitomized the music of the "rent party," a party thrown in an apartment in Harlem to help the tenant pay Harlem's high rents.

In addition to the writers, musicians, and artists, social thinkers such as W. E. B Du Bois were important advocates of black rights and education. Whites, too, were active in the Harlem Renaissance; the photographer Carl Van Vechten, for example, was a close friend of Langston Hughes's who supported the renaissance and admired the work of blacks, though at the time most of the black population was not touched by this cultural awakening.

"Negro Vogue"

"Madame is of the opinion that little of artistic merit is now being produced in America except that which is being done by Negroes," wrote Countee Cullen after meeting with the (white) Claire Goll. Indeed, whites were drawn to African-American culture, and particularly the night life of Harlem—so much so that one of Harlem's most famous clubs, the Cotton Club, catered to an exclusively white clientele. While this interest in black culture brought national attention to the work of black artists, people like Du Bois feared that it might fuel stereotypes of black society. Still, new venues such as *Crisis* and *Opportunity*—both important magazines for black audiences staffed by leading writers of the Harlem Renaissance—offered an unprecedented outlet for thought and literature.

Duke Ellington (1899–1974), one of America's most influential jazz composers, and the Duke Ellington Orchestra, with its growling trumpet, street rhythms, and the influence of classical music, were broadcast from the Cotton Club. Ellington called it simply "the American Music."

Langston Hughes (1902–1967)

For Langston Hughes, life was—as he put it—"no crystal stair." Hughes was born in Joplin, Missouri, in 1902; his parents divorced when he was quite young. His father left for Mexico, hoping to find a society less hostile to blacks, and his mother moved away to pursue her personal interests. Hughes was raised by his grandmother in Kansas, who told him her first husband had been killed with John Brown's men raiding Harper's Ferry; sometimes she wrapped his bullet-torn shawl around the child. Although this may have helped nurture Hughes's sense of pride in his race, his childhood was a lonely one, marked by longing for his mother. After his grandmother's death, he moved at age thirteen to Illinois and then to Cleveland to live with his mother, who never provided the maternal love that Hughes so desired.

Cleveland, where he attended high school, set the stage for the rest of his life in two central ways. First, he was active in many clubs at school and immensely popular. Second, he published poems while still in high school. "The Negro Speaks of Rivers" appeared just after his graduation at age nineteen. Still in his early twenties, he won the admiration of poet Vachel Lindsay when, as a busboy at a Washington, D.C., hotel, he put three of his poems next to Lindsay's plate. Even a small sampling of Hughes's poetry—such as we include in this chapter—makes clear the talent and ambition Hughes demonstrated from an early age. He wanted to be a poet, following his favorite forefathers, Walt Whitman and Carl Sandburg, but more, he wanted to celebrate his race, to show whites and blacks alike the beauty and integrity of the common African-American masses.

The year 1926 was an important one for Hughes. After traveling abroad—in France, Spain, and the Soviet Union—and holding a variety of jobs, Hughes entered Lincoln University, from which he would earn his bachelor's degree three years later. He then settled in Harlem, an African-American section of New York City. Hughes lived there during the time of the Harlem Renaissance, when black culture thrived and produced great artists, musicians, and writers, who were for the first time reaching black and white audiences alike. Foremost among these artists was Hughes, who had two early publications of major importance. His first collection of poems, *The Weary Blues,* earned much acclaim, and an essay appeared in *The Nation* called "The Negro Artist and the Racial Mountain," an essay that was both Hughes's personal manifesto and the manifesto of his generation of Harlem Renaissance artists. In it, he speaks against what he calls the "high-class Negro"—blacks who adopt a white way of life and try to fit in with the conventions of white middle-class culture. Instead, he celebrates the "low-down folks, the so-called common element." To Hughes, blacks who are genuine in their way of life are preferable; as he writes, "they still hold their own individuality in the face of American standardizations." The essay concludes with a clear statement of intention: "We younger Negro artists who create now intend to express our individual dark-skinned selves without fear or shame. If white people are pleased we are glad. If they are not, it doesn't matter."

Hughes followed his own dictum as stated in these last lines of "The Negro Artist and the Racial Mountain," for his poetry celebrates black identity, particularly the "low-down folks," in several ways. First, the "I" in these poems is not meant as a specific person but embodies the entire black race by claiming all their experiences—the difficult and admirable alike—in personal terms. "The Negro Speaks of Rivers", "I, Too," and "A New Song" are all written by adopting the voice of a "collective consciousness"—that is, a single speaker who transcends time and place as he recounts the experiences of an entire group. Second, Hughes's poetry is characterized by the directness of his thoughts, a "plain style" (see casebook on Dickinson and Frost) reflecting a long tradition in American literature that extends back to the Puritans, who favored simplicity over adornment. Third, Hughes's poetry consciously salutes and imitates the musical forms of blues and jazz. Hughes describes his 1951 collection *Montage of a Dream Deferred* as growing from popular African-American music. He explains "this poem on contemporary Harlem, like be-bop, is marked by conflicting changes, sudden nuances, sharp and impudent interjections, broken rhythms, and passages sometimes in the manner of a jam session, sometimes the popular song, punctuated by the riffs, runs, breaks, and distortions of the music of a community in transition."

Hughes expressed his black identity in poetry, fiction, nonfiction, children's books, plays, librettos, and a popular newspaper column featuring the character Jesse B. Semple, nicknamed "Simple." In all his work, Hughes celebrated African-American identity, focusing on the urban black population and mimicking what he saw to be at the heart of that population: blues and jazz. Despite Hughes's innovation using dialect, jazz, blues, and black culture in his poetry, he was barely able to make a living with his pen. He once referred to himself as a "literary sharecropper" as he pieced together a career filled with great accomplishments and occasional critical failures. Although in later years Hughes became controversial because of his far left political views, those around him invariably knew him to be a kind man with a celebratory sense of humanity, and he remained popular with readers and audiences throughout his life; even being ordered by Senator Joseph McCarthy to appear before his infamous committee on un-American activities because of socialist political views did not diminish his career. Hughes's credo can be summed up as "to my mind, it is the duty of the younger Negro artist, if he accepts any duties at all from outsiders, to change through the force of his art that old whispering 'I want to be white,' hidden in the aspirations of his people, to 'Why should I want to be white? I am Negro—and beautiful.'"

The Poetry of Langston Hughes

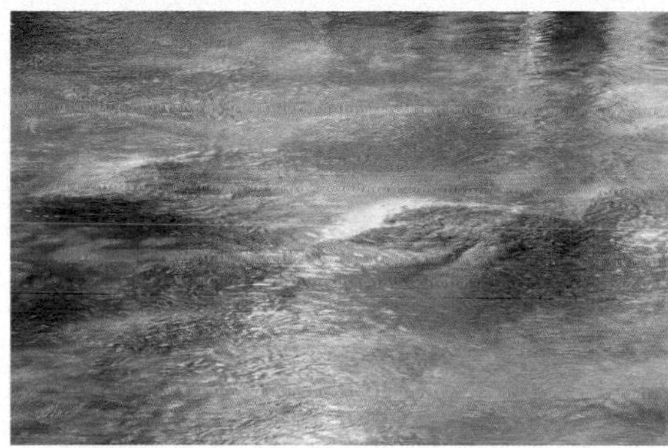

The Negro Speaks of Rivers (1921)

I've known rivers:
I've known rivers ancient as the world and older than the flow of human blood in human veins.

My soul has grown deep like the rivers.

I bathed in the Euphrates when dawns were young.
I built my hut near the Congo and it lulled me to sleep.
I looked upon the Nile and raised the pyramids above it.
I heard the singing of the Mississippi when Abe Lincoln went down to New Orleans, and I've seen its muddy bosom turn all golden in the sunset.

I've known rivers:
Ancient, dusky rivers.

My soul has grown deep like the rivers.

Questions for Critical Thinking

1. Highlight the repeated phrases and lines in this poem. What effect does Hughes achieve with these repetitions?
2. Make a list of everything the word *rivers* connotes to you. How do these connotations enhance your reading of the poem?

Mother to Son (1922)

Well, son, I'll tell you:
Life for me ain't been no crystal stair.
It's had tacks in it,
And splinters,
And boards torn up,
And places with no carpet on the floor—
Bare.
But all the time
I'se been a-climbin' on,
And reachin' landin's,
And turnin' corners,
And sometimes goin' in the dark
Where there ain't been no light.
So boy, don't you turn back.
Don't you set down on the steps
'Cause you finds it's kinder hard.
Don't you fall now
For I'se still goin', honey,
I'se still climbin',
And life for me ain't been no crystal stair.

Questions for Critical Thinking

1. Review what you learned about persona in chapter 20. How does this poem compare to one of Robert Browning's dramatic monologues such as "My Last Duchess" (in chapter 16)?
2. What is the controlling metaphor in this poem?

Negro (1922)

I am a Negro:
  Black as the night is black,
  Black as the depths of my Africa.

I've been a slave:
  Caesar told me to keep his door-steps clean.
  I brushed the boots of Washington.

I've been a worker:
  Under my hand the pyramids arose.
  I made mortar for the Woolworth Building.

I've been a singer:
  All the way from Africa to Georgia
  I carried my sorrow songs.
  I made ragtime.

I've been a victim:
  The Belgians cut off my hands in the Congo.
  They lynch me still in Mississippi.

I am a Negro:
  Black as the night is black,
  Black like the depths of my Africa.

Questions for Critical Thinking

1. Describe the relation between the repeated statement in the first and last stanzas and the specific descriptions.
2. Could you substitute other racial or ethnic identities and still have the same poem? Why or why not?

I, Too (1925)

I, too, sing America.

I am the darker brother.
They send me to eat in the kitchen
When company comes,
But I laugh,
And eat well,
And grow strong.

Tomorrow,
I'll be at the table
When company comes.
Nobody'll dare
Say to me,
"Eat in the kitchen,"
Then.

Besides,
They'll see how beautiful I am
And be ashamed—

I, too, am America.

Questions for Critical Thinking

1. "I sing America" is a phrase from Walt Whitman's "I Hear America Singing." Why is Hughes tipping his cap to his white predecessor, and how is he stressing a kind of separate identity when he writes "I, too, sing America"?
2. Scan this poem's meter. Even though it is free verse, what patterns do you see within the poem? What do you think is the significance of where those patterns fall?

The Weary Blues (1925)

Droning a drowsy syncopated tune,
Rocking back and forth to a mellow croon,
  I heard a Negro play.
Down on Lenox Avenue the other night
By the pale dull pallor of an old gas light
  He did a lazy sway. . . .
  He did a lazy sway. . . .
To the tune o' those Weary Blues.
With his ebony hands on each ivory key
He made that poor piano moan with melody.
  O Blues!
Swaying to and fro on his rickety stool
He played that sad raggy tune like a musical fool.
  Sweet Blues!
Coming from a black man's soul.
  O Blues!
In a deep song voice with a melancholy tone
I heard that Negro sing, that old piano moan—
  "Ain't got nobody in all this world,
    Ain't got nobody but ma self.
    I's gwine to quit ma frownin'
    And put ma troubles on the shelf."

Thump, thump, thump, went his foot on the floor.
He played a few chords then he sang some more—
  "I got the Weary Blues
    And I can't be satisfied.
    Got the Weary Blues
    And can't be satisfied—
    I ain't happy no mo'
    And I wish that I had died."

And far into the night he crooned that tune.
The stars went out and so did the moon.
The singer stopped playing and went to bed
While the Weary Blues echoed through his head.
He slept like a rock or a man that's dead.

Questions for Critical Thinking

1. How does the voice shift after the last blues stanza? What effect does this have on your response to the poem?
2. How is the Harlem street scene that Hughes creates here typical or idealized?

Po' Boy Blues (1926)

When I was home de
Sunshine seemed like gold.
When I was home de
Sunshine seemed like gold.
Since I come up North de
Whole damn world's turned cold.

I was a good boy,
Never done no wrong.
Yes, I was a good boy,
Never done no wrong,
But this world is weary
An' de road is hard an' long.

I fell in love with
A gal I thought was kind.
Fell in love with
A gal I thought was kind.
She made me lose ma money
An' almost lose ma mind.

Weary, weary,
Weary early in de morn.
Weary, weary,
Early, early in de morn.
I's so weary
I wish I'd never been born.

Questions for Critical Thinking

1. In what ways does this poem interact with the blues?
2. Given the colloquial quality of this poem, which word choices seem important to you and why?

Song for a Dark Girl (1927)

Way Down South in Dixie
  (Break the heart of me)
They hung my black young lover
  To a cross roads tree.

Way Down South in Dixie
  (Bruised body high in air)
I asked the white Lord Jesus
  What was the use of prayer.

Way Down South in Dixie
  (Break the heart of me)
Love is a naked shadow
  On a gnarled and naked tree.

Questions for Critical Thinking

1. How would you describe the character the poet has created to sing these lines?
2. How does the historical and social material work with or against the musical aspect of the poem?

The Dream Keeper (1932)

Bring me all of your dreams,
You dreamers,
Bring me all of your
Heart melodies
That I may wrap them
In a blue cloud-cloth
Away from the too-rough fingers
Of the world.

Questions for Critical Thinking

1. How does one wrap a heart melody in a cloud-cloth, and why should the world have fingers? Attack or defend the use of figurative language here.
2. Freewrite a page or two comparing this poem to "Harlem (Dream Deferred)." Pay particular attention to differences in tone, imagery, and diction.

Minstrel Man (1932)

Because my mouth
Is wide with laughter
And my throat
Is deep with song,
You do not think
I suffer after
I have held my pain
So long?

Because my mouth
Is wide with laughter,
You do not hear
My inner cry?
Because my feet
Are gay with dancing,
You do not know
I die?

Questions for Critical Thinking

1. What patterns do you see in this poem's structure? In its metric foot? In its rhyme?
2. How is this poem a particular discussion of a particular form of entertainment, a general statement about the black man's role in society, or both?

Quiet Girl (Ardella) (1926)

I would liken you
To a night without stars
Were it not for your eyes.
I would liken you
To a sleep without dreams
Were it not for your songs.

Questions for Critical Thinking

1. How would you describe the form of this poem? Does it remind you of a traditional form, or is it closer to the blues?
2. Compare this poem to such love songs as Leonard Cohen's "For Anne" (chapter 15) or William Shakespeare's "Shall I compare thee to a summer's day?" (chapter 18). What is different, what similar in tone?

Let America Be America Again (1936)

Let America be America again.
Let it be the dream it used to be.
Let it be the pioneer on the plain
Seeking a home where he himself is free.

(America never was America to me.)

Let America be the dream the dreamers dreamed—
Let it be that great strong land of love
Where never kings connive nor tyrants scheme
That any man be crushed by one above.

(It never was America to me.)

O, let my land be a land where Liberty
Is crowned with no false patriotic wreath,
But opportunity is real, and life is free,
Equality is in the air we breathe.

(There's never been equality for me,
Nor freedom in this "homeland of the free.")

Say, who are you that mumbles in the dark?
And who are you that draws your veil across the stars?

I am the poor white, fooled and pushed apart,
I am the Negro bearing slavery's scars.
I am the red man driven from the land,
I am the immigrant clutching the hope I seek—
And finding only the same old stupid plan
Of dog eat dog, of mighty crush the weak.

I am the young man, full of strength and hope,
Tangled in that ancient endless chain
Of profit, power, gain, of grab the land!
Of grab the gold! Of grab the ways of satisfying need!
Of work the men! Of take the pay!
Of owning everything for one's own greed!

I am the farmer, bondsman to the soil.
I am the worker sold to the machine.
I am the Negro, servant to you all.
I am the people, humble, hungry, mean—
Hungry yet today despite the dream.
Beaten yet today—O, Pioneers!
I am the man who never got ahead,
The poorest worker bartered through the years.

Yet I'm the one who dreamt our basic dream
In the Old World while still a serf of kings,
Who dreamt a dream so strong, so brave, so true,
That even yet its mighty daring sings
In every brick and stone, in every furrow turned
That's made America the land it has become.
O, I'm the man who sailed those early seas
In search of what I meant to be my home—
For I'm the one who left dark Ireland's shore,
And Poland's plain, and England's grassy lea,
And torn from Black Africa's strand I came
To build a "homeland of the free."

The free?

Who said the free? Not me?
Surely not me? The millions on relief today?
The millions shot down when we strike?
The millions who have nothing for our pay?
For all the dreams we've dreamed
And all the songs we've sung
And all the hopes we've held
And all the flags we've hung,
The millions who have nothing for our pay—
Except the dream that's almost dead today.

O, let America be America again—
The land that never has been yet—
And yet must be—the land where *every* man is free.
The land that's mine—the poor man's, Indian's, Negro's, ME—
Who made America,
Whose sweat and blood, whose faith and pain,
Whose hand at the foundry, whose plow in the rain,
Must bring back our mighty dream again.

Sure, call me any ugly name you choose—
The steel of freedom does not stain.
From those who live like leeches on the people's lives,
We must take back our land again,
America!

O, yes,
I say it plain,
America never was America to me,
And yet I swear this oath—
America will be!

Out of the rack and ruin of our gangster death,
The rape and rot of graft, and stealth, and lies,
We, the people, must redeem
The land, the mines, the plants, the rivers.
The mountains and the endless plain—
All, all the stretch of these great green states—
And make America again!

Questions for Critical Thinking

1. Highlight the parts of this poem that use repetition. What is the effect of repetition here? You might want to compare your answer to your response to the first question that accompanies "The Negro Speaks of Rivers" to get a better understanding of how Hughes uses the device.
2. Examine the punctuation in this poem. How does Hughes build the emotion of the poem with punctuation?

A New Song (1938)

I speak in the name of the black millions
Awakening to action.
Let all others keep silent a moment.
I have this word to bring,
This thing to say,
This song to sing:

Bitter was the day
When I bowed my back
Beneath the slaver's whip.

That day is past.

Bitter was the day
When I saw my children unschooled,
My young men without a voice in the world,
My women taken as the body-toys
Of a thieving people.

That day is past.

Bitter was the day, I say,
When the lyncher's rope
Hung about my neck,
And the fire scorched my feet,
And the oppressors had no pity,
And only in the sorrow songs
Relief was found

That day is past.

I know full well now
Only my own hands,
Dark as the earth,
Can make my earth-dark body free.
O, thieves, exploiters, killers,
No longer shall you say
With arrogant eyes and scornful lips:
"You are my servant,
Black man—
I, the free!"

That day is past—

For now,
In many mouths—
Dark mouths where red tongues burn
And white teeth gleam—
New words are formed,
Bitter
With the past
But sweet
With the dream.
Tense,
Unyielding,
Strong and sure,
They sweep the earth—

Revolt! Arise!

The Black
And White World
Shall be one!
The Worker's World!

The past is done!

A new dream flames
Against the
Sun!

Questions for Critical Thinking

1. Compare the overall message of this poem with the message in "Let America Be America Again." Which do you find more compelling for Hughes's social context? Which do you find more compelling for today's society?
2. Remembering that Hughes had far left political views—that is, like many of his generation, he sympathized with socialism—where do you see his political views reflected in this poem? Which parts, if any, seem above politics to you?

Ballad of the Landlord (1940)

Landlord, landlord,
My roof has sprung a leak.
Don't you 'member I told you about it
Way last week?

Landlord, landlord,
These steps is broken down.
When you come up yourself
It's a wonder you don't fall down.

Ten Bucks you say I owe you?
Ten Bucks you say is due?
Well, that's Ten Bucks more'n I'll pay you
Till you fix this house up new.

What? You gonna get eviction orders?
You gonna cut off my heat?
You gonna take my furniture and
Throw it in the street?

Um-huh! You talking high and mighty.
Talk on—till you get through.
You ain't gonna be able to say a word
If I land my fist on you.

Police! Police!
Come and get this man!
He's trying to ruin the government
And overturn the land!

Copper's Whistle!
Patrol bell!
Arrest.

Precinct Station.
Iron cell.
Headlines in press:

MAN THREATENS LANDLORD
TENANT HELD NO BAIL
JUDGE GIVES NEGRO 90 DAYS IN COUNTY JAIL

Questions for Critical Thinking

1. Where do you think the poet might have found the material for the story within his poem?
2. Describe the situation that the poet makes use of, and discuss the process by which he transforms the "news" into his subject here.

Dream Boogie (1951)

Good morning, daddy!
Ain't you heard
The boogie-woogie rumble
Of a dream deferred?
Listen closely:
You'll hear their feet
Beating out and beating out a—

You think
It's a happy beat?

Listen to it closely:
Ain't you heard
something underneath
like a—

What did I say?

Sure,
I'm happy!
Take it away!

Hey, pop!
Re-bop!
Mop!

Y-e-a-h!

Questions for Critical Thinking

1. Does such playfulness as we find in these lines have its place in good poetry? Why or why not?
2. How does the poet bend a traditional musical form to his own purposes? Why does he do it?

Harlem (Dream Deferred) (1951)

What happens to a dream deferred?

Does it dry up
like a raisin in the sun?
Or fester like a sore—
And then run?
Does it stink like rotten meat?
Or crust and sugar over—
like a syrupy sweet?

Maybe it just sags
like a heavy load.

Or does it explode?

Questions for Critical Thinking

1. How would you describe the rhyme in this poem? What effect does it create?
2. What impact does the last line have on your understanding of the rest of the poem?

Motto (1951)

I play it cool
And dig all jive.
That's the reason
I stay alive.

My motto,
As I live and learn,
is:
Dig And Be Dug
In Return.

Questions for Critical Thinking

1. Rewrite this poem without using slang. What does this reveal about the voice in the poem?
2. Compare your new version with Hughes's version. What is gained by using slang?

Night Funeral In Harlem (1951)

Night funeral
In Harlem:

Where did they get
Them two fine cars?

Insurance man, he did not pay—
His insurance lapsed the other day—
Yet they got a satin box
For his head to lay.

Night funeral
In Harlem:

Who was it sent
That wreath of flowers?

Them flowers came
from that poor boy's friends—
They'll want flowers, too,
When they meet their ends.

Night funeral
In Harlem:

Who preached that
Black boy to his grave?

Old preacher-man
Preached that boy away—
Charged Five Dollars
His girl friend had to pay.

Night funeral
In Harlem:

When it was all over
And the lid shut on his head
and the organ had done played
and the last prayers been said
and six pallbearers
Carried him out for dead
And off down Lenox Avenue
That long black hearse done sped,
The street light
At his corner
Shined just like a tear—

That boy that they was mournin'
Was so dear, so dear
To them folks that brought the flowers,
To that girl who paid the preacher-man—
It was all their tears that made
That poor boy's
Funeral grand.

Night funeral
In Harlem.

Questions for Critical Thinking

1. How does this poem achieve a musical effect? Keep in mind that it comes from the jazz-inspired collection *Montage of a Dream.*
2. There are several speakers here, and a kind of chorus. Who are the speakers, and what does each contribute to the narrative of the poem?

Theme for English B (1951)

The instructor said,

Go home and write
a page tonight.
And let that page come out of you—
Then, it will be true.

I wonder if it's that simple?
I am twenty-two, colored, born in Winston-Salem.
I went to school there, then Durham, then here
to this college on the hill above Harlem.
I am the only colored student in my class.
The steps from the hill lead down into Harlem,
through a park, then I cross St. Nicholas,
Eighth Avenue, Seventh, and I come to the Y,
the Harlem Branch Y, where I take the elevator
up to my room, sit down, and write this page:

It's not easy to know what is true for you and me
at twenty-two, my age. But I guess I'm what
I feel and see and hear, Harlem, I hear you:
hear you, hear me—we two—you, me, talk on this page.
(I hear New York, too.) Me—who?
Well, I like to eat, sleep, drink, and be in love.
I like to work, read, learn, and understand life.
I like a pipe for a Christmas present,
or records—Bessie, bop, or Bach.
I guess being colored doesn't make me *not* like
the same things other folks like who are other races.
So will my page be colored that I write?
Being me, it will not be white.

But it will be
a part of you, instructor.
You are white—
yet a part of me, as I am a part of you.
That's American.
Sometimes perhaps you don't want to be a part of me.
Nor do I often want to be a part of you.
But we are, that's true!
As I learn from you,
I guess you learn from me—
although you're older—and white—
and somewhat more free.

This is my page for English B.

Questions for Critical Thinking

1. Given the sentence-like and conversational quality of many of the lines, what elements make this a poem, rather than an essay?
2. Given your knowledge of the facts of Hughes's life, it's obvious that the "I" who speaks in this poem is neither directly autobiographical nor the "I" of the poet himself. Who, then, is the speaker?

Hughes wrote the following essay in 1926, the same year that his first collection of poetry, The Weary Blues, *appeared to great acclaim. "The Negro Artist and the Racial Mountain" stands as his personal manifesto even as it speaks to the entire generation of the Harlem Renaissance. It celebrates the "so-called common element," the genuine black artists who stay true to their heritage. At the same it serves as a call to arms for all Negro artists and intellectuals to resist white middle-class standards and express their individuality.*

The Negro Artist and the Racial Mountain (1926)

1 One of the most promising of the young Negro poets said to me once, "I want to be a poet—not a Negro poet," meaning, I believe, "I want to write like a white poet"; meaning subconsciously, "I would like to be a white poet"; meaning behind that, "I would like to be white." And I was sorry the young man said that, for no great poet has ever been afraid of being himself. And I doubted then that, with his desire to run away spiritually from his race, this boy would ever be a great poet. But this is the mountain standing in the way of any true Negro art in America—this urge within the race toward whiteness, the desire to pour racial individuality into the mold of American standardization, and to be as little Negro and as much American as possible.

2 But let us look at the immediate background of this young poet. His family is of what I suppose one would call the Negro middle class: people who are by no means rich yet never uncomfortable nor hungry—smug, contented, respectable folk, members of the Baptist church. The father goes to work every morning. He is a chief steward at a large white club. The mother sometimes does fancy sewing or supervises parties for the rich families of the town. The children go to a mixed school. In the home they read white papers and magazines. And the mother often says "Don't be like niggers" when the children are bad. A frequent phrase from the father is, "Look how well a white man does things." And so the word white comes to be unconsciously a symbol of all virtues. It holds for the children beauty, morality, and money. The whisper of "I want to be white" runs silently through their minds. This young poet's home is, I believe, a fairly typical home of the colored middle class. One sees immediately how difficult it would be for an artist born in such a home to interest himself in interpreting the beauty of his own people. He is never taught to see that beauty. He is taught rather not to see it, or if he does, to be ashamed of it when it is not according to Caucasian patterns. . . .

3 But then there are the low-down folks, the so-called common element, and they are the majority—may the Lord be praised! The people who have their hip of gin on Saturday nights and are not too important to themselves or the community, or too well fed, or too learned to watch the lazy world go round. They live on Seventh Street in Washington or State Street in Chicago and they do not particularly care whether they are like white folks or anybody else. Their joy runs, bang! into ecstasy. Their religion soars to a shout. Work maybe a little today, rest a little tomorrow. Play awhile. Sing awhile. O, let's dance! These common people are not afraid of spirituals, as for a long time their more intellectual brethren were, and jazz is their child. They furnish a wealth of colorful, distinctive material for any artist because they still hold their own individuality in the face of American standardizations. And perhaps these common people will give to the world its truly great Negro artist, the one who is not afraid to be himself. Whereas the better-class Negro would tell the artist what to do, the people at least let him alone when he does appear. And they are not ashamed of him—if they know he exists at all. And they accept what beauty is their own without question. . . .

Most of my own poems are racial in theme and treatment, derived from the life I know. In many of them I try to grasp and hold some of the meanings and rhythms of jazz. I am as sincere as I know how to be in these poems and yet after every reading I answer questions like these from my own people: Do you think Negroes should always write about Negroes? I wish you wouldn't read some of your poems to white folks. How do you find anything interesting in a place like a cabaret? Why do you write about black people? You aren't black. What makes you do so many jazz poems? 4

But jazz to me is one of the inherent expressions of Negro life in America; the eternal tom-tom beating in the Negro soul—the tom-tom of revolt against weariness in a white world, a world of subway trains, and work, work, work; the tom-tom of joy and laughter, and pain swallowed in a smile. Yet the Philadelphia clubwoman is ashamed to say that her race created it and she does not like me to write about it. The old subconscious "white is best" runs through her mind. Years of study under white teachers, a lifetime of white books, pictures, and papers, and white manners, morals, and Puritan standards made her dislike the spirituals. And now she turns up her nose at jazz and all its manifestations—likewise almost everything else distinctly racial. She doesn't care for the Winold Reiss' portraits of Negroes because they are "too Negro." She does not want a true picture of herself from anybody. She wants the artist to flatter her, to make the white world believe that all Negroes are as smug and 5 as near white in soul as she wants to be. But, to my mind, it is the duty of the younger Negro artist, if he accepts any duties at all from outsiders, to change through the force of his art that old whispering "I want to be white," hidden in the aspirations of his people, to "Why should I want to be white? I am a Negro—and beautiful."

6 So I am ashamed for the black poet who says, "I want to be a poet, not a Negro poet," as though his own racial world were not as interesting as any other world. I am ashamed, too, for the colored artist who runs from the painting of Negro faces to the painting of sunsets after the manner of the academicians because he fears the strange unwhiteness of his own features. An artist must be free to choose what he does, certainly, but he must also never be afraid to do what he must choose.

7 Let the blare of Negro jazz bands and the bellowing voice of Bessie Smith singing the Blues penetrate the closed ears of the colored near intellectuals until they listen and perhaps understand. Let Paul Robeson singing "Water Boy," and Rudolph Fisher writing about the streets of Harlem, and Jean Toomer holding the heart of Georgia in his hands, and Aaron Douglas's drawing strange black fantasies cause the smug Negro middle class to turn from their white, respectable, ordinary books and papers to catch a glimmer of their own beauty. We younger Negro artists who create now intend to express our individual dark-skinned selves without fear or shame. If white people are pleased we are glad. If they are not, it doesn't matter. We know we are beautiful. And ugly too. The tom-tom cries and the tom-tom laughs. If colored people are pleased we are glad. If they are not, their displeasure doesn't matter either. We build our temples for tomorrow, strong as we know how, and we stand on top of the mountain, free within ourselves.

Questions for Critical Thinking

1. Hughes identifies two groups within the African-American race. What are these groups? List their characteristics, then state which group Hughes admires more. Why?
2. Describe Hughes's feelings toward jazz. According to Hughes, why is jazz important? What does it express?
3. Based on this essay, write a one-paragraph summary of Hughes's mission as a black artist.

Countee Cullen (1903–1946)

A prominent voice of the Harlem Renaissance, Cullen rivaled and at times surpassed Langston Hughes in his lifetime. Although he was immensely popular in the 1920s and early 1930s, relatively little is known about the childhood of the boy who would grow up to become the "black Keats." He was most likely born in Louisville, Kentucky. Although he went by the name Countee Porter early in life, by early adolescence, he had been adopted by the Cullen family, and he enjoyed a close relationship with his Cullen father, who led a church in Harlem, and spent his young adulthood in Harlem.

Early success with his poetry collections *Color* (1925), *Copper Sun* (1927), *The Ballad of the Brown Girl* (1927), and *The Black Christ* (1929), all published in a four-year period; his receipt of a Guggenheim Fellowship that allowed him to live in France for a year and write; and his high-profile marriage to Yolande Du Bois, the only daughter of the famous African-American activist W. E. B. Du Bois, all promised the making of an exceptional poet and role model and cemented his reputation as the great "crossover" poet—a black man who wrote in the style of classically white poetry. While Hughes made it clear in "The Negro Artist and the Racial Mountain" that he planned to be a poet who celebrated his race, Countee Cullen made the following statement in the *Brooklyn Eagle:*

> If I am going to be a poet at all, I am going to be POET and not NEGRO POET. This is what has hindered the development of artists among us. Their one note has been the concern with their race. That is all very well, none of us can get away from it. I cannot at times. You will see it in my verse. The consciousness of this is too poignant at times. I cannot escape it. But what I mean is this: I shall not write of negro subjects for the purpose of propaganda. That is not what a poet is concerned with. Of course, when the emotion rising out of the fact that I am a negro is strong, I express it. But that is another matter.

Cullen's career peaked early; he began writing less, and his marriage ended in divorce a year after it began. He took a job teaching French and English at a junior high school where he taught until his death at age forty-two.

Incident (1925)

Once riding in old Baltimore,
Heart-filled, head-filled with glee,
I saw a Baltimorean
Keep looking straight at me.

Now I was eight and very small,
And he was no whit bigger,
And so I smiled, but he poked out
His tongue, and called me, "Nigger."

I saw the whole of Baltimore
From May until December;
Of all the things that happened there
That's all that I remember.

Questions for Critical Thinking

1. This poem is more straightforward than other classical poems that Cullen wrote. Why do you think Cullen chose to make it that way? How would its impact change if it were written in elevated language or a more complex form?
2. Discuss the difference in the rhyme pattern, in these four-line stanzas, between the first and third lines and the second and fourth. Also discuss the enjambment in lines 7 and 8. How does the conversational "tone" here get supported or undermined by the poem's formal structure?

Helene Johnson (1907–1995)

Helene Johnson came to New York in 1926 to attend the awards ceremony for the winners of *Opportunity* magazine's poetry contest—she had received an honorable mention—and stayed. Langston Hughes's friend and collaborator on "Mule Bone," Zora Neale Hurston (see chapter 14, Stories for Further Reading), lived in the same apartment building, and her cousin, the writer Dorothy West, was nearby in Harlem. Johnson was close to many writers during this time, and Countee Cullen published her work in his anthology *Caroling Dusk*. After her marriage to William Warner Hubbel and the birth of their daughter, she wrote less. When they separated, she moved back home to Boston but later returned to New York, where she died. The subject of race and identity is framed in Johnson's work by lyrical formal verse, as it is in the following poem, "Sonnet to a Negro in Harlem."

Sonnet to a Negro in Harlem (1927)

You are disdainful and magnificent—
Your perfect body and your pompous gait,
Your dark eyes flashing solemnly with hate;
Small wonder that you are incompetent
To imitate those whom you so despise—
Your shoulders towering high above the throng,
Your head thrown back in rich, barbaric song,
Palm trees and mangoes stretched before your eyes.
Let others toil and sweat for labor's sake
And wring from grasping hands their meed of gold.
Why urge ahead your supercilious feet?
Scorn will efface each footprint that you make.
I love your laughter arrogant and bold.
You are too splendid for this city street!

Questions for Critical Thinking

1. Do you find this description in the poem similar to that of an actual painting? List the details you learn from the poem. Which details would you also learn from an actual painting, and which are unique to verse? Are any details missing that you would get only from a real picture?
2. How critical is this depiction of the subject? Do you find elements of admiration along with the negative elements?

Claude McKay (1889–1948)

Jamaican-born Claude McKay brought in a more defiant tone than that of Langston Hughes, but like Hughes his subject was race. He had grown up hearing from his father about his West African Ashanti traditions and how his grandfather had been enslaved by whites. He published two collections while still living in Jamaica, *Songs of Jamaica* (1912), celebrating the life of Jamaican farmers, and *Constab Ballads* (1912), deriding the treatment of dark-skinned blacks by whites and mulattos. These books earned him the medal of the Jamaican Institute of the Arts and Sciences. McKay arrived in the United States, where he studied agriculture first at Booker T. Washington's Tuskegee Institute in Alabama and later at Kansas State College. After two years, he decided instead to make his living as a writer and moved to Harlem. He was close to radicals, often publishing his work in Greenwich Village political magazines, and he lived for a time in England, where he worked at *Workers' Dreadnought*. He returned to America in 1921. Writers like Hughes and McKay were "The New Writers" that Alain Locke described in his essay "The New Negro." McKay shaped the imagination and subject matter of black writers and did so by writing his unflinching condemnations of bigotry in formal verse, as he does in the following sonnet, "The White City."

The White City (1922)

I will not toy with it nor bend an inch.
Deep in the secret chambers of my heart
I muse my life-long hate, and without flinch
I bear it nobly as I live my part.
My being would be a skeleton, a shell,
If this dark Passion that fills my every mood,
And makes my heaven in the white world's hell,
Did not forever feed me vital blood.
I see the mighty city through a mist—
The strident trains that speed the goaded mass,
The poles and spires and towers vapor-kissed,
The fortressed port through which the great ships pass,
The tides, the wharves, the dens I contemplate,
Are sweet like wanton loves because I hate.

Questions for Critical Thinking

1. What does the title tell you about the subject of the somewhat difficult poem? What is its subject?
2. How difficult is it to interpret this poem once you identify the subject? What is your interpretation?

Jessie Redmon Fauset (1884–1961)

Jessie Redmon Fauset was raised by her father, the Reverend Redmon Fauset, and his wife, Annie, outside Philadelphia. She went to public schools in Philadelphia until she graduated with a scholarship to Cornell. She was the first woman to graduate Phi Beta Kappa at Cornell and the first black woman to be admitted to that prestigious academic organization nationally. After teaching Latin and French in Baltimore and Washington, D.C. (where her race did not bar her from getting a teaching job), Fauset went back to school at the University of Pennsylvania to earn her master's degree. She began working for the magazine *Crisis* under W. E. B. Du Bois in 1918 and became its literary editor in 1919. She nurtured the talents of many, including Langston Hughes, whom she recognized early in his career. When she invited him to lunch, he was so nervous he asked if he could bring his gregarious mother (which he did) to make sure the lunch went smoothly. Fauset's home was often the meeting place for literary discussions, sometimes held in French. She had exacting standards as an editor and was of central importance in shaping the talent that was burgeoning in this time in Harlem.

Touché (1927)

Dear, when we sit in that high, placid room,
"Loving" and "doving" as all lovers do,
Laughing and leaning so close in the gloom,—

What is the change that creeps sharp over you?
Just as you raise your fine hand to my hair,
Bringing that glance of mixed wonder and rue?

"Black hair," you murmur, "so lustrous and rare,
Beautiful too, like a raven's smooth wing;
Surely no gold locks were ever more fair."

Why do you say every night that same thing?
Turning your mind to some old constant theme,
Half meditating and half murmuring?

Tell me, that girl of your young manhood's dream,
Her you loved first in that dim long ago—
Had *she* blue eyes? Did *her* hair goldly gleam?

Does *she* come back to you softly and slow,
Stepping wraith-wise from the depths of the past?
Quickened and fired by the warmth of our glow?

There, I've divined it! My wit holds you fast.
Nay, no excuses; 'tis little I care,
I knew a lad in my own girlhood's past,—
Blue eyes he had and such waving gold hair!

Questions for Critical Thinking

1. What role does race play in this affair between two dark-haired and, presumably, dark-skinned lovers? How does the matter of race engender doubt in the lover's mind?
2. How does the formal and even archaic diction and tone (words like "rue" and "nay") compare with the writing of Toomer or Hughes? What do these aesthetic choices reveal about Redmon Fauset's work?

Jean Toomer (1894–1967)

Jean Toomer insisted that he was "of no race," a mix of "Scotch, Welsh, German, English, French, Dutch, Spanish and some dark blood," but his great work *Cane* (1923) is a modernist study by turns of black life in rural Georgia and black life in urban Chicago and Washington, D.C., and an autobiographical synthesis of the two. It includes poems and sketches as well as prose and immediately became a central text for African Americans of his time. Toomer was born in Washington, D.C.; his father abandoned the family a year after he was born. He and his mother moved in with her parents, where Toomer spent his early years. Race was an issue early on but with a twist; Toomer's maternal grandfather had achieved some success as a politician in southern Louisiana, and though he claimed to be black, Toomer himself did not believe it was true. When Toomer's mother remarried, they relocated to New Rochelle, New York. He never graduated from college, though he attended several, and claimed Alain Locke had "tricked" him into including his work in *The New Negro*. In the 1920s he began a long association with George I. Gurdjieff, a Greek-Armenian spiritualist, and he tried to recruit his friends, African-American writers such as Nella Larsen and Wallace Thurman, to Gurdjieff's Unitism. In later life, Toomer moved away from Gurdjieff, married, and became a Quaker. The following poem, "Reapers," appears in *Cane*.

Reapers (1923)

Black reapers with the sound of steel on stones
Are sharpening scythes. I see them place the hones
In their hip-pockets as a thing that's done,
And start their silent swinging, one by one.
Black horses drive a mower through the weeds,
And there, a field rat, startled, squealing bleeds,
His belly close to ground. I see the blade,
Blood-stained, continue cutting weeds and shade.

Questions for Critical Thinking

1. The poet observes workers in the field. How does he use language and rhythm to convey a sense of danger?
2. How does Toomer use the word *reaper* to raise the physical activity in the poem to a higher level of meaning?

Angelina Weld Grimké (1880–1958)

Angelina Weld Grimké's paternal great-aunts were white Southern abolitionists; she and her sister publicly acknowledged their brother's child from a union with a slave, Nancy Weston. Her father, a lawyer with a Harvard law degree, had married their mother, Sarah Stanly of Boston, though Sarah's father, a clergyman, disapproved of the match, and she eventually abandoned the marriage and her children. She never saw Angelina again. Angelina's father doted on her, and she continued her family tradition in her first work, a play, *Rachel,* which, according to the playbill, was "the first attempt to use the stage for race propaganda in order to enlighten the American people relative to the lamentable condition of ten million of Colored citizens in this free republic." Her output was small, but her poetry is characterized by lyricism and the address of life as a woman. She married Theodore Dwight Weld and remained close friends with a widely published African-American writer of the time, Georgia Douglas Johnson.

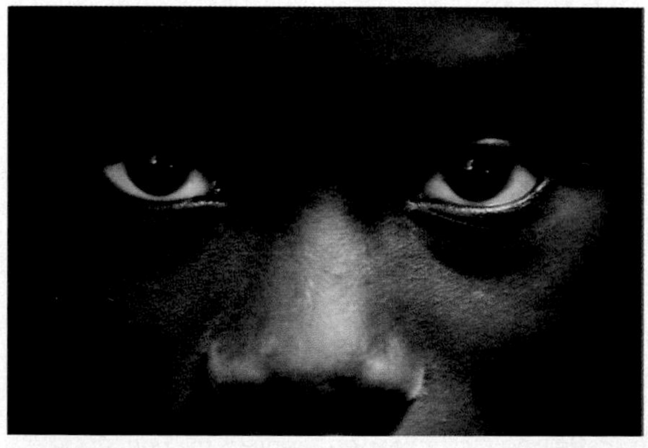

Fragment (c. 1930)

I am the woman with the black black skin
I am the laughing woman with the black black face
I am living in the cellars and in every crowded place
  I am toiling just to eat
  In the cold and in the heat
    And I laugh
I am the laughing woman who's forgotten how to weep
I am the laughing woman who's afraid to go to sleep

Questions for Critical Thinking

1. Does the ironic juxtaposition of laughter and destitution seem evident to you?
2. Why does the poet employ irony here? What does she gain? What do you gain as a reader?

Getting Started: A Research Project

Research is a skill that will carry you through your college career. To help acquaint you with the research process, the materials you need for this project are made available on our website (**www.mhhe.com/delbanco1e**). Other ideas for research projects and sources appear at the end of this chapter.

Although a popular and iconic figure for the Harlem Renaissance, Langston Hughes did share the spotlight with other outspoken literary figures during the period. One such person was Countee Cullen, whose poem "Incident" appears earlier in this chapter. Like Hughes, Cullen was not raised by his biological parents, he was very successful in high school, and he was a published poet in his late teenage years. Although both would become prominent voices of the Harlem Renaissance, their messages were not always the same.

Information on Cullen's background and a timeline of his accomplishments can be found at **www.mhhe.com/delbanco1e**. You will also find a variety of essays related to Cullen, Hughes, and the other writers of their generation. As you conduct your research, ask yourself what ties these diverse writers together as voices of the Harlem Renaissance, and consider how their messages resonate in modern society.

The Harlem Renaissance and the poets associated with it often dealt with race, and it was in many ways a racial movement, but it was more than that. It was a cultural awakening, a celebration of music like blues and jazz, an explosion of new art and theater and political thinking. In the same way, the key players like Langston Hughes or Countee Cullen were not just poets. They wrote essays, plays, and novels. They worked in colloquialisms and formal voices. They wrote about private experiences as well as public issues.

Go to **www.mhhe.com/delbanco1e** for essays and resources on topics centered on Langston Hughes and the poets of his time.

1. Focus on one pair of poets, such as Hughes and Cullen. Read the quote from Cullen's brief biography earlier in this chapter. Contrast Cullen's statement with Hughes's arguments in his essay "The Negro Artist and the Racial Mountain." Note how Hughes refers to a "Negro poet" in the first line of the essay. Compare Hughes's and Cullen's ideas about being a "Negro poet." Write a definition of "Negro poet" from each man's point of view. Now consider how the two definitions compare, and how they are different.
2. Discuss how blues and jazz influenced literature during the Harlem Renaissance.
3. Both Hughes and Cullen experienced highs and lows of popularity. Consider the timelines of their lives and careers, as well as the social atmosphere of their era, and discuss the various factors surrounding each figure's prominence and decline.

Further Suggestions for Writing and Research

1. If you have an interest in music, particularly in blues and jazz, reread Hughes's poem "Harlem (Dream Deferred)" and some of the blues poems in preparation for reading at least two of the articles listed below—including one from the Hughes scholar Onwuchekwa Jemie. Drawing upon these articles, write an essay in which you present a critical reading of "Harlem," interweaving the significance of its form as a jazz poem.
   - Johnson, Charles S. "Jazz Poetry and Blues." *Critical Essays on Langston Hughes*. Ed. Edward J. Mullen. Boston: G. K. Hall & Co., 1986. See pages 143–147.
   - Jemie, Onwuchekwa. "Jazz, Jive, and Jam." *Langston Hughes: An Introduction to the Poetry*. New York: Columbia UP, 1976. 57–96. Print.

2. Look up Wallace Thurman in the *Encyclopedia of the Harlem Renaissance.* Read selections from Thurman's novel *The Blacker the Berry* (1929) and from his satirical critique of the Harlem Renaissance in *Infants of the Spring* (1932). Argue a case for the complexity of the years of the Harlem Renaissance, in which not all the artists and writers making up this so-called movement take a positive view of the world in which they move.
3. Look up the paintings of Jacob Lawrence, a painter who was another of Langston Hughes's contemporaries during the Harlem Renaissance. The word *renaissance* means, literally, "born again." This is not a religious term but a cultural one; in the European Renaissance of the fifteenth and sixteenth centuries the ideals of antiquity were rediscovered, and artists and writers tried to express the "classical" ideals as derived from Greece and Rome. The name Harlem comes from the Dutch city of Haarlem, the home of many of the first settlers of New Amsterdam (New York City's original name). To what degree do artists like Langston Hughes and Jacob Lawrence pay conscious attention to their own history, and what are they suggesting should be "born again" in this new/old form of art? What's innovative and what's traditional in their work; how much influence do African or Caribbean roots have in the flowering of the Harlem Renaissance? Cite specific examples. What role did music play?
4. There are several other twentieth-century examples of artists in community. To pick a few, there's expatriate Paris (Gertrude Stein, Ernest Hemingway, F. Scott Fitzgerald, Pablo Picasso, etc.), London's Bloomsbury (Virginia Woolf, Vanessa Stephen, E. M. Forster, Lytton Strachey, etc.), and a group of novelists near the southern English town of Rye (Henry James, Joseph Conrad, Ford Madox Ford, and Stephen Crane). How does the idea of collegiality—a shared aesthetic, shared pleasure in each other's company—pertain to the Harlem Renaissance? How does the idea of regionalism (discussed in the Case Studies on Regionalism in chapter 12) play a role in the work—from music to literature—of the Harlem Renaissance? When Josephine Baker sings "Harlem on My Mind" in Paris, or James Baldwin (whose story "Sonny's Blues" can be found in chapter 14) goes to Paris with recordings of Billie Holiday and Bessie Smith, what does that say about the value and power of place?

Some Sources for Research

Online Sources:

1. Alexander, Elizabeth. "The Black Poet as Canon-Maker: Langston Hughes, New Negro Poets, and American poetry's segregated past." *PoetryFoundation.org.* 2004. Web. <http://www.poetryfoundation.org/archive/feature.html?id=177377>.

2. Giaimo, Paul. "Ethnic outsiders: the hyper-ethnicized narrator in Langston Hughes and Fred L. Gardaphe." *MELUS* 28 (2003): 133-147. Web. 18 March 2009. <http://www.articlearchives.com/humanities-social-science/literature-literature/942664-1.html>.

3. Graham, Maryemma. "The beat goes on." *The New Crisis* Jan/Feb (2002). Web. 29 March 2009. <http://findarticles.com/p/articles/mi_qa3812/is_200201/ai_n9041756>.

4. Lamb, Robert Paul. "'A Little Yellow Bastard Boy': Paternal Rejection, Filial Insistence, and the Triumph of African American Cultural Aesthetics in Langston Hughes's 'Mulatto.'" *College Literature* 35.2 (2008): 126-153. Web. 18 March 2009. <http://findarticles.com/p/articles/mi_qa3709/is_200804/ai_n25419543?tag=content;col1>.

5. The Poetry Foundation. "Langston Hughes." *PoetryFoundation.org*. 2009. Web. <http://www.poetryfoundation.org/archive/poet.html?id=3340>.

6. Scott, Jonathan. "Advanced, repressed, and popular: Langston Hughes during the cold war." *College Literature* 33.2 (2006): 30-51. Web. 19 March 2009. <http://www.accessmylibrary.com/coms2/summary_0286-15272890_ITM>.

Print Sources:

1. Beckman, Wendy Hart. *Artists and Writers of the Harlem Renaissance*. Berkeley Heights, NJ: Enslow Publishers, 2002. Print.
2. Bloom, Harold, ed. *The Harlem Renaissance*. Philadelphia: Chelsea House Publishers, 2004. Print.
3. Carroll, Anne Elizabeth. *Word, Image, and the New Negro: Representation and Identity in the Harlem Renaissance*. Bloomington: Indiana UP, 2005. Print.
4. Douglas, Ann. *Terrible Honesty: Mongrel Manhattan in the 1920's*. Farrar, Strauss, and Giroux, 1995. Print.
5. Harper, Donna Akiba Sullivan. *Not So Simple: The "Simple" Stories By Langston Hughes*. Columbia, MO: University of Missouri Press, 1995. Print.
6. Jones, Sharon L. *Rereading the Harlem Renaissance: Race, Class, and Gender in the Fiction of Jessie Fauset, Zora Neale Hurston, and Dorothy West*. Westport, CT: Greenwood Press, 2002. Print.
7. Krasner, David. *A Beautiful Pageant: African American Theatre, Drama, and Performance in the Harlem Renaissance, 1910-1927*. New York: Palgrave Macmillan, 2002. Print.
8. Rampersad, Arnold. *The Life of Langston Hughes*. 2 vols. New York: Oxford UP, 2002. Print.
9. Schumacher, Julie A., ed. *The Harlem Renaissance*. Logan, IA: Perfection Learning, 2001. Print.

For examples of student papers, see chapter 3, "Common Writing Assignments" and chapter 5, "Writing the Research Paper," in the Handbook for Writing from Reading.

27 Art & Poetry A Case Study on *William Blake*

Songs of Innocence

Songs of Experience

"I have this morning been reading a strange publication—viz. Poems with very wild and interesting pictures, as the swathing, etched (I suppose) but it is said—printed and painted by the Author, W. Blake. He is a man of Genius . . . certainly a mystic emphatically. You may perhaps smile at my calling another Poet, a Mystic; but verily I am in the very mire of commonplace common-sense compared with Mr. Blake."

—Samuel Taylor Coleridge upon reading *Songs of Innocence and of Experience*
(from a letter written by Coleridge, February 1818)

Blake in Context

Eighteenth-Century London

With the exception of three years, William Blake lived his entire life in London. As the center of British commerce and culture, London—like the rest of England—experienced much change in the late eighteenth and early nineteenth centuries. Blake's poetry and art show an acute consciousness of the social changes and problems of his day, a consciousness that appears in poems like "London," "The Chimney Sweeper," "The Little Black Boy," and "The Sick Rose."

Social Unrest

Both the American Revolution (1775–1783) and the French Revolution (1789–1799) took place in the late eighteenth century, and in each case, the monarchy was overthrown in favor of creating a republic. The British government responded by more tightly regulating its subjects and cracking down on treasonous speech and behavior. Blake himself faced a treason trial in 1803 after a British soldier accused him of cursing the crown. Although Blake's innocence was proven and he was acquitted, the experience continued to haunt him.

Slavery

In 1788, parliament began an investigation of the slave trade, and a year later, Olaudah Equiano published his best-selling autobiography, which revealed how he had risen from slavery and earned an education. By 1792, the House of Commons was in favor of ending slavery, and in 1807, the law officially ending slavery in Britain was passed. However, many free blacks who lived in London struggled with extreme poverty and racial prejudice from whites. In "The Little Black Boy," Blake captures the voice of a child who has suffered from inequality; it is only in heaven that he and the white boy will be brought together.

Industry

The Industrial Revolution—that is, the change from an agricultural, rural society to the urban world of manufacturing—began in this time period. The

A photo of chimney sweeps, taken in 1877.

first cotton mill in Britain appeared in 1771, and by the beginning of the nineteenth century, the rise of industry had created a large population of poor urban laborers. Among these laborers who faced long shifts, unsafe conditions, and stifling tasks were children who worked because they were orphans or belonged to an impoverished family.

The chimney sweeping trade was particularly notorious for its maltreatment of child laborers. Children as young as four years old, and more commonly around six to eight years old, were sold as apprentices to master chimney sweepers, many of whom did not provide for the children but made them subsist by begging. Jonas Hanway, an active protester against child labor, gave a picture of the deplorable condition of child chimney sweepers in his 1767 letter published in the *London Chronicle:* "Chimney-sweepers ought to breed their own children to the business, then perhaps they will wash, clothe and feed them. As it is, they do neither, and these poor black urchins have no protectors and are treated worse than a humane person would treat a dog. . . . They often beg in the streets, and seem to be in much more real need than common beggars." Children were popular with the chimney sweeping profession because their small bodies allowed them to climb into fireplace flues; this occupation, however, almost certainly led to an early death—if not from suffocation in the flue, then from cancer and other diseases resulting from constant exposure to soot. Note that "poor black urchins" refers not to skin color but to skin blackened by soot.

A portrait of Mary Wollstonecraft, pregnant with her daughter, painted by John Opie in 1797.

Women's Rights

Women had almost no rights in the late eighteenth century. When a woman married, she and all her possessions became her husband's property. Further, she was not allowed to initiate a court case, and thus had no form of redress for any abuses she suffered at the hands of her husband or others. Although there were some voices that began to call for more equal treatment—most notably Mary Wollstonecraft, whose 1792 *Vindication of the Rights of Women* argued that men as well as women had been corrupted by the inequality of the genders—women were educated only in domestic accomplishments, like music, drawing, and Romance languages. Furthermore, a girl's virginity before marriage was essential to her worth, and therefore women were expected to be pure and modest. Only a few occupations—such as those of governess or nurse—were considered appropriate for women, making marriage necessary to their economic stability.

William Blake (1757–1827)

"Genius," "mad," "mystic"—each of these words was applied to William Blake by his contemporaries. Although he lived in relative obscurity and died completely misunderstood, Blake has come to be recognized as one of the most imaginative writers and artists ever to have lived. A lifelong resident of London, Blake was writing poetry by age twelve. At fourteen, he began an apprenticeship with James Brasire, an engraver who taught in a classical style considered out-of-date by most of his colleagues. A few years after completing his seven-year apprenticeship, Blake married Catherine Boucher. Boucher was illiterate, but Blake soon taught her both to read and to be his assistant in producing art that accompanied his own writing.

Unlike that of most other poets, William Blake's craft includes the tangible aspect of visual art—painting, drawing, engraving, and printing. His poems—themselves small masterpieces of symbol and sound—are best studied in conjunction with the illustrations and illuminated designs that Blake made to accompany them in a time-consuming process of etching the words and image backward on a copper plate so that the printed page would turn out the proper way, ready for Blake to paint it by hand. His collection of poems *Songs of Innocence and of Experience* (1794), for example, includes elaborate illustrations that Blake made by etching wax on copper plates, then printing from those plates, and finally painting the printed images by hand. Blake earned a meager living by illustrating children's books and accepting patronage from wealthy benefactors, but for the most part he lived his life in poverty.

Further, his craft is notable because of the singularity of the mind behind the works. In contemporary terms, we might call Blake "antiestablishment"—against the conventional philosophy, politics, and religion of his day. Blake was also a supporter of the French Revolution, which began in 1789 and which many of the English regarded as a threat to their own system of government. At the same time, Blake, a dreamer with a strong interest in mythology and the Bible, valued the imagination over all else and therefore found himself in conflict with the prevailing philosophy of his day, known as The Enlightenment, which valued the authority of rational thought over religious belief. Despite his adherence to Christian views and his love of the Bible, he portrayed the institution of the church of his time as a repressive force. In his poem "The Garden of Love" (which appears later in this chapter), for example, the church is associated with binding people's desires with its forbidding presence.

Blake wrote a series of prophetic works, consciously engaging in the tradition of great English writers like Edmund Spenser (1552–1599) and John Milton (1608–1674), both of whom had written book-length poems of their own. *America: A Prophecy* and *Europe: A Prophecy* show Blake's hatred of social and political tyranny, while *The Book of Urizen* attacks religious tyranny. These themes appear in earlier works as well, particularly *Songs of Innocence and of Experience,* which Blake subtitled "showing the two contrary states of the human soul." Originally, Blake composed just *Songs of Innocence* in 1789, but he added *Songs of Experience* five years later. Just as the two books can stand separately, so does each poem have its individual merit. But, just as Blake combined the two books, so, too, are there parallels connecting the poems: a version of "The Chimney Sweeper" appears in *Innocence* and another appears in *Experience;* "The Tyger" in *Experience* is the counterpart to "The Lamb" in *Innocence;* the "Introduction" in each section achieves a similar purpose but with an opposing view.

> "Of all the conditions which arouse the interest of the psychologist, none assuredly is more attractive than the union of genius and madness in single remarkable minds, which, while on the one hand they compel our admiration by their great mental powers, yet on the other move our pity by their claims to supernatural gifts. Of such is the whole race of ecstatics, mystics, seers of visions, and dreamers of dreams, and to their list we have now to add another name, that of William Blake."
>
> —H. C. Robinson, 1811
> (from his essay "William Blake, artist, poet, and religious mystic" published 1811)

Title page from *Songs of Innocence*.

Selected Poems from *Songs of Innocence*

The Ecchoing Green

The Sun does arise,
And make happy the skies;
The merry bells ring
To welcome the Spring;
The sky-lark and thrush,
The birds of the bush,
Sing louder around
To the bells' chearful sound,
While our sports shall be seen
On the Ecchoing Green.

Old John, with white hair,
Does laugh away care,
Sitting under the oak,
Among the old folk.
They laugh at our play,
And soon they all say:
"Such, such were the joys
When we all, girls & boys,
In our youth time were seen
On the Ecchoing Green."

Till the little ones, weary,
No more can be merry;
The sun does descend,
And our sports have an end.
Round the laps of their mothers
Many sisters and brothers,
Like birds in their nest,
Are ready for rest,
And sport no more seen
On the darkening Green.

Question for Critical Thinking

Underline the imagery in "The Ecchoing Green." How would you describe the imagery? Does it change or remain the same throughout the poem?

(1794)

They laugh at our play.
And soon they all say
Such such were the joys.
When we all girls & boys.
In our youth-time were seen,
On the Ecchoing Green.

Till the little ones weary
No more can be merry
The sun does descend,
And our sports have an end:
Round the laps of their mothers.
Many sisters and brothers,
Like birds in their nest.
Are ready for rest:
And sport no more seen,
On the darkening Green.

The Lamb

Little lamb, who made thee?
Dost thou know who made thee?
Gave thee life, & bid thee feed
By the stream & o'er the mead;
Gave thee clothing of delight,
Softest clothing, wooly, bright;
Gave thee such a tender voice,
Making all the vales rejoice?
Little Lamb, who made thee?
Dost thou know who made thee?

Little Lamb, I'll tell thee,
Little Lamb, I'll tell thee:
He is called by thy name,
For he calls himself a Lamb.
He is meek & he is mild;
He became a little child.
I a child, & thou a lamb.
We are called by his name.
Little Lamb, God bless thee!
Little Lamb, God bless thee!

Question for Critical Thinking

Make a list of all the things you associate with a lamb. You might want to think about literal lambs as well as the symbol of the lamb in Christian tradition. In general, are these pleasant connotations? Or are there darker connotations as well? If so, how does the poem deal with these darker undercurrents?

The Little Black Boy

My mother bore me in the southern wild,
And I am black, but O! my soul is white;
White as an angel is the English child,
But I am black as if bereav'd of light.

My mother taught me underneath a tree,
And, sitting down before the heat of day,
She took me on her lap and kissed me,
And pointing to the east, began to say:

"Look on the rising sun: there God does live,
And gives his light, and gives his heat away;
And flowers and trees and beasts and men receive
Comfort in morning, joy in the noonday.

"And we are put on earth a little space,
That we may learn to bear the beams of love;
And these black bodies and this sunburnt face
Is but a cloud, and like a shady grove.

"For when our souls have learn'd the heat to bear,
The cloud will vanish; we shall hear his voice,
Saying: 'Come out from the grove, my love & care,
And round my golden tent like lambs rejoice.'"

Thus did my mother say, and kissed me;
And thus I say to little English boy:
When I from black and he from white cloud free,
And round the tent of God like lambs we joy,

I'll shade him from the heat, till he can bear
To lean in joy upon our father's knee;
And then I'll stand and stroke his silver hair,
And be like him, and he will then love me.

Question for Critical Thinking

Refer to the "Blake in Context" section, and after reading it, summarize "The Little Black Boy," being sure to use the historical context to figure out what is being said in this poem.

The Chimney Sweeper

When my mother died I was very young,
And my father sold me while yet my tongue
Could scarcely cry "'weep! 'weep! 'weep! 'weep!"
So your chimneys I sweep, & in soot I sleep.

There's little Tom Dacre, who cried when his head,
That curl'd like a lamb's back, was shav'd: so I said
"Hush, Tom! never mind it, for when your head's bare
You know that the soot cannot spoil your white hair."

And so he was quiet, & that very night,
As Tom was a-sleeping, he had such a sight!
That thousands of sweepers, Dick, Joe, Ned & Jack,
Were all of them lock'd up in coffins of black.

And by came an Angel who had a bright key,
And he open'd the coffins & set them all free;
Then down a green plain leaping, laughing, they run,
And wash in a river, and shine in the Sun.

Then naked & white, all their bags left behind,
They rise upon clouds and sport in the wind;
And the Angel told Tom, if he'd be a good boy,
He'd have God for his father, & never want joy.

And so Tom awoke; and we rose in the dark,
And got with our bags & our brushes to work.
Tho' the morning was cold, Tom was happy & warm;
So if all do their duty they need not fear harm.

Question for Critical Thinking

Victor N. Paananen argues that "The finest poems of the *Songs of Innocence* are those in which there is some admission of the hardships actually faced by the innocents . . . but in these poems the innocent view can be seen as easily rising above adversity." In what ways does Tom Dacre's dream raise the chimney sweepers from their harsh reality? Do you see any patterns of imagery present in his dream?

The Little Boy Lost

"Father! father! where are you going?
O do not walk so fast.
Speak, father, speak to your little boy,
Or else I shall be lost."

The night was dark, no father was there;
The child was wet with dew;
The mire was deep, & the child did weep,
And away the vapour flew.

Question for Critical Thinking

Brainstorm several different ways you understand "father" in this poem. In other words, what might "father" represent beyond the child's biological parent?

The Little Boy Found

The little boy lost in the lonely fen,
Led by the wand'ring light,
Began to cry; but God, ever nigh,
Appear'd like his father in white.

He kissed the child & by the hand led
And to his mother brought,
Who in sorrow pale, thro' the lonely dale,
Her little boy weeping sought.

Question for Critical Thinking

Many critics argue that "The Little Boy Lost" and "The Little Boy Found" are two parts of the same poem; in other words, something is lost if a person reads just one half. In what ways does "The Little Boy Found" answer "The Little Boy Lost"? Does it change your understanding of "father"? Of the enigmatic "vapour" in "The Little Boy Lost"?

Holy Thursday

'Twas on a Holy Thursday, their innocent faces clean,
The children walking two & two, in red & blue & green,
Grey-headed beadles walk'd before, with wands as white as snow,
Till into the high dome of Paul's they like Thames' waters flow

O what a multitude they seem'd, these flowers of London town!
Seated in companies they sit with radiance all their own.
The hum of multitudes was there, but multitudes of lambs,
Thousands of little boys & girls raising their innocent hands.

Now like a mighty wind they raise to heaven the voice of song,
Or like harmonious thunderings the seats of Heaven among.
Beneath them sit the aged men, wise guardians of the poor;
Then cherish pity, lest you drive an angel from your door.

Question for Critical Thinking

Scan this poem, being sure to identify the meter and rhyme scheme. Then underline places where Blake deviates from the established pattern. What significance do you see to these changes? In your opinion, what certain ideas does Blake highlight with these deviations?

The Divine Image

To Mercy, Pity, Peace, and Love
All pray in their distress;
And to these virtues of delight
Return their thankfulness.

For Mercy, Pity, Peace, and Love
God, our father dear,
And Mercy, Pity, Peace, and Love
Man, his child and care.

For Mercy has a human heart,
Pity a human face,
And Love, the human form divine,
And Peace, the human dress.

Then every man, of every clime
That prays in his distress,
Prays to the human form divine,
Love, Mercy, Pity, Peace.

And all must love the human form,
In heathen, turk, or jew;
Where Mercy, Love, & Pity dwell
There God is dwelling too.

Question for Critical Thinking

Summarize the message you believe Blake conveys in this poem. (Hint: You might pay particular attention to the second and fifth stanzas.) You might also consider how it resonates with or mirrors Christian beliefs.

Title page from *Songs of Experience.*

Selected Poems from *Songs of Experience* (1794)

Holy Thursday

Is this a holy thing to see
In a rich and fruitful land,
Babes reduc'd to misery,
Fed with cold and usurous hand?

Is that trembling cry a song?
Can it be a song of joy?
And so many children poor?
It is a land of poverty!

And their sun does never shine,
And their fields are bleak & bare,
And their ways are fill'd with thorns:
It is eternal winter there.

For where-e'er the sun does shine,
And where-e'er the rain does fall,
Babe can never hunger there,
Nor poverty the mind appall.

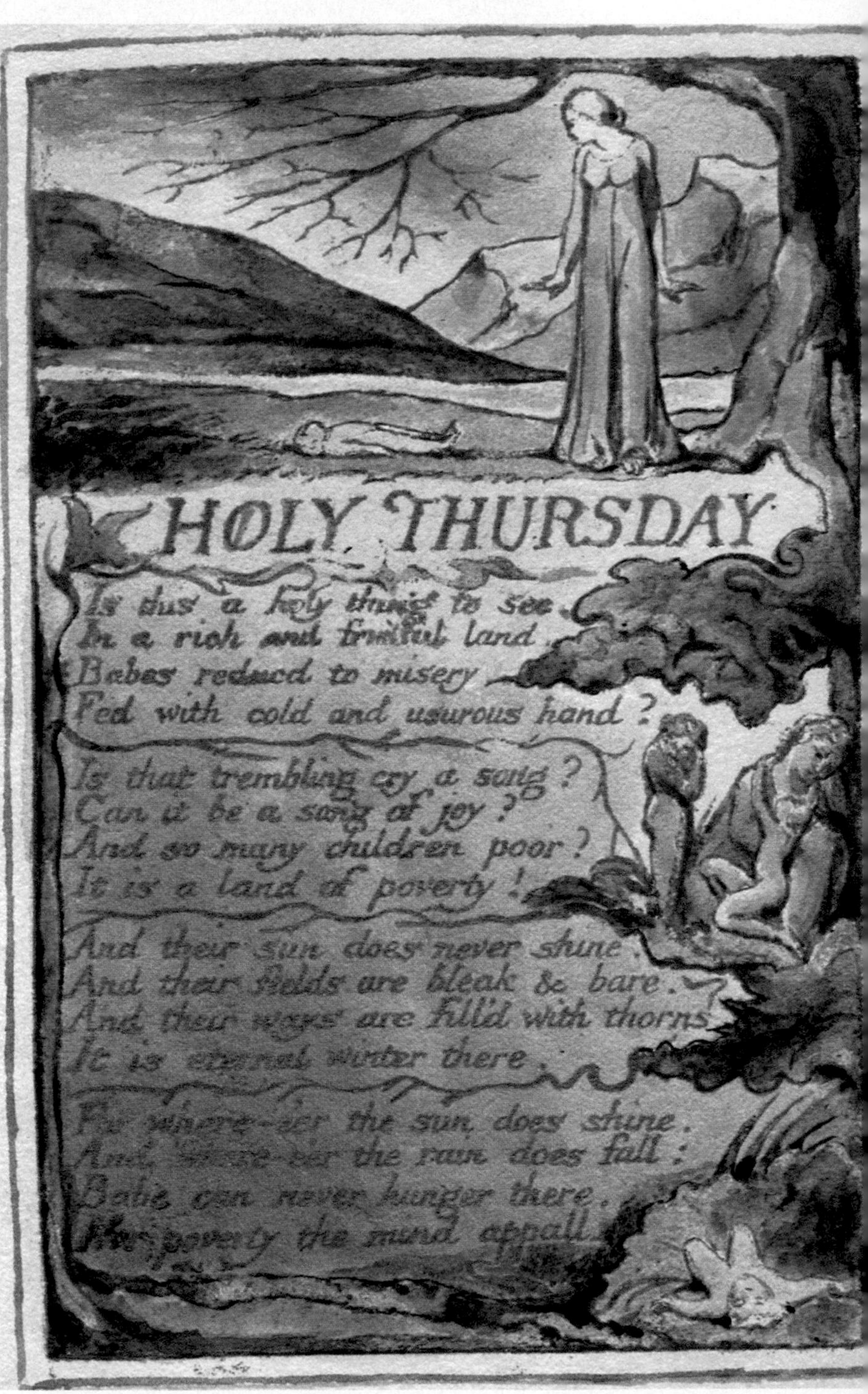

Question for Critical Thinking

Underline the imagery that Blake associates with the impoverished children. How would you characterize this imagery? What does it suggest about the children's lives?

The Chimney Sweeper

A little black thing among the snow,
Crying "'weep! 'weep!" in notes of woe!
"Where are thy father & mother? say?"
"They are both gone up to the church to pray.

"Because I was happy upon the heath,
And smil'd among the winter's snow,
They clothed me in the clothes of death,
And taught me to sing the notes of woe.

"And because I am happy & dance & sing,
They think they have done me no injury,
And are gone to praise God & his Priest & King,
Who make up a heaven of our misery."

Question for Critical Thinking

What words contribute to the overall idea that others live well because the chimney sweeps perform miserable labor? In your response, consider the connotations of color and seasons.

The Sick Rose

O Rose, thou art sick!
The invisible worm
That flies in the night,
In the howling storm,

Has found out thy bed
Of crimson joy,
And his dark secret love
Does thy life destroy.

Question for Critical Thinking

The rose and the worm act as symbols in this poem. What might they represent?

The Tyger

Tyger! Tyger! burning bright
In the forests of the night,
What immortal hand or eye
Could frame thy fearful symmetry?

In what distant deeps or skies
Burnt the fire of thine eyes?
On what wings dare he aspire?
What the hand dare sieze the fire?

And what shoulder, & what art,
Could twist the sinews of thy heart?
And when thy heart began to beat,
What dread hand? & what dread feet?

What the hammer? what the chain?
In what furnace was thy brain?
What the anvil? what dread grasp
Dare its deadly terrors clasp?

When the stars threw down their spears,
And water'd heaven with their tears,
Did he smile his work to see?
Did he who made the Lamb make thee?

Tyger! Tyger! burning bright
In the forests of the night,
What immortal hand or eye,
Dare frame thy fearful symmetry?

Question for Critical Thinking

Describe the tone of this poem. What word choices help create this mood?

London

I wander thro' each charter'd street,
Near where the charter'd Thames does flow,
And mark in every face I meet
Marks of weakness, marks of woe.

In every cry of every Man,
In every Infant's cry of fear,
In every voice, in every ban,
The mind-forg'd manacles I hear.

How the Chimney-sweeper's cry
Every black'ning Church appalls;
And the hapless Soldier's sigh
Runs in blood down Palace walls.

But most thro' midnight streets I hear
How the youthful Harlot's curse
Blasts the new born Infant's tear,
And blights with plagues the Marriage hearse.

Question for Critical Thinking

Make a list of the people mentioned in this poem. How does each act as a symbol? In other words, what part of society does each represent?

The Human Abstract

Pity would be no more
If we did not make somebody Poor;
And Mercy no more could be
If all were as happy as we.

And mutual fear brings peace,
Till the selfish loves increase:
Then Cruelty knits a snare,
And spreads his baits with care.

He sits down with holy fears,
And waters the ground with tears;
Then Humility takes its root
Underneath his foot.

Soon spreads the dismal shade
Of Mystery over his head;
And the Catterpiller and Fly
Feed on the Mystery.

And it bears the fruit of Deceit,
Ruddy and sweet to eat;
And the Raven his nest has made
In its thickest shade.

The Gods of the earth and sea
Sought thro' Nature to find this Tree;
But their search was all in vain:
There grows one in the Human Brain.

Question for Critical Thinking

As this poem progresses, it develops a complex metaphor. In a paragraph, explain the metaphor, exploring how it is appropriate for talking about abstract concepts like Humility, Mystery, and Deceit.

A Little Boy Lost

"Nought loves another as itself,
Nor venerates another so,
Nor is it possible to Thought
A greater than itself to know:

"And Father, how can I love you
Or any of my brothers more?
I love you like the little bird
That picks up crumbs around the door."

The Priest sat by and heard the child,
In trembling zeal he siez'd his hair:
He led him by his little coat,
And all admir'd the Priestly care.

And standing on the altar high,
"Lo! what a fiend is here!" said he,
"One who sets reason up for judge
Of our most holy Mystery."

The weeping child could not be heard,
The weeping parents wept in vain;
They strip'd him to his little shirt,
And bound him in an iron chain;

And burn'd him in a holy place,
Where many had been burn'd before:
The weeping parents wept in vain.
Are such things done on Albion's shore?

Question for Critical Thinking

As the introduction to this chapter points out, Blake, who subscribed to Christian beliefs, thought the church was a negative force because it was repressive. How does he develop that idea in this poem? You might pay particular attention to the images he uses.

A Little Girl Lost

Children of the future Age
Reading this indignant page,
Know that in a former time
Love! sweet Love! was thought a crime.

In the Age of Gold,
Free from winter's cold,
Youth and maiden bright
To the holy light,
Naked in the sunny beams delight.

Once a youthful pair,
Fill'd with softest care,
Met in garden bright
Where the holy light
Had just remov'd the curtains of the night.

There, in rising day
On the grass they play;
Parents were afar,
Strangers came not near,
And the maiden soon forgot her fear.

Tired with kisses sweet,
They agree to meet
When the silent sleep
Waves o'er heaven's deep,
And the weary tired wanderers weep.

To her father white
Came the maiden bright;
But his loving look,
Like the holy book,
All her tender limbs with terror shook.

"Ona! pale and weak!
To thy father speak:
O, the trembling fear!
O, the dismal care!
That shakes the blossoms of my hoary hair."

Question for Critical Thinking

How would you describe the poem's attitude toward sexual activity? What poetic devices suggest this attitude? You might also want to read the paragraph on women's rights in the "Blake in Context" section.

The Voice of the Bard

Youth of delight, come hither,
And see the opening morn,
Image of truth new-born.
Doubt is fled & clouds of reason,
Dark disputes & artful teazing.
Folly is an endless maze,
Tangled roots perplex her ways.
How many have fallen there!
They stumble all night over bones of the dead,
And feel they know not what but care,
And wish to lead others, when they should be led.

Question for Critical Thinking

What does "Image of truth new-born" describe? After you have formed your answer, ask yourself whether the lines that follow surprise you. Describe the contrast between the opening three lines and the rest of the poem.

The Clod & the Pebble

"Love seeketh not Itself to please,
Nor for itself hath any care,
But for another gives its ease,
And builds a Heaven in Hell's despair."

So sang a little Clod of Clay
Trodden with the cattle's feet,
But a Pebble of the brook
Warbled out these metres meet:

"Love seeketh only Self to please,
To bind another to Its delight,
Joys in another's loss of ease,
And builds a Hell in Heaven's despite."

Question for Critical Thinking

In a single sentence, summarize what the Clod says in the first four lines; then do the same for the Pebble's statement in the last four lines. Which has the more optimistic point of view?

The Garden of Love

I went to the Garden of Love,
And saw what I never had seen:
A Chapel was built in the midst,
Where I used to play on the green.

And the gates of this Chapel were shut,
And "Thou shalt not" writ over the door;
So I turn'd to the Garden of Love
That so many sweet flowers bore;

And I saw it was filled with graves,
And tomb-stones where flowers should be;
And Priests in black gowns were walking
    their rounds,
And binding with briars my joys & desires.

Questions for Critical Thinking

Reread the last two lines of the poem, noting how they do not follow the meter or rhyme scheme of the rest of the poem. What is the effect of deviating from the pattern in these last lines? How does the new pattern mirror what takes place in these lines?

Making Connections

Songs of Innocence and of Experience

Review the poems, one from *Innocence* and one from *Experience,* in the following order: "The Ecchoing Green" and "The Garden of Love"; "The Lamb" and "The Tyger"; "The Chimney Sweeper" and "The Chimney Sweeper"; "The Divine Image" and "The Human Abstract"; "Holy Thursday" and "Holy Thursday." Then, pick one pair that you find particularly interesting and make a list of the differences between the two poems, paying particular attention to diction, imagery, rhyme, meter, and the speaker's point of view. How do these differences change the meaning of the poems between *Innocence* and *Experience*?

Reading Text and Image

1. Consider the illustration for "The Garden of Love." Does the tone of the illustration match the tone of the poem? Explain your answer, being sure to mention specific details from the illustration.
2. Examine the illustration for "Holy Thursday." Then, in a few sentences, summarize what appears to be taking place at the top and sides of the illustration. Is this narrative the same as the poem's? If not, what new ideas does the illustration introduce that are not present in the poem?
3. What symbols in the illustration for "The Ecchoing Green" represent leisure? How do the decorative portions—rather than the main illustrations—support the idea of the poem?
4. Examine the frontispieces to *Songs of Innocence* and *Songs of Experience.* Compare and contrast these pages and ask yourself, "What statement does Blake make about innocence versus experience?"

Frontispiece from *Songs of Innocence.*

Frontispiece from *Songs of Experience.*

Getting Started: A Research Project

As suggested earlier, research is a skill that will carry you through your college career. To help acquaint you with the research process, the materials you need for this project are available on our website (**www.mhhe.com/delbanco1e**). Other ideas for research projects and sources appear at the end of this chapter.

Learning to Read Images

Critical Readings on William Blake's "The Fly"

- The William Blake Archive. Ed. Morris Eaves, Robert Essick, and Joseph Viscomi. 8 Sept. 2003. 17 Sept. 2003 <www.blakearchive.org/main.html>.
- Simpson, Michael. "Who Didn't Kill Blake's Fly: Moral Law and the Rule of Grammar in 'Songs of Experience.'" *Style* 30.2 (1996): 220–40.
- The William Blake Archive at www.blakearchive.org.

After looking at G. S. Morris's reading of "The Fly," examine the artwork from the title page of *Songs of Innocence* and the title page of *Songs of Experience* as printed in this chapter. Use the questions to guide your interpretation of the images.

1. Summarize what each picture portrays. Speculate on what the woman's role is—mother, governess, or something else.
2. After you've created a summary you feel is accurate, explain how the concepts of innocence and experience relate to the story the pictures tell.
3. Compare the foliage surrounding the words. What differences do you notice? What might these differences represent about the states of innocence and experience?
4. Compare the lettering. Is the font appropriate for the words? Why or why not?
5. Thinking of all the elements listed above—lettering, ornamentation, and pictoral narrative—what statements can you make about innocence versus experience? (Begin by listing all the words that come to mind when you look at each picture, for example, innocence = happy, experience = sad.)

The Fly

Little Fly,
Thy summer's play
My thoughtless hand
Has brush'd away.

Am not I
A fly like thee?
Or art not thou
A man like me?

For I dance,
And drink, & sing,
Till some blind hand
Shall brush my wing.

If thought is life
And strength & breath,
And the want
Of thought is death;

Then am I
A happy fly,
If I live
Or if I die.

Further Suggestions for Writing and Research

Many critics argue that we cannot achieve a full understanding of Blake's poems without "reading" the illustrations that go along with them. To see the complete set of illustrations, visit the William Blake Archive at www.blakearchive.org, a website maintained by the nation's leading Blake scholars. Which common Blakean themes do these pictures represent, like innocence and experience, the portrayal of religion, the portrayal of British society, the portrayal of nature, and the portrayal of mythological or religious figures?

Some Sources for Research

Online Sources:

1. Eaves, Morris, Robert Essick, and Joseph Viscomi. *The William Blake Archive.* Web. <www.blakearchive.org>.

Print Sources:

1. Bentley, G. E., Jr. *Blake Books: Annotated Catalogues of William Blake's Writings in Illuminated Printing, in Conventional Typography and in Manuscript.* Oxford: Clarendon Press, 1977. Print.
2. Bentley, G. E., Jr. *The Stranger from Paradise: A Biography of William Blake.* New Haven, CT: Yale UP, 2001. Print.
3. Bentley, G. E., Jr., ed. *William Blake: The Critical Heritage.* London: Routledge, 1975. Print.
4. Bindman, David. "Blake as a Painter." *The Cambridge Companion to William Blake.* Ed. Morris Eaves. Cambridge: Cambridge University Press, 2003. 85–109. Print.
5. Bloom, Harold. *The Visionary Company: a Reading of English Romantic Poetry.* Ithaca, NY: Cornell University Press, 1971. Print.
6. Cervo, Nathan A. "Blake's 'The Garden of Love.'" *Explicator,* 59.3 (2001): 121–122. Print.
7. Eaves, Morris, ed. *The Cambridge Companion to William Blake.* Cambridge: Cambridge University Press, 2003. Print.
8. Graves, Roy Neil. "Blake's 'London.'" *Explicator,* 63.3 (2005): 131–136. Print.
9. Lambert, Stephen, Jr. "Blake's 'London.'" *Explicator,* 53.3 (1995): 141–143. Print.
10. Rawlinson, Nick. *William Blake's Comic Vision.* New York: Palgrave Macmillan, 2003. Print.

For examples of student papers, see chapter 3, Common Writing Assignments, and chapter 5, Writing the Research Paper, in the Handbook for Writing from Reading.

28

American Plain Style

A Case Study on *Emily Dickinson and Robert Frost*

"It seems to me that in great poems, in the great poems of Frost, in the great poems of Dickinson . . . they're actually thinking in poetry, they're not taking some idea and poeticizing it; or they're not taking some idea and embellishing it. . . . What's manifested is thinking by imagination."

Conversation with Li-Young Lee

Emily Dickinson

Robert Frost

The Roots of American Plain Style

No one was more reclusive than Emily Dickinson; no one more widely recognized than Robert Frost. However, they have much in common. Both gave the best parts of their lives to their art; both worked at it unceasingly. Each was eloquent as a letter writer; each was described by others as a "Yankee crank." More importantly, both were original makers and forgers of the American Plain Style. As you have likely observed from the examples so far in this textbook, there are many different approaches to poetry. However, studying plain style allows us to get at the heart of a major split within the genre—"two roads" that, as Robert Frost observes, "diverged."

In American poetry, the divergence in style occurred between poets who write highly symbolic and complex verse in the vein of Wallace Stevens and those who write distilled or pared-down work that focuses on the world around us, such as William Carlos Williams. Think of the difference between Stevens's "jar in Tennessee" (chapter 20) and Williams's "red wheelbarrow" (chapter 20), and you'll get some sense of what we mean. However, this American split has its origin much further back; it came ashore with the Puritan settlers who first inhabited New England. The Puritans, as you may recollect from history, sought religious freedom from what they saw as corruption in the English church. They eschewed the formal pomp and ceremony associated with worship in the Catholic church in favor of a simple and "pure" devotion to God. In other words, "plain"-ness was a way of life, as reflected in their plain clothes, their plain houses of worship, and their simple forms of entertainment—all aspects that allowed them to focus not on a worldly existence but on a godly one.

This belief in plainness as the best way of approaching God permeated Puritan discourse as well. Remember Anne Bradstreet's comparison of her book to her child (chapter 19) or the noticing eye ("I") of Walt Whitman (chapter 24); their use of domestic particulars would not have seemed appropriate before. In early American sermons, you can see a wide embrace of the language of everyday speech. In a sermon titled "Sinners in the Hands of an Angry God," the eighteenth-century New England minister Jonathan Edwards declared, "The God that holds you over the pit of hell, much as one holds a spider, or some loathsome insect, over the fire, abhors you, and is dreadfully provoked; his wrath towards you burns like fire." Here Edwards uses earthy images of spiders and fire to great rhetorical effect.

"Robert Frost . . . is the most cunning and uncanny American poet who ever lived. . . . He refuses to say something is something when it isn't. . . . To rest in that is such a pleasure."

Conversation with Marie Howe

Given the strong Puritan influence in New England, which shaped the society surrounding Emily Dickinson, it's relatively easy to trace that tradition of plain speech in America. Dickinson—along with Whitman and later, Frost—brought an early turn in poetry to plain style. These poets, who confronted the American wilderness and understood that their ancestors had literally done so, brought a view of nature as concrete rather than as an abstract entity. Plain style, then, brought a split from both florid poetic language and elevated treatment of nature: In short, it brought poetry "down to earth."

The Plain Style

Through plain style, both Dickinson and Frost have left their separate yet shared imprint on the contemporary mode of utterance in verse. By this we mean a way of *saying* that involves a way of *seeing:* straightforward, uncluttered language shaped into poetical form. Enjambment is common, since it makes the poem's line breaks seem less obvious or end-stopped, and rhyme, though widespread, feels unforced. The tone is unpretentious and the vocabulary serviceable; it's the surprising shift of emphasis, not the surprising (or obscure, or arcane) word that counts. Nothing they write is hard to read, but much of it demands close reading before we understand. What's sometimes difficult to follow in this pair of poets is the thought process itself, the sudden leap of intuition or juxtaposition—in Dickinson's case by way of dashes—of what might seem disconnected.

Dickinson rarely glories in the play of "wit" for its own sake. She does love wordplay and the way sounds edge up against each other, but there's an almost confessional impulse in her truth-telling work. Frost, too, is schooled in poetic tradition and studiously familiar with those who wrote before. Although his "homespun" style was always intended to seem offhand and conversational; no matter how intricate the form or thought, the manner of speaking is *plain.*

In the largest sense this style is democratic. Best read aloud, the poems that follow have the rhythms of natural speech (we've included twice as many by Dickinson, because her work is brief). Between them, these two artists provide a portrait of America in its period of growth and maturation, its increasing sense of what's at risk, what's still to be discovered, and what must be preserved.

Emily Dickinson (1830–1886)

Like other writers whose eccentricities turn into legend over time, Emily Dickinson lives in the popular imagination as a recluse who dressed in all white and never left her room. While it is true that she dressed in white, and that she preferred living in her father's house her entire life, she cultivated relationships with people both near—like her sister-in-law, Susan Gilbert, who lived next door—and far, like her literary critic friend Thomas Wentworth Higginson, with whom she maintained a correspondence for more than twenty years.

Born in Amherst, Massachusetts, she lived her life in almost total obscurity. Raised in a Puritan, New England atmosphere, and in a devoutly religious family, Dickinson herself did not give the public confession of her faith that was expected of her and eventually refused to attend conventional church services. She attended Mount Holyoke Female Seminary—a few miles from Amherst—but returned home after her first year because she was acutely homesick. Though her family was prosperous and prominent, she became a kind of hermit, remaining in the village and writing her "odd" poetry for herself alone. She spent her days reading, writing letters, and composing more than 2,000 poems. Only a handful of these poems were published in her lifetime, and those by the initiative of family and friends, not her own effort. Dickinson preferred self-publication, which for her meant binding by hand forty volumes of her handwritten poetry. She did conceive of the work as a "letter to the world," but it was delivered posthumously; her present fame would not have been imagined and could not have been predicted at the time. When her poems were discovered upon her death, her younger sister, Lavinia, was instrumental in getting them published; however, the editors normalized much of Dickinson's punctuation (they eliminated her characteristic dashes) and syntax so that it read much like any other nineteenth-century verse.

It was not until the 1950s that her original intention was restored by an editor working with her fascicles (handwritten manuscripts). Today, along with Whitman, Dickinson is recognized for creating a uniquely American poetic voice—hers marked by its simplicity of structure and diction, its hymn-like rhythms, and its odd punctuation.

Success is counted sweetest (c. 1859)

Success is counted sweetest
By those who ne'er succeed.
To comprehend a nectar
Requires sorest need.

Not one of all the purple Host
Who took the Flag today
Can tell the definition
So clear of Victory

As he defeated—dying—
On whose forbidden ear
The distant strains of triumph
Burst agonized and clear!

Questions for Critical Thinking

1. What does the speaker mean by "To comprehend a nectar / Requires sorest need"? Paraphrase these lines.
2. If Dickinson had ended the poem after the first stanza, the overall meaning of the poem (which you paraphrased in the question above) would still come across. What, then, would be lost by removing the last two stanzas? In other words, how do those stanzas expand upon the meaning set up in the first stanza?

I taste a liquor never brewed— (c. 1860)

I taste a liquor never brewed—
From Tankards scooped in Pearl—
Not all the Vats upon the Rhine
Yield such an Alcohol!

Inebriate of Air—am I—
And Debauchee of Dew—
Reeling—thro endless summer days—
From inns of Molten Blue—

When "Landlords" turn the drunken Bee
Out of the Foxglove's door—
When Butterflies—renounce their "drams"—
I shall but drink the more!

Till Seraphs swing their snowy Hats—
And Saints—to windows run—
To see the little Tippler
Leaning against the—Sun—

Questions for Critical Thinking

1. On what is this speaker drunk? Underline where you find the answer, and then paraphrase it in your own words.
2. Scan this poem to discover its meter. Keeping in mind that a typical hymn stanza has alternating lines of eight syllables and six syllables, consider how this poem relates to a hymn. Does this relation enhance the meaning of this poem?

Some keep the Sabbath going to Church— (c. 1860)

Some keep the Sabbath going to Church—
I keep it, staying at Home—
With a Bobolink for a Chorister—
And an Orchard, for a Dome—

Some keep the Sabbath in Surplice—
I just wear my Wings—
And instead of tolling the Bell, for Church,
Our little Sexton—sings.

God preaches, a noted Clergyman—
And the sermon is never long,
So instead of getting to Heaven, at last—
I'm going, all along.

Questions for Critical Thinking

1. In line 6, the speaker says "I just wear my Wings." What does she mean?
2. Highlight all the words that have to do with the church. Then underline the words that have to do with nature. How does diction support the message of this poem?

Safe in their Alabaster Chambers— (1861)

Safe in their Alabaster Chambers—
Untouched by Morning—
And untouched by Noon—
Lie the meek members of the Resurrection—
Rafter of Satin—and Roof of Stone!

Grand go the Years—in the Crescent—above them—
Worlds scoop their arcs—
And Firmaments—row—
Diadems—drop—and Doges—surrender—
Soundless as dots—on a Disc of Snow—

Questions for Critical Thinking

1. Who are the safe ones?
2. Does nature seem sympathetic to their condition, or indifferent?
3. The second stanza suggests a relation between time and history and the subjects of the poem. How would you describe it?
4. Interpret the line in the second stanza "Soundless as dots—on a disc of snow—" in relation to the first three lines of the stanza. Are the dots the years, worlds, jewels, and rulers referred to there? If so, what does the line mean?

I like a look of Agony (c. 1861)

I like a look of Agony,
Because I know it's true—
Men do not sham Convulsion,
Nor simulate, a Throe—

The Eyes glaze once—and that is Death—
Impossible to feign
The Beads upon the Forehead
By homely Anguish strung

Questions for Critical Thinking

1. What does the speaker mean by the beads "Anguish" strings on the forehead? Describe the mental image you get from the last two lines.
2. Describe the speaker's tone in this poem. Is his or her stance toward suffering surprising to you? How does it affect the way you read the poem?

Wild Nights—Wild Nights! (c. 1861)

Wild Nights—Wild Nights!
Were I with thee
Wild Nights should be
Our luxury!

Futile—the Winds—
To a Heart in port—
Done with the Compass—
Done with the Chart!

Rowing in Eden—
Ah, the Sea!
Might I but moor—Tonight
In Thee!

Questions for Critical Thinking

1. What is the effect of repeating the phrase "Wild Nights"?
2. Discuss the erotic component of this poem. Does the speaker describe physical love or yearn for spiritual union with something abstract? Or both?

There's a certain Slant of light (c. 1861)

There's a certain Slant of light,
Winter Afternoons—
That oppresses, like the Heft
Of Cathedral Tunes—

Heavenly Hurt, it gives us—
We can find no scar,
But internal difference,
Where the Meanings, are—

None may teach it—Any—
'Tis the Seal Despair—
An imperial affliction
Sent us of the Air—

When it comes, the Landscape listens—
Shadows—hold their breath—
When it goes, 'tis like the Distance
On the look of Death—

Questions for Critical Thinking

1. Explain the central metaphor—the oppressive nature of a certain way the light falls on a winter afternoon. Can you link this feeling created in the poet by the light with any modern condition or state of mind?
2. Interpret the meaning of the listening landscape. Is it only in New England that such a condition might occur? Could a poet in Florida or Texas or California make a similar poem?

I felt a Funeral, in my Brain (c. 1861)

I felt a Funeral, in my Brain,
And Mourners to and fro
Kept treading—treading—till it seemed
That Sense was breaking through—

And when they all were seated,
A Service, like a Drum—
Kept beating—beating—till I thought
My Mind was going numb—

And then I heard them lift a Box
And creak across my Soul
With those same Boots of Lead, again,
Then Space—began to toll,

As all the Heavens were a Bell,
And Being, but an Ear,
And I, and Silence, some strange Race
Wrecked, solitary, here—

And then a Plank in Reason, broke,
And I dropped down, and down—
And hit a World, at every plunge,
And Finished knowing—then—

Questions for Critical Thinking

1. Read the poem a second time. As you do so, underline any place where a particular sound comes to mind. What techniques allow Dickinson to create a sense of hearing what the speaker hears?
2. Paying particular attention to the last stanza, explain what you think "happens" in this poem. What clues in the poem lead you to your conclusion?
3. The brain surfaces in several of Dickinson's poems. Describe the brain as it is portrayed in this poem (i.e., does it feel claustrophobic or expansive? what type of activity does it harbor? what types of words does Dickinson use in relation to the brain?, etc.). Then do the same for her poem "The Brain—is wider than the Sky" (p. 409). What are the similarities and differences? In your analysis, examine the significance of using "the brain" rather than "the heart" or "the soul."

I'm Nobody! Who are you? (c. 1861)

I'm Nobody! Who are you?
Are you—Nobody—Too?
Then there's a pair of us!
Don't tell! they'd advertise—you know!

How dreary—to be—Somebody!
How public—like a Frog—
To tell one's name—the livelong June—
To an admiring Bog!

Questions for Critical Thinking

1. To whom is the poet speaking? Who is "they"? Why would they "advertise" the speaker and the addressee of the poem? What would they advertise about the two?
2. Do you find the pairing of "Somebody" and "Frog" jarring or sensible?
3. How do frogs "tell" their names to the bog?
4. What effect does the adjective "admiring" have on "Bog," or vice versa?

The Soul selects her own Society— (c. 1862)

The Soul selects her own Society—
Then—shuts the Door—
To her divine Majority—
Present no more—

Unmoved—she notes the Chariots—
pausing—
At her low Gate—
Unmoved—an Emperor be kneeling
Upon her Mat—

I've known her—from an ample nation—
Choose One—
Then—close the Valves of her attention—
Like Stone—

Questions for Critical Thinking

1. Paraphrase this poem. What statement is the speaker making about the soul?
2. Without reviewing the poem, make a list of images you remember in it. Now read the poem again, and make a list of images that are in it. Compare the two lists. How does Dickinson's use of imagery enhance the meaning of the poem?

After great pain, a formal feeling comes— (c. 1862)

After great pain, a formal feeling comes—
The Nerves sit ceremonious, like Tombs—
The stiff Heart questions was it He, that bore,
And Yesterday, or Centuries before?

The Feet, mechanical, go round—
Of Ground, or Air, or Ought—
A Wooden way
Regardless grown,
A Quartz contentment, like a stone—

This is the Hour of Lead—
Remembered, if outlived,
As Freezing persons, recollect the Snow—
First—Chill—then Stupor—then the letting go—

Questions for Critical Thinking

1. What pain might the poet be trying to describe? How many varieties of metaphor does the poet employ here to describe it?
2. Who is the "He" of line 3?
3. Do you find any possibility for hope in the final stanza?

Much madness is divinest Sense— (c. 1862)

Much Madness is divinest Sense—
To a discerning Eye—
Much Sense—the starkest Madness—
'Tis the Majority
In this, as All, prevail—
Assent—and you are sane—
Demur—you're straightway
dangerous—
And handled with a Chain—

Questions for Critical Thinking

1. Circle any of the words that you need to double-check in the dictionary. You may want to choose words that are critical to the poem, such as "madness" and "sense," even if you believe you know their meaning. Then write the dictionary definition on a separate sheet of paper. Are the words' shades of meaning different from what you had expected?
2. The argument of this poem is based on a paradox: "Much Madness is divinest Sense . . . Much Sense—the starkest Madness." In your own words, what does the speaker mean by this contradiction?
3. Can you think of fictional characters who act in a way that appears mad to others, but which is actually sane? Going further, can you think of people you know, either personally or at large, whose "madness" leads them to go against the majority?

I died for Beauty—but was scarce (c. 1862)

I died for Beauty—but was scarce
Adjusted in the Tomb
When One who died for Truth, was lain
In an adjoining Room—

He questioned softly "Why I failed"?
"For Beauty", I replied—
"And I—for Truth—Themself are One—
We Brethren, are," He said—

And so, as Kinsmen, met a Night—
We talked between the Rooms—
Until the Moss had reached our lips—
And covered up—Our names—

Questions for Critical Thinking

1. Given that one of Dickinson's major influences was the English poet John Keats, read Keats's "Ode on a Grecian Urn" (chapter 18). How do the two relate? Can you find any evidence that Dickinson may have had Keats's poem in mind when she wrote hers, or is there insufficient support for that conclusion?
2. What is the mood of this poem? Which words and images lead to your reading of the tone?

I heard a Fly buzz—when I died— (c. 1862)

I heard a Fly buzz—when I died—
The Stillness in the Room
Was like the Stillness in the Air—
Between the Heaves of Storm—

The Eyes around—had wrung them dry—
And Breaths were gathering firm
For that last Onset—when the King
Be witnessed—in the Room—

I willed my Keepsakes—Signed away
What portion of me be
Assignable—and then it was
There interposed a Fly—

With Blue—uncertain stumbling Buzz—
Between the light—and me—
And then the Windows failed—and then
I could not see to see—

Questions for Critical Thinking

1. What effect does the last line have? Why do you think "I could not see to see" fits better than simply "I could not see"?
2. Why does Dickinson select a fly as opposed to, say, a bird or a bee?

The Brain—is wider than the Sky— (c. 1862)

The Brain—is wider than the Sky—
For—put them side by side—
The one the other will contain
With ease—and You—beside—

The Brain is deeper than the sea—
For—hold them—Blue to Blue—
The one the other will absorb—
As Sponges—Buckets—do—

The Brain is just the weight of God—
For—Heft them—Pound for Pound—
And they will differ—if they do—
As Syllable from Sound—

Questions for Critical Thinking

1. How does the "weight of God" relate to the brain? What does the speaker suggest by making this comparison?
2. What techniques does Dickinson use to *illustrate* the vastness of the brain as well as describe it?

I started Early—Took my Dog— (1862)

I started Early—Took my Dog—
And visited the Sea—
The Mermaids in the Basement
Came out to look at me—

And Frigates—in the Upper Floor
Extended Hempen Hands—
Presuming Me to be a Mouse—
Aground—upon the Sands—

But no Man moved Me—till the Tide
Went past my simple Shoe—
And past my Apron—and my Belt
And past my Bodice—too—

And made as He would eat me up—
As wholly as a Dew
Upon a Dandelion's Sleeve—
And then—I started—too—

And He—He followed—close behind—
I felt His Silver Heel
Upon my Ankle—Then my Shoes
Would overflow with Pearl—

Until We met the Solid Town—
No One He seemed to know—
And bowing—with a Mighty look—
At me—The Sea withdrew—

Questions for Critical Thinking

1. Some critics read this as a poem about a sexual encounter. Which lines support such a reading? Which images seem to stand for something other than merely a surreal landscape?
2. Besides the sexual encounter theory we suggested in question 1, what else might the poem be about? How does the meaning of the symbols change as your reading changes?

Because I could not stop for Death— (1863)

Because I could not stop for Death—
He kindly stopped for me—
The Carriage held but just Ourselves—
And Immortality.

We slowly drove—He knew no haste
And I had put away
My labor and my leisure too,
For His Civility—

We passed the School, where Children strove
At Recess—in the Ring—
We passed the Fields of Gazing Grain—
We passed the Setting Sun—

Or rather—He passed Us—
The Dews drew quivering and chill—
For only Gossamer, my Gown—
My Tippet—only Tulle—

We paused before a House that seemed
A Swelling of the Ground—
The Roof was scarcely visible—
The Cornice—in the Ground—

Since then—'tis Centuries—and yet
Feels shorter than the Day
I first surmised the Horses' Heads
Were toward Eternity—

Questions for Critical Thinking

1. Is there a rhyme scheme in this poem? If not, how do the words work together to create the semblance of such a scheme?
2. Using two different colors, highlight the words you don't know; then highlight the words that you think Dickinson has used to the best possible effect. Do you find that "difficult" diction is the most effective, or simpler phrasing? Explain your answer.

One need not be a Chamber— to be Haunted— (c. 1863)

One need not be a Chamber—to be Haunted—
One need not be a House—
The Brain has Corridors—surpassing
Material Place—

Far safer, of a Midnight Meeting
External Ghost
Than its interior Confronting—
That Cooler Host.

Far safer, through an Abbey gallop,
The Stones a'chase—
Than Unarmed, one's a'self encounter—
In lonesome Place—

Ourself behind ourself, concealed—
Should startle most—
Assassin hid in our Apartment
Be Horror's least.

The Body—borrows a Revolver—
He bolts the Door—
O'erlooking a superior spectre—
Or More—

Questions for Critical Thinking

1. What psychological state might have prompted the poet to make this poem?
2. List the metaphors—what does the fact that they are architectural suggest about the poet and the poem? Does she derive the idea only from the traditional myths about haunted houses?
3. Who or what is the ghost in this little ghost story?
4. Do you find her assumptions to be antiquated or modern enough for you to sympathize with?

A narrow Fellow in the Grass (c. 1865)

A narrow Fellow in the Grass
Occasionally rides—
You may have met him—did you not
His notice instant is—

The Grass divides as with a Comb—
A spotted shaft is seen—
And then it closes at your feet
And opens further on—

He likes a Boggy Acre
A Floor too cool for Corn—
Yet when a Boy, and Barefoot
I more than once at Noon

Have passed, I thought, a Whip lash
Unbraiding in the Sun
When stooping to secure it
It wrinkled, and was gone—

Several of Nature's People
I know, and they know me—
I feel for them a transport
Of Cordiality—

But never met this Fellow
Attended, or alone
Without a tighter breathing
And Zero at the Bone.

Questions for Critical Thinking

1. Underline the rhyming words in this poem. Then identify what type of rhyme occurs in each instance (i.e., end rhyme, internal rhyme, assonance, consonance, eye rhyme, etc.). What does the rhyme scheme contribute to the poem?
2. Although the speaker never states who or what the "narrow Fellow" is, you can figure it out from context clues. What is the "narrow Fellow"?

The Bustle in a House (c. 1866)

The Bustle in a House
The Morning after Death
Is solemnest of industries
Enacted upon Earth—

The Sweeping up the Heart
And putting Love away
We shall not want to use again
Until Eternity.

Questions for Critical Thinking

1. How are the near rhymes of lines 2 and 4, and lines 6 and 8, appropriate to that which is taking place? In other words, why do you think Dickinson did not use exact rhymes in those lines?
2. Many of Dickinson's two-stanza poems put forth something concrete in the first stanza and something abstract in the second stanza. Identify how this poem follows that pattern. How does thinking of the concrete action in the first stanza enhance your understanding of the metaphor in the second stanza?

Tell all the Truth but tell it slant— (c. 1868)

Tell all the Truth but tell it slant—
Success in Circuit lies
Too bright for our infirm Delight
The Truth's superb surprise

As Lightning to the Children eased
With explanation kind
The Truth must dazzle gradually
Or every man be blind—

Question for Critical Thinking

1. Paraphrase what the speaker means by telling the truth "slant." This famous phrase has often been used as a working definition of Dickinson's poetry in particular and of the art of poetry in general. What does the phrase suggest about the value of the poet's understanding of the word?

There is no Frigate like a Book (c. 1873)

There is no Frigate like a Book
To take us Lands away
Nor any Coursers like a Page
Of prancing Poetry—
This Traverse may the poorest take
Without oppress of Toll—
How frugal is the Chariot
That bears the Human soul.

Questions for Critical Thinking

1. Explain how the idea expressed in the last two lines is appropriate for a plain-style poet (see chapter 25).
2. Notice how all the comparisons suggest movement. How is the idea of movement appropriate to reading? Explore your ideas in a short essay.

Robert Frost (1874–1963)

Like Emily Dickinson, Robert Frost, too, lived in New England—mostly New Hampshire and Vermont. Unlike her, however, he died when much celebrated at the age of nearly ninety. By then he was the nation's unofficial laureate, had garnered every prize worth having (among them the Bollingen Prize, a Congressional Medal) and had recited "The Gift Outright" for an audience of millions at President John F. Kennedy's inauguration. Robert Frost, known as a New England poet, was born in San Francisco, where he spent his childhood until age eleven. His family then relocated to Massachusetts, where they traced their roots back several generations. Frost determined as a teenager that he would be a poet, and that he would marry his high school sweetheart and co-valedictorian Elinor White. But their courtship was not fairy-tale: They separated for college, and she twice refused his marriage proposals before at last agreeing in 1895. He and Elinor taught school after they were married, and Frost then spent two years studying at Harvard. He did not take a degree and spent the next decade farming and composing many of the poems that would make up his early collections. In 1912, Frost relocated (with Elinor and their four children) to England, with the express purpose of writing poetry. His first two collections, *A Boy's Will* and *North of Boston,* were published in England to great success. By the time Frost returned to New England, his poetry had been published in both England and the United States, and his reputation as a leading poet was secure.

From 1917 onward, Frost spent his career as a "bardic" figure—his way of referring to the public recitations of his poetry he liked to give—and as a professor at Amherst College. Yet while his rural New England imagery and easy manner of public appearance won him a large audience and a reputation as a simple New England farmer, the reality of Frost's life was grimmer. His poetry shows a constant struggle to find order in chaos. On a more literal level, his personal life fell apart in the 1930s: His favorite daughter died after giving birth, he lost his beloved Elinor to a heart attack, one of his sons committed suicide in 1940, and another daughter was committed to a mental institution. Still, by the time of his death in 1963, Frost had won four Pulitzer Prizes, received more than forty honorary degrees, and was perhaps the best-known and most widely respected poet of the time, a status confirmed by John F. Kennedy's request that Frost recite a poem at his inauguration.

> "Well, you know, I remember finally reading Frost as other than a folksy poet, [as] somebody who is essentially a philosophical poet, I thought, which was exciting." Conversation with Stephen Dunn

Mowing (1913)

There was never a sound beside the wood but one,
And that was my long scythe whispering to the ground.
What was it it whispered? I knew not well myself;
Perhaps it was something about the heat of the sun,
Something, perhaps, about the lack of sound—
And that was why it whispered and did not speak.
It was no dream of the gift of idle hours,
Or easy gold at the hand of fay or elf:
Anything more than the truth would have seemed too weak
To the earnest love that laid the swale in rows,
Not without feeble-pointed spikes of flowers
(Pale orchises), and scared a bright green snake.
The fact is the sweetest dream that labor knows.
My long scythe whispered and left the hay to make.

Questions for Critical Thinking

1. A scythe whispering in the grass brings to mind an auditory image. Read the poem aloud and identify words and phrases that mimic this whispering.
2. The penultimate line contains simple diction but a complex thought: "The fact is the sweetest dream that labor knows." Write a paragraph in which you reflect on this statement.

After Apple-Picking (1914)

My long two-pointed ladder's sticking through a tree
Toward heaven still,
And there's a barrel that I didn't fill
Beside it, and there may be two or three
Apples I didn't pick upon some bough.
But I am done with apple-picking now.
Essence of winter sleep is on the night,
The scent of apples: I am drowsing off.
I cannot rub the strangeness from my sight
I got from looking through a pane of glass
I skimmed this morning from the drinking trough
And held against the world of hoary grass.
It melted, and I let it fall and break.
But I was well
Upon my way to sleep before it fell,
And I could tell
What form my dreaming was about to take.
Magnified apples appear and disappear,
Stem end and blossom end,
And every fleck of russet showing clear.
My instep arch not only keeps the ache,
It keeps the pressure of a ladder-round.
I feel the ladder sway as the boughs bend.
And I keep hearing from the cellar bin
The rumbling sound
Of load on load of apples coming in.
For I have had too much
Of apple-picking: I am overtired
Of the great harvest I myself desired.
There were ten thousand thousand fruit to touch,
Cherish in hand, lift down, and not let fall.
For all
That struck the earth,
No matter if not bruised or spiked with stubble,
Went surely to the cider-apple heap
As of no worth.
One can see what will trouble
This sleep of mine, whatever sleep it is.
Were he not gone,
The woodchuck could say whether it's like his
Long sleep, as I describe its coming on,
Or just some human sleep.

Questions for Critical Thinking

1. Looking at the subject, where does the story of the speaker's work end and the story of his dreaming begin?
2. How does the ice on the surface of the drinking trough follow a progression to what he sees in the dream?

Mending Wall (1914)

Something there is that doesn't love a wall,
That sends the frozen-ground-swell under it
And spills the upper boulders in the sun;
And makes gaps even two can pass abreast.
The work of hunters is another thing:
I have come after them and made repair
Where they have left not one stone on a stone,
But they would have the rabbit out of hiding,
To please the yelping dogs. The gaps I mean,
No one has seen them made or heard them made,
But at spring mending-time we find them there.
I let my neighbor know beyond the hill;
And on a day we meet to walk the line

And set the wall between us once again.
We keep the wall between us as we go.
To each the boulders that have fallen to each.
And some are loaves and some so nearly balls
We have to use a spell to make them balance:
"Stay where you are until our backs are turned!"
We wear our fingers rough with handling them.
Oh, just another kind of outdoor game,
One on a side. It comes to little more:
There where it is we do not need the wall:
He is all pine and I am apple orchard.
My apple trees will never get across
And eat the cones under his pines, I tell him.
He only says, "Good fences make good neighbors."
Spring is the mischief in me, and I wonder
If I could put a notion in his head:
"*Why* do they make good neighbors? Isn't it
Where there are cows? But here there are no cows.
Before I built a wall I'd ask to know
What I was walling in or walling out,
And to whom I was like to give offense.
Something there is that doesn't love a wall,
That wants it down." I could say "Elves" to him,
But it's not elves exactly, and I'd rather
He said it for himself. I see him there
Bringing a stone grasped firmly by the top
In each hand, like an old-stone savage armed.
He moves in darkness as it seems to me,
Not of woods only and the shade of trees.
He will not go behind his father's saying,
And he likes having thought of it so well
He says again, "Good fences make good neighbors."

Questions for Critical Thinking

1. This poem has some beautiful imagery. Highlight two or three of the images you like best. What in those images draws you to them?
2. Identify where the mood shifts in this poem. Does it change more than once? Do you think the last line is consistent with what leads up to it?

Birches (1915)

When I see birches bend to left and right
Across the lines of straighter darker trees,
I like to think some boy's been swinging them.
But swinging doesn't bend them down to stay.
Ice-storms do that. Often you must have seen them
Loaded with ice a sunny winter morning
After a rain. They click upon themselves
As the breeze rises, and turn many-coloured

As the stir cracks and crazes their enamel.
Soon the sun's warmth makes them shed crystal shells
Shattering and avalanching on the snow-crust
Such heaps of broken glass to sweep away
You'd think the inner dome of heaven had fallen.
They are dragged to the withered bracken by the load,
And they seem not to break; though once they are bowed
So low for long, they never right themselves:
You may see their trunks arching in the woods
Years afterwards, trailing their leaves on the ground,
Like girls on hands and knees that throw their hair
Before them over their heads to dry in the sun.
But I was going to say when Truth broke in
With all her matter-of-fact about the ice-storm,
I should prefer to have some boy bend them
As he went out and in to fetch the cows—
Some boy too far from town to learn baseball,
Whose only play was what he found himself,
Summer or winter, and could play alone.
One by one he subdued his father's trees
By riding them down over and over again
Until he took the stiffness out of them,
And not one but hung limp, not one was left
For him to conquer. He learned all there was
To learn about not launching out too soon
And so not carrying the tree away
Clear to the ground. He always kept his poise
To the top branches, climbing carefully
With the same pains you use to fill a cup
Up to the brim, and even above the brim.
Then he flung outward, feet first, with a swish,
Kicking his way down through the air to the ground.
So was I once myself a swinger of birches.
And so I dream of going back to be.
It's when I'm weary of considerations,
And life is too much like a pathless wood
Where your face burns and tickles with the cobwebs
Broken across it, and one eye is weeping
From a twig's having lashed across it open.
I'd like to get away from earth awhile
And then come back to it and begin over.
May no fate wilfully misunderstand me
And half grant what I wish and snatch me away
Not to return. Earth's the right place for love:
I don't know where it's likely to go better.

I'd like to go by climbing a birch tree—
And climb black branches up a snow-white trunk
Toward heaven, till the tree could bear no more,
But dipped its top and set me down again.
That would be good both going and coming back.
One could do worse than be a swinger of birches.

Questions for Critical Thinking

1. The poem starts in the first person ("When I see birches . . .") and ends with a general—even impersonal—assertion ("One could do worse . . ."). How and where does the voice shift?
2. Why does the poet capitalize "Truth" in line 21? And how would you describe the tone of the phrase "I don't know where it's likely to go better" (line 53)?

"Out, Out—" (1916)

The buzz-saw snarled and rattled in the yard
And made dust and dropped stove-length sticks of wood,
Sweet-scented stuff when the breeze drew across it.
And from there those that lifted eyes could count
Five mountain ranges one behind the other
Under the sunset far into Vermont.
And the saw snarled and rattled, snarled and rattled,
As it ran light, or had to bear a load.
And nothing happened: day was all but done.
Call it a day, I wish they might have said
To please the boy by giving him the half hour
That a boy counts so much when saved from work.
His sister stood beside them in her apron
To tell them "Supper." At the word, the saw,
As if to prove saws knew what supper meant,
Leaped out at the boy's hand, or seemed to leap—
He must have given the hand. However it was,
Neither refused the meeting. But the hand!
The boy's first outcry was a rueful laugh,
As he swung toward them holding up the hand
Half in appeal, but half as if to keep
The life from spilling. Then the boy saw all—
Since he was old enough to know, big boy
Doing a man's work, though a child at heart—
He saw all spoiled. "Don't let him cut my hand off—
The doctor, when he comes. Don't let him, sister!"
So. But the hand was gone already.
The doctor put him in the dark of ether.
He lay and puffed his lips out with his breath.
And then—the watcher at his pulse took fright.
No one believed. They listened at his heart.
Little—less—nothing!—and that ended it.
No more to build on there. And they, since they
Were not the one dead, turned to their affairs.

Questions for Critical Thinking

1. Rewrite this poem as a short story and then compare your work with Frost's. What is emphasized in your version that is not in Frost's, and vice versa?
2. How is nature portrayed in this poem? Describe the relationship between the nature description and the events of the poem.

The Road Not Taken (1916)

Two roads diverged in a yellow wood,
And sorry I could not travel both
And be one traveler, long I stood
And looked down one as far as I could
To where it bent in the undergrowth;

Then took the other, as just as fair,
And having perhaps the better claim,
Because it was grassy and wanted wear;
Though as for that the passing there
Had worn them really about the same,

And both that morning equally lay
In leaves no step had trodden black.
Oh, I kept the first for another day!
Yet knowing how way leads on to way,
I doubted if I should ever come back.

I shall be telling this with a sigh
Somewhere ages and ages hence:
Two roads diverged in a wood, and I—
I took the one less traveled by,
And that has made all the difference.

Questions for Critical Thinking

1. Explain the larger meaning of this poem. What do the paths stand for? What does it mean that one is less traveled than the other?
2. Write a short profile of the speaker, based on clues from the poem. Is he daring? Individualistic? Indecisive? For each trait you mention, cite the line or lines that support your inference.

Fire and Ice (1923)

Some say the world will end in fire,
Some say in ice.
From what I've tasted of desire
I hold with those who favor fire.
But if it had to perish twice,
I think I know enough of hate
To say that for destruction ice
Is also great
And would suffice.

Questions for Critical Thinking

1. Scan this poem for both rhyme and meter. Identify places where the irregularities in rhyme or meter emphasize what is being said.
2. If you were given the text of the poem without the poet's name, would you be able to identify it as Frost's? Why or why not? In other words, what in this poem seems characteristic of Frost, and what deviates from his typical poem?

Nothing Gold Can Stay (1923)

Nature's first green is gold,
Her hardest hue to hold.
Her early leaf's a flower;
But only so an hour.
Then leaf subsides to leaf.
So Eden sank to grief.
So dawn goes down to day.
Nothing gold can stay.

Questions for Critical Thinking

1. There's a stanza in Thomas Nashe's sixteenth-century poem "Elegy in Times of Pestilence" that reads:

   Brightness falls from the air
   Queens have died young and fair
   Beauty is but a flower
   Which wrinkles must devour
   Dust hath closed Helen's eye
   I am sick, I must die.
   Lord have mercy upon us

   To what degree does Frost's "Nothing Gold Can Stay" echo this refrain? Compose your answer in a short essay.
2. Scan this poem for rhyme and meter. What is the relationship between the form and what is being said?

Acquainted with the Night (1928)

I have been one acquainted with the night.
I have walked out in rain—and back in rain.
I have outwalked the furthest city light.

I have looked down the saddest city lane.
I have passed by the watchman on his beat
And dropped my eyes, unwilling to explain.

I have stood still and stopped the sound of feet
When far away an interrupted cry
Came over houses from another street,

But not to call me back or say good-by;
And further still at an unearthly height,
One luminary clock against the sky

Proclaimed the time was neither wrong nor right
I have been one acquainted with the night.

Questions for Critical Thinking

1. What is the tone? Which words create this tone?
2. On a literal level, the poem ends with a clock against the night sky. How do you interpret this image on a metaphorical level? Going further, what do you think it means to be "acquainted with the night"?

Desert Places (1936)

Snow falling and night falling fast, oh, fast
In a field I looked into going past,
And the ground almost covered smooth in snow,
But a few weeds and stubble showing last.

The woods around it have it—it is theirs.
All animals are smothered in their lairs,
I am too absent-spirited to count;
The loneliness includes me unawares.

And lonely as it is, that loneliness
Will be more lonely ere it will be less—
A blanker whiteness of benighted snow
With no expression, nothing to express

They cannot scare me with their empty spaces
Between stars—on stars where no human race is.
I have it in me so much nearer home
To scare myself with my own desert places.

Questions for Critical Thinking

1. Frost in the fourth stanza refers to a statement by the sixteenth-century French philosopher Blaise Pascal—"The infinite spaces between the stars frightens me." How does the landscape he creates in the poem align with that statement?
2. What can you learn from Frost's style of making complex ideas clear that may help you with your own poetry or prose?

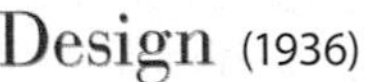

Design (1936)

I found a dimpled spider, fat and white,
On a white heal-all, holding up a moth
Like a white piece of rigid satin cloth—
Assorted characters of death and blight
Mixed ready to begin the morning right,
Like the ingredients of a witches' broth—
A snow-drop spider, a flower like a froth,
And dead wings carried like a paper kite.

What had the flower to do with being white,
The wayside blue and innocent heal-all?
What brought the kindred spider to that height,
Then steered the white moth thither in the night?
What but design of darkness to appall?—
If design govern in a thing so small.

Questions for Critical Thinking

1. How would you define "design" in the context of this poem? What connotations does it have?
2. What significance does the speaker give to the color white in this poem? What does the all-white imagery bring to mind for you?

The Gift Outright (1942)

The land was ours before we were the land's.
She was our land more than a hundred years
Before we were her people. She was ours
In Massachusetts, in Virginia,
But we were England's, still colonials,
Possessing what we still were unpossessed by,
Possessed by what we now no more possessed.
Something we were withholding made us weak
Until we found out that it was ourselves
We were withholding from our land of living,
And forthwith found salvation in surrender.

Such as we were we gave ourselves outright
(The deed of gift was many deeds of war)
To the land vaguely realizing westward,
But still unstoried, artless, unenhanced,
Such as she was, such as she would become.

Questions for Critical Thinking

1. Frost once called "The Gift Outright" "a history of the United States in sixteen lines." What does he mean by this, and do you agree?
2. Do you read the last line as optimistic or pessimistic? Explain your answer.

The Silken Tent (1942)

She is as in a field a silken tent
At midday when a sunny summer breeze
Has dried the dew and all its ropes relent,
So that in guys it gently sways at ease,
And its supporting central cedar pole,
That is its pinnacle to heavenward
And signifies the sureness of the soul,
Seems to owe naught to any single cord,
But strictly held by none, is loosely bound
By countless silken ties of love and thought
To everything on earth the compass round,
And only by one's going slightly taut
In the capriciousness of summer air
Is of the slightest bondage made aware.

Questions for Critical Thinking

1. Who is the subject of the poem? How does the speaker make his feelings toward and understanding of her known?
2. Why a tent? Why silk? Why a suggestion of a tie between earth and heaven? What goes "taut"? What does that signify?

Getting Started: A Research Project

Choose Emily Dickinson or Robert Frost and examine the poet by exploring his or her biography, historical context, and select critical perspectives on his or her work; then make connections among the three.

Emily Dickinson

Critical Readings on Emily Dickinson

The Letters of Emily Dickinson. Thomas H. Johnson. Cambridge, MA: Harvard University Press, 1986.
Dickinson's "The soul selects her own society." Bernhard Frank. *The Explicator,* January 1, 2000.
Comic Power in Emily Dickinson. Suzanne Juhasz, Cristanne Miller, and Martha Nell Smith. Austin: University of Texas Press, 1993.

Exploring Biography

Emily Dickinson's sole literary confidant and critic was an editor at the *Atlantic Monthly,* Thomas Wentworth Higginson. Dickinson initiated contact with him after reading an article in which Higginson called for new writers. Her hunger for responses to her work and literary discourse is clear from her reply to his first letter, but Dickinson and Higginson did not meet face-to-face for more than eight years after their initial correspondence when Higginson at last made a trip to Amherst in 1870. He wrote a letter to his wife describing his meeting with Dickinson. Dickinson and Higginson continued to exchange letters, however, and Dickinson describes herself in several of her early letters to him. These self-descriptions offer a unique glimpse of her home life and self-image. Based on Dickinson's account of her family life and the comments Higginson relays about her father and mother, what type of home life did Dickinson seem to have? How might this have impacted her poetry, in terms of both content and the act of creating it?

Exploring Historical Context

Although Dickinson excludes herself in her letters when she says her family is religious, what statements does she make that indicate her Puritan background?

Exploring Critical Perspectives

Based on any prior knowledge of Emily Dickinson you may have and on your current reading of her in these select articles, are you surprised by Juhasz, Miller, and Smith's reading of Dickinson as comic? How does this challenge or agree with your conception of Dickinson? Do you agree with their view?

Making Connections

Select one of Dickinson's quotations that Higginson recorded. Review her poems and see if the sentiment in her quote is reflected in one of them. When you have found one that resonates, write an essay connecting the personal philosophy with the poetic expression.

Robert Frost

Critical Readings on Robert Frost

Selected Letters of Robert Frost. Lawrence Thompson, ed. New York: Holt, 1964.
Robert Frost and the Darkness of Nature, Roberts W. French. Critical Essays on Robert Frost. *The English Record,* 1978: 155–62.
"Frost's 'Mending Wall,'" A. R. Coulthard. *The Explicator* 45, no. 2 (1987): 40–42.

Exploring Biography

From these two letters to his friends John T. Bartlett and Sidney Cox, in which Frost describes his poetic technique, how would you characterize Frost's personality? Is there anything in the letter that surprises you, or challenges your perception of Frost as a person?

Exploring Historical Context

In the letter to Sidney Cox, Frost says that poetry should not "tell all to the last scrapings of the brain pan." What contemporary trend in poetry does he seem to be railing against? You might review the work of such poets as Sylvia Plath, Anne Sexton, and Robert Lowell with an eye to secrets told.

Exploring Critical Perspectives

Coulthard argues that Frost himself was unaware of the negative portrayal of the speaker. Does this seem like a solid claim to you? Why or why not? Write a short essay evaluating the fairness of Coulthard's conjecture on Frost's intent.

Given what you know about Frost as a person, and given what you have read of his letters, evaluate Coulthard's conclusion that the poem "exposes Frost's cold mind posing as a warm heart." Do you see evidence of this in other poems? Or does this seem to be another image of the poet that is not necessarily true? Compose your thoughts in an essay.

Making Connections

Based on just these two letters, what would you imagine Frost's manifesto on poetry to be? Which of his poems seem to follow his dictates?

Further Suggestions for Writing and Research

1. Emily Dickinson's publication history is uniquely complex, because of the heavy editing done in the 1890s, which scholars then undid in the 1950s to create a version more faithful to her original poems. Research the progression of editions of Dickinson's work, along with the critical reception—that is, how critics and the public reacted to her poetry as each edition appeared. Write your findings into an essay, being sure to cite your sources. You may want to consult the resources listed below, although you can certainly find a host of information on Dickinson at your college's library:
   - *Guide to Emily Dickinson's Collected Poems.* Online resource: www.poets.org/page.php/prmID/308
   - *Critical Essays on Emily Dickinson.* Paul J. Ferlazzo, ed. Boston: G. K. Hall, 1984.
     - Two anonymous reviews from 1890, pp. 28–29.
     - Anonymous review of British edition, 1904, pp. 50–52.
     - "Emily Dickinson Complete" by Arlin Turner, 1956, pp. 113–16.
   - *A Companion to Emily Dickinson.* Martha Nell Smith and Mary Loeffelholz, eds. Malden, MA: Blackwell, 2008.
     - "Reading Dickinson in Her Context: The Fascicles" by Eleanor Elson Heginbotham, pp. 288–307.
2. Robert Frost appeals to an odd mix of audience—on the one hand, he is known and recited by the general public, including schoolchildren, while on the other, he is recognized in literary circles for his sophisticated versification and hauntingly dark subtext. This research topic asks you to find out how he was received by yet another group: other poets who were his contemporaries. The following three articles give a glimpse of how Ezra Pound, Amy Lowell, and Randall Jarrell reacted to Frost. Read their essays, noting the specific strengths and weaknesses each points to in Frost. Then write your own essay evaluating their reactions. Is Pound's opinion more accurate than Lowell's? Do you agree with Jarrell the most? This is the type of question you will answer in your essay, being sure to use support from Frost's poems in your discussion of his identified strengths and weaknesses. Finally, you may find it useful to review some of Pound's, Lowell's, and Jarrell's own poetry (these poets have work of their own in *Literature: Craft and Voice*) and see how it compares. Each of the following essays appears in *Critical Essays on Robert Frost,* Philip L. Gerber, ed., Boston: G. K. Hall, 1982.
   - "Modern Georgics," Ezra Pound, pp. 19–21.
     - Original Source: *Poetry* (December 1914).
   - "North of Boston," Amy Lowell, pp. 22–25.
     - Original Source: *The New Republic,* February 20, 1915, pp. 81–82.
   - "Tenderness and Passive Sadness," Randall Jarrell, pp. 112–13.
     - Original Source: *The New York Times Book Review,* June 1, 1947.

Some Sources for Research

Emily Dickinson

Online Source:

The Emily Dickinson Journal. Project MUSE. The John Hopkins UP, 2009. Web. <http://muse.jhu.edu/journals/emily_dickinson_journal/>.

Print Sources:

1. Ferlazzo, Paul J., ed. *Critical Essays on Emily Dickinson.* Boston: G. K. Hall, 1984. Print.
2. Higginson, Thomas Wentworth. "An Open Portfolio." *Critical Essays on Emily Dickinson.* Ed. Paul J. Ferlazzo. Boston: G. K. Hall, 1984. 23. Print.
3. Johnson, Thomas H., ed. *The Letters of Emily Dickinson.* Cambridge: Harvard UP, 1986. Print.
4. Loeffelholz, Mary. *Dickinson and the Boundaries of Feminist Theory.* Urbana Chicago: University of Illinois Press, 1991. Print.
5. Whicher, George Frisbie. *This Was a Poet: Emily Dickinson.* Charles Scribner's Sons: New York, 1938. Print.
6. Wolff, Cynthia Griffin. *Emily Dickinson.* Knopf: New York, 1986. Print.
7. Mudge, Jean McClure. *Emily Dickinson and the Image of Home.* Amherst: University of Massachusetts Press, 1975. Print.
8. Patterson, Rebecca. *Emily Dickinson's Imagery.* Amherst: University of Massachusetts Press, 1979. Print.
9. Sewall, Richard. *The Life of Emily Dickinson.* New York: Harvard UP: 1980. Print.

Robert Frost

Online Source:

The Poetry Foundation. "Robert Frost." *PoetryFoundation.org.* 2009. Web. <http://www.poetryfoundation.org/archive/poet.html?id=2361>.

Print Sources:

1. Brower, Reuben A. *The Poetry of Robert Frost: Constellations of Intention.* New York: Oxford UP, 1963. Print.
2. Brodsky, Joseph, Seamus Heaney, and Derek Walcott. *Homage to Robert Frost.* New York: Farrar, Straus, and Giroux, 1996. Print.
3. Gerber, Philip L., ed. *Critical Essays on Robert Frost.* Boston: G. K. Hall, 1982. Print.
4. Meyers, Jeffrey. *Robert Frost: A Biography.* Boston: Houghton Mifflin, 1996. Print.
5. Parini, Jay. *Robert Frost: A Life.* New York: Henry Holt, 1999. Print.
6. Poirier, Richard. *Robert Frost, the Work of Knowing.* New York: Oxford UP, 1977. Print.
7. Sergeant, Elizabeth Shipley. *Robert Frost, The Trial by Existence.* New York: Holt, Rinehart & Winston, 1966. Print.
8. Thompson, Lawrence, ed. *Selected Letters of Robert Frost.* New York: Holt, Rinehart and Winston, 1964. Print.

For examples of student papers, see chapter 3, Common Writing Assignments, and chapter 5, Writing the Research Paper, in the Handbook for Writing from Reading.

29

An Anthology of Poetry for Further Reading

Kim Addonizio (b. 1954)

First Poem for You (1994)

I like to touch your tattoos in complete
darkness, when I can't see them. I'm sure of
where they are, know by heart the neat
lines of lightning pulsing just above
your nipple, can find, as if by instinct, the blue
swirls of water on your shoulder where a serpent
twists, facing a dragon. When I pull you
to me, taking you until we're spent
and quiet on the sheets, I love to kiss
the pictures in your skin. They'll last until
you're seared to ashes; whatever persists
or turns to pain between us, they will still
be there. Such permanence is terrifying.
So I touch them in the dark; but touch them, trying.

Gloria Anzaldúa (1942–2004)

To live in the Borderlands means you (1987)

are neither *hispana india negra española*
ni gabacha, eres mestiza, mulata, half-breed
caught in the crossfire between camps
while carrying all five races on your back
not knowing which side to turn to, run from;

To live in the Borderlands means knowing
that the *india* in you, betrayed for 500 years,
is no longer speaking to you,
that *mexicanas* call you *rajetas,*
that denying the Anglo inside you
is as bad as having denied the Indian or the Black;

Cuando vives en la frontera
people walk through you, the wind steals your voice,
you're a *burra, buey,* scapegoat,
forerunner of a new race,
half and half—both woman and man, neither—
a new gender;

To live in the Borderlands means to
put *chile* in the borscht,
eat whole wheat *tortillas,*
speak Tex-Mex with a Brooklyn accent;
be stopped by *la migra* at the border checkpoints;

Living in the Borderlands means you fight hard to
resist the gold elixir beckoning from the bottle,
the pull of the gun barrel,
the rope crushing the hollow of your throat;

In the Borderlands
you are the battleground
where enemies are kin to each other;
you are at home, a stranger,
the border disputes have been settled
the volley of shots have shattered the truce
you are wounded, lost in action
dead, fighting back;

To live in the Borderlands means
the mill with the razor white teeth wants to shred off
your olive-red skin, crush out the kernel, your heart
pound you pinch you roll you out
smelling like white bread but dead;

To survive the Borderlands
you must live *sin fronteras*
be a crossroads.

W. H. Auden (1907–1973)

For a brief biography of W. H. Auden, see chapter 18.

The Unknown Citizen (1940)

(To JS/07/M/378
This Marble Monument
Is Erected by the State)

He was found by the Bureau of Statistics to be
One against whom there was no official complaint,
And all the reports on his conduct agree
That, in the modern sense of an old-fashioned word, he
was a saint,
For in everything he did he served the Greater Community.
Except for the War till the day he retired
He worked in a factory and never got fired,
But satisfied his employers, Fudge Motors Inc.
Yet he wasn't a scab or odd in his views,
For his Union reports that he paid his dues,
(Our report on his Union shows it was sound)
And our Social Psychology workers found
That he was popular with his mates and liked a drink.
The Press are convinced that he bought a paper every day
And that his reactions to advertisements were normal in
every way.
Policies taken out in his name prove that he was fully
insured,

And his Health-card shows he was once in hospital but
left it cured.
Both Producers Research and High-Grade Living declare
He was fully sensible to the advantages of the Instalment
Plan
And had everything necessary to the Modern Man,
A phonograph, a radio, a car and a frigidaire.
Our researchers into Public Opinion are content
That he held the proper opinions for the time of year;
When there was peace, he was for peace; when there was
war, he went.
He was married and added five children to the population,
Which our Eugenist says was the right number for a
parent of his generation,
And our teachers report that he never interfered with
their education.
Was he free? Was he happy? The question is absurd:
Had anything been wrong, we should certainly have
heard.

Anne Bradstreet (1612–1672)

For a brief biography of Anne Bradstreet, see chapter 19.

To my Dear and Loving Husband (1678)

If ever two were one, then surely we.
If ever man were lov'd by wife, then thee;
If ever wife was happy in a man,
Compare with me ye women if you can.
I prize thy love more than whole Mines of gold,
Or all the riches that the East doth hold.
My love is such that Rivers cannot quench,
Nor ought but love from thee, give recompence.
Thy love is such I can no way repay,
The heavens reward thee manifold I pray.
Then while we live, in love lets so persever,
That when we live no more, we may live ever.

Emily Brontë (1818–1848)

Come Walk with Me (1902)

Come, walk with me,
There's only thee,
To bless my spirit now.
We used to love on winter nights,
To wander through the snow;
Can we not woo back old delights?
The clouds rush dark & wild.
They fleck with shade our mountains bright
The same as long ago,
And on the horizon rest at last
In looming masses piled;
While moonbeams flash & fly so fast
We scarce can say they smiled.

Come walk with me, come walk with me,
We were not once so few;
But death has stolen our company,
As sunshine steals the dew.
He took them one by one, and we
Are left, the only two;
So closer would my feelings twine
Because they have no stay but thine.

"Nay call me not; it may not be;
Is human love so true?
Can friendship's flower droop for years
And then revive anew?
No; though the soil be wet with tears,
How fair soe're it grew;
The vital sap once perished
Will never flow again.
And surer than that dwelling dread,
The narrow dungeon of the dead,
Time parts the hearts of men.

Robert Browning (1812–1889)

For a brief biography of Robert Browning, see chapter 16.

Meeting at Night (1845)

I

The gray sea and the long black land;
And the yellow half-moon large and low;
And the startled little waves that leap
In fiery ringlets from their sleep,
As I gain the cove with pushing prow,
And quench its speed i' the slushy sand.

II

Then a mile of warm sea-scented beach;
Three fields to cross till a farm appears;
A tap at the pane, the quick sharp scratch
And blue spurt of a lighted match,
And a voice less loud, through its joys and fears,
Than the two hearts beating each to each!

Parting at Morning (1845)

Round the cape of a sudden came the sea,
And the sun looked over the mountain's rim:
And straight was a path of gold for him,
And the need of a world of men for me.

George Gordon, Lord Byron (1788–1824)

For a brief biography of Lord Byron, see chapter 16.

She Walks in Beauty (1815)

I

She walks in beauty, like the night
  Of cloudless climes and starry skies;
And all that's best of dark and bright
  Meet in her aspect and her eyes:
Thus mellowed to that tender light
  Which heaven to gaudy day denies.

II

One shade the more, one ray the less,
  Had half impaired the nameless grace
Which waves in every raven tress,
  Or softly lightens o'er her face;
Where thoughts serenely sweet express
  How pure, how dear their dwelling place.

III

And on that cheek, and o'er that brow,
  So soft, so calm, yet eloquent,
The smiles that win, the tints that glow,
  But tell of days in goodness spent,
A mind at peace with all below,
  A heart whose love is innocent!

John Ciardi (1916–1986)

Most Like an Arch This Marriage (1958)

Most like an arch—an entrance which upholds
and shores the stone-crush up the air like lace.
Mass made idea, and idea held in place.
A lock in time. Inside half-heaven unfolds.

Most like an arch—two weaknesses that lean
into a strength. Two fallings become firm.
Two joined abeyances become a term
naming the fact that teaches fact to mean.

Not quite that? Not much less. World as it is,
what's strong and separate falters. All I do
at piling stone on stone apart from you
is roofless around nothing. Till we kiss
I am no more than upright and unset.
It is by falling in and in we make
the all-bearing point, for one another's sake,
in faultless failing, raised by our own weight.

Judith Ortiz Cofer (b. 1952)

Quinceañera (1987)

My dolls have been put away like dead
children in a chest I will carry
with me when I marry.
I reach under my skirt to feel
a satin slip bought for this day. It is soft
as the inside of my thighs. My hair
has been nailed back with my mother's
black hairpins to my skull. Her hands
stretched my eyes open as she twisted
braids into a tight circle at the nape
of my neck. I am to wash my own clothes
and sheets from this day on, as if
the fluids of my body were poison, as if
the little trickle of blood I believe
travels from my heart to the world were
shameful. Is not the blood of saints and
men in battle beautiful? Do Christ's hands
not bleed into your eyes from His cross?
At night I hear myself growing and wake
to find my hands drifting of their own will
to soothe skin stretched tight
over my bones.
I am wound like the guts of a clock,
waiting for each hour to release me.

Samuel Taylor Coleridge (1772–1834)

For a brief biography of Samuel Taylor Coleridge, see chapter 22.

Kubla Khan (1797–1798)
Or A Vision in a Dream. A Fragment

In Xanadu did Kubla Khan
A stately pleasure dome decree:
Where Alph, the sacred river, ran
Through caverns measureless to man
  Down to a sunless sea.
So twice five miles of fertile ground
With walls and towers were girdled round:

And there were gardens bright with sinuous rills,
Where blossomed many an incense-bearing tree;
And here were forests ancient as the hills,
Enfolding sunny spots of greenery.

But oh! that deep romantic chasm which slanted
Down the green hill athwart a cedarn cover!
A savage place! as holy and enchanted
As e'er beneath a waning moon was haunted
By woman wailing for her demon lover!
And from this chasm, with ceaseless turmoil seething,
As if this earth in fast thick pants were breathing,
A mighty fountain momently was forced:
Amid whose swift half-intermitted burst
Huge fragments vaulted like rebounding hail,
Or chaffy grain beneath the thresher's flail:
And 'mid these dancing rocks at once and ever
It flung up momently the sacred river.
Five miles meandering with a mazy motion
Through wood and dale the sacred river ran,
Then reached the caverns measureless to man,
And sank in tumult to a lifeless ocean:
And 'mid this tumult Kubla heard from far
Ancestral voices prophesying war!

    The shadow of the dome of pleasure
    Floated midway on the waves;
    Where was heard the mingled measure
    From the fountain and the caves.
It was a miracle of rare device,
A sunny pleasure dome with caves of ice!

    A damsel with a dulcimer
    In a vision once I saw:
    It was an Abyssinian maid,
    And on her dulcimer she played,
    Singing of Mount Abora.
    Could I revive within me
    Her symphony and song,
    To such a deep delight 'twould win me,
That with music loud and long,
I would build that dome in air,
That sunny dome! those caves of ice!
And all who heard should see them there,
And all should cry, Beware! Beware!
His flashing eyes, his floating hair!
Weave a circle round him thrice,
And close your eyes with holy dread,
For he on honey-dew hath fed,
And drunk the milk of Paradise.

e. e. cummings (1894–1962)

For a brief biography of e. e. cummings, see chapter 24.

l(a (1923)

l(a
le
af
fa

ll

s)
one
l

iness

anyone lived in a pretty how town (1940)

anyone lived in a pretty how town
(with up so floating many bells down)
spring summer autumn winter
he sang his didn't he danced his did.

Women and men(both little and small)
cared for anyone not at all
they sowed their isn't they reaped their same
sun moon stars rain

children guessed(but only a few
and down they forgot as up they grew
autumn winter spring summer)
that noone loved him more by more

when by now and tree by leaf
she laughed his joy she cried his grief
bird by snow and stir by still
anyone's any was all to her

someones married their everyones
laughed their cryings and did their dance
(sleep wake hope and then)they
said their nevers they slept their dream

stars rain sun moon
(and only the snow can begin to explain
how children are apt to forget to remember
with up so floating many bells down)

one day anyone died i guess
(and noone stooped to kiss his face)
busy folk buried them side by side
little by little and was by was

all by all and deep by deep
and more by more they dream their sleep
noone and anyone earth by april
wish by spirit and if by yes.

Women and men(both dong and ding)
summer autumn winter spring
reaped their sowing and went their came
sun moon stars rain

Buffalo Bills (1923)

Buffalo Bill's
defunct
        who used to
        ride a watersmooth-silver
                                                stallion
and break onetwothreefourfive pigeonsjustlikethat
                                                                        Jesus

he was a handsome man
                                    and what i want to know is
how do you like your blueeyed boy
Mister Death

John Donne (1572–1631)

For a brief biography of John Donne, see chapter 25.

Death Be Not Proud (c. 1610)

Death, be not proud, though some have callèd thee
Mighty and dreadful, for thou art not so;
For those whom thou think'st thou dost overthrow
Die not, poor Death, nor yet canst thou kill me.
From rest and sleep, which but thy pictures be,
Much pleasure; then from thee much more must flow,
And soonest our best men with thee do go,
Rest of their bones, and soul's delivery.
Thou art slave to fate, chance, kings, and desperate men,
And dost with poison, war, and sickness dwell,
And poppy or charms can make us sleep as well
And better than thy stroke; why swell'st thou then?
One short sleep past, we wake eternally
And death shall be no more; Death, thou shalt die.

The Flea (1633)

Mark but this flea, and mark in this,
How little that which thou deniest me is;
Me it sucked first, and now sucks thee,
And in this flea our two bloods mingled be.
Thou know'st that this cannot be said
A sin, or shame, or loss of maidenhead,
  Yet this enjoys before it woo,
  And pampered swells with one blood made of two,
  And this, alas, is more than we would do.

Oh stay, three lives in one flea spare,
Where we almost, nay more than married are.
This flea is you and I, and this
Our marriage bed and marriage temple is;
Though parents grudge, and you, we are met,
And cloistered in these living walls of jet.
  Though use make you apt to kill me,
  Let not to that, self-murder added be,
  And sacrilege, three sins in killing three.

Cruel and sudden, hast thou since
Purpled thy nail in blood of innocence?
Wherein could this flea guilty be,
Except in that drop which it sucked from thee?
Yet thou triumph'st, and say'st that thou
Find'st not thyself nor me the weaker now;
  'Tis true; then learn how false fears be:
  Just so much honor, when thou yield'st to me,
  Will waste, as this flea's death took life from thee.

The Sun Rising (1633)

    Busy old fool, unruly Sun,
    Why dost thou thus
Through windows, and through curtains call on us?
Must to thy motions lovers' seasons run?
    Saucy pedantic wretch, go chide
    Late schoolboys and sour prentices,
  Go tell court huntsmen that the King will ride,
  Call country ants to harvest offices;
Love, all alike, no season knows nor clime,
Nor hours, days, months, which are the rags of time.

    Thy beams, so reverend and strong
    Why shouldst thou think?
I could eclipse and cloud them with a wink,
But that I would not lose her sight so long;
    If her eyes have not blinded thine,
    Look, and tomorrow late, tell me,
  Whether both th' Indias of spice and mine
  Be where thou leftst them, or lie here with me.
Ask for those kings whom thou saw'st yesterday,
And thou shalt hear, All here in one bed lay.

    She is all states, and all princes I,
    Nothing else is.
Princes do but play us; compared to this,
All honor's mimic, all wealth alchemy.

Thou, sun, art half as happy as we,
In that the world's contracted thus;
Thine age asks ease, and since thy duties be
To warm the world, that's done in warming us.
Shine here to us, and thou art everywhere;
This bed thy center is, these walls thy sphere.

H.D. (Hilda Doolittle) (1886–1961)

For a brief biography of H.D., see chapter 20.

Heat (1916)

O wind, rend open the heat.
cut apart the heat,
rend it to tatters.

Fruit cannot drop
through this thick air—
fruit cannot fall into heat
that presses up and blunts
the points of pears
and rounds the grapes.

Cut the heat—
plough through it,
turning it on either side
of your path

T. S. Eliot (1888–1965)

The Love Song of J. Alfred Prufrock (1915)

S'io credesse che mia risposta fosse
A persona che mai tornasse al mondo,
Questa fiamma staria senza più scosse.
Ma perciocche giammai di questo fondo
Non tornò vivo alcun, s'i'odo il vero,
Senza tema d'infamia ti rispondo.°

Let us go then, you and I,
When the evening is spread out against the sky
Like a patient etherized upon a table;
Let us go, through certain half-deserted streets,
The muttering retreats
Of restless nights in one-night cheap hotels
And sawdust restaurants with oyster-shells:
Streets that follow like a tedious argument
Of insidious intent
To lead you to an overwhelming question . . .
Oh, do not ask, "What is it?"
Let us go and make our visit.

In the room the women come and go
Talking of Michelangelo.

The yellow fog that rubs its back upon the window-panes
The yellow smoke that rubs its muzzle on the window-panes
Licked its tongue into the corners of the evening,
Lingered upon the pools that stand in drains,
Let fall upon its back the soot that falls from chimneys,
Slipped by the terrace, made a sudden leap,
And seeing that it was a soft October night,
Curled once about the house, and fell asleep.

And indeed there will be time
For the yellow smoke that slides along the street,
Rubbing its back upon the window-panes;
There will be time, there will be time
To prepare a face to meet the faces that you meet;
There will be time to murder and create,
And time for all the works and days of hands
That lift and drop a question on your plate;
Time for you and time for me,
And time yet for a hundred indecisions,
And for a hundred visions and revisions,
Before the taking of a toast and tea.

In the room the women come and go
Talking of Michelangelo.

And indeed there will be time
To wonder, "Do I dare?" and, "Do I dare?"
Time to turn back and descend the stair,
With a bald spot in the middle of my hair—
[They will say: "How his hair is growing thin!"]
My morning coat, my collar mounting firmly to the chin,
My necktie rich and modest, but asserted by a simple pin—
[They will say: "But how his arms and legs are thin!"]
Do I dare
Disturb the universe?
In a minute there is time
For decisions and revisions which a minute will reverse.

For I have known them all already, known them all:
Have known the evenings, mornings, afternoons,
I have measured out my life with coffee spoons;
I know the voices dying with a dying fall
Beneath the music from a farther room.
So how should I presume?

°If I believed that my reply were made
To one to who the world would e'er return,
The flame without more flickering would stand still;
But inasmuch as never from this depth
Did anyone return, if I hear true,
Without the fear of infamy I answer.

And I have known the eyes already, known them all—
The eyes that fix you in a formulated phrase,
And when I am formulated, sprawling on a pin,
When I am pinned and wriggling on the wall,
Then how should I begin
To spit out all the butt-ends of my days and ways?
And how should I presume?

And I have known the arms already, known them all—
Arms that are braceleted and white and bare
[But in the lamplight, downed with light brown hair!]
Is it perfume from a dress
That makes me so digress?
Arms that lie along a table, or wrap about a shawl.
And should I then presume?
And how should I begin?

. . . . .

Shall I say, I have gone at dusk through narrow streets
And watched the smoke that rises from the pipes
Of lonely men in shirt-sleeves, leaning out of windows? . . .

I should have been a pair of ragged claws
Scuttling across the floors of silent seas.

. . . . .

And the afternoon, the evening, sleeps so peacefully!
Smoothed by long fingers,
Asleep . . . tired . . . or it malingers,
Stretched on the floor, here beside you and me.
Should I, after tea and cakes and ices,
Have the strength to force the moment to its crisis?
But though I have wept and fasted, wept and prayed,
Though I have seen my head [grown slightly bald] brought in upon a platter,
I am no prophet—and here's no great matter;
I have seen the moment of my greatness flicker,
And I have seen the eternal Footman hold my coat, and snicker,
And in short, I was afraid.

And would it have been worth it, after all,
After the cups, the marmalade, the tea,
Among the porcelain, among some talk of you and me,
Would it have been worth while,
To have bitten off the matter with a smile,
To have squeezed the universe into a ball
To roll it toward some overwhelming question,
To say: "I am Lazarus, come from the dead,
Come back to tell you all, I shall tell you all"—
If one, settling a pillow by her head,
Should say: "That is not what I meant at all.
That is not it, at all."

And would it have been worth it, after all,
Would it have been worth while,
After the sunsets and the dooryards and the sprinkled streets,
After the novels, after the teacups, after the skirts that trail along the floor—
And this, and so much more?—
It is impossible to say just what I mean!
But as if a magic lantern threw the nerves in patterns on a screen:
Would it have been worth while
If one, settling a pillow or throwing off a shawl,
And turning toward the window, should say:
"That is not it at all,
That is not what I meant, at all."

. . . . .

No! I am not Prince Hamlet, nor was meant to be;
Am an attendant lord, one that will do
To swell a progress, start a scene or two,
Advise the prince; no doubt, an easy tool,
Deferential, glad to be of use,
Politic, cautious, and meticulous;
Full of high sentence, but a bit obtuse;
At times, indeed, almost ridiculous—
Almost, at times, the Fool.

I grow old . . . I grow old . . .
I shall wear the bottoms of my trousers rolled.

Shall I part my hair behind? Do I dare to eat a peach?
I shall wear white flannel trousers, and walk upon the beach.
I have heard the mermaids singing, each to each.

I do not think that they will sing to me.

I have seen them riding seaward on the waves
Combing the white hair of the waves blown back
When the wind blows the water white and black.

We have lingered in the chambers of the sea
By sea-girls wreathed with seaweed red and brown
Till human voices wake us, and we drown.

Louise Erdrich (b. 1954)

Dear John Wayne (1984)

August and the drive-in picture is packed.
We lounge on the hood of the Pontiac
surrounded by the slow-burning spirals they sell

at the window, to vanquish the hordes of mosquitoes.
Nothing works. They break through the smoke screen for
blood.

Always the lookout spots the Indian first,
spread north to south, barring progress.
The Sioux or some other Plains bunch
in spectacular columns, ICBM missiles,
feathers bristling in the meaningful sunset.

The drum breaks. There will be no parlance.
Only the arrows whining, a death-cloud of nerves
swarming down on the settlers
who die beautifully, tumbling like dust weeds
into the history that brought us all here
together: this wide screen beneath the sign of the bear.

The sky fills, acres of blue squint and eye
that the crowd cheers. His face moves over us,
a thick cloud of vengeance, pitted
like the land that was once flesh. Each rut,
each scar makes a promise: *It is*
not over, this fight, not as long as you resist.

Everything we see belongs to us.

A few laughing Indians fall over the hood
slipping in the hot spilled butter.
The eye sees a lot, John, but the heart is so blind.
Death makes us owners of nothing.
He smiles, a horizon of teeth
the credits reel over, and then the white fields

again blowing in the true-to-life dark.
The dark films over everything.
We get into the car
scratching our mosquito bites, speechless and small
as people are when the movie is done.
We are back in our skins.

How can we help but keep hearing his voice,
the flip side of the sound track, still playing:
Come on, boys, we got them
where we want them, drunk, running.
They'll give us what we want, what we need.
Even his disease was the idea of taking everything.
Those cells, burning, doubling, splitting out of their skins.

Rhina Espaillat (b. 1932)

Bilingual/Bilingüe (1998)

My father liked them separate, one there,
one here (allá y aquí), as if aware

that words might cut in two his daughter's heart
(el corazón) and lock the alien part

to what he was—his memory, his name
(su nombre)—with a key he could not claim.

"English outside this door, Spanish inside,"
he said, "y basta." But who can divide

the world, the word (mundo y palabra) from
any child? I knew how to be dumb

and stubborn (testaruda); late, in bed,
I hoarded secret syllables I read

until my tongue (mi lengua) learned to run
where his stumbled. And still the heart was one.

I like to think he knew that, even when,
proud (orgulloso) of his daughter's pen,

he stood outside mis versos, half in fear
of words he loved but wanted not to hear.

Linda Gregg (b. 1942)

Something Scary (1985)

Over the phone Joel tells me
his marriage is suddenly miraculous.
That his wife is glad now about us.
Is even grateful.
"We have crossed a border," he says.
I listen, knowing myself too far gone
to last more than a day.
Remembering him in that dark room
with the shades down saying,
"You don't need the sun. You carry
a brightness in you." And me saying
nothing, burning alone lying there
like the terrible brightness of heaven.

Kimiko Hahn (b. 1955)

The Details We Fall For (1994)

Shifting to fifth and swinging behind a Harley
he could be you: black helmet, gloved fists—
on that spin down some LA boulevard,
the heat of February sweating the streets,
my hands around your waist in our first contact
since I married a second time still not to you.

What were those weird trees,
Dr. Seuss illustrations, cocktail mixers?
and what about all that pink—
bungalows, latex buns, tanning billboards—
details instructing the interior landscape
we ride through even, or especially in sleep.
I'm back in New York.
So to the driver behind me:
don't tail the woman behind the guy on the motorcycle.
She's working on a rough draft.

Donald Hall (b. 1928)

Letter with No Address (1996)

Your daffodils rose up
and collapsed in their yellow
bodies on the hillside
garden above the bricks
you laid out in sand, squatting
with pants pegged and face
masked like a beekeeper's
against the black flies.
Buttercups circle the planks
of the old wellhead
this May while your silken
gardener's body withers or moulds
in the Proctor graveyard.
I drive and talk to you crying
and come back to this house
to talk to your photographs.

There's news to tell you:
Maggie Fisher's pregnant.
I carried myself like an egg
at Abigail's birthday party
a week after you died,
as three-year-olds bounced
uproarious on a mattress.
Joyce and I met for lunch
at the mall and strolled weepily
through Sears and B. Dalton.

Today it's four weeks
since you lay on our painted bed
and I closed your eyes.
Yesterday I cut irises to set
in a pitcher on your grave;
today I brought a carafe
to fill it with fresh water.
I remember the bone-pain,
vomiting, and delirium. I remember
the pond afternoons.

My routine
is established: coffee;
the *Globe;* breakfast;
writing you this letter
at my desk. When I go to bed
to sleep after baseball,
Gus follows me into the bedroom
as he used to follow us.
Most of the time he flops
down in the parlor
with his head on his paws.

Once a week I drive to Tilton
to see Dick and Nan.
Nan doesn't understand much
but she knows you're dead;
I feel her fretting. The tune
of Dick and me talking
seems to console her.

You know now
whether the soul survives death.
Or you don't. When you were dying
you said you didn't fear
punishment. We never dared
to speak of Paradise.

At five a.m., when I walk outside,
mist lies thick on hayfields.
By eight, the air is clear,
cool, sunny with the pale yellow
light of mid-May. Kearsarge
rises huge and distinct,
each birch and balsam visible.
To the west the waters
of Eagle Pond waver
and flash through popples just
leafing out.

Always the weather,
writing its book of the world,
returns you to me.
Ordinary days were best,
when we worked over poems
in our separate rooms.
I remember watching you gaze
out the January window
into the garden of snow
and ice, your face rapt
as you imagined burgundy lilies.

Your presence in this house
is almost as enormous
and painful as your absence.
Driving home from Tilton,
I remember how you cherished
that vista with its center
the red door of a farmhouse
against green fields.
Are you past pity?
If you have consciousness now,
if something I can call
"you" has something
like "consciousness," I doubt
you remember the last days.
I play them over and over:
I lift your wasted body
onto the commode, your arms
looped around my neck, aiming
your bony bottom so that
it will not bruise on a rail.
Faintly you repeat,
"Momma, Momma."

You lay
astonishing in the long box
while Alice Ling prayed
and sang "Amazing Grace"
a capella. Three times today
I drove to your grave.
Sometimes, coming back home
to our circular driveway,
I imagine you've returned
before me, bags of groceries upright
in the back of the Saab,
its trunklid delicately raised
as if proposing an encounter,
dog-fashion, with the Honda.

Thomas Hardy (1840–1928)

For a brief biography of Thomas Hardy, see chapter 19.

The Darkling Thrush (1900)

I leant upon a coppice gate
  When Frost was specter-gray,
And Winter's dregs made desolate
  The weakening eye of day.
The tangled bine-stems scored the sky
  Like strings of broken lyres,
And all mankind that haunted nigh
  Had sought their household fires.

The land's sharp features seemed to be
  The Century's corpse outleant,
His crypt the cloudy canopy,
  The wind his death-lament.
The ancient pulse of germ and birth
  Was shrunken hard and dry,
And every spirit upon earth
  Seemed fervorless as I.

At once a voice arose among
  The bleak twigs overhead
In a full-hearted evensong
  Of joy illimited;
An aged thrush, frail, gaunt, and small,
  In blast beruffled plume,
Had chosen thus to fling his soul
  Upon the growing gloom.

So little cause for carolings
  Of such ecstatic sound
Was written on terrestrial things
  Afar or nigh around,
That I could think there trembled through
  His happy good night air
Some blessed Hope, whereof he knew
  And I was unaware.

George Herbert (1593–1633)

For a brief biography of George Herbert, see chapter 24.

Love (1633)

Love bade me welcome: yet my soul drew back,
  Guilty of dust and sin.
But quick-eyed Love, observing me grow slack
  From my first entrance in,
Drew nearer to me, sweetly questioning
  If I lacked anything.

"A guest," I answered, "worthy to be here":
  Love said, "You shall be he."
"I, the unkind, ungrateful? Ah, my dear,
  I cannot look on thee."
Love took my hand, and smiling did reply,
  "Who made the eyes but I?"

"Truth, Lord; but I have marred them; let my shame
  Go where it doth deserve."
"And know you not," says Love, "who bore the blame?"
  "My dear, then I will serve."
"You must sit down," says Love, "and taste my meat."
  So I did sit and eat.

Robert Herrick (1591–1674)

Upon Julia's Clothes (1648)

Whenas in silks my Julia goes,
Then, then, methinks, how sweetly flows
The liquefaction of her clothes.

Next, when I cast mine eyes and see
That brave vibration each way free,
Oh, how that glittering taketh me!

Delight in Disorder (1648)

A sweet disorder in the dress
Kindles in clothes a wantonness.
A lawn about the shoulders thrown
Into a fine distraction;
An erring lace, which here and there
Enthralls the crimson stomacher;
A cuff neglectful, and thereby
Ribbons to flow confusedly;
A winning wave, deserving note,
In the tempestuous petticoat;
A careless shoestring, in whose tie
I see a wild civility:
Do more bewitch me than when art
Is too precise in every part.

To the Virgins, to Make Much of Time (1646)

Gather ye rosebuds while ye may,
  Old time is still a-flying;
And this same flower that smiles today,
  Tomorrow will be dying.

The glorious lamp of heaven, the sun,
  The higher he's a-getting,
The sooner will his race be run,
  And nearer he's to setting.

That age is best which is the first,
  When youth and blood are warmer;
But being spent, the worse, and worst
  Times still succeed the former.

Then be not coy, but use your time,
  And while ye may, go marry;
For having lost but once your prime,
  You may forever tarry.

Gerard Manley Hopkins (1844–1889)

For a brief biography of Gerard Manley Hopkins, see chapter 22.

God's Grandeur (1877)

The world is charged with the grandeur of God.
  It will flame out, like shining from shook foil;
  It gathers to a greatness, like the ooze of oil
Crushed. Why do men then now not reck his rod?
Generations have trod, have trod, have trod;
  And all is seared with trade; bleared, smeared with toil;
  And wears man's smudge and shares man's smell:
    the soil
Is bare now, nor can foot feel, being shod.

And for all this, nature is never spent;
  There lives the dearest freshness deep down things;
And though the last lights off the black West went
  Oh, morning, at the brown brink eastward, springs—
Because the Holy Ghost over the bent
  World broods with warm breast and with ah! bright
    wings.

The Windhover (1877)

To Christ our Lord

I caught this morning morning's minion, king-
  dom of daylight's dauphin, dapple-dawn-drawn
    Falcon, in his riding
  Of the rolling level underneath him steady air, and
    striding
High there, how he rung upon the rein of a wimpling
  wing
In his ecstasy! then off, off forth on swing,
  As a skate's heel sweeps smooth on a bow-bend: the
    hurl and gliding
  Rebuffed the big wind. My heart in hiding
Stirred for a bird,—the achieve of, the mastery of the thing!

Brute beauty and valour and act, oh, air, pride, plume, here
  Buckle! AND the fire that breaks from thee then,
    a billion
Times told lovelier, more dangerous, O my chevalier!

  No wonder of it: shéer plód makes plough down sillion
Shine, and blue-bleak embers, ah my dear,
  Fall, gall themselves, and gash gold-vermillion.

A. E. Housman (1859–1936)

Loveliest of trees, the cherry now (1896)

Loveliest of trees, the cherry now
Is hung with bloom along the bough,
And stands about the woodland ride
Wearing white for Eastertide.

Now, of my threescore years and ten,
Twenty will not come again,
And take from seventy springs a score,
It only leaves me fifty more.

And since to look at things in bloom
Fifty springs are little room,
About the woodlands I will go
To see the cherry hung with snow.

When I was one-and-twenty (1896)

When I was one-and-twenty
  I heard a wise man say,
"Give crowns and pounds and guineas
  But not your heart away;
Give pearls away and rubies
  But keep your fancy free."
But I was one-and-twenty,
  No use to talk to me.

When I was one-and-twenty
  I heard him say again,
"The heart out of the bosom
  Was never given in vain;
'Tis paid with sighs a plenty
  And sold for endless rue."
And I am two-and-twenty,
  And oh, 'tis true, 'tis true.

Ben Jonson (1573?–1637)

For a brief biography of Ben Jonson, see chapter 19.

To Celia (1616)

Drink to me only with thine eyes,
  And I will pledge with mine;
Or leave a kiss but in the cup,
  And I'll not look for wine.
The thirst that from the soul doth rise
  Doth ask a drink divine;
But might I of Jove's nectar sup,
  I would not change for thine.
I sent thee late a rosy wreath,
  Not so much honoring thee,
As giving it a hope that there
  It could not withered be.
But thou thereon didst only breathe,
  And sent'st it back to me;
Since when it grows and smells, I swear,
  Not of itself, but thee.

John Keats (1795–1821)

For a brief biography of John Keats, see chapter 18.

La Belle Dame sans Merci (1819)

Ah, what can ail thee, wretched wight,
  Alone and palely loitering?
The sedge is wither'd from the lake,
  And no birds sing.

Ah, what can ail thee, wretched wight,
  So haggard and so woe-begone?
The squirrel's granary is full,
  And the harvest's done.

I see a lily on thy brow,
  With anguish moist and fever dew;
And on thy cheek a fading rose
  Fast withereth too.

I met a lady in the meads
  Full beautiful—a faery's child;
Her hair was long, her foot was light,
  And her eyes were wild.

I set her on my pacing steed,
  And nothing else saw all day long,
For sideways would she lean, and sing
  A faery's song.

I made a garland for her head,
  And bracelets too, and fragrant zone;
She look'd at me as she did love,
  And made sweet moan.

She found me roots of relish sweet,
  And honey wild, and manna dew;
And sure in language strange she said—
  "I love thee true."

She took me to her elfin grot,
And there she gazed, and sighed deep,
And there I shut her wild wild eyes
So kiss'd to sleep.

And there we slumber'd on the moss,
And there I dream'd—Ah! woe betide!
The latest dream I ever dream'd
On the cold hill side.

I saw pale kings, and princes too,
Pale warriors, death-pale were they all;
They cried—"La Belle Dame sans Merci
Hath thee in thrall!"

I saw their starved lips in the gloam,
With horrid warning gaped wide,
And I awoke, and found me here
On the cold hill side.

And this is why I sojourn here,
Alone and palely loitering,
Though the sedge is wither'd from the lake,
And no birds sing.

Yusef Komunyakaa (b. 1947)

Facing It (1988)

My black face fades,
hiding inside the black granite.
I said I wouldn't
dammit: No tears.
I'm stone. I'm flesh.
My clouded reflection eyes me
like a bird of prey, the profile of night
slanted against morning. I turn
this way—the stone lets me go.
I turn that way—I'm inside
the Vietnam Veterans Memorial
again, depending on the light
to make a difference.
I go down the 58,022 names,
half-expecting to find
my own in letters like smoke.
I touch the name Andrew Johnson;
I see the booby trap's white flash.
Names shimmer on a woman's blouse
but when she walks away
the names stay on the wall.
Brushstrokes flash, a red bird's
wings cutting across my stare.
The sky. A plane in the sky.
A white vet's image floats
closer to me, then his pale eyes
look through mine. I'm a window.
He's lost his right arm
inside the stone. In the black mirror
a woman's trying to erase names:
No, she's brushing a boy's hair.

Emma Lazarus (1849–1887)

The New Colossus (1883)

Not like the brazen giant of Greek fame,
With conquering limbs astride from land to land;
Here at our sea-washed, sunset gates shall stand
A mighty woman with a torch, whose flame
Is the imprisoned lightning, and her name
Mother of Exiles. From her beacon-hand
Glows world-wide welcome; her mild eyes command
The air-bridged harbor that twin cities frame.
"Keep, ancient lands, your storied pomp!" cries she
With silent lips. "Give me your tired, your poor,
Your huddled masses yearning to breathe free,
The wretched refuse of your teeming shore.
Send these, the homeless, tempest-tost to me,
I lift my lamp beside the golden door!"

Thomas Lynch (b. 1948)

For a brief biography of Thomas Lynch, see chapter 22.

Liberty (1998)

Some nights I go out and piss on the front lawn
as a form of freedom—liberty from
porcelain and plumbing and the Great Beyond
beyond the toilet and the sewage works.
Here is the statement I am trying to make:
to say I am from a fierce bloodline of men
who made their water in the old way, under stars
that overarched the North Atlantic where
the River Shannon empties into sea.
The ex-wife used to say, "Why can't you pee
in concert with the most of humankind
who do their business tidily indoors?"
It was gentility or envy, I suppose,
because I could do it anywhere, and do
whenever I begin to feel encumbered.
Still, there is nothing, here in the suburbs,
as dense as the darkness in West Clare
nor any equivalent to the nightlong wind
that rattles in the hedgerow of whitethorn there
on the east side of the cottage yard in Moveen.

It was market day in Kilrush, years ago:
my great-great-grandfather bargained with tinkers
who claimed it was whitethorn that Christ's crown was
made from.
So he gave them two and six and brought them home—
mere saplings then—as a gift for the missus,
who planted them between the house and garden.
For years now, men have slipped out the back door
during wakes or wedding feasts or nights of song
to pay their homage to the holy trees
and, looking up into that vast firmament,
consider liberty in that last townland where
they have no crowns, no crappers and no ex-wives.

Archibald MacLeish (1892–1982)

Ars Poetica (1926)

A poem should be palpable and mute
As a globed fruit,

Dumb
As old medallions to the thumb,

Silent as the sleeve-worn stone
Of casement ledges where the moss has grown—

A poem should be wordless
As the flight of birds.

-

A poem should be motionless in time
As the moon climbs,

Leaving, as the moon releases
Twig by twig the night-entangled trees,

Leaving, as the moon behind the winter leaves,
Memory by memory the mind—

A poem should be motionless in time
As the moon climbs.

-

A poem should be equal to:
Not true.

For all the history of grief
An empty doorway and a maple leaf.

For love
The leaning grasses and two lights above the sea—

A poem should not mean
But be.

Andrew Marvell (1621–1678)

To His Coy Mistress (1681)

Had we but world enough, and time,
This coyness, lady, were no crime.
We would sit down, and think which way
To walk, and pass our long love's day.
Thou by the Indian Ganges' side
Shouldst rubies find; I by the tide
Of Humber would complain. I would
Love you ten years before the Flood,
And you should, if you please, refuse
Till the conversion of the Jews.
My vegetable love should grow
Vaster than empires, and more slow;
An hundred years should go to praise
Thine eyes, and on thy forehead gaze;
Two hundred to adore each breast,
But thirty thousand to the rest:
An age at least to every part,
And the last age should show your heart.
For, lady, you deserve this state,
Nor would I love at lower rate.

But at my back I always hear
Time's wingèd chariot hurrying near;
And yonder all before us lie
Deserts of vast eternity.
Thy beauty shall no more be found,
Nor, in thy marble vault, shall sound
My echoing song, then worms shall try
That long-preserved virginity,
And your quaint honor turn to dust,
And into ashes all my lust:
The grave's a fine and private place,
But none, I think, do there embrace.
Now therefore, while the youthful hue
Sits on thy skin like morning dew,
And while thy willing soul transpires
At every pore with instant fires,
Now let us sport us while we may,
And now, like amorous birds of prey,
Rather at once our time devour
Than languish in his slow-chapped power.
Let us roll all our strength and all
Our sweetness up into one ball,
And tear our pleasures with rough strife
Thorough the iron gates of life:
Thus, though we cannot make our sun
Stand still, yet we will make him run.

Gerda Mayer (b. 1927)

Narcissus (1980)

What he liked in her voice
was his name
called over & over
and the mirrorlike look
in the weeping eyes of his lover;
in the end, left her
on a chill mountain shelf,
in a damp cave
with her wits and her words astray,
to devote himself
to himself.

Then the gods with indolent yawns
took a high hand with him for
such eNOR
mous self-love
was considered by others a bore.

Changed to a flower
he stood by the river
a sad case
of rooted vanity;
he never forgave
the reflecting water
for rippling his face.

James Merrill (1926–1995)

The Victor Dog (1972)

For Elizabeth Bishop

Bix to Buxtehude to Boulez,
The little white dog on the Victor label
Listens long and hard as he is able.
It's all in a day's work, whatever plays.

From judgment, it would seem, he has refrained.
He even listens earnestly to Bloch,
Then builds a church upon our acid rock.
He's man's—no—he's the Leiermann's best friend,

Or would be if hearing and listening were the same.
Does he hear? I fancy he rather smells
Those lemon-gold arpeggios in Ravel's
"Les jets d'eau du palais de ceux qui s'aiment."

He ponders the Schumann Concerto's tall willow hit
By lightning, and stays put. When he surmises
Through one of Bach's external boxwood mazes
The oboe pungent as a bitch in heat,

Or when the calypso decants its raw bay rum
Or the moon in *Wozzeck* reddens ripe for murder,
He doesn't sneeze or howl; just listens harder.
Adamant needles bear down on him from

Whirling of outer space, too black, too near—
But he was taught as a puppy not to flinch,
Much less to imitate his bête noire Blanche
Who barked, fat foolish creature, at King Lear.

Still others fought in the road's filth over Jezebel,
Slavered on hearths of horned and pelted barons.
His forebears lacked, to say the least, forbearance.
Can nature change in him? Nothing's impossible.

The last chord fades. The night is cold and fine.
His master's voice rasps through the grooves' bare groves.
Obediently, in silence like the grave's
He sleeps there on the still-warm gramophone

Only to dream he is at the première of a Handel
Opera long thought lost—*Il Cane Minore.*
Its allegorical subject is his story!
A little dog revolving round a spindle

Gives rise to harmonies beyond belief,
A cast of stars . . . Is there in Victor's heart
No honey for the vanquished? Art is art.
The life it asks of us is a dog's life.

W. S. Merwin (b. 1927)

For the Anniversary of My Death (1967)

Every year without knowing it I have passed the day
When the last fires will wave to me
And the silence will set out
Tireless traveller
Like the beam of a lightless star

Then I will no longer
Find myself in life as in a strange garment
Surprised at the earth
And the love of one woman
And the shamelessness of men
As today writing after three days of rain
Hearing the wren sing and the falling cease
And bowing not knowing to what

John Milton (1608–1674)

[Of Man's first disobedience]

—from "Paradise Lost" (1667)

Of Man's first disobedience, and the fruit
Of that forbidden Tree, whose mortal taste
Brought death into the world, and all our woe,
With loss of Eden, till one greater Man
Restore us, and regain the blissful seat,
Sing, Heavenly Muse, that on the secret top
Of Oreb, or of Sinai, didst inspire
That shepherd, who first taught the chosen seed
In the beginning how the Heavens and Earth
Rose out of Chaos: or, if Sion hill
Delight thee more, and Siloa's brook that flowed
Fast by the oracle of God, I thence
Invoke thy aid to my adventurous song,
That with no middle flight intends to soar
Above the Aonian mount, while it pursues
Things unattempted yet in prose or rhyme.
And chiefly thou, O Spirit, that dost prefer
Before all temples the upright heart and pure,
Instruct me, for thou know'st; thou from the first
Wast present, and, with mighty wings outspread,
Dove-like sat'st brooding on the vast Abyss,
And mad'st it pregnant: what in me is dark
Illumine, what is low raise and support;
That to the highth of this great argument
I may assert Eternal Providence,
And justify the ways of God to men.

When I consider how my light is spent (1655?)

When I consider how my light is spent,
  Ere half my days, in this dark world and wide,
  And that one talent which is death to hide
  Lodged with me useless, though my soul more bent
To serve therewith my Maker, and present
  My true account, lest he returning chide;
  "Doth God exact day-labor, light denied?"
  I fondly ask; but Patience to prevent
That murmur, soon replies, "God doth not need
  Either man's work or his own gifts; who best
  Bear his mild yoke, they serve him best. His state
Is kingly. Thousands at his bidding speed
  And post o'er land and ocean without rest:
  They also serve who only stand and wait."

Wilfred Owen (1893–1918)

For a brief biography of Wilfred Owen, see chapter 19.

Anthem for Doomed Youth (1917)

What passing-bells for these who die as cattle?
  Only the monstrous anger of the guns.
  Only the stuttering rifles' rapid rattle
Can patter out their hasty orisons.
No mockeries now for them; no prayers nor bells,
  Nor any voice of mourning save the choirs,—
The shrill, demented choirs of wailing shells;
  And bugles calling for them from sad shires.
What candles may be held to speed them all?
  Not in the hands of boys, but in their eyes
Shall shine the holy glimmers of good-byes.
  The pallor of girls' brows shall be their pall;
Their flowers the tenderness of patient minds,
And each slow dusk a drawing-down of blinds.

Grace Paley (1922–2007)

Here (2001)

Here I am in the garden laughing
an old woman with heavy breasts
and a nicely mapped face

how did this happen
well that's who I wanted to be

at last   a woman
in the old style   sitting
stout thighs apart under
a big skirt   grandchild sliding
on   off my lap   a pleasant
summer perspiration

that's my old man across the yard
he's talking to the meter reader
he's telling him the world's sad story
how electricity is oil or uranium
and so forth   I tell my grandson
run over to your grandpa   ask him
to sit beside me for a minute   I
am suddenly exhausted by my desire
to kiss his sweet explaining lips

Linda Pastan (b. 1932)

For a brief biography of Linda Pastan, see chapter 21.

Ethics (1980)

In ethics class so many years ago
our teacher asked this question every fall:
if there were a fire in a museum
which would you save, a Rembrandt painting
or an old woman who hadn't many
years left anyhow? Restless on hard chairs
caring little for pictures or old age
we'd opt one year for life, the next for art
and always half-heartedly. Sometimes
the woman borrowed my grandmother's face
leaving her usual kitchen to wander
some drafty, half-imagined museum.
One year, feeling clever, I replied
why not let the woman decide herself?
Linda, the teacher would report, eschews
the burdens of responsibility.
This fall in a real museum I stand
before a real Rembrandt, old woman,
or nearly so, myself. The colors
within this frame are darker than autumn,
darker even than winter—the browns of earth,
though earth's most radiant elements burn
through the canvas. I know now that woman
and painting and season are almost one
and all beyond saving by children.

Molly Peacock (b. 1947)

Desire (1984)

It doesn't speak and it isn't schooled,
like a small foetal animal with wettened fur.
It is the blind instinct for life unruled,
visceral frankincense and animal myrrh.
It is what babies bring to kings,
an eyes-shut, ears-shut medicine of the heart
that smells and touches endings and beginnings
without the details of time's experienced *part-*
fit-into-part-fit-into-part. Like a paw,
it is blunt; like a pet who knows you
and nudges your knee with its snout—but more raw
and blinder and younger and more divine, too,
than the tamed wild—it's the drive for what is real,
deeper than the brain's detail: the drive to feel.

Sylvia Plath (1932–1963)

For a brief biography of Sylvia Plath, see chapter 19.

Mirror (1963)

I am silver and exact. I have no preconceptions.
Whatever I see I swallow immediately
Just as it is, unmisted by love or dislike.
I am not cruel, only truthful—
The eye of a little god, four-cornered.
Most of the time I meditate on the opposite wall.
It is pink, with speckles. I have looked at it so long
I think it is a part of my heart. But it flickers.
Faces and darkness separate us over and over.

Now I am a lake. A woman bends over me,
Searching my reaches for what she really is.
Then she turns to those liars, the candles or the moon.
I see her back, and reflect it faithfully.
She rewards me with tears and an agitation of hands.
I am important to her. She comes and goes.
Each morning it is her face that replaces the darkness.
In me she has drowned a young girl, and in me an old
  woman
Rises toward her day after day, like a terrible fish.

Edgar Allan Poe (1809–1849)

Annabel Lee (1849)

It was many and many a year ago,
  In a kingdom by the sea,
That a maiden there lived whom you may know
  By the name of Annabel Lee;
And this maiden she lived with no other thought
  Than to love and be loved by me.

She was a child and *I* was a child,
  In this kingdom by the sea,
But we loved with a love that was more than love—
  I and my Annabel Lee—
With a love that the wingéd seraphs of Heaven
  Coveted her and me.

And this was the reason that, long ago,
  In this kingdom by the sea,
A wind blew out of a cloud by night
  Chilling my Annabel Lee;
So that her highborn kinsmen came
  And bore her away from me,

To shut her up in a sepulchre
  In this kingdom by the sea.

The angels, not half so happy in Heaven,
  Went envying her and me:
Yes! that was the reason (as all men know,
  In this kingdom by the sea)
That the wind came out of the cloud, chilling
  And killing my Annabel Lee.

But our love it was stronger by far than the love
  Of those who were older than we—
  Of many far wiser than we—
And neither the angels in Heaven above
  Nor the demons down under the sea,
Can ever dissever my soul from the soul
  Of the beautiful Annabel Lee:

For the moon never beams without bringing me dreams
  Of the beautiful Annabel Lee;
And the stars never rise but I see the bright eyes
  Of the beautiful Annabel Lee;
And so, all the night-tide, I lie down by the side
Of my darling, my darling, my life and my bride,
  In her sepulchre there by the sea—
  In her tomb by the side of the sea.

Ezra Pound (1885–1972)

For a brief biography of Ezra Pound, see chapter 20.

The River-Merchant's Wife: A Letter (1915)

While my hair was still cut straight across my forehead
I played about the front gate, pulling flowers.
You came by on bamboo stilts, playing horse,
You walked about my seat, playing with blue plums.
And we went on living in the village of Chokan:
Two small people, without dislike or suspicion.

At fourteen I married My Lord you.
I never laughed, being bashful.
Lowering my head, I looked at the wall.
Called to, a thousand times, I never looked back.

At fifteen I stopped scowling,
I desired my dust to be mingled with yours
Forever and forever and forever.
Why should I climb the lookout?

At sixteen you departed,
You went into far Ku-tō-en, by the river of swirling eddies,
And you have been gone five months.
The monkeys make sorrowful noise overhead.

You dragged your feet when you went out.
By the gate now, the moss is grown, the different mosses,
Too deep to clear them away!
The leaves fall early this autumn, in wind.
The paired butterflies are already yellow with August
Over the grass in the West garden;
They hurt me. I grow older.
If you are coming down through the narrows of the river
  Kiang,
Please let me know beforehand,
And I will come out to meet you
As far as Chō-fū-Sa.

Sir Walter Raleigh (1552–1618)

The Nymph's Reply to the Shepherd (1600)

If all the world and love were young,
And truth in every shepherd's tongue,
These pretty pleasures might me move
To live with thee and be thy love.

Time drives the flocks from field to fold
When rivers rage and rocks grow cold,
And Philomel becometh dumb;
The rest complains of cares to come.

The flowers do fade, and wanton fields
To wayward winter reckoning yields;
A honey tongue, a heart of gall,
Is fancy's spring, but sorrow's fall.

The gowns, thy shoes, thy beds of roses,
Thy cap, thy kirtle, and thy posies
Soon break, soon wither, soon forgotten—
In folly ripe, in reason rotten.

Thy belt of straw and ivy buds,
Thy coral clasps and amber studs,
All these in me no means can move
To come to thee and be thy love.

But could youth last and love still breed,
Had joys no date nor age no need,
Then these delights my mind might move
To live with thee and be thy love.

Dudley Randall (1914–2000)

The Ballad of Birmingham (1969)

(On the bombing of a church in Birmingham, Alabama, 1963)

"Mother dear, may I go downtown
Instead of out to play,
And march the streets of Birmingham
In a Freedom March today?"

"No, baby, no, you may not go,
For the dogs are fierce and wild,
And clubs and hoses, guns and jails
Aren't good for a little child."

"But, mother, I won't be alone.
Other children will go with me,
And march the streets of Birmingham
To make our country free."

"No, baby, no, you may not go,
For I fear those guns will fire.
But you may go to church instead
And sing in the children's choir."

She has combed and brushed her night-dark hair,
And bathed rose petal sweet,
And drawn white gloves on her small brown hands,
And white shoes on her feet.

The mother smiled to know that her child
Was in the sacred place,
But that smile was the last smile
To come upon her face.

For when she heard the explosion,
Her eyes grew wet and wild.
She raced through the streets of Birmingham
Calling for her child.

She clawed through bits of glass and brick,
Then lifted out a shoe.
"O, here's the shoe my baby wore,
But, baby, where are you?"

Ishmael Reed (b. 1938)

beware: do not read this poem (1972)

tonite, *thriller* was
abt an ol woman, so vain she
surrounded herself w/
  many mirrors

It got so bad that finally she
locked herself indoors & her
whole life became the
  mirrors

one day the villagers broke
into her house, but she was too
swift for them. she disappeared
  into a mirror
each tenant who bought the house
after that, lost a loved one to
  the ol woman in the mirror:
  first a little girl
  then a young woman
  then the young woman/s husband

the hunger of this poem is legendary
it has taken in many victims
back off from this poem
it has drawn in yr feet
back off from this poem
it has drawn in yr legs
back off from this poem
it is a greedy mirror
you are into this poem. from
  the waist down
nobody can hear you can they?
this poem has had you up to here
    belch
this poem aint got no manners
you cant call out frm this poem
relax now & go w/ this poem
move & roll on to this poem

    do not resist this poem
    this poem has yr eyes
    this poem has his head
    this poem has his arms
    this poem has his fingers
    this poem has his fingertips

this poem is the reader & the
reader this poem

statistic: the US bureau of missing persons reports
that in 1968 over 100,000 people disappeared
leaving no solid clues
nor trace only
a space in the lives of their friends

Henry Reed (1914–1986)

Naming of Parts (1946)

Today we have naming of parts. Yesterday,
We had daily cleaning. And tomorrow morning,
We shall have what to do after firing. But today,
Today we have naming of parts. Japonica
Glistens like coral in all of the neighboring gardens,
And today we have naming of parts.

This is the lower sling swivel. And this
Is the upper sling swivel, whose use you will see,
When you are given your slings. And this is the piling swivel,
Which in your case you have not got. The branches
Hold in the gardens their silent, eloquent gestures,
Which in our case we have not got.

This is the safety-catch, which is always released
With an easy flick of the thumb. And please do not let me
See anyone using his finger. You can do it quite easy
If you have any strength in your thumb. The blossoms
Are fragile and motionless, never letting anyone see
Any of them using their finger.

And this you can see is the bolt. The purpose of this
Is to open the breech, as you see. We can slide it
Rapidly backwards and forwards: we call this
Easing the spring. And rapidly backwards and forwards
The early bees are assaulting and fumbling the flowers:
They call it easing the Spring.

They call it easing the Spring: it is perfectly easy
If you have any strength in your thumb: like the bolt,
And the breech, and the cocking-piece, and the point of balance,
Which in our case we have not got; and the almond-blossom
Silent in all of the gardens and the bees going backwards and forwards,
For today we have the naming of parts.

Adrienne Rich (b. 1929)

Aunt Jennifer's Tigers (1951)

Aunt Jennifer's tigers prance across a screen,
Bright topaz denizens of a world of green.
They do not fear the men beneath the tree;
They pace in sleek chivalric certainty.

Aunt Jennifer's fingers fluttering through her wool
Find even the ivory needle hard to pull.
The massive weight of Uncle's wedding band
Sits heavily upon Aunt Jennifer's hand.

When Aunt is dead, her terrified hands will lie
Still ringed with ordeals she was mastered by.
The tigers in the panel that she made
Will go on prancing, proud and unafraid.

Diving into the Wreck (1973)

First having read the book of myths,
and loaded the camera,
and checked the edge of the knife-blade,
I put on
the body-armor of black rubber
the absurd flippers
the grave and awkward mask.
I am having to do this
not like Cousteau with his
assiduous team
aboard the sun-flooded schooner
but here alone.

There is a ladder.
The ladder is always there
hanging innocently
close to the side of the schooner.
We know what it is for,
we who have used it.
Otherwise
it is a piece of maritime floss
some sundry equipment.

I go down.
Rung after rung and still
the oxygen immerses me
the blue light
the clear atoms
of our human air.

I go down.
My flippers cripple me,
I crawl like an insect down the ladder
and there is no one
to tell me when the ocean
will begin.

First the air is blue and then
it is bluer and then green and then
black I am blacking out and yet
my mask is powerful
it pumps my blood with power
thc sca is anothcr story
the sea is not a question of power
I have to learn alone
to turn my body without force
in the deep element.

And now: it is easy to forget
what I came for
among so many who have always
lived here
swaying their crenellated fans
between the reefs
and besides
you breathe differently down here.

I came to explore the wreck.
The words are purposes.
The words are maps.
I came to see the damage that was done
and the treasures that prevail.
I stroke the beam of my lamp
slowly along the flank
of something more permanent
than fish or weed

the thing I came for:
the wreck and not the story of the wreck
the thing itself and not the myth
the drowned face always staring
toward the sun
the evidence of damage
worn by salt and away into this threadbare beauty
the ribs of the disaster
curving their assertion
among the tentative haunters.

This is the place.
And I am here, the mermaid whose dark hair
streams black, the merman in his armored body.
We circle silently
about the wreck
we dive into the hold.
I am she: I am he

whose drowned face sleeps with open eyes
whose breasts still bear the stress
whose silver, copper, vermeil cargo lies
obscurely inside barrels
half-wedged and left to rot
we are the half-destroyed instruments
that once held to a course
the water-eaten log
the fouled compass

We are, I am, you are
by cowardice or courage
the one who find our way
back to this scene
carrying a knife, a camera
a book of myths
in which
our names do not appear.

Wendy Rose (b. 1948)

Leaving Port Authority for the St. Regis Rezz (1989)

I saw a mesa
between two buildings,
a row of tall
thin houses on top
bare like the desert I know,
the roofs occurring
in clumps like greasewood. O Wendy, he said,
looking at his fingernails,
that's Weehawken.

Well
one way or anothcr
we'll get some
where soon
for I have seen crow
dancing on the snow,
a hawk on Henry Street,
smoke plumes on the lips
of streetkids,
mesas
along the Hudson.
I am getting ready.

Christina Rossetti (1830–1894)

Echo (1862)

Come to me in the silence of the night;
Come in the speaking silence of a dream;
Come with soft rounded cheeks and eyes as bright
As sunlight on a stream;
Come back in tears,
O memory, hope, love of finished years.

O dream how sweet, too sweet, too bitter sweet,
Whose wakening should have been in Paradise,
Where souls brimful of love abide and meet;
Where thirsting longing eyes
Watch the slow door
That opening, letting in, lets out no more.

Yet come to me in dreams, that I may live
My very life again though cold in death:
Come back to me in dreams, that I may give
Pulse for pulse, breath for breath:
Speak low, lean low,
As long ago, my love, how long ago.

Carl Sandburg (1878–1967)

Fog (1916)

The fog comes
on little cat feet.

It sits looking
over harbor and city
on silent haunches
and then moves on.

Anne Sexton (1928–1974)

Letter Written on a Ferry while Crossing Long Island Sound (1961)

I am surprised to see
that the ocean is still going on.
Now I am going back
and I have ripped my hand
from your hand as I said I would
and I have made it this far
as I said I would
and I am on the top deck now
holding my wallet, my cigarettes
and my car keys
at 2 o'clock on a Tuesday
in August of 1960.

Dearest,
although everything has happened,
nothing has happened.
The sea is very old.
The sea is the face of Mary,
without miracles or rage
or unusual hope,
grown rough and wrinkled
with incurable age.

Still,
I have eyes.
These are my eyes:
the orange letters that spell
ORIENT on the life preserver
that hangs by my knees;
the cement lifeboat that wears
its dirty canvas coat;
the faded sign that sits on its shelf
saying KEEP OFF.
Oh, all right, I say,
I'll save myself.

Over my right shoulder
I see four nuns
who sit like a bridge club,
their faces poked out
from under their habits,
as good as good babies who
have sunk into their carriages.
Without discrimination
the wind pulls the skirts
of their arms.
Almost undressed,
I see what remains:
that holy wrist,
that ankle,
that chain.

Oh God,
although I am very sad,
could you please
let these four nuns
loosen from their leather boots
and their wooden chairs
to rise out

over this greasy deck,
out over this iron rail,
nodding their pink heads to one side,
flying four abreast
in the old-fashioned side stroke;
each mouth open and round,
breathing together
as fish do,
singing without sound.

Dearest,
see how my dark girls sally forth,
over the passing lighthouse of Plum Gut,
its shell as rusty
as a camp dish,
as fragile as a pagoda
on a stone;
out over the little lighthouse
that warns me of drowning winds
that rub over its blind bottom
and its blue cover;
winds that will take the toes
and the ears of the rider
or the lover.

There go my dark girls,
their dresses puff
in the leeward air.
Oh, they are lighter than flying dogs
or the breath of dolphins;
each mouth opens gratefully,
wider than a milk cup.
My dark girls sing for this.
They are going up.
See them rise
on black wings, drinking
the sky, without smiles
or hands
or shoes.
They call back to us
from the gauzy edge of paradise,
good news, good news.

William Shakespeare (1564–1616)

For a brief biography of William Shakespeare, see chapter 18.

Let me not to the marriage of true minds (1609)

Let me not to the marriage of true minds
Admit impediments; love is not love
Which alters when it alteration finds,
Or bends with the remover to remove:
O, no, it is an ever-fixèd mark,
That looks on tempests and is never shaken;
It is the star to every wand'ring bark,
Whose worth's unknown, although his highth be taken.
Love's not Time's fool, though rosy lips and cheeks
Within his bending sickle's compass come;
Love alters not with his brief hours and weeks,
But bears it out even to the edge of doom.
  If this be error and upon me proved,
  I never writ, nor no man ever loved.

Not marble, nor the gilded monuments (1609)

Not marble, nor the gilded monuments
Of princes, shall outlive this powerful rhyme;
But you shall shine more bright in these contents
Than unswept stone, besmeared with sluttish time.
When wasteful war shall statues overturn,
And broils root out the work of masonry,
Nor Mars his sword nor war's quick fire shall burn
The living record of your memory.
'Gainst death and all-oblivious enmity
Shall you pace forth; your praise shall still find room
Even in the eyes of all posterity
That wear this world out to the ending doom.
  So, till the judgment that yourself arise,
  You live in this, and dwell in lovers' eyes.

That time of the year thou mayest in me behold (1609)

That time of year thou mayest in me behold
When yellow leaves, or none, or few, do hang
Upon those boughs which shake against the cold,
Bare ruined choirs, where late the sweet birds sang.
In me thou seest the twilight of such day
As after sunset fadeth in the west;
Which by and by black night doth take away,
Death's second self that seals up all in rest.
In me thou seest the glowing of such fire
That on the ashes of his youth doth lie,
As the deathbed whereon it must expire,
Consumed with that which it was nourish'd by.
  This thou perceiv'st, which makes thy love more strong,
  To love that well, which thou must leave ere long.

Percy Bysshe Shelley (1792–1822)

Ozymandias (1818)

I met a traveller from an antique land
Who said: Two vast and trunkless legs of stone
Stand in the desert. . . Near them, on the sand,
Half sunk, a shattered visage lies, whose frown,
And wrinkled lip, and sneer of cold command,
Tell that its sculptor well those passions read
Which yet survive, stamped on these lifeless things,
The hand that mocked them, and the heart that fed:
And on the pedestal these words appear:
"My name is Ozymandias, king of kings:
Look on my works, ye Mighty, and despair!"
Nothing beside remains. Round the decay
Of that colossal wreck, boundless and bare
The lone and level sands stretch far away.

Jane Shore (b. 1947)

My Mother's Chair (2004)

Coming home late, I'd let myself in
with my key, tiptoe up the stairs,
and there she was, in the family room,
one lamp burning, reading her newspaper
in her velvet-and-chrome swivel chair

as though it were perfectly natural
to be wide awake at 2 A.M.,
feet propped on the matching
ottoman, her orthopedic shoes
underneath, two empty turtle shells.

Like a mummy equipped for the afterlife,
she'd have her ashtray and Kents handy,
her magnifying mirror,
and tweezers and eyeglass case,
her crossword puzzle dictionary.

Glancing up and down, she never
appeared to be frisking me, even when,
just seconds before, coming home
from a date, at the front door,
I'd stuck my tongue into a boy's mouth.

I'd sit on the sofa and bum her cigarettes,
and as the room filled up with smoke,
melding our opposite temperaments,
we'd talk into the night, like diplomats
agreeing to a kind of peace.

I'd feign indifference—so did she—
about what I was doing out so late.
When I became a mother myself,
my mother was still the sentry at the gate,
waiting up, guarding the bedrooms.

After her funeral, her chair sat empty.
My father, sister, husband, and I
couldn't bring ourselves to occupy it.
Only my daughter climbed up its base
and spun herself round and round.

In the two years my father lived alone
in the apartment over their store,
I wonder, did he ever once
sit down on that throne, hub
around which our family had revolved.

After my father died, the night
before I left the place for good,
the building sold, the papers signed,
before the moving vans drove away,
dividing the cartons and the furniture

between my sister's house and mine,
a thousand miles apart,
I sat on the sofa—my usual spot—
and stared at the blank TV, the empty chair;
then I rose, and walked across the room,

and sank into her ragged cushions,
put my feet up on her ottoman,
rested my elbows on the scuffed armrests,
stroked the brown velvet like fur.
The headrest still smelled like her!

Swiveling the chair to face the sofa,
I looked at things from her point of view:
What do you need it for?
So I left it behind, along with the blinds
the meat grinder, the pressure cooker.

Gary Soto (b. 1952)

Saturday at the Canal (1991)

I was hoping to be happy by seventeen.
School was a sharp check mark in the roll book,
An obnoxious tuba playing at noon because our team
Was going to win at night. The teachers were
Too close to dying to understand. The hallways

Stank of poor grades and unwashed hair. Thus,
A friend and I sat watching the water on Saturday,
Neither of us talking much, just warming ourselves
By hurling large rocks at the dusty ground
And feeling awful because San Francisco was a postcard
On a bedroom wall. We wanted to go there,
Hitchhike under the last migrating birds
And be with people who knew more than three chords
On a guitar. We didn't drink or smoke,
But our hair was shoulder length, wild when
The wind picked up and the shadows of
This loneliness gripped loose dirt. By bus or car,
By the sway of train over a long bridge,
We wanted to get out. The years froze
As we sat on the bank. Our eyes followed the water,
White-tipped but dark underneath, racing out of town.

Wallace Stevens (1879–1955)

For a brief biography of Wallace Stevens, see chapter 18.

Disillusionment of Ten O'Clock (1923)

The houses are haunted
By white night-gowns.
None are green,
Or purple with green rings,
Or green with yellow rings,
Or yellow with blue rings.
None of them are strange,
With socks of lace
And beaded ceintures.
People are not going
To dream of baboons and periwinkles.
Only, here and there, an old sailor,
Drunk and asleep in his boots,
Catches tigers
In red weather.

Thirteen Ways of Looking at a Blackbird (1917)

I

Among twenty snowy mountains,
The only moving thing
Was the eye of the blackbird.

II

I was of three minds,
Like a tree
In which there are three blackbirds.

III

The blackbirds whirled in the autumn winds.
It was a small part of the pantomime.

IV

A man and a woman
Are one.
A man and a woman and a blackbird
Are one.

V

I do not know which to prefer—
The beauty of inflections
Or the beauty of innuendoes,
The blackbird whistling
Or just after.

VI

Icicles filled the long window
With barbaric glass.
The shadow of the blackbird
Crossed it, to and fro.
The mood
Traced in the shadow
An indecipherable course.

VII

O thin men of Haddam,
Why do you imagine golden birds?
Do you not see how the blackbird
Walks around the feet
Of the women about you?

VIII

I know noble accents
And lucid, inescapable rhythms;
But I know, too,
That the blackbird is involved
In what I know.

IX

When the blackbird flew out of sight,
It marked the edge
Of one of many circles.

X

At the sight of blackbirds
Flying in a green light,
Even the bawds of euphony
Would cry out sharply.

XI

He rode over Connecticut
In a glass coach.
Once, a fear pierced him,
In that he mistook
The shadow of his equipage
For blackbirds.

XII

The river is moving.
The blackbird must be flying.

XIII

It was evening all afternoon.
It was snowing
And it was going to snow.
The blackbird sat
In the cedar-limbs.

Sir Philip Sydney (1554–1586)

To the Sad Moon (1591)

With how sad steps, O Moon, thou climb'st the skies!
How silently, and with how wan a face!
What! may it be that even in heavenly place
That busy archer his sharp arrows tries?
Sure, if that long-with-love-acquainted eyes
Can judge of love, thou feel'st a lover's case;
I read it in thy looks; thy languished grace
To me, that feel the like, thy state descries.
Then, even of fellowship, O Moon, tell me,
Is constant love deemed there but want of wit?
Are beauties there as proud as here they be?
Do they above love to be loved, and yet
Those lovers scorn whom that love doth possess?
Do they call virtue there ungratefulness?

Alfred, Lord Tennyson (1809–1892)

Ulysses (1842)

It little profits that an idle king,
By this still hearth, among these barren crags,
Matched with an aged wife, I mete and dole
Unequal laws unto a savage race,
That hoard, and sleep, and feed, and know not me.
I cannot rest from travel; I will drink
Life to the lees. All times I have enjoyed
Greatly, have suffered greatly, both with those
That loved me, and alone; on shore, and when
Through scudding drifts the rainy Hyades
Vexed the dim sea. I am become a name;
For always roaming with a hungry heart
Much have I seen and known—cities of men
And manners, climates, councils, governments,
Myself not least, but honored of them all,—
And drunk delight of battle with my peers,
Far on the ringing plains of windy Troy.
I am a part of all that I have met;
Yet all experience is an arch wherethrough
Gleams that untraveled world whose margin fades
Forever and forever when I move.
How dull it is to pause, to make an end,
To rust unburnished, not to shine in use!
As though to breathe were life! Life piled on life
Were all too little, and of one to me
Little remains; but every hour is saved
From that eternal silence, something more,
A bringer of new things; and vile it were
For some three suns to store and hoard myself,
And this gray spirit yearning in desire
To follow knowledge like a sinking star,
Beyond the utmost bound of human thought.
  This is my son, mine own Telemachus,
To whom I leave the scepter and the isle,
Well-loved of me, discerning to fulfill
This labor, by slow prudence to make mild
A rugged people, and through soft degrees
Subdue them to the useful and the good.
Most blameless is he, centered in the sphere
Of common duties, decent not to fail
In offices of tenderness, and pay
Meet adoration to my household gods,
When I am gone. He works his work, I mine.
  There lies the port; the vessel puffs her sail;
There gloom the dark, broad seas. My mariners,
Souls that have toiled, and wrought, and thought with me,
That ever with a frolic welcome took
The thunder and the sunshine, and opposed
Free hearts, free foreheads—you and I are old;
Old age hath yet his honor and his toil.
Death closes all; but something ere the end,
Some work of noble note, may yet be done,
Not unbecoming men that strove with gods.
The lights begin to twinkle from the rocks;
The long day wanes; the slow moon climbs; the deep
Moans round with many voices. Come, my friends,
'Tis not too late to seek a newer world.
Push off, and sitting well in order smite

The sounding furrows; for my purpose holds
To sail beyond the sunset, and the baths
Of all the western stars, until I die.
It may be that the gulfs will wash us down;
It may be we shall touch the Happy Isles,
And see the great Achilles, whom we knew.
Though much is taken, much abides; and though
We are not now that strength which in old days
Moved earth and heaven, that which we are, we are,
One equal temper of heroic hearts,
Made weak by time and fate, but strong in will
To strive, to seek, to find, and not to yield.

Anne Waldman (b. 1945)

Bluehawk (1991)

Monk's gone
blown
those keys
his
alone
unlock

a heart-mind

sway
swipe those tears away

Monk's gone
Monk's gone

(pause)
a minor chord
asymmetry
(accent on the "try")
push limits
all his own
&
music of the spheres
(song the gong)
gone
Monk's gone
old Buddha fingers gone
bluehawk

in the sky
soars high

Phyllis Wheatley (1753–1784)

On Being Brought from Africa to America (1773)

'Twas mercy brought me from my *Pagan* land,
Taught my benighted soul to understand
That there's a God, that there's a *Saviour* too:
Once I redemption neither sought nor knew.
Some view our sable race with scornful eye,
"Their colour is a diabolic die."
Remember, *Christians*, *Negros*, black as *Cain*,
May be refin'd, and join th' angelic train.

Richard Wilbur (b. 1921)

The Writer (1976)

In her room at the prow of the house
Where light breaks, and the windows are tossed with linden,
My daughter is writing a story.

I pause in the stairwell, hearing
From her shut door a commotion of typewriter-keys
Like a chain hauled over a gunwale.

Young as she is, the stuff
Of her life is a great cargo, and some of it heavy:
I wish her a lucky passage.

But now it is she who pauses,
As if to reject my thought and its easy figure.
A stillness greatens, in which

The whole house seems to be thinking,
And then she is at it again with a bunched clamor
Of strokes, and again is silent.

I remember the dazed starling
Which was trapped in that very room, two years ago;
How we stole in, lifted a sash

And retreated, not to affright it;
And how for a helpless hour, through the crack of the door,
We watched the sleek, wild, dark

And iridescent creature
Batter against the brilliance, drop like a glove
To the hard floor, or the desk-top,

And wait then, humped and bloody,
For the wits to try it again; and how our spirits
Rose when, suddenly sure,

It lifted off from a chair-back,
Beating a smooth course for the right window
And clearing the sill of the world.

It is always a matter, my darling,
Of life or death, as I had forgotten. I wish
What I wished you before, but harder.

William Carlos Williams (1883–1963)

For a brief biography of William Carlos Williams, see chapter 20.

Spring and All (1923)

By the road to the contagious hospital
under the surge of the blue
mottled clouds driven from the
northeast—a cold wind. Beyond, the
waste of broad, muddy fields
brown with dried weeds, standing and fallen

patches of standing water
the scattering of tall trees

All along the road the reddish
purplish, forked, upstanding, twiggy
stuff of bushes and small trees
with dead, brown leaves under them
leafless vines—

Lifeless in appearance, sluggish
dazed spring approaches—

They enter the new world naked,
cold, uncertain of all
save that they enter. All about them
the cold, familiar wind—

Now the grass, tomorrow
the stiff curl of wildcarrot leaf
One by one objects are defined—
It quickens: clarity, outline of leaf

But now the stark dignity of
entrance—Still, the profound change
has come upon them: rooted they
grip down and begin to awaken

William Wordsworth (1770–1850)

For a brief biography of William Wordsworth, see chapter 15.

London, 1802 (1802)

Milton! thou shouldst be living at this hour:
England hath need of thee: she is a fen
Of stagnant waters: altar, sword, and pen,
Fireside, the heroic wealth of hall and bower,
Have forfeited their ancient English dower
Of inward happiness. We are selfish men;
Oh! raise us up, return to us again;
And give us manners, virtue, freedom, power.
Thy soul was like a Star, and dwelt apart;
Thou hadst a voice whose sound was like the sea:
Pure as the naked heavens, majestic, free,
So didst thou travel on life's common way,
In cheerful godliness; and yet thy heart
The lowliest duties on herself did lay.

The World Is Too Much with Us (1807)

The world is too much with us; late and soon,
Getting and spending, we lay waste our powers;
Little we see in Nature that is ours;
We have given our hearts away, a sordid boon!
This Sea that bares her bosom to the moon,
The winds that will be howling at all hours,
And are up-gathered now like sleeping flowers,
For this, for everything, we are out of tune;
It moves us not.—Great God! I'd rather be
A Pagan suckled in a creed outworn;
So might I, standing on this pleasant lea,
Have glimpses that would make me less forlorn;
Have sight of Proteus rising from the sea;
Or hear old Triton blow his wreathéd horn.

The Solitary Reaper (1807)

Behold her, single in the field,
Yon solitary Highland Lass!
Reaping and singing by herself;
Stop here, or gently pass!
Alone she cuts and binds the grain,
And sings a melancholy strain;
O listen! for the Vale profound
Is overflowing with the sound.

No Nightingale did ever chaunt
More welcome notes to weary bands
Of travelers in some shady haunt,
Among Arabian sands;
A voice so thrilling ne'er was heard
In springtime from the Cuckoo bird,
Breaking the silence of the seas
Among the farthest Hebrides.

Will no one tell me what she sings?—
Perhaps the plaintive numbers flow
For old, unhappy, far-off things,
And battles long ago;
Or is it some more humble lay,
Familiar matter of today?
Some natural sorrow, loss, or pain,
That has been, and may be again?

Whate'er the theme, the Maiden sang
As if her song could have no ending;
I saw her singing at her work,
And o'er the sickle bending—
I listened, motionless and still;
And, as I mounted up the hill,
The music in my heart I bore,
Long after it was heard no more.

James Wright (1927–1980)

For a brief biography of James Wright, see chapter 18.

Lying in a Hammock at William Duffy's Farm in Pine Island, Minnesota (1963)

Over my head, I see the bronze butterfly,
Asleep on the black trunk,
Blowing like a leaf in green shadow.
Down the ravine behind the empty house,
The cowbells follow one another
Into the distances of the afternoon.
To my right,
In a field of sunlight between two pines,
The droppings of last year's horses
Blaze up into golden stones.
I lean back, as the evening darkens and comes on.
A chicken hawk floats over, looking for home.
I have wasted my life.

William Butler Yeats (1865–1939)

For a brief biography of William Butler Yeats, see chapter 15.

The Second Coming (1921)

Turning and turning in the widening gyre
The falcon cannot hear the falconer;
Things fall apart; the center cannot hold;
Mere anarchy is loosed upon the world,
The blood-dimmed tide is loosed, and everywhere
The ceremony of innocence is drowned;
The best lack all conviction, while the worst
Are full of passionate intensity.

Surely some revelation is at hand;
Surely the Second Coming is at hand:
The Second Coming! Hardly are those words out
When a vast image out of *Spiritus Mundi*
Troubles my sight: somewhere in sands of the desert
A shape with lion body and the head of a man,
A gaze blank and pitiless as the sun,
Is moving its slow thighs, while all about it
Reel shadows of the indignant desert birds.
The darkness drops again; but now I know
That twenty centuries of stony sleep
Were vexed to nightmare by a rocking cradle,
And what rough beast, its hour come round at last,
Slouches towards Bethlehem to be born?

When You Are Old (1893)

When you are old and grey and full of sleep,
And nodding by the fire, take down this book,
And slowly read, and dream of the soft look
Your eyes had once, and of their shadows deep;

How many loved your moments of glad grace,
And loved your beauty with love false or true,
But one man loved the pilgrim soul in you,
And loved the sorrows of your changing face;

And bending down beside the glowing bars,
Murmur, a little sadly, how Love fled
And paced upon the mountains overhead
And hid his face amid a crowd of stars.

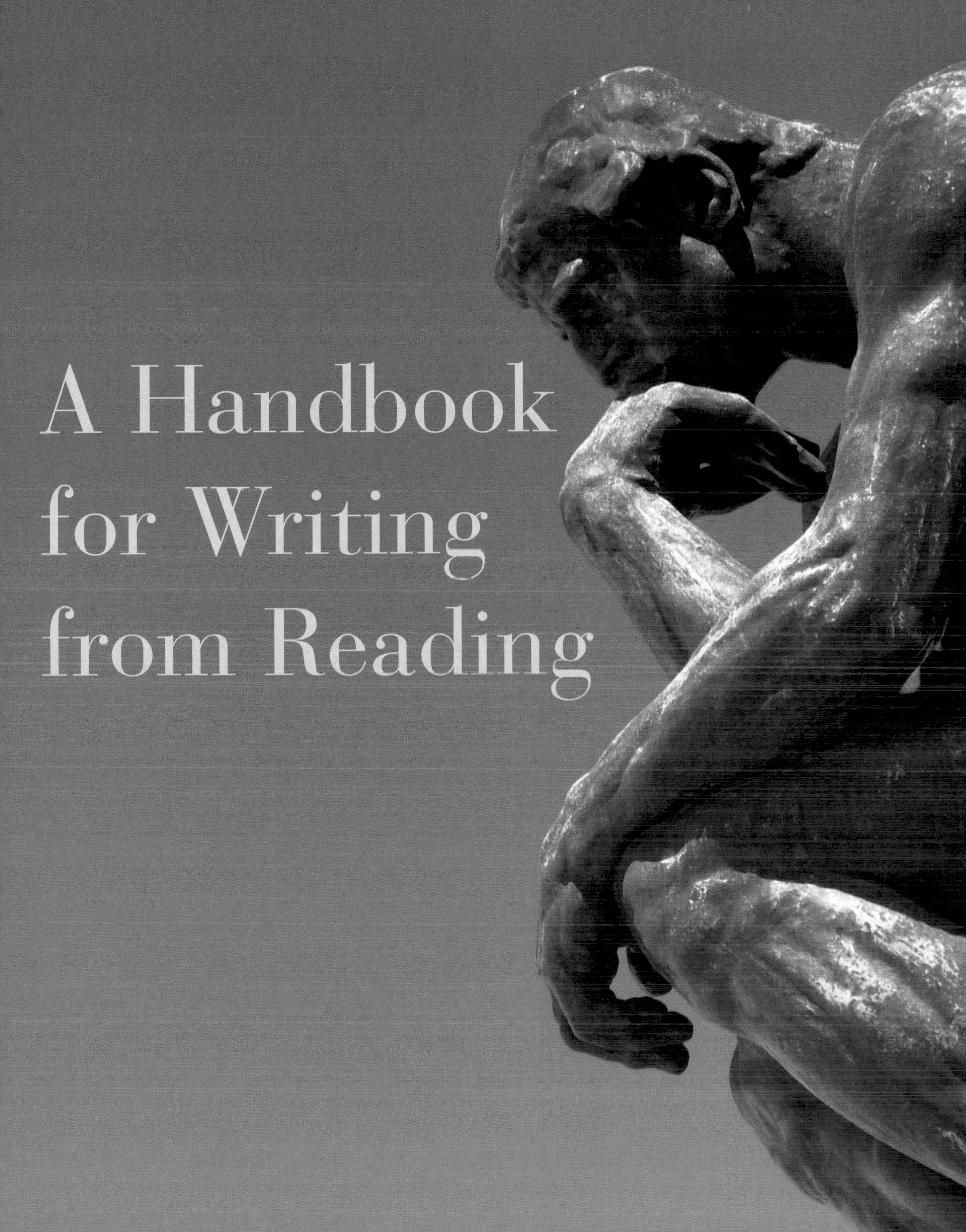
A Handbook
for Writing
from Reading

Handbook Contents

1 Critical Approaches to Literature

1a APPROACH CRITICISM AS AN ONGOING CONVERSATION

Literary theorist Kenneth Burke famously described literary criticism as an ongoing conversation, one that began before we arrived and will continue after we leave. If the thought of engaging in literary criticism intimidates you, think of it instead as adding your voice to those of others who have read the same work of literature and want to talk about it. You need not interpret the work as if you've been the first to read it, and you certainly don't have to feel as though you must deliver the final response. You need only contribute to the conversation.

Whenever we discuss literature, whether we acknowledge our appreciation or disdain for a text, interpret its meanings and mysteries, or cite it as an example of a larger trend in culture, we engage in an act of **literary criticism.** Such responsiveness is all around us and probably has its origins in the genesis of literature itself. The classical philosophers Plato and Aristotle laid the foundations for studying the creation, interpretation, and impact of the written and spoken word—in a sense, they began the conversation we now join.

1b USE A CRITICAL APPROACH AS A LENS FOR EXAMINATION

While these classical theories are still relevant, approaches to literature have changed with new developments in human thought. Literary critics and theorists are almost inevitably influenced by major shifts in philosophy, politics, history, science, technology, and economics. For example, the advent of Freud's theories of psychology opened up a way of examining literature by applying psychoanalytic concepts to characters and authors. Later in the century, the feminist movement led critics to apply ideas about gender roles to literary criticism. These borrowings from other fields are particularly influential for twentieth-century theory and criticism, as our discussion of the major approaches to criticism will show.

It may be helpful to think of each of the critical approaches described here as a *lens* through which a piece of literature can be examined. Any work can be looked at from several different points of view, but the lens itself cannot do the interpreting—a reader must do that. Still, the lens provides the reader with a set of guiding principles with which to limit all of the possible questions the reader might ask. For students engaging in literary criticism for the first time, these lenses can be enormously helpful because they narrow down the overwhelming array of possibilities, providing specific approaches to take and questions to ask. Studying and understanding the work of readers who have come before us can make the task of coming up with our own ideas less daunting.

1c CONSIDER MULTIPLE APPROACHES

Many of the critical schools described here initially defined themselves in opposition to the dominant theories of their times. It is important to keep in mind, though, that in current practice many critics are comfortable adopting methods from several critical approaches. For example, a reader who considers herself a Marxist critic may draw on historical and deconstructionist theories to help her analyze a work. Each approach described here has its own merits and shortcomings, proponents, and skeptics. These approaches are not necessarily mutually exclusive, and it is possible for critics to choose the most useful strategies from several approaches in their own writing. Though we will refer to "feminist critics" and "formalist critics" in the descriptions below, there are very few scholars who confine themselves solely to one theory without sometimes turning to other approaches.

What follows is an overview of different major critical methods.

Formalist Criticism

Formalist criticism emerged in Russia in the early twentieth century in the work of critics like Boris Eikhenbaum, Viktor Shklovsky, and Mikhail Bakhtin. Their ideas were adopted and further developed in the United States and Great Britain under the heading of **new criticism** by critics such as John Crowe Ransom, Allen Tate, Robert Penn Warren, I. A. Richards, William Wimsatt, T. S. Eliot, and Cleanth Brooks.

Formalists/new critics consider a successful text to be a complete, independent, unified artifact whose meaning and value can be understood purely by analyzing the interaction of its formal and technical components, such as plot, imagery, structure, style, symbol, and tone. Rather than drawing their textual interpretations from *extrinsic* factors such as the historical, political, or biographical context of the work, formalist critics focus on the text's *intrinsic* formal elements. As Cleanth Brooks explains in his article, "The Formalist Critic," published in 1951 in the *Kenyon Review,*

> *. . . the formalist critic is concerned primarily with the work itself. Speculation on the mental processes of the author takes the critic away from the work into biography and psychology. There is no reason, of course, why he should not turn away into biography and psychology. Such explorations are very much worth making. But they should not be confused with an account of the work.*

Formalist criticism relies heavily on **close reading** or explication of the text in order to analyze the ways in which distinct formal elements combine to create a unified artistic experience for the reader. A major tenet of formalism is the notion that form and content are so intertwined that in a successful work of art they cannot be dissevered or separated out.

For formalist or new critics the study and interpretation of literature is an intrinsically valuable intellectual activity rather than a means to advance moral, religious, or political ideologies. There are those who consider this approach to be a limited one—they have argued that formalism can be elitist, willfully dismissive of historical and biographical factors in the work. *All* study of literature has to include at least a component of close reading; the question other critics raise is whether it suffices as a way to approach a text.

Boris Eikhenbaum (1886–1959)

The Theory of the Formal Method (1926)

The organization of the Formal method was governed by the principle that the study of literature should be made specific and concrete. All efforts were directed toward terminating the earlier state of affairs, in which literature, as A. Veselovskij observed, was *res nullius.*[1] That was what made the Formalists so intolerant of other "methods" and of eclectics. In rejecting these "other" methods, the Formalists actually were rejecting (and still reject) not methods but the gratuitous mixing of different scientific disciplines and different scientific problems. Their basic point was, and still is, that the object of literary science, as literary science, ought to be the investigation of the specific properties of literary material, of the properties that distinguish such material from material of any other kind, notwithstanding the fact that its secondary and oblique features make that material properly and legitimately exploitable, as auxiliary material, by other disciplines. The point was consummately formulated by Roman Jakobson:

> The object of study in literary science is not literature but "literariness," that is, what makes a given work a *literary* work. Meanwhile, the situation has been that historians of literature act like nothing so much as policemen, who, out to arrest a certain culprit, take into custody (just in case) everything and everyone they find at the scene as well as any passers-by for good measure. The historians of literature have helped themselves to everything—environment, psychology, politics, philosophy. Instead of a science of literature, they have worked up a concoction of home-made disciplines. They seem to have forgotten that those subjects pertain to their own fields of study—to the history of philosophy, the history of culture, psychology, and so on, and that those fields of study certainly may utilize literary monuments as documents of a defective and second-class variety among other materials.

To establish this principle of specificity without resorting to speculative aesthetics required the juxtaposing of the literary order of facts with another such order. For this purpose one order had to be selected from among existent orders, which, while contiguous with the literary order, would contrast with it in terms of functions. It was just such a methodological procedure that produced the opposition between "poetic" language and "practical" language. This opposition [. . .] served as the activating principle for the Formalists' treatment of the fundamental problems of poetics. Thus, instead of an orientation toward a

[1] A legal term describing something that has no ownership.

> history of culture or of social life, towards psychology, or aesthetics, and so on, as had been customary for literary scholars, the Formalists came up with their own characteristic orientation toward linguistics, a discipline contiguous with poetics in regard to the material under investigation, but one approaching that material from a different angle and with different kinds of problems to solve.
>
> from *The Theory of the Formal Method*

Biographical Criticism

Biographical criticism emphasizes the belief that literature is created by authors whose unique experiences shape their writing and therefore can inform our reading of their work. Biographical critics research and use an author's biography to interpret the text as well as the author's stated *intentions* or comments on the process of composition itself. These critics often consult the author's memoirs to uncover connections between the author's life and the author's work. They may also study the author's rough drafts to trace the evolution of a given text or examine the author's library to discern potential influences on the author's work.

Knowledge of an author's biography can surely help readers interpret or understand a text. For example, awareness of Flannery O'Connor's devout Catholicism will make the religious elements of her stories and novels more meaningful to readers. However, as we have just seen, formalist critics reject biographical criticism, arguing that any essential meaning in a text should be discernable to readers purely through close reading. They reject the notion that an author's thought processes and stated *intentions* for a text necessarily define the work's meaning. They call this emphasis on discerning or trusting an author's own stated purpose the **intentional fallacy** and believe a text's meaning must be contained in and communicated only by the text as such.

While biographical criticism was once quite common, in recent decades it is more often used as *part* of a larger critical approach than as the primary critical strategy.

Gary Lee Stonum (b. 1947)

Dickinson's Literary Background (1998)

> Books and reading were [Emily] Dickinson's primary access to a world beyond Amherst. We can thus at least be reasonably confident that the cultural contexts of Dickinson's writing are primarily literary, particularly if that term is defined inclusively. Her surviving letters are filled with references to favorite authors, and some of the poems allude in one way or another to recognizable elements of her reading (Pollak, "Allusions"). To be sure, she is by no means a learned poet in the vein of Milton or Pope, writers who can hardly be appreciated without understanding their allusions and allegiances. Yet she is also surely not the unlettered author Richard Chase once unguardedly deemed her, uninfluenced by literary sources in either style or thought.
>
> A few cautions need to be kept in mind as we examine various claims about Dickinson's literary milieu. First, we know very little about how or even whether Dickinson imagined her work as participating in any public enterprise. By con-

trast to Keats, who dreamed of being among the English poets after his death, or a James Joyce, who schemed tirelessly to shape his own reputation, Dickinson hardly trafficked in any cultural arena. We do possess information about the books she read or admired, and we know from the persistent testimony of her letters and poems that she regarded poetry as an exalted calling. Yet, although we can reasonably infer from this a certain broad ambition, we simply do not know if Dickinson regarded her vocation as entailing some sense of a role in literary history or as obliging her to bargain in the cultural marketplace. We do not, for example, know whether or in what respect she regarded herself as a woman poet, in spite of a number of lively arguments supposing that she did.

[. . .] At the writerly end of the spectrum lie the sources Dickinson drew upon or referred to as she wrote, which are of varying importance. Dickinson's regard for Elizabeth Barrett Browning makes it likely that her "Vision of Poets" is a source of "I died for Beauty," as well as or even rather than Keats's now more famous "Ode on a Grecian Urn." On the other hand, the identification is by no means crucial to an understanding of the poem.

The more interesting cases are those in which the source is disputed and identification would make some difference to our reading. Dickinson was notably fond of exotic place-names, most of which she must have come upon in her reading and some of which may carry thematic associations. The reference to "Chimborazo" in "Love—thou are high" may well derive incidentally from Edward Hitchcock's *Elementary Geology,* where it stands among a list of the world's tallest mountains, or it may originate from similarly casual uses in Barrett Browning and Emerson. On the other hand, if we heed Judith Farr's investigations into the influence of contemporary painting, then we might recall that Frederic Church's mammoth painting of Chimborazo was one of the most celebrated luminist canvases of the day. If the poem is read in the latter context, then the "Love" addressed by the poem as like the mountain would function more insistently as a figure of sublime theophany. (The poem also clearly alludes to Exodus 33, the chief biblical commonplace for such an event.)

[. . .] Many of the references in Dickinson's writings are discussed in Jack Capps's indispensable *Emily Dickinson's Reading,* which includes a detailed index of the books and authors she mentions in poems or letters. Capps also surveys the contents of the family library, much of which is now at Harvard. Unfortunately, the usefulness of the library "is limited by the fact that books from the Austin Dickinson and Edward Dickinson household have been mixed and, in most cases, dates of acquisition and individual ownership are uncertain." Likewise, although these volumes include inscriptions, marginalia, and other evidence of use, few of the markings can be confidently traced to the poet herself.

from *Dickinson's Literary Background*

Historical Criticism

Historical criticism emphasizes the relationship between a text and its historical context. When interpreting a text, historical critics highlight the cultural, philosophical, and political movements and ideologies prevalent during the text's creation and reception. Such critics may also use literary texts as a means of studying or promoting a particular movement in history—cultural , political, or otherwise.

Historical critics do extensive research to uncover the social and intellectual trends that influenced the life and work of the author and his or her original audience. This research brings to light allusions, concepts, and vocabulary or word usage that would have been easily understood by the author or the original audience but may elude contemporary readers. Historical critics also study the ways in which the meanings of a given text change over time, looking, for example, at the ways in which Victorians staged or responded to Shakespeare's *A Midsummer Night's Dream*.

One frequent objection to historical criticism is that these methods can reveal more about the context surrounding a text than about the meaning or value of the text itself. Another objection is that historical criticism sometimes views literature simply as an expression of the historical trends of a given era, rather than viewing texts as autonomous, idiosyncratic expressions of a particular author's views. Historical criticism, some argue, oversimplifies the relationship between a text and the prevailing or dominant cultural context, overlooking the possibility that the text may have a subversive, distorted, distanced, or anachronistic relationship to the dominant culture of the author's time.

Carl Van Doren (1885–1950)

Mark Twain (1921)

Of the major American novelists Mark Twain derived least from any literary, or at any rate from any bookish, tradition. Hawthorne had the example of Irving, and Cooper had that of Scott, when they began to write; Howells and Henry James instinctively fell into step with the classics. Mark Twain came up into literature from the popular ranks, trained in the school of newspaper fun-making and humorous lecturing, only gradually instructed in the more orthodox arts of the literary profession. He seems to most eyes, however, less indebted to predecessors than he actually was, for the reason that his provenance has faded out with the passage of time and the increase of his particular fame. Yet he had predecessors and a provenance. As a printer he learned the mechanical technique of his trade of letters; as a jocose writer for the newspapers of the Middle West and the Far West at a period when a well established mode of burlesque and caricature and dialect prevailed there, he adapted himself to a definite convention; as a raconteur he not only tried his methods on the most diverse auditors but consciously studied those of Artemus Ward, then the American master of the craft; Bret Harte, according to Mark Twain, "trimmed and trained and schooled me"; and thereafter, when the "Wild Humorist of the Pacific Slope," as it did not at first seem violent to call him, came into contact with professed men of letters, especially Howells, he had already a mastership of his own, though in a second rank.

To be a "humorist" in the United States of the sixties and seventies was to belong to an understood and accepted class. It meant, as Orpheus C. Kerr and John Phœnix and Josh Billings and Petroleum V. Nasby and Artemus Ward had recently and typically been showing, to make fun as fantastically as one liked but never to rise to beauty; to be intensely shrewd but never profound; to touch pathos at intervals but never tragedy. The humorist assumed a name not his own, as Mark Twain did, and also generally a character—that of some rustic sage or adventurous eccentric who discussed the topics of the moment keenly and drolly. Under his assumed character, of which he ordinarily made fun, he claimed a wide license of speech, which did not, however, extend to indecency or to any very serious satire. His fun was the ebullience of a strenuous society, the laughter of escape from difficult conditions. It was rooted fast in that optimism

> which Americans have had the habit of considering a moral obligation. It loved to ridicule those things which to the general public seemed obstacles to the victorious progress of an average democracy; it laughed about equally at idlers and idealists, at fools and poets, at unsuccessful sinners and unsuccessful saints. It could take this attitude toward minorities because it was so confident of having the great American majority at its back, hearty, kindly, fair-intentioned, but self-satisfied and unspeculative. In time Mark Twain partly outgrew this type of fun—or rather, had frequent intervals of a different type and also of a fierce seriousness—but the origins of his art lie there. So do the origins of his ideas lie among the populace, much as he eventually outgrew the evangelical orthodoxy and national complacency and personal hopefulness with which he had first been burdened.
>
> from *The American Novel*

Psychological or Psychoanalytic Criticism

Psychoanalytic criticism originally stemmed, like psychoanalysis itself, from the work of Sigmund Freud. That revolutionary thinker sought to analyze the conscious and subconscious mental workings of his patients by listening to them discuss their dreams, their erotic urges, and their childhoods. Psychoanalytical critics in a sense study characters and authors as they would patients, looking in the text for evidence of childhood trauma, repressed sexual impulses, preoccupation with death, and so on. Through the lens of psychology they attempt to explain the motivations and meanings behind characters' actions. Such critics have, for example, noted Hamlet's Oedipus complex, his desire to kill his (step)father and possess his mother.

At the same time, psychological critics use textual and biographical evidence as a means to better understand the *author's* psychology. They may attribute the somber tone of a group of poems to the poet's contemporaneous loss of a spouse, or may look for patterns in several texts to identify an author's subconscious preoccupations, fears, or motivations. Psychological critics have, for example, attributed sexist tendencies to Hemingway by arguing that women rarely play major roles in his fiction and are often manipulative or emasculating when they do. Others disagree, noting that Hemingway's female characters, while not dominant, frequently offer the story's wisest, most lucid perspectives through what are often the story's most memorable lines of dialogue. To relate these issues to Hemingway's conflicted love for his mother is to consider the work in psychological as well as biographical terms.

Finally, psychoanalytical critics also examine the process and nature of literary creation, studying the ways in which texts create an emotional and intellectual effect for readers and authors. Here too the strategy is most effective when inclusive as opposed to exclusive; this is a useful tool for reading when it's not the *only* approach to a text.

Kenneth Burke (1897–1993)

The Poetic Process (1925)

> If we wish to indicate a gradual rise to a crisis, and speak of this as a climax, or a crescendo, we are talking in intellectualistic terms of a mechanism which can often be highly emotive. There is in reality no such general thing as a crescendo. What does exist is a multiplicity of individual artworks each of which

may be arranged as a whole, or in some parts, in a manner which we distinguish as climactic. And there is also in the human brain the potentiality for reacting favorably to such a climactic arrangement. Over and over again in the history of art, different material has been arranged to embody the principle of the crescendo; and this must be so because we "think" in a crescendo, because it parallels certain psychic and physical processes which are at the roots of our experience. The accelerated motion of a falling body, the cycle of a storm, the procedure of the sexual act, the ripening of crops—growth here is not merely a linear progression, but a fruition. Indeed, natural processes are, inevitably, "formally" correct, and by merely recording the symptoms of some physical development we can obtain an artistic development. Thomas Mann's work has many such natural forms converted into art forms, as, in *Death in Venice,* his charting of a sunrise and of the progressive stages in a cholera epidemic. And surely, we may say without much fear of startling anyone, that the work of art utilizes climactic arrangement because the human brain has a pronounced potentiality for being arrested, or entertained, by such an arrangement.

[. . .] Whereupon, returning to the Poetic Process, let us suppose that while a person is sleeping some disorder of the digestion takes place, and he is physically depressed. Such depression in the sleeper immediately calls forth a corresponding psychic depression, while this psychic depression in turn translates itself into the invention of details which will more or less adequately symbolize this depression. If the sleeper has had some set of experiences strongly marked by the feeling of depression, his mind may summon details from this experience to symbolize his depression. If he fears financial ruin, his depression may very reasonably seize upon the cluster of facts associated with this fear in which to individuate itself. On the other hand, if there is no strong set of associations in his mind clustered about the mood of depression, he may invent details which, on waking, seem inadequate to the mood. This fact accounts for the incommunicable wonder of a dream, as when at times we look back on the dream and are mystified at the seemingly unwarranted emotional responses which the details "aroused" in us. Trying to convey to others the emotional overtones of this dream, we laboriously recite the details, and are compelled at every turn to put in such confessions of defeat as "There was something strange about the room," or "For some reason or other I was afraid of this boat, although there doesn't seem to be any good reason now." But the details were not the cause of the emotion; the emotion, rather, dictated the selection of the details. Especially when the emotion was one of marvel or mystery, the invented details seem inadequate—the dream becoming, from the standpoint of communication, a flat failure, since the emotion failed to individuate itself into adequate symbols. And the sleeper himself, approaching his dream from the side of consciousness after the mood is gone, feels how inadequate are the details for conveying the emotion that caused them, and is aware that even for him the wonder of the dream exists only in so far as he still remembers the quality pervading it. Similarly, a dreamer may awaken himself with his own hilarious laughter, and be forthwith humbled as he recalls the witty saying of his dream. For the delight in the witty saying came first (was causally prior) and the witty saying itself was merely the externalization, or individuation, of this delight. Of a similar nature are the reminiscences of old men, who recite the facts of their childhood, not to force upon us the trivialities and minutiae of these experiences, but in the forlorn hope of conveying to us the "overtones" of their childhood, overtones which, unfortunately, are beyond reach of the details which they see in such an incommunicable light, looking back as they do upon a past which is at once themselves and another.

The analogy between these instances and the procedure of the poet is apparent. In this way the poet's moods dictate the selection of details and thus individuate themselves into one specific work of art.

from *The Poetic Process*

Archetypal, Mythic, or Mythological Criticism

Archetypal or **mythological criticism** focuses on the patterns or features that recur through much of literature, regardless of its time period or cultural origins. The archetypal approach to criticism stems from the work of Carl Jung, a Swiss psychoanalyst (and contemporary of Freud) who argued that humans share in a **collective unconscious,** or a set of characters, plots, symbols, and images that each evoke a universal response. Jung calls these recurring elements **archetypes** and likens them to *instincts*—knowledge or associations with which humans are born. Some examples of archetypes are the quest story, the story of rebirth, or the initiation story; others are the good mother, the evil stepmother, the wise old man, the notion that a desert symbolizes emptiness or hopelessness, or that a garden symbolizes fertility or paradise.

Archetypal or mythological critics analyze the ways in which such archetypes function in literature and attempt to explain the power that literature has over us or the reasons why certain texts continue to hold power over audiences many centuries after their creation.

Northrop Frye (1912–1991)

The Archetypes of Literature (1951)

We say that every poet has his own peculiar formation of images. But when so many poets use so many of the same images, surely there are much bigger critical problems involved than biographical ones. As Mr. Auden's brilliant essay *The Enchafèd Flood* shows, an important symbol like the sea cannot remain within the poetry of Shelley or Keats or Coleridge: it is bound to expand over many poets into an archetypal symbol of literature. And if the genre has a historical origin, why does the genre of drama emerge from medieval religion in a way so strikingly similar to the way it emerged from Greek religion centuries before? This is a problem of structure rather than origin, and suggests that there may be archetypes of genres as well as of images.

It is clear that criticism cannot be systematic unless there is a quality in literature which enables it to be so, an order of words corresponding to the order of nature in the natural sciences. An archetype should be not only a unifying category of criticism, but itself a part of a total form, and it leads us at once to the question of what sort of total form criticism can see in literature. [. . .] the search for archetypes is a kind of literary anthropology, concerned with the way that literature is informed by pre-literary categories such as ritual, myth and folk tale. We next realize that the relation between these categories and literature is by no means purely one of descent, as we find them reappearing in the greatest classics—in fact there seems to be a general tendency on the part of great classics to revert to them.

[. . .] In the solar cycle of the day, the seasonal cycle of the year, and the organic cycle of human life, there is a single pattern of significance, out of

> which myth constructs a central narrative around a figure who is partly the sun, partly vegetative fertility and partly a god or archetypal human being. [. . .] I supply the following table of its phases:
>
> 1. The dawn, spring and birth phase. Myths of the birth of the hero, of revival and resurrection, of creation and (because the four phases are a cycle) of the defeat of the powers of darkness, winter and death. Subordinate characters: the father and the mother. The archetype of romance and of most dithyrambic and rhapsodic poetry.
> 2. The zenith, summer, and marriage or triumph phase. Myths of apotheosis, of the sacred marriage, and of entering into Paradise. Subordinate characters: the companion and the bride. The archetype of comedy, pastoral and idyll.
> 3. The sunset, autumn and death phase. Myths of fall, of the dying god, of violent death and sacrifice and of the isolation of the hero. Subordinate characters: the traitor and that siren. The archetype of tragedy and elegy.
> 4. The darkness, winter and dissolution phase. Myths of the triumph of these powers; myths of floods and the return of chaos, of the defeat of the hero[. . .] Subordinate characters: the ogre and the witch. The archetype of satire (see, for instance, the conclusion of *The Dunciad*).
>
> from *The Archetypes of Literature*

Marxist Criticism

Marxist criticism is one of the most significant types of **sociological criticism.** Sociological criticism is the study of literary texts as products of the cultural, political, and economic context of the author's time and place. Critics using this approach examine practical factors such as the ways in which economics and politics influence the publishing and distribution of texts, shaping the audience's reception of a text and therefore its potential to influence society. Such factors, of course, may also affect the author's motives or options while writing the text. Sociological critics also identify and analyze the sociological content of literature, or the ways in which authors or audiences may use texts directly or indirectly to promote or critique certain sociological views or values.

Marxist or **economic determinist criticism** is based on the writings of Karl Marx, who argued that economic concerns shape lives more than anything else, and that society is essentially a struggle between the working classes and the dominant capitalist classes. Rather than assuming that culture evolves naturally or autonomously out of individual human experience, Marxist critics maintain that culture—including literature—is shaped by the interests of the dominant or most powerful social class.

Although Marxist critics do not ignore the artistic construction of a literary text, they tend to focus more on the ideological and sociological content of literary texts—such as the ways in which a character's poverty or powerlessness limits his or her choice of actions in a story, making his or her efforts futile or doomed to failure. These critics use literary analysis to raise awareness about the complex and powerful relationship between class and culture. At the same time, some Marxist critics also promote literature or interpretations of literature that can *change* the balance of power between social classes, often by subverting the values of the dominant class, or by inspiring the working classes to heroic or communal rebellion. As Marx wrote, "The philosophers have only *interpreted* the world in various ways; the point is to *change* it."

Leon Trotsky (1879–1940)

Literature and Revolution (1924)

The form of art is, to a certain and very large degree, independent, but the artist who creates this form, and the spectator who is enjoying it are not empty machines, one for creating form and the other for appreciating it. They are living people, with a crystallized psychology representing a certain unity, even if not entirely harmonious. This psychology is the result of social conditions. The creation and perception of art forms is one of the functions of this psychology. And no matter how wise the Formalists try to be, their whole conception is simply based upon the fact that they ignore the psychological unity of the social man, who creates and who consumes what has been created.

The proletariat has to have in art the expression of the new spiritual point of view which is just beginning to be formulated within him, and to which art must help him give form. This is not a state order, but an historic demand. Its strength lies in the objectivity of historic necessity. You cannot pass this by, nor escape its force. [. . .] It is unquestionably true that the need for art is not created by economic conditions. But neither is the need for food created by economics. On the contrary, the need for food and warmth creates economics. It is very true that one cannot always go by the principles of Marxism in deciding whether to reject or to accept a work of art. A work of art should, in the first place, be judged by its own law, that is, by the law of art. But Marxism alone can explain why and how a given tendency in art has originated in a given period of history; in other words, who it was who made a demand for such an artistic form and not for another, and why.

It would be childish to think that every class can entirely and fully create its own art from within itself, and, particularly, that the proletariat is capable of creating a new art by means of closed art guilds or circles, or by the Organization for Proletarian Culture, etc. Generally speaking, the artistic work of man is continuous. Each new rising class places itself on the shoulders of its preceding one. But this continuity is dialectic, that is, it finds itself by means of internal repulsions and breaks. New artistic needs or demands for new literary and artistic points of view are stimulated by economics, through the development of a new class, and minor stimuli are supplied by changes in the position of the class, under the influence of the growth of its wealth and cultural power. Artistic creation is always a complicated turning inside out of old forms, under the influence of new stimuli which originate outside of art. In this sense of the word, art is a handmaiden. It is not a disembodied element feeding on itself, but a function of social man indissolubly tied to his life and environment.

from *Literature and Revolution*

Structuralist Criticism

Structuralism emerged in France in the 1950s, largely in the work of scholars like Claude Levi-Strauss and Roland Barthes. They were indebted in part to the earlier work of the Swiss linguist Ferdinand de Saussure, who emphasized that the meanings of words or signs are shaped by the overarching structure of the language or system to which they belong. Similarly, structuralist literary critics work from the belief that a given work of literature can be fully understood only when a reader considers the system of conventions, or the *genre* to which it belongs or responds.

Structuralist critics therefore define and study systematic patterns or structures exhibited by many texts in a given genre. A classic example of this type of study is Vladimir Propp's *Morphology of the Folktale*, in which the critic identifies several key patterns in the plots of folk tales (the hero leaves home, the hero is tested, the hero gains use of a magic agent, etc.). Structuralists thus study the relationship between a given literary text and the larger system of meanings and expectations in the genre or culture from which that text emerges. They also look to literature to study the ways in which meaning is created across culture by means of a system of signs—for example, the pattern of associations that has developed around the images of light (purity, good) and darkness (evil, somber). Here the study of **semiotics** is germane; the way a thing looks to the individual reader or how and what a word *signifies* can change our understanding of a text.

The structuralist approach has been used more frequently and successfully in the study of fiction than poetry. Because of its emphasis on the commonalities within a genre, the structuralist approach has also been helpful to critics attempting to compare works from different time periods or cultures.

Vladimir Propp (1895–1970)

Fairy Tale Transformations (1928)

The study of the fairy tale may be compared in many respects to that of organic formation in nature. Both the naturalist and the folklorist deal with species and varieties which are essentially the same. The Darwinian problem of the origin of species arises in folklore as well. The similarity of phenomena both in nature and in our field resists any direct explanation which would be both objective and convincing. It is a problem in its own right. Both fields allow two possible points of view: either the internal similarity of two externally dissimilar phenomena does not derive from a common genetic root—the theory of spontaneous generation—or else this morphological similarity does indeed result from a known genetic tie—the theory of differentiation owing to subsequent metamorphoses or transformations of varying cause and occurrence.

In order to resolve this problem, we need a clear understanding of what is meant by similarity in fairy tales. Similarity has so far been invariably defined in terms of a plot and its variants. We find such an approach acceptable only if based upon the idea of the spontaneous generation of species. Adherents to this method do not compare plots; they feel such comparison to be impossible or, at the very least, erroneous. Without our denying the value of studying individual plots and comparing them solely from the standpoint of their similarity, another method, another basis for comparison may be proposed. Fairy tales can be compared from the standpoint of their composition or structure; their similarity then appears in a new light.

We observe that the actors in the fairy tale perform essentially the same actions as the tale progresses, no matter how different from one another in shape, size, sex, and occupation, in nomenclature and other static attributes.

> This determines the relationship of the constant factors to the variables. The functions of the actors are constant; everything else is a variable. For example:
>
> 1. The king sends Ivan after the princess; Ivan departs.
> 2. The king sends Ivan after some marvel; Ivan departs.
> 3. The sister sends her brother for medicine; he departs.
> 4. The stepmother sends her stepdaughter for fire; she departs.
> 5. The smith sends his apprentice for a cow; he departs.
>
> The dispatch and departure on a quest are constants. The dispatching and departing actors, the motivations behind the dispatch, and so forth, are variables. In later stages of the quest, obstacles impede the hero's progress; they, too, are essentially the same, but differ in the form of imagery.
>
> The functions of the actors may be singled out. Fairy tales exhibit thirty-one functions, not all of which may be found in any one fairy tale; however, the absence of certain functions does not interfere with the order of appearance of the others. Their aggregate constitutes one system, one composition. This system has proved to be extremely stable and widespread. The investigator, for example, can determine very accurately that both the ancient Egyptian fairy tale of the two brothers and the tale of the firebird, the tale of *Morozka*, the tale of the fisherman and the fish, as well as a number of myths follow the same general pattern. An analysis of the details bears this out.
>
> from *Fairy Tale Transformations*

New Historicism

Both **new historicism** and structuralism owe a debt to the work of the influential French philosopher Michel Foucault. Among other things, Foucault studied the ways in which power dynamics affect human society and, more important, the acquisition and spread of knowledge. Individuals and institutions in positions of power have greater potential to shape the discourse in their field and thus to influence human knowledge and shape the "truth." New historicists look in literary history for "sites of struggle"—developments or texts that illustrate or seek to shift the balance of power.

New historicism emerged as a reaction to new criticism's disregard of historical context, but also in response to the perceived shortcomings of older methods of historical criticism. Rather than focusing on canonical texts as representations of the most powerful or dominant historical movements, new historicists give equal or more attention to marginal texts and non-literary texts (newspapers, pamphlets, legal documents, medical documents, etc.). New historicists attempt to highlight overlooked or suppressed texts, particularly those that express deviation from the dominant culture of the time. In this way, new historicists study not just the historical context of a major literary text, but the complex relationship between texts and culture, or the ways in which literature can challenge as well as support a given culture.

A weakness of this method is implicit in its strength. Those who disagree with Foucault and his followers would stress that the plays of William Shakespeare are more important documents than laundry lists or tax rolls from Elizabethan and Jacobean England—that a work of individual excellence can tell us more about a period than does its census or burial records. Again, it's useful here to remember that critical approaches need not be exclusive, and a sophisticated critic will likely use more than a single strategy when dealing with a text.

Stephen Greenblatt (b. 1943)
The Power of Forms in the English Renaissance (1982)

The earlier historicism tends to be monological; that is, it is concerned with discovering a single political vision, usually identical to that said to be held by the entire literate class or indeed the entire population ("In the eyes of the later middle ages," writes Dover Wilson, Richard II "represented the type and exemplar of royal martyrdom" [p. 50]). This vision, most often presumed to be internally coherent and consistent, though occasionally analyzed as the function of two or more elements, has the status of an historical fact. It is not thought to be the product of the historian's interpretation, nor even of the particular interests of a given social group in conflict with other groups. Protected then from interpretation and conflict, this vision can serve as a stable point of reference, beyond contingency, to which literary interpretation can securely refer. Literature is conceived to mirror the period's beliefs, but to mirror them, as it were, from a safe distance.

The new historicism erodes the firm ground of both criticism and literature. It tends to ask questions about its own methodological assumptions and those of others [. . .].

Moreover, recent criticism has been less concerned to establish the organic unity of literary works and more open to such works as fields of force, places of dissension and shifting interests, occasions for the jostling of orthodox and subversive impulses. [. . .] The critical practice represented in this volume challenges the assumptions that guarantee a secure distinction between "literary foreground" and "political background" or, more generally, between artistic production and other kinds of social production. Such distinctions do in fact exist, but they are not intrinsic to the texts; rather they are made up and constantly redrawn by artists, audiences, and readers. These collective social constructions on the one hand define the range of aesthetic possibilities within a given representational mode and, on the other, link that mode to the complex network of institutions, practices, and beliefs that constitute the culture as a whole. In this light, the study of genre is an exploration of the poetics of culture.

from *The Power of Forms in the English Renaissance*

Gender Criticism

Feminist criticism also focuses on sociological determinants in literature, particularly the ways in which much of the world's canonical literature presents a patriarchal or male-dominated perspective. Feminist critics highlight the ways in which female characters are viewed with prejudice, are subjugated to male interests, or are simply overlooked in literature. They highlight these injustices to women and seek to reinterpret texts with special attention to the presentation of women. Feminist critics also study the ways in which women *authors* have been subjected to prejudice, disregard, or unfair interpretation. They attempt to recover and champion little-known or little-valued texts by women authors—who have been marginalized by the male establishment since the formal study of literature began.

Gay and lesbian studies are, if not directly related to feminist criticism, similar in operational strategy. Interpretation of recognized classics may bring a new vantage to bear and cast a new light on old writings; a discussion of "cross-dressing in Shakespeare" or "male bonding in Melville" would belong to this mode of analysis. Here the critic focuses on submerged or hidden aspects of a text, as well as more overt referents; here too a part of the project is to recover lost or little known works of art from earlier generations.

While the focus on overt prejudice is the easiest feature of feminist criticism to recognize, the approach as a whole actually involves much more subtle and nuanced interpretations of texts. As the passage below from Judith Fetterley indicates, feminist critics in some cases find the more subtle traces of male dominance in literature to be the most insidious, because they so easily can go overlooked and pass for the universal or true experience. This puts female readers in the awkward position of doubting the very validity of a female perspective.

Queer theory emerged from **gay and lesbian criticism** partly in response to the AIDS epidemic and owes much to Michel Foucault's work on power and discourse and how language itself shapes our sense of who we are. He argues that the idea of being a "homosexual" would have been impossible without psychoanalytic institutions and discourse that created the category of homosexuality. Sexuality is looked upon as straight (or *normative*) or queer (or *non-normative*) and as a social construction rather than an essential component of one's identity. Some believe this undermines a critique of oppression and prejudice toward gays and lesbians.

Judith Fetterley (b. 1938)

On the Politics of Literature (1978)

> Literature is political. It is painful to have to insist on this fact, but the necessity of such insistence indicates the dimensions of the problem. John Keats once objected to poetry "that has a palpable design upon us." The major works of American fiction constitute a series of designs on the female reader, all the more potent in their effect because they are "impalpable." One of the main things that keep the design of our literature unavailable to the consciousness of the woman reader, and hence impalpable, is the very posture of the apolitical, the pretense that literature speaks universal truths through forms from which all the merely personal, the purely subjective, has been burned away or at least transformed through the medium of art into the representative. When only one reality is encouraged, legitimized, and transmitted and when that limited vision endlessly insists on its comprehensiveness, then we have the conditions necessary for that confusion of consciousness in which impalpability flourishes. It is the purpose of this book to give voice to a different reality and different vision, to bring a different subjectivity to bear on the old "universality." To examine American fictions in light of how attitudes toward women shape their form and content is to make available to consciousness that which has been largely left unconscious and thus to change our understanding of these fictions, our relation to them, and their effect on us. It is to make palpable their designs.

> American literature is male. To read the canon of what is currently considered classic American literature is perforce to identify as male. Though exceptions to this generalization can be found here and there—a Dickinson poem, a Wharton novel—these exceptions usually function to obscure the argument and confuse the issue: American literature is male. Our literature neither leaves women alone nor allows them to participate. It insists on its universality at the same time that it defines that universality in specifically male terms. "Rip Van Winkle" is paradigmatic of this phenomenon. While the desire to avoid work, escape authority, and sleep through the major decisions of one's life is obviously applicable to both men and women, in Irving's story this "universal" desire is made specifically male. Work, authority, and decision making are symbolized by Dame Van Winkle, and the longing for flight is defined against her. She is what one must escape from, and the "one" is necessarily male. In Mailer's *An American Dream,* the fantasy of eliminating all one's ills through the ritual of scapegoating is equally male: the sacrificial scapegoat is the woman/wife and the cleansed survivor is the husband/male. In such fictions the female reader is co-opted into participation in an experience from which she is explicitly excluded; she is asked to identify with a selfhood that defines itself in opposition to her; she is required to identify against herself.
>
> from *On the Politics of Literature*

Ethnic Studies and Postcolonialism

Ethnic studies emerged after the Civil Rights movement in the United States, but you can find its roots in the pioneering work of W.E.B. DuBois and others of the black arts movement and the Harlem Renaissance. Ethnic studies employs a cross-curricular analysis that is concerned with the social, economic, and cultural aspects of ethnic groups and an approach to literature that includes artistic and cultural traditions that are often pushed to the margins or considered only in relation to a dominant culture. Asian American, Native American, Afro-Caribbean, Italian American, and Latinos are a few of many examples of groups that ethnic studies might explore. Ethnic studies seeks to give voice to literature that has previously been overlooked in the traditionally Eurocentric worldview by reclaiming literary traditions and taking on subjects that explore identity outside the Eurocentric mainstream. But even works that are not written by ethnic writers lend themselves to ethnic studies. For example, a critic wishing to analyze William Faulkner's work from an ethnic studies perspective might focus on his portrayal of African Americans.

Ethnic studies has helped open the American literary **canon**—works deemed essential milestones in a literary tradition—to works by authors outside the white majority. Another far-reaching effect of ethnic studies is that it questions applying traditional modes of literary inquiry (such as feminist and Marxist approaches) to all literature. It suggests that we might be able to learn something more if we approach a text by examining the cultural and social conventions and realities out of which it was created. With the publication in the 1950s of work by Caribbean poet and legislator Aimée Césaire and North African writer Frantz Fanon, the discipline of **postcolonialism** found its beginnings, offering views of relations between the colonizing West and colonized nations and regions that differed sharply from the conventional Western perspectives. The field's modern American academic roots go back to the 1978 publication of *Orientalism* by the late Columbia University scholar Edward Said, a Palestinian by birth, who posits that the concept of the Orient was a projection of the West's ideas of the "other." Many of today's major writers have come out of the old British colonies, from Chinua Achebe to V.S. Naipal to Salman Rushdie, to name a few.

One of the major practitioners of this mode of criticism, Harvard scholar Henry Louis Gates, places such variety of study in a cultural context in which the urgency of the matter becomes plain to hear.

Henry Louis Gates (b. 1950)

Loose Canons: Notes on the Culture Wars (1992)

There's no denying that the multicultural initiative arose, in part, because of the fragmentation of American society by ethnicity, class, and gender. To make it the culprit for this fragmentation is to mistake effect for cause. [. . .] Perhaps we should try to think of American culture as a conversation among different voices—even if it's a conversation that some of us weren't able to join until recently. Perhaps we should think about education, as the conservative philosopher Michael Oakeshott proposed, as "an invitation into the art of this conversation in which we learn to recognize the voices," each conditioned, as he says, by a different perception of the world. Common sense says that you don't bracket 90 percent of the world's cultural heritage if you really want to learn about the world.

To insist that we "master our own culture" before learning others only defers the vexed question: What gets to count as "our" culture? What makes knowledge worth knowing? Unfortunately, as history has taught us, an Anglo-American regional culture has too often masked itself as universal, passing itself off as our "common culture," and depicting different cultural traditions as "tribal" or "parochial." So it's only when we're free to explore the complexities of our hyphenated American culture that we can discover what a genuinely common American culture might actually look like. Common sense . . . reminds us that we're all ethnics, and the challenge of transcending ethnic chauvinism is one we all face.

Granted, multiculturalism is no magic panacea for our social ills. We're worried when Johnny can't read. We're worried when Johnny can't add. But shouldn't we be worried, too, when Johnny tramples gravestones in a Jewish cemetery or scrawls racial epithets on a dormitory wall? It's a fact about this country that we've entrusted our schools with the fashioning and refashioning of a democratic policy; that's why the schooling of America has always been a matter of political judgment. But in America, a nation that has theorized itself as plural from its inception, our schools have a very special task.

The society we have made simply won't survive without the values of tolerance. And cultural tolerance comes to nothing without cultural understanding. In short, the challenge facing Americans in the next century will be the shaping, at long last, of a truly common public culture, one responsive to the long-silenced cultures of color. If we relinquish the ideal of America as a plural nation, we've abandoned the very experiment that America represents.

From *Loose Canons: Notes on the Cultural Wars*

Reader-Response Criticism

The **reader-response** approach emphasizes the role of the reader in the writer-text-reader transaction. Reader-response critics believe a literary work is not complete until someone reads and interprets it. Such critics acknowledge that each reader has a different set of experiences and views; therefore, each reader's response to a text may be different. (Moreover, a single reader may have several and contradictory responses to a work of art depending on the reading-context: a good dinner, a bad breakfast, a single flickering fluorescent bulb—all these affect the way we look at and absorb a page.) This plurality of interpretations is acceptable, even inevitable, since readers are not interpreting a fixed, completed text, but rather *creating* the text as they read it. Reader-response critics do stress that texts limit the possibilities of interpretation; it is not correct for readers to derive an interpretation that textual evidence does not support. So, for instance, it's inappropriate to claim that the character in a story is a vampire because she only ever appears during nighttime scenes in the story—but it's appropriate to compare the housewife in Susan Glaspell's play *Trifles* (chapter 30), to a "caged" bird once we understand the nature of her plight.

Reader-response criticism, moreover, acknowledges the subjectivity of interpretation and aims to discover the ways in which cultural values affect readers' interpretations. Rather than only emphasizing values embodied in an author or literary work, this approach examines the values embodied in the *reader*.

Wolfgang Iser (1926–2007)

Interplay between Text and Reader (1978)

Textual models designate only one aspect of the communicatory process. Hence textual repertoires and strategies simply offer a frame within which the reader must construct for himself the aesthetic object. Textual structures and structured acts of comprehension are therefore the two poles in the act of communication, whose success will depend on the degree in which the text establishes itself as a correlative in the reader's consciousness. This "transfer" of text to reader is often regarded as being brought about solely by the text. Any successful transfer however—though initiated by the text—depends on the extent to which this text can activate the individual reader's faculties of perceiving and processing. Although the text may well incorporate the social norms and values of its possible readers, its function is not merely to *present* such data, but, in fact, to use them in order to secure its uptake. In other words, it offers guidance as to what is to be produced, and therefore cannot itself be the product. This fact is worth emphasizing, because there are many current theories which give the impression that texts automatically imprint themselves on the reader's mind of their own accord. This applies not only to linguistic theories but also to Marxist theories, as evinced by the term "Rezeptionsvorgabe"[1] (structured

---

[1]See Manfred Naumann et al., *Gesellschaft—Literatur—Lesen. Literaturrezeption in theoretischer Sicht* (Aufbau-Verlog, Berlin and Weimar, 1973), p. 35.

prefigurement) recently coined by East German critics. Of course, the text is a "structured prefigurement," but that which is given has to be received, and the *way* in which it is received depends as much on the reader as on the text. Reading is not a direct "internalization," because it is not a one-way process, and our concern will be to find means of describing the reading process as a dynamic *interaction* between text and reader. We may take as a starting-point the fact that the linguistic signs and structures of the text exhaust their function in triggering developing acts of comprehension. This is tantamount to saying that these acts, though set in motion by the text, defy total control by the text itself, and, indeed, it is the very lack of control that forms the basis of the creative side of reading.

This concept of reading is by no means new. In the eighteenth century, Laurence Sterne was already writing in *Tristram Shandy:* ". . . no author, who understands the just boundaries of decorum and good-breeding, would presume to think all: The truest respect which you can pay to the reader's understanding, is to halve this matter amicably, and leave him something to imagine, in his turn, as well as yourself. For my own part, I am eternally paying him compliments of this kind, and do all that lies in my power to keep his imagination as busy as my own."[2] Thus author and reader are to share the game of the imagination, and, indeed, the game will not work if the text sets out to be anything more than a set of governing rules. The reader's enjoyment begins when he himself becomes productive, i.e., when the text allows him to bring his own faculties into play. There are, of course, limits to the reader's willingness to participate, and these will be exceeded if the text makes things too clear or, on the other hand, too obscure: boredom and overstrain represent the two poles of tolerance, and in either case the reader is likely to opt out of the game.

from *Interplay Between Text and Reader (1978)*

Poststructuralism and Deconstruction

The poststructuralist approach (**poststructuralism**) was primarily developed in France in the late 1960s by Roland Barthes and Jacques Derrida. Poststructuralists believe that texts do not have a single, stable meaning or interpretation, in part because language itself is filled with ambiguity, multiple meanings, and meanings that can change with time or context. Even a simple dictionary definition reveals several multiple uses for each word, and we know that context and tone can expand the number of possible meanings. Moreover, within any work of literature, authors intentionally and unintentionally create even more multiple meanings through sound sense, connotation, or patterns of usage. Poststructuralists revel in the possibility of so many interpretations not just for words but for every element of a text's construction.

Like formalists, poststructuralists use the technique of close reading to focus very precisely on the language and construction of a text. Yet whereas formalists do this in order to develop a sense of the text as a unified artistic whole, poststructuralists "deconstruct" the text, deliberately seeking to reveal the inevitable *inconsistency* or *lack of unity* in even the most successful and revered texts (**deconstruction**). Poststructuralists do not believe that interpretation can reconstruct an author's intentions; they do not even privilege an author's intentions, believing that the text stands apart from the author and may well contain meanings unintended by its maker. These meanings are, in the eyes of poststructuralists, as valid as any other, if textual evidence supports them.

[2]Laurence Sterne, *Tristram Shandy II,* 11 (Everyman's Library; London, 1956), p. 79.

Poststructuralists thus reject the notion of "privileged" or standard interpretations and embrace what might sometimes seem like a chaotic approach to literary interpretation. In his book *The Pleasure of the Text,* for example, Roland Barthes presents his random observations on narrative *in alphabetical order,* rather than in the form of a methodically unified argument, since the notion of textual unity is, in his eyes, an illusion.

Roland Barthes (1915–1980)

The Death of the Author (1967)

In his story *Sarrasine,* Balzac, describing a castrato disguised as a woman, writes the following sentence: "This was woman herself, with her sudden fears, her irrational whims, her instinctive worries, her impetuous boldness, her fussings, and her delicious sensibility." Who is speaking thus? Is it the hero of the story bent on remaining ignorant of the castrato hidden beneath the woman? Is it Balzac the individual, furnished by his personal experience with a philosophy of Woman? Is it Balzac the author professing "literary" ideas on femininity? Is it universal wisdom? Romantic psychology? We shall never know, for the good reason that writing is the destruction of every voice, of every point of origin. Writing is that neutral, composite, oblique space where our subject slips away, the negative where all identity is lost, starting with the very identity of the body of writing.

No doubt it has always been that way. As soon as a fact is *narrated* no longer with a view to acting directly on reality but intransitively, that is to say, finally outside of any function other than that of the very practice of the symbol itself, this disconnection occurs, the voice loses its origin, the author enters into his own death, writing begins. [. . .] The *author* still reigns in histories of literature, biographies of writers, interviews, magazines, as in the very consciousness of men of letters anxious to unite their person and their work through diaries and memoirs. The image of literature to be found in ordinary culture is tyrannically centered on the author, his person, his life, his tastes, his passions [. . .] The *explanation* of a work is always sought in the man or woman who produced it, as if it were always in the end, through the more or less transparent allegory of the fiction, the voice of a single person, the *author* "confiding" in us.

[. . .] We know now that a text is not a line of words releasing a single "theological" meaning (the "message" of the Author-God) but a multi-dimensional space in which a variety of writings, none of them original, blend and clash. The text is a tissue of quotations drawn from the innumerable centres of culture. [. . .] the writer can only imitate a gesture that is always anterior, never original. His only power is to mix writings, to counter the ones with the others, in such a way as never to rest on any one of them. Did he wish to *express himself,* he ought at least to know that the inner "thing" he thinks to "translate" is itself only a ready-formed dictionary, its words only explainable through other words, and so on indefinitely [. . .]. Succeeding the Author, the scriptor no longer bears within him passions, humours, feelings, impressions, but rather this immense dictionary from which he draws a writing that can know no halt: life never does more than imitate the book, and the book itself is only a tissue of signs, an imitation that is lost, infinitely deferred.

Once the Author is removed, the claim to decipher a text becomes quite futile. To give a text an Author is to impose a limit on the text, to furnish it with a final signified, to close the writing. Such a conception suits criticism very well, the latter then allotting itself the important task of discovering the Author (or its hypostases: society, history, psyche, liberty) beneath the work: when the Author has been found, the text is "explained"—victory to the critic. Hence there is no surprise in the fact that, historically, the reign of the Author has also been that of the Critic, nor again in the fact that criticism (be it new) is today undermined along with the author. In the multiplicity of writing, everything is to be *disentangled,* nothing *deciphered;* the structure can be followed, "run" (like the thread of a stocking) at every point and at every level, but there is nothing beneath: the space of writing is to be ranged over, not pierced; writing ceaselessly posits meaning ceaselessly to evaporate it, carrying out a systematic exemption of meaning. In precisely this way literature (it would be better from now on to say *writing*), by refusing to assign a "secret," an ultimate meaning, to the text (and to the world as texts), liberates what may be called an anti-theological activity, an activity that is truly revolutionary since to refuse to fix meaning is, in the end, to refuse God and his hypostases—reason, science, law.

from *The Death of the Author*

Cultural Studies

The critical perspective usually referred to as **cultural studies** developed mainly in England in the sixties by such New Left writers and sociologists as Raymond Williams, Richard Hoggart, and Stuart Hall. These critics took a sociological approach to literature and their views were colored by the philosophical leftism of such social philosophers as the Italian Antonio Gramsci. The movement grew mainly out of the desire to view social life and social movements from an analytical perspective somewhat akin to the analysis of film and literature.

The American academic branch of this form of criticism also incorporated (mainly in translation) the formal philosophical and critical approaches of a number of French academics including Foucault and other so-called deconstructionists. (Novelist Saul Bellow, affronted by this method, called these writings "Stale chocolates, imported from France. . . ."). Whatever good the English approach might have produced was muted, if not negated, by the French influence, which emphasized viewing society as comprised of various "texts" and imbuing everything from literature to the placement of traffic lights with equal value.

Twentieth-century sociological criticism has been a productive and interesting variety of criticism, as in, for example, studies of the relation of the literacy rate and the rise of the English novel or the effects of the rise of the dime novel in nineteenth-century America or the elevation of film studies to a high place within the university curriculum. Cultural criticism cheerfully blurs the boundaries among the disciplines and acts with a vengeance to blur the lines between high art and popular culture.

Vincent B. Leitch (b. 1944)
Poststructuralist Cultural Critique (1992)

Whereas a major goal of New Criticism and much other modern formalistic criticism is aesthetic evaluation of freestanding texts, a primary objective of cultural criticism is cultural critique, which entails investigation and assessment of ruling and oppositional beliefs, categories, practices, and representations, inquiring into the causes, constitutions, and consequences as well as the modes of circulation and consumption of linguistic, social, economic, political, historical, ethical, religious, legal, scientific, philosophical, educational, familial, and aesthetic discourses and institutions. In rendering a judgment on an aesthetic artifact, a New Critic privileges such key things as textual coherence and unity, intricacy and complexity, ambiguity and irony, tension and balance, economy and autonomy, literariness and spatial form. In mounting a critique of a cultural "text," an advocate of postructuralist cultural criticism evaluates such things as degrees of exclusion and inclusion, of complicity and resistance, of domination and letting-be, of abstraction and situatedness, of violence and tolerance, or monologue and polylogue, of quietism and activism, of sameness and otherness, of oppression and emancipation, or centralization and decentralization. Just as the aforementioned system of evaluative criteria underlies the exegetical and judgmental labor of New Criticism, so too does the above named set of commitments undergird the work of poststructuralist cultural critique.

Given its commitments, poststructuralist cultural criticism is, as I have suggested, suspicious of literary formalism. Specifically, the trouble with New Criticism is its inclination to advocate a combination of quietism and asceticism, connoisseurship and exclusiveness, aestheticism and apoliticism. [. . .] The monotonous practical effect of New Critical reading is to illustrate the subservience of each textual element to a higher, overarching, economical poetic structure without remainders. What should be evident here is that the project of poststructuralist cultural criticism possesses a set of commitments and criteria that enable it to engage in the enterprise of cultural critique. It should also be evident that the cultural ethicopolitics of this politics is best characterized, using current terminology, as "liberal" or "leftist," meaning congruent with certain socialist, anarchist, and libertarian ideals, none of which, incidentally, are necessarily Marxian. Such congruence, derived from extrapolating a generalized stance for poststructuralism, constitutes neither a party platform nor an observable course of practical action; avowed tendencies often account for little in the unfolding of practical engagements.

from *Cultural Criticism, Literary Theory, Poststructuralism*

2 Writing from Reading

2a CONSIDER THE VALUE OF READING IN A DIGITAL AGE

If you want to savor a cup of coffee or a good meal, you will have to linger over it; you can't just gulp it down. In this supercharged world of instant access and the Internet, reading literature helps you slow down long enough to feel, almost firsthand, the experience of characters from nations, cultures, religions, genders, social classes, and temperaments different from your own. Complexity involves consciously sensing multiple aspects of an experience at one time, and reading literature is a training ground for understanding complex situations. In an era when the global economy makes the world smaller every day, this experience can enhance your ability to work with diverse groups of people—both in college and in your career—by helping you see others' points of view clearly. It will also help prepare you for most of the writing you will do in college, where understanding a variety of viewpoints is fundamental to academic thinking.

2b MASTER WRITING FROM READING FOR COLLEGE SUCCESS

Not only will you have required reading for almost all courses in college, you will likely be required to write about what you read. Your success will depend on how well you can turn your reading into writing. College writing assignments have a variety of specific purposes, but one of their main benefits is that when you write about what you read you become a better reader as well as a better writer. Your personal reaction causes you to be more attentive to the text, and this focused response contributes to your ability to remember what you've read, clarify your observations, and explore complex relationships. In this chapter you will find a step-by-step approach to any text-based writing assignment, from a short response to a research paper. In the handbook chapter 4, you will find several sample papers for a variety of common writing assignments.

2c USE READING STRATEGIES THAT SUPPORT WRITING

Critical reading is a process of digesting and understanding a text so you can appreciate not just the ideas it presents or the story it tells but how it presents those ideas, why it presents them, and the way those ideas exist in a certain context. Below are the three steps for successful critical reading.

1. Preview the text. The process of gathering information about a piece of literature before you read it is called *previewing*. When you **preview,** look for information that will help you know how to approach the text. This information can be found in or on the book itself and includes:

- *Date of publication.* Check the copyright page—or, for older classics, you may need to consult the book's introduction or the author's biographical note—to find out when the book or story was published. This will help you determine whether the author was writing about his or her own time, or about a historical period. It might surprise you, for example, to find that Tolstoy wrote *War and Peace* more than fifty years after the time in which the story takes place.
- *Genre.* Sometimes you can tell genre simply from the cover. If it shows a shirtless man gazing at the attractive woman he holds in his arms, you can bet you're in for a romance novel. Knowing whether what you are about to read is fiction or nonfiction, and if it is science fiction, crime, literary, or another form of fiction will help you focus your expectations of your reading experience.
- *The foreword, preface, or other introductory material.* Read the introductory notices to help prepare for your reading. If the selection is part of an anthology or textbook, the surrounding text and questions will be especially helpful in giving your reading direction.
- *The epigraph,* if there is one. An epigraph is a quotation that the author selects and places at the beginning of a work, and it usually alerts you to an important theme.

Previewing Non-Literary Works

If you are reading something that is not a piece of literature, say for another of your college courses or for research on a piece of literature, previewing is still an important step. For non-literary works,

- Try to identify the purpose of a work and the audience for which it was intended. This information can be found, often in great detail, in the foreword or introduction.
- Also, read the author's biographical note to see if you can identify a bias or school of thought, if the author has one.
- Finally, take note of the context of the work. Scan the copyright page to see where a work was published and by whom. Note how many editions the text has had and if the one you have is current.

2. Interact with the text: Annotate, keep a journal, take notes. Reading closely is the first step to writing about literature. A careful reading and simple markup leads to observations that can form the basis of a written response. Annotating a text is a very basic process of noting impressions as they occur throughout a reading. Annotation should be as simple as circling repeated words, underlining interesting phrases, and jotting down brief sets of words. Remember that annotation is a process of *observation;* deeper analysis and interpretation will come later.

Look back at the student's annotation of Jamaica Kincaid's story "Girl" in chapter 3, and notice that this student does not come up with any actual *ideas* in his annotation. Instead, he makes *observations* about what he noticed as he read the story. This is an important distinction. For example, our student, Andrew, noticed that the narrator repeats certain phrases in the story, but he doesn't yet ask why. In fact, by comparing Andrew's original annotation to his final draft, you can see that most of his observations did not make their way into the final paper. He first had to notice many details about the story's tone, patterns, words, and his own reactions before he could start narrowing down the details that would be helpful in firming up his interpretation.

Annotation is a skill that improves with practice like any other. The skill of annotating is best described as learning to *notice what you notice.* Everyone has had the experience of reading a story, poem, or play for the first time and coming across something odd or jarring. Maybe while reading John Updike's "A&P" (chapter 1) you were surprised or even offended by the narrator's comparison of the female mind to a "little buzz like a bee in a glass jar." Students new to reading literature are often tempted to ignore that feeling of surprise, blaming themselves for the disruption. "I must not get what the author is trying to do," they tell themselves, or, "I just don't understand literature." In fact, those feelings are useful, the beginnings of your ideas. Don't ignore them. Even feeling bored by what you read is worth noticing.

Interactive Readings

Annotated selections can be found in the following chapters:

- Anton Chekhov's story "Rapture" (chapter 2)
- Jamaica Kincaid's story "Girl" (chapter 3)
- Carolyn Forché's poem "The Museum of Stones" (chapter 15)
- William Shakespeare's poem "My mistress' eyes are nothing like the sun" (chapter 16)
- Li-Young Lee's poem "Eating Alone" (chapter 17)
- Susan Glaspell's play *Trifles* (chapter 30)
- Edward Albee's play *Zoo Story* (chapter 31)

Keeping a reading journal is a great way to develop all kinds of skills—your observational skills, your writing skills, and even your skill for appreciating literature. Often, instructors will ask you to keep a journal and give you prompts to which you will respond. But whether or not you have that kind of guidance, you can keep your own journal in which you record what you have read, what you thought about it, and what you felt about it. There is no one right way to keep a journal; you may choose to fill it with personal reactions to literature, with ideas for paper topics, or with quotes that you liked and a description of what that quote means to you.

For samples of journal entries as part of the entire writing process, see chapter 3 (Writing about Fiction), chapter 17 (Writing about Poetry), and chapter 32 (Writing about Drama). Our student models from chapters 3 and 17 used their journals as a place to write a slightly more formal and focused response. Their strategy is worth emulating: By focusing their ideas in their journals, each student will be able to look back later in the semester if he or she has an exam—or later in their college career when they want to revisit literature that they enjoyed—and will immediately have a springboard into remembering the Jamaica Kincaid story or the Li-Young Lee poem and what makes it effective.

3. Read the text again for craft and context. Reading a good piece of literature is like getting to know somebody new: Your first impression is meaningful, but your second and third impressions can reveal to you entirely different aspects of the work. For a second reading, take into account how the elements of craft work together to create the selection you are reading, and for a third reading, put the selection into context. When was it written? What does its theme say about the perspective of the author on issues or circumstances of the day? It is important to make note of these impressions as well, because they will become the body of information you draw from when you write your responses. The practice of annotation and note taking will not only produce a fuller, more informed response, but will also save you time later.

2d MOVE FROM SUMMARY TO INTERPRETATION

When you start to write down your thoughts about a piece of literature, first make sure you understand the basics: What has happened in the selection, who is the main character or speaker, and whose point of view is at stake? This is a summary. Building on summary, you will want to think about the tone and style of the work, to analyze how the story, poem, or play is told. As you analyze, look for the role of the setting (particularly if you're reading a story), or important symbols, repeated words or sounds (which is critical when reading a poem), and the way dialogue pushes the plot forward (a central element in analyzing a play). Your analysis should take special note of who is telling the story; in a poem, identifying the speaker allows you to get underneath the hood of the "machine of words."

When you look at what was said (summary) and how it was said (analysis), you can put these together, bring in the context in which a work was written, and synthesize the work of literature to find themes and subthemes that the substance and style mutually support. You are now prepared to interpret the selection and support your interpretation with points taken from the selection itself. You may take a particular approach (see the preceding chapter on Critical Approaches to Literature) or point of view, and this framework can be useful as you interpret anything you read, whether it is literature or basic prose. Whether or not you take a particular point of view, this approach to reading will set you up to express your thoughts on what is important and meaningful to you in a literary work.

1. Summarize. After a first reading, solidify your understanding of the text by *summarizing* what you have read. **Summary** involves condensing a story, poem, or play into your own words, making sure to capture the text's main points. In the case of prose, a summary is much shorter than the original source and is often no more than a paragraph or two in length. For poetry, it may take a line-by-line paraphrase to result in the information you need to condense into the summary of a poem. Before summarizing, you might reread your annotations and notes with an eye toward picking out important points to include.

Remember that summary should be *objective*—focused more on what you saw happen in the work than on how you reacted to it. It should also not get bogged down with details and examples, but should focus on capturing the main events of the story or the main idea if it is a poem or an article.

One easy approach to summarizing is outlined below:

- *Pinpoint the main idea and write it in a sentence.* For a scholarly article, a main idea usually emerges in the thesis or is stated concisely in the conclusion. When you are summarizing a story, the main idea is often contained in the broad trajectory of the main character. For example: "In Alice Munro's *An Ounce of Cure,* the main character embarrasses herself while babysitting by getting drunk to ease her heartache."
- *Break the text into its sections.* Some scholarly sources might already have headings that divide the text for you. In a story or poem, identify the places where shifts occur—scene changes, a change in tone, or other points where the work takes a new direction.
- *Summarize each section's main idea.* As you did in the first step, write a sentence describing the key point the author makes in each section—or for a piece of literature, the key action or idea of the section. Think of this step as writing a topic sentence for each section. For example, the student who wrote the paper on Albee's *Zoo Story,* which appears in chapter 32, summarizes the beginning of Peter and Jerry's conversation and makes a point about the significance of animals in the play. In her discussion, she includes the following summary to support her point that Peter is associated with domesticated animals:

  > *After learning that Peter has a wife and two daughters, Jerry is eager to know what type of pets Peter owns. The animals he guesses are typical house pets: dogs and cats.*

Summaries are sometimes their own goal. See the chapter on Common Writing Assignments for help if your assignment is to write a **summary paper** or a **précis.** For that assignment, your professor is looking for a short paper that represents the main ideas of the text as the writer has presented it—*not* your own ideas or interpretation.

2. Analyze craft and voice. Summary helps you understand *what* happened in the text, and you will likely use your summary to support a point. The next step is to **analyze** the text by determining *how* the author created the work. When you analyze, you take the text apart and examine its elements: the different writing devices the author uses (such as point of view, plot, and imagery) and the voice the author brings to the piece (tone, word choice).

3. Synthesize summary and analysis. The goal of **synthesis** is to bring together the ideas and observations you've generated in your reading and analysis in order to make a concrete statement about the work you've read. The secret ingredients to synthesis are your own personal opinions and perspectives. (In a research paper, you will want to include the opinions and perspectives from academic sources as well.) Thus, synthesis takes the *what* happened from summary and the *how* it was accomplished from analysis and shapes them into an argument or statement.

4. Interpret the text. By *analyzing* a text and *synthesizing* your thoughts into a statement on the text, you will set yourself up to **interpret** a particular element of a work by suggesting what that element means. **Interpretation** means striving to increase understanding of some aspect of a work to illuminate its meaning. Interpretation does not mean identifying one correct answer, one key to unlock a text. Rather, it means taking an argument or statement you've generated through synthesis and using it as an angle from which to enter a work and explore some new, insightful aspect. It is important to remember that an interpretation must have a strong foundation of evidence from the text itself.

Other Strategies for Exploring Ideas

A walkthrough of the entire writing process from exploring ideas to writing the final draft can be found in chapter 3 (Writing about Fiction), chapter 17 (Writing about Poetry), and chapter 32 (Writing about Drama). When you're stuck, here are some additional strategies that might get you going again.

Freewriting

1 It is all right to start with obvious impressions. Try to answer some of the questions that you asked yourself while annotating the text. Don't worry about finding the "right" answer, and don't limit yourself to just one—there are probably many possible interpretations. *Freewriting* is private writing, just for you. You need not worry about proper spelling or grammar, or even proper sentences and paragraphs.

Talking

2 Try explaining a story, poem, or play to someone who has never read it before, and encourage that person to ask you questions. If this sounds odd to you, consider what you do after seeing a new movie you had looked forward to seeing.

Brainstorming

3 If you find it simpler to think in diagrams, your freewrite might take the shape of a web or cluster of related or unrelated impressions. Start with a central idea, literary device, or character that you wish to explore and place that in the center. Then, draw lines to the elements or characteristics associated with your central term.

Charting

4 Another way to draw connections between your observations is by charting them. This is an especially helpful method if you have identified opposites of some sort in the text, whether it be a hero and a villain, rainy weather and fair weather, or light images and dark images.

2e DEVELOP AN ARGUMENT

A literary analysis builds a complex argument around a particular aspect of a work of literature. Summarizing, analyzing, and synthesizing might help you come up with an interpretation that could be your paper's topic, but when you're looking for a topic for a paper, you probably wonder: Where do ideas come from? For all of us, coming up with ideas—and developing those ideas into claims worth writing about—is a challenge.

Claim: An argument is based on a claim that requires a defense. It isn't an opinion ("I liked the characters in this story"), and it isn't a fact or a generally recognized truth ("Langston Hughes is one of the most important American poets"). Your essay's claim will be reflected in your thesis (see the following section for guidance on creating a defendable thesis).

Persuasion: Aristotle, the same great philosopher who defined tragedy in ancient Greek theater (chapter 33) also defined logic and the art of persuasion. What we call *logic* today Aristotle would have called *analytics,* as in *to analyze.* When we refer to an academic argument, therefore, we are not referring to a fight but rather to a well-reasoned, logical analysis that is based on evidence.

Evidence: For literature, the text itself is your most convincing evidence; other kinds of evidence might be statistics, expert opinions, and anecdotes.

Different Kinds of Source-Based Evidence
Summary vs. Paraphrase vs. Quotation

Reference to a source is a form of evidence, and it can take many forms.

Summary: A boiled down analysis of the line of action or thought in a passage or full text, a summary is used not only to represent your understanding of a text but also as a point of reference that provides context for your argument. See the summary paper in the next chapter on Common Writing Assignments.

Paraphrase: Using your own words, a paraphrase is a restatement ("in other words") of someone else's language that makes a point more clearly than could be made by using the quotation itself. A paraphrase, therefore, may blend your own view with the words of the source. A paraphrase can help you understand a passage, particularly in poetry. Make sure you mention the source when you paraphrase. Use phrases like "According to," "As said in," "We know from."

Quotation: When the meaning of what was said would be distorted or changed in any other words, a quotation needs to be used to make your point. Do not avoid making a point by overusing quotations. A quotation is your evidence out of which you should build a point, using the quotation as a springboard for your own ideas.

You will need to show details, patterns, and ideas from the text when you present your evidence. The tips that follow are possible ways of developing or refining your ideas and then finding the evidence to support them. Together with the critical approaches outlined in the preceding chapter, they offer ways to generate new possibilities to develop an effective argument.

1. Follow your interests and expertise whenever possible. If you are a psychology major and the family's interactions in *Death of a Salesman* (chapter 35) remind you of a theory you have just studied in a psychology seminar, don't be afraid to use that knowledge to aid in your interpretation. If you are an avid sailor and that makes you especially interested in analyzing the "open boat" scenes in Stephen Crane's short story (chapter 9), take advantage of your knowledge in creating your argument.

2. Acknowledge your gut reactions, but then analyze them. If you found a given text or page extremely frustrating to read, it is absolutely legitimate to admit this to yourself and others. But don't stop there. Ask yourself,

- *What was it that frustrated me so much about this passage?*
- *Was it the slow pace of the action?*
- *Was it my own lack of familiarity with the language used at the time the piece was written?*
- *Was it the fact that the character I most identified with died in the previous scene?*
- *Was it the wordy prose style?*
- *What might have motivated the author to use such convoluted language?*
- *Are there any benefits to it?*

Certainly some works of art will appeal to you more than others; elements of taste and personal preference affect every reading. It is legitimate to say, "I hated that story," and intelligent analysis can come from that reaction if you analyze the ways in which the text creates specific impressions on readers.

Similarly, if you enjoy a text and feel a deep personal connection with it, keep in mind that you will have to ask yourself questions similar to those above to make sure you are being specific in examining the attributes you admire. You need not try to develop negative observations, but make sure that your affection isn't clouding your ability to see all aspects of the work clearly.

3. Choose a single aspect of the genre to examine. For instance, look at meter in poetry, voice in fiction, or stage directions in drama. Reread the text closely, looking only at that one aspect. It may be counterintuitive, but it can be especially useful to choose an aspect of the genre that is *not* the most noticeable in the particular text. For instance, most readers notice right away that Elizabeth Bishop's poem "One Art" (chapter 23) is a villanelle, a tricky form that requires a complex rhyme scheme and repetition. It would be easy to comment on her use of the form, but it might be more fruitful, and certainly more original, to think about something less obvious, like the poem's use of images or its rhythm.

4. Pay attention to detail. It is a convention of literary criticism to assume that *every* element of a text is potentially significant, no matter how small it seems. Whether or not the author specifically intended everything we notice, once it is written down, everything is fair game for interpretation. When a literary argument does go too far, it is generally *not* because the argument depended on minor details for its support but because it failed to present sufficient evidence or to form a coherent, logical argument. Some of the most insightful interpretations sound as though they are "reading too deeply" into the text until we hear all the supporting evidence and analysis.

Of course, this does not mean that we can arbitrarily assign meaning to any single detail in a text. It is not convincing, for instance, to argue that "Bartleby" (chapter 14) is Melville's rallying cry for Marxism, since there is little evidence for that interpretation in Melville's biography or his other works. The details, however, that might lead to this conclusion—Bartleby's escalating refusal to make copies, his boss's obliviousness to his condition, and the depressing metaphor of Bartleby staring at the brick wall—*could* work together to support a more subtle, complex claim about work and social class in the story. Each of these details on its own does not necessarily carry meaning, but a good paper will *note* them *and put them together* to form a meaningful interpretation.

So, do not be nervous about "reading too deeply" into a text. No claim is too outlandish, no detail too random or seemingly insignificant, no conclusion too far-fetched or implausibly small if your literary argument provides sufficient evidence. "Did Herman Melville *really* mean to use the brick wall as a symbol of class struggle?" you might ask. "Is every tiny detail really so important?" Keep in mind that some interpretations that seemed to be reading too much into the text when they first appeared later became widely accepted. Today's audacious argument might be tomorrow's commonplace one, so don't be afraid to add to the conversation.

5. Compare the text with other things you have read. Even if your assignment does not require or allow you to discuss more than one work of art, you may still find it helpful to compare your text to others while in the process of developing your topic. Comparing the spare, straightforward prose of Ernest Hemingway (chapter 7) with the more elaborate prose style of James Joyce (chapter 4), for example, may lead you to useful conclusions about the ways each of these authors uses language. It often helps to look at texts in juxtaposition or opposition; the differences are as important as the similarities.

6. Pay attention to the things a text does *not* contain. Thinking about what an author decides to leave out of a text is as revealing as considering what he or she includes. Painters talk about the blank space surrounding an object in a composition, and literary critics often do the same. Looking at the blank space, or what *isn't there,* will cast our subject in relief, enabling us to see it more clearly. Consider which events a play summarizes through dialogue rather than staging; consider whose points of view are left out of a short story; consider why a poet writes without using rhyme. What are the possible motivations for and consequences of those decisions?

7. Try lumping ideas together. Sometimes two (or more) minor ideas can combine into one strong one. Let's say your freewrite about Thomas Lynch's poem "Liberty" (chapter 29) turns up an interesting observation: the appearance of the "ex-wife" in line ten tells us that she and the speaker are divorced, which makes the light argument between them suddenly seem more serious. Much later in your freewrite, you notice that it was the great-great-grandfather who bought the plant, but it was "the missus" who planted it.

Neither of these ideas on its own is enough to generate much more, but what if you try putting them together? The ex-wife and the great-great-grandmother are the only two women in a poem about men taking the "liberty" of urinating outside. You find it interesting that the two women seem so different, and they might represent two different responses to male "nature," one American and one Irish. By *lumping* your two separate observations together, you stumble upon a complex and specific idea for an essay.

8. Or try splitting ideas apart. You might *split* an unwieldy idea into two or more by narrowing or qualifying it. Narrow a broad observation to just one character, scene, or metaphor. For example, in Flannery O'Connor's "A Good Man Is Hard to Find" (chapter 12) you might notice that every scene in the story contains a moment of foreshadowing that the family will encounter the Misfit. This is a useful observation, but too broad for a short essay. If you instead concentrate on how descriptions of objects foreshadow the end (the car that looks like a hearse, for example), you will find it more manageable to gather evidence and make a clear argument.

9. Look for patterns. If an author repeats an image, word, metaphor, gesture, or setting, make note of it. A poem might use words with "sh" sounds in many lines, a story might include images of animals repeatedly, or a play might have two important scenes set in kitchens. Notice these patterns and ask yourself how they are working—is the pattern emphasizing something, providing a sense of comfort, showing the ineffectuality of characters' attempts to change things? Repetition often works together with other aspects of the work and can serve as evidence that the author wanted to emphasize a point.

10. Look for breaks in the pattern. Once an author establishes a given pattern, he or she may also disrupt that pattern in a way that compels a reader's attention. If there is a part that seems quite different from the rest of the text, don't ignore it! You can safely assume that such a passage merits special consideration. If a poem is in perfect sonnet form, conforming exactly to the traditional meter and rhyme scheme *except for one line,* it is likely the author wanted this line to disrupt the pattern and create a sense of surprise. If two characters seem alike in almost every regard, look more closely to discover what *distinguishes* them. If a play contains two scenes in the same setting, with nearly the same action, pay attention to the *differences* in these scenes.

Developing an Argument for Robert Pinsky's "Shirt" (chapter 23)

Follow your interests and expertise whenever possible.	Maybe your Gender Studies course has been discussing the treatment of women who work in sweatshops; a research paper could combine information about how clothes are made now with Pinsky's description of garment workers in the twentieth century. Or: Let's say your Journalism course has been studying newspaper stories from the turn of the twentieth century. You could use your new knowledge about how stories were written to compare and contrast the *New York Times* coverage of the Triangle Factory fire with the description of the fire in Pinsky's poem.
Acknowledge your gut reactions, but then analyze them.	This poem at first seems like a mishmash of depressing situations: the sweatshop workers, the girls jumping to their deaths in the Triangle fire, Scottish workers tricked into believing in a fake heritage, slaves growing cotton. All of this is disturbing when combined with the speaker's satisfaction with his new shirt—in the face of the workers' suffering, that satisfaction seems shallow. But these histories are not just tragic, because many of the people in the stories are behaving nobly (like the man who helped girls jump out of the burning building). Maybe Pinsky is saying that every object we own has this kind of tragic history or that our belongings' histories are also positive, because people like Irma are proud of doing good work even if they are exploited.
Choose a single aspect of the genre to examine.	Some of the more obvious aspects of this poem to write about are Pinsky's use of lists and his inclusion of stories and images from history. Those might lead to good essay topics, but it might be more interesting to look at a less obvious aspect of the poem, such as Pinsky's use of sound. For example, compare the hard, iambic words in the lists of objects with the longer, softer sounds of words in the stories.
Pay attention to detail.	The speaker's comparison of the matching pattern to "a strict rhyme" makes it seem as though he finds rhyme pleasing—but this poem does not rhyme, which would seem to suggest that its own speaker wouldn't like it. It would be going too far to argue that the speaker of "Shirt" dislikes the poem and is presenting it ironically, based on this one word. However, the observation of the word *rhyme* in an unrhymed poem is intriguing—maybe it could lead to looking for other kinds of rhyme, for instance combinations such as "the back, the yoke" and "sizing and facing."
Compare the text with other things you have read.	It might be useful to compare this poem to other poems by Robert Pinsky ("To Television," chapter 21) other poems about work ("The Fisherman," chapter 21), or to other poems that closely examine a single object ("The Red Wheelbarrow," chapter 20 and "Anecdote of the Jar," chapter 20).
Pay attention to the things a text does *not* contain.	You might notice that the poem doesn't contain any information about the speaker except that he has a new shirt. The poem offers no name, no history of the speaker, and no other people in the poem except those he imagines sewing shirts. You might come up with some ideas about what effect this anonymity has on the poem—how would it be different if we knew the speaker's name, his occupation, his tastes and preferences, etc.?
Try lumping and splitting your ideas.	Let's say you noticed the repeated use of jargon (vocabulary specialized to a specific profession)—terms like *yoke* and *navvy* that most readers will not be familiar with. You are also struck by the detail about Scottish workers being tricked into believing a false story about their heritage. Neither of these observations on its own is very useful, so you try *lumping* them: both the jargon and the lies about heritage are instances of people being left out of some important knowledge because of language. *continued*

	Or you noticed that all the workers in the poem seem to be somehow exploited. Your first idea is to write a research paper exploring the situations of garment workers Pinsky mentions—Koreans and Malaysians, labor unions, the Triangle Factory, Scottish workers, and slaves in the American South. Then you realize this is too much even for a long essay and decide to *split* these possibilities and focus on only one, the Triangle Factory workers' union.
Look for patterns.	You might notice that most of the poem is made up of sentences that are not grammatically complete but just noun phrases—even some long sentences, like the second one (48 words) are just noun phrases, even though they span multiple stanzas.
Look for breaks in the pattern.	The pattern breaks in the fourth stanza with "One hundred and forty-six died in the flames . . ." The verb "died" jumps out and seems even more disturbing because it's the first verb in the poem.

2f FORM A DEFENDABLE THESIS

A thesis is not the topic of the paper or the topic sentence to the entire paper. Unlike a topic sentence, a thesis must be more than just a statement of fact. A **thesis** is the writer's argument about the topic of the paper, the controlling idea that he or she will show and develop in the body of the essay. Your interpretation will need to be set forth in a strong arguable thesis. Two strategies may be useful in developing your thesis:

- **Do a focused freewrite.** For example, if you are interested in how Shakespeare uses the seasons symbolically, you might want to highlight all the lines in the sonnets you are addressing that have to do with spring, summer, fall, or winter. It would also be a good idea to write a few sentences about your initial impressions of his handling of the seasons: Does he mention more than one season in a given poem, or does he limit it to one? What details of the season does he incorporate? Is the season mentioned a principal subject of the poem or a subpoint?
- **Write an observation as a sentence.** Then ask yourself which part of the observation you made is arguable. Try to imagine the opposite of your statement. If there is an opposite, you are well on your way to having a thesis. If not, you might try writing another of your observations as a statement, and then see if there is an opposite or argument in your new sentence.

Often, you may find it difficult to know exactly what your argument is until you have made it in the course of writing the paper. That's perfectly fine. Although you want to give yourself the best start possible with a well-planned thesis, don't worry too much about getting your thesis right the first time. Instead, look at the thesis in your first draft as a *working thesis,* one that serves as a diving board to launch you into a draft of your paper. At the end of the paper, chances are you'll have come to a more nuanced understanding of your topic. At that point, you'll want to revise your thesis so that it accurately reflects what you ended up saying in the paper itself. The defendable thesis that follows is arguable, supportable, complex, and purpose-driven.

1. A thesis must be arguable. A thesis is not just a statement of fact. Rather, a thesis is your argument, or to put it another way, a meaning you see in the story that not every other reader will necessarily see. Since your idea is not readily apparent to every reader, it is your job over the course of the paper to show why and how you have formed your interpretation. A good way to test whether you have a thesis statement or simply a statement of fact is to ask, "What is the opposite side of this statement? Is that opposite equally arguable?" If it is, you have a good thesis. If not, you either have a statement of fact or a weak argument, one that is widely accepted as true without needing to be explored in a paper.

INEFFECTIVE THESIS:

Some of Langston Hughes's poetry was inspired by jazz.

➡ *The statement is a widely accepted fact. Although this particular sentence may function as a good topic sentence or a sentence in the introduction to the paper, it is not an effective thesis statement because there is nothing about it that the writer has to defend.*

ARGUABLE THESIS:

Beyond being a jazz poet, Hughes understood the significance of jazz—even as it was being created—and used only those aspects of jazz that express the African-American experience.

➡ *As you will see this arguable thesis is also supportable, complex, and purpose driven. This statement takes a widely accepted fact—that Hughes is a jazz poet—and offers a particular and original interpretation of the significance of jazz in Hughes's poetry. Notice that the sentence is arguable: one could say that Hughes's interest in jazz was for another reason altogether—perhaps that it served the type of free verse he wanted to write or that it gave a popular appeal to his poetry. This thesis promises to show how race is the prominent factor in determining Hughes's use of jazz, and in so doing, it also promises a nuanced discussion of the elements of jazz present in Hughes's poetry.*

2. A thesis must be supported by the text. In a good thesis, the writer puts forth a statement that is arguable, or, in other words, a statement of the writer's opinion. It may seem, then, that the writer can say whatever he or she wants in a thesis, but on the contrary, a thesis must be supportable. This support will come primarily from the text itself. You don't want to take your idea and quote the text in a way that misrepresents it, simply to make your idea work. Instead, your thesis should be a reflection of your broad and open reading of the text in question. Although you must ultimately settle on an opinion in your thesis, you must reach that opinion through observation, not through fabrication.

INEFFECTIVE THESIS:

Beyond being a jazz poet, Hughes understood the significance of jazz—even as it was being created—and deliberately used very specific elements of jazz to exclude non-musical audiences.

SUPPORTABLE THESIS:

> Beyond being a jazz poet, Hughes understood the significance of jazz—even as it was being created—and used only those aspects of jazz that express the African-American experience.

➡ *You may choose to support this with poems that come from Hughes's* Montage of a Dream Deferred *collection, which Hughes identified as being "like be-bop." Also, since the thesis has to do with all of Hughes's jazz poetry, you would want to choose support from poems written at different times in Hughes's career. Whichever poems you choose, you will need to explicate sections of those poems to show how their elements are primarily influenced by race.*

3. A thesis must be complex, yet focused. You may not perfect this aspect of your thesis until a later draft, but your goal is to write a thesis that points you toward a topic with enough material to fill a paper. However, it should also be refined enough that the scope of your topic is manageable—that is, in a paper about Shakespeare's sonnets, you need not address the entire evolution of the sonnet form, just one aspect that interests you, such as Shakespeare's symbolic use of the seasons.

INEFFECTIVE THESIS:

> Beyond being a jazz poet, Hughes understood the significance of jazz—even as it was being created—and aspects of the jazz form can be found in every one of his poems.

COMPLEX, YET FOCUSED THESIS:

> Beyond being a jazz poet, Hughes understood the significance of jazz—even as it was being created—and used only those aspects of jazz that express the African-American experience.

➡ *This thesis has plenty of potential for a long paper. The author can easily limit the scope, however, by choosing a few key poems to use in his or her discussion.*

4. A thesis must be purpose-driven and significant. If your thesis is doing its job well, it should lead the reader to answer the question "So what?" As the writer of the paper, you'll want to answer this question yourself over the course of the paper and perhaps more explicitly in your conclusion. But the seed of the answer to "So what?" or "Why is this significant?" lies in the thesis. A good thesis leads the writer (and the reader) to a particular perspective of an aspect of the text, or the writers' oeuvre, or literature in general.

INEFFECTIVE THESIS:

> Beyond being a jazz poet, Langston Huges was also a big fan of listening to jazz music.

PURPOSE-DRIVEN THESIS:

> Beyond being a jazz poet, Hughes understood the significance of jazz—even as it was being created—and used only those aspects of jazz that express the African-American experience.

➡ *The purpose of this thesis is to better understand the role of race and jazz in Hughes's poems—an endeavor that may lead to a greater appreciation of Hughes's achievement and a deeper understanding of how to read his poems.*

2g CREATE A PLAN

If you have ever printed road directions from websites like MapQuest or Google Maps, you know that they provide step-by-step instructions for how to get from point A to point B. Some students may have such a finely tuned sense of direction that they are able to dive directly into writing a first draft. Or maybe a lucky few simply prefer to see where their writing takes them. Most, however, need some kind of a road map for their paper. An outline provides you with step-by-step instructions on how to get from your introduction (Point A) to your conclusion (Point B). It might help to sketch out an informal plan.

- introduction (includes your thesis and why the thesis is important to you and why you want to explore it in your paper)
- body (indicates the points you will use to support your thesis in a series of paragraphs)
- conclusion (adds a final comment that connects your thesis to a larger issue or places your thesis in a larger context that will make it more meaningful to the person who reads your paper)

Outlines can be very brief and simple or longer and in-depth. You might just write a **scratch outline,** or a list of topics you want to cover. If you're writing a shorter paper that analyzes one work, a **topic outline** might be enough. Topic outlines simply provide the order in which you plan to talk about your broad topics. Look at the student outline in chapter 17, Emma Baldwin's paper on Li-Young Lee's "Eating Alone."

I. Introduction
   A. confusing because last lines contradict
   B. thesis: A close reading shows the entire poem is created out of contradictory elements. Through contrasts of imagery, tone, and the literal events of the poem, Lee uses paradox to give full expression to the grief his speaker feels about his father's death.

II. Imagery
    A. imagery that suggests life
    B. imagery that suggests death
III. Tone
    A. plain language
    B. syntax is not complicated . . .
    C. . . . but subject matter is. This = understatement
IV. Time/Literal Events
    A. present, past "years back," past "this morning"
    B. talk about contrast in time
V. Conclusion
    A. address contrast in last lines
    B. we can understand them in context of poem

Notice how the major headers following the Roman numerals are the topics Emma plans to address: imagery, tone, and events. Supporting ideas can be listed with the alphabet (*A, B, C*). Evidence (quotations, for example) could be numbered in a third level as *1., 2., 3.*

I. Topic
    A. Supporting Idea
        1. Evidence
        2. More Evidence
    B. Second Supporting Idea

Instead of single words or phrases, you might find it more helpful to state every idea in a complete sentence, giving you a **sentence outline** to work from.

Until you have written many papers and learned more about the way your own writing process works best for you, an outline can help you to organize your thoughts and to understand where your paper is headed. Generally, the longer or more complex your paper, the more useful a detailed outline will be. For example, before writing a research paper, you may want to make an outline so detailed that it includes the quotes you plan to integrate. In fact, you may find a full formal outline absolutely necessary.

A more detailed outline example follows for a research paper on Langston Hughes and jazz. The final draft is found in the chapter on Writing the Research Paper. Compare this slice of outline with the third and fourth paragraphs of that paper. Notice how the outline is so detailed that the author had only to flesh out the outline points into complete sentences when writing the actual paper.

II. Blues in the Jazz Age
    A. "The Dream Keeper" and the Jazz Age
        1. Hughes's *The Weary Blues* published in 1925
            a. 1925 was middle of Jazz Age
                1. Marked by energy and optimism
                2. Jazz connoted rebellion
        2. "The Dream Keeper" influenced by blues, not jazz
            b. Part of *The Weary Blues* collection
                1. "The Dream Keeper" reads like abbreviated blues lyrics
                2. Compound words "cloud-cloth" and "too-rough" slow pacing to slow blues pace
    B. The Jazz Age and African-American experience
        1. Jazz Age and the blues have contrasting relationship
            a. Blues related to jazz; jazz grew out of blues roots
            b. Jazz exuberant, blues melancholy

2. Historical context is key
   a. Jazz Age "unprecedented prosperity" ("Roaring Twenties" article) for whites
   b. Great Migration—10% of blacks moved from South to North
      (1) low wages, poor housing conditions
      (2) disease

2h DRAFT YOUR PAPER

The word *draft* is used here to help keep the pressure down. Don't worry about spelling and grammar at this stage. Get your thoughts out on paper. *Draft* connotes that what you are writing is not final, that it is a work-in-progress. You will likely revise your first draft, so you will want to save your drafts early and often. Label your drafts so that you can retrace your steps (*draft l, draft 2* . . . or use specific dates to show what the most current draft is). Print the original. Having a hard copy may free you up to tinker and explore.

Introductions, Conclusions, and Body Paragraphs. You may find you want to write your introduction last or right before your conclusion but after you've developed the supporting points of the paper. If you do, these two framing paragraphs can speak to each other more obviously, with the introduction stating your thesis and why it matters to you and the conclusion bringing in your thesis and why it might matter to your reader.

Drafting Body Paragraphs

- Focus each paragraph on one idea.
- State the main idea of each paragraph in a topic sentence.
- Connect the information clearly in each paragraph to support the topic.
- Make sure the paragraph clearly supports your thesis.

2i REVISE YOUR DRAFT

Once you've finished a draft you feel is complete, take a break from your paper—distance can sometimes help you see if your ideas flow as naturally as you thought when you first wrote them. Distance can also help you catch editing mistakes you miss in the heat of developing your ideas. It is also good to get some feedback from a fellow student in your class or a friend. When you come back to your paper, annotate the issues you find. (It is great if you can get your peer to annotate your paper as well.) As you write and revise your paper you have a chance to re-envision how to make your argument clearer and to support it more effectively. In the chapter on Writing the Research Paper you will find the entire final paper for the paragraphs that follow.

Draft Introductory Paragraph

Jazz poetry, according to the American Academy of Poets website, is "a literary genre defined as poetry necessarily informed by jazz music—that is, poetry in which the poet responds to and writes about jazz." By this definition, Langston Hughes was a jazz poet. Many critics point to specific techniques that Hughes employs to create the effect of jazz. Although the observations are true, such technical readings fail to show the full extent of Hughes's achievement in jazz poetry. More than just a jazz poet, Hughes understood the significance of jazz as it was being created, and he used only the aspects of jazz that expressed the African-American experience.

In what way? Back up this assertion.

Which critics? What techniques? May be a good place for an outside source.

Used how? Maybe back this up. Is there an existing critical argument my claim could respond to in order to create a stronger thesis?

Revised Introductory Paragraph

Jazz poetry, according to the American Academy of Poets website, is "a literary genre defined as poetry necessarily informed by jazz music—that is, poetry in which the poet responds to and writes about jazz." Langston Hughes was a jazz poet in that his poetry often captured jazz in a literary form. Many critics point to specific techniques that Hughes employs to create the effect of jazz. One such critic is Lionel Davidas, who writes:

> Langston Hughes, in his collection of poems, lavishly uses such characteristics of jazz as repetitions, choruses, riffs, scats, and nonsensical onomatopoeia to achieve musical success as well as audience participation. It is also significant to note that Hughes's poems are often marked by dissonance, discordance, and line irregularity, which all contribute to the representation of the jazz spirit in verse forms. (268)

Although these observations are true, readings like Davidas's fail to show the full extent of Hughes's achievement in jazz poetry. Beyond being a jazz poet, Hughes understood the significance of jazz—even as it was being created—and used only those aspects of jazz that express the African-American experience.

Draft Supporting Paragraph (Body)

"The Dream Keeper" was published in 1925. At that time, America was in the midst of the "Jazz Age," the period from 1920-1930 marked by energy and optimism. Jazz itself was popular and connoted rebellion. However, Hughes's collection *The Weary Blues* was influenced more by (obviously) the blues than by this new form of jazz. ~~While~~ "The Dream Keeper" doesn't have as obvious a connection to the blues as Hughes's poems that copy blues lyrics directly—such as "Po' Boy Blues"—the repetition early in the poem bears echoes of the repetition characteristic of the blues. Consider the repetition of "Bring me all of your" in the first three lines; typical blues lyrics follow a pattern where the first couplet repeats before a third couplet resolves it, and here half the couplet is repeated and half resolved in both instances. Since Hughes was writing in the "Jazz Age," it may seem surprising that so many of his poems in *The Weary Blues* reflect the blues (lines 1, 3). His decision may in part have been informed by the fact that jazz grew out of the blues, and they were closely related enough that Hughes could use blues and be safe in the jazz realm. But whereas blues are "blue" and melancholy, jazz is "jazzy." The solution to this puzzle is in the historical context. The Roaring Twenties brought "unprecedented prosperity" to the United States ("Roaring Twenties") but it was also the era of the Great Migration, when many African Americans left the south and moved north. Times were difficult for blacks, who faced low wages and poor housing conditions (Marks). So, at the time that Hughes was writing these poems, jazz had two forms: the exuberant, new jazz, and the blues roots it came from. Hughes chose the form—the blues—that best reflected the state of the common black man at the time.

Maybe need some more here—how did jazz, just a music form, connote rebellion?

The discussion here is a little unfounded . . . maybe I need a researched source.

This is too informal! Need to keep an eye out for these.

This explanation is cluttered and a bit confusing; illustrate or clarify.

Reads like a topic sentence. Break the paragraph here?

Cute, but is it meaningful?

Are these common knowledge? Maybe include a brief description.

Maybe I need more research here, since understanding historical context is so important to my argument.

Didn't I see a good image for this when I was researching online? That might help engage the reader here and enrich the discussion of historical context.

Could this point have its own paragraph?

Revised Supporting Paragraphs (Body)

Hughes first published "The Dream Keeper" in 1925 and included it in his collection *The Weary Blues* the following year (Rampersad 617). At that time, America was in the midst of the "Jazz Age," the period from 1920–1930 marked by energy and optimism. Jazz itself was popular and connoted rebellion as it was associated with nightclubs, sex, and drinking (Tucker, screen 4). But Hughes's collection was clearly influenced more by the blues than by this new form of jazz. The title of the collection suggests the blues takes center stage in these poems, and indeed, "The Dream Keeper" is no exception. While it does not have as overt a connection to the blues as Hughes's poems that replicate blues lyrics directly—such as "Po Boy Blues"—the repetition early in the poem bears echoes of the repetition characteristic of the blues. "Bring me all of your" is repeated twice within the first three lines; the object the addressee is told to bring, however, varies (lines 1, 3). In a way, lines one through three are a compounded version of blues lyrics. Typical blues lyrics follow a pattern where the first couplet repeats before a third couplet resolves it. Here, half the couplet is repeated and half resolved in both instances. Blues also has a hand in the pace of the poem. Compound phrases like "cloud-cloth" and "too-rough" slow the pace of reading, as does the high number of line breaks compared to the small number of words (6, 7).

Draft Concluding Paragraph

Too familiar, not the right tone for a research paper.

As you can see, "The Dream Keeper" and "Harlem [2]" demonstrate how Hughes effectively incorporated new forms of jazz as they arose. While he does successfully use technical elements of jazz music, to end a reading there would be to miss Hughes's larger achievement. He did not simply adopt jazz technique; he selected only

Embellish conclusion to include new arguments based on content. Remember to restate the argument.

the trends that reflected the African-American experience. He leaves out the "white" sounds of swing and opts instead for the forms of blues and bebop. In so doing, Hughes's poetry captures both the music, as it evolved from blues to bebop, and the African-American experience.

Elaborate or change wording; doesn't sound right.

Tie in history and time period with this, since it's the basis for the argument.

Revised Concluding Paragraph

As "The Dream Keeper" and "Harlem [2]" demonstrate, Hughes effectively incorporated new forms of jazz as they arose. While he does successfully use formal elements of jazz music, to end a reading there would be to miss Hughes's larger achievement. Hughes did not simply adopt jazz technique; he selected only those trends in jazz that reflected the African-American experience of the time in which he wrote. There is no room in his poetry for the smooth sounds of swing at the hands of whites; instead, he used the true African-American forms of blues and bebop. In so doing, Hughes's poetry captures both the music, as it evolved from blues to bebop, and the African-American experience, as it moved from the blues of the Great Migration to the bitter conflict of continued discrimination.

Revising

- *Rethink your introduction:* Have you drawn your readers in by explaining how the topic of your paper is meaningful to you?
- *Rethink your thesis:* Have you changed your mind? Can you make your thesis clearer?
- *Rethink your structure:* Do you have a beginning, a middle, and an end? Do they flow naturally and logically into each other, with each paragraph focusing on an idea that supports your thesis? Are your transitions between ideas and paragraphs effective?
- *Rethink your argument:* Do you have sufficient and convincing evidence to prove your thesis? Does the evidence build logically to your conclusion?
- *Rethink your conclusion:* Have you made your case? Have you connected your thesis to a larger issue that gives it more meaning for your reader?

2i EDIT AND FORMAT YOUR PAPER

After you have looked at your paper as a whole, take one more look at its sentence structure, spelling, and formatting. These simple matters, if not done correctly, can interfere with your instructor's good opinion of a well thought-out paper. You may have been making small corrections all along, but consider this last edit your dress rehearsal for making your paper public.

Questions to Guide Editing

1. Are my sentences wordy?
2. Have I dropped a word out of a sentence?
3. Is my point of view consistent?
4. Does each sentence make sense?
5. Do I have any sentence fragments?
6. Are my commas in the right places?
7. Do my subjects and verbs agree—*single to single/plural to plural?*
8. Are my apostrophe's used correctly—**'s** for singular possession (this *critic's* opinion; Hughes's work); ***s'*** for plural possession when the word ends in **s** (the *singers'* music)?
9. Do my quotation marks represent the exact words of the writer?
10. Have I paraphrased without giving credit to the source?

In addition to formatting your paper with a heading and a title, you will need to follow the formatting guidelines your professor prefers, particularly as you cite sources in your papers:

- *The Modern Language Association* (MLA) provides guidelines for formatting papers and citing sources for courses in the humanities (see handbook chapter 6, MLA Documentation Style Guide).
- *The Chicago Manual of Style* (Chicago or Turabian) is sometimes required for humanities courses where an instructor requires that footnotes be used.
- *The American Psychological Association* (APA) has a different set of formatting guidelines for citing sources in the social sciences.
- *The Council of Science Editors* (CSE) have put together guidelines for papers in mathematics, engineering, computer sciences, and the natural sciences.

Whatever form your instructor wishes you to follow, pay close attention to the conventions for quoting and citing sources that are provided. Mistakes can be misconstrued as plagiarism, and following the correct form will have the added benefit of making your paper consistent and clear. This is the effect you want your paper's design to convey. Variety is the spice of life but not the spice you need for your paper. Be consistent with the features of your design, and make your paper look clean, clear, and serious.

Formatting

1. Include a heading on the left with your name, the professor's name, your class, and the date.
2. Center your title (it can be larger than the rest of the type in your paper).
3. Headings within the paper should be the same style and typeface each time.
4. Make your margins wide enough to make the paper easy to read and not so wide as to make your professor suspect you are stretching out thin content.
5. Make your type big enough to be read easily (12-point type is fairly standard) and not so big your professor suspects you are stretching out thin content.
6. Select a common typeface that is easy to read (Times New Roman, for example).
7. Include a caption with any visual in the paper.
8. Double-space your paper.
9. Number the pages.
10. Print on standard 8½ by 11 paper with an ink-jet or laser printer.

3 Common Writing Assignments across the Curriculum

3a CONNECT WRITING IN COLLEGE TO WRITING BEYOND COLLEGE

In our digital age, we actually write more than ever, and our writing is quite public—on Facebook pages, blogs, or email. Writing after college becomes even more public. Writing for success—especially in the business world—must be succinct, logical, and persuasive. Most professions demand excellent writing skills, even if the job does not seem to depend on writing. According to a recent survey, more than half of major corporations say they take writing skills into consideration when hiring salaried employees—and exceptional writing skills are required for advancement. While it is unlikely you will be asked to write an essay on Coleridge's "Kubla Khan" or Shakespeare's *Hamlet* after graduation, you will very likely be asked to articulate an argument that reveals a better understanding of a complex situation and a complex text or set of texts. Writing about literature is a training ground in dealing with complexity and expressing yourself with clarity

3b WRITE TO LEARN ACROSS THE CURRICULUM

The ability to summarize, analyze, synthesize, and critique information is also essential for college writing. In almost all your college courses, you will be asked to respond to something you have read, whether it be a piece of literature, a textbook, a critical article or book, a primary source, a blog, or a website. You may find these sources in a library, in your bookstore, or on the Internet, but whatever the particular assignment, you will have to *show that you understand* the text and *explain* it clearly, and you will have to *develop your own ideas* about how it works and *persuade* your reader that your interpretation is correct.

As you interpret a work of literature, you will use critical thinking skills—from summary to analysis, synthesis, and critique—that require you to look more carefully at how the text has been put together and whether the text effectively accomplishes its purpose. You will use your critical thinking skills in a summary to determine what details to leave out and which ones to keep or in a research paper when you synthesize your research into your presentation. The interpretations that you create in writing about literature employ a number of strategic skills that will prepare you to write throughout your college career:

- Summary
- Analysis
- Synthesis
- Critique

3c USE SUMMARY TO DISTILL A TEXT

Summary is used across the curriculum. It is used to condense a whole passage or text and may be a specific part of another paper (where a summary is a necessary reference point for your readers to understand your analysis) or the purpose of your paper as a whole. A summary is useful whenever you need to communicate the content of a text and represent the ideas behind any article or complex essay accurately. Summary is a mainstay of academic writing and is used in a variety of ways in all your courses, including some of the following:

- To summarize a source in order to critique it (as you would in a book review)
- To summarize several sources to reveal the body of knowledge on a particular topic (as in a report)
- To summarize the evidence you have compiled in an argument
- To summarize a critical perspective you are using to analyze a work

The goal of a summary paper (or précis or abstract) is to boil down into a few of your own words a whole text, without using your opinion or commentary. While you do have to decide what to include and what to leave out, your presentation should strive to be fair-minded and neutral. The summary paper is a way for you and your instructor to make sure you understand the main trajectory of action or thought in a reading.

Throughout this text, summary has been invoked to enhance learning, to help you make sure you have understood what has happened in a reading. The summary, therefore, needs to show that you have understood the overarching idea of what you've read. Begin by distilling the text to its single most compelling issue. Unlike a paraphrase, which is something said in another way (see the box on Summary vs. Paraphrase vs. Quotation in the handbook chapter 2 on Writing from Reading), a summary begins with a sentence that is a general condensation of all the *somethings* that were said and done in a text.

Your *interaction* with the text—the notes and annotations you have made while reading—will guide you as you identify how the story, play, or poem unfolds. You may find it useful to break the text into parts and write down each part's main idea. Use your notes or annotations to help you understand the text's twists and turns, its patterns and its allusions, and to explain comprehensively, concisely, and coherently how the main idea is supported by the entire reading.

TIP

Writing a Summary: Just the Facts

- Be neutral; don't include your opinion.
- Begin with a summary sentence of the whole text.
- Be concise; do not paraphrase the whole text.
- Explain how the elements in the reading work with the main idea.
- Look for repetitions and variations that provide insight into the main idea of the text.
- Check the text's context: When was it written? What form does it use?

Sample Student Summary

Solis 1

Lily Solis

Professor Bennett

Composition 102

30 September 2009

Précis of "Bartleby, the Scrivener"

Begins with a neutral statement that presents the basis for all plot elements in the story.

Important element identified specifically.

Concise statements introduce major characters and define their roles in the story.

Concise, neutral statements explain the sequence of action

Herman Melville's short story "Bartleby, the Scrivener" presents a businessman narrator who hires an unusual employee named Bartleby, and who consequently struggles with what to do about Bartleby's behavior. The first-person narrator introduces himself as an elderly gentleman who owns a law office. His three employees, Turkey, Nippers, and Ginger Nut, are so temperamental that the narrator is forced to hire a fourth man to fill in the gaps of their work. He hires Bartleby, who at first works industriously. However, when the narrator asks him to fulfill tasks beyond copying, Bartleby consistently replies "I would prefer not to." This pattern continues, with the narrator becoming more annoyed at Bartleby's refusals and yet feeling unwilling to turn him out. When the narrator discovers that Bartleby is living at the office, he makes an attempt at befriending Bartleby, which Bartleby evades with his usual "prefer not to" responses. Soon, Bartleby stops working entirely, due to damaged eyesight, but even when his eyes improve, Bartleby does nothing but stand all day in the office. The narrator gives Bartleby a friendly ultimatum that he must leave in six days. However, at the end of six days, Bartleby is still there, and the narrator—out of Christian charity—decides to let him remain. Still, Bartleby's presence is a nuisance, and the narrator at last decides to move his offices to another building. He receives complaints from the new tenants, asking him to remove the man he left behind. The narrator

Solis 2

returns to the old building and offers to Bartleby that he come to the narrator's private home and live there, but Bartleby refuses. A short time later, the narrator learns that Bartleby has been taken to prison as a vagrant. Although the narrator makes provisions for Bartleby to be well-fed in prison, Bartleby refuses to eat, and the narrator visits one day to find him dead. The narrator concludes the story by offering a rumor that Bartleby previously worked in a Dead Letter Office.

Gives story's resolution without offering reader's interpretation.

Work Cited

Melville, Herman. "Bartleby, the Scrivener." *Literature: Craft & Voice*. Eds. Nicholas Delbanco and Alan Cheuse. Vol. 1. New York: McGraw-Hill, 2009. 553–572. Print.

3d USE ANALYSIS TO EXAMINE HOW THE PARTS CONTRIBUTE TO THE WHOLE

Like summary, analysis is critical to college writing. In an analysis, you break the selection down into its parts and examine how the parts of a work contribute to the whole. Whether you are writing about irony in Flannery O'Connor or the impact of gunpowder on warfare, your analysis will look at how your source has put together its case, and you will use the source itself as evidence for your analysis. Your thesis will point specifically to the scope of your analysis. Possible analyses include:

- An explication of several aspects of how language is used—most often line by line—to point out the connotations and denotations of words as well as the reinforcing images that are used (see the following paper on William Blake's "The Garden of Love").
- An analysis of one aspect of a specific text, like dialect in Gish Jen's "Who's Irish?" or parallelism in The Museum of Stones by Carolyn Forché (see the Interactive Reading in chapter 15).
- A card report on the various elements of a story, generally only what you can fit on a 5" x 8" index card (see the sample card report at the end of this section).

1. Explication. An explication is a kind of analysis that shows how words, images, or other textual elements relate to each other and how these relationships make the meaning of the text clearer. Outside literature, an explication is a close reading of any text where the goal is to logically analyze details within the text itself to uncover deeper meanings or contradictions. According to *Merriam-Webster*, the definition of explicate is "to give a detailed explanation of" or "to develop the implications of; analyze logically." An explication paper does both of these things, as it *gives a detailed* *explanation of* the devices present in order to *analyze logically* the work in question. In other words, the goal of an explication is to unpack the elements of a poem, short passage of fiction or drama, or other text. The thesis statement in an explication is usually a summary of the central idea that all the devices combine to create.

Many explications take a line-by-line or sentence-by-sentence approach. Others organize the paper according to a few elements of craft that seem most meaningful to the work. However you decide to tailor your paper, remember that an explication should touch on more than one element. When explicating fiction or drama, pay attention to character, diction, and tone, and how those connect with larger thematic concerns. In the following paper on a poem, you will see an explanation of the significance of elements like rhyme, meter, diction, simile, metaphor, symbol, imagery, tone, and allusion. Although the author doesn't exactly move line by line through the poem, she does start where the poem starts and walks through it to the end. She organizes her paper in light of the shift she identifies in the poem, which she addresses in the introduction. Notice, too, that her thesis states the sum total of the devices explicated: an overall shift from an innocent state to a repressed state.

Sample Student Explication

Brown 1

Deborah Brown

Dr. Cranford

English 200

16 September 2007

Title introduces the poem and poet.

Repression and the Church: Understanding Blake's "The Garden of Love"

William Blake's "The Garden of Love" is seemingly appropriate for either *Songs of Innocence* or *Songs of Experience,* for it contains elements of both states. In publishing the poem under the latter, however, Blake suggests that beneath the singsong, child-like quality is a serious message. While the poem begins with colorful imagery and nursery-rhyme rhythm, there is a marked shift as it progresses with an increasingly dark setting and disrupted meter. This shift is triggered by the appearance of a chapel. It is only when considering how this shift occurs that we can fully appreciate how "The Garden of Love" inverts the idea of the church as good, aligning it instead with oppression.

Thesis statement that gives the central idea conveyed by the elements to be explicated.

At the beginning of the poem, several poetic factors work together to create the impression of youthfulness, and therefore a sense of innocence. The meter consists of an iamb followed by two anapestic feet, which makes a beat reminiscent of a nursery rhyme recitation. This nursery rhyme quality is supported by the rhyme scheme which, until the last stanza, follows a regular pattern of abcb. In addition to the structure of the poem, Blake's diction contributes to the child-like voice of the speaker, for he selects

Discuses how each poetic device—meter, rhyme, diction, simile, and imagery—contributes to theme of innocence.

simple words that are, for the most part, monosyllabic. At the most, the words contain two syllables, the longest being "garden" (lines 1, 7), "chapel" (3, 5), and "tombstones" (10). Furthermore, the syntax follows in accord with the simplicity of the diction, as the words are organized in a straightforward, sentence-like manner. The tone comes across as particularly child-like when we consider that seven of the twelve lines in this poem begin with "And," creating the effect of a child who is incapable of forming complex sentences and so advances his story by adding onto the same sentence time and again. The absence of simile and metaphor also lends a lack of complexity to the speaker (although this is certainly not to say that there is a lack of complexity in the poem). In fact, the seeming simplicity of the poem is furthered by the way in which the speaker offers observations rather than reflections. This is set up in the second line when the speaker says, "And saw what I never had seen." The rest of the poem, then, is merely a description of the scene without offering any interpretation. The innocence of the speaker is also established through the imagery at the beginning of the poem. Blake describes the Garden of Love as full of "so many sweet flowers" (8), and he also mentions "the green" (4). These images suggest growth and spring, both of which connote youth. Green especially holds connotations with innocence or a lack of maturity, since both wood that is not yet mature and un-ripened fruit are green.

Specific support from the poem.

Topic sentences identify the shift in the poem.

All of these elements that are associated with childhood and innocence are found at the beginning of the poem. In the second stanza, there is a change in meter with the line, "And the gates of the Chapel were shut" (5). Here, just before the first hint of repression found in the word "shut," Blake has omitted the iamb and included three anapests instead of two. Although still predominantly anapestic, Blake continues to vary the meter, such as in lines 11 and 12 in which he alternates an iamb with an anapest and further deviates from his original form by changing from the abcb end rhyme scheme to internal rhyme—"And binding with *briars* my joys & *desires*" (emphasis added, 12). This altered structure is significant because it indicates that something has changed from the beginning of the poem. To understand this shift, we must first note where the disruptions occur.

Discusses how meter contributes to shift identified in topic sentence.

Specific support from the poem.

The first major disruption of meter comes when Blake writes, "And 'Thou shalt not' writ over the door" (6). Because there are so many monosyllabic words, it is ambiguous where the stresses should lie, yet it is clearly impossible to read this as

Brown 3

strictly anapestic. The result is that "thou shalt not" is emphasized, a message that contrasts the carefree state of "play" (4) in the first stanza. Blake again disrupts the meter when he writes, "And I saw it was filled with graves" (9), which draws attention to the word "graves." Here, too, Blake creates a stark contrast between the image of a garden full of life and the image of a garden filled with graves. Furthermore, the change in the color of Blake's imagery from the first stanza to the last represents a loss of the vibrant nature of youth. What began as a green is now filled with the bleak, monochromatic image of "tombstones where flowers should be" (10) while the priests add to the gloom of the scene by wearing "black gowns" (11). While all these changes are important to note, the key to understanding this poem can be found in the source that sparked this change of setting: a Chapel.

Discusses symbol.

The Chapel in the poem acts as a symbol, a metonymical device that can be taken as a representative of the church as an institution. The shut doors and the phrase "thou shalt not" written over them suggest that the Chapel represents repression. Blake writes that, "A Chapel was built [in the garden's] midst, / Where I used to play on the green" (3, 4), furthering the Chapel—a symbol of religion—as a repressive force by implying that it impedes playing and all the carefree ways that accompany playing. The Priests, who enter the scene with the Chapel, enforce the repression dictated by the church, for they are the ones who end up "binding with briars [the speaker's] joys & desires" (12). Blake's choice of the word "binding" is significant because it implies passivity and restraint; the same qualities are evoked in the idea of routine found in the image of the priests "walking their rounds" (11).

Topic sentence moves discussion towards the thesis.

Further explication of symbol.

In addition to the Chapel and the Priests, there are several religious elements that suggest that this poem is making a statement about the church. To begin with, the Garden of Love is in many ways reminiscent of the Garden of Eden. Both house abundant growth and are originally places of innocence. However, they each contain something forbidden which brings a loss of innocence and death. In Eden, it was the forbidden fruit from the Tree of Knowledge that led to sin and ultimately death. The forbidden part in the Garden of Love is the implication of "thou shalt not." The appearance of this forbidding message—a statement of repression—is accompanied by an appearance of graves (representative of death) instead of flowers (representative of growth/life). A second religious element in the poem is the phrase "thou shalt not"

Identifies allusion.

Brown 4

itself, which alludes to the Bible, and more specifically, the Ten Commandments. These commandments are statements of what man should not do; thus the phrase automatically echoes with connotations of restraint and repression. Another element reminiscent of religion is Blake's use of capitalization. Just as "He" is capitalized as a sign of respect when used in reference to God, so too does Blake capitalize only those words which are related to religion: Garden of Love, Chapel, and Priests. The poem becomes ironic when one considers that it is the Chapel and the Priests, the very objects that the capitalization suggests we should revere, that bring about the change from a place of life and play to a place of restraint and death. It is through these religious allusions that Blake allows the reader to connect the repressive, restrictive setting wrought by the appearance of a Chapel to the church at large as an institution.

Explains significance of Biblical allusions; ties elements previously discussed to thesis.

The diction, imagery, symbols, and allusions used in "The Garden of Love" work together to create a contrast between the energy and youthfulness of innocence found in the first stanza and the repression and death that is increasingly present after the chapel's appearance. In this way, Blake shows that the church turns happy innocence into dark forbidding, creating in a mere twelve lines of poetry a statement against the repressive nature of the church in his time.

Reviews key points of the discussion; re-statement and refinement of thesis.

Work Cited

Blake, William. "The Garden of Love." *Literature: Craft & Voice*. Eds. Nicholas Delbanco and Alan Cheuse. Vol. 2. New York: McGraw-Hill, 2009. 396. Print.

2. Card report. A card report asks you to represent in a condensed space the various elements of a story. Most instructors require that your report not exceed the amount of information you can fit on a 5" x 8" inch note card, and therefore you must make every word count. As you take apart the pieces of the story, you will naturally forge a deeper understanding of it, and likely a new opinion of the work as a whole. Card reports are a great way to keep track of what you have read and can be an invaluable tool in preparing for exams.

In the following card report, our student, Tessa Harville, was instructed to include the list of information that appears below:

1. Title of the story and date of publication

2. Author's name, dates of birth and death, and the nationality or region (if applicable) with which he/she is associated
3. The name and a brief description of the main character, especially important personality traits
4. Additional characters who play important roles and their major traits
5. The setting, including time and place
6. The type of narration or point of view
7. A summary of the story's major events in the order in which they occur
8. The tone or voice in which the author relates the story
9. The overall style of the work, including (if space allows) short quotes that exemplify the style
10. A brief analysis of irony in the story
11. The theme of the story
12. The major symbols in the story and a brief explanation of what you think each means
13. A critique of the story in which you give your evaluation or opinion of the story in question

As you look at the following model, note the amount of thought and effort to refine language that the student put into the "Critique" portion. Although it is brief, your critique should reflect the amount of thought you might put into a three-page paper.

Sample Student Card Report

Front of Card

Tessa Harville

English 101, Section 2

Title: "A Good Man Is Hard to Find" (1955)

Author: Flannery O'Connor, 1925-1964, American, Southern writer

Main Character: The grandmother, who lives with her son's family and refuses to be ignored. She considers herself a lady, but is stubborn, talkative, and insists on her own way.

Other Characters: Bailey, the father of the family, who is grumpy and sullen; Bailey's unnamed wife, who quietly tends the children and is ineffectual; John Wesley and June Star, Bailey's son and daughter who are typical children that bluntly speak their minds and are excited by adventure; and The Misfit, an escaped murderer who philosophizes with the grandmother.

Setting: Georgia, presumably around the 1950s, when the story was written. Much of the story recounts a car trip so the scenery changes.

Narration: Third-person omniscient; primarily follows grandmother.
Summary: 1. The grandmother tries to convince Bailey to take the family to Tennessee for vacation, rather than Florida, and uses the newspaper article she reads about The Misfit as a reason not to travel toward Florida. 2. The family leaves for Florida. The car trip is full of bickering and a restaurant stop where the grandmother talks with the owners about how bad people have become. 3. Back on the road, the grandmother convinces Bailey to take a detour so she can see a plantation she visited years ago. 4. The grandmother's cat, which she snuck into the car, causes an accident while they are on a deserted road looking for the plantation. 5. Three men arrive to help the family. The grandmother recognizes one as The Misfit, and as a result, he has his men shoot the family, one by one. The grandmother is shot last, after a moment of connection with The Misfit in which she sees him as "one of [her] own children" (437).
Tone/Voice: The tone is deadpan, with no comments from the narrator. This makes for a reportorial voice with the precision of an acute observer.

Back of Card

Style: The sentences are straightforward and often declarative: "The grandmother didn't want to go to Florida" (429). The description is vivid but concise: "The car raced roughly along in a swirl of pink dust" (433).
Irony: Becomes most apparent after reading the story and looking back, making it dramatic irony. The family does not know to heed the grandmother's preposterous warning about The Misfit before taking the vacation, but the reader knows she is right. The dramatic irony is aided by the large amount of foreshadowing, such as the grandma's remembering the plantation outside of "Toombsboro" (432). The grandmother's behavior is at times ironic—she is concerned with being a lady, but talks too much; she says people should be more respectful, but then uses biased language as she ogles a "pickaninny" (430). The way she causes her own trouble is ironic.

Theme: A feeling of connection can transcend the shocking reality of life's brutality.

Symbols: The grandmother could symbolize the South: her vanity and pretense to being a lady cause a violent downfall. The family burial ground with "five or six graves" seen from the car is both a foreshadowing tool and symbolic of the family's impending death (431).

Critique: Although the story relies on wild coincidence, elements including highly believable characters, perfectly placed description, and economic movement of the plot make this story gripping and a representation of life with all its vanity, surprises, and connections.

3e USE A SYNTHESIS TO SHOW RELATIONSHIPS

Synthesis requires two or more sources and shows significant relationships among those sources. The classic synthesis in college writing is the research project, which asks you to look at a topic in depth and from multiple perspectives. The next chapter will follow closely a research paper on the poetry of Langston Hughes, from finding a topic to selecting sources. Here we will look at how that research project is an argument. Another synthesis across the curriculum could be a report on a body of information (on, for example, the effect of AIDS on Africa). The comparison-contrast paper, like the research project, is found in almost every area of college study.

1. Argument. The primary goal of an argument paper is to take a position on an issue or form an opinion about a piece of literature and defend that position/opinion using evidence. In a single-source paper (such as the critique of Chekhov's "Rapture" discussed under critique in this chapter), your evidence will be examples and quotations from the text itself. Most of the time, however, an argument paper will be an assignment that involves outside or secondary sources. Secondary sources, such as literary criticism, report, describe, comment on, or analyze a written work other than itself. You can use secondary sources to see what people have learned and written about a topic or an existing work of literature.

Nearly every sample paper cited in this chapter is an argument paper in some sense—a thesis statement in most papers is a type of argument because it posits an opinion that the writer must then support. The best examples of argument papers are the Chekhov student paper, which appears in chapter 2, and the model research project, which appears in the next chapter. In the Chekhov paper, the student argues that the story is incomplete and unsatisfying. Because the student responds to a single source, he supports his argument by citing Chekhov's text directly.

In the research paper on Langston Hughes in the next chapter, the student argues that Langston Hughes uses only those aspects of jazz that reflect the African-American experience. In that paper, the student uses multiple sources to make her argument. To support her points about jazz, she uses secondary sources that provide historical context. To support her reading of jazz devices in Hughes's poems, she relies on quotes taken directly from two of Hughes's poems.

2. Comparison and contrast. A compare/contrast paper asks you to consider two works side-by-side and highlight the similarities and differences between them in order to make a point about one or both texts. When you are selecting texts to compare, you must make sure that there is some basis for the comparison—perhaps the works share a common theme; or, they may be vastly different but both products of the same region.

Let's break that definition down a little bit, using the example of comparing *Beowulf* the epic poem with *Beowulf* the 2007 movie version (see chapter 13, Fiction and the Visual Arts, for these two works). The basis for comparison of these sources is self-evident: they are two versions of the same story. After reading the epic and watching the movie, you would ask yourself what the major similarities are and list them. In this case, you might make a list of the characters that the two have in common or the scenes that are common to both text and movie. Then, you should do the same for differences. In the *Beowulf* example, you might note the major plot change that Grendel's mother seduces King Hrothgar and Beowulf, so that they are the fathers of monsters.

As you make your lists, you might further think if some of the items you listed under similarities might in fact hold small differences when examined closely. Continuing with the *Beowulf* example, you might first have noted that Grendel appears in both versions and is a monster in both versions. But as you think about the movie, you might see that, in fact, he seems more distressed than evil.

The following student paper grew out of just such a comparison. Our author, Anthony Melmott, used the similarities and particularly the differences he saw in the two versions of Grendel to make a point about the role of the villain in today's world. Notice how he moves through the paper: after an introduction and an overview of the characters' similarities, Anthony delves into a detailed analysis of how the two differ. He then ties his entire discussion together in the concluding paragraph, and impressively broadens it to make a statement about contemporary society.

Sample Student Comparison/Contrast Paper

Melmott 1

Anthony Melmott

Professor Wallace

English 150

30 November 2008

Visions of the Villain:

The Role of Grendel in *Beowulf* the Epic and the Movie

Opening sentence establishes the works that will be compared.

In the movie version of *Beowulf,* directed by Robert Zemeckis and released in 2007, there are obvious deviations from the plot of the original epic. Most viewers who are familiar with the epic will readily recognize a major change: Beowulf does not kill Grendel's mother but is instead seduced by her. Clearly, Beowulf in the movie

Melmott 2

version is no longer the hero that he was in the original epic. But what many viewers might miss is that the movie changes more than the hero. Grendel, too, is no longer the evil villain he was in the original epic. Whereas the poem leaves no question that Grendel is a demon with evil intent, the movie portrays him as a tortured, childish soul through differences in his motivation, his power status, and his lineage.

Thesis statement. Also, the mention of three points sets up the organization of the paper.

Discussion of similarities.

The reason that many *Beowulf* movie viewers might miss the change to Grendel's character is that in many respects, he is similar to the original Grendel. In both versions, Grendel is a monster who eats and kills men. His overall trajectory does not change from the epic to the movie: in each, he attacks Hereot's hall and gets away with it until Beowulf comes and tears off his arm, thereby killing him. Even certain details of Grendel's portrayal in the movie echo the original epic. For example, the epic introduces Grendel by calling him an inhabitant of "the abode of monster kind" (14). The movie visually represents him as a monster by making him tall and hideous: his body—which drips with slime—looks as if it is turned inside out. As in the original epic, Grendel appears at night, thus aligning him with darkness in both versions. In these ways, he is meant to be seen as a terrible being in each.

Transition into discussion of differences.

But a little digging suggests otherwise. A major difference between the epic and the movie is that Grendel does not speak in the epic but does speak in the movie. Since Grendel does not speak, and since he is portrayed through narrative rather than visual effect, the epic uses a variety of language to describe Grendel. He is called a "fiend of hell"; "wrathful spirit"; "mighty stalker of the marches" (14); "creature of destruction, fierce and greedy, wild and furious" (15); and a "terrible monster, like a dark shadow of death" (17). All of this language reinforces Grendel's evilness and angry mode of existence. Grendel's fearsome appearance in the movie might lead a viewer to imagine him as the above list describes. However, the movie version allows Grendel to speak, and when he does, we hear a different story. Grendel speaks in Old English, even though the other characters speak in contemporary English, so his lines are difficult to understand. But listening closely reveals that when Beowulf says to Grendel, whose arm is caught in the door, "Your bloodletting days are finished, demon," Grendel replies, "I am not a demon."

Textual support.

Support from the movie.

Melmott 3

On its own, this example could be explained as Grendel lacking the self-awareness that he is a demon. But other details corroborate Grendel's statement. Both of Grendel's attacks are triggered by the loud rollicking of the men in Hereot. As the scene pans from the meadhall to Grendel's underground lair, the noise of the chanting sounds as if it has been submerged. The effect is that we are hearing the men as Grendel hears them—a constant, throbbing, bass line that makes Grendel's membranous ears quiver. When Grendel bursts into full view, his screams are more like cries of anguish than roars meant to frighten. The attention given to Grendel's sensitive ears, his clutching at his head as he screams, and his posture all suggest that he is in physical agony from the parties at Heorot, and thus bursts in to put a stop to it. This is a far less demoniac motivation than that cited in the epic.

In the original, Grendel's first attack reads, "The creature of destruction, fierce and greedy, wild and furious, was ready straight. He seized thirty thanes upon their bed" (15). Nothing in this suggests any sort of pain or anguish that Grendel experiences, as he appears to in the movie. Further, while the movie shows him as provoked, the epic clearly states after that first attack, "It was no longer than a single night ere he wrought more deeds of murder; he recked not of the feud and the crime—he was too fixed in them!" (16). According to the *Oxford English Dictionary,* "reck" means "To take heed or have a care of some thing (or person), so as to be alarmed or troubled thereby, or to modify one's conduct or purpose on that account." In other words, this quote shows that Grendel's killings do not bother him or give him pause because he is so set in his evil ways. Hence, even if Grendel could speak in the original epic, he certainly wouldn't say "I am no demon" and even if he did, we would know by his actions that this was not true. On the contrary, when Grendel utters that line in the movie, we have seen that, indeed, his motivation is not naturally demonic but provocation.

Defines unknown word to add textual support.

Transition sentence that leads into the second point of the thesis.

Consistent with the change in motivation is the change in Grendel's power status from the epic to the movie. In the epic, Grendel holds a reign of terror. Although it is difficult to analyze language in a translation, it is safe to say that the text refers to Grendel in several places as a ruling authority of sorts. One example follows Grendel's

Textual support.

Melmott 4

first series of attacks in which the poem reads, "Thus he tyrannized over them" (16). In another translation, that of Seamus Heaney, the same line reads "So Grendel ruled" (35). Both "rule" and "tyranny" are ways of describing an all-powerful governing body. Later, when he fights Beowulf, Grendel is described as the "master of evils" (43), and in the Heaney translation as "the captain of evil" (47). "Master" and "captain" both refer to someone in charge, someone with power, and both are applied to Grendel in the original epic.

Yet for all the power the epic accords to Grendel, the movie portrays Grendel as child-like. While Grendel has a mother in both versions, only the movie shows Grendel interact with her like a child. After his first attack in the movie, he returns to his lair and speaks with his mother. Throughout their dialogue, he lays on the floor of the cave in a position reminiscent of a fetus. The words he speaks are likewise childish; at one point, he cries out, "The men screamed! The men bellowed and screamed! The men hurt me, hurt my ear." Not only do his simple, repetitive sentences suggest a child's voice, but his fear of and dismay at the men show him to be the opposite of their tyrant, ruler, master, or captain.

Support from the movie.

Transition sentence that leads into the third point of the thesis.

The reduction of Grendel's evilness and power can perhaps be traced to the biggest difference between the epic and the movie's Grendel: that of Grendel's lineage. As mentioned in the introduction, the movie portrays Grendel's mother as a seductress, with the premise that she once seduced King Hrothgar, making Grendel the offspring of Hrothgar and the mother. On the other hand, the original epic is very clear—and frequently emphasizes—that Grendel is a descendent of Cain, who committed the first murder. Referring to Cain, the epic reads, "From him there woke to life all the evil broods, monsters and elves and sea-beasts, and giants too, who long time strove with God" (14–15). There is no room for a human in this description, and certainly not Hrothgar, whom the epic praises as being a "good king." By changing Grendel's parentage, the movie shifts the root of evil from Grendel to Hrothgar. It is because of Hrothgar's past weakness that his kingdom is plagued by the fruit of that very weakness. Grendel, then, is a by-product, a mere pawn in the struggle between Hrothgar's kingdom and the mother's corrupting ways. The mother uses Grendel's

Melmott 5

death as a way to further corrupt the kingdom through her seduction of Beowulf—and Beowulf succumbs.

Brief reiteration of the three points made in the paper.

In the retelling of an existing story—whether that retelling be in the form of a story, a poem, or a movie—there will always be similarities and differences. But the difference in the role of the villain between an epic written in 1000 and a movie filmed in 2007 tells us something about our contemporary society. As we noted briefly in the introduction, Beowulf's seduction makes him less heroic; likewise, we have seen that the movie makes Grendel less villainous in motivation, in power, and in lineage. We might ask ourselves: What does it mean to live in an age where we see heroes as fallible and villains as innocent? The difference between the epic Grendel and the movie Grendel offers an answer: the original villain has been turned into a product of human vice, suggesting that true villainy lies in human behavior. Or, to put it another way, in a world where human deeds are monstrous, there isn't much room for a monster.

Conclusion broadens significance to our own society.

Conclusion explains the implication of the thesis; answers the "so what?" question.

Works Cited

Beowulf. Dir. Robert Zemeckis. Perf. Crispin Glover, Anthony Hopkins, Angelina Jolie, and Ray Winstone. Paramount Pictures, 2007. Film.

Beowulf. Trans. Seamus Heaney. *The Norton Anthology of English Literature.* 7th ed. Ed. M.H. Abrams and Stephen Greenblatt. New York: W.W. Norton, 2000. 32–99. Print.

Beowulf. Trans. Chauncey Brewster Tinker. New York: Newson & Co., 1902. Print.

"Reck." Def. 1b. *The Oxford English Dictionary.* 2nd ed. 1989. Print.

3f USE CRITIQUE TO BRING IN YOUR OWN EVALUATION

We define a critique as a summary with your own reasonable opinion. Whether you are asked to critique a reading for an essay exam, the accuracy of a website as a source, or respond to an argument, in most of your courses, you will be required to evaluate the presentation of information.

- What is the work (or performance) trying to accomplish?
- Does it achieve its purpose?
- Do you agree or disagree with the piece, like or dislike it?
- How has the piece created this reaction in you?

Review. A critique is a formal evaluation of a text, and one of the most common forms of critique in literature is the review. In a review, you—as the reviewer—get to evaluate the text or, in the case of live theatre, a performance. For an example of a review, see the response to Anton Chekhov's early story "Rapture" in chapter 2. After a few general, opening sentences, the discussion becomes more specific as the student asserts that the main character's lack of change makes the story unsatisfying. The student continues by analyzing the various parts of the story. As your review progresses and you begin to make evaluative statements—such as *The story begins on a strong note but deteriorates; The casting was so well-done that it carries the play from start to finish; The poem's sonnet form is perfect for its content*—you will also need to analyze why you are reacting to the text in that particular way. Particularly strong is his division of the story into three parts:

> *Part one: the clerk runs in, announcing himself, disrupting the household, waking his brothers. Part two: Mitya takes out the newspaper and urges his father to read it aloud. In the closing sequence, a reader may expect something to happen as a result of Mitya's "rapture" that he has become famous because his name is in the paper and on the police record. However, as the ancient philosopher and critic Aristotle might put it, what is the dramatic purpose here? . . . His parents and his siblings humor him instead of contradicting or berating him; thus making change less likely for Mitya. The reader is left to wonder what the point is, and without that concluding action, the dramatic purpose is unclear, and the story is incomplete and ultimately unsatisfying.*

Notice here that the author is not afraid to make bold claims: that the story is incomplete and unsatisfying. You may feel a little intimidated the first time you write a review, especially if the author is well known. Take the Chekhov paper to heart; the validity of an evaluation rests not on how highly you are ranking a noted author but on how your analysis of the story supports your evaluation. In this case, the student has analyzed the structure of the story, and found that in a story set up for a three-part movement, the third part is missing. Therefore, when he claims that the story is incomplete and unsatisfying, we see the author's point.

Guidelines for Writing Reviews

Introduce What You Are Evaluating

- Include the title and author.
- For a live performance, include who performed, when, and under what circumstances (a full house? an outdoor amphitheater?).
- Be clear about what you are evaluating.

Set Up Your Review with a Summary

- Your summary is to be used as a reference point for your discussion; you may not want to give the ending away, however.

Put the Piece into Context

- What type of work is it? A comedy? A tragedy?
- When was it written?
- If it is a well-known play such as Shakespeare, include any unusual information on the "take" of the director (what's the director's purpose in staging Shakespeare's "Hamlet" in Pakistan, for example).

Analyze the Text

- For a play, note the staging, lighting, and costuming as well as the acting.
- Note how the work is structured.
- Look at the individual elements: plot, character, dialogue.
- Determine the purpose of the work.

Include Your Reasoned Opinion: This Is Your Evaluation

- Did the work achieve its purpose?
- What is your response to the selection and why?
- Agree or disagree with the presentation of information (whether or not it achieved its purpose).
- Base your agreement or disagreement on evidence.

End with a Balanced Conclusion

- Recap the pros and cons of the piece.
- Give your overall reaction.

3g FIND AN EFFECTIVE APPROACH TO THE ESSAY EXAM

Timed writing on an exam may seem like an intimidating prospect. Reviewing the tips below will help you learn an effective approach to essay exams, whether you are taking one for a class in English, political science, or psychology.

1. Prepare. If you have been diligent in annotating the texts you read and keeping a journal or freewriting exercises, be sure to review these materials before the day of your exam. Jog your memory about each story, poem, novel, or play you have read for the class by reviewing major characters and events of the work, as well as any important information about the authors.

2. Pace yourself. When you receive the exam, glance through it to see approximately how much time you should spend on each section. Remember that if an essay is worth, say, 70 percent of the grade, you want to make it a priority to spend sufficient time on it.

3. Read the assignment carefully. When you arrive at the essay question, circle key words as you read the assignment. Pay particular attention to the verbs your instructor uses: common choices are *explain, discuss, analyze, compare, contrast, interpret,* and *argue*. Your understanding of the different types of assignments addressed in this chapter can help you here.

TIP

Understanding Essay Exam Assignments

The words explain *or* discuss *ask you to engage in a detailed way, much like an explication or a close reading.*

Analyze *should remind you of what you know about an analysis paper—that your job is to explore one element of the text and show how it contributes to the overall work.*

Compare *and* contrast *asks you to find similarities and differences between two items and to suggest what those similarities or differences emphasize or illuminate.*

Argue *is a way of asking you to take a position about an issue, or in the case of a literary text, to defend what you see in the work that may not be readily apparent to others.*

4. Form a thesis. In an essay exam, your thesis will likely be a simpler statement than the type of complex argument you would form in a longer research paper or analysis. Look at the phrasing of the question itself to help you shape your thesis.

EXAMPLE OF AN ESSAY EXAM ASSIGNMENT

➡ *Analyze Frost's use of imagery in "Stopping By Woods on a Snowy Evening."*

EXAMPLE OF A THESIS THAT RESPONDS TO THE ASSIGNMENT

Frost uses idyllic, New England imagery to disguise a more serious statement about death.

5. Outline briefly. Even if you don't typically work from an outline when writing a paper, take a few moments to jot down a brief outline. In an essay exam, even a brief outline will keep you from freezing up entirely. And, if you find you are spending too much time on the first paragraph, you can quickly wrap it up to move on to the next point in your outline. In short, an outline can help you budget time and space in your essay while eliminating the stressful feeling of not knowing where to go next.

6. Check your work. Try your best to allow a little extra time in which to read over what you have written. Time constraints often make even the best students leave out words or write sentences that make no sense. Rereading your work will allow you to fix these problems.

Follow our model student, Renee Knox, as she completes the following essay assignment on a timed exam.

Notes for a Sample Student Essay Exam

Renee identifies key words in the prompt. Already, she knows her paper must focus on the significance of the imagery.

Assignment: Analyze Frost's use of imagery in "Stopping By Woods on a Snowy Evening," reproduced below.

Renee underlines the imagery in the poem and highlights phrases she finds significant.

Renee numbers the lines for easy reference when she quotes in the essay.

Stopping By Woods On A Snowy Evening

Whose woods these are I think I know.
His house is in the village though;
He will not see me stopping here
To watch his woods fill up with snow.
My little horse must think it queer
To stop without a farmhouse near
Between the woods and frozen lake
The darkest evening of the year.
He gives his harness bells a shake
To ask if there is some mistake.
The only other sound's the sweep
Of easy wind and downy flake.
The woods are lovely, dark and deep.
But I have promises to keep,
And miles to go before I sleep,
And miles to go before I sleep.

Renee notes that many of her underlined phrases bring to mind a farm-like, New England setting. Then she separates out the other images and names their connotations.

Important images: woods, snow, horse, house, village, dark, wind, snowflakes, dark

woods, snow, horse, farmhouse, village=New England; ideal Christmas scene
no farmhouse near, dark, deep, winter=cold, alone, death??
sleep=death?

Renee formulates a thesis based on her observations.

Thesis: Frost uses pretty New England imagery to disguise a more serious statement about death.

Renee generates a brief outline to follow. In constructing her essay, she will use a 5 paragraph structure.

I. Introduction and thesis
II. Set up "pretty" imagery
  A. Mention horse
  B. Mention farmhouse
  C. Mention woods
  D. Mention snow
  E. Adds up to ideal Christmas village scene
III. Set up dark imagery and cold effect
  A. Snow
  B. Woods
  C. Wind
  D. Solitary
IV. Discuss symbolic significance of images
  A. Snow=winter=death
  B. Woods=wild, easily lose your way
  C. Sleep=form of death
V. Conclusion—why would Frost do this?

Sample Student Essay Exam

Knox 1

Renee Knox

Professor Giordano

ENGL 1203

5 November 2008

Renee uses a simple but complete title, in order not to spend too much time on it.

Imagery in Frost's "Stopping By Woods on a Snowy Evening"

Many times in literature, as in life, something appears to be one thing but is actually another. One need only think of tales like "Little Red Riding Hood" in which the woman who appears to be her grandmother turns out to be a wolf. In a similar way, Robert Frost's "Stopping By Woods on a Snowy Evening" appears to be a simple and charming experience. Instead, Frost uses idyllic New England imagery to disguise a more serious statement about death.

Thesis statement. When Renee reread her essay, she changed "pretty" to "idyllic" for more sophisticated diction.

Renee stays on topic by following her outline.

Even in the poem's title, Frost is already using imagery, for the title presents woods, snow, and evening. We can picture an evening scene in which snow is softly falling on woods. And indeed, the speaker is there with his "little horse" (line 5) that wears "harness bells" (9). The mention of a village (2) and a farmhouse (6), even though the speaker is not near them, suggests that villages and farmhouses dot the landscape in which the speaker moves. Put all together—snow, a horse with harness bells, a village, and a farmhouse—Frost's imagery conjures a New England scene that is so quaint, it is exactly the type of scene many people replicate with porcelain villages at Christmas time—it is that perfect.

Renee helps her paper flow by using "however" to signal her transition to her next point.

However, if we look at the nature imagery, we get a much darker picture. While evening might connote a soothing time of leisure after the day's work is done, it is also the time of oncoming dark, as Frost's imagery indicates when he describes it as "the darkest evening of the year" (8). In fact, Frost calls attention to the fact that it is the darkest evening by placing that description in line 8, the exact center of the 16-line poem. Furthermore, he repeats "dark" again when he describes the woods as "dark and deep" (13), adding emphasis to the imagery of dark through repetition. We also know that the evening is cold, and although snow is a part of an idyllic New England Christmas scene, it is equally an unpleasant feeling with bleak connotations. If the world is cold, it means that it is not treating you well. Beyond this kind of cold, there

Knox 2

is the sensory imagery of the only sound being "the sweep / of easy wind and downy flake" (11-12). In other words, the narrator is not only out in the cold, but he is so alone that he actually hears the snowflakes falling in the wind. When put together with the dark, this is a bleak and lonely scene.

Renee supports her point with specific examples from the text.

Renee further analyzes the imagery she set up in the previous paragraph to ensure she sufficiently answers the prompt.

Beyond the sensory unpleasantness of dark and cold, these images have symbolic meaning when placed in the context of other literature. Frost's imagery clearly places this moment in winter, which traditionally symbolizes death, much as spring symbolizes rebirth. Moreover, even though the woods are "lovely," they are also "dark and deep," a place where in much of literature, like Shakespeare's "A Midsummer Night's Dream," characters easily lose themselves or succumb to supernatural forces. Perhaps the woods are "lovely" because their darkness tantalizes the narrator to lose himself, but if you followed such an idea through, the speaker would end up lost and frozen in the dark woods. The last lines reinforce the idea that he is being tempted by death. When recalling himself from gazing into the cold, dark woods, the speaker gives his reason as having "miles to go before I sleep" (15). Sleep, like winter, is another way of suggesting death, for much of literature speaks of death as a type of eternal sleep.

Thus, while the scene's first impression is one of a quaint New England night—an impression built through imagery of horse, village, farmhouse, and snow—the cold and dark nature imagery tells another story of death and the temptation to remain in the presence of death. By bringing these two types of imagery together in one poem, Frost perhaps suggests that death is always near, even when we think we are looking at a vivid scene of comfort. Or, to put a more optimistic spin on things, since some of the images overlap (snowy woods are both beautiful and dangerous), Frost might be trying to tell us that death is nothing to fear, that even on the darkest evening, there is still loveliness in the dark of the woods and the sweep of the flake.

Renee transitions to a brief but insightful conclusion.

In reading Renee's essay, you may have noticed that there were places that sounded a little rough or colloquial and other spots that weren't perfectly explained, such as the end of the fourth paragraph. However, her main ideas are clear and her conclusion compelling. She also used specific support and stayed exactly on topic with what the assignment asked her to do. For these reasons, Renee's essay is well done because the constraints of a timed setting often force the writer to leave a few rough spots. If you have time, do your best to revise, but remember that a timed essay will almost never have the same polished quality as a paper you have had time to think about, draft, and revise.

4 Quoting, Paraphrasing, Summarizing, and Avoiding Plagiarism

4a KNOW WHAT INFORMATION REQUIRES DOCUMENTATION

When writing from sources—whether a single source, as when you respond to a story, poem, or play you have just read, or multiple sources, as when you include research—you will need to effectively use quotation, paraphrase, and summary in your paper. Quotation, paraphrase, and summary are the evidence you use for your interpretation of a work, and it is common for all three to be employed in the same paper. **Plagiarism** occurs when this material isn't presented accurately. In this chapter, you will find information on how to keep track of the author, title, or URL for any source you have consulted (see also Writing the Research Paper, Avoiding Plagiarism, and Documenting Sources). Keeping track of sources is critical, because how you present your evidence determines more than just how convincing your paper is; it keeps your paper honest by giving your readers

- A framework (who, what, when, where, and how) for your response.
- The specifics in the source that led you to your observations, thoughts, and connections.

Marginal annotations, underlined and highlighted passages, or notes in a reading journal help you trace your response back to specific source material. Your interaction with one text or many provides the basis of your interpretation and the thesis of your paper. Whether you base your paper on a single source or you work with multiple sources, you will likely need to summarize a work to provide your reader with a framework for your analysis. When working with multiple sources, you may also need to summarize a number of critical opinions. It is likely you will paraphrase a short passage to give your reader context for your assessment or the point of view of a scholarly work. Should you be writing about drama, you'll likely quote from the play; should you be discussing a poem, it's almost inevitable that several lines of poetry will be included in your discussion. The guidelines provided here will keep you from plagiarizing when you have summarized, paraphrased, or quoted sources. You will always want to document in your paper where you found the kinds of information listed in the following box.

Information Requiring Documentation

- Lines from a story, poem, or play
- Opinions, observations, interpretations by writers, critics, and scholars
- Information from expert and/or sponsored sites
- Visual materials, including tables, charts, or graphs
- Footnotes from printed sources
- Statements that are open to debate
- Historical information that is not commonly known
- Statistics, or surveys, census or poll results if you use them

SAMPLES OF TYPES OF INFORMATION REQUIRING DOCUMENTATION

The whaling industry in nineteenth-century America collapsed when flexible steel hoops replaced whalebone in women's corsets.

A twenty-year Swiss study of organic farming found that organic farms yielded more produce per unit of energy consumed than farms that did not use organic farming methods.

Smoking kills over 418,000 people every year in the United States.

The easiest way to avoid plagiarism is to remember that you must tell your reader the sources of all facts, ideas, and opinions that are taken from others that are not considered common knowledge. If a number of sources contain the same information and that information is widely considered to be true, it is considered common knowledge. For example, in biology, the structure of DNA and the process of cell division or photosynthesis are considered common knowledge. A recent scientific discovery about genetics, however, would not be common knowledge, so you would need to cite the source of this information. When in doubt cite your source; citing is never incorrect.

COMMON KNOWLEDGE (DOCUMENTATION NOT REQUIRED)

Millions of soldiers died in the trenches of the Western front in World War I.

Mohandas K. Gandhi was assassinated in 1948.

The cheetah is the fastest-moving land animal.

Tip for Avoiding Plagiarism and the Web. What you find on the Web requires extra precaution to make sure you document correctly where you got your information. Do not assume that what you find on the Web is common knowledge. Write in your notes the URL as well as *the date* that you accessed the site. Websites are notoriously prone to change, so this helps you keep your source clear. In your notes, put quotation marks around anything that is a direct quotation (wherever you found the information, print or online) so that you can easily see when you are using another's words. It is easy to cut whole passages from the Internet and paste them into your paper, or to think you have paraphrased when you have quoted if your notes aren't effective. This is plagiarism. Diligence is needed to avoid cobbling together a patchwork of sources without complete and accurate source information.

4b USE SOURCES TO SUPPORT YOUR COMMENTARY

Your paper is your own independent thought. A quotation, paraphrase, or summary should be used only if you are going to comment on it in your paper. You can expand upon a quotation, paraphrase, or summary. You can interpret it. You can indicate what you believe the work implies. You can refer to a quotation, paraphrase, or a summary. You can even disagree. Your instructor is looking at your work to make sure you have understood a selection and to see what you have discovered for yourself. So, do not worry that you don't have anything original to say. Few do, even among professionals. *How* you say what you have to say is original to you. Don't apologize by suggesting this is only your opinion ("it seems to me" or "in my opinion"). Make your case. Be confident that, if you have discovered something that is interesting to you, it will also be interesting to your reader.

- A paper with too few references to sources does not provide the evidence you need to support your case.
- A paper with too many references to sources prevents you from making your case because it is overshadowed by the ideas of others.

Use Quotation, Summary, Paraphrase

- To support a point
- To present your source's point of view
- To disagree with your source
- To generalize from examples
- To reason through examples
- To make comparisons
- To distinguish fact from opinion
- To provide context

1. Quotation: *A word-for-word copy from an original source.* Direct quotation is especially useful when you are writing about literature because the way a writer uses words is central to an understanding of the text You will use quotations as examples of the way a writer uses language. However, you can also use a quotation from another source if a technical term is used that is not easily rephrased or if rephrasing it would change its meaning. You may want to use a quotation when the ideas are so vividly and beautifully expressed that you prefer to avoid paraphrase. Even if you do, a direct quotation is not to be used as a conclusion or summation of your main point in your work. It doesn't stand on its own. You must expand upon any quotation—or paraphrase or summary—that you include in your paper.

Tip on Avoiding Plagiarism in a Quotation: Using quotation marks around information from a source while changing or omitting information from that source is a serious error. Use *brackets* **[ ]** around a word or words you insert in a quotation. Use three periods in succession (**ellipses**) **. . .** to show that you have omitted something that was in the original quotation: "He turned green **. . .** but he went on [to steer the ship]."

ORIGINAL SOURCE (from page 7 of *The Metaphysical Club* by Louis Menand).

> We think of the Civil War as a war to save the union and to abolish slavery, but before the fighting began most people regarded these as incompatible ideals. Northerners who wanted to preserve the union did not wish to see slavery extended into the territories; some of them hoped it would wither away in the states where it persisted. But many Northern businessmen believed that losing the South would mean economic catastrophe, and many of their employees believed that freeing the slaves would mean lower wages. They feared secession far more than they disliked slavery, and they were unwilling to risk the former by trying to pressure the South into giving up the latter.

➡ ***For more practice with quotation, paraphrase, and summary using this example and many others, visit www.mhhe.com/delbancole.***

SERIOUS ERROR

> Menand notes that "many Northern businessmen and many of their employees feared secession far more than they disliked slavery, and they were unwilling to risk the former by trying to pressure the South into giving up the latter" (7).

➡ *This sentence is unacceptable because the writer has not used ellipses to indicate where words have been omitted from the quotation.*

CORRECT QUOTATION

> Menand notes that "many Northern businessmen . . . and many of their employees . . . feared secession far more than they disliked slavery, and they were unwilling to risk the former by trying to pressure the South into giving up the latter" (7).

2. Paraphrase: *Someone else's ideas in your own words.* When writing about literature, you may paraphrase some of the story line in order to get to the point you want to make. In research, paraphrase is most often used when you are referring to the work of critics and scholars. If you find that the language you are trying to put into your words is already broken down to its most simple form, or that the language is too perfectly worded to change, you may want to use a quotation instead of a paraphrase. Don't paraphrase if you are not entirely sure you understand the original or you risk misrepresenting its original meaning. One test of a good paraphrase is if you can restate what you are trying to paraphrase without looking at the source.

Tip on Avoiding Plagiarism in a Paraphrase: A true paraphrase is not just a few different words, even if you feel the scholar has said something better than you could have said it yourself. *Your words* are the words that matter to your instructor. Just changing a few words—*even when you indicate the source of the paraphrase*—is still plagiarism. In a true paraphrase, the sentence structure is your own. It doesn't sound like the original; it sounds like you.

PLAGIARISM

> Menand observes that before the Civil War, many Northerners feared secession far more than they disliked slavery, and they were unwilling to risk the former by trying to pressure the South into giving up the latter (7).

➡ *This quotation is plagiarized because it uses the exact words of the source—most of a sentence—without quotation marks.*

CORRECT PARAPHRASE

> Menand observes that before the Civil War, many Northerners were afraid that secession would be worse for the country than slavery, and they were not willing to try and force the South to give up slavery for fear that a disastrous Southern secession would follow (7).

3. Summary: *A condensation of the main idea or action that includes only the supporting details related directly to that main idea.* Unlike a paraphrase, where a concept or action from a brief passage is explained in your own words, a summary lays out a long passage (such as an act in a play or a whole poem, story, play, or other work). When writing about literature, a plot summary is not enough. A summary sets the stage for an analysis, providing your readers with enough information for them to understand your commentary. In a research paper, summary can also be used to provide examples of a variety of points of view on your topic. Make comparisons between two points of view, then summarize several sources to build upon for your conclusion. (See the chapter on Common Writing Assignments for a discussion of the summary paper.)

Tip on Avoiding Plagiarism in a Summary: When you summarize information, you must include information on the source or it will appear as if you are using someone else's ideas as your own. Omitting information in a summary that alters the source's meaning is also unacceptable. Offering an inaccurate interpretation of your source in a summary is not satisfactory either. If the source's words or meaning do not support your argument as fully as you might like, find another source that does.

PLAGIARISM

> People believed that the Civil War was a war to save the union and to abolish slavery, but before the fighting began most people regarded these as incompatible ideals.

➡ *The sentence does not acknowledge that the idea comes from a source and is, therefore, an example of plagiarism. Ideas and words from a source cannot be included as if they are your own. You must give credit to the original writer.*

CORRECT SUMMARY

> According to Menand, during the Civil War people did not believe both that slavery could be abolished and the union could be saved (7).

4c ACKNOWLEDGE YOUR SOURCES

In the case of paraphrases, summaries, and direct quotations, your paper itself must include information about your source (an in-text citation), including an introductory phrase with the author and title, and the page number(s), URL, or line numbers (for a poem or play) placed immediately following the cited material and usually preceding any punctuation marks that divide or end the sentence. (See block quotation later in the next section, p. H-79.)

IN-TEXT CITATION

> According to Louis Menand in his book on the Civil War, *The Metaphysical Club,* people believed that "the Civil War was a war to save the union and to abolish slavery, but before the fighting began most people regarded these as incompatible ideals" (7).

Professional organizations (such as the Modern Language Association or the American Psychological Association) provide guidelines for how sources should be acknowledged in a paper. MLA guidelines are commonly used in writing for the humanities, and those guidelines are followed here. For more information on how to properly cite electronic and print sources using the MLA documentation styles, see the chapters on Writing the Research Paper and MLA Documentation.

Keep a running list of your sources. The more accurate and complete the information on your sources, the easier it will be to present that source accurately and completely in your paper. In addition to in-text citation, you must also provide a complete and accurate list of all the texts you have consulted in a list at the end of your paper called a **bibliography.** Anything you have cited in your paper must be included in the final bibliography for that paper. Other works, not referenced in your paper, can be included as well. The best way to prevent plagiarism is to make sure you keep precise records of the sources you consult while preparing your paper in a **working bibliography**—a list of all the sources you've used, as well as all the information you'll use to cite them later. For your working bibliography, make sure to include this information:

- The names of all the authors, editors, and/or translators of the piece
- The complete title of the work and relevant chapter title or heading; for Web pages, the name of the site and the page on which the information appears
- The publisher, copyright date, edition, and place of publication should be recorded for sources from books.
- The date, volume, issue, and page number should be included for all sources from periodicals or journals (including those you have pulled up from an online database).
- The URL (complete web address), the date the page was updated, and the date you viewed the page should be recorded for all sources from the Internet.

Plagiarism can be intentional or unintentional. Professors are adept at recognizing papers obtained via the Web—they've likely seen them before! However, unintentional plagiarism carries the same penalties. This chapter should help you avoid plagiarizing unintentionally, and you will soon be found out if your plagiarism is of the other kind.

Two Kinds of Plagiarism

Intentional plagiarism	Intentional plagiarism occurs when you buy someone else's work or copy something from a source, usually word for word, and use it without quotation marks or acknowledgment of the source, as if it were your own words.
Unintentional plagiarism	Unintentional plagiarism can result from careless note taking, such as forgetting to put quotation marks around material you copy, cutting and pasting from the web, and using material you have summarized or paraphrased and forgetting to tell readers the source of that material.

4d FORMAT QUOTATIONS TO AVOID PLAGIARISM

When you integrate your ideas with those of your sources, you will want to format your quotations so that they flow naturally into your sentences and build toward your conclusion. Where possible, keep your quotation brief, four or fewer lines for prose and no more than three for poetry or drama, since you will comment on the entire quotation in your paper. If you include a long quotation (five lines or more for prose or four or more for poetry or drama) make sure you include the entire quotation for your interpretation or analysis. Otherwise, the quotation overshadows your argument instead of supporting it. Introducing a direct quotation into a text can happen in two ways depending on whether it is short or long; each is formatted differently.

- A short quotation within a sentence is identified by quotation marks.
- A long quotation formatted in an indented block of text separated out from a sentence does not use quotation marks.

1. Refer to your source in an introductory phrase. Whether your quotation is short or long, however, you will need to introduce it with an introductory (*signal*) phrase. You need to identify the source and the author *before* the quotation. An in-text citation requires that you include the author's full name (without Mr., Miss, Mrs., or Ms.) the first time you quote from the source. Unless there is a long lapse between references to the source, the second time you quote from the same source you should use only the author's last name. Treat women and men equally when you cite them as authors, using the last name only for the second citation and no *Miss, Mrs.,* or *Ms.* Avoid the repetition of *the author says.*

Verbs to Use in an Introductory Phrase

according to	considers	notes
adds		
admits	declares	observes
aknowledges	denies	
agrees	describes	points out
asks	disagrees	proposes
asserts		proves
argues	emphasizes	
	establishes	refutes
believes	explains	rejects
	expresses	remarks
charges		reports
claims	finds	responds
comments		
compares	holds	shows
complains		states
concedes	implies	speculates
concludes	insists	suggests
contends	interprets	
continues		warns
	maintains	

2. Integrate a short quotation in a sentence and always use quotation marks. Always put a short quotation into quotation marks. Not to do so constitutes plagiarism. Keep your quotations to the point. The source material you quote as a reference should provide backup for the argument you have made. Avoid the temptation to use sources to make your arguments for you, however well the source is worded. References from outside sources, whether they are paraphrased or quoted, are *evidence* or *support* for your own arguments.

You should not use outside sources to make arguments for you.

- Use an introductory phrase to identify the source.
- If the quotation flows into the natural wording of the sentence, begin the quotation with a lowercase letter whether or not the original is capitalized.
- If your introductory phrase ends with a comma, use a capital letter.
- Use quotation marks.
- When quoting poetry in a sentence, use the format of the lines in the poem and break the lines exactly as they appear in the poem with a slash / mark.
- Place periods and commas inside the quotation marks.
- Semicolons, colons, and dashes are placed outside the quotation marks.
- Question marks and exclamation points are sometimes placed inside the quotation marks and sometimes placed outside. If the quotation is itself a question or exclamation, the question mark/exclamation point goes inside the quotation marks.
- Include page numbers for prose, line numbers for poems, act, scene, and line numbers for plays written in verse and page numbers for plays written in prose.

A SHORT QUOTATION FROM A POEM

> In Robert Frost's "Stopping by Woods on a Snowy Evening," the hypnotic rhythm of the poem is reinforced through the repetition of the speaker's last lines, "And I have miles to go before I sleep / And I have miles to go before I sleep" (lines 15-16).

INTEGRATING A QUOTATION WITH A LOWERCASE LETTER

> Even certain details of Grendel's portrayal in the movie echo the original epic. For example, the epic introduces him by calling him an inhabitant of "the abode of monster kind" (line 14).

PERIOD INSIDE QUOTATION MARK

> Blake again disrupts the meter when he writes, "And I saw it was filled with graves" (line 9), which draws attention to the word "graves."
>
> —from the student paper on William Blake's "The Garden of Love" in Common Assignments across the Curriculum.

SEMICOLON OUTSIDE QUOTATION MARKS

He is called a "fiend of hell"; "wrathful spirit"; "mighty stalker of the marches" (line 14); "creature of destruction, fierce and greedy, wild and furious" (15); and a "terrible monster, like a dark shadow of death" (17).

—from the student paper on the role of Grendel in *Beowulf,* the epic and the movie, in Common Assignments across the Curriculum.

3. Set off a long quotation in a block, and don't use quotation marks. Quotations in block format should be used sparingly because they break up your discussion and can be distracting. If you find that you do not need to refer back to a long quote in several instances, consider using a paraphrase or more precise direct quotation to present the information. If you use a long quotation to support your point, you must set the quote apart:

- Use an introductory phrase to identify the source.
- Punctuate the end of an introductory phrase with a comma or a colon.
- Leave a line of space before and after the long quotation.
- Do not use quotation marks.
- Indent each line of the quotation by ten spaces from the left margin (right margin is not indented).
- Capitalize the first word whether or not it is capitalized in the original unless quoting poetry.
- When quoting poetry, follow the line format exactly as it appears in the poem.
- Double-space.
- Include a page number (or line numbers for a poem) in parentheses after the final punctuation in the quotation.

BLOCK QUOTATION

As her spirit wanes, our heroine in Charlotte Perkins Gilman's "Yellow Wallpaper" gives her soliloquy:

> I lie down ever so much now. John says it is good for me, and to sleep all I can. Indeed he started the habit by making me lie down for an hour after each meal. It is a very bad habit, I am convinced, for you see, I don't sleep. And that cultivates deceit, for I don't tell them I'm awake—oh, no! The fact is I'm getting a little afraid of John. (226)

4e FORMAT A PARAPHRASE TO AVOID PLAGIARISM

Using paraphrase in your paper is similar to using quotation, but there are some areas that require extra care. Make sure you have understood the text you are paraphrasing; your paraphrase must be true to the original meaning of the text. Don't guess at the meaning of a text by changing a few words and letting it stand for your own idea. This is plagiarism. Even if one part of the text can be construed to support your argument, don't use it if that part doesn't represent the whole source accurately. Make it clear where your ideas end and the ideas of others begin. In addition to giving credit to others for their ideas, a clear transition from your own work to your source materials gives your writing credibility.

- Keep your paraphrase brief.
- Refer to the source in an introductory phrase.
- Include the page number in parentheses after the paraphrase.
- A period, question mark, or exclamation point goes after the page number when the page number is at the end of a sentence.

ORIGINAL SOURCE MATERIAL

Although Emily Dickinson was a noted wit in her circle of friends and family, and although her poetry is surely clever, frequently downright funny, and as we shall argue, throughout possessed of a significant comic vision, criticism has paid little attention to her humor. Dickinson's profound scrutiny of life-and-death matters has usually taken precedence in the analysis and evaluation of her work. Yet comedy is a part of that profundity.

—from "Comedy and Audience in Emily Dickinson's Poetry" by Suzanne Juhasz, Cristanne Miller, and Martha Nell Smith (See the McGraw-Hill website for the full text of this article that accompanies the Frost/Dickinson case studies.)

PARAPHRASE

Because Emily Dickinson's poetry concerns itself with serious issues like mortality, critics have long overlooked the comedy that aids her poems' success. Those who knew Dickinson personally recognized her smart humor, which shines through her poems but has since gone unnoticed. The authors of the article wish to reverse this trend of neglect, as Dickinson's witty touches are important to understanding her oeuvre.

4f FORMAT SUMMARY TO AVOID PLAGIARISM

Summary and paraphrase are certainly related, but they are not the same thing. In general, paraphrase is used for a smaller portion of the original source, and your goal is to capture the spirit of the passage you are paraphrasing, without exactly copying the sentence structure or word choice. Summary is useful for relating a larger idea that you gained from a longer passage of text, as the above example shows.

Paraphrase	Summary
• a relatively short passage	• a passage of any length
• covers every point in the passage	• condenses main idea and support
• takes up points consecutively	• changes order when necessary
• includes no interpretation	• explains point of passage

When you write a summary, introduce your source and identify the main ideas of the text. Break the discussion of those ideas into sections, and then write a sentence or two in your own words that captures each section.

ORIGINAL SOURCE

> A figure who played a major role in popularizing swing in the mid-1930s was Benny Goodman. Like Whiteman earlier and Elvis Presley a few decades later, Goodman was a white musician who could successfully mediate between a black American musical tradition and the large base of white listeners making up the majority population in the USA. Wearing glasses and conservative suits—"looking like a high school science teacher,"according to one observer (Stowe 45)—Goodman appeared to be an ordinary, respectable white American. Musically he was anything but ordinary: a virtuoso clarinetist, a skilled improviser who could solo "hot" on up tempo numbers and "sweet" on ballads, and a disciplined bandleader who demanded excellence from his players. [. . .]
>
> In the guise of swing, jazz became domesticated in the 1930s. Earlier, jazz had been associated with gin mills and smoky cabarets, illegal substances (alcohol and drugs) and illicit sex. Swing generally enjoyed a more wholesome reputation, although some preached of the dangers it posed to the morals of young people. This exuberant, extroverted music performed

> by well-dressed ensembles and their clean-cut leaders entered middle-class households through everyday appliances like the living-room Victrola and the kitchen radio. It reached a wider populace as musicians transported it from large urban centers into small towns and rural areas. Criss-crossing North America by bus, car, and train, big bands played single night engagements in dance halls, ballrooms, theatres, hotels, night clubs, country clubs, military bases, and outdoor pavilions. They attracted hordes of teenagers who came to hear the popular songs of the day and dance the jitterbug, lindy hop and Susie Q. The strenuous touring schedule of big bands was far from glamorous. Nevertheless, musicians who played in these ensembles could symbolize achievement and prove inspirational, as the writer Ralph Ellison recalled from his early years growing up in Oklahoma City. . . .
>
> Mark Tucker and Travis A. Jackson. "Jazz." *Grove Music Online*. Oxford UP. Web. 11 May 2008.

EXAMPLE OF SUMMARY

> Swing, which became the popular dance music in more reputable venues than just bars and clubs, was usually performed by big bands under the direction of white leaders like Benny Goodman and Glenn Miller. Thus, jazz became mainstream and middle class, unlike the "hot jazz" of the twenties.

5 Writing the Research Paper, Avoiding Plagiarism, and Documenting Sources

5a UNDERSTAND RESEARCH TODAY

Research today often makes its first stop at the World Wide Web. You might even access the library through your computer. Navigating the research process, therefore, requires critical skills not asked of your predecessors for one of the most common assignments across the curriculum. While the Web makes it more convenient to do your research at three o'clock in the morning if you like, it also brings with it a new set of challenges. Today you don't just find sources, you have to manage the thousands of hits you might get when you google a topic. The Web also makes it more difficult to see what is credible and valid when every site looks largely the same on the computer screen. Plus, the Web makes it easy to create a patchwork cut-and-paste of sources that can lead to unintentional plagiarism. Plagiarism occurs when a source is not properly acknowledged, and whenever you conduct research from outside sources, you run the risk of taking credit for another person's ideas. For more information on acknowledging sources, see our chapter on Quoting, Paraphrasing, Summarizing, and Avoiding Plagiarism.

This chapter will get you started on your research project and also provide guidelines for documentation that keep you from unintentionally plagiarizing someone else's work. How you take notes is more important than ever if you are to distinguish your own work from the work you have found online (or in print). In literature, your instructor is likely to want a variety of sources, not just online references. There are three basic kinds of sources with which you will be working:

- Books
- Print magazines, newspapers, or scholarly journals
- Non-print online sources

The type of source you want to use depends on the type of project you are working on. If you are approaching a piece of literature from a particular critical perspective—like the feminist, Marxist, or psychoanalytical schools of thought discussed in our chapter on Critical Approaches to Literature—your research will likely involve reading literary criticism. If you are embarking on historical criticism or biographical criticism, you will need to gear your research to sources that inform you about a time period or your author's life. This chapter provides a step-by-step walkthrough of the research process. Read the student research paper on Langston Hughes at the end of this chapter to see how these steps look in action.

5b CHOOSE A TOPIC

Often, your instructor will assign a topic or provide some guidance. Or, you can find several research topics in this textbook, especially at the end of each case study. We have provided not only the topics, but also a list of good sources to get you started. In addition, there are many relevant secondary sources that you can find for each case study on our website at www.mhhe.com/delbanco1e. Research projects require a considerable amount of reading and a good deal of thinking. Your job is to make your process and the research project fun. Explore a topic that interests you, and discover new ideas that will help inform your own idea. Break the topic down so that you can manage your research and create a project that teaches you about a subject you enjoy.

1. Identify what interests you. Choose your topic, or choose how you want to address your assigned topic, by considering what strikes you as important or interesting in the work of literature you are researching.

> **Example:** Our student author, Christine Keenan, was assigned to write a research paper on Langston Hughes. To find a topic, she thought of what she knew about Hughes that interested her. Since Christine loves music, she decided she would like to know more about how jazz influenced Langston Hughes.

2. Form a question. Once you have a topic in mind, explore how that aspect of the work is meaningful to you. Do some of the brainstorming exercises that students used to get started in chapter 3, Writing about Fiction, chapter 17, Writing about Poetry, and chapter 32, Writing about Drama. Turn this aspect into a question. Christine made a list of words that she associated with jazz.

> *improvisation, be-bop, Duke Ellington, and nightclubs*

She also considered that jazz has several forms including blues, swing, be-bop, and cool jazz. Based on this, she formed the question.

Example: "What elements of jazz influenced Langston Hughes when he wrote his poems?"

3. Narrow your topic. She then decided to narrow her question further by picking two poems influenced by jazz, an early poem, "The Dream Keeper," and a later poem, "Harlem [2]."

5c FIND AND MANAGE PRINT AND ONLINE SOURCES

The sources you cite in your research should be *reliable* and *relevant*—significant in the context of your current discussion. Refining your keyword search can help prevent information overload and find sources that are pertinent to your topic. Your instructor may have some recommendations for good sources on a topic, and there are also sources listed in this textbook as good starting places. The Web does not offer any guarantees about the accuracy of its content. However, some websites and search engines are better than others for trustworthiness. If your website ends in *.org*, *.edu*, or *.gov*, it's like having a good character reference for the content on the site. If your search engine has preselected source material (such as GoogleScholar) or if you have accessed a library database, you will have saved yourself the painful weeding through of hits that cannot help you. Some tips for finding reliable and relevant sources include:

- *Title.* In a scholarly article or book, the title and subtitle will usually be designed to convey the topic of the piece as specifically as possible. If the title doesn't seem relevant to your topic, that author or piece of work might not be the best source for your discussion.
- *Date of publication.* For print sources, this will often be found on the copyright page of the book. Note not just the copyright of the current edition, but the original copyright. Journals will have dates printed with their issue numbers and often on individual articles themselves to inform the reader when the article's research was originally conducted. A reliable web page will usually print the date last modified at the bottom of the page. Bear in mind that "relevant" doesn't always mean "current." A classic source is one that is a hallmark in the field. If you see a source cited when you're reading sources elsewhere, you've likely come upon a classic work. A current source is just what the word suggests, something written about a topic within the past five years.
- *Abstract.* Most research papers in journals will have **abstracts,** or summaries, that explain the research done, briefly detail the findings, and state the conclusion of the research.
- *Chapter titles or headings.* A perusal of a print source's detailed table of contents can help you determine if the source will contain information useful and relevant to your research. If you are searching for an interpretation of Shakespeare's *Romeo & Juliet* and the index of the book indicates that all mentions of that play occur in a chapter called "Shakespeare: The Fraud," that text might be biased toward a perspective beyond the scope of your paper.

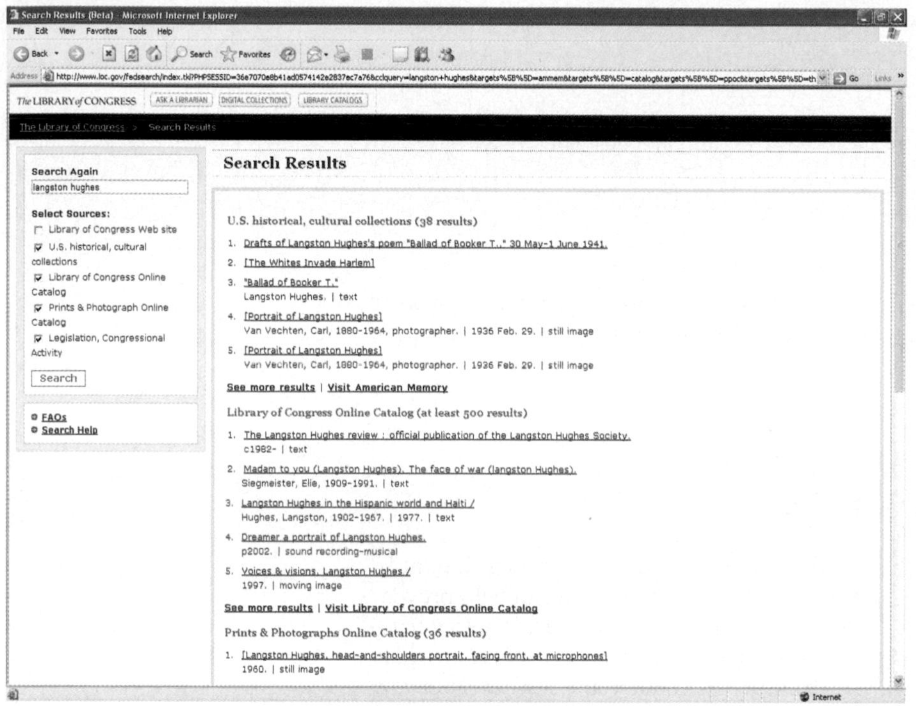

(Library of Congress search for "Langston Hughes")

1. Refine your keyword search. Whether you are searching one of your library's databases or the Web, refine your key words by grouping words together, e.g. "Harlem Renaissance." Use *and* or + to bring up sites that have both topics together. Use *or* when you list sites that are for either topic. Two words are better than one to help you narrow the number of sites that come up; use quotation marks around titles or parentheses around key phrases to manage the number of hits as well. To find information on Web pages and avoid the information flood, a good key word search is essential. Experiment with the phrasing of your keyword.

2. Use more than one search engine. The Internet brings the world to your door, but don't just google. Use at least three general search engines to locate the sources you need. In addition to Google, you may want to try Yahoo! (http://www.yahoo.com) or WebCrawler (http://www.webcrawler.com). Some sites search several different search engines at once: Library of Congress (http://www.loc.gov) or the Librarian's Index to the Internet (http://www.lii.org). You even have search sites that have already been vetted by experts, such as GoogleScholar (http://scholar.google.com), About.com (http://www.about.com), and Looksmart (http://www.looksmart.com).

Google Advanced Scholar Search - Microsoft Internet Explorer

Google Scholar BETA — Advanced Scholar Search

Advanced Search Tips | About Google Scholar

Find articles — with all of the words: langston hughes — 10 results — Search Scholar
with the exact phrase
with at least one of the words
without the words
where my words occur: anywhere in the article

Author — Return articles written by — e.g., "PJ Hayes" or McCarthy

Publication — Return articles published in — e.g., J Biol Chem or Nature

Date — Return articles published between — e.g., 1996

Subject Areas — Return articles in all subject areas. / Return only articles in the following subject areas:
Biology, Life Sciences, and Environmental Science
Business, Administration, Finance, and Economics
Chemistry and Materials Science
Engineering, Computer Science, and Mathematics
Medicine, Pharmacology, and Veterinary Science
Physics, Astronomy, and Planetary Science
Social Sciences, Arts, and Humanities

©2008 Google

(Google Scholar Advanced Search Page)

3. Use the library, on campus and online. Check out your library's website. Talk to your librarian. The library is not just a collection of printed texts anymore. Your librarian can help you find the library's computerized catalog of books and discipline-specific encyclopedias, bibliographies, and almanacs, such as the *MLA International Bibliography of Books and Articles on Modern Language and Literature* (also available online) or the *Oxford History of English Literature*. In addition, the librarian can help you locate the library's database of scholarly journals and other electronic resources.

Databases, Online Periodicals

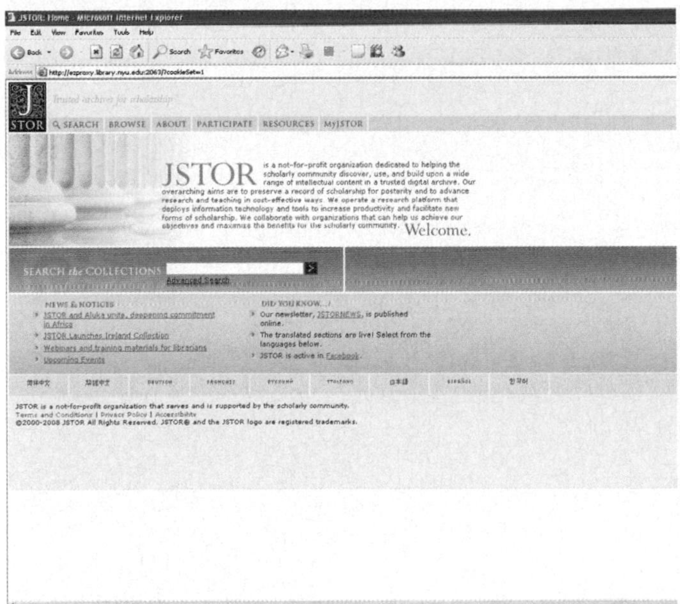

(JSTOR Online Database)

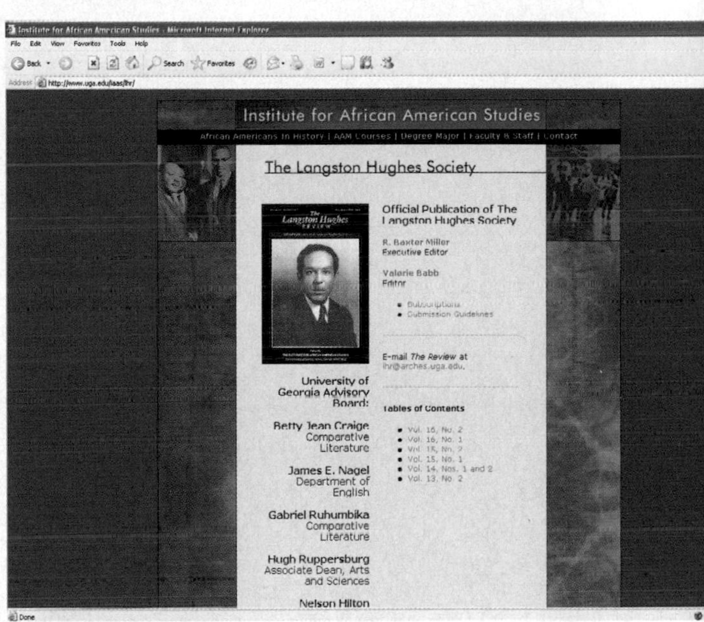

(Langston Hughes Society online Periodical)

Library searches can help you find the kinds of sources your professor wants to see on your topic.

Example: Christine used a database through her university's library to do keyword searches using the words "Langston Hughes" and "jazz." She skimmed the results and picked a few that seemed most related to her topic.

TIP

Searching the Internet

When you go online for help, you may feel all the information is the same. It only looks that way. The Internet serves up information in a couple of ways that it is important for you to differentiate.

- A *general search* from the entire World Wide Web includes everything that anyone has posted on your topic, from very personal blogs to news groups. You will need to carefully evaluate anything you find in a general search to determine if it is providing information that is reliable.
- An *online database* from your library searches through a collection of reliable published articles and electronic journals. The results of a database search will include only publications and will connect you to abstracts, summaries, or full text (that is, the entire article).

These film shots illustrate portrayals of the Grendel monster and the Beowulf hero in the movie Beowulf *(top) and the movie* The 13th Warrior *(bottom).*

5d EVALUATE VISUAL SOURCES

A picture is worth a thousand words, or so the old proverb goes. We live in a visual world and visual data is now as easy as a cut-and-paste job off GoogleImage. Like all source information, however, it must be relevant and reliable. Visuals must serve a specific purpose in your paper. A graph or chart can be a useful snapshot of quantitative data. A diagram is a useful flowchart to explain a process. A picture is qualitative evidence that is used to strengthen or amplify your point. If you have taken your visual from the Web or another source, it must be documented in your bibliography and identified in your paper with a caption. The example here is evidence for a paper on adapting the *Beowulf* epic.

5e EVALUATE TEXT SOURCES

Sources can be popular or scholarly. A popular source is something you could buy easily at a store, such as *Time* magazine. It will likely have advertisements in it or be advertised to the general public (such as a self-help book like *Rich Dad, Poor Dad*). A scholarly source is generally found through a library rather than a store. The writers focus on discipline-specific rather than broad, general topics and are usually affiliated with a university. These books are likely to have footnotes or include citations to sources and bibliographies. When considering whether a print publication is popular or scholarly, follow these guidelines:

- *Note the publisher of the book, magazine, or journal.* A commercial publisher will probably suggest a popular aim, whereas an academic publisher such as a university press will suggest a scholarly aim.
- *Consider the authors of the articles.* Take note of both the authors' names and their affiliations (generally universities for scholarly articles), and consider how their titles match up with the topic of their article. For instance, Alton Brown might be a name you recognize as an authority from The Food Network, but he would not be a trustworthy expert to cite in a paper on comparative politics.
- *Notice the range of topics in the publication.* A popular publication will usually cover a range of topics to appeal to a wide readership, whereas a scholarly publication will focus on various aspects of one topic.
- *Observe the visual presentation of the publication.* Is it flashy and full of ads and cartoons? Or is it mostly text-based, with fewer but higher quality captioned images?
- *Evaluate the articles themselves.* Academic articles will often be preceded by abstracts that summarize their findings and followed by bibliographies or listings of works cited. Popular articles, on the other hand, may lead in with a catchy line that leaves an unanswered question and will seldom list references.
- *Ask whether the source is refereed or peer reviewed.* A publication may or may not specify this, but most trustworthy scholarly publications accept articles only after they have been reviewed, debated, and accepted by a body of experts in the field. Some research databases will allow you to filter for peer-reviewed publications; or, when in doubt, you can ask your librarian whether a publication has been refereed.

You may find it difficult when using the Web to tell the difference not only between a popular and a scholarly site, but also between a reliable site and one that is biased. The Library of Congress website can be counted on, as can its search engine, so don't just google. Find search engines that will save you the time by leading you to reliable sites. Many of the same guidelines you use for evaluating print sources can apply to evaluating an online publication as well. Some other things you can pay attention to when considering whether an electronic source like a website is reliable include

- *The Web address.* As mentioned earlier, often reliable content will be found on websites with the domains *.org* (non-profit organization), *.edu* (educational institution), *.mil* (military), or *.gov* (United States government). Keep in mind that not all information on a *.org* or *.edu* (or sometimes *.gov* or *.mil*) is reliable. Information on these pages may be biased; or, sometimes, the information might be from a personal page hosted by that specific domain. In this case, you will often notice a tilde (~) followed by a name or personalized "handle" (such as your school ID or AIM screen name) in the Web address.
- *The host of the page.* Is the Web page hosted by a university or academic association? Is it an article of an online encyclopedia? Be careful of sites like Wikipedia, which can claim to be "encyclopedias" or "dictionaries" but may not be accurate. Do not use Wikipedia as a citation in a college paper. You will need to verify the content you find on Wikipedia through another source, and if it is common knowledge (a birth date, for example), it won't need a citation.
- *The visual presentation.* As with print sources, you can tell a lot about a Web page's content and intended audience just by looking at how it is presented. Flashy ads, pop-up windows, intricate backgrounds, complex layouts, and funky colors are all indications that a website might not contain reliable content. A reliable Web page, created by an academic for academic use, will be laid out functionally, without intricate designs or distracting colors.

- *The tone of the information.* Tone is a major indicator of scholarliness and bias. Avoid Web pages that use poor grammar or punctuation or employ colloquial Internet shorthand. Scholarly information will seldom be presented so informally. Also take note of aggravated tone of voice, or hyperbolic claims, or a failure to consider more than one point of view. These are indicators of bias—which might support your point of view, but will detract from the legitimacy of the source as support.

Whenever you are conducting research, if an opinion or piece of information seems fishy or flimsy, you should double-check. If you find that information or point of view in only one place, there's a good chance it is unsupported or not widely agreed upon by the academic community. Many databases now provide information on where an article or book has been cited by other academics in their research; this can be a valuable resource in confirming the reliability of a research source.

5f RECOGNIZE UNRELIABLE WEBSITE WARNING SIGNS

The following example shows two websites containing the text of Langston Hughes's poem "Harlem," one unreliable and one reliable. Note the striking differences between the two. Likely your eye will go first to the unreliable site; whereas the reliable site by the Poetry Foundation is designed as a resource, the unreliable site hosted by PoemHunter.com is designed to attract attention and amass visits to the page.

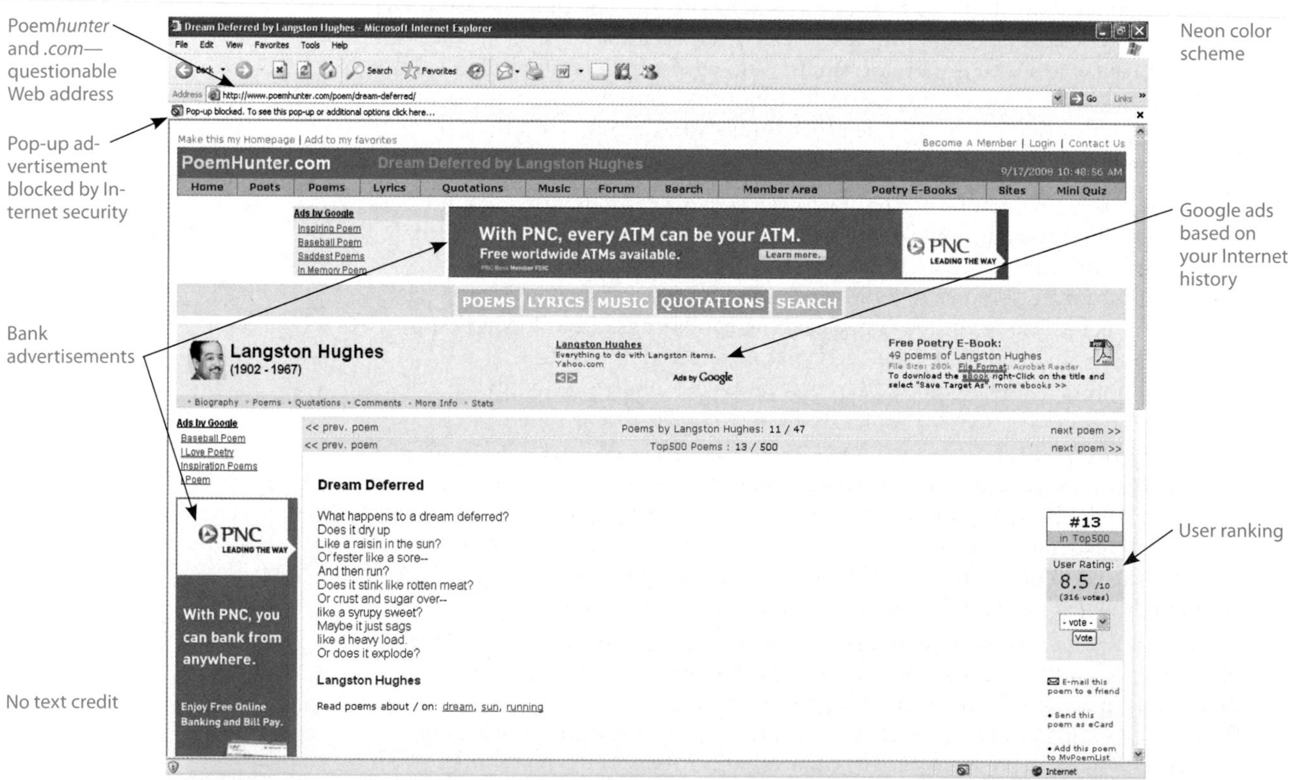

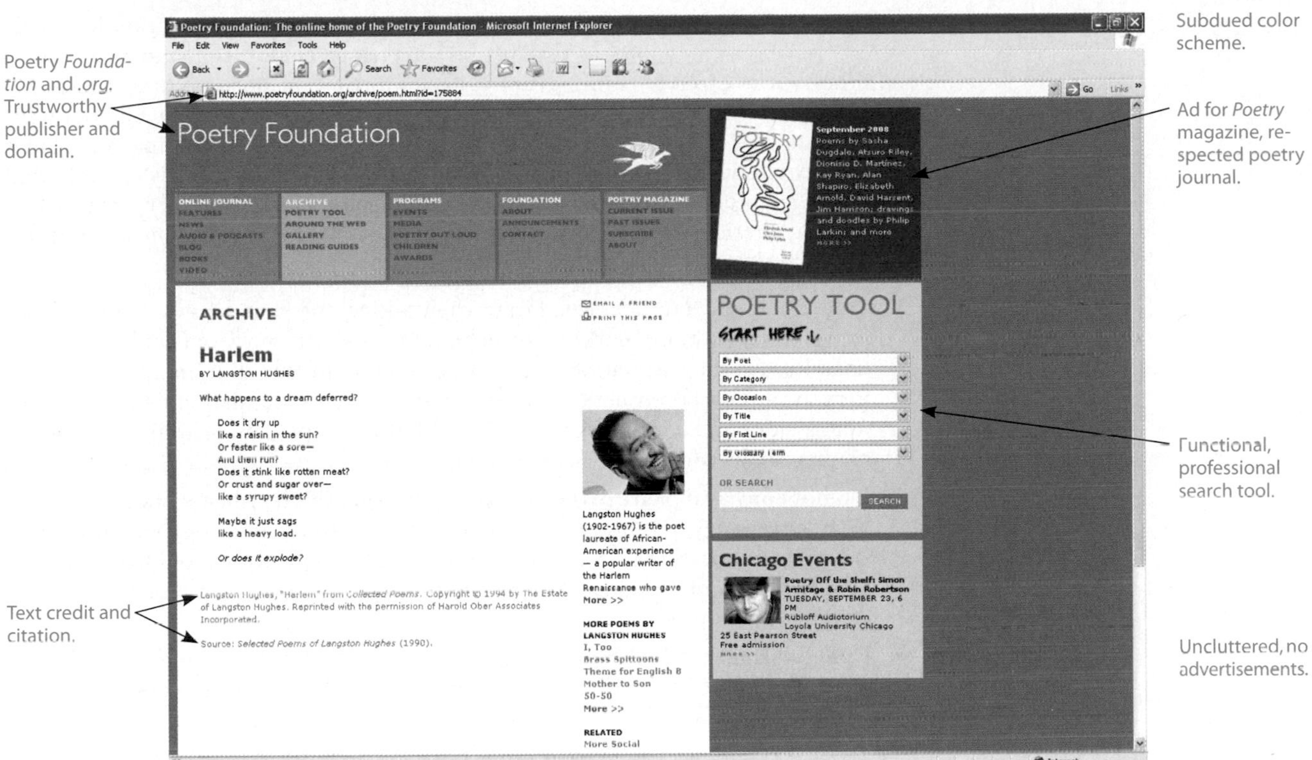

Besides flashy colors and design, there are other major differences between the two. Whereas PoemHunter.com has bank ads (don't ignore that blocked pop-up ad, it's a major clue to unreliability), the Poetry Foundation website advertises only its own publication, *Poetry* magazine, a well-known and respected journal of poetry. Notice also the references that follow the poem text: PoemHunter.com does attribute the author of the poem but does not cite any permission or original publication information.

It will save you time if you can quickly recognize the difference between reliable and unreliable sites. A google search for Langston Hughes's "Harlem" will list PoemHunter.com before the Poetry Foundation, so strong searching skills and judgment are your keys to efficient, effective Web research.

5g WORK WITH SOURCES TO AVOID PLAGIARISM

As you collect your sources for your papers, your source notes will protect you from plagiarism. Take careful notes as you read your sources. You may want to use sticky notes to flag specific quotes or passages that you find interesting or of particular relevance to your topic. A necessary part of writing a research paper is the inclusion and citation of outside sources, usually scholarly works from books, journals, and trustworthy Web pages. Because of the risk of plagiarism (taking credit for another's words or ideas), it is important to know the several appropriate ways to include outside information.

There are two different approaches to including outside information into your own research paper, and both require **in-text parenthetical citation** and documentation in the **Works Cited** (or **Bibliography,** depending on the documentation style you are working within) at the end of your paper. Always be sure to copy the bibliographical information of the source so you can easily return to it when writing your paper and properly cite it (for more on this, see the MLA Documentation Style Guide that follows this chapter). All works that have been included in your paper with in-text parenthetical citations must be included in your Works Cited page. Some general tips to avoid plagiarism during research are:

- **Take notes on your sources.** First, when taking notes, make sure to underline or put into quotation marks all direct quotations you copy from books or journals. Record the page numbers and other source information that you'll need for your in-text parenthetical citation. This will help you distinguish your own impressions and conclusions from those that you copied directly and to avoid plagiarism by correctly citing your sources.
- **Do not copy and paste directly into your paper.** Next, when working with Web sources, try not to copy and paste directly into the body of your work; consider instead pasting into a separate document and printing it out to consult alongside your other notes. It's much easier to catch yourself retyping whole passages from another source.
- **Keep bibliographical information.** Finally, choose a documentation style (MLA, APA) early and stick to it as you create the body of your work. Usually your instructor will have assigned you a style for the assignment. If you cannot cite as you write, make sure to note "citation needed" in appropriate places, such as after paraphrases, figures, or direct quotations.

5h REFERENCE CITATIONS WITHIN THE PAPER IN THE END-OF-PAPER WORKS CITED PAGE

When you use sources in an MLA -style paper, you must include a parenthetical reference in the body of your paper (for more information, see our chapter on Quoting, Paraphrasing, Summarizing, and Avoiding Plagiarism) and a corresponding entry in a Works Cited page at the end of your paper. The idea is simple: full information about the books, journals, or websites you used in writing your paper appears in a list (the Works Cited page) at the end of your paper. Including all that information in the body of your paper would bog down both you and your reader. Instead, insert a brief reference in parentheses after the word or idea you have borrowed from an outside source. This parenthetical citation does two jobs: (1) It shows your reader exactly which sentences of your paper include ideas that are not your own, and (2) It points the reader to the original source by corresponding with the full citation that occurs in the Works Cited page.

1. In-text parenthetical reference. Here, the parenthetical citation tells the reader that the student author has summarized or paraphrased an idea that she found on pages 61 and 62 of a source with an author whose last name is Borshuk.

SENTENCE FROM STUDENT PAPER:

Also, the traditionally African-American art form had now been taken over and turned into a commercial success largely by whites, with a few exceptions like Duke Ellington and Count Basie (Borshuk 61-62).

2. Corresponding entry from works cited page. Turning to the Works Cited page at the end of the paper, the reader can find the entry beginning with "Borshuk" and know that the information following it is the source from which it came. In this case, the source is a book called *Swinging the Vernacular* by Michael Borshuk. The parenthetical citation and the works cited entry have worked together to inform the reader of the original source of the idea.

Borshuk, Michael. Swinging the Vernacular. New York: Routledge, 2006.

5i ORGANIZE YOUR RESEARCH AND DEVELOP A THESIS

1. Connect your interpretation of a text to various sources. Consider what each source tells you about your topic. Particularly if you are reading literary criticism, decide whether or not you agree with the critic. If you agree, you may want to use what that critic says to corroborate your reading. If you disagree, use that critic's perspective as a springboard into talking about your own perspective.

Example: Christine read the following quote in one of her sources:

> Langston Hughes, in his collection of poems, lavishly uses such characteristics of jazz as repetitions, choruses, riffs, scats, and nonsensical onomatopoeia, to achieve musical success as well as audience participation. It is also significant to note that Hughes's poems are often marked by dissonance, discordance, and line irregularity, which all contribute to the representation of the jazz spirit in verse forms.

Although this quote directly related to her topic, Christine found that she was dissatisfied with the vague way in which most sources—like this one—talked about the jazz elements in Hughes's poems. She began to consider the historical reasons why Hughes might have chosen these specific elements.

2. Form a working thesis. Once you have gathered your own ideas and taken notes on your sources, try to state your overall idea in a sentence or two. Most likely, your thesis will have the kernel of the idea that you started with, but it will have become more nuanced by your research. (See more on thesis in our chapter on Writing from Reading.)

Example: Christine's original idea was to talk about jazz elements in Hughes's poems. Her research showed her that most critics approach his jazz poetry from a general angle. As a result, she formed the following thesis, which shows a very specific interpretation of why Hughes chose certain jazz elements.

> ***Working thesis:*** Hughes used jazz in a significant way. More than simply feeling jazz's influence generally, Hughes felt the influence of African-American jazz specifically.

3. Choose your best support. Review the notes you took on your sources and on the primary text. Select a few quotes that best illustrate a point you want to make. Note ideas that you will want to paraphrase or summarize in your paper, and remember that these are important forms of support as well. For examples of successful summary, paraphrase, and direct quotation refer to our chapter on Quoting, Paraphrasing, Summarizing, and Avoiding Plagiarism and the sample research paper in this chapter.

5j DRAFT AND REVISE YOUR DRAFT

Now that you have conducted your research and developed a thesis, you are ready to draft your paper. This is just a first draft, so leave yourself time to revise.

- **Introduction.** Your introduction sets up the rest of your paper.
- **Body.** The body of your paper presents your supporting evidence.
- **Conclusion.** Your conclusion relates your paper to a larger issue.

You may want to share your first draft with a friend or classmate. Then put your draft away and return to it fresh. You may see things you hadn't seen before. When you think through your thesis and look at the supporting evidence for your thesis, you may even find that you've changed your mind. Your thesis can be refined in response to your writing. To see revisions of the introduction, body, and conclusion in the paper on Langston Hughes, go to our Chapter on Writing from Reading. There you will find more on the drafting and revising process.

You can see in-text references and a properly formatted Works Cited page by looking at the student research paper that follows. Other student papers, like the explication of William Blake's "The Garden of Love," which appear in Common Writing Assignments, can also serve as models for in-text references. In that particular paper, note the proper parenthetical citation of lines of poetry rather than page numbers.

Remember, too, that even if you respond to a single source, you should still cite that work. This is especially important when many versions of the same text exist—for example, if you are reading Charlotte Bronte's classic *Jane Eyre* from a Penguin Classics edition, the pagination will be different from the *Jane Eyre* edition published by Oxford World's Classics. Only a full citation in a Works Cited page will tell your reader from which version you are reading. For an example of a single source, see the final draft of the student paper in chapter 3 on Jamaica Kincaid's "Girl."

Sample Student Research Paper

Christine Keenan

Professor Jackson

English 200

15 May 2008

Title centered; no underline.

From Dream Keeper to Dream Deferred:

Langston Hughes and Jazz Poetry

Quote from website source.

Jazz poetry, according to the American Academy of Poets website, is "a literary genre defined as poetry necessarily informed by jazz music—that is, poetry in which the poet responds to and writes about jazz" ("A Brief Guide to Jazz Poetry"). Langston Hughes was a jazz poet in that his poetry often captured jazz in a literary form. Many critics point to specific techniques that Hughes employs to create the effect of jazz. One such critic is Lionel Davidas, who writes:

Block quote (more than four lines long) from a periodical source.

> Langston Hughes, in his collection of poems, lavishly uses such characteristics of jazz as repetitions, choruses, riffs, scats, and nonsensical onomatopoeia, to achieve musical success as well as audience participation. It is also significant to note that Hughes's poems are often marked by dissonance, discordance, and line irregularity, which all contribute to the representation of the jazz spirit in verse forms. (268)

Establishes a critical reading to which the student responds.

Thesis statement

Although these observations are true, readings like Davidas's fail to show the full extent of Hughes's achievement in jazz poetry. Beyond being a jazz poet, Hughes understood the significance of jazz—even as it was being created—and used only those aspects of jazz that express the African-American experience.

Author maps out how she will support her thesis.

Two of Hughes's collections that have an overt connection to music are *The Weary Blues,* published in 1926, and *Montage of a Dream Deferred,* published in 1951. In the twenty-five years between their publications, jazz music changed dramatically. Two poems, "The Dream Keeper" from *The Weary Blues* and "Harlem [2]" from *Montage of a Dream Deferred,* show how Hughes effectively responded to the current trends in jazz from an African-American perspective.

Topic sentence introduces first poem to be analyzed.

Hughes first published "The Dream Keeper" in 1925 and included it in his collection *The Weary Blues* the following year (Rampersad 617). At that time, America was in the midst of the "Jazz Age," the period from 1920-1930 marked by energy and optimism. Jazz itself was popular and connoted rebellion as it was associated with nightclubs, sex, and drinking (Tucker, screen 4). But Hughes's collection was clearly influenced more by the blues than by this new form of jazz. The title of the collection suggests the blues takes center stage in these poems, and indeed, "The Dream Keeper" is no exception. While it does not have as overt a connection to the blues as Hughes's poems that replicate blues lyrics directly—such as "Po Boy Blues"—the repetition early in the poem bears echoes of the repetition characteristic of the blues. "Bring me all of your" is repeated twice within the first three lines; the object the addressee is told to bring, however, varies (lines 1, 3). In a way, lines one through three are a compounded version of blues lyrics. Typical blues lyrics follow a pattern where the first couplet repeats before a third couplet resolves it. Here, half the couplet is repeated and half resolved in both instances. Blues also has a hand in the pace of the poem. Compound phrases like "cloud-cloth" and "too-rough" slow the pace of reading, as does the high number of line breaks compared to the small number of words (6, 7).

Example of paraphrase.

Student's own analysis.

Since Hughes was writing in the Jazz Age, it may seem surprising that so many of his poems in *The Weary Blues* reflect the blues. In part, his decision may have been informed by the fact that jazz grew out of the blues, and the close relationship of the two forms of music allowed Hughes to use blues and still be in the realm of jazz. But blues is marked by a "blue" or melancholy frame of mind (Oliver, screen 1), not the exuberance of the Jazz Age. Examining the historical context offers an answer for why Hughes chose blues over jazz. While the Roaring Twenties brought "unprecedented prosperity" to the United States ("Roaring Twenties"), it was also the era of the Great Migration, the movement in which ten percent of African Americans left the South and moved North. These were difficult times for blacks, as they faced low wages, poor housing conditions, and disease in the northern cities to which they relocated (Marks). Also, while positive advances did occur in the African-American community, such as the Harlem Renaissance, Emily Bernard has noted that most blacks were not affected

Example of summary.

by the Renaissance—only a so-called talented tenth participated, leaving most blacks to face everyday problems (Bernard xvi-xvii).

Transition paragraph. The first two sentences conclude the blues discussion. The last sentence segues into discussion of the second poem.

To put it simply, jazz at the time that Hughes was writing poems for *The Weary Blues* had two forms: the exuberant new jazz and the blues roots from which it came. Hughes chose the form of music—the blues—that best reflected the state of the common black man. By the time Hughes was writing the poems for *Montage of a Dream Deferred,* however, jazz had changed and once again offered two new forms.

Example of summary.

The 1930s and 40s brought a change to jazz: ensembles of about twelve players began to change the rhythms of jazz into swing. Swing, which became the popular dance music in more reputable venues than just bars and clubs, was usually performed by big bands under the direction of white leaders like Benny Goodman and Glenn Miller.[1] Thus, jazz became mainstream and middle class, unlike the "hot jazz" of the 20s (Tucker, screen 5). Also, the traditionally African-American art form had now been taken over and turned into a commercial success largely by whites, with a few exceptions like Duke Ellington and Count Basie (Borshuk 61-62).

Example of paraphrase.

Fig. 1 The Glenn Miller Orchestra Source: Photo Gallery. Glenn Miller Orchestra Online. Glenn Miller Productions, Inc. Web. 12 May 2008.

Jazz underwent another major change in the 1940s. Young African-American musicians in Harlem met in informal jam sessions where they began to experiment with nearly every aspect of the music—melody, harmony, and rhythm.[2] Musicians such as Dizzy Gillespie, Thelonious Monk, and Charlie Parker increasingly championed improvisation and creativity over the organized big band aesthetic. Their innovations included "rapid tempo, irregular phrase groups . . . sudden, sharp drum accents, [and] chromatically altered notes" (Tucker, screen 7). This new form of jazz became known as bebop, a form of music that many critics see as "the revolt of young black musicians of the ghetto against the commercialization of 'swing music' of the time" (Lenz 274). In other words, bebop made jazz into a predominantly African-American art once more.

Citation of both paraphrase and direct quote.

Fig. 2 Tommy Potter, Charlie Parker, Dizzy Gillespie, and John Coltrane—leaders of the bebop movement—pictured at the famous jazz club Birdland, c. 1951. Source: "Charlie Parker, Uptown and Down." *New York Times on the Web. The New York Times*. Web. 12 May 2008.

Topic sentence introduces the second poem to be analyzed.

When Langston Hughes penned "Harlem [2]," two types of jazz existed: the mellow, organized sound of swing and the creative, frantic sound of bebop. For *Montage of a Dream Deferred,* Hughes chose to use the latter jazz form, as his preface to the collection suggests:

Example of paraphrase.

> In terms of current Afro-American popular music and the sources from which it has progressed—jazz, ragtime, swing, blues, boogie-woogie, and be-bop—this poem on contemporary Harlem, like be-bop, is marked by conflicting changes, sudden nuances, sharp and impudent interjections, broken rhythms, and passages sometimes in the manner of the jam session, sometimes the popular song, punctuated by the riffs, runs, breaks, and disc-tortions [sic] of the music of a community in transition. (Rampersad 387)

Citation of line in poem.

Conclusion that shows significance of student's preceding analysis.

Indeed, these bebop-like traits are present in "Harlem [2]": "conflicting changes" and "sudden nuance" can be seen in the series of images Hughes selects; "sharp and impudent interjections" occur in the form of the last line, "*Or does it explode?*" (line 11); and "broken rhythms" are created by the space after the first line and the space before the last line. Hughes, then, successfully reflects bebop technique in his poetry, and in so doing, uses the form of jazz aligned with African Americans, rather than the form of mainstream, middle-class whites.

Topic sentence that Introduces a new thread of discussion and analysis.

Reiteration that citation is to poetic line. Avoids confusion with source page numbers found in other citations.

More significant than the blues and bebop form, however, is Hughes's use of blues and bebop content. "The Dream Keeper" and "Harlem [2]" share the theme of dreams, yet each reflects the mindset of the music that influenced it—music that in turn was influenced by the historical events of its day. "The Dream Keeper" is itself dreamy in its imagery of "blue cloud-cloth" and the diction of phrases like "heart melodies" (6, 7). Despite these whimsical elements, the act of tucking away one's dreams so the world will not harm them is a sad one. In fact, the tone of the poem is melancholy, or "blue." Even the one color mentioned in the poem is "blue," which

Student's analysis.

Example of summary.

guides the reader toward blue (i.e., sad) feelings (6). This laying aside of dreams is more than the material of blues music; it was also, for many blacks, the reality of the Great Migration. Reading "The Dream Keeper" with the Great Migration in mind makes the poem seem as if it is directly about the blues created by the migration. Blacks were motivated to migrate by the promise of opportunity and freedom from the South's discrimination; once in the North, however, blacks often found limited advancement possibilities in their jobs and continued to suffer from segregation (Marks). In a sense, then, African Americans of the Great Migration often had to lay aside their dreams from the "too-rough fingers" of reality (7).

Student's synthesis of poem and historical context.

Student's analysis.

Similarly, "Harlem [2]" captures the mindset and historical context that gave rise to bebop. Although the dream theme is the same as in "The Dream Keeper," its imagery of "fester[ing] like a sore" and "stink[ing] like rotten meat" suggests an uglier, bitterer side of dreams than anything that appears in "The Dream Keeper" (4, 6). John Lowney's characterization of Harlem is helpful in understanding this shift; he writes, "By the 1940s, Harlem was of course no longer the center of refuge and hope associated with the New Negro Renaissance. Although still a major destination for poor migrant blacks during the Great Depression, Harlem had become better known nationally as an explosive site of urban racial conflict, first in 1935 and then in 1943" (362). Those years saw race riots in Harlem, and racial tension continued to grow as blacks faced discrimination even in the World War II era (362). Lowney notes that "the agitated sound of *Montage* struck many of [Hughes's] contemporaries as a radical departure from the more straightforward 'populist' rhetoric of his best-known work" (369). Indeed, in reflecting bebop's dramatic change from swing, Hughes's poetry also takes a dramatic shift from earlier modes. This shift shows the rising frustration of

Example of direct quotation.

Student's synthesis of poem and historical context.

African Americans whose dreams were no longer the root of melancholy from being tucked away, but were now the product of dreams that continued to be deferred, nearly halfway into the twentieth century.

As "The Dream Keeper" and "Harlem [2]" demonstrate, Hughes effectively incorporated new forms of jazz as they arose. While he does successfully use formal elements of jazz music, to end a reading there would be to miss Hughes's larger achievement. Hughes did not simply adopt jazz technique; he selected only those trends in jazz that reflected the African-American experience of the time in which he wrote. There is no room in his poetry for the smooth sounds of swing at the hands of whites; instead, he used the true African-American forms of blues and bebop. In so doing, Hughes's poetry captures both the music, as it evolved from blues to bebop, and the African-American experience, as it moved from the blues of the Great Migration to the bitter conflict of continued discrimination.

Topic sentence that signals conclusion.

Reiteration of thesis and broadening to encompass Hughes's overall achievement.

Broadens thesis to include historical discussion presented in the body of the paper

Notes

Properly formatted "Notes" section for additional information.

[1]Fig. 1 shows Glenn Miller's orchestra, which exemplifies the white, mainstream big band associated with swing of the 1930s and 1940s.

[2] Fig. 2 represents the smaller, black ensembles associated with bebop in the early 1940s. Comparing the two figures gives a visual representation of the stark difference between the two forms of jazz.

Works Cited

Introduction to a book.

Bernard, Emily. Introduction. *Remember Me to Harlem: The Letters of Langston Hughes and Carl Van Vechten, 1925-1964*. Ed. Bernard. New York: Knopf, 2001. Print.

Book.

Borshuk, Michael. *Swinging the Vernacular.* New York: Routledge, 2006. Print.

"A Brief Guide to Jazz Poetry." *Poets.org*. The American Academy of Poets. Web. 8 May 2008.

Article on a website.

Visual from Web.

"Charlie Parker, Uptown and Down." *New York Times on the Web. The New York Times*. Web. 12 May 2008.

Davidas, Lionel. " 'I, Too, Sing America': Jazz and Blues Techniques and Effects in Some of Langston Hughes's Selected Poems." *Dialectical Anthropology* 26 (2001): 267-272. Print.

Print periodical.

Book.

Hughes, Langston. *Montage of a Dream Deferred.* New York: Henry Holt, 1951. Print.

Hughes, Langston. *The Weary Blues*. New York: Knopf, 1926. Print.

Book.

Article from a database.

Lenz, Gunter. "The Riffs, Runs, Breaks, and Distortions of the Music of a Community in Transition." *The Massachusetts Review* 44.1-2 (Spring 2003): 269-282. *ProQuest*. Web. 11 May 2008.

Lowney, John. "Langston Hughes and the 'Nonsense' of Bebop." *American Literature Online*. Duke University. Web. 11 May 2008.

Online periodical.

Article on a scholarly website.

Marks, Carole. "The Great Migration: African Americans Searching for the Promised Land, 1916-1930." *In Motion: The African-American Migration Experience*. Ed. Howard Dodson and Sylviane A. Diouf. Schomburg Center for Research in Black Culture. Web. 11 May 2008.

Oliver, Paul. "Blues." *Grove Music Online*. Oxford UP. Web. 11 May 2008.

Online music dictionary.

Visual from web.

Photo Gallery. *Glenn Miller Orchestra Online*. Glenn Miller Productions, Inc. Web. 12 May 2008.

Rampersad, Arnold, ed. *The Collected Poems of Langston Hughes*. New York: Knopf, 1995. Print.

Book, emphasis on editor.

Article on a website.

"Roaring Twenties." *JAZZ: A Film by Ken Burns*. PBS. Web. 11 May 2008.

Tucker, Mark and Travis A. Jackson. "Jazz." *Grove Music Online*. Oxford UP. Web. 11 May 2008.

Online music dictionary.

6 MLA Documentation Style Guide

6a DOCUMENT SOURCES CONSISTENTLY IN APPROPRIATE STYLE

Anytime you use a direct quotation, paraphrase, or summary from a source—in other words, any text or idea that is not your own—you must indicate the author and work from which it came. This is called citing your sources. Different fields of study follow different guidelines for how to format citation. Psychology, for example, requires APA style, while anthropology typically uses the *Chicago Manual of Style*. English and most humanities, however, use MLA style, a format developed and maintained by the Modern Language Association. (For more on documentation styles, see p. H-108.)

This chapter will provide a quick overview and an abbreviated guide to MLA style. For a full description of how to properly cite works, you will want to consult the *MLA Handbook for Writers of Research Papers* (often referred to as simply the *MLA Handbook*), which is the authoritative guide to MLA style. Be sure to consult the 6th edition, which is the most current, as the rules vary slightly from edition to edition.

6b DOCUMENT IN-TEXT CITATIONS, MLA STYLE

1. Author Named in Parenthesis

A parenthetical reference in MLA consists of the author's last name and the page number from which you are quoting, summarizing, or paraphrasing. The reference comes at the end of the sentence *before* the period. Do *not* insert a comma, hyphen, or other punctuation between the last name and the page number.

Example: While documenting sources may take extra time, it is worth it because "your reader might want to see the source for his or her own research" (Smith 42-43).

When you need to cite a page range, simply put a hyphen between the start and end pages, as in the example above. When citing two different pages, separate them with a comma.

Example: (Smith 42, 51)

2. Author Named in Sentence

If you mention the author's name in the text surrounding the sentence, you need insert only the page number in parentheses.

Example: As John Smith points out, "Your reader might want to see the source for his or her own research" (42).

3. Two or More Works by the Same Author

If you use two books or articles by John Smith in your paper, you must let your reader know which source you are using by inserting the title of the work into your sentence *or* by abbreviating the title and inserting it in the parenthetical reference as shown below.

Example: As John Smith points out in his article "Using Sources," "Your reader might want to see the source for his or her own research" (42).

Example: While documenting sources may take extra time, it is worth it because "your reader might want to see the source for his or her own research" (Smith, "Sources" 42).

*For parenthetical references for works with two, three, or more authors, see p. H-108.

4. Source of a Long Quotation

When citing a block quotation—one that is four lines or longer in poetry or five lines or longer in prose—indent by one inch and do not include quotation marks. The citation comes *after* the period.

Example: Many critics point to specific techniques that Hughes employs to create the effect of jazz. One such critic is Lionel Davidas, who writes:

> Langston Hughes, in his collection of poems, lavishly uses such characteristics of jazz as repetitions, choruses, riffs, scats, and nonsensical onomatopoeia to achieve musical success as well as audience participation. It is also significant to note that Hughes's poems are often marked by dissonance, discordance, and line irregularity, which all contribute to the representation of the jazz spirit in verse forms. (268)

6c DOCUMENT LIST OF WORKS CITED, MLA STYLE

To properly format a Works Cited page:

- Begin on a new page, following the end of your paper. If your paper ends on page 5, your Works Cited page will begin on page 6.
- Just like your paper itself, a Works Cited page should be double spaced with one-inch margins.

- At the top of the page, type "Works Cited" and center it. Do not include quotation marks around the words "Works Cited."
- Do not skip spaces. Drop down one double-spaced line, and align your entry to the left.
- If an entry runs longer than one line, indent every line one-half inch (or five spaces) after the first line.
- Put a period at the end of each entry.
- Alphabetize your Works Cited list by the first word of the entry. In most cases, this will be the author's last name.

For an example of a Works Cited page, see the model research paper in the previous chapter on Writing the Research Paper.

Common Formatting Errors

- Single spacing a Works Cited page
- Adding extra spaces between entries
- Numbering entries

What goes in an entry on a Works Cited page? First determine what type of source it is—a book, a periodical, an online resource. Then follow the instructions in the appropriate section, as follows:

Citing Book Sources

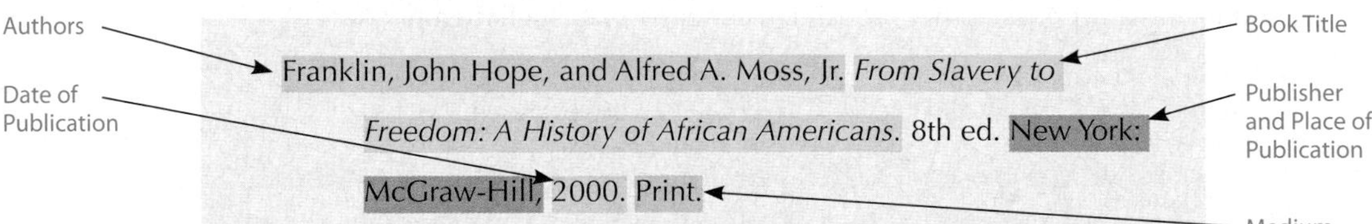

1. Book with One Author. Reverse the author's name for alphabetizing, adding a comma after the last name and a period after the first name. The book title follows in italics, followed by a period. Then list the city of publication, followed by a colon. Then the publisher, followed by a comma, then the year, followed by a period. Then list the medium. For how to abbreviate the publisher's name, see Additional Tips, p. H-111.

Borshuk, Michael. *Swinging the Vernacular.* New York: Routledge, 2006. Print.

Elements in Works Cited Entry: Books

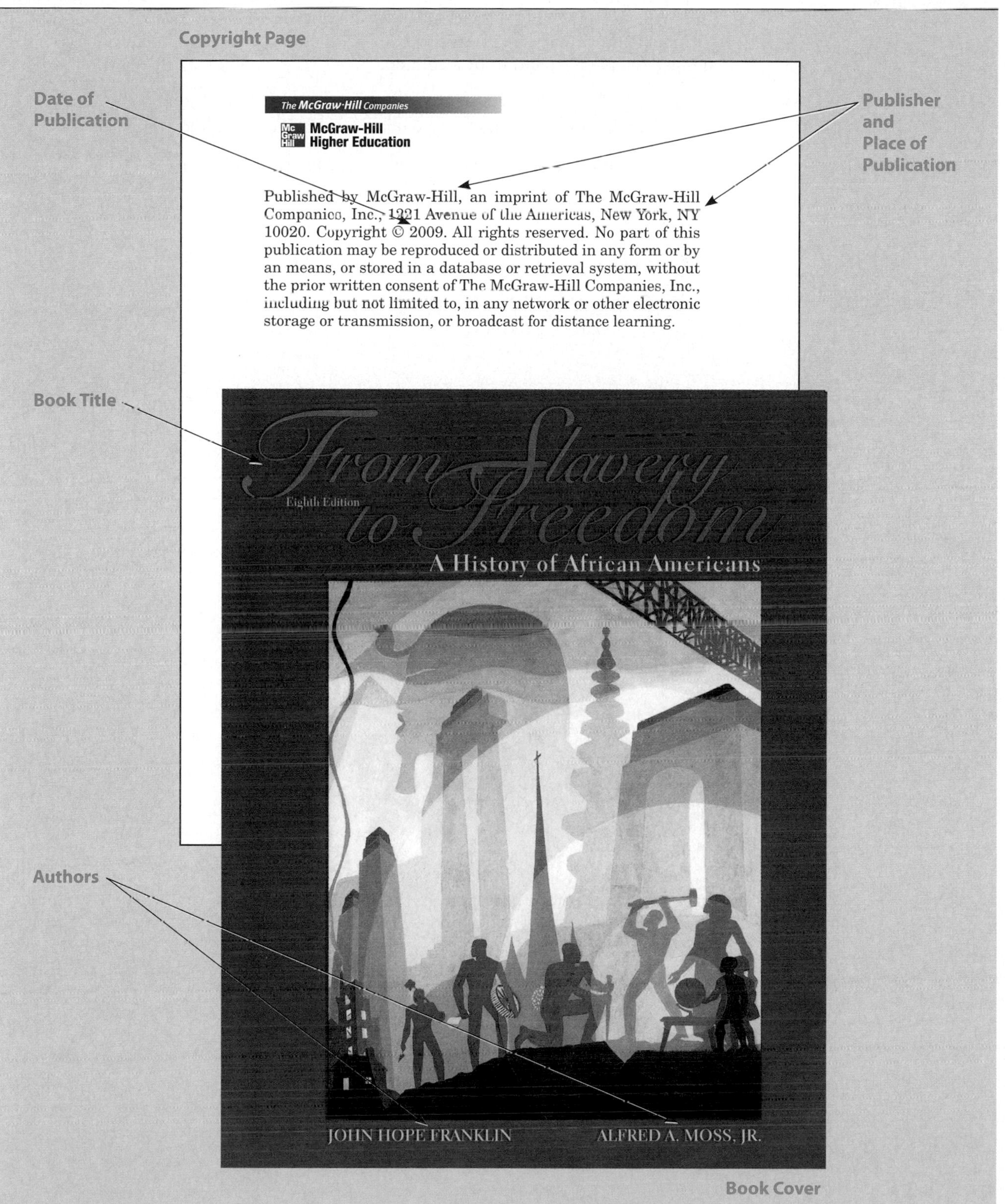
Copyright Page
Date of Publication
Publisher and Place of Publication
The McGraw-Hill Companies
McGraw-Hill Higher Education
Published by McGraw-Hill, an imprint of The McGraw-Hill Companies, Inc., 1221 Avenue of the Americas, New York, NY 10020. Copyright © 2009. All rights reserved. No part of this publication may be reproduced or distributed in any form or by an means, or stored in a database or retrieval system, without the prior written consent of The McGraw-Hill Companies, Inc., including but not limited to, in any network or other electronic storage or transmission, or broadcast for distance learning.
Book Title
From Slavery to Freedom
Eighth Edition
A History of African Americans
Authors
JOHN HOPE FRANKLIN
ALFRED A. MOSS, JR.
Book Cover

2. Book with Two or Three Authors. This entry follows the same formula as a book with a single author *except* that you will name the authors in the order listed on the title page. Reverse only the name of the first author. Then add a comma and list additional authors by first name followed by last name. Separate each author's complete name from the next author by a comma.

Gilbert, Sandra M., and Susan Gubar. *The Madwoman in the Attic: The Woman Writer and the Nineteenth-Century Literary Imagination.* New Haven: Yale UP, 2000. Print.

*A parenthetical reference for **two** authors should look like this:

(Gilbert and Gubar 34)

*A parenthetical reference for **three** authors should look like this:

(Gilbert, Gilbert, and Gubar 34)

3. Book with Four or More Authors. Indicate the name of the first author appearing on the title page, followed by "et al." (the Latin abbreviation for "and others"). As an alternative, however, you may list the names of all the authors *if convenient.*

Jordan, Frank, et al. *The English Romantic Poets: A Review of Research and Criticism.* New York: MLA, 1985. Print.

*A parenthetical reference for **four or more** authors would look like this:

(Gilbert et al. 34)

4. Two or More Books by the Same Author. Follow the same formula as the single book entry, but in this case, you need not repeat the author's name. Instead, indicate the same author with three hyphens and a period.

Bloom, Harold. *The Art of Reading Poetry.* New York: Perennial, 2005. Print.

---. *How to Read and Why.* New York: Scribner, 2000. Print.

5. Book with an Editor. In place of an author's name, put the editor's name, followed by a comma and the abbreviation "ed." If there is more than one editor, follow the format for "Book with more than one author" but place a comma and the abbreviation "eds." after the final editor's name listed.

Rampersad, Arnold, ed. *The Collected Poems of Langston Hughes.* New York: Knopf, 1995. Print.

6. Book with Two Editors. Use the abbreviation "eds." after the names of the editors.

Opie, Iona, and Peter Opie, eds. *The Oxford Book of Children's Verse.* New York: Oxford, 1973. Print.

7. Book with an Author and an Editor. Start with the name of the author, followed by the book title and a period. Then write "Ed." followed by the editor's name in normal order.

Twain, Mark. *Adventures of Huckleberry Finn.* Ed. Henry Nash Smith. Boston: Houghton, 1958. Print.

8. Book by an Unknown Author. Begin with the title of the book, followed by the translator or editor (if appropriate). Follow with the publication information. Remember to alphabetize such a book in your Works Cited list by the first major word in the title, *not* by an article (*a, an,* or *the*).

The Bhagavad Gita. Trans. Eknath Easwaran. Berkeley: Blue Mountain Center for Meditation, 2007. Print.

9. Work in an Anthology or Chapter in an Edited Book. Selection author's last name, first name. "Selection or Chapter Title." *Book Title.* Editor's name. City: Publisher, Year. Page numbers of selection. Medium.

Fox, Paula. "The Broad Estates of Death." *The O. Henry Prize Stories.* Ed. Laura Furman. New York: Anchor, 2006. 46-58. Print.

10. Translation of a Text. Author's last name, first name. *Title of Book.* Abbreviation "Trans." for "translator." City of publication; publisher, year. Medium.

Alighieri, Dante. *The Divine Comedy.* Trans. John Ciardi. New York: Norton, 1970. Print.

11. Introduction/Preface/Foreword/Afterword to a Text If the introduction, preface, foreword, or afterword was written by *someone other than the book's author,* start with the writer and the title of *this* part. Then, indicate the book's title, followed by the word "By" and the name of the book's author in normal order. In the following example, Anita Brookner wrote the introduction to Edith Wharton's novel *The House of Mirth.*

Brookner, Anita. Introduction. *The House of Mirth.* By Edith Wharton. New York: Scribner, 1977. ii- ix. Print.

If the introduction, preface, foreword, or afterword *was written by the author,* use **only** his or her last name preceded by the word "By." In the following example, Thomas Hardy wrote both the book itself and the introduction.

Hardy, Thomas. Introduction. *Tess of the D'Urbervilles.* By Hardy. New York: Barnes and Noble, 1993. Print.

12. Multivolume Work If you have taken information from only one of the work's volumes, indicate the number of that volume and abbreviate to "Vol" (no period after "Vol").

Poe, Edgar Allan. *The Collected Works of Edgar Allan Poe.* Ed. Thomas Ollive Mabboth. Vol 2. Cambridge: Harvard UP, 1969. Print.

If you have taken information from more than one volume, indicate the total number of volumes used, abbreviate to "vols" and follow with a period.

Poe, Edgar Allan. *The Collected Works of Edgar Allan Poe.* Ed. Thomas Ollive Mabboth. 2 vols. Cambridge: Harvard UP, 1969. Print.

13. Book in a Series Place the name of the series after the medium. Indicate the book's number in the series if available.

Franchere, Hoyt C., ed. *Edwin Arlington Robinson.* New York: Twayne, 1968. Print. Twaynes's United States Authors Series 137.

14. Encyclopedia Article

Signed A signed article is one that is attributed to an author.

Invert author's name. "Title of the Article." *Title of the Encyclopedia.* Editor(s). Volume number (if appropriate). City of publication; publisher, year. Page number(s). Medium.

Merlan, Philip. "Athenian School." *The Encyclopedia of Philosophy.* Ed. Paul Edwards. Vol. 1. New York: Macmillan, 1967. 192-93. Print.

Unsigned An unsigned article is not attributed to an author. Start with the title of the article. Then proceed as above.

"Pericles." *The Columbia Concise Encyclopedia.* Eds. Judith S. Levey and Agnes Greenhall. New York: Columbia UP, 1983. 655. Print.

15. Dictionary Definition "Title of Entry." *Title of Dictionary.* Edition. Year of publication. Medium.

"Fresco." *Merriam-Webster's Collegiate Dictionary.* 11th ed. 2003. Print.

Additional Tips

When a book lists multiple cities in which the publisher exists, choose the closest one geographically to put in your citation. For W. W. Norton & Company, which lists New York and London, you would use New York as the city for publication. Also, if the city is relatively unknown, or if there is more than one U.S. city with the same name, indicate the state in addition to the city, as in the following examples:

Durham, NC: Duke UP

Springfield, IL: Charles C Thomas

You will want to abbreviate or condense the publisher's name. Anytime you see "University Press," you can abbreviate it as "UP." For Southern Methodist University Press, write Southern Methodist UP. Alfred A. Knopf can be condensed to simply "Knopf."

If a book has multiple years on the copyright page, put only the most recent year in your Works Cited entry.

Citing Periodical Sources

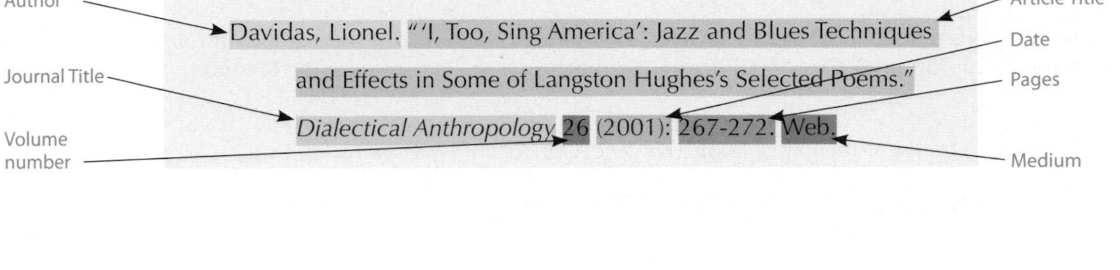

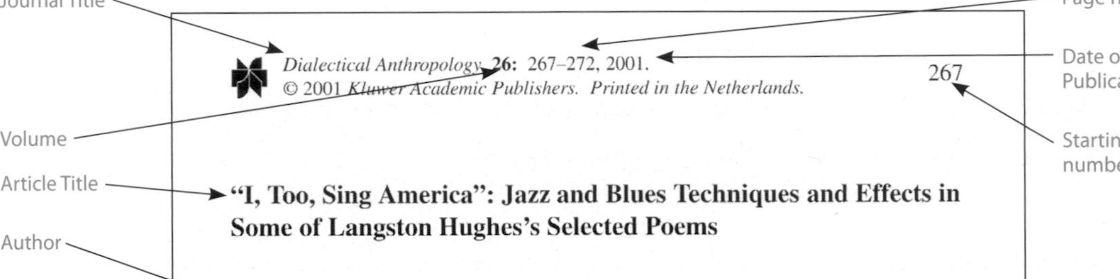

Dialectical Anthropology **26:** 267–272, 2001.
© 2001 *Kluwer Academic Publishers. Printed in the Netherlands.*

267

"I, Too, Sing America": Jazz and Blues Techniques and Effects in Some of Langston Hughes's Selected Poems

LIONEL DAVIDAS
Université des Antilles et de la Guyane, Martinique, West Indies

It is commonly accepted that oral poetry has been greatly influenced by jazz and blues, a phenomenon that developed mainly in the USA. In light of this, we may infer that such poems should logically be considered as mere scores to be deciphered and performed, or records that should be heard rather than read, and that have many of the dynamics of "the music" about them.[1] In point of fact, a significant number of jazz techniques are to be found within the framework of poetry and combine with it to produce a highly personalized mode of free expression, which is the essence and spirit of of jazz creation. As it appears, Langston Hughes's outstanding collection of poems exemplifies the greatest of those qualities of jazz and blues, and his talent truly makes these poems come alive in the same way that jazz and blues music comes alive for the audience as well as for the musicians.

To those who are familiar with such music, it is quite clear that *Selected Poems of Langston Hughes*, a book which reveals the author's personal choice, unquestionably includes blues poetry, as evidenced by the many characteristics of blues music that pervade most of the selected pieces. To start with, it is significant to note that Hughes's poems are not at all static. They are pervaded with lively and active repetitions, and we notice a series of variations within each poem which closely resemble the variations present in a blues song. Many of Hughes's poems exhibit a slow tempo and rhythm which is a common trait to most styles of blues. What is more, there exists some degree of internal variation in breath rhythm that contributes to the blues effect. In addition, those poems definitely seek the interaction of call-and-response, making the reader feel an active participant in the "concert" provided by the poet as musician, as performer.

Periodicals include scholarly journals, magazines, and newspapers. For print periodicals (as opposed to online periodicals), use the following citation formulas.

1. Article in a Scholarly Journal Author's last name, first name. "Article Title." *Journal Title* Volume. Issue (Year): Page numbers of article. Medium.

> Davidas, Lionel. "'I, Too, Sing America': Jazz and Blues Techniques and Effects in Some of Langston Hughes's Selected Poems." *Dialectical Anthropology* 26 (2001): 267-272. Print.

Note that not all journals have an issue number, as in the example above. If that is the case, simply include the volume and the year.

2. Article in a Magazine Author's last name, first name. "Article Title." *Magazine Title* Day Month Year: Page numbers of article. Medium.

> Lehrer, Jonah. "The Eureka Hunt." *The New Yorker* 28 July 2008: 40-45. Print.

Note that monthly magazines will not have a day with the month; in that case, simply list the month. Also, abbreviate months except for May, June, and July.

3. Article in a Newspaper Author's last name, first name. "Article Headline." *Newspaper's Name* Day Month Year: Section letter Page number +. Medium.

> Svrluga, Barry. "Phelps Earns Eighth Gold." *The Washington Post* 17 Aug. 2008: A1+. Print.

Use the plus sign after the page number only if the article is continued on nonconsecutive pages.

4. Book Review Start with the reviewer's name, followed by the title of the review (if it has one) in quotation marks. Follow with "Rev. of" (the abbreviation for "review of"), the title of the book, and the name of the book's author preceded by the word "by." The author's name should be in normal order.

In the following example, the reviewer is Robert Kelly; the author of the book is Umberto Eco.

> Kelly, Robert. "Castaway." Rev. of *The Island of the Day Before,* by Umberto Eco. *New York Times* 22 Oct. 1995: BR7. Print.

Citing Online Resources

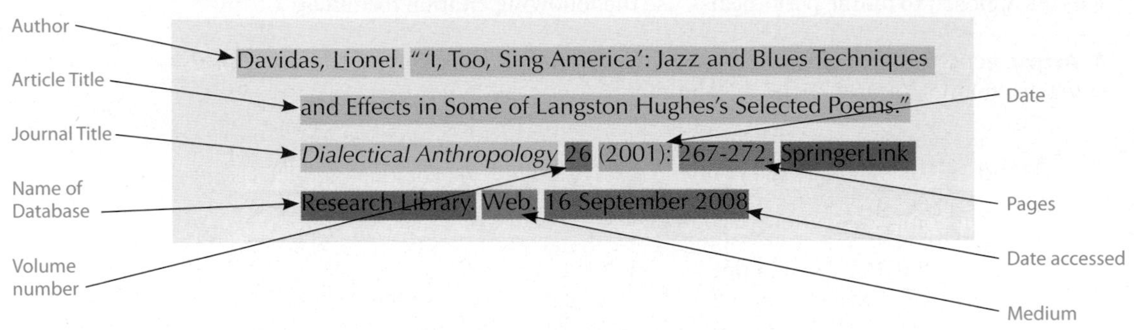

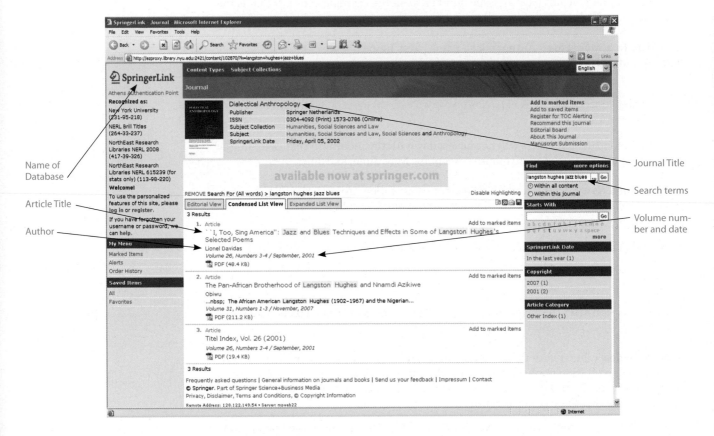

Name of Database
Article Title
Author
Journal Title
Search terms
Volume number and date

SpringerLink - Journal - Microsoft Internet Explorer
File Edit View Favorites Tools Help
Address http://ezproxy.library.nyu.edu:2421/content/102870/?k=langston+hughes+jazz+blues
SpringerLink
Athens Authentication Point
Recognized as:
New York University (231-95-218)
NERL Brill Titles (264-33-237)
NorthEast Research Libraries NERL 2008 (417-39-326)
NorthEast Research Libraries NERL 615239 (for stats only) (113-98-220)
Welcome!
To use the personalized features of this site, please log in or register.
If you have forgotten your username or password, we can help.
My Menu
Marked Items
Alerts
Order History
Saved Items
All
Favorites
Content Types Subject Collections
Journal
Dialectical Anthropology
Publisher Springer Netherlands
ISSN 0304-4092 (Print) 1573-0786 (Online)
Subject Collection Humanities, Social Sciences and Law
Subject Humanities, Social Sciences and Law, Social Sciences and Anthropology
SpringerLink Date Friday, April 05, 2002
Add to marked items
Add to saved items
Register for TOC Alerting
Recommend this journal
Editorial Board
About This Journal
Manuscript Submission
available now at springer.com
REMOVE Search For (All words) > langston hughes jazz blues
Disable Highlighting
Editorial View | Condensed List View | Expanded List View
3 Results
1. Article
"I, Too, Sing America": Jazz and Blues Techniques and Effects in Some of Langston Hughes's Selected Poems
Lionel Davidas
Volume 26, Numbers 3-4 / September, 2001
PDF (48.4 KB)
2. Article
The Pan-African Brotherhood of Langston Hughes and Nnamdi Azikiwe
Obiwu
...nbsp; The African American Langston Hughes (1902-1967) and the Nigerian...
Volume 31, Numbers 1-3 / November, 2007
PDF (211.2 KB)
3. Article
Titel Index, Vol. 26 (2001)
Volume 26, Numbers 3-4 / September, 2001
PDF (19.4 KB)
3 Results
Find more options
langston hughes jazz blues
Within all content
Within this journal
Starts With
SpringerLink Date
In the last year (1)
Copyright
2007 (1)
2001 (2)
Article Category
Other Index (1)
Frequently asked questions | General information on journals and books | Send us your feedback | Impressum | Contact
© Springer. Part of Springer Science+Business Media
Privacy, Disclaimer, Terms and Conditions, © Copyright Information

1. Web Site. The amount of source information provided varies from Web site to Web site. Include as much of the information below as you can. Remember, too, to choose your online resources wisely. If there is little or no information on the person or institution that created it, you may want to reconsider using it in your paper.

Last name of person responsible for site, first name. *Name of Web site.* Name of publisher, date of publication or last update. Medium. Day you accessed site—Month Year. Note: If no publisher is listed, use the abbreviation "n.p."

> Souther, Randy. *Celestial Timepiece: A Joyce Carol Oates Homepage.* N.p., Web. 8 Oct. 2007.

2. Article on a Web Site/Part of an Online Scholarly Project. Segment author's last name, first name. "Title of the Part of the Project." Ed. Name of person responsible for project. Date of publication or update. Name of sponsoring institution. Medium. Date you accessed site.

> "Roaring Twenties." *JAZZ: A Film by Ken Burns.* PBS. Web. 11 May 2008.

*Note that in the above example, the date of the Web site's publication was not available, so the student simply put the date she accessed the site.

3. Article in an Online Periodical. Article author's last name, first name. "Article Title." *Periodical's Web site.* Web site sponsor (if available). Day Month Year of publication. Medium. Date you accessed site.

> Lowney, John. "Langston Hughes and the 'Nonsense' of Bebop." *American Literature Online.* June 2000. Web. 11 May 2008.

4. Article from a Database. Cite the article as you normally would for a print article, but at the end of your entry add the following information:

Database Name. Medium. Date of access.

> Lenz, Gunter. "The Riffs, Runs, Breaks, and Distortions of the Music of a Community in Transition." *The Massachusetts Review* 44.1-2 (Spring 2003): 269-282. *ProQuest.* Web. 11 May 2008.

5. Online Book.

The entire online book. Start with the information you would include for any printed book. Follow with the name of the database, project, or other entity in which you found the book. Then, indicate the medium and the date you accessed the book.

> Hardy, Thomas. *Wessex Poems and Other Verses.* New York: Harper, 1898. *Bartleby.com.* Web. 30 Sept. 2008.

Part of an online book. Start with the name of the author, followed by the title of the part of the book you have cited. Then, proceed as above. The following example is an entry for Thomas Hardy's poem "Neutral Tones," which appears in an online book entitled *Wessex Poems and Other Verses.*

Hardy, Thomas. "Neutral Tones." *Wessex Poems and Other Verses.* New York: Harper, 1898. *Bartleby.com.* Web. 30 Sept. 2008.

6. Online Posting. Treat an online posting as you would a Web site.

Brantley, Ben. "London Theater Journal: Hitting Bottom." *Artsbeat. New York Times.* 17 July 2008. Web. 29 Sept. 2008.

Citing Other Media

1. Audio Recording. Start with the name of the composer, performer, or conductor—depending on whom you have discussed in your paper. Then, indicate the title of the recording, followed by the name(s) of the composer (s), performer(s), and/or conductor (if they were not mentioned earlier). Follow this with the distributor, the date, and the medium.

Chopin. Frederic. *Chopin: Etudes.* Maurizio Pollini. Deutsche Grammaphon, 1972. CD.

2. Film. Begin with the title of the film. Then, write the name of the director preceded by "Dir." (the abbreviation for "director"). Next indicate the name(s) of the principal performer(s) preceded by "Perf." (the abbreviation for "performers"). Follow this with the distributor, the date, and the medium.

Cinema Paradiso. Dir. Giuseppe Tornatore. Perf. Phillipe Noiret, Jacques Perrin, Antonella Attilli, Pupella Maggio, and Salvatore Cascio. Miramar, 1988. Film.

3. Television Program. Start with the title of the episode in quotation marks. Then, list the title of the program. Follow with the name of the network or channel, the city, the date you viewed the program, and the medium.

"Noah: Myth or Fact." *Into the Unknown with Josh Bernstein.* Discovery Channel, Silver Springs, MD. 15 Aug. 2008. Television.

Glossary of Literary Terms

Abstract A short **summary** at the beginning of a scholarly article that states the **thesis,** the major points of **evidence,** and the **conclusion** of the article.

Abstract Diction Language referring to a general or conceptual thing or quality, such as *progress,* or *justice.*

Accent The vocal emphasis on a syllable in a word. Often used interchangeably with **stress,** which sometimes refers to emphasis within a line of poetry, rather than a single word.

Accentual Meter A kind of **meter** or verse measure that uses a fixed number of stressed syllables in each line, although based on a number of unstressed syllables may vary. Accentual meters often can be heard in rap music and children's rhymes.

Accentual-Syllabic Verse A verse form that uses a fixed number of **stresses** and syllables per line. This is the most common verse form in English poetry, and includes, for example, **iambic pentameter,** where each line has five **stressed** syllables and five unstressed syllables.

Act A subdivision of the action of a play, similar to a chapter in a book. Acts generally occur during a change in **scenery,** cast of **characters,** or mood, and the end of an act usually suggests the advancement of time in the play. Acts are often divided into subunits called **scenes.**

Allegory A story in which major elements such as **characters** and settings represent universal truths or moral lessons in a one-to-one correspondence.

Alliteration The repetition of the initial consonant sounds of a sequence of words.

Allusion A reference to another work of art or literature, or to a person, place, or event outside the text.

Amphibrach A syllable pattern characterized by three syllables in the order *unstressed, stressed, unstressed.*

Amphitheater A stage surrounded on all sides by the audience, who watch the action from above.

Anagnorisis In **tragedy,** a change from ignorance to knowledge, producing love or hate between the persons destined by the poet for good or bad fortune.

Anagram A word or phrase created using the letters that spell a different word or phrase. For example, *dirty room* is an anagram for *dormitory.*

Analyze To take a text apart and examine its elements: the different written devices the author uses (such as **point of view, plot,** and imagery) and the **voice** the author brings to the piece (**tone,** word choice).

Anapestic Meter A **meter** using feet with two unstressed syllables followed by a **stressed** syllable.

Anecdote A personal remembrance or brief story.

Antagonist A **character** in **conflict** with the **protagonist.** A story's **plot** often hinges on a protagonist's conflict with an antagonist.

Anticlimax The opposite of a **climax;** a point in a narrative that is striking for its *lack* of excitement, intensity, or emphasis. An anticlimax generally occurs at a point of high action where a true climax is expected to occur.

Antihero A main **character** who acts outside the usual lines of heroic behavior (brave, honest, true).

Apostrophe A **figure of speech** in which a writer directly addresses an unseen person, force, or personified idea. The term *apostrophe* derives from the Greek term meaning *turning away* and often marks a digression.

Approximate Rhyme *See* **Slant Rhyme.**

Archetypal Criticism *See* **Mythological Criticism.**

Archetype An **image** or **symbol** with a universal meaning that evokes a common emotional reaction in readers.

Arena Theater Also called *Theater in the Round,* an arena stage is surrounded on all sides by the audience, with all the action taking place on a stage in the center.

Argument A position or perspective based on a **claim** that can be supported with **evidence.**

Aside In drama, a remark made by an actor to the audience, which the other **characters** do not hear. This convention is sometimes discernable in fiction writing, when a self-conscious **narrator** breaks the flow of the narrative to make a remark directly to the reader.

Assonance A repetition of vowel sounds or patterns in neighboring words.

Auditory Imagery **Images** that appeal to a reader's sense of hearing.

Augustan Age A distinct period in early-eighteenth-century neoclassical English literature characterized by formal structure and diction. This Augustan Age is named after the great period of Roman literature during Emperor Augustus's reign, when Ovid, Horace, and Virgil were writing. Famous writers of the English Augustan Age were Alexander Pope, Thomas Gray, and Jonathan Swift.

Authorial Intrusion *See* **Editorial Omniscience.**

Ballad Stanza A **quatrain** in which the first and third lines possess four stresses, while the second and fourth have three stresses. The **rhyme scheme** is often *abcb.*

Ballad A song or poem that tells a lively or tragic story in simple language using rhyming four-line **stanzas** and a set **meter.**

Bathos An error that occurs when a writer attempts elevated language but is accidentally trite or ridiculous; a sort of **anticlimax.**

Beat Generation A group of writers in the 1950s and '60s who represented the counterculture to 1950s American prosperity. The word "beat" comes from the slang for being down and worn out, suggesting their weariness with mainstream culture and their adoption of a freespirited attitude. Jack Kerouac's *On the Road* and Allen Ginsberg's poem "Howl" are major works of the Beat Generation.

Bibliography A list of the works consulted in the preparation of a paper, containing adequate information for readers to locate the source materials themselves.

Bildungsroman A **coming of age story** that details the growth or maturity of a youth, usually an adolescent. The term is German, meaning "**novel** of formation."

Biographical Criticism **Literary criticism** that emphasizes the belief that literature is created by authors whose unique experiences shape their writing and therefore can inform our reading of their work. Biographical critics research and use an author's biography to interpret the text as well as the author's stated intentions or comments on the process of composition itself. These critics often consult the author's memoirs to uncover connections between the author's life and the author's work. They may also study the author's rough drafts to trace the evolution of a given text or examine the author's library to discern potential influences on the author's work.

Biography The factual account of a person's life.

Blank Verse Unrhymed **iambic pentameter,** often used in Shakespeare's plays or for epic subject matter, as in Milton's *Paradise Lost.*

Blues A form of music that originated in the Deep South. Descended from African-American spirituals and work songs, the blues reflects the hardships of life and love in its lyrics. Most blues songs follow a form made of three phrases equal in length: a first phrase, a second that repeats the first phrase, and a third phrase different from the first two that concludes the verse.

Box Set *See* **Proscenium Stage.**

Brainstorming A process of generating and collecting ideas on a topic.

Burlesque A work of drama or literature that ridicules its subject matter through exaggerated mockery and broad **comedy.**

Cacophony Harsh-sounding, grating, or even hard-to-pronounce language.

Caesura A pause, usually in the middle of a line, that marks a kind of rhythmic division.

Canon In a literary context, the group of works considered by academics and scholars to be essential to and representative of the body of respected literature.

Carpe diem Latin for *seize the day.* A phrase used commonly in poetry that emphasizes the brevity of life and the importance of living in the moment.

Catharsis The purging of emotions which the audience experiences as a result of the powerful **climax** of a classical **tragedy**; the sense of relief and renewal experienced through art.

Central Intelligence Henry James's term for the **narrator** of a story—distinct from the author—whose impressions and ideas shape the telling of the story and determine the details revealed.

Character The depiction of human beings (and nonhumans) within a story.

Characters The actors (human and nonhuman) in a story.

Characteristics The physical and mental attributes of a **character,** established through **characterization.**

Characterization The way a writer crafts and defines a **character**'s personality to give an insight into that character's thoughts and actions.

Charting A technique for generating ideas that involves placing related concepts and themes in a chart to view their relationships.

Chorus A group of amateurs and trained actors who participated in traditional Greek plays. The chorus represents a group of citizens with worries and questions, expressed in poetry and music and dance movement.

Claim An idea or stance on a particular subject; a defendable claim is necessary for a strong **thesis.**

Classifications of Drama These four categories are generally assigned to Shakespeare's theater, but are commonly used in reference to the works of other **playwrights. Histories** focus on the reign of kings from the past, from Julius Caesar to Henry V. Because histories naturally contain very astute and sometimes troubling political commentaries, playwrights had to limit their subjects to rulers of the distant past. **Comedies** are plays for entertainment, and as a convention end in the marriage of two main **characters.** A comedic **plot** generally begins with a complication or misunderstanding between two lovers, which is complicated by further scheming and misunderstandings until finally a **resolution** is attained and the two are wed. **Tragedies** are darker plays, with more complex **characters** and more dire consequences, usually dramatizing the fall from a high state of life of a royal or special **character. Romances** (from the French *roman,* which means an "extended narrative") involve lovers whose potential happiness is complicated by misunderstandings, mistaken identities, and any number of other difficulties. Although similar in plot to a **comedy,** a romance play does not guarantee a happy ending.

Cliché A **figure of speech** that has been used so commonly that it has become trite. The use of cliché may suggest an ironic tone.

Climax The narrative's turning point in a struggle between opposing forces. The point of highest **conflict** in a story.

Close Reading The **explication** of a text in order to **analyze** the ways in which distinct formal elements interact to create a unified artistic experience for the reader.

Closed Couplet A pair of rhymed lines that capture one complete idea. If the couplet is **end-stopped** and in **iambic pentameter,** it is called a **heroic couplet.**

Closed Denouement A **resolution** to a story that leaves no loose ends.

Closed Form *See* **Fixed Form.**

Closet Drama A piece of literature written as though for the stage, but intended only to be read.

Collective Unconscious A set of **characters, plots, symbols,** and **images** that each evoke a universal response.

Colloquial Speech Familiar and conversational speech.

Comedy A type of drama that deals with light or humorous subject matter and usually includes a happy ending. The opposite of **tragedy.** *See* **Classifications of Drama.**

Comedy of Manners A work of **satire** that pokes fun at human behavior in particular social circles. Since a comedy of manners concerns itself with social interactions, it tends to reveal the **characters'** foibles or follies as they try to appear or act in a certain way.

Comic Relief A **character** or situation that provides humor in the midst of a work that is predominantly serious. A classic example is the bumbling Falstaff, a character in Shakespeare's *Henry IV* who makes the audience laugh, even as England's fate hangs in the balance.

Coming of Age Story A story that follows a **character's** physical, emotional, or spiritual maturation, often from youth into adulthood. *See* ***Bildungsroman.***

Common Measure A variation on **ballad** meter that uses **iambic quatrains** with the first and third lines containing four feet (**tetrameter**) and the second and fourth containing three feet (**trimeter**). The rhyme scheme is often *abab* rhyme. Common measure, also called *common meter,* is the **meter** most associated with hymns.

Comparison Looking at two or more texts, **characters,** authors, or other items side by side to draw similarities between them.

Conceit A complex comparison or **metaphor** that extends throughout a poem

Conclusion The final idea and **resolution** of a text. In a good essay, the conclusion not only reiterates the **thesis** but offers a reason for its significance or a reflection that pushes it toward a broader meaning beyond the essay itself. In a story or play, the conclusion refers to the resolution or **dénouement.**

Concrete Diction Language referring to a specific, definite thing or quality, such as *lawn mower* or *street light.*

Concrete Poetry Also called *visual poetry.* Poetry written in the shape of something it describes.

Confessional Poetry Poetry that includes pieces of a poet's autobiography or personal experience. This mode of poetry was prevalent in the mid-twentieth century with poets like Sylvia Plath, Anne Sexton, and Robert Lowell.

Conflict The central problem in a story. The source of tension between the **protagonist** and **antagonist.**

Connotation The associations a word carries beyond its literal meaning. Connotations are formed by the context of the word's popular usage; for example, *green*, aside from being a color, connotes money. The opposite of **denotation.**

Consonance A repetition of consonant sounds or similar patterns in neighboring words.

Context The literary, historical, biographical, or poetical situation that influences the writing of a work of literature.

Contextual Reading Reading and interpreting a story while mindful of its author, the time and place it was written, the traditions of its form, and the criticism it explicitly or implicitly responds to.

Contrast Looking at two or more texts, **characters,** authors, or other items side by side to highlight the differences between them.

Convention In literature, a feature or element of a **genre** that is commonly used and therefore widely accepted—and expected—by readers and writers alike. For example, it is a convention of Shakespearean **comedy** to end with a marriage.

Conventional Symbols **Symbols** that have accrued a widely accepted **interpretation** through their repeated use in literature and the broader culture. For example, spring and winter are conventional symbols of birth and death, as they appear with that meaning in Shakespeare's works through Frost's poetry. Colors, too, can be used as conventional symbols; in contemporary society, a pink ribbon is a conventional symbol of breast cancer awareness.

Cosmic Irony A literary convention where forces beyond the control of **characters**—such as God or fate or the supernatural—foil plans or expectations.

Couplet Two lines of poetry forming one unit of meaning. Couplets are often **rhymed,** strung together without a break, and share the same **meter.**

Cothurni Tall boots, worn by actors in the Ancient Greek theater, which served both to elevate an actor and make him more visible to the massive crowds, and also to make the **character**s seem larger than life.

Craft As a noun, craft refers to the elements that comprise a story; as a verb, craft refers to the process of making or fashioning a story out of those elements.

Cretic Also called *Amphimacer.* A syllable pattern characterized by three syllables in the order *stressed, unstressed, stressed.*

Crisis *See* **Climax.**

Critical Reading A process of digesting and understanding a text so you can appreciate not just the ideas it presents or the story it tells, but how it presents those ideas, why it presents them, and how those ideas exist in a certain context. Critical reading involves **summary, analysis, synthesis,** and **interpretation.**

Critique A **summary** accompanied by one's own personal opinion and perspectives.

Cultural Studies This critical perspective was developed mainly in England in the sixties by New Left writers, social philosophers, and sociologists. Cultural studies incorporates the techniques of literary analysis to **analyze** social life and social movements as though they were written texts.

Dactylic Meter A **meter** in which the foot contains a stressed syllable followed by two unstressed syllables.

Deconstruction A critical approach to analyzing literature based on the idea that texts do not have a single, stable meaning or **interpretation.** Deconstructionists seek to break down literature to reveal the inevitable inconsistency or lack of unity in even the most successful and revered texts, believing that the author's intentions have no bearing on the meaning of the text to the reader.

Decorum A certain level of propriety appropriate to a given text. As well as demanding a certain level of **diction,** decorum can also have bearing on the **characters, setting,** and **plot** events of a piece of literature.

Denotation The literal meaning of a word. The opposite of **connotation.**

Denouement The period after the story's **climax** when **conflicts** are addressed and/or resolved. Includes the **falling action** and **resolution** of a story.

Deus ex machina Latin for *God from the machine;* a literary device, often seen in drama, where a **conflict** is resolved by unforeseen and often far-fetched means.

Dialect **Dialogue** written to phonetically or grammatically replicate a particular **sound,** cadence, **rhythm,** or emphasis in a **character's** speech.

Dialogue Spoken interaction between two or more **characters.** A **characterization** technique that can signal class, education, intelligence, ethnicity, and attitude in the characters involved.

Diction An author's or **character's** distinctive choice of words and style of expression.

Didactic Literature Literature, such as a fable or **allegory,** written to instruct or teach a moral.

Dimeter A poetic **meter** comprised of two poetic feet.

Dirge A funeral song.

Doggerel An obviously patterned piece of **rhyme,** often lunging or twisting word order in order to get a rhyme. Doggerel can sometimes seem almost childish and, when extensive, boring.

Drama A term that comes from the Greek word for doing or acting and refers to a literary work that is represented through performance.

Dramatic Irony A situation in which an author or **narrator** lets the reader know more about a situation than a **character** does.

Dramatic Monologue A poem in which a **character** addresses another character or the reader. Dramatic monologues are offshoots of the epic form.

Dramatic Poetry Poetry in which the speaker of the poem is not the poet. Dramatic poetry often tells a story.

Dramatic Point of View A **third-person point of view** in which the **narrator** presents only bare details and the **dialogue** of other **characters.**

Dramatic Question The overarching challenge or issue in a piece of drama—the complication which the events of a play work to resolve.

Dynamic Character A **character** whose personality and behavior alter over the course of the action in response to challenges and changing circumstances.

Dramatis Personae "People of the play"; a list of the **characters** in a play, usually one of the first elements of a script.

Echo Verse Poetry in which words at the ends of lines or **stanzas** are repeated, mimicking an echo.

Economic Determinist Criticism *See* **Marxist Criticism.**

Editorial Omniscience A **narrator** inserts his or her own commentary about **character**s or events into the narrative.

Electra Complex The female version of the **Oedipus Complex,** the Electra Complex suggests that female children are hostile toward their mothers because of subconscious sexual attraction to their fathers.

Elegy A poem of lamentation memorializing the dead or contemplating some nuance of life's melancholy. Early Greek elegies employed a fixed form of **dactylic hexameter** and **iambic pentameter couplets.**

Elision The omission of a vowel or consonant sound within or between words, such as "ne'er" for "never" and "o'er" for "over." Elision dramatizes language and allows for flexibility within a poem's **meter.**

Ellipses Three periods placed in succession (. . .) to illustrate that something has been omitted.

End Rhyme **Rhyme** that occurs at the end of two or more lines of poetry. An example of end rhyme can be found in "The Love Song of J. Alfred Prufrock": "Let us go through certain half-deserted streets, / The muttering retreats."

End-stopped Line A line that ends with a full stop or period.

Endnote Information placed at the end of a text in an explanatory note. In a research paper, endnotes are used to comment on sources or provide additional analysis that is slightly tangential to the focus of your paper. An endnote is indicated by a superscript number ([1]) in the text itself, which corresponds to a numbered explanatory note at the end.

English Sonnet *See* **Shakespearean Sonnet.**

Enjambment The running over of a phrase from one line into another so that closely related words belong to different lines.

Envoi The final **stanza** of a **sestina,** which summarizes the entire poem. Envoi is French for *farewell.*

Epic A long **narrative poem,** traditionally recited publicly, whose subject matter reflects the values of the culture from which it came by portraying important legends or heroes. Classical epics include the *Odyssey* and the *Aeneid,* while English epics include *Beowulf* and *Paradise Lost.*

Epigram A short, often satirical observation on a single subject.

Epigraph A quotation or brief passage from another source, included at the beginning of a piece of literature. Writers use epigraphs to suggest a major theme or idea in their work.

Epiphany A sudden realization or new understanding achieved by a **character** or speaker. In many short stories, the character's epiphany is the **climax** of the story.

Episode A unified event or incident within a longer narrative.

Episodia The scenes of a Greek tragedy, divided by ***stasimon*** from the **Chorus.**

Epistolary Novel A novel written in the form of letters between two or more **characters,** or in the form of diary entries. Epistolary novels were particularly popular in the eighteenth century.

Ethnic Studies A critical approach to literature that seeks to give voice to literature that has previously been overlooked in the traditionally Euro-centric worldview—not simply by including ethnically diverse literature in the **canon,** but by attention to historically underrepresented groups, like African Americans and Native Americans.

Euphony Musically pleasing poetic language.

Evidence Reliable information, such as statistics, expert opinions, and anecdotes, used to support a **claim** in an **argument.**

Exact Rhyme A rhyme in which the final vowel and consonant sounds are identical, regardless of spelling. Also called *pure rhyme, perfect rhyme,* and *true rhyme.*

Exodos The concluding scene of a Greek **tragedy.**

Explication a **close reading** of any text where the goal is to logically **analyze** details within the text itself to uncover deeper meanings or contradictions.

Exposition: The narrative presentation of necessary information about the **character, setting,** or character's history provided to make the reader care what happens to the characters in the story.

Expressionism A mode of theater in which the playwright attempts to portray his or her subjective emotions in a symbolic way on stage.

Extended Metaphor A figurative analogy that is woven through a poem.

Eye Rhyme Words that share similar spellings but—when spoken—have different sounds. For example, *lint* and *pint.* Also called *Sight Rhyme.*

Fables A short narrative in which the **characters** (often animals or inanimate things) illustrate a lesson. The characters in fables are *actors* rather than **symbols.**

Fairy Tale A story, usually for children, that involves magical creatures or circumstances and usually has a happy ending.

Falling Action The events following the **climax** and leading up to the **resolution.** These events reveal how the **protagonist** has been impacted by and dealt with the preceding **conflicts** of the story.

Falling Meter A **meter** comprised of feet that begin with a stressed syllable, followed by an unstressed syllable or syllables. **Trochaic** and **dactylic** feet both create falling meter, which is named for the effect of *falling* from the initial stressed syllable to the unstressed.

Fantasy A literary **genre** that uses magical **characters** or circumstances.

Farce A work of drama or literature that uses broad, often physical **comedy,** exaggerated **characters,** absurd situations, and improbable **plot** twists to evoke laughter without intending social criticism.

Feminine Rhyme Rhymes between multisyllable words in which the final syllable is unstressed, such as *bother* and *father.* Also called *falling rhyme.*

Feminist Criticism An approach to literary criticism that highlights literature written by women and the exploration of the experience of female **characters;** also a critical examination of the ways in which female characters are viewed with prejudice, are subjugated to male interests, or are simply overlooked in literature.

Fiction A genre of literature that describes events and **characters** invented by the author.

Figurative Language Language that describes one thing by relating it to something else.

Figure of Speech A technique of using language to describe one thing in terms of another, often comparing two unlike objects, such as *the sun* and *the face of the beloved,* to condense and heighten the effect of language, particularly the effect of **imagery** or **symbolism** in a poem.

First-Person Narrator The story is narrated by a **character** in the story, identified by use of the pronoun *I* or the plural first-person, *we.*

Fixed Form An arrangement of text that requires a poet to obey set written combinations, including line length, **meter, stanza** structure, and **rhyme scheme.** Also called ***closed form.***

Flashback The device of moving back in time to a point before the primary action of the story.

Flat Character A **character** with a narrow range of speech or action. Flat characters are predictable and do not develop over the course of the **plot.**

Foil A **character** who contrasts with the central character, often with the purpose of emphasizing some trait in the central character. For example, a cruel sister emphasizes the other sister's kindness.

Folklore A traditional **canon** of stories, sayings, and **characters.**

Folktale A short, often fantastic tale passed down over time.

Foot The smallest unit of measure in poetic **meter.** A foot usually contains a stressed syllable and one or two unstressed syllables. **Meter** is formed when the same foot repeats more than once. For example, in **iambic pentameter,** *iambic* refers to the type of foot (an unstressed syllable followed by a stressed syllable), while *pentameter* tells us that there are five (pent) iambic feet in each line.

Footnote Like an **endnote,** a way to include commentary on sources or other information tangential to the focus of a text. A footnote occurs at the bottom of the page on which the subject is most closely addressed. To create a footnote, a superscript number ([1]) is placed in the text itself and corresponds to the number of the explanatory note at the bottom of the page.

Foreshadowing A hint about **plot** elements to come, both to advance the plot and build **suspense.**

Form The shape, structure, and style of a poem, as distinguishable from, but integral to, the content or substance of the poem.

Formal Diction Complex, grammatically proper, and often polysyllabic language in writing. It sounds grandiloquent—a *formal* word—and tends not to resemble the sort of talk heard in daily life.

Formalist Criticism An approach to literary criticism that considers a successful text to be a complete, independent, unified artifact whose meaning and value can be understood purely by analyzing the interaction of its formal and technical components, such as **plot, imagery,** structure, style, **symbol,** and **tone.** Rather than drawing their textual interpretations from *extrinsic* factors such as the historical, political, or biographical context of the work, formalist critics focus on the text's *intrinsic* formal elements.

Found Poem A poem created from already existing text that the poet reshapes and presents in poetic form. Text may come from advertisements, labels on household items, newspapers, magazines, or any other printed source not intended originally as poetry. A poet may piece together several sources like a collage, or he/she might take a short text exactly as it is and insert line breaks.

Fourth Wall The *invisible wall* of the stage, through which the audience views the action.

Free Verse Poetry in which the poet does not adhere to a preset metrical or **rhyme scheme.** Free verse has become increasingly prevalent since the nineteenth century, when it was first used. *See* **Open Form.**

Freewrite Writing continuously to generate ideas, without worrying about mistakes.

Gay and Lesbian Criticism A critical approach that is similar to **feminist criticism** in its quest to uncover previously overlooked undertones and themes in literature. Gay and lesbian criticism seeks to identify underlying homosexual themes in literature.

Gender Criticism A critical approach to literature that seeks to understand how gender and sexual identity reflect upon the interpretation of literary works. Feminist criticism and gay and lesbian criticism are derivatives of gender criticism.

Genre A literary category or form, such as the short story or novel, or a specific type of fiction, such as science fiction or mystery.

Groundlings "Standing room only" spectators in the Elizabethan theater who paid a penny to stand on the ground surrounding the stage.

Haiku A poetic form containing seventeen syllables in three lines of five, seven, and five syllables each. Haiku traditionally contain a natural-world reference or central **image.**

Hamartia A tragic flaw or weakness in a tragic **character** that leads to his or her downfall. **Hubris** is a type of *hamartia.*

Heptameter A poetic **meter** that consists of seven feet in each line.

Hero/Heroine The **protagonist** of a story, often possessing positive traits such as courage or honesty.

Heroic Couplet Two successive rhyming lines in **iambic pentameter.**

Hexameter A poetic **meter** that consists of six feet in each line. If the six feet are **iambic,** the line is known as an alexandrine, which was the preferred line of French epic poetry.

High Comedy **Comedy,** often a satire of upper-class society, that relies on sophisticated wit and **irony.**

Hip Hop An intensely rhythmical form of popular music developed by African-Americans and Latinos in the 1970s in which vocalists deploy rhyme—known as rap—over the rhythm.

Historical Criticism An approach to **literary criticism** that emphasizes the relationship between a text and its historical context. When interpreting a text, historical critics highlight the cultural, philosophical, and political movements and ideologies prevalent during the text's creation and reception.

Historical Fiction A type of fiction writing wherein the author bases his or her **characters, plot,** or **setting** on actual people, events, or places.

Histories *See* **Classifications of Drama.**

Hubris Excessive arrogance or pride. In classical literature, the hero's tragic flaw was often hubris, which caused his downfall in the tragedy.

Hyperbole A type of figurative speech that uses verbal exaggeration to make a point. Hyperbole is sometimes called ***overstatement.***

Iamb A poetic **foot** consisting of an unstressed syllable followed by a stressed syllable.

Iambic Meter A poetic **meter** created when each line contains more than one **iamb** (a unit with an unstressed syllable followed by a stressed syllable).

Iambic Pentameter A poetic **meter** in which each line contains five feet, predominantly iambs. Iambic pentameter is the most commonly used meter in English poetry, comprising **sonnets,** much of Shakespeare's plays, Milton's *Paradise Lost*, Wordsworth's *The Prelude* and Wallace Stevens' "Sunday Morning."

Iconography **Symbols** that commonly engender a certain meaning. For example, a skull equals *death,* and a dove equals *peace.*

Image A sensory impression created by language. Not all images are visual pictures; an image can appeal to any of the five senses, emotions, or the intellect.

Imagism A poetic practice wherein the *thing itself*—the object seen and not discussed or **analyzed**—becomes the poet's focus and the poem's primary concern. Imagism is associated with poets like Ezra Pound and William Carlos Williams.

Impartial Omniscience A **narrator** who remains neutral, relating events and **characters'** thoughts without passing judgment or offering an opinion.

Implied Metaphor A suggested comparison that is never stated plainly.

Impressionism In literature, a style of writing that focuses on a **protagonist**'s reactions to external events rather than the events themselves.

Indirect Discourse A **narrator**'s description of an action or event as experienced by a **character** in the story.

Informal Diction An author's use of words that are conversational or easily understood, as opposed to elevated or formal language. For example, using *you* instead of *thou.*

Initial Alliteration The repetition of consonant or vowel sounds in the middle of a line of poetry.

Initiation Story *See* **Coming of Age Story** and ***Bildungsroman.***

In medias res Latin for *in the middle of things.* A term applied when a story begins with relevant story events already having occurred.

Innocent Narrator *See* **Naïve Narrator.**

Intentional Fallacy The practice by **formalist** critics of discerning or trusting an author's own stated purpose for the meaning of a text.

Interior Monologue A **character's** conscious or unconscious thought processes, narrated as they occur, with only minimal-seeming guidance from the **narrator.**

Internal Alliteration The repetition of consonant or vowel sounds in the middle of a line of poetry.

Internal Refrain The repetition of words or phrases within the lines of a poem.

Internal Rhyme **Rhyme** that occurs within a line. The placement of internal rhyme can vary; for example, a word in the middle of the line might rhyme with the word at the end of that same line, or both rhyming words might occur in the middle of two consecutive lines.

Interpret The act of **interpretation.**

Interpretation The process of contributing to the overall understanding of some aspect of a work in order to illuminate its meaning.

In-Text Parenthetical Citation A reference within the body of a paper that links a **quotation, paraphrase,** or **summary** from another source to its full citation in the list of **works cited.**

In the Round *See* **Arena Theater.**

Inverted Syntax A reversal of expected or traditional word order, often used to aid a poem's sounds, **rhyme,** and/or **meter.**

Ironic Point of View Describes a **narrator** who does not understand the significance of the events of a story.

Irony A **tone** characterized by a distance between what occurs and what is expected to occur, or between what is said and what is meant.

Italian Sonnet *See* **Petrarchan Sonnet.**

Jargon Words used with specific meaning for a particular group of people. For example, *starboard* in nautical jargon refers to the right side of a ship.

Journal Entry A writing exercise that expands **freewriting** into a more focused discussion that reflects a growing understanding of a topic.

Language, Tone, and Style The elements that conjure a story's particular flavor and **voice,** as achieved by means of the words the author chooses and the **rhythm** with which he or she puts the words together

Language The words of a story, including **syntax** (how words or other elements of the sentence are arranged) and **diction** (what words the author chooses).

Levels of Diction Refers to the three major categories of diction: high, middle, and low diction. The level of diction a writer uses determines whether the words in the work will be formal or informal, poetic or conversational, etc.

Limerick A light, often humorous verse form consisting of five **anapestic** (two short syllables followed by one long one) lines, with a rhyme scheme of *aabba*. The first, second, and fifth lines consist of three feet, while lines three and four consist of two feet.

Limited Omniscient Narrator A **third-person narrator** who enters into the mind of only one **character** at a time. This narrator serves more as an interpreter than a source of the main **character's** thoughts.

Line A row of words containing phrases and/or sentences. The line is a defining feature of poetry, in which there are often set amounts of syllables or poetic feet in each line.

Literary Ballad A story told in **ballad** form.

Literary Criticism The acts of analyzing, interpreting, and commenting on literature.

Literary Epic *See* **Epic.**

Literary Theory The body of criticism and schools of thought (such as **Feminist, Deconstructionist,** or **Biographical** Criticism) that govern how we study literature.

Low Comedy An informal brand of **comedy** that uses crude humor and **slapstick.**

Lyric A short poem with a central pictorial **image** written in an uninflected (direct and personal) **voice.**

Madrigal A variety of contrapuntal song that originated in 16th-century Italy. Madrigal features secular verse sung by two or more voices without instrumental accompaniment.

Magic Realism A type of fiction in which something "magical" happens in an otherwise realistic world. The form is particularly associated with Latin American writers like Gabriel García Márquez. Unlike **fantasy** or science fiction, magic realism generally has only one fantastical element and the rest relies on realistic **characters** and settings. Notable examples in this book are Franz Kafka's *The Metamorphosis* and Aimee Bender's "The Rememberer."

Marxist Criticism Marxist or Economic Determinist Criticism is based on the writings of Karl Marx, who argued that economic concerns shape lives more than anything else, and that society is essentially a struggle between the working classes and the dominant capitalist classes. Rather than assuming that culture evolves naturally or autonomously out of individual human experience, Marxist critics maintain that culture—including literature—is shaped by the interests of the dominant or most powerful social class.

Masculine Rhyme The **end rhymes** of multisyllable words with a stressed final syllable, such as *remove* and *approve*. Also called rising rhyme.

Melodrama A literary work, mainly a stage play, movie, or television play or show in which **characters** display exaggerated emotions and the **plot** takes sensational turns, sometimes accompanied by music intended to lead the audience's feelings.

Melody The linear succession of various musical pitches recognized as a unit.

Metafiction A work of fiction that self-consciously draws attention to itself as a work of fiction. Rather than upholding the standard pretense, prevalent in realist fiction, that a story creates or refers to a "real world" beyond the text, metafiction self-consciously reveals the fact and sometimes the manner of its own construction. Metafiction is often associated with **postmodernism,** but examples of metafiction also occur in many other literary movements.

Metaphor A close comparison of two dissimilar things that creates a fusion of identity between the things that are compared. A metaphor joins two dissimilar things *without* using words such as *like* or *as*. While a **simile** suggests that X is *like* Y a metaphor states that X *is* Y.

Meter A measure of verse, based on regular patterns of sound.

Metonymy A **figure of speech** that uses an identifying emblem or closely associated object to represent another object. For example, the phrase *the power of the purse* makes little sense literally (there is no purse that has power), but in the metonymical sense, *purse* stands for money.

Middle Diction Poetic language characterized by sophisticated word usage and grammatical accuracy. Middle diction reads as educated, cultured language but is not extravagant like **poetic diction.**

Mime The act of performing a play without words.

Miracle Plays During the tenth century, when drama was suppressed by the church, these anonymous plays were acted out as religious instruction for the benefit of spectators who could not read the Bible.

Mixed Metaphor A failed comparison that results when a writer uses at least two separate, mismatched comparisons in one statement—to confusing, and sometimes comical effect. For example, *The early bird strikes when the iron's hot!*

Monologue A single **character's** discourse, without interaction or interruption by other **characters.**

Monometer A poetic **meter** comprised of one poetic foot.

Monosyllabic A word with one syllable.

Moral The lesson taught by a piece of **didactic literature** such as a fable. A moral is often phrased simply and memorably.

Morality Play A form of drama in which the figures on stage taught right and proper behavior—morality—to those who watched.

Motif A pattern of **imagery** or a concept that recurs throughout a work of literature.

Motivation A **character's** reason for doing something.

Mystery Play A play that enacted stories of the Bible, such as the Creation or the Crucifixion. These plays appeared during the tenth century, when drama was suppressed in England.

Myth The pre-Classical Greek word for sacred story or religious narrative, which by the Classical period had come to mean **plot,** as used in Aristotle's *Poetics*.

Mythological Criticism Also called the *archetypal approach,* mythological criticism stems from the work of Carl Jung, a Swiss psychoanalyst (and contemporary of Freud) who argued that humans share in a **collective unconscious,** or a set of **characters,** plots, symbols, and **images** that each evoke a universal response. Jung calls these recurring elements **archetypes,** and likens them to *instincts*—knowledge or associations with which humans are born. Mythological critics analyze the ways in which such archetypes function in literature and attempt to explain the power that literature has over us or the reasons why certain texts continue to hold power over audiences many centuries after their creation.

Naïve Narrator An unreliable **narrator** who remains unaware of the full complexity of events in the story being told, often due to youth, innocence, or lack of cultural awareness.

Narrative Poem A poem that tells a story. Examples include Tennyson's "The Charge of the Light Brigade," Longfellow's "The Midnight Ride of Paul Revere," and most ballads.

Narrator The **character** or consciousness that tells a story. For specific types of narrators, see **First-Person Narrator, Second-Person Narrator, Third-Person narrator, Omniscient Narrator, Limited Omniscient Narrator, Impartial Omniscience, Editorial Omniscience, Naïve Narrator,** and **Unreliable Narrator.**

Naturalistic Theater Drama that shines a light on the painful realities and problems of everyday life.

Near Rhyme *See* **Slant Rhyme.**

New Criticism *See* **Formalist Criticism.**

New Historicism A critical approach that emerged as a reaction to **new criticism**'s disregard of historical context, but also in response to the perceived shortcomings of older methods of **historical criticism.** Rather than focusing on texts in the **canon** as representations of the most powerful or dominant historical movements, new historicists give equal or greater attention to less dominant texts and non-literary texts (newspapers, pamphlets, legal documents, medical documents, etc.). New historicists attempt to highlight overlooked or suppressed texts, particularly those that express deviation from the dominant culture of the time. In this way, new historicists study not just the historical context of a major literary text, but the complex relationship between texts and culture, or the ways in which literature can challenge as well as support a given culture.

Nonfiction Novel A presentation of real events using the craft and technique of a fiction novel.

Novel A long fictional work. Because of their greater length, novels are typically complex and may follow more than one **character** or **plot.**

Novella A short novel, which generally means it has more complexity than a short story but without the usual length of a novel.

Objective Point of View The story is told by an observer who relates only facts, providing neither commentary nor insight into the **character's** thoughts or actions.

Observer A **first-person narrator** who does not participate in the action of the story.

Octameter A poetic **meter** that consists of eight feet in each line.

Octave Eight lines of poetry grouped together in a **stanza** or a unit of thought, as in the **Petrarchan sonnet** where the octave sets up a thought or feeling that the following **sestet** resolves.

Ode An elevated, formal **lyric** poem often written in ceremony to someone or to an abstract subject. In Greek **tragedy,** a song and dance performed by the **Chorus** between ***episodia***.

Oedipus Complex: Sigmund Freud's theory of behavior (derived from the **plot** of Sophocles's *Oedipus the King*) which holds that male children are jealous of the father because of their sexual attraction to the mother. In *Oedipus the King,* Oedipus kills his father and sleeps with his mother.

Off Rhyme *See* **Slant Rhyme.**

O. Henry Ending A short story ending that consists of a sudden surprise, often ironic or coincidental in nature, named for the short story writer O. Henry, who frequently ended his stories in this way. A classic example is O. Henry's "The Gift of the Magi" in which a husband and wife each give something precious of theirs to purchase a gift for the other; the ending reveals that each has sacrificed the very thing that would have allowed him or her to enjoy the gift received from their spouse.

Omniscient Narrator A **third-person narrator** who observes the thoughts and describes the actions of multiple **characters** in the story. The omniscient narrator can see beyond the physical actions and **dialogue** of **characters** and is able to reveal the inner thoughts and emotions of anyone in the story.

One-Act Play A play that consists of a single act that contains the entire action of the play. One-act plays usually portray a single **scene** with an exchange among a smaller number of **characters**; for example, Edward Albee's *The Zoo Story*.

Onomatopoeia The use of words that imitate the sounds they refer to, such as *buzz* or *pop*.

Open Denoument A **resolution** to a story that leaves loose ends and does not completely resolve the overarching **conflict.**

Open Form Poetry ungoverned by metrical or rhyme schemes. Also called free verse.

Orchestra The open area in front of the stage (or ***skene***) in the Greek **amphitheater.**

Overstatement *See* **Hyperbole.**

Oxymoron A version of **paradox** that combines contradictory words into a compact, often two-word term, such as *jumbo shrimp* or *definitely maybe*.

Paean The final choral **ode** of a Greek **tragedy.**

Pantoum A variation on the **villanelle,** consisting of an unspecified number of **quatrains** with the rhyme scheme *abab*. The first line of each quatrain repeats the second line of the preceding quatrain, and the third line repeats the final line of the preceding quatrain. In the final quatrain, the second line repeats the third line of the first quatrain, and the last line of the poem repeats the first line of the poem.

Parable A short narrative that illustrates a lesson using comparison to familiar **characters** and events. The characters and events in parables often have obvious significance as **symbols** and **allegories.**

Parados The **Chorus**' first **ode** in a Greek **tragedy.**

Paradox Seemingly contradictory statements that, when closely examined, have a deeper, sometimes complicated, meaning.
Parallelism The arrangement of words or phrases in a grammatically similar way.
Paraphrase Condensing a passage or idea from an existing text into your own words. Paraphrase does not mean simply changing the words from the original; rather, it should re-present the original in a way that demonstrates your understanding of it.
Parody Mimicking another author or work of literature in such a way as to make fun of the original, often by exaggerating its characteristic aspects.
Participant narrator A **first-person narrator** who takes part in the action of the story.
Pastoral Poetry A variety of poem in which life in the countryside, mainly among shepherds, is glorified and idealized.
Pentameter A poetic **meter** that consists of five feet in each line.
Peripeteia An element of Greek **tragedy,** *peripeteia* occurs when an action has the opposite result of what was intended. In a **tragedy,** this generally occurs at a turning point for the **hero** and signals his downfall.
Persona A poem's speaker, which may or may not use the **voice** of the poet.
Personae Masks, often representative of certain **iconography** and familiar **characters,** worn by actors in the Ancient Greek theater to enable one actor to perform as many **characters.** *Personae* often were designed to project an actor's voice to the far rows of the **amphitheater.**
Personification A **figure of speech** in which a writer ascribes human traits or behavior to something inhuman.
Persuasion The process of using **analysis** and logical **argument** to prove the validity of a certain **interpretation** or **point of view.**
Petrarchan (Italian) Sonnet A sonnet consisting of an **octave** and a **sestet,** all in **iambic pentameter,** with the rhyme scheme *abbaabba cdecde* or *abbaabba cdcdcd.* The **volta,** or turn, typically occurs between the octave and sestet, around line nine of the poem.
Plagiarism The act of taking credit for another's work or ideas.
Play A work of drama, usually performed before an audience.
Players Traveling actors, men and boys, who spoke their lines for pay.
Play Review The critique of a play.
Playwright The author of a dramatic work.
Plot The artful arrangement of incidents in a story, with each incident building on the next in a series of causes and effects.
Poetic Diction Lofty and elevated language, used traditionally in poetry written before the nineteenth century to separate poetic speech from common speech.
Point of View The perspective from which the story is told to the reader.
Polysyllabic A word that has many syllables.
Portmanteau Word A word invented by combining two other words to achieve the effect of both. Lewis Carroll's poem "Jabberwocky" is comprised largely of portmanteau words such as *slithy,* which means *slimy* and *lithe.*
Postcolonialism A critical approach to **literary criticism** that seeks to offer views of relations between the colonizing West and colonized nations and regions that differed sharply from the conventional Western perspectives.
Poststructuralist Criticism Criticism based on the belief that texts do not have a single, stable meaning or **interpretation,** in part because language itself is filled with ambiguity, multiple meanings, and meanings that can change with time or context.
Precís *See* **Summary Paper.**
Preview The process of gathering information about a piece of literature before you read it.
Problem Play A play about a social problem, written with an aim to create awareness of the problem.
Prologue The introduction to a literary work.
Proscenium Stage A realistic **setting** with three flat walls (two flat sides, and a ceiling) that simulates a room; the audience views the action through the missing **fourth wall.**
Prose Poem A poem that uses the devices and **imagery** characteristic of traditionally lined poetry, but in compact units without clearly defined line breaks.
Prosody The analysis of a poem's rhythm and metrical structures.
Protagonist The main figure (or principal actor) in a work of literature. A story's **plot** hinges equally on the protagonist's efforts to realize his or her desires and to cope with failure if and when plans are thwarted and desires left unfulfilled.
Psalm A sacred song, usually written to or in honor of a deity.
Psychoanalytic Criticism Also called *psychological criticism,* this approach in a sense studies **characters** and authors as one would patients, looking in the text for evidence of childhood trauma, repressed sexual impulses, preoccupation with death, and so on. Through the lens of psychology critics attempt to explain the motivations and meanings behind characters' actions. Psychological critics also use textual and biographical evidence as a means to better understand the author's psychology, as well as examine the process and nature of literary creation, studying the ways in which texts create an emotional and intellectual effect for their readers and authors.
Pun A play on words that reveals different meanings in words that are similar or even identical.
Pyrrhic A poetic foot characterized by two unstressed syllables.

Quantitative Meter A type of poetry that counts the length of syllables, rather than the emphasis they receive (as in **accentual meter** and syllabic verse). Quantitative meter primarily appears in Greek and Latin poetry and is rarely used in English since English vowel lengths are not clearly quantified.
Quatrain A four-line **stanza.** Quatrains are the most popular stanzaic form in English poetry because they are easily varied in **meter,** line length, and **rhyme scheme.**
Queer Theory The idea that power is reflected in language and that discourse itself shapes our sense of who we are and how we define ourselves sexually.

Rap An oral form of poetry that is akin to spoken word, but distinguished by musical qualities and choral repetitions. *See* **Hip Hop.**
Reader-Response Criticism The reader-response approach emphasizes that the reader is central to the writer-text-reader interaction. Reader-response critics believe a literary work is not complete until someone reads and **interprets** it. Such critics acknowledge that because each reader has a different set of experiences and views, each reader's response to a text may be different.
Realism A mode of literature in which the author depicts **characters** and scenarios that could occur in real life. Unlike **fantasy** or **surrealism,** realism seeks to represent the world as it is.
Recognition The moment in a **tragedy** when the **hero** comes to recognize the actuality of events and is no longer under illusion.
Refrain A line or **stanza** that is repeated at regular intervals in a poem or song.
Resolution The end of the story, where the **conflict** is ultimately resolved and the effects of the story's events on the **protagonist** become evident.
Restoration Comedy A bawdy play about fallen virtue and infidelity that

became popular after the Puritans were displaced in England in the mid-seventeenth century.

Retrospect *See* **Flashback.**

Reversal *See* ***Peripeteia.***

Rhyme The echoing repetition of sounds in the end syllables of words, often (though not always) at the end of a line of poetry.

Rhyme Scheme The pattern of **rhyme** throughout a particular poem.

Rhythm The sequence of stressed and unstressed sounds in a poem.

Rising Action Story events that increase tension and move the plot toward the climax.

Rising Meter A **meter** comprised of feet that begin with an unstressed syllable, followed by a stressed syllable or syllables. **Iambic** and **anapestic** feet both create rising meter, which is named for the effect of *rising* from the initial unstressed syllable to the stressed.

Romance *See* **Classifications of Drama.**

Romantic Comedy A type of **comedy** in which two would-be/should-be lovers find each other after a series of misunderstandings and false starts.

Round Character A **character** with complex, multifaceted characteristics. Round characters behave as real people. For example, a round **hero** may suffer temptation, and a round **villain** may show compassion.

Run-On Line A line of poetry that, when read, does not come to a natural conclusion where the line breaks. *See* **Enjambment.**

Sarcasm Verbal irony that is intended in a mean-spirited, malicious, or critical way.

Satire An artistic critique, sometimes heated, on some aspect of human immorality or absurdity.

Satiric Comedy A derisive and dark **comedy** in which there is no promise that good will prevail.

Satyr Play An often obscene satirical fourth play, provided after a trilogy of tragedies, meant to provide **comic relief.**

Scansion The process of determining the metrical pattern of a line of poetry by marking its stresses and feet.

Scene A defined moment of action or interaction in a story usually confined to a single **setting.** Scenes are the building blocks of a story's **plot.**

Scenery The set pieces and stage decorations onstage during the performance of a play.

Scratch Outline A multi-tiered, ordered list of topics that should be covered in a paper. A scratch outline goes into deeper detail than a topic outline.

Screenplay A script that is specifically tailored and structured for television or film rather than the stage.

Script The written text of a play, which may include set descriptions and actor cues.

Second-Person Narrator A **narrator** who addresses the character as *you*, often involving the reader by association.

Semiotics The study of how meaning is attached to and communicated by symbols.

Sentence Outline An outline that uses complete sentences instead of brief words or phrases.

Sestet Six lines of poetry grouped together in a stanza or a unit of thought, as in the **Petrarchan sonnet** where the last six lines of the poem resolve the idea or question set up by the initial **octave.**

Sestina A poem of six six-line **stanzas** and a three-line **envoi,** usually unrhymed, in which each stanza repeats the end words of the lines of the first stanza, but in different order, the envoi using the six words again, three in the middle of the lines and three at the end.

Setting The time and place where the story occurs. Setting creates expectations for the types of **characters** and situations encountered in the story.

Shakespearean (English) Sonnet A **sonnet** form composed of three quatrains and a final couplet, all in **iambic pentameter** and rhymed *abab cdcd efef gg.* The **volta,** or turn, occurs in the final **couplet** of the poem.

Short Story A brief fictional narrative that attempts to dramatize or illustrate the effect or meaning of a single incident or small group of incidents in the life of a single **character** or small group of characters.

Simile A direct comparison of two dissimilar things using the words *like* or *as.*

Situational Irony A situation portrayed in a poem when what occurs is the opposite or very different from what's expected to occur.

Skene The stage in the Greek **amphitheater.**

Slam Poetry in a variety of styles, performed competitively in clubs and halls.

Slant Rhyme A case in which vowel or consonant sounds are similar but not exactly the same, such as *heap* and *rap* and *tape.* Also called *near rhyme, imperfect rhyme* and *off rhyme.*

Slapstick A type of low **comedy** characterized by unexpected, often physical humor. A classic example of slapstick is the man walking along who accidentally slips on a banana peel.

Social Environment A study of **setting** that considers era and location as well as a **character's** living and working conditions.

Sociological Criticism The study of literary texts as products of the cultural, political, and economic context of the author's time and place.

Soliloquy A **monologue** delivered by a **character** in a play who is alone onstage. Soliloquies generally have a **character** revealing his or her thoughts to the audience.

Sonnet A poem of fourteen lines of **iambic pentameter** in a recognizable pattern of **rhyme.** Sonnets contain a **volta,** or turn, in which the last lines resolve or change direction from the controlling idea of the preceding lines.

Sound The rhythmic structure of the lines of a poem, which draws the reader in, often utilizing **rhyme** and created through word choice and word order.

Spoken Word Poetry Poetry that derives from the **Beat** poets, characterized by emphasis of the *performance* of a poem over the written form. Spoken word often employs improvisation.

Spondee A poetic foot characterized by two stressed syllables.

Stage Directions Cues, included by the playwright in the script of a play, which inform the actions of the actors during the play.

Stanza A unit of two or more lines, set off by a space, often sharing the same **rhythm** and **meter.**

Stasimon In Greek **tragedy,** an ode performed by the **Chorus** which interprets and responds to the preceding scene.

Static Character A **character,** often flat, who does not change over the course of the story.

Stock Character A **character** who represents a concept or type of behavior, such as a "mean teacher" or "mischievous student," and offers readers the comfort of repetition and reliability.

Stream of Consciousness: A **character's** thoughts are presented flowing by in free association, and the literary convention that rules is that there is no writer mediating the consciousness of the subject.

Stress The vocal emphasis on a syllable in a line of verse, largely a matter of pitch.

Structuralism Structuralist literary critics work from the belief that a given work of literature can be fully understood only when a reader considers the system of conventions, or the *genre* to which it belongs or responds.

Style The characteristic way in which any writer uses language.

Subplot A **plot** that is not the central plot of the work, but nonetheless appears in the same work. Longer works, like **novels** and plays, tend to have subplots that might follow side **characters** or somehow affect the action of the main plot.

Summary Restating concisely the main ideas of a text without adding opinion or commentary. The best approach to summary is to divide the text into its major sections and then write a sentence for each section stating its main idea.

Summary Paper A short paper that represents the main ideas of the text as the author has presented them, excluding any subjective ideas or interpretations.

Surrealism A technique of the modern theater in which the realms of conscious and unconscious experience are fused together to create a total reality. In this way the fiction writer, poet, and **playwright,** tap into the resources of the unconscious mind and the imagination and portray in story on the page or on the modern stage the stuff of human desire, hope, and dreams.

Suspense A sense of anticipation or excitement about what will happen and how the **characters** will deal with their newfound predicament.

Syllabic verse A verse form that uses a fixed number of syllables per line or stanza, regardless of the number of stressed or unstressed syllables.

Symbol Any object, **image, character,** or action that suggests meaning beyond the everyday literal level.

Symbolic Act A gesture or action beyond the everyday practical definition.

Synecdoche A **figure of speech** that uses a piece or part of a thing to represent the thing in its entirety. For example, in the Biblical saying that man does not live by bread alone, *bread* stands for the larger concept of food or physical sustenance.

Synopsis A **summary** or **précis** of a work.

Syntax The meaningful arrangement of words and phrases. Syntax can refer to word placement and order, as well as the overall length and shape of a sentence.

Synthesis The act of bringing together the ideas and observations generated by reading and analysis in order to make a concrete statement about a work.

Tactile Imagery Imagery that appeals to a reader's sense of touch.

Tercet A group of three lines of poetry, sometimes called a **triplet** when all three lines rhyme.

Terminal Refrain Repeated lines which appear at the end of each **stanza** in a poem.

Terza Rima A **tercet** fixed form featuring the interlocking rhyme scheme *aba, bcb, cdc, ded,* etc.

Tetrameter A poetic **meter** that contains four feet in each line.

Theme The central or underlying meanings of a literary work.

Thesis Statement A sentence, usually but not always included in a paper's introductory paragraph, that defines a paper's purpose and argument.

Thesis A paper's purpose and **argument,** defined by the **thesis statement** and proved by the paper's **conclusion.**

Third-Person Narrator A **narrator** who is outside the story. The narrator refers to all the **characters** in the story with the pronouns *he, she,* or *they.*

Tiring House In the Elizabethan theater, a room, adjoined to the stage, in which actors changed their costumes.

Tone The author's attitude toward his or her **characters** or subject matter.

Topic Outline A multi-tiered organization of a paper's topics and **arguments,** used to structure a paper.

Tragedy A dramatic form in which **characters** face serious and important challenges that end in disastrous failure or defeat for the **protagonist.** *See* **Classifications of Drama.**

Tragic Flaw In classical literature, the hero's weakness that causes his downfall.

Tragic Hero A heroic **protagonist** who from the beginning, due to some innate flaw in his **character** or some unforeseeable mistake (*see* **Tragic Flaw**), is doomed. The inevitability of a tragic hero's demise inspires sympathy in the audience.

Tragic Irony The situation in a **tragedy** where the audience is aware of the **tragic hero's** fate although the **character** has not yet become aware.

Tragicomedy A play with the elements of **tragedy** that ends happily.

Transferred Epithet A description that pairs an adjective with a noun that does not logically follow, such as *silver sounds.*

Trimeter A poetic **meter** that contains three feet in each line.

Triplet A **tercet** of three rhymed lines.

Trochaic Meter: A poetic **meter** created when each line contains more than one **trochee** (a unit with a stressed syllable followed by an unstressed syllable). Trochaic meter is a type of **falling meter.**

Trochee A poetic **foot** consisting of a stressed syllable followed by an unstressed syllable. The opposite of an **iamb,** and so sometimes called an "inverted foot," often beginning a line of **iambic pentameter.**

Understatement A purposeful underestimation of something, used to emphasize its actual magnitude.

Unreliable Narrator A **narrator** who cannot be trusted to present an undistorted account of the action because of inexperience, ignorance, personal bias, intentional deceptiveness, or even insanity.

Verbal Irony A statement in which the stated meaning is very different (sometimes opposite) from the implied meaning.

Verisimilitude How alike an imitation is to its original. The goal of literature, especially when written in the mode of realism, is to provide a likeness, or a verisimilitude, of real life.

Verse A broad term to describe poetic lines.

Vers libre *See* **Free Verse.**

Villanelle A poem consisting of five **tercets** and a concluding **quatrain.** Each tercet rhymes *aba* and the final quatrain rhymes *abaa.* The poem's opening line repeats as the final line of the second and fourth stanzas, and in the second-to-last line of the poem. The last line of the first **stanza** repeats as the final line of the third and fifth stanzas and is also the final line of the poem overall.

Visual imagery **Imagery** and descriptions that appeal to a reader's sense of sight.

Voice The unique sound of an author's writing, created by elements such as **diction, tone,** and sentence construction.

Volta In a sonnet, the turn where a shift in thought or emotion occurs. In the **Petrarchan sonnet,** the **volta** occurs between the **octave** and the **sestet;** in the **Shakespearean sonnet,** the ending couplet provides the volta.

Vulgate A term to describe the common people, often used in reference to a level of speech or **diction.**

Well-made Play A type of theater popularized in France. Well-made plays feature a three-act sequence that *poses* a problem, *complicates* and then *resolves* it; usually that **resolution** comes when a **character's** past is revealed. The first act offers *exposition,* the second a *situation,* the third an unraveling or *completion.* Meticulous plotting and **suspense** are components of this mode of theater.

Working Bibliography A list of all the sources consulted in preparing a paper, as well as all the information necessary to cite them in the final list of works cited.

Works Cited A list of all the primary and secondary sources consulted in the creation of a paper.

Credits

Kim Addonizio: "First Poem for You" from *The Philosopher's Club*. Reprinted by permission of Kim Addonizio.

Ai: "Riot Act, April 29, 1992" from *Greed* by Ai. Copyright © 1993 by Ai. Used by permission of W. W. Norton & Company, Inc.

Sherman Alexie: "Defending Walt Whitman" reprinted from *The Summer of Black Widows*, © 1996 by Sherman Alexie, by permission of Hanging Loose Press.

Miguel Algarín: "HIV" from *Love is Hard*. Reprinted by permission of the author.

Julia Alvarez: "Woman's Work" from *Homecoming*. Copyright © 1984, 1996 by Julia Alvarez. Published by Plume, an imprint of Penguin Group (USA); originally published by Grove Press. Reprinted by permission of Susan Bergholz Literary Services, New York, NY and Lamy, NM. All rights reserved.

A. R. Ammons: "Their Sex Life," "Small Song," from *The Really Short Poems of A. R. Ammons* by A. R. Ammons. Copyright © 1990 by A. R. Ammons. Used by permission of W. W. Norton & Company, Inc.

Gloria Anzaldúa: "To live in the borderlands means you" from *Borderlands/LaFrontera: The New Mestiza*. Copyright © 1987, 1999 by Gloria Anzaldúa. Reprinted by permission of Aunt Lute Books www.auntlute.com.

Margaret Atwood: "you fit into me" from *Power Politics* copyright © 1971, 1996 by Margaret Atwood. Reprinted by permission of House of Anansi Press, Toronto.

W. H. Auden: "Funeral Blues," "Musée des Beaux Arts," "The Unknown Citizen," "In Memory of W. B. Yeats" all copyright 1940 and renewed 1968 by W. H. Auden from *Collected Poems by W. H. Auden*. Used by permission of Random House, Inc.

Jimmy Santiago Baca: "Choices" is reprinted by permission of the author.

Frank Bidart: "Herbert White" from *In the Western Night: Collected Poems 1965–1990* by Frank Bidart. Copyright © 1990 by Frank Bidart. Reprinted by permission of Farrar, Straus and Giroux, LLC.

Elizabeth Bishop: "The Fish" and "One Art" from *The Complete Poems 1927–1979* by Elizabeth Bishop. Copyright © 1979, 1983 by Alice Helen Methfessel. Reprinted by permission of Farrar, Straus and Giroux, LLC.

Robert Bly: "Driving to Town Late to Mail a Letter" from *Silence in the Snowy Field*, reprinted by permission of the author.

Louise Bogan: "Changed Woman" from *The Blue Estuaries* by Louise Bogan. Copyright © 1968 by Louise Bogan. Copyright renewed1996 by Ruth Limmer. Reprinted by permission of Farrar, Straus and Giroux, LLC.

Gwendolyn Brooks: "We Real Cool" and "Sadie and Maud" from *Blacks* by Gwendolyn Brooks. Reprinted by consent of Brooks Permissions.

Kenneth Carroll: "So What!" (for the White Dude who said dis ain't poetry) from *So What! (for the White Dude who said this ain't poetry)*, reprinted by permission of Bunny and the Crocodile Press.

Anne Carson: "Automat" from *Men in the Off Hours* by Anne Carson, copyright © 2000 by Anne Carson. Used by permission of Alfred A. Knopf, a division of Random House, Inc.

Kelly Cherry: "The Raiment We Put On" from *Hazard and Prospect*. Reprinted by permission of Louisiana State University Press.

Marilyn Chin: "Turtle Soup" from The *Phoenix Gone, The Terrace Empty* (Minneapolis: Milkweed Editions, 1994). Copyright © 1994 by Marilyn Chin. Reprinted with permission from Milkweed Editions.

John Ciardi: "Most Like an Arch This Marriage" from *Collected Poems* by John Ciardi. Reprinted by permission of The Estate of John Ciardi.

Sandra Cisneros: "Pumpkin Eater" from *Loose Woman*. Copyright © 1994 by Sandra Cisneros. Published by Vintage Books, a division of Random House, Inc. and originally in hardcover by Alfred A. Knopf, Inc. Reprinted by permission of Susan Bergholz Literary Services, New York, NY and Lamy, NM. All rights reserved.

Amy Clampitt: "John Donne in California" from *The Collected Poems of Amy Clampitt* by Amy Clampitt, copyright © 1997 by the Estate of Amy Clampitt. Introduction copyright © 1997 by Mary Jo Salter. Used by permission of Alfred A. Knopf, a division of Random House, Inc.

Lucille Clifton: "homage to my hips" copyright © 1980 by Lucille Clifton. First appeared in *Two-Headed Woman*, published by The University of Massachusetts Press. Reprinted by permission of Curtis Brown, Ltd.

Judith Ortiz Cofer: "Quinceañera" is reprinted with permission from the publisher of *Terms of Survival* by Judith Ortiz Cofer (© 1987 Arte Publico Press—University of Houston).

Leonard Cohen: "For Anne" from *The Spice-Box of Earth* by Leonard Cohen. Copyright © 1961 by Leonard Cohen. Reprinted by permission of R K Management, LLC.

Wanda Coleman: "The ISM" from *Imagoes*. Reprinted by permission of the author.

Billy Collins: "The Names" reprinted by permission of the author.

Countee Cullen: "Incident" from *Color*, Copyright 1925 by Harper & Bros., NY. Copyrights held by the Amistad Research Center, Tulane University, Administered by Thompson and Thompson, Brooklyn, NY.

E.E. Cummings: "next to of course god america i," "l(a", "since feeling is first", "Buffalo Bill's," "in Just-," "anyone lived in a pretty how town" from Complete Poems: 1904–1962 by E.E. Cummings, edited by George J. Firmage. Copyright 1923, 1925, 1926, 1931, 1935, 1938, 1939, 1940, 1944, 1945, 1946, 1947, 1948, 1949, 1950, 1951, 1952, 1953, 1954, © 1955, 1956, 1957, 1958, 1959, 1960, 1961, 1962, 1963, 1966, 1967, 1968, 1972, 1973, 1974, 1975, 1976, 1977, 1978, 1979, 1980, 1981, 1982, 1983, 1984, 1985, 1986, 1987, 1988, 1989, 1990, 1991 by the Trustees for the E. E. Cummings Trust. Copyright © 1973, 1976, 1978, 1979, 1981, 1983, 1985, 1991 by George James Firmage. Used by permission of Liveright Publishing Corporation.

J.V. Cunningham: Epigram #9 and #24 from *The Poems of J.V. Cunningham*, edited with an Introduction and Commentary by Timothy Steele. Reprinted with the permission of Swallow Press/Ohio University Press, Athens, Ohio (www.ohioswallow.com).

William Dickey: "Therefore" from *The Rainbow Grocery*.

Emily Dickinson: "Because I could not stop for death," "I'm nobody! Who are you?" One need not be a chamber to be haunted," "There is no frigate like a book," "There's a certain slant of light," "I heard a fly buzz when I died," "Tell all the truth, but tell it slant," "The brain is wider than the sky," "A narrow fellow in the grass," "The difference between despair," "Safe in their alabaster chambers," "I died for beauty but was scarce," "Much madness is divinest sense," "Some keep the Sabbath going to church," "I started early, took my dog," "Wild nights! Wild nights!" "I felt a funeral in my brain," "The soul selects her own society," "I taste a liquor never brewed," "The bustle in a house," "Success is counted sweetest," "After great pain a formal feeling comes" reprinted by permission of the publishers and the Trustees of Amherst College from *The Poems of Emily Dickinson*, Thomas H. Johnson, ed., Cambridge, Mass: The Belknap Press of Harvard University Press, Copyright © 1951, 1955, 1979, 1983 by the President and Fellows of Harvard College.

Mark Doty: "Golden Retrievals" from *Sweet Machine* by Mark Doty. Copyright © 1998 by Mark Doty. Reprinted by permission of HarperCollins Publishers.

Rita Dove: "Flash Cards" from *Grace Notes* by Rita Dove. Copyright © 1989 by Rita Dove. Used by permission of the author and W. W. Norton & Company, Inc.

Alan Dugan: "Love Song: I and Thou" from *Poems Seven: New and Complete Poetry.* Copyright © 2001 by Alan Dugan. Reprinted with the permission of Seven Stories Press, www.sevenstories.com.

Stephen Dunn: "Poem for People That Are Understandably Too Busy to Read Poetry" from *Work and Love* by Stephen Dunn. Reprinted by permission of the author. "To a Terrorist" from *Between Angels* by Stephen Dunn. Copyright © 1989 by Stephen Dunn. "After" from *Different Hours* by Stephen Dunn. Copyright © 2000 by Stephen Dunn. Used by permission of W. W. Norton & Company, Inc.

T.S. Eliot: "The Love Song of J. Alfred Prufrock" from *Prufrock and Other Observations,* reprinted by permission of Faber and Faber Ltd.

Emily XYZ: "Ship of State of Fools" reprinted by permission of the author.

Louise Erdrich: "Dear John Wayne" from *Jacklight* by Louise Erdrich. Copyright © 1984 by Louise Erdrich, reprinted with permission of The Wylie Agency, Inc.

Rhina P. Espaillat: "Bilingual/Bilingue" from *Where Horizons Go.* Reprinted by permission of the author.

Mari Evans: "Spectrum" from *Where Is All the Music?*(1968). Copyright © Mari Evans.

Jesse Redmond Fauset: "Touché" in *Caroling Dusk,* edited, and with a foreword by Countee Cullen.

Kenneth Fearing: "AD" is reprinted by the permission of Russell & Volkening as agents for the author. Copyright © 1938 by Kenneth Fearing, renewed in 1966 by the Estate of Kenneth Fearing.

Carolyn Forché: "The Colonel" from *The Country Between Us* by Carolyn Forché. Copyright © 1981 by Carolyn Forché. Originally appeared in *Women's International Resource Exchange.* Reprinted by permission of HarperCollins Publishers. "The Museum of Stones" from *The New Yorker* March 26, 2007. Copyright © 2007 by Carolyn Forché. Reprinted by permission of William Morris Agency, LLC on behalf of the author.

Robert Frost: "Design," "Nothing Gold Can Stay," "Acquainted with the Night," "The Gift Outright," "Fire and Ice," "The Silken Tent," "Desert Places," "and "Come In" from *The Poetry of Robert Frost* edited by Edward Connery Lathem. Copyright 1923, 1928, 1969 by Henry Holt and Company, copyright 1936, 1942, 1951, 1956 by Robert Frost, copyright 1964, 1970 by Lesley Frost Ballantine. Reprinted by permission of Henry Holt and Company, LLC.

Erica Funkhouser: "First Pantoum of Summer" from *Earthly: Poems by Erica Funkhouser.* Copyright © 2008 by Erica Funkhouser. Reprinted by permission of Houghton Mifflin Harcourt Publishing Company. All rights reserved.

Allen Ginsberg: "A Supermarket in California" from *Collected Poems 1947–1980* by Allen Ginsberg. Copyright © 1955 by Allen Ginsberg. Reprinted by permission of HarperCollins Publishers.

Nikki Giovanni: "Knoxville, Tennessee" by Nikki Giovanni, reprinted by permission of the author.

Bhagavad Gita: "The Arjuna Speech" translated by Stephen Mitchell from *Bhagavad Gita* translated by Stephen Mitchell, copyright © 2000 by Stephen Mitchell. Used by permission of Harmony Books, a division of Random House, Inc.

Louise Glück: "Song of Obstacles" from *The First Four Books of Poems* by Louise Glück. Copyright 1968, 1971, 1972, 1973, 1974, 1975, 1976, 1977, 1978, 1979, 1980, 1985, 1995 by Louise Glück. Reprinted by permission of HarperCollins Publishers. *Firstborn, Descending Figure, House on Marshland, Triumph of Achilles,* Ecco Press.

Ray Gonzalez: "Corn Face Mesilla" from *Human Crying Daisies* by Ray Gonzalez. Reprinted by permission of Red Hen Press.

Lorna Goodison: "On Becoming a Tiger" from *Women's Worlds* by Lorna Goodison. Reprinted by permission of the author.

Linda Gregg: "Something Scary" Copyright © 2001 Linda Gregg. Reprinted from *Too Bright to See & Alma* by Linda Gregg with the permission of Graywolf Press, Saint Paul, Minnesota.

Angelina Weld Grimke: "Fragment" reprinted by permission of the Moorland-Spingarn Research Center, Howard University.

H.D. (Hilda Doolittle): "Heat" from *Collected Poems, 1912–1944,* copyright © 1982 by The Estate of Hilda Doolittle. Reprinted by permission of New Directions Publishing Corp.

Robert Hass: "Meditation at Lagunitas" from *Praise* by Robert Hass. Copyright © 1979 by Robert Hass. "Dragonflies Mating" from *Sun Under Wood: New Poems* by Robert Hass. Copyright © 1996 by Robert Hass. Reprinted by permission of HarperCollins Publishers." Tethered Horse" by Buson, "Don't worry, spiders" by Issa and "Kyoto," "a caterpillar" and "Deep autumn" by Basho from *The Essential Haiku: Versions of Basho, Buson & Issa,* edited with an Introduction by Robert Hass. Introduction and selection copyright © 1994 by Robert Hass. Unless otherwise noted, all translations copyright © 1994 by Robert Hass. All reprinted by permission of HarperCollins Publishers.

Marilyn Hacker: "Elektra on Third Avenue." Copyright © 1974 by Marilyn Hacker from *Selected Poems: 1965–1990* by Marilyn Hacker. Used by permission of W. W. Norton & Company, Inc.

Kimiko Hahn: "The Details We Fall For" from *Volatile.* Copyright ©1999 by Kimiko Hahn. Reprinted by permission of Hanging Loose Press.

Donald Hall: "Letter with No Address" from *Without: Poems* by Donald Hall. Copyright © 1998 by Donald Hall. Reprinted by permission of Houghton Mifflin Company. All rights reserved.

Joy Harjo: "Morning Song" from *A Map to the Next World: Poems and Tales* by Joy Harjo. Copyright © 2000 by Joy Harjo. Used by permission of W.W. Norton & Company, Inc.

Robert Hayden: "Those Winter Sundays," Copyright © 1966 by Robert Hayden, from *Collected Poems of Robert Hayden* by Robert Hayden, edited by Frederick Glaysher. Used by permission of Liveright Publishing Corporation.

Samuel Hazo: "Just Words" from *As They Sail.* Copyright © 1999 by Samuel Hazo. Reprinted with the permission of the University of Arkansas Press, www.uapress.com.

Seamus Heaney: "Digging" and "Mid-Term Break" from *Opened Ground: Selected Poems 1966–1996* by Seamus Heaney. Copyright © 1998 by Seamus Heaney. Reprinted by permission of Farrar, Straus and Giroux, LLC and Faber and Faber Limited.

Anthony Hecht: "The Dover Bitch" from *Collected Earlier Poems* by Anthony Hecht, copyright © 1990 by Anthony E. Hecht. Used by permission of Alfred A. Knopf, a division of Random House, Inc.

Gil Scott-Heron: "The Revolution Will Not Be Televised." Written by Gil Scott-Heron. Used by permission of Bienstock Publishing Company.

Juan Felipe Herrera: "Autobiography of a Chicano Teen Poet" from *187 Reasons Mexicans Cross the Border* by Juan Felipe Herrera. Reprinted by permission of City Lights Books.

Edward Hirsch: "My First Theology Lesson" from *Lay Back the Darkness: Poems* by Edward Hirsch. Copyright © 2003 by Edward Hirsch. Used by permission of Alfred A. Knopf, a division of Random House, Inc.

Hirshfield, Jane: "Tree" and "Button" from *Given Sugar, Given Salt* by Jane Hirshfield. Copyright © 2001 by Jane Hirshfield. Reprinted by permission of HarperCollins Publishers.

John Hollander: "Swan and the Shadow" from *Types of Shape* by John Hollander. Reprinted by permission of Yale University Press.

Marie Howe: "What the Living Do" from *What the Living Do* by Marie Howe. Copyright © 1997 by Marie Howe. Used by permission of W. W. Norton & Company, Inc.

Andrew Hudgins: "Elegy for My Father, Who Is Not Dead" from *The Never-Ending: New Poems* by Andrew Hudgins. Copyright © 1991 by Andrew Hudgins. Reprinted by permission of Houghton Mifflin Harcourt Publishing Company. All rights reserved.

Langston Hughes: "Po' Boy Blues," "The Dream Keeper," "I, Too," "Theme for English B," "The Negro Speaks of Rivers," "Mother to Son," "Let America Be America Again," "Harlem (2), " "Negro, " "Prayer [1]," "Motto," "Ballad of the Landlord," "A New Song," "Dream Boogie, "The Weary Blues,"

"Song for a Dark Girl," "Minstrel Man," "Night Funeral in Harlem," "The Blue," "Ardella" edited by Arnold Rampersad with David Roessel, Associate Editor, from *The Collected Poems of Langston Hughes* by Langston Hughes, edited by Arnold Rampersad with David Roessel, Associate Editor, copyright © 1994 by The Estate of Langston Hughes. Used by permission of Alfred A. Knopf, a division of Random House, Inc. Excerpt from "The Negro Artist and the Racial Mountain" Copyright 1926 by Langston Hughes. Reprinted by permission of Harold Ober Associates Incorporated. First published in *The Nation*.

Lawson Fusao Inada: "Grandmother" from *Drawing the Line* copyright © 1997 by Lawson Fusao Inada. Reprinted with the permission of Coffee House Press, Minneapolis, MN www.coffeehousepress.org.

Issa: "On a branch" by Kobayashi Issa, translation © 2004 Jane Hirshfield; used by permission of Jane Hirshfield.

Randall Jarrell: "The Death of the Ball Turret Gunner" from *The Complete Poems* by Randall Jarrell. Copyright © 1969, renewed, 1997 by Mary von S. Jarrell. Reprinted by permission of Farrar, Straus and Giroux, LLC.

Louis Jenkins: "Football" from *An Almost Human Gesture,* Eighties Press and Ally Press, 1987. Reprinted by permission of Louis Jenkins.

Donald Justice: "Pantoum of the Great Depression" from *New and Selected Poems* by Donald Justice, coypright © 1995 by Donald Justice. Used by permission of Alfred A. Knopf, a division of Random House, Inc.

Jane Kenyon: "The Suitor" and "The Blue Bowl" copyright © 1997 The Estate of Jane Kenyon. Reprinted from *Otherwise: New & Selected Poems* with the permission of Graywolf Press, Saint Paul, Minnesota.

Galway Kinnell: "After Making Love We Hear Footsteps" from *Mortal Acts, Mortal Words* by Galway Kinnell. Coyright © 1980 by Galway Kinnell. Reprinted by permission of Houghton Mifflin Harcourt Publishing Company. All rights reserved.

Yusef Komunyakaa: "Facing It" from *Dien Kai Dau.* © 1988 by Yusef Komunyakaa and reprinted by permission of Wesleyan University Press.

Maxine Kumin: "Saga" from *Poetry,* Fall 1991, reprinted by permission of Maxine Kumin and the Anderson Literary Agency, Inc.

J.D. Landis: "Starvation Diet" from *Cars on Mars,* reprinted by permission of the author.

Philip Larkin: "Aubade" from *Collected Poems* by Philip Larkin. Copyright © 1988, 2003 by the Estate of Philip Larkin. Reprinted by permission of Farrar, Straus and Giroux, LLC and Faber and Faber Limited.

Dorianne Laux: "The Shopfitter's Wife" from *Smoke.* Copyright © 2000 by Dorianne Laux. Reprinted with the permission of BOA Editions, Ltd., www.boaeditions.org.

Li-Young Lee: "Eating Together" and "Eating Alone" from *Rose.* Copyright © 1986 by Li-Young Lee. Reprinted by permission of BOA Editions, Ltd., www.boaeditions.org.

Denise Levertov: "The Ache of Marriage" by Denise Levertov from *Poems 1960–1967,* copyright © 1966 by Denise Levertov. Reprinted by permission of New Directions Publishing Corp.

Chen Li: "A War Symphony" from *The Edge of the Island* by Chen Li.

Shirley Geok-lin Lim: "Scavenging on a Double Bluff" from *Tilting the Continent* by Shirley Geok-lin Lim is reprinted by permission of the author.

Audre Lorde: "The Electric Slide Boogie" from *The Marvelous Arithmetics of Distance: Poems 1987–1992* by Audre Lorde. Copyright © 1993 by Audre Lorde. Used by permission of W. W. Norton & Company, Inc.

Thomas Lynch: "Liberty" and "Iambs for the day of burial" by Thomas Lynch. Reprinted by permission of the author.

Archibald MacLeish: "Ars Poetica" from *Collected Poems 1917–1982* by Archibald MacLeish. Copyright © 1985 by The Estate of Archibald MacLeish. Reprinted by permission of Houghton Mifflin Harcourt Publishing Company. All rights reserved.

Cleopatra Mathis: "Lilacs" from *Crazyhorse,* Spring 1982 is reprinted by permission of the author.

Gerda Mayer: "Narcissus" from *Monkey on the Analyst's Couch* by Gerda Mayer. Ceolfrith Press, 1980.

James Merrill: "The Victor Dog" from *Collected Poems* by James Merrill, edited by J. D. McClatchy and Stephen Yesner, copyright © 2001 by the Literary Estate of James Merrill at Washington University. Used by permission of Alfred A. Knopf, a division of Random House, Inc.

W.S. Merwin: "For the Anniversary of My Death" from *The Second Four Books of Poems* by W. S. Merwin. Copyright © 1967 by W. S. Merwin. Reprinted with permission of The Wylie Agency, Inc.

Charlotte Mew: "I So Liked Spring" from *Collected Poems & Selected Prose* by Charlotte Mew. Reprinted by permission of Carcanet Press Limited.

Edna St. Vincent Millay: "Not In A Silver Casket Cool With Pearls" copyright © 1921, 1931, 1948, 1958 by Edna St. Vincent Millay and Norma Millay Ellis. All rights reserved. Reprinted by permission of Elizabeth Barnett, Literary Executor, The Millay Society.

Czeslaw Milosz: "Encounter" from *The Collected Poems: 1931–1987* by Czeslaw Milosz. Copyright © 1988 by Czeslaw Milosz Royalties, Inc.

Gabriella Mistral: "Fugitive Woman" from *Madwomen,* reprinted by permission of the University of Chicago Press.

Marianne Moore: "The Fish" reprinted with the permission of Scribner, a Division of Simon & Schuster, Inc., from *The Collected Poems of Marianne Moore* by Marianne Moore. Copyright © 1935 by Marianne Moore. Copyright renewed © 1963 by Marianne Moore & T.S. Eliot. All rights reserved.

Paul Muldoon: "Symposium" from *Poems: 1968–1998* by Paul Muldoon. Copyright © 2001 by Paul Muldoon. Reprinted by permission of Farrar, Straus and Giroux, LLC. This poem originally appeared in *The New Yorker.*

Marilyn Nelson Waniek: "Chopin" from *The Homeplace,* reprinted by permission of Louisiana State University Press from *The Homeplace: Poems by Marilyn Nelson Waniek.* Copyright © 1990 by Marilyn Nelson Waniek.

Howard Nemerov: "The Blue Swallows" from *The Blue Swallows: The Collected Poems of Howard Nemerov.* Reprinted by permission of Margaret Nemerov.

Pablo Neruda: "Sonnet LXVI" from *100 Love Sonnets: Cien Sonetos De Amor* by Pablo Neruda, translated by Stephen Tapscott. Copyright © Pablo Neruda 1959 and Fundacion Pablo Neruda, Copyright © 1986 by the University of Texas Press. By permission of the University of Texas Press. "The Stolen Branch" by Pablo Neruda, translated by Donald D. Walsh, from *The Captain's Verses,* copyright © 1972 by Pablo Neruda and Donald D. Walsh. Reprinted by permission of New Directions Publishing Corp.

Naomi Shihab Nye: "The World in Translation" from *Words Under the Words: Selected Poems,* by Naomi Shihab Nye. Reprinted by permission of the author.

Sharon Olds: "Sex Without Love" from *The Dead and the Living* by Sharon Olds, copyright © 1987 by Sharon Olds. Used by permission of Alfred A. Knopf, a division of Random House, Inc.

Mary Oliver: "At Blackwater Pond" from *New and Selected Poems* by Mary Oliver. Copyright © 1992 by Mary Oliver. Reprinted by permission of Beacon Press, Boston.

Michael Ondaatje: "Sweet Like a Crow" from *Running in the Family,* copyright © 1982 Michael Ondaatje. Reprinted by permission of Michael Ondaatje. Trident Media Group, LLC.

Jacqueline Osherow: "Sonnet for the Music in the Warsaw Ghetto" from *With a Moon in Transit* by Jacqueline Osherow. Copyright © 1996 by Jacqueline Osherow. Used by permission of Grove/Atlantic.

Grace Paley: "Here" from *Begin Again: Collected Poems* by Grace Paley. Copyright © 2000 by Grace Paley. Reprinted by permission of Farrar, Straus and Giroux, LLC.

Dorothy Parker: "Sonnet for the End of a Sequence" from *The Portable Dorothy Parker* by Dorothy Parker, edited by Marion Meade, copyright 1928, renewed © 1956 by Dorothy Parker. Used by permission of Viking Penguin, a division of Penguin Group (USA) Inc.

Linda Pastan: "Jump Cabling" from *Light Year 85* by Linda Pastan. Reprinted by permission of Jean V. Naggar Literary Agency, Inc. "Ethics" from *Waiting for My Life* by Linda Pastan. Copyright © 1981 by Linda Pastan. Used by permission of W. W. Norton & Company, Inc.

Octavio Paz: "Motion" translated by Eliot Weinberger, from *The Collected Poems of Octavio Paz 1957–1987,* copyright © 1986 by Octavio Paz and

Eliot Weinberger. Reprinted by permission of New Directions Publishing Corp.

Molly Peacock: "Desire" from *Cornucopia: New and Selected Poems* by Molly Peacock. Copyright © 2000 by Molly Peacock. Used by permission of W. W. Norton & Company, Inc.

Willie Perdomo: "Postcards of El Barrio" from *Where a Nickel Costs a Dime* by Willie Perdomo. Copyright © 1996 by Willie Perdomo. Used by permission of W. W. Norton & Company, Inc. NA

Laurence Perrine: "The limerick's never averse" reprinted by permission of Doug Perrine.

Marge Piercy: "The secretary chant" from *Circles on the Water* by Marge Piercy, copyright © 1982 by Marge Piercy. Used by permission of Alfred A. Knopf, a division of Random House, Inc.

Robert Pinsky: "Shirt" from *The Want Bone* by Robert Pinsky. Copyright © 1990 by Robert Pinsky. Pinsky. Reprinted by permission of HarperCollins Publishers. "Sonnet" from *The Figured Wheel: New and Collected Poems 1966–1996* by Robert Pinsky. Copyright © 1996 by Robert Pinsky. "To Television" from *Jersey Rain* by Robert Pinsky. Copyright © 2000 by Robert Pinsky. Reprinted by permission of Farrar, Straus and Giroux, LLC.

Sylvia Plath: "Daddy" from *Ariel* by Sylvia Plath. Copyright © 1963 by Ted Hughes. "Metaphors" and "Mirrors" from *Crossing the Water* by Sylvia Plath. Copyright © 1971 by Ted Hughes. Reprinted by permission of HarperCollins Publishers and Faber and Faber Ltd.

Dudley Randall: "Ballad of Birmingham" from *Cities Burning* by Dudley Randall. Reprinted by permission of Broadside Press.

Henry Reed: "Naming of Parts" from *A Map of Verona*. Reprinted by permission of The Royal Literary Fund.

Adrienne Rich: "Aunt Jennifer's Tigers" copyright © 2002, 1951 by Adrienne Rich. "Living in Sin" copyright © 2002, 1955 by Adrienne Rich. "Diving into the Wreck" copyright © 2002 by Adrienne Rich. Copyright © 1973 by W. W. Norton & Company, Inc. from *The Fact of a Doorframe: Selected Poems 1950–2001* by Adrienne Rich. Used by permission of the author and W. W. Norton & Company, Inc.

Ranier Maria Rilke: "Archaic Torso of Apollo" from *The Selected Poetry of Ranier Maria Rilke* by Ranier Maria Rilke, translated by Stephen Mitchell. Used by permission of Random House, Inc.

Alberto Rios: "Nani" from *Whispering to Fool the Wind* by Alberto Ríos. Reprinted by permission of the author.

Theodore Roethke: "My Papa's Waltz", copyright 1942 by Hearst Magazines, Inc. "Root Cellar" copyright 1943 by Modern Poetry Association, Inc. "Elegy for Jane," copyright 1950 by Theodore Roethke, from *Collected Poems of Theodore Roethke* by Theodore Roethke. Used by permission of Doubleday, a division of Random House, Inc.

Wendy Rose: "Leaving Port Authority for the St. Regis Rez" from *What the Mohawk Made the Hopi Say* by Wendy Rose. Reprinted by permission of the author.

Rumi: "Some Kiss We Want" from *The Soul of Rumi: A New Collection of Ecstatic Poems,* translated by Coleman Barks. Copyright © 2001 by Coleman Barks. Reprinted by permission of HarperCollins Publishers.

Mary Jo Salter: "Video Blues" from *A Kiss in Space: Poems* by Mary Jo Salter, copyright © 1999 by Mary Jo Salter. Used by permission of Alfred A. Knopf, a division of Random House, Inc.

Sonia Sanchez: "Poem at Thirty" from *I've Been a Woman,* copyright © 1978, 1985 by Sonia Sanchez. Reprinted by permission of Third World Press, Inc., Chicago, Illinois

Carole Satyamurti: "I Shall Paint My Nails Red" from Carole Satyamurti, *Stitching the Dark: New & Selected Poems* (Bloodaxe Books, 2005). Reprinted by permission of Bloodaxe Books.

Gjertrud Schnackenberg: "Snow Melting" from *Supernatural Love: Poems 1976–1992* by Gjertrud Schnackenberg. Copyright © 2000 by Gjertrud Schnackenberg. Reprinted by permission of Farrar, Straus and Giroux, LLC.

Anne Sexton: "Letter Written on a Ferry While Crossing Long Island Sound" from *All My Pretty Ones* by Anne Sexton. Copyright © 1962 by Anne Sexton, renewed 1990 by Linda G. Sexton. Reprinted by permission of Houghton Mifflin Harcourt Company.

Julie Sheehan: "Hate Poem" from *Orient Point* by Julie Sheehan. Copyright © 2006 by Julie Sheehan. Used by permission of W. W. Norton & Company, Inc.

Jane Shore: "My Mother's Chair" from *A Yes or No Answer: Poems* by Jane Shore. Copyright © 2008 by Jane Shore. Reprinted by permission of Houghton Mifflin Harcourt Company. All rights reserved

Marc Smith: "Dusty Blues" and "The Father Has Faded" from *Crowdpleaser* by Marc Smith. Copyright © 1996. Reprinted by permission of the author.

Cathy Song: "Girl Powdering Her Neck" from *Picture Bride* by Cathy Song. Copyright © 1983. Reprinted by permission of Yale University Press.

Gary Soto: "Mexicans Begin Jogging" from *New and Selected Poems* © 1995 by Gary Soto. Used with permission of Chronicle Books LLC, San Francisco. ChronicleBooks.com. "Saturday at the Canal" from *A Fire in My Hands* by Gary Soto. Copyright © 2006, 1999 by Gary Soto. Reprinted by permission of Houghton Mifflin Harcourt Company. All rights reserved.

William Stafford: "Traveling Through the Dark" copyright 1998 The Estate of William Stafford. Reprinted from *The Way It Is: New & Selected Poems* with the permission of Graywolf Press, Saint Paul, Minnesota.

Robert Sward: "God is in the Cracks" from *God is in the Cracks* by Robert Sward. Reprinted by permission of the author.

The Last Poets: "My People" by The Last Poets.

Dylan Thomas: "Vision and Prayer (part I)" copyright © 1946 by New Directions Publishing Corp. "Do Not Go Gentle Into That Good Night" copyright © 1952 by Dylan Thomas. Both poems from *The Poems of Dylan Thomas*. Reprinted by permission of New Directions Publishing Corp.

Jean Toomer: "Reapers" from *Cane* by Jean Toomer. Copyright 1923 by Boni & Liveright, renewed 1951 by Jean Toomer. Used by permission of Liveright Publishing Corporation.

Natasha Trethewey: "Letter Home" copyright 2002 Natasha Trethewey. Reprinted from *Bellocq's Ophelia* with the permission of Graywolf Press, Saint Paul, Minnesota.

Quincy Troupe: "Poem Reaching Toward Something" from *Transcircularities: New & Selected Poems*. Copyright © 2001 Quincy Troupe. Reprinted with the permission of Coffee House Press, www.coffeehousepress.com.

Diane Wakoski: "Inside Out" from *Emerald Ice: Selected Poems 1962–1987* by Diane Wakoski. Reprinted by permission of Black Sparrow Books, an imprint of David R. Godine, Publishers, Inc. Copyright © 1988 by Diane Wakoski.

Anne Waldman: "Bluehawk" is reprinted by permission of the author.

Richard Wilbur: "The Writer" from *The Mind-Reader,* copyright © 1971 and renewed 1999 by Richard Wilbur, reprinted by permission of Houghton Mifflin Harcourt Publishing Company.

Nancy Willard: "Saint Pumpkin" from *Swimming Lessons: New and Selected Poems* by Nancy Willard, copyright © 1966 by Nancy Willard. Used by permission of Alfred A. Knopf, a division of Random House, Inc.

William Carlos Williams: "Spring and All: Section I" "The Red Wheelbarrow," and "This Is Just to Say" by William Carlos Williams, from *The Collected Poems: Volume I 1909–1939,* copyright © 1938 by New Directions Publishing Corp. Reprinted by permission of New Directions Publishing Corp.

C.K. Williams: "Tar" from *Collected Poems* by C.K. Williams. Copyright © 2006 by C.K. Williams Reprinted by permission of Farrar, Straus and Giroux, LLC.

David Wojahn: "The Assassination of John Lennon as Depicted by the Madame Tussaud Wax Museum, Niagara Falls, Ontario, 1987" from *Mystery Train,* by David Wojhan, © 1990. Reprinted by permission of the University of Pittsburgh Press.

James Wright: "Lying in a Hammock at William Duffy's Farm in Pine Island, Minnesota" from *Above the River: The Complete Poems* © 1963 by James Wright and reprinted by permission of Wesleyan University Press. "Autumn Begins in Martin's Ferry, Ohio" and "A Blessing" from *The Branch Will Not Break*. © 1963 by James Wright and reprinted by permission of Wesleyan University Press.

W. B. Yeats: "Leda and the Swan" and "Sailing to Byzantium" reprinted with the permission of Scribner, a Division of Simon & Schuster Adult Publishing Group, from *The Complete Works of W.B. Yeats, Volume I: The Poems,* edited by Richard J Finneran, copyright © 1928 by The Macmillan Company. Copyright renewed © 1956 by Georgie Yeats. "Crazy Jane Talks with the Bishop" from *The Complete Works of W. B. Yeats, Volume I: The Poems,* edited by Richard J. Finneran. Copyright © 1933 by The Macmillan Company. Copyright renewed © 1961 by Bertha Georgie Yeats. "The Second Coming" from *The Complete Works of W. B. Yeats, Volume I: The Poems,* edited by Richard J. Finneran. Copyright © 1924 by The Macmillan Company. Copyright renewed © 1952 by Bertha Georgie Yeats. All rights reserved.

Kevin Young: "Jook" from *Jelly Roll* by Kevin Young, copyright © 2003 by Kevin Young. Used by permission of Alfred A. Knopf, a division of Random House, Inc.

Al Young: "Doo Wop: The Moves" from *Coastal Nights and Inland Afternoons: Poems 2001–2006* by Al Young. Angel City Press. Reprinted by permission of the author.

Photo Credits

Page ii–iii: (Red Door) Mark Lewis/Getty Images, (Field of Sunflowers) Herbert Kehrer/Zefa/Corbis, (Sunflower) Brand X Pictures/Punchstock, (Woman) Photo of Jasmin Tokatlian courtesy of Miroslav Wiesner; **2:** 2002 Watson & Spierman/Jupiterimages; **3:** Tim McGuire/Corbis; **5:** Brand X Pictures/PunchStock; **5:** The McGraw-Hill Companies, Inc/Ken Karp photographer; **9:** LOC [LC-USZ62-42949]; **10:** Pach Brothers/Corbis; **11:** Kaz Chiba/Getty Images; **12T:** EclectiCollections/Fotosearch; **12B:** Royalty-Free/Corbis; **14T:** University of Texas' Perry Castaneda collection; **14B:** Getty Images; **16T:** Jon Chase photo/Harvard News Office; **16B:** Ingram Publishing/AGE Fotosearch; **17:** Library of Congress (LOC) [LC-USZ62-87604]; **20:** The McGraw-Hill Companies, Inc./Ken Cavanagh Photographer; **21:** Stockbyte; **22:** Robert Levin/Corbis; **23:** DLILLC/Corbis; **27:** AP Photo; **28:** Ingram Publishing/SuperStock; **29:** LOC [LC-USZ62-87604]; **30:** Fototeca Storica Nazionale/Getty Images; **32:** LOC [LC-USZ61-307]; **33:** Kaz Chiba/Getty Images; **35T:** LOC [LC-USZ62-123319]; **35B:** Ingram Publishing/Alamy; **39:** Design Pics/PunchStock; **41:** LOC [LC USZ62 40902]; **42:** Royalty-Free/Corbis; **46:** Gay Bumgarner/Getty Images; **47:** 2008 Jupiterimages; **49T:** Burke Triolo Productions/Getty Images; **49B:** C Squared Studios/Getty Images ; **64:** Eiji Yanagi/Photonica/Getty Images; **65:** Photodisc/PunchStock; **69:** LOC [LC-USZ62-70369]; **72T:** LOC [LC-USZ62-93465]; **72B:** Digital Vision/Getty Images; **74:** Royalty-Free/Corbis; **75:** LOC [LC-USZC4-6527]; **76:** C Squared Studios/Getty Images; **77:** LOC [LC-USZ62-36767]; **79:** Image Club ; **83:** PhotoLink/Getty Images; **84:** Stockbyte; **85:** Imagestate Media (John Foxx)/Imagestate; **87T:** LOC [LC-USZ62-120744]; **87B:** Brand X Pictures/PunchStock; **90:** The McGraw-Hill Companies, Inc./Lars A. Niki; **91T:** LOC [LC-DIG-cwpbh-00752]; **91B:** LOC [LC-DIG-ppmsca-08969]; **92:** Royalty-Free/Corbis; **94:** Library of Congress, Prints and Photographs Division [LC-DIG-ppmsca-09854] ; **105:** Jupiterimages/Imagesource; **102:** Drew Kelly Photography/zefa/Corbis; **103:** Bananastock/Jupiterimages; **110:** Imagestate Media (John Foxx)/Imagestate; **111:** Digital Vision/PunchStock ; **113:** iStockphoto.com/Viktor Pravdi; **116T:** LOC [SWANN - no. 775f]; **116B:** Photodisc; **119:** Brand X Pictures/PunchStock; **120:** Photodisc/Getty Images; **121T:** Photo by Fred Viebahn; **121B:** Chet Phillips/Getty Images; **122:** Photo by Mark Lacy; **123:** Brand X Pictures/PunchStock; **124:** Photo by Charlie M. P. Sirait; **125:** Brand X Pictures; **126T:** LOC [LC-USZ62-87604]; **126B:** Royalty-Free/Corbis; **131:** LOC [LC USZ62-108239]; **133:** JupiterImages ; **134:** LOC [LC-USZ62-108026]; **135:** Royalty-Free/Corbis; **136:** iStockphoto.com/Diana Didyk; **138:** Iceberg: Digital Vision/Getty Images; **138:** Jewel: Brand X Pictures/PunchStock; **144:** Huntstock, Inc/Alamy; **144:** Tooga/The Image Bank/Getty Images; **144:** Andy Ryan/Riser/Getty Images; **147:** 1995 Zedcor, Inc.; **148:** iStockphoto.com/Once Upon a Time Creations; **149:** Anthony Ise/Getty Images; **154:** LOC [LC-USZ62-109601]; **155:** iStockphoto.com/Radient Byte; **157:** Courtesy of Donald Hall; **158:** Hemera Technologies/Alamy; **159:** LOC [LC-USZ62-93465]; **160:** Brueghel, Pieter the Elder (c.1525-1569). Landscape with the Fall of Icarus. Musee d'Art Ancien, Musees Royaux des Beaux-Arts, Brussels, Belgium. Photo Credit : Scala/Art Resource, NY; **161:** Courtesy of Peter Smith; **162:** Edward Hopper (American, 1882-1967). Automat. 1927. Oil on canvas; 36 x 28 1/8 in. Des Moines Art Center Permanent Collections; Purchased with fund from the Edmundson Art Foundation, Inc., 1958.2.; **163:** Courtesy of Douglas Davenport; **164:** Kitagawa Utamaro (1753-1806). Woman Powdering Her Neck. Musee des Arts Asiatiques-Guimet, Paris, France. Photo Credit: Réunion des Musées Nationaux/Art Resource, NY; **176:** Rick Lew/Getty Images; **177:** Bill Stormont/Corbis; **179:** LOC [LC-USZ62-93789] ; **180:** The McGraw-Hill Companies, Inc./Lars A. Niki, photographer; **182:** IT Stock/PunchStock; **183B:** Purestock/PunchStock; **185:** Glenn Mitsui/Getty Images; **186T:** Photo by Donald Hall; **186B:** Rim Light/PhotoLink/Getty Images; **187:** Imagestate Media (John Foxx)/Imagestate; **189T:** Courtesy of Oliver Pastan; **189B:** Comstock/JupiterImages; **190T:** Courtesy of Paul Muldoon; **190B:** Royalty-Free/Corbis; **192:** image100/PunchStock; **195T :** University of Texas' Perry Castaneda Collection; **195B:** Andrew Ward/Life File/Getty Images; **196T:** LOC [LC-USZ62-103583]; **196B:** Don Bishop/Getty Images; **198:** Kaz Chiba/Getty Images; **199:** Burke/Triolo Productions/Getty Images; **200T:** LOC [LC-USZ62-87604]; **202T:** Courtesy of the Division of Rare and Manuscript Collections, Cornell University Library; **202B:** Ryan McVay/Getty Images; **203:** Photo by Miles Thorsen.; **204:** Ingram Publishing/AGE Fotostock; **210:** Tom Grill/Corbis; **211R:** simple stock shots/Getty; **211L:** Guy Thouvenin/Photolibrary; **213:** D. Normark/PhotoLink/Getty Images; **217:** iStockphoto.com/Robert Pinna; **223:** LOC [LC-USZ62-101955]; **224:** Royalty-Free/Corbis; **225:** LOC [LC-USZ62-90564]; **226:** Photodisc/Getty Images; **230:** Nick Koudis/Getty Images; **235:** Digital Vision/PunchStock; **242:** Chris Stein/Digital Vision/Getty Images; **243:** Gil Cohen Magen/Reuters/Corbis; **245:** PhotoLink/Getty Images; **250T:** LOC [LC-DIG-ggbain-03571]; **250B:** Digital Vision/PunchStock; **251:** LOC [LC-USZ62-70369]; **252:** Brand X Pictures/PunchStock; **253:** LOC [LC-USZC4-6527]; **254:** Mel Curtis/Getty Images; **255B:** Sharon Hudson/Corbis; **258T:** LOC [LC-USZ62-70369]; **258B:** ©iStockphoto.com/René Mansi; **260:** Laurent Hamels/Photoalto/PictureQuest; **261:** Creatas Images/Punchstock; **263B:** LOC, FSA/OWI Collection, [LC-DIG-fsa-8a26538]; **264:** Photo by Nubar Alexanian; **265:** Punchstock/Image Source; **267:** Harnett/Hanzon/Getty Images; **268B:** Royalty-Free/Corbis; **269T:** Kaz Chiba/Getty Images; **269M:** Courtesy of the Division of Rare and Manuscript Collections, Cornell University Library; **269B:** Creatas/PunchStock; **271:** 1995 Zedcor, Inc.; **273:** Ingram Publishing/SuperStock; **274:** LOC [LC-USZ62-93465]; **275:** Doug Sherman/Geofile; **277:** iStockphoto.com/AJ Studios; **278:** NPS photo by R. Lake; **279:** iStockphoto.com/

Cunfek; **288:** Fresh Food Images/Photolibrary; **289:** Visuals Unlimited/ Getty Images; **291:** PhotoAlto/PunchStock; **293T:** LOC [LC-DIG-cwpbh-00752]; **293B:** Royalty-Free/Corbis; **295:** Kim Steele/Getty Images; **296:** LOC [LC-USZC4-5181]; **298T:** LOC [LC-USZ62-111603]; **298B:** PhotoAlto/Glasshouse Images; **299:** Courtesy of Wild Duck Review; **300:** Adam Crowley/Getty Images; **301:** Photo by Catherine Mauger; **302:** Brand X Pictures/PunchStock; **303:** Don Hamerman Photography; **304:** Digital Vision/Getty Images; **305:** MedioImages/PunchStock; **307:** iStockphoto.com/Eric Etman; **313:** LOC [LC-USZ62-78972]; **315B:** iStockphoto.com/Lepas2004; **316:** Comstock/PunchStock; **317T:** Courtesy of Ray Gonzalez; **317B:** PhotoLink/Getty Images; **326:** Blend Images/Hill Street Studios/Veer; **327:** Michael Ochs Archives/Getty Images; **329:** Jupiterimages/Brand X Pictures; **331:** Andy Sotiriou/Getty Images; **333:** Digital Vision; **335:** The Palma Collection/Getty Images; **336T:** LOC [LC-USZC4-6527]; **336B:** Royalty-Free/Corbis; **338:** Angelo Cavalli/Getty Images; **339T:** Photo by Paul Abdoo; **339B:** PhotoLink/Getty Images; **341:** Tim Hall/Getty Images; **342:** Digital Vision; **343:** Courtesy of Marc Smith; **344:** Darren Hopes/Getty Images; **345:** Courtesy of Kenneth Carroll; **346:** Fancy/Veer; **347T:** Darren Hopes/Getty Images; **347B:** © Richard Green; **348T:** Pixtal/SuperStock; **348B:** Courtesy of Emily XYZ; **349:** MIXA/ PunchStock; **356:** Ingram Publishing/AGE Fotostock; **358L:** Michael Ochs Archives/Getty Images; **358R:** Michael Ochs Archives/Getty Images; **359L:** LOC [LC-USZ62-123107]; **359R:** LOC [LC-USZ62-129808]; **360:** LOC [LC-USZ62-111447]; **361T:** Bruce Heinemann/Getty Images; **361B:** Philip Coblentz/Brand X Pictures/PictureQuest; **362:** Punchstock/Stockbyte; **363T:** Digital Vision/Getty Images; **363B:** Brand X Pictures/PunchStock; **364T:** LOC [LC-USZC4-2814]; **364B:** Getty Images/Stockbyte; **365:** Steve Hamblin/Alamy; **366:** Lisa Zador/Getty Images; **367T:** PhotoAlto; **367B:** Darren Hopes/Getty Images; **368:** D. Falconer/PhotoLink/ Getty Images; **371:** LOC [LC-USZ62-42529]; **372:** Image Source/PunchStock; **373T:** Lifesize/Getty Images; **373B:** LOC [LC-USZ62-105919]; **374:** Jack Hollingsworth/Corbis; **375:** Anthony Saint James/Getty Images; **376:** iStockphoto.com/Peeter Viisimaa; **369:** Royalty-Free/Corbis; **370:** Brian Barneclo; **380 - 381:** LOC, The Lessing J. Rosenwald Collection; **381:** LOC, The Lessing J. Rosenwald Collection; **382:** NMPFT/RPS/SSPL/The Image Works;**383:** LOC [LC-USZ62-64309]; **384:** LOC [LC-USZ62-103583]; **386 - 397:** LOC, The Lessing J. Rosenwald Collection; **400:** James Marshall/Corbis; **401:** Time & Life Pictures/Getty Images; **402:** Royalty-Free/ Corbis; **403:** Digital Vision/PunchStock; **404T:** LOC [LC-USZ62-90564]; **404B:** Digital Vision/Getty Images; **405L:** Creatas/Punchstock; **405R:** Royalty-Free/Corbis; **406:** Ingram Publishing/SuperStock; **407T:** Ingram Publishing/AGE Fotostock; **407B:** Digital Vision/PunchStock; **408:** Getty Images; **409L:** IT Stock Free/Alamy; **409R:** Royalty-Free/Corbis; **410:** Royalty-Free/Corbis; **411L:** Corbis; **411R:** Ryan McVay/Getty Images; **412T:** Digital Vision Ltd./SuperStock; **412B:** LOC [LC-USZ62-120744]; **413:** Pixtal/age fotostock; **414:** PhotoLink/Getty Images; **415:** Brand X Pictures/Punchstock; **416T:** Design Pics/PunchStock; **416B:** Royalty-Free/Corbis; **417L:** iStockphoto.com/kirschbam; **417R:** Digital Vision; **421:** Raymond Forbes/AGE Fotostock/Photolibrary; **H-1:** Andre Jenny/ Alamy; **H-97:** Michael Ochs Archives /Getty Images; **H-98:** Frank Driggs Collection/Getty Images; **H-107:** "Book Cover" © 2000 from, FROM SLAVERY TO FREEDOM BY John H. Franklin and Evelyn Higginbotham. Used by permission of the McGraw-Hill Companies.

Index

Note: Page references in **boldface** refer to literary works included in their entirety.